SMART CITIES CYBERSECURITY AND PRIVACY

SMART CITIES CYBERSECURITY AND PRIVACY

Edited by

DANDA B. RAWAT
Howard University, Washington, DC, United States

KAYHAN ZRAR GHAFOOR
Shanghai Jiao Tong University, Shanghai, China
Department of Computer Science, Faculty of Science, Cihan University-Erbil, Kurdistan, Iraq

ELSEVIER

Elsevier
Radarweg 29, PO Box 211, 1000 AE Amsterdam, Netherlands
The Boulevard, Langford Lane, Kidlington, Oxford OX5 1GB, United Kingdom
50 Hampshire Street, 5th Floor, Cambridge, MA 02139, United States

Notices
Knowledge and best practice in this field are constantly changing. As new research and experience broaden our understanding, changes in research methods, professional practices, or medical treatment may become necessary.

Practitioners and researchers must always rely on their own experience and knowledge in evaluating and using any information, methods, compounds, or experiments described herein. In using such information or methods they should be mindful of their own safety and the safety of others, including parties for whom they have a professional responsibility.

To the fullest extent of the law, neither the Publisher nor the authors, contributors, or editors, assume any liability for any injury and/or damage to persons or property as a matter of products liability, negligence or otherwise, or from any use or operation of any methods, products, instructions, or ideas contained in the material herein.

Library of Congress Cataloging-in-Publication Data
A catalog record for this book is available from the Library of Congress

British Library Cataloguing-in-Publication Data
A catalogue record for this book is available from the British Library

ISBN: 978-0-12-815032-0

For information on all Elsevier publications visit our website at
https://www.elsevier.com/books-and-journals

Working together
to grow libraries in
developing countries

www.elsevier.com • www.bookaid.org

Publisher: Joe Hayton
Acquisition Editor: Brian Romer
Editorial Project Manager: Emily Thomson
Production Project Manager: Sujatha Thirugnana Sambandam
Cover Designer: Matthew Limbert

Typeset by SPi Global, India

Dedication

To our families.

Contents

Contributors

Mohamed Abdallah   College of Science and Engineering, Hamad bin Khalifa University, Doha, Qatar

Yousra Abdul Alsahib S. Aldeen   Department of Computer Science, College of Science for Women, University of Baghdad, Baghdad, Iraq; Faculty of Computing, University Technology Malaysia, Skudai, Malaysia

Ahmad Alsharif   Department of Electrical and Computer Engineering, Tennessee Tech University, Cookeville, TN, United States

Ala' M. Al-Zoubi   Business Information Technology Department, King Abdulla II School for Information Technology, The University of Jordan, Amman, Jordan

Aniruddha Bhattacharjya   Beijing National Research Center for Information Science and Technology, Department of Electronic Engineering, Tsinghua University, Beijing, China

Muhammad Bima   Department of Electrical and Computer Engineering, Tennessee Tech University, Cookeville, TN, United States

Gedare Bloom   Howard University, Washington, DC, United States

Guihai Chen   Shanghai Jiao Tong University, Shanghai, China

Lei Cui   School of IT, Deakin University, Geelong, Australia

Amardeep Das   C.V. Raman College of Engineering, Bhubaneswar, India

Ronald Doku   Cybersecurity and Wireless Networking Innovation (CWiNs) Lab, Department of Electrical Engineering and Computer Science, Howard University, Washington, DC, United States

Zouina Doukha'   USTHB University, Algiers, Algeria

Neil Eliot   Department of Computer and Information Sciences, Northumbria University, Newcastle Upon Tyne, United Kingdom

Noe Elisa   Department of Computer and Information Sciences, Northumbria University, Newcastle Upon Tyne, United Kingdom

Hossam Faris   Business Information Technology Department, King Abdulla II School for Information Technology, The University of Jordan, Amman, Jordan

Raj Gaire   CSIRO Data61, Canberra, ACT, Australia

Kayhan Zrar Ghafoor   School of Electronic, Information and Electrical Engineering, Shanghai Jiao Tong University, Shanghai, China; Department of Computer Science, Faculty of Science, Cihan University-Erbil, Kurdistan, Iraq

Ratan K. Ghosh   Department of Computer Science and Engineering, Indian Institute of Technology (IIT) Kanpur, Kanpur, India

Surya Gunukula   Department of Electrical and Computer Engineering, Tennessee Tech University, Cookeville, TN, United States

Junqin Huang   Shanghai Jiao Tong University, Shanghai, China

Willaim Johnson   Department of Electrical and Computer Engineering, Tennessee Tech University, Cookeville, TN, United States

Anupam Joshi   University of Maryland Baltimore County, Baltimore, MD, United States

Kush Khanna   Indian Institute of Technology Delhi, New Delhi, India

Jongkil Kim   School of Computing and Information Technology, University of Wollongong, Wollongong, NSW, Australia

Linghe Kong   Shanghai Jiao Tong University, Shanghai, China

Alexander Krumpholz   CSIRO Data61, Canberra, ACT, Australia

Xing Li   Beijing National Research Center for Information Science and Technology, Department of Electronic Engineering, Tsinghua University, Beijing, China

Iman Loumachi   USTHB University, Algiers, Algeria

C. Louw   University of Johannesburg, Johannesburg, South Africa

Mohamed Mahmoud   Department of Electrical and Computer Engineering, Tennessee Tech University, Cookeville, TN, United States

Seyedali Mirjalili   Institute for Integrated and Intelligent Systems, Griffith University, Brisbane, Australia

Deepak Mishra   Department of Electrical Engineering (ISY), Linköping University, Linköping, Sweden

Mahmoud Nabil   Department of Electrical and Computer Engineering, Tennessee Tech University, Cookeville, TN, United States

Sandeep Nair Narayanan   University of Maryland Baltimore County, Baltimore, MD, United States

Surya Nepal   CSIRO Data61, Epping, NSW, Australia

Mohammad Reza Nosouhi   School of IT, Deakin University, Geelong, Australia

Habeeb Olufowobi   Howard University, Washington, DC, United States

Bijaya Ketan Panigrahi   Indian Institute of Technology Delhi, New Delhi, India

Youyang Qu   School of IT, Deakin University, Geelong, Australia

Rajiv Ranjan   School of Computing, Urban Sciences Building, Newcastle University, Newcastle upon Tyne, United Kingdom

Stefan Rass   Institute of Applied Informatics, System Security Group, University of Klagenfurt, Klagenfurt, Austria

Bikram Kesari Ratha   Utkal University, Bhubaneswar, India

Danda B. Rawat   Cybersecurity and Wireless Networking Innovation (CWiNs) Lab, Department of Electrical Engineering and Computer Science, Howard University, Washington, DC, United States

Ali Safa Sadiq   School of Information Technology, Monash University, Bandar Sunway, Malaysia

Ravikant Saini   Department of Electrical Engineering, Indian Institute of Technology Jammu, Jammu, India

Mazleena Salleh   Faculty of Computing, University Technology Malaysia, Skudai, Malaysia

Azadeh Sarkheyli   Department of Informatics, Dalarna University, Falun, Sweden

Elnaz Sarkheyli   Faculty of Art and Architecture, Kharazmi University,Tehran, Iran

Peter Schartner   Institute of Applied Informatics, System Security Group, University of Klagenfurt, Klagenfurt, Austria

Sumanta Chandra Mishra Sharma   C.V. Raman College of Engineering, Bhubaneswar, India

R.K. Shyamasundar   Department of Computer Science and Engineering, Indian Institute of Technology (IIT) Bombay, Mumbai, India

Nicolas Sklavos   SCYTALE Group, Computer Engineering & Informatics Department, University of Patras, Patras, Greece

Sophocles Theodorou   Open University of Cyprus, Nicosia, Cyprus

B. Von Solms   University of Johannesburg, Johannesburg, South Africa

Jing Wang   Beijing National Research Center for Information Science and Technology, Department of Electronic Engineering, Tsinghua University, Beijing, China

Longzhi Yang   Department of Computer and Information Sciences, Northumbria University, Newcastle Upon Tyne, United Kingdom

Shui Yu   School of IT, Deakin University, Geelong, Australia

Xiaofeng Zhong   Department of Electronic Engineering, Tsinghua University, Beijing, China

Quanyan Zhu'   Beijing National Research Center for Information Science and Technology, Department of Electrical and Computer Engineering, New York University, New York, NY, United States

About the Editors

Danda B. Rawat is an Associate Professor in the Department of Electrical Engineering & Computer Science, and Founding Director of the Data Science and Cybersecurity Center (DSC^2) at Howard University, Washington, DC, United Sates. Rawat's research focuses on cybersecurity, machine learning, and wireless networking for emerging networked systems, including cyber-physical systems (energy, transportation, water, UAV), smart cities, software defined systems, and vehicular networks. His professional career comprises more than 10 years in academia, government, and industry. He has secured more than $3 million in research funding from the US National Science Foundation, US Department of Homeland Security, and private foundations. Rawat was the recipient of the NSF Faculty Early Career Development (CAREER) Award in 2016, the US Air Force Research Laboratory (AFRL) Summer Faculty Visiting Fellowship in 2017, the Outstanding Research Faculty Award (Award for Excellence in Scholarly Activity) at GSU in 2015, and the Best Paper Award from BWCCA in 2010. He has delivered more than 10 keynotes and invited speeches at international conferences and workshops. Rawat has published more than 150 scientific/technical articles and 8 books. He has been serving as an Editor/Guest Editor for more than 20 international journals. He has been on organizing committees for several IEEE flagship conferences, such as IEEE INFOCOM 2015–2019, IEEE CNS 2017, IEEE CCNC 2016–2019, ICNC 2017/2018, IEEE AINA 2015/2016, and so on. He served as a technical program committee (TPC) member for several international conferences, including IEEE INFOCOM, IEEE GLOBECOM, IEEE CCNC, IEEE GreenCom, IEEE AINA, IEEE ICC, IEEE WCNC, and IEEE VTC. He served as a Vice Chair of the Executive Committee of the IEEE Savannah Section from 2013 to 2017. He is the Founding Director of the Cyber-security and Wireless Networking Innovations (CWiNs) Research Lab. He received a PhD in Electrical and Computer Engineering (Wireless Networking and Security) from Old Dominion University, Norfolk, Virginia. Rawat is a Senior Member of IEEE and ACM, and a member of ASEE. Rawat is a Fellow of the Institution of Engineering and Technology (IET).

Kayhan Zrar Ghafoor received the BSc degree in Electrical Engineering from Salahaddin University, the MSc degree in Remote Weather Monitoring from Koya University, and a PhD degree in Wireless Networks from University Technology Malaysia in 2003, 2006, and 2011, respectively. He is working as a senior lecturer in the Department of Software Engineering at Salahaddin University-Erbil, Kurdistan Region. He was visiting Shanghai Jiao Tong University, Shanghai, China as a postdoctoral fellow. He has published more than 50 scientific/research papers in prestigious international journals and at conferences. He has served as an editor of several journals and books. He has also served as a workshop general chair for international workshops and conferences, and worked as a TPC member for more than 40 international conferences. He is the recipient of the UTM Chancellor Award 48th UTM convocation in 2012. He was also awarded the UTM International Doctoral Fellowship (IDF) and Kurdistan Regional Government (KRG) scholarship (Ahmad Ismail Foundation). His current research interests include Big Data in VANET and the Smart City, Network Function Virtualization, Cybersecurity, and Vehicular Cloud Computing. He is a member of the IEEE Vehicular Technology Society, IEEE Communications Society, Internet Technical Committee (ITC), and International Association of Engineers (IAENG).

Preface

Over the past few years, we have witnessed a rapid growth in the Internet of Things (IoT) that provides ubiquitous connectivity between physical components and cyberspace. Recent advances in hardware, software, and networking technologies have fueled the deployment of IoT technologies. This advancement has led to smart cities that have also become a promising field of study that encompasses distributed large-scale sensing, data acquisition, information processing, and heterogeneous networking. Smart cities aim to improve the quality of life of citizens in several areas, such as energy usage, healthcare, the environment, water, and transportation. However, smart cities will not only impact the private information of citizens, but will also have a direct effect on city services that are directly related to the daily life of citizens. The connectivity of billions of IoT devices opens many security vulnerabilities and threats that must be deterred, prevented, detected, and mitigated. Thus, it is becoming increasingly important to develop adaptive, robust, scalable, reliable security, and privacy mechanisms in smart city applications. The security mechanisms are required to mitigate negative implications associated with cyberattacks and privacy issues in the smart city.

This book aims to provide the latest research developments and results in the areas of security and privacy for smart cities. It presents insights into networking and security-related architectures, designs, and models for smart city applications that will ultimately enable the secure operation of smart cities. This book is expected to be a valuable resource for students, researchers, engineers, and policy makers who are working in various areas related to cybersecurity and privacy for smart cities.

This book includes chapters entitled "New Era of Smart Cities, from the Perspective of the Internet of Things," "Community-Based Security for the Internet of Things," "Blockchain-Based Security and Privacy in Smart Cities," "Privacy-aware Physical Layer Security Techniques for Smart Cities," "Crowdsensing and Privacy in Smart City Applications," "Privacy Preservation in Smart Cities," "Privacy and Security Aspects of E-government in Smart Cities," "Big Data-enabled Cybersecurity for Smart City Applications," "Free Public Wi-Fi Security in a Smart City Context—an End User Perspective," "Techniques for Privacy-preserving Data Publication in the Cloud," "Security in Smart Cyber-Physical Systems: A Case Study on Smart Grids and Smart Cars," "Priority-based and Privacy-preserving Electric Vehicle Dynamic Charging System with Divisible E-Payment," "Secure IoT Structural Design for Smart Homes," "Outlier Discrimination and Correction in Intelligent Transportation Systems," "Secure Data Dissemination for Smart Transportation Systems," "Connected Cars: Automotive Cybersecurity and Privacy for Smart Cities," "Fraud Detection Model Based on Multi-Verse Features Extraction Approach for Smart City Applications," "Privacy-preserving Date Utility Mining Architecture," and "Evaluation of Mega Projects' Effects in Smart Cities Using a Sustainable Development Approach."

This book provides state-of-the-art of research results, current issues, challenges, solutions, and recent trends related to cybersecurity and privacy for smart cities. We expect this book to be of significant importance, not only to researchers and practitioners in academia, government agencies and industries, but also for policy makers and system managers. We anticipate this book to be a valuable resource for all those working in this new and exciting area, and a "must have" for all university libraries.

Danda B. Rawat
Howard University, Washington, DC, United States

Kayhan Zrar Ghafoor
Shanghai Jiao Tong University, Shanghai, China
Department of Computer Science, Faculty of Science, Cihan University-Erbil, Kurdistan, Iraq

Acknowledgements

This book would not have been published without the contribution of several people. First and foremost, we would like to express our warm appreciation to the authors who worked hard to contribute the chapters, who have chosen this book as a platform to publish their research findings. Special thanks go to the contributors' universities and organizations who allowed them valuable time and resources toward the effort of writing the chapters. We would also like to express our warm appreciation to the reviewers who gave their valuable time to review chapters, and helped select these high-quality chapters.

Finally, we want to thank our families who supported and encouraged us in spite of all the time it took us away from them. Last and not least: we beg forgiveness of all whose names we have failed to mention.

Danda B. Rawat
Howard University, Washington, DC, United States

Kayhan Zrar Ghafoor
Shanghai Jiao Tong University, Shanghai, China
Department of Computer Science, Faculty of Science, Cihan University-Erbil, Kurdistan, Iraq

1

The New Era of Smart Cities, From the Perspective of the Internet of Things

Amardeep Das, Sumanta Chandra Mishra Sharma*, and
Bikram Kesari Ratha†*

*C.V. Raman College of Engineering, Bhubaneswar, India
†Utkal University, Bhubaneswar, India

1 INTRODUCTION

It is difficult to find the proper meaning of "smart" from the perspective of information and communication technology (ICT). This term is trendy in the global market, and is considered anything that is new and intelligent. The term "smart" has lots of synonyms, including acute, clever, astute, perspicacious, and so forth. However, when smart is associated with devices, it means efficient and knowledgeable. The word "smart" refers to thoughts that offer intelligent insights, but nowadays it has been adopted in developing cities with smart tools. With the application of smart technology, an overall growth has been seen in population, economy, and the efficiency of city life.

Similar to "smart," it is tough to find a unique definition for the term "city." It depends on the experience and considerations of individuals to specify a meaning and identify the properties that a locality should satisfy to become a city. In general, a city is a well-thought-out urban area where the population density depends upon the geographical region or countries to which it belongs. As per the UN world urbanization report, it is expected that around 67% of the world's population will be in urban areas in 2050. When the populations exceed 1.5 million, the cities will be considered megacities.

There are some global or international cities that influence and invite peoples from outside the nation, or even from all over the world. Most of the time, these cities compete with each other for resources [2]. An alternative analytic explanation says that the "city is an urban community falling under a specific administrative boundary" [3, 4].

Apart from their size and importance, cities can also be classified as new and existing, based on their urban growth and establishment. New cities come into existence to satisfy economic growth of the country. Some researchers suggested that a city is a complex system that includes physical (building, bridges, etc.) and social (people, institutions, etc.) components for society's development [5]. Some researchers described the physical component as a hard component, and the social component as a soft component of development [2, 6].

If we want to find the meaning of "smart city," then we can say that it is the combination of "smart" and "city." It can be represented as an urban area that uses smart systems to make day-to-day life easier. Here, smartness of the city defines the capability to combine all its resources, to successfully and flawlessly attain the goals, and achieve the purposes that have been set before [4]. However, if somebody looks for a perfect definition for smart city, he or she will fail to find it, and instead, will find many substitutes that result in an uncertain meaning.

2 EVOLUTION OF THE SMART CITY

The phrase "smart city" was coined in the early 1990s to illustrate the use of technology and innovation in urban development [1]. More precisely, it can be stated that in the 1990s, researchers examined cities and their ongoing IT

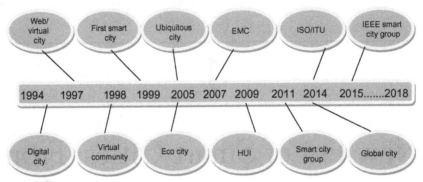

FIG. 1   Smart city evolution timeline.

projects from different viewpoints, and using slightly different terms, described IT and communication-based project initiation in urban spaces (Fig. 1).

The smart city evolved into a digital city in 1994 in Amsterdam. In 1997, it was claimed that there were 2000 virtual urban areas in the world [7]. These virtual cities introduced a local ICT network, which permitted the growth of local cyber-based (virtual) communities. These virtual urban areas were treated as electronic and web-based representations of the real urban areas, and were housed with the help of the world wide web (WWW).

Virtual cities were treated as the first effort to make use of the Internet to support native democracy, and allowed urban promotion, Internet-based municipal operation, and social development within cities. However, a deficiency of citizen feedback was documented.

After the introduction of the virtual city, the virtual community came into existence in 1998 [8]. The virtual community enables communication between individuals through shared norms. This virtual community network had a narrow scope of digitalization, because it was associated with a community. People outside the community had no direct access to the community network.

The facts discussed herein show that virtual and digital cities intended to form communities using ICT to socialize residents, to digitalize local government policy, and to make use of virtual space to remove the barrier of public space. By this perspective, the Internet, in collaboration with the city system and the WWW, was used to build up city websites that present substitute smart services, including information rescue, and official and general communication. These two smart city approaches pretend the metropolitan spaces are either a connected communities, or two/three dimensional virtual spaces.

In 1999, the first smart city concept was considered in Dubai [9]. Another well-known digital city system was Kyoto [10], which was developed in 1998, and resulted in 2D and 3D spaces, where inhabitant communications were collected with sensors, and their behavior was animated.

The digital city model became identical to an information city, which was understood as a metropolitan location where the ICT is the key driver to deliver innovative online services [11]. The idea of an information city later evolved into the ubiquitous city, where data is available through implanted urban communications [12]. The intelligent city focuses on the city performance, which depends on innovation in the following areas (i) intelligence, creativity, and originality; (ii) communal intelligence; and (iii) artificial intelligence [11].

The preceding smart city types evolved progressively into a more complicated environment, which was able to present more services and enable scientific embeddedness. Anttiroiko et al. [13] explain scientific embeddedness as the capability of technology to embed itself into social systems in order to attain a smart service delivery. The level of embeddedness ranges from simple information delivery to intelligent system implementation, then from implementations to systems that deal with social and human concerns, and to ecological systems that deal with sustainability [13]. In comparison, the city ecosystems are generally defined as communities of interacting organisms and their environments, and are typically described as complex networks formed because of resource interdependencies [14].

An ecosystem can be seen as "an interdependent social system of actors, organizations, material infrastructures, and symbolic resources" [15]. In this respect, ecosystems, like other kinds of systems, are comprised of elements, interconnections, and a function/purpose; but are special types of systems, in that their elements are intelligent, autonomous, adaptive agents that often form communities, and also because of the way they adapt to elements being added or removed. According to this definition, four critical elements exist in ecosystems: (1) interaction/engagement; (2) balance; (3) loosely coupled actors with shared goals; and, (4) self-organization [14].

Today, almost all cities claim to be more or less smart with an underlying self-congratulatory tendency [16], obviously with regard to a different level of technology embedded, or due to the existing intelligent capacity that a city holds.

The era of the smart city deals with huge storage and processing issues. To get such storage, processing, and data availability, the smart architecture needs the help of cloud computing. Researchers have proposed different methods to distribute the work load of a cloud milieu [17]. Researchers also suggested some smart methods [18] that help build the smart city.

2.1 Components of a Smart City

The smart city has a collection of smart components. These components help to solve the problems in an intelligent way, and also provide facilities to its users to build a smart society. Fig. 2 shows how the components are interrelated, and the impact of data and communications in building the smart city. Following are the smart components:

- *Smart Infrastructure*: This includes the use of sensors and smart grid technologies to facilitate smart infrastructure, such as water and energy networks, streets, buildings, and so forth.
- *Smart Transportation (or Smart Mobility)*: This includes transportation networks with improved, embedded real time monitoring and control systems.
- *Smart Environment*: This component provides a smart innovation and ICT to incorporate natural resource protection and supervision, such as a waste product management system, sensor based pollution control, and so on.
- *Smart Services*: Smart services utilize the technology and ICT for health, education, tourism, safety, and so forth.
- *Smart Governance*: This component introduces smart government in the urban space, associated with technology for service delivery and resource utilization with respect to government policy.
- *Smart People*: This component deals with creativity and innovation introduced by individuals in the society.
- *Smart Living*: This refers to the advancements that improve lifestyles and quality of life in the urban area.
- *Smart Economy*: This is the technology and innovation that escalate business growth, employment, and urban growth.

The preceding components are interconnected to provide smart services to people of the city. Apart from that, smart government systems help to successfully execute smart city missions.

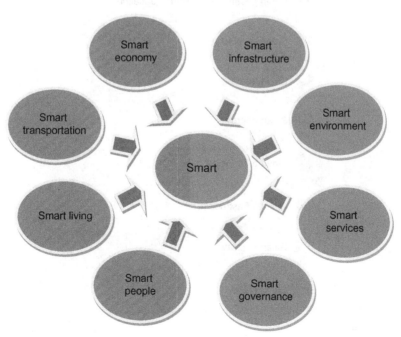

FIG. 2   Components of a smart city.

3 SMART CITY AN URBAN DEVELOPMENT

The World Foundation for Smart Communities encouraged the use of information technology in smart cities to meet the challenges in a global economy. However, the recent attention in smart cities can be recognized to the strong concern for sustainability and rise of new Internet technologies, such as mobile technologies, the semantic web, cloud computing, and the Internet of Things (IoT) for improving real world user interfaces.

The theory of smart cities has been seen from the viewpoint of technologies and components that have some specific properties within the digital and intelligent cities literature. It focuses on the most recent developments in mobile and persistent computing, and agent technologies, as they become embedded into the physical spaces of cities. The emphasis on smart embedded devices represents a distinctive characteristic of smart cities compared with intelligent cities, which create territorial innovation systems combining knowledge-intensive activities, institutions for cooperation and learning, and web-based applications of collective intelligence. The most critical challenge of the smart city environment is to address the troubles and improvement priority of cities within a global and innovation-led world. The first task that cities must address in becoming smart is to create a rich environment of broadband networks that support digital applications.

This includes: (1) the development of broadband infrastructure combining cable, optical fiber, and wireless networks, offering high connectivity and bandwidth to citizens and organizations located in the city, (2) the enrichment of the physical space and infrastructures of cities with embedded systems, smart devices, sensors, and actuators, offering real-time data management, alerts, and information processing, and (3) the creation of applications enabling data collection and processing, web-based collaboration, and actualization of the collective intelligence of citizens.

The latest developments in cloud computing and the emerging the Internet of Things, open data, semantic web, and future media technologies have much to offer. These technologies can assure economies of scale in infrastructure, standardization of applications, and turn-key solutions for software as a service, which dramatically decrease the development costs while accelerating the learning curve for operating smart cities.

The second task consists of initiating large-scale participatory innovation processes for the creation of applications that will run and improve every sector of activity, city cluster, and infrastructure. All city economic activities and utilities can be seen as innovation ecosystems in which citizens and organizations participate in the development, supply, and consumption of goods and services. Fig. 3 presents three application areas of smart cities in the fields of economy, infrastructure, and governance.

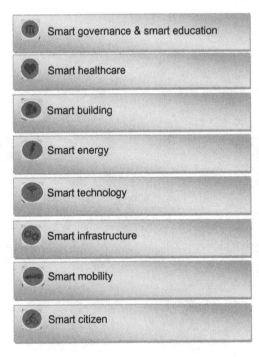

FIG. 3   Application areas of smart cities.

4 SMART CITY ARCHITECTURE

The term "architecture" describes several technological aspects, which range from information structure to technology delivery, or, ICT. However, the most familiar use for the term concerns the formulation of physical structures such as systems or buildings. In this respect, architecture concerns a definition of the structure, relationships, views, assumptions, and rationale of a system.

Following up on the preceding definition, an ICT system also has an architecture, which offers the following features:

- It is used to define a single "system."
- It describes the functional aspects of the system.
- It concentrates on describing the structure of the system.
- It describes both the intra-system and inter-system relationships.
- It defines guidelines, policies, and principles that govern the system's design, development, and evolution over time.

The smart city architecture definition consists of the following components:

- Smart city meta-architecture
- Smart city multilayer communication architecture
- Smart city modular architecture

The smart city multi-tier, meta-architecture consists of the following Fig. 4 layers:

Layer 1—Natural Environment: This includes all the environmental features where the city is located.
Layer 2—Hard Infrastructure (Non ICT-based): This includes all the urban facilities (e.g., buildings, roads, bridges, energy-water-waste-heat utilities, etc.).
Layer 3—Hard Infrastructure (ICT-based): This concerns all hardware with which smart services are being produced and delivered to the end-users (e.g., datacenters, telecommunication networks, IoT, sensors, etc.).
Layer 4—Smart Services: These are the smart services that are being offered via both the hard and soft infrastructure (e.g., smart safety, intelligent transportation, smart government, smart water management, etc.).
Layer 5—Soft Infrastructure: This includes individuals and groups of people living in the city, business processes, software applications and data with which the smart services are executed and being realized.

The communications view of the architecture is also multi-tiered, and consists of the following Fig. 5 layers:

- *Sensing Layer*: This layer consists of the terminal node and capillary network. Terminals (sensors, transducers, actuators, cameras, RFID readers, barcode symbols, GPS trackers, etc.) sense the physical world. They provide the superior "environment-detecting" ability and intelligence for monitoring and controlling the physical infrastructure within the city. The capillary network (including SCADA, sensor networks, HART, WPAN, video surveillance, RFID, GPS-related networks, etc.) connects various terminals to network layers, providing ubiquitous and omnipotent information and data.
- *Network Layer*: indicates facilities that are being provided by telecommunication operators, as well as other metropolitan networks provided by city stakeholders and/or enterprise private communication networks. It is the

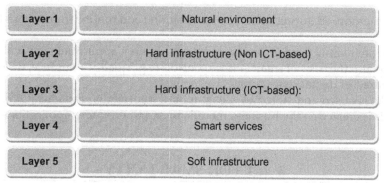

FIG. 4 Meta architecture of a smart city.

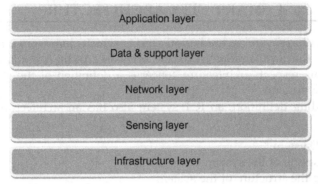

FIG. 5   Smart city multilayer communication architecture.

"Infobahn," the network layer data and support layer: The data and support layer makes the city "smarter," its main purpose is to ensure support capabilities of various city-level applications and services. The data and support layer contains data centers from industries, departments, and enterprises, as well as the municipal dynamic data center and data warehouse, among others, established for the realization of data processes and application support.

- *Application Layer*: The application layer includes various applications that enable smart city management and deliver smart services.
- *Operation, Administration, Maintenance and Provisioning, and Security (OAM & P & security) Framework*: This layer ensures operation, administration, maintenance and provisioning, and security function for the ICT systems.

The third type of architecture, also known as "modular architecture," consists of the following modules:

- *Smart City Networking Infrastructure and Communications Protocol*: This module addresses the necessary network infrastructure (telecommunications networks and IoT) to deploy smart services and enhance living inside the city.
- *Applications*: This concerns all the smart applications that are available inside the smart city ecosystem. These applications could be classified in the 6 smart city components (people, mobility, government, economy, environment, and living).
- *Business*: This refers to all business groups, which are available inside the smart city ecosystem, and use smart applications. This particular module deals with the following information management issues:
  - User information for consumer behavior recognition.
  - Business intelligence for statistical and feasibility studies.
- *Management*: This module contains all rules and procedures for managing a smart city. The primary elements of this module concern:
  - *Information management*: information collection and dissemination across the smart city.
  - *Process management*: ICT management from a business transaction perspective.
  - *People management*: human and workflow management in terms of a sequence of operations within the city, such as a single organization and visualization.
- *Data*: Data is crucial in smart cities, and can be either used or produced, while they can be stored centrally or in a distributed manner (locally). It is analyzed in the following components:
  - *People data*: This is individual information, which is produced by inhabitants and mostly preserved with privacy issues.
  - *Process data*: This is produced during smart service execution and routine transactions between machines and/ or people.
  - *Documents*: These are mainly used or produced by government applications, or within the business sectors. Documents can be also the basis of smart service controls (e.g., quality assurance, disaster recovery plans, etc.) and can be organized in digital repositories.
  - *Geospatial*: This data is used and stored by Geographical Information Systems (GIS).
  - *Business data*: This is created in the business module by smart economy applications.

5 IoT FOR SMART CITY

The Internet of Things (IoT) is the network of devices that are connected together and communicate with each other to perform certain tasks, without requiring human-to-human or human-to-computer interaction. The Internet of

Things is about installing sensors (RFID, IR, GPS, laser scanners, etc.) for everything, and connecting them to the Internet through specific protocols for information exchange and communications, in order to achieve intelligent recognition, location, tracking, monitoring, and management. With the technical support from IoT, a smart city needs to be instrumented, interconnected, and intelligent.

The Internet of Things examples extend from smart connected homes, to wearables, to healthcare. It is not wrong to suggest that IoT is now becoming part of every aspect of our lives. Not only are the Internet of Things applications enhancing the comforts of our lives, but also they are giving us more control by simplifying routine work life and personal tasks.

The recent hype about the future prospects of the IoT has forced companies to take the initiative of coming up with basic building blocks of the Internet of Things, that is, hardware, software, and support to enable developers to deploy applications that can connect anything within the scope of the Internet of Things. Following are the different application areas where the IoT works:

- Smart homes
- Connected cars
- Wearables
- Industrial Internet
- Smart cities
- IoT in agriculture
- Smart retail
- Energy engagement
- IoT in healthcare
- IoT in poultry and farming

6 CYBER SECURITY AND PRIVACY IN SMART CITIES

All together, the smart-city market is expected to exceed $1.7 trillion in the next 20 years. But the interconnectivity across the virtual and physical infrastructure that makes a smart city work also creates new and substantial cyber security risks. With each additional access point, sensitive data exposure vulnerabilities expand. Smart cities can be susceptible to numerous cyberattack techniques, such as remote execution and signal jamming, as well as traditional means, including malware, data manipulation, and DDoS. To overcome these risks, a critical infrastructure needs to be designed that involves all parties (from individual citizens to large public and private institutions).

Security is a global idea tied to safety (life, property, and rights) as an assurance that a person may go about their life without injury.

Cyber security is a subset of security that focuses on the computing systems, data exchange channels, and the information they process. Information security is interlaced with cyber security, with the focus being on information processed. Cyber security is a critical issue due to the increasing potential of cyberattacks and incidents against critical sectors in smart cities. When we think about cyberthreats in smart cities, we come across data and system threats. The data threats include personally identifiable information (PII) being put at risk, natural disasters, and malicious activities and DDoS attacks.

To overcome these cyber risks, we need to develop a clear structure for risk assessment and management. The following actions should be taken to help reduce cyber risk in a smart city:

- Use threat modeling to assess threats.
- Document and review risk acceptance and exceptions.
- Make risk assessment and management an ongoing process.
- Educate city leaders to understand and support the principles, and to manage priorities.
- Consider resilience.
- Leverage procurement processes to reflect priorities and risks.
- Establish minimum security baselines.
- Define clear responsibilities for supporting a security baseline.
- Establish a system for continuous security monitoring.
- Set expectations for sharing threat and vulnerability information.
- Create a cross-city mechanism for sharing.
- Run cyber drills to test game plans.
- Emphasize privacy and civil liberty protections in threat information sharing.

- Apply relevant national or international standards for information sharing.
- Create a Computer Emergency Response Team (CERT).
- Create clear ownership.
- Engage private sector and national resources.
- Enable consistent incident classification.
- Test incident response capabilities and processes.
- Develop public awareness campaigns.
- Cultivate employee development and workforce training programs.

7 FUTURE OF THE SMART CITY WITH RESPECT TO THE IoT

The Internet of Things (IoT) carries the potential to transform communities around the world into "smart cities," creating a new era of urban living. The benefits include increased safety, reduced traffic, lower levels of pollution, more efficient use of energy, and a better overall quality of life for future city dwellers.

Smart cities of the future will allow IoT systems to revolutionize the way we live and conduct business, with sensors attached to virtually every vehicle, device, or piece of equipment that a city uses on a daily basis. The possibilities are almost endless, as IoT produces invaluable data for a multitude of business intelligence systems, such as emergency services, crime prevention, parking management, and much, much more. And according to Smart America, city governments will invest more than $41 trillion over the next two decades to upgrade their infrastructures to benefit from the IoT. Here are some of the initiatives taking place in smart cities today:

- Smart roads to optimize and adapt to changing traffic patterns.
- Smart buildings to optimize energy, lighting, and resources.
- Smart lighting with adaptive street lights.
- Smart waste management to monitor and optimize collection.
- Smart grids to manage energy consumption with monitoring and allocation for dynamic conditions.

8 CONCLUSION

There are a lot of benefits of smart cities that can make citizens' daily lives more comfortable and convenient. The Smart Cities Mission is a bold new worldwide initiative to drive economic growth and improve the quality of life of people by enabling local development and harnessing technology as a means to create smart outcomes for citizens.

References

[1] D.V. Gibson, G. Kozmetsky, R.W. Smilor (Eds.), The Technopolis Phenomenon: Smart Cities, Fast Systems, Global Networks, Rowman& Littlefield, New York, 1992.
[2] M. Angelidou, Smart city policies: a spatial approach, Cities 41 (2014) S3–S11.
[3] International Standards Organization (ISO), ISO 37120:2014: Sustainable development of scommunities—indicators for city services and quality of life, 2014.
[4] International Standards Organization (ISO), Smart Cities Preliminary Report 2014, 2014.
[5] K.C. Desouza, T.H. Flanery, Designing, planning, and managing resilient cities: a conceptual framework, Cities 35 (2013) 88–89.
[6] P. Neirotti, A. De Marco, A.C. Cagliano, G. Mangano, Current trends in smart city initiatives: some stylised facts, Cities 38 (2014) 25–36.
[7] S. Graham, A. Aurigi, Urbanising cyberspace? City 2 (7) (1997) 18–39.
[8] P. van den Besselaar, D. Beckers, Demographics and sociographics of the digital city, in: T. Ishida (Ed.), Community Computing & Support Systems, Lecture Notes in Computer Science (LNCS), vol. 1519, Springer-Verlag, Berlin, Heidelberg, 1998, , pp. 108–124.
[9] L.G. Anthopoulos, The rise of the smart city, in: Understanding Smart Cities: A Tool for Smart Government or an Industrial Trick? Public Administration and Information Technology, vol. 22, Springer, Cham, 2017.
[10] T. Ishida, In: Digital city, smart city and beyond, The Proceedings of the 26th World Wide Web International Conference (WWW17), Perth, Australia, 2017.
[11] J.H. Lee, M.G. Hancock, M.-C. Hu, Towards an effective framework for building smart cities: lessons from Seoul and San Francisco, Technol. Forecast. Soc. Change 89 (2014) 80–99.
[12] L. Anthopoulos, P. Fitsilis, Smart cities and their roles in city competition: a classification, Int. J. Electron. Gov. Res. (IJEGR) 10 (1) (2014) 67–81.
[13] A.-V. Anttiroiko, P. Valkama, S.J. Bailey, Smart cities in the new service economy: building platforms for smart services, Artif. Intell. Soc. 29 (2014) 323–334.
[14] U. Gretzel, H. Werthner, C. Koo, C. Lamsfus, Conceptual foundations for understanding smart tourism ecosystems, Comput. Hum. Behav. 50 (2015) 558–563.

[15] D. Maheshwari, M. Janssen, Reconceptualizing measuring, benchmarking for improving interoperability in smart ecosystems: the effect of ubiquitous data and crowdsourcing, Gov. Inf. Q. 31 (2014) S84–S92.

[16] R. Hollands, Will the real smart city stand up? Creative, progressive, or just entrepreneurial? City 12 (3) (2008) 302–320.

[17] S.C. Mishra Sharma, A.K. Rath, Multi-rumen anti-grazing approach of load balancing in cloud network, Int. J. Inf. Technol. 9 (2017) 129–138, https://doi.org/10.1007/s41870-017-0022-y.

[18] A. Das, P.K. Dash, B.K. Mishra, An intelligent parking system in smart cities using IoT, in: Exploring the Convergence of Big Data and the Internet of Things, IGI Global, Hershey, PA, 2018, pp. 155–180.

2

Community-Based Security for the Internet of Things

Quanyan Zhu'*, Stefan Rass[†], and Peter Schartner[†]
*Department of Electrical and Computer Engineering, New York University, New York, NY, United States
[†]Institute of Applied Informatics, System Security Group, University of Klagenfurt, Klagenfurt, Austria

1 INTRODUCTION

The potential of services offered by the future Internet of Things (IoT) is accompanied by an equally strong growing potential of new threats. The IoT induces the trend of turning special-purpose devices such as TVs, radios, and so forth into universal platforms able to execute arbitrary pieces of software, with strong communication abilities. This new power makes them vulnerable to the same types of malware that were previously only seen in classical computer networks. One of them is ransomware, which, although dating back to the 1980s, is seeing a revival, and is a major pillar of the cybercrime ecosystem today [1]. Ransomware is typically a weapon against the masses, with the goal of pressing money. Advanced persistent threats are the opposite, being highly targeted attacks against specific victims, and typically not about monetary gain, but to demonstrate power and to cause maximal damage. The common denominator of both extremes, and most that live between these two, is their focus on the weakest element, which is typically the human. Nature itself teaches that flocks (in general communities) have much higher chances to survive than any of their individuals would have on their own. Why not adopt and systematize this well-proven behavior in security and the IoT? Awareness of humans is a notoriously volatile state because the press and media have an undoubted power in sensitizing people to a topic, but this regards every topic on which news is reported. So, more recent news tends to supersede older news, and hence, awareness about threats is continuously fading away due to the mass of information that people are confronted with every day.

In that sense, the IoT and, more generally, the information society itself, creates one of the biggest dangers, by constantly overloading individuals with information, so that recognizing the real danger, when it occurs, is harder than ever to detect. Can we find a way out of this? There is surely no easy answer, and societal changes toward better awareness should be expected to solve the problem in the near future. But human communities are not the only ones that we can create, and the IoT, which basically is a community, offers much more controllable dynamics than any human society.

Speaking more concretely, let us look at a documented case of ransomware having locked a TV screen [2]. The issue was apparently due to the installation of a mysterious app. More critically, viruses are usually able to jump between different devices, partly also due to the strong prevalence of only a few platforms. For example, Android is running on tablets, mobile phones, eBook readers, TVs, and many others. So, there is no technical barrier for a virulent app to pass from one device to the other. The links are exactly what IoT provides, so the world is open to any number of viruses to be fruitful and multiply and infect the world. Indeed, why not turn IoT devices themselves into a community in which individuals (devices) mutually inform each other about threats and countermeasures, and securely share apps? Because trust of humans in technology seems to be high already, why not let the awareness be up to the devices, rather than the people? Fig. 1 sketches the vision on this smart community living in the IoT.

With apps obtainable from various sources, only one of which is the trusted official app store, drive-by downloads have become a common way of injecting malware on mobile platforms, and perhaps also the future IoT. In a drive-by download attack, the adversary obtains a legitimate copy of an app installation file (on Android, this would be an

FIG. 1   Turning the IoT into a smart community.

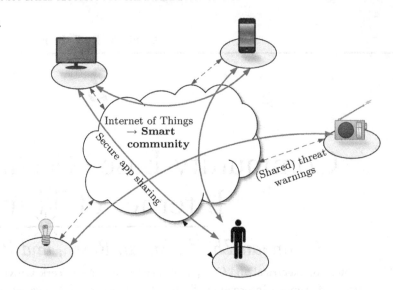

apk-file), unpacks it (as it is basically a compressed archive), adds the malware, and repacks everything back into the harmless looking app installation file. The unaware victim obtains the apk-file from some source and installs the app, but also the malware that unknowingly ships with it. Official key stores run by platform vendors (such as Google, Apple, etc.) perform lots of screenings and security checks, and a drive-by download is most unlikely for these sources. Still, one attack vector on IoT and mobile platforms is to disconnect the user from the official app store (say, by redirecting or blocking the connection somehow), to force the user to look for alternative sources. There are usually many of them, but not all are equally trustworthy.

More specifically, mobile platforms can be used with mobile device management systems that let anyone (primarily enterprises) run their own app stores, so why not turn the community itself into a trusted app store for itself? While app stores enjoy the luxury of cryptographic security (digital signatures to verify the originality of the app), those cryptographic security precautions are not easily established inside a loose community that cannot perform a proper and decent key management.

Fortunately, there may not even be a strong need for a full-fledged public key infrastructure to endow an IoT user community with the cryptographic assurance of mutual authentication, and hence trustworthiness, in the shared apps! Indeed, past research has come up with proposals on how to use keys shared only with friends (or more generally, the local neighborhood), to establish end-to-end authentication (and security) even with strangers with which no public key data is shared. The community, in turn, should be formed so that everyone in it has an incentive to contribute, that is, actively communicate potential threat discoveries, and actively serve as a trusted source of data, software, and information for others. The challenge herein is building the community in the proper way to achieve (cryptographic) security for everyone. This creates two problems; one of community formation, and the other related to security establishment. The community can be formed based on incentives so that it is the best option for everyone in the community to contribute to it. Suitable mechanisms to this end can be constructed from game theory, as we will discuss later in this chapter.

2 STATE OF THE ART ON APP SECURITY

Taking mobile platforms as templates as to how IoT devices may look in the future, the security of mobile devices rests on four main pillars:

1. Screening of apps at app stores: Before an app goes online for download, most app stores scan for malicious code or patterns (similar to what a virus scanner would do).
2. Access restrictions and permissions by the operating systems: When an app is installed, usually the required access privileges are displayed so that the user can explicitly consent. An informed decision hereby judges the combination of permissions and apps rather than each one individually, because the sum of permissions is typically much more powerful (dangerous) than each permission is on its own. At this point, care is up to the user

(e.g., in becoming suspicious if a torchlight app asks for network access; even if this app has no network access rights, it could share sensitive information via the clipboard with a "befriended" app from the same vendor that can send away the data). Newer versions of Android, for example, also allow such rights to be revoked, even after installation.

3. App sandboxing: The mobile device prevents apps from mutually accessing each other's memory space or the process itself. Still, there are several possibilities to let apps talk to each other and exchange data, which can be exploited maliciously (similar to how the heartbleed exploit worked for SSL).

4. User awareness: The checks done at the app stores and everything that the operating system does hinge on the user acting carefully. This care includes an original (especially not jailbroken) copy of the platform, as well as a careful decision on which app to install. If the app's purpose is inconsistent with the privileges that it requires, then this is an indication of potential danger.

The last pillar is where the community can help the most: it is not always obvious why an app should not need some privilege, and some paid apps may have free-of-charge siblings that are simply unofficial and may thus not be found in an official app store. In both cases, community knowledge can aid and guide the user. For example, if an app is reported (to the community) as asking for strange privileges, then a warning could be issued to a new user. Likewise, untrusted sources can be replaced by the community acting as a team, thus making it more difficult for the adversary to spread its malicious content.

Using opinions is already standard in app stores, where apps get user ratings to help others find the best app for their needs. Establishing a similar system for security appears as a natural next step, and can be achieved using simple means. In fact, the cryptographic assurance that users get when retrieving an app over official channels can, in a similar way, be provided by (and to) the whole user community, by proper incentive and authentication mechanisms; the former resting on game theory, the latter rooted in cryptography. Hereafter, we will thus look at ways to safely distribute apps with cryptographic assurance.

3 COMMUNITY-BASED SECURITY

The basic goal to accomplish for an attacker is tricking an unaware user into installing an app from a distrusted source. While app stores can easily certify the genuineness of their items by public key cryptography (digital signatures), not all software is obtained from these stores, and certificate management is typically a challenge of its own (despite rich and useful theory behind it).

Usually, communities rely on one or more authorities for the authentic distribution of software and threat information (warning) communication. Why not have the community do that job collaboratively? The conventional approach to authentication via public key cryptography would require a fully pervasive public key management in all devices. While this is certainly possible, the cryptographic operations are expensive (maybe too expensive for some IoT devices) and the variety of vendors will probably render the entire architecture quite complex. Symmetric cryptography, on the other hand, is lightweight and can be used for authentication based on keys that need to be established only in the local neighborhood of a device. This simplifies matters and takes out at least one of the central authorities toward a more decentralized approach.

Also, the method of sharing threat notifications and patches can be determined by the community, potentially by centralized news distribution mechanisms. Essentially, the community can engage in multipeer credibility checking toward an early warning system about drive-by downloads.

3.1 Multipeer Credibility Checking

A drive-by download occurs if an installation package is modified by an attacker to contain malicious code in addition to the actual (legitimate) app code. Adding the malware is the simple part, the tricky bit is getting someone else to download the now malicious app. One way of enforcing this is disconnecting people from the app store (temporarily), to enforce the search for alternate sources for an app.

Assume that an app has been originally distributed from a trusted source in the first place, which is—in any case— the app store (hence, its role is equally crucial in a community-based security approach, as it acts as the initial point of trust before the decentralized security can come into play). Once the app—in its legitimate form—has reached some outspread, suppose a user wants to install it from a given installation package. The open source domain offers a simple and effective security precaution in the form of fingerprints: usually, an installation package is accompanied by several

FIG. 2   Multipeer credibility checking.

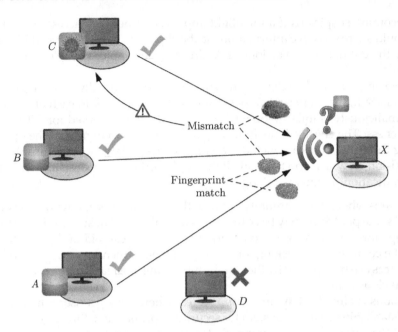

mirrors and a (cryptographic) hash-sum (often, MD5 or SHA-1). The genuineness of the downloaded file can be checked by verifying the checksum on the website. For this to work, the checksum and installation package should come from different sources, so that the confidence in the verification can be based on the unlikely event of the attacker having conquered both the data and the checksum host(s) at the same time.

Some software systems (such as the statistical software R or the package manager Chocolatey) by default do such a verification, which is no more expensive than one hash-and-compare operation. IoT devices will not have much difficulty in offering the necessary computational power to achieve security by the same technique, by relying on the community.

Fig. 2 gives an example of this process, where a user X seeks to install some app on a smart TV. To get the installation package, it issues a callout asking for others who have installed the app on their (similar) devices. Suppose devices A, B, and C have the app, while device D sees the request, but must remain silent because the app is not available on this device. The peers A, B, and C, however, respond by sending back a fingerprint (hash checksum) of their locally installed apps. Among the three incoming fingerprints, those from B and C match, while that of A is different. This is already an indication that either B and C, or A, must have some malicious version of the app installed. Going with a majority vote (based on the hypothesis that fewer infections are more likely than a pandemic outbreak of the malware), the user would thus request the app from either B or C (making a random choice), and inform A about its suspicion to have malware there. In this way, A is informed, and can, upon the next possibility, retrieve either a clean version of the app from the store, or communicate this fingerprint to others to check their own copies of the app (similar to a signature-based virus scan). Similar techniques are also deployed for public key management, such as for trust management in PGP and GPG [3, 4].

Once the user has found a source to get the app from, it must authentically retrieve it. This can be done by multipath authentication [5].

3.2 Incentive-Based Community Formation

It is apparent that the credibility checking proposed relies on community building, because IoT peers need to establish a trusted neighborhood to ask for credibility, and also to help with the authentication if software will be deployed. Mechanisms to form these trust clusters can be understood using agent-based models and game-theoretic tools. The formation of the community is dynamic and arises from a network formation process or a cooperative game. The formation of a trustworthy IoT community plays an essential role in enabling the collaboration among devices. The community formation is naturally a dynamic problem in which nodes can join and depart the network and form communities of their interest. This process can be modeled using a network formation process in which each node is characterized by its type, preferences, trust, and utility. The type of the nodes refers to the functionalities, the age, and the version of the devices. Devices of the same type often benefit more from the collaboration. However, devices of different types can also learn about emerging cyber threats and protection mechanisms from devices of similar types. Each device has a preference over the devices that it wants to communicate with. The preferences are dependent on the trustworthiness of the information received from other nodes and the utility of the collaboration. Based on the preferences, each node can choose a subset of existing nodes to initiate a request of connections, and a link is formed between two nodes if the request is accepted. The acceptance of a request can be determined by a node through a cost-and-benefit evaluation; that is, a node can determine the collaboration devices through its own preferences. This request-and-approval process is implemented at each node at every stage. As a result, a large-scale network is formed in a distributed fashion. As the parameters of the system change, nodes can terminate their collaboration with other nodes and establish new collaborations over time. In addition, new nodes will join the network, and the existing nodes can leave the system. Hence, the networks formed are highly dynamic. The emergence of the community of the dynamic network indicates the formation of the collaboration community. One important phenomenon that we observe is the homophily, in which nodes of the same types often form a community and share information together. Game-theoretic methods can be used to form an agent-based model to predict the structure of the network and the emergence of the communities by analyzing the Nash equilibrium of the game.

Incentive mechanism design is an important tool to create incentives in the network so that nodes actively share information with other nodes trustfully, and untrustworthy devices or free riders will be isolated and disconnected from the network. In the recent work of [6], mechanism design tools enable the system to reach a desirable and unique Nash equilibrium that allows devices to communicate in a conducive environment in which nodes endeavor to contribute knowledge and resources to assist connected nodes in the community. Any selfish or free-riding behavior will receive a tit-for-tat response from the nodes in the community as a consequence. In this way, healthy and growing collaborative communities will be achieved and maintained. Mechanism design tools can also shape the size and the structure of the network. With an appropriate design of incentive parameters, the network can grow to a desirable size by encouraging the participation of new devices. The connectivity and clustering of the community network can also be controlled by creating supernodes that behave as information hubs and incentivizing nodes to reach unconnected devices that can benefit from joining the community.

3.3 Multipath Authentication

When an IoT device makes contact with its neighborhood in the network, any "surrounding" device will respond upon some sort of "Hello-Message" being sent out upon the first connection (a direct connection could, e.g., use a time-to-live set to 1 in order to get only the adjacent network devices; but farther distances are equally possible and legitimate here).

Suppose that a new IoT device makes a handshake with its network neighbors, and establishes a shared secret for later authentication. The pairing can be done by any means, such as via firmware, Bluetooth, near-field communication, and so forth. Preferably, it can even be done during manufacturing for a whole production lot, to achieve distribution in (geographic) proximity, but in highly diverse networks (different homes, distinct enterprises, etc.). In (smart) homes, for example, this avoids all paired devices communicating over the same potentially compromised hub, because the paired devices are located in different areas and under the control of independent users. The mutual location of two IoT devices can, relative to network segmentation, firewalls or other logical barriers, happen as a particular service on the application layer, which needs to be allowed to run over the IoT. However, communicating devices are the main purpose of IoT anyway.

In any case, note that unlike for general public key schemes, our schemes do not require key updates as frequently over their lifetimes as an IoT device. For mobile phones, as an example, an expected lifetime of 2–3 years (until it is replaced by a more modern version) could make a key update even unnecessary at all.

The idea of multipath authentication is the following: if B wants to send an authentic message to A, but has neither a shared key nor public key certificate from A, it employs its network neighbors to certify B's identity to A. To this end, B shares a (distinct) key with each of its neighbors, and attaches a set of message authentication codes (MACs) to the data for A, indicating who A should contact to have each MAC verified. Upon reception of the data and MACs, A can contact each neighbor of B and ask for a verification of the MACs. This validation process somewhat resembles how handwritten signatures are verified in real life upon leaving a signature sample that can be compared with the handwritten signature in question. Electronically, the processes can be run just alike, with the appeal of being cheap, because the most expensive operation is the key exchange (done only once), but all subsequent operations are fast and efficient algorithms from symmetric cryptography.

The security of the scheme, unlike that of public key cryptography, can be made independent of unproven mathematical conjectures and rests only on the assumption of a "sufficiently small" portion of the network having been compromised. In that sense, the achievable security is "unconditional." This avoids complicated assumptions that can make public key cryptography somewhat opaque to people outside the expert community (thus, adding negatively to the trust in these feelingly black boxes); see Koblitz and Menezes [7] for an excellent introduction and discussion of the issue. Finally, we remark that the way of proving security uses game theory at the core [5].

Experimental Implementations

The concept of multipath authentication has previously been implemented and demonstrated to work on layer 7. In Rass et al. [8], a demonstrator has been reported that implements arbitrary secure end-to-end communication (confidential and authentic) between devices where only locally paired ones share a common secret (in an IoT setting, exchanging these is possible in various ways, such as QR codes, near-field communication, etc.). The main assumption upon which the security rests is multipath source routing, where paths do not intersect. Given a sufficiently dense network and accurate information on the topology, it is not difficult to let the devices do the routing on the application layer (as was shown in Rass et al. [8], where a local Java client was used to handle these matters). Fig. 3 shows a screenshot of the past prototype, which is (cryptographically) lightweight and implemented in Java to run on all platforms. The screenshot shows parts of the log of a protocol run where node 2 was asked by node 5 to verify the MACs that node 2 received from node 1. Node 5 shares a secret with node 1 so that it can confirm (see the "boxed" part on the bottom of the window) that the MAC it computed using the secret shared with 1 matches what it received from 2 upon the authentication request. Thus, node 1's "signature" is verified by node 2, and this is told to node 5.

FIG. 3   Multipath authentication prototype from Rass et al. [8].

4 PROPOSED ARCHITECTURE

Suppose a user wants to install an app. The user has retrieved the app from somewhere (not the app store), so that the source is distrusted (typically indicated by a digital signature verification failure). What if the user, for whatever reason, decides to get the app anyway? Where to get it from? Apps retrieved from the Internet directly are usually not subject to the thorough screenings that app stores apply. In that case, the risk is fully taken by the user. Why not rely on community knowledge and resources in that case? The idea is the following: To retrieve the app (from elsewhere than the app store but still from a trusted source), the user (device) X performs the following steps:

1. Callout to the community "Who's got 'this app'?"
2. Some (perhaps many) devices may respond by sending a confirmation that they have the app, and sending the fingerprint (hash of the app file), upon which a set of $h_1, ..., h_n$ arrives at the user. Devices that are too old should be abandoned from that list, for example, if their key length (for calculating the MACs in Step 5) is less than the current recommendations.
3. The user X goes for a majority vote and uses the hash that appears the most among $h_1, ..., h_n$, following the hypothesis that the malware has not yet affected a large part of the community. Let h_i be that majority value received from the ith respondent. Let the user having sent h_i be called B (as in Fig. 4).
4. If any of the hashes mismatches another, then we have an indication of malware potentially being in the community.
5. To retrieve the app, X contacts B to send the app with fingerprint h_i as known from Step 4. User B then runs multipath authentication to send an authentic version of the app. In Fig. 4, B attaches MACs using the keys shared with its neighbors and sends the app file with the MACs to X. This one compares the fingerprint of the received app to match what it should be (namely h_i), and asks then (indicated) neighbors of B to verify the hash of the app and the MAC attached to it. This prevents B from sending a correct fingerprint, but a malicious version of the app later (because the fingerprints would mismatch then), and assures X the authenticity of B's app packet.

The plain protocol can be adapted toward a less stringent, yet no less informed, behavior, in case users are willing to accept a certain residual risk in the retrieval process. If so, then quantifying that risk is the major objective, and is done as follows.

Let $N = \{1, 2, 3, ...\}$ represent the community, with physical member IDs being numbers. To each member $i \in N$ of the community, we associate a trust value based on the following intuition: in the preceding protocol, a user X may query another user B asking to respond to an MAC verification. Ultimately, the user X is interested in the trustworthiness of the retrieved app; let us call this event $T \in \{0, 1\}$, where $T = 0$ is zero trust and $T = 1$ is full trust. We are interested in the distribution of T over the unit interval $[0, 1]$, conditional on the information available to X, that is, our trust measure is $\tau = \Pr(\text{app is trustworthy}|\text{user } i \text{ says so})$, or more compactly, $\tau = \Pr(T = 1|R)$. Note that X polls only a subset of app sources/users $u_1, ..., u_n \in N$, so that the probability space in which T lives will not be partitioned by

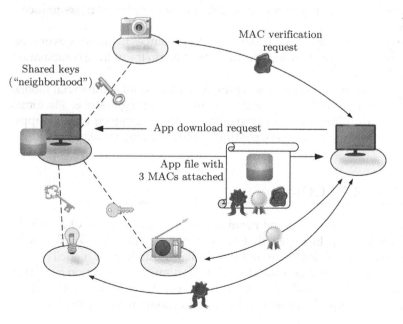

FIG. 4 Multipath authentication.

MAC verification request

Shared keys ("neighborhood")

App download request

App file with 3 MACs attached

the events R_i associated with the peers in the protocol. To fix this, we replace T by $T_{X, B}$, as being the *subjective* trust level that user X assigns to the app retrieved from user B, based on the information available. This (conditional) random variable has its probability space partitioned by the users that X contacts, but the fix comes with the caveat of the objective trust T remaining out of reach, with only the subjective trust $T_{X, B}$ assigned by X being computable. The distribution of $T_{X, B}$, however, follows from the law of total probability,

$$\Pr(T_{X,B}) = \sum_{i=1}^{n} \Pr(T_{X,B} = 1 | R_i) \Pr(R_i). \tag{1}$$

Mechanism design is herein concerned with the question of *why* a user should be willing to honestly participate in the protocol. The *incentive* for user i to respond correctly, by Eq. (1) is positively correlated to the subjective trust that user X obtains from asking user i. Because i is, by construction, B's neighbor, whatever i reports back depends on the trust that i has in B. But the situation is symmetric: i has an incentive to answer faithfully about B, because whichever information or app is ever retrieved from i, B is perhaps among the neighbors to be queried, so if i refrains from responding or responds incorrectly, it may indirectly damage its own reputation in the long run. The same symmetry, however, cannot be straightforwardly used by a malicious i to damage B's reputation, because there is still the set of other neighbors that may indicate B's honesty (recall that the protocol goes for the majority vote among all the replies).

Practically, we have a triple of trust values, which X maintains about the community:

1. The likelihood $\Pr(R_i)$ that user i responds. Based on whether or not i participated in the preceding protocol, X can update the trust value for i accordingly. If i refuses to reply about B, B can later refuse to tell about i, which is i's indirect incentive to become active.
2. The likelihood $\Pr(T_{X,B} = 1 | R_i)$ that user i's reply was correct and helpful. This value is updated upon the outcome of the majority vote made along the protocol, as discussed earlier.
3. The trust value $\Pr(T_{X,B} = 1)$ computed from Eq. (1), based on the previous two items.

This form of app retrieval is designed to be simple and secure at the same time: note that the community—by collecting and comparing app fingerprints—continuously builds up some sort of threat intelligence. Note that the hash in Step 1 and the MAC in Step 5 cryptographically link the app discovery and the app download. Otherwise, a malicious device may present one (harmless) app at Step 1 and another (malicious) one at Step 5 (cf. time of check to time of use— TOCTTOU [9]).

The bandwidth increase is the primary price to pay for this scheme to work, but remember that all we need to exchange are cryptographic hash values, which are only a few bytes long. For a quick calculation: using a 224-Bit SHA-3 checksum (state of the art) and with 10 peers contacted, the following bandwidth is required: we have 10×224 bit ≈ 2 kBit for the initial callout. Now, if the app sender, upon request, uses 10 of its neighbors to verify its authenticity, we end up with a total of 2 kBit for the 10 MACs, and another $10 \times 2 \times 224$ bit ≈ 4.5 kBit for all verifications. Thus, a total of less than 10 kBit of overhead is required for 10 neighbors (more or fewer peers induce a proportional increase or decrease, respectively).

We finally stress that this entire scheme can be constructed on Layer 7, that is, no deep changes to the devices or their network stack is necessary. In fact, a demonstration prototype of multipath authentication (in the natural combination with multipath transmission) has been successful already.

The local management of keys is herein aligned with the app sandboxing implemented on all commercial mobile phone platforms. General IoT devices are expected to run the same (or at least similar) operating systems. Platforms such as Android enforce sandboxing to preventing apps from accessing the memory blocks assigned to other apps. Thus, the cryptographic keys are essentially locally safe by logic access control by the operating system.

5 OUTLOOK

The system discussed in this article already has close relatives up and running to warn users about malicious websites or changed/outdated public key certificates [10–12]. Provided that such technology does not itself exhibit unwanted behavior otherwise (like unauthorized data collection), why not use similar technology in the IoT?

Hacking and threat intelligence are community actions, and so should security and mutual protection be. Large (animal) populations protect themselves by forming herds, and IoT devices can do similar things to harden the whole community against external threats. We believe that a comprehensive security concept should not exclusively rest on cryptographic mechanisms, but should, to a wide extent, include incentive and credibility-driven mechanisms to let users (devices) collaborate to the good of everyone. A combination of mechanism design [13], game theory, and cryptography can make a start here, but the diversity of the IoT seems to call for a scientific treatment with tools that are equally diverse.

References

[1] E. Maor, Cybercrime ecosystem: everything is for sale, 2015. https://securityintelligence.com/cybercrime-ecosystem-everything-is-for-sale/ (Retrieved 15 November 2017).

[2] C. Cimpanu, Android ransomware infects LG smart TV, 2016. https://www.bleepingcomputer.com/news/security/android-ransomware-infects-lg-smart-tv/ (Retrieved 15 November 2017).

[3] J. Callas, H. Donnerhacke, H. Finney, D. Shaw, R. Thayer, OpenPGP message format, 2007. https://tools.ietf.org/html/rfc4880 (Retrieved 15 November 2017).

[4] H.P. Penning, Analysis of the strong set in the PGP web of trust, 2016. https://pgp.cs.uu.nl/plot/ (Retrieved 15 November 2017).

[5] S. Rass, P. Schartner, Multipath authentication without shared secrets and with applications in quantum networks, in: Proceedings of the International Conference on Security and Management (SAM), vol. 1, CSREA Press, 2010, pp. 111–115.

[6] Q. Zhu, C. Fung, R. Boutaba, T. Basar, GUIDEX: a game-theoretic incentive-based mechanism for intrusion detection networks, IEEE J. Sel. Areas Commun. 30 (11) (2012) 2220–2230.

[7] N. Koblitz, A.J. Menezes, Another look at "Provable Security", J. Cryptol. 20 (1) (2007) 3–37.

[8] S. Rass, B. Rainer, M. Vavti, J. Göllner, A. Peer, S. Schauer, Secure communication over software-defined networks, Mob. Netw. Appl. 20 (1) (2015) 105–110.

[9] C. Mulliner, B. Michéle, Read it twice! A mass-storage-based TOCTTOU attack, Presented as Part of the 6th USENIX Workshop on Offensive Technologies, USENIX, Bellevue, WA, 2012. https://www.usenix.org/conference/woot12/workshop-program/presentation/Mulliner.

[10] D. Wendlandt, D. Anderson, A. Perrig, Perspectives project (Firefox browser add-on), 2015. https://perspectivessecurity.wordpress.com/ (Retrieved 15 November 2017).

[11] W.O.T. Services, MyWOT/WOT: website reputation rating (Firefox browser add-on), 2015. https://addons.mozilla.org/EN-us/firefox/addon/wot-safe-browsing-tool/ (Retrieved 15 November 2017).

[12] C. von Loesch, Certificate patrol, v.2.0.16 (Firefox browser add-on), 2015. https://addons.mozilla.org/de/firefox/addon/certificate-patrol (Retrieved 15 November 2017).

[13] T. Börgers, D. Krähmer, R. Strausz, An Introduction to the Theory of Mechanism Design, Oxford University Press, Oxford, 2015.

3

Blockchain-Based Security and Privacy in Smart Cities

Sophocles Theodorou* and Nicolas Sklavos[†]

*Open University of Cyprus, Nicosia, Cyprus
[†]SCYTALE Group, Computer Engineering & Informatics Department, University of Patras, Patras, Greece

1 INTRODUCTION

A quick overview of technology websites and relevant conference proceedings is sufficient to identify a technology trend that dominates the interest of the internet and communication technologies (ICT) community: blockchain technology is on a track to change the way information is stored, secured, and transported. It would be interesting to take a step back to understand the causes that led the ICT community to look for new technologies and solutions. Needless to say, a list of root causes cannot be exhaustive; however, a first glance would shed some light on the emergence of blockchain.

Modern cities are constantly growing, and in conjunction with the dawn of the era of the Internet of Things (IoT), we have experienced the gradual development of smart cities. Not long down the road, we will be called to inhabit such cities. The IoT model was launched reluctantly at the beginning of the century. Despite the initial enthusiasm and optimism from all involved parties, there is a significant delay in its widespread implementation. Nevertheless, today, we witness a complete shift in dynamics on this: the progressive increase of companies and corporations developing applications and devices that could be connected in the broader network. For example, automotive corporations invest a vast proportion of their budget to deploy applications that will allow control of the vehicle via a mobile application. On a broader scale, many researchers propose algorithms that aim to eliminate traffic congestion through real-time traffic control and smart parking [1]. Complete security seems like an unachievable venture; hence, security should be unified with the network in order to eliminate any obstacles between reliability and security [2]. There are efforts toward even more delicate technologies, such as SCADA, to provide solutions in industrial environments, that is, highly critical industries that will implement and control those technologies. Considered to be highly sensitivity, they mainly deal with electrical grids, and power and transportation plants. These industries, regardless of how critical they are, demonstrate increasing efforts to implement a platform based on IoT that will allow the instant control and supervision of the security of an entire SCADA network [3].

These developments create new requirements in terms of security, speed, and analysis of information. The ICT community is called upon to respond to several questions and revert with practical solutions that could be implemented immediately. For example, so far, the majority of companies have no obligation to include information security in the design of their products. Will these companies be able to cope with the new developments? Until recently, a washing machine was just a standalone node that had to comply with some basic security standards. In this new context, this device will be part of the broader network, in which, without the necessary security design, it could be the weakest link. There are many well-known examples that involve electrical devices, such as washing machines, surveillance cameras, and GPS navigators with security vulnerabilities. Some of them concern devices with default ethernet interfaces, which allow a plethora of attacks, such as web server directory traversal [4]. To strengthen these vulnerabilities, FORTINET published a white paper that analyzes the impact on business security from the transition to the IoT [5]. Among others, it is indicated that the majority of IoT devices are headless – in other words, they have no traditional operating system, or even the necessary memory capacity and processing power for building a secure environment or installing a secure client.

On this matter, there are plenty of other questions that arise concerning the storage and transportation of the information. Are the existing solutions ready to face the new challenges imposed by the millions of connected nodes in smart cities? As mentioned at the outset of this chapter, blockchain technology is gaining momentum to provide the answers needed. Based on a decentralized and distributed model of storing information, blockchain is introduced as an alternative solution to bridge the security gaps from the transition toward the era of the IoT and smart cities. Specifically, blockchain provides the opportunity to abandon the current technologies used for information storage in third-party ledgers. As it stands, a vast amount of resources is consumed to ensure their security [6]. Information is stored in various locations in the form of a block. Each location holds a true copy of the stored information. The absence of a third party significantly reduces the needed resources, and increases the transaction speed. In the following chapters, we will have a thorough look at the application and implementation of blockchain technology, and how this could stand as the vehicle to smart cities.

Smart contracts are among the groundbreaking changes that blockchain technology will introduce. Smart contracts aim to perform fast, autonomous transactions within the chaotic environment of big data. What is more, they will reduce the processing power needed for everyday transactions, as a consequence of the millions of connected nodes. Smart contracts are based on the blockchain of the Ethereum platform. Through their code, they have the capacity to take decisions, interact, and store information as soon as the network is active. The various transactions are executed only when the conditions of each contract are met. As a precursor to the theory of smart contracts, Nick Szabo published an article in 1997 titled "The Idea of Smart Contracts," which is still used today as the main reference on the concept of smart contracts.

In this chapter, we will mainly focus on the areas of e-governance in conjunction with smart contracts. Some countries, such as Estonia, have already adopted an e-governance scheme. In other countries, we have observed the implementation of some aspects of the concept, which mainly focus on digital signatures, and will facilitate faster and more secure transactions with governmental authorities. Smart contracts aim to push the concept of e-governance a step further, as they provide the end user with the opportunity to establish mutual agreements with relevant parties, or even between each other. The agreed-upon contracts will be registered in a public ledger. To this end, users manage to avoid third parties, as the smart contract is directly accessible by all relevant parties. Consequently, not only are the needed resources decreased dramatically, but also transaction speed increases. It is important to stress that blockchain technology, and especially the application of smart contracts in e-governance, cannot be the only solution to the existing security issues, which we will attempt to illustrate in this chapter. In particular, we will examine some already known vulnerabilities that appear in currently functioning smart contracts. Moreover, we will try to recommend a smart contract that we believe has practical applications in the overall scheme of e-governance.

2 THE INTERNET OF THINGS IN SMART CITIES

As stated in the introduction, our societies are rapidly marching toward the era of the IoT. It has been only in the past few years that we have seen the IoT movement start to gain credibility; hence, the literature on this matter is very scarce. Nowadays, we see some serious steps being taken in the right direction, demonstrating a genuine desire to achieve a full implementation of the IoT, rather than just some individual efforts from specific communities. In brief, the IoT is considered an "environment where internet capabilities are applied to everyday objects that have earlier not been considered as computers to provide a network connectivity that will enable these objects to generate, exchange, and consume data" [7]. Based on the preceding definition, the IoT relies on a wide range of protocols, technologies, and applications to meet its ultimate goal, which is a real value to society. Fig. 1 shows the IoT lifecycle, starting from the point when a node is connected in the network, up until real value is delivered as an outcome to the user.

Observing Fig. 1, it would be useful to look closely at points 2, 3, and 4. Input, analysis, and processing in real time are some of the operations that ought to be implemented at minimum latency. Let us have a look at a practical example. Nowadays, it is very common to receive or transmit real-time incidents through a car processing unit. These incidents could be traffic jam alerts, accidents, road closures, and anything that could be newsworthy to drivers. In the overall model of the smart city, this information should be available to whoever is active in the network. Therefore, in order to maximize the value to the end user, information has to be delivered with minimum delay. Hence, the speed of processing and delivering the information is of great importance—especially when the analysis will be operated in the ocean of information of Big Data. By observing the preceding simple example, there are already some basic issues that the ICT community has to address to give the necessary initiative to the industry for investing in the IoT. To make it even more

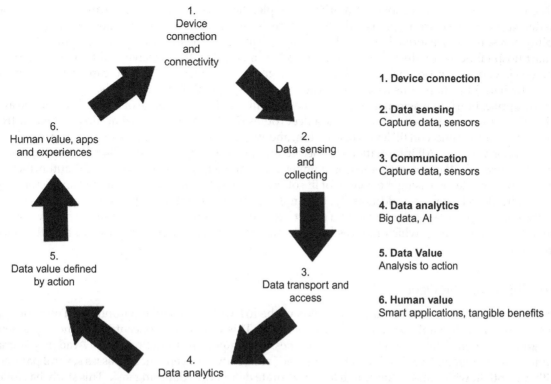

FIG. 1 IoT cycle. *Source: i-scoop.eu, The Internet of Things (IoT) – Essential IoT Business Guide. Retrieved from i-sccop.eu: https://www.i-scoop.eu/internet-of-things-guide/#The_Internet_of_Things_in_an_ (2017).*

complicated, the cost of the answers should not be restrictive, as it would discourage companies from investing in relation to the returned value. It is not a coincidence that the IoT Business Index 2017 of the Economist specifies the following main drawbacks for the full implementation of the IoT [8]:

- High cost for new technologies
- Lack of resources with technical knowledge in IoT matters
- Security

Security, the last item on the preceding list, will be examined later in this chapter. Regarding the other two items, there is one major question that arises: Why are cost and the lack of resources major drawbacks in the implementation of the IoT? It should be stated that all of the drawbacks on the list are closely associated. For example, there are various companies that deploy updated applications of their products in preparation for the IoT era. Gradually, the companies observe that this exercise is an expensive investment. Meanwhile, the older versions of the same products should be either substituted or introduced in the IoT model. Usually, the former is very costly; hence, the companies opt for the latter option, which is the most cost-effective of the two. As a result, there are outdated applications on the market that are exposed to vulnerabilities. Security has a big part to play in the model implementation of each company, and especially on which products should be in the market. Products with outdated firmware and a lack of security-by-design will be ticking time bombs within the network. Hence, the companies should either accept the financial burden for substituting new ones, or live with the risk of any potential security breach. The Economist survey indicates that various devices in the market use outdated protocols and software that are not deigned to be IP-enabled. These devices can be disabled by a simple network scan [8].

The practical implementation of the IoT could be applied in various sectors, such as the industrial, consumer, or commercial sectors. For example, the IoT implementation in the commercial sector will improve the process and image of the supply chain. Products will be able to provide information regarding the weight, load, temperature, time of arrival, and destination, among many others. This specific matter will be discussed further later in this chapter. Sometimes, there is an interaction between two affected sectors in which the industrial IoT will provide results that have applications relevant to the consumer's IoT. For example, the compliance of the automobile industry (industrial IoT) facilitates the transmission of traffic data in real time. This will have an immediate effect on the end user, as there will be real-time traffic management (consumer's IoT). The role of the IoT in the creation of smart cities is paramount, and there is an abundance of applications. As a prime example, the most significant applications are in the healthcare sector. The development of smart hospitals will allow the real-time exchange of information on the status of patients, the availability of resources (consumables, etc.), the access to health data outside office hours, among many other applications. Smart hospital beds are already a reality; they allow medical staff to receive real-time information on each patient's status via various sensors enabled on the bed. As a general conclusion, the healthcare sector has made serious steps toward the harmonization of its basic infrastructure to comply with the IoT's needs.

Another IoT application is in waste management. The IoT will enable an exchange of information on the availability and capacity of each station, as well as on collection fleet routes [7]. In Denmark, citizens already benefit from smart bins, which provide information on fill levels of each bin, and increase in illumination as soon as someone is approaching the bin in a poorly lit area. All information is collected and processed in newly installed software, developed specifically for this purpose. Waste management is gaining great momentum, as it allows local authorities to reduce administration costs, while increasing the quality of life of the citizens [9]. These are very significant factors in persuading investors to fund such projects. Additionally, the implementation of smart waste management systems involves fewer security-related concerns, compared with a smart healthcare system, due to the minimal involvement of sensitive personal data in the former, which reduces implementation costs, and therefore provides a further incentive to potential investors.

2.1 Smart Cities and Big Data

In the previous section we examined the application of the IoT within the city environment. The main question is whether smart cities are achievable in our age at a broader level. This section will concentrate on the implementation of the IoT within a smart city. Before discussing smart cities, it is important to define them. Academic literature has already made several attempts at a suitable definition. The "smart city" concept encompasses several parameters that interact with each other, which makes the search for an accurate definition a daunting task. This study has followed the definition of IBM, which refers to smart cities as "the smart usage of technology in order to collect, examine, process, and implement large amounts of useful data directly from the already functioning cities" [10]. On the same note, Amjad [11] explains that the most important obejctives of smart cities are the maintainance of the sustainability of the services, the improvement of the quality of living, and the creation of a more suitable liveable environment. There are many cities that are heading in this direction by implementing various programs that will allow them to activate the necessary mechanisms and relevant authorities. The main challenge of this initiative is the obligatory interaction of various sectors and providers that specialize in security, telecommunications, and data processing, among other areas. Fig. 2 lists the main sectors that will be the spine of smart cities.

All sectors mentioned in Fig. 2 should be able to interact and cooperate in harmony within an already established environment. As a result, the issues that will emerge will be manifold, and most will be predominantly security-related. The next subsections attempt to highlight them.

The speed of processing data within the Big Data environment is one of the most critical issues that experts are called to address. Thus far, the collection and storage of data is local; as a result, the users/providers can adjust data processing according to their needs. In smart cities, the data will be distributed in a way (and speed) that is beneficial to the entire network. We have already explained the example of data distribution in cars. Using the same example, let us imagine a case where there is severe latency in data distribution that could affect the smart transportation scheme: traffic lights and congestion. Such an incident would have catastrophic consequences in the greater scale of megacities such as London, Paris, or New York, thereby creating confusion, frustration, and even despair in millions of citizens. To make this even more complicated, any solution used for this issue should not jeopardize the three major pillars of

Smart cities

Smart commerce	Banking, property, finance
Smart environment	Waste management, water, energy
Smart management	Governance, security, education, health
Smart communication	Telecoms, identification
Smart transportation	Transport, traffic

FIG. 2   Basic sectors of IoT.

security: confidentiality, integrity, and availability. In 2001, Laney developed the model of three (3) Vs, which applies to Big Data [12]. The 3Vs are volume, variety, and velocity, which smart cities are challenged to handle. In other words, smart cities should be able to gather, process, and analyze an abundance of data, as an output of a plethora of sources at maximum velocity.

It is evident that the processing of vast amounts of data in real time might pose some serious challenges from a security perspective. The main source of these challenges is the lack of tools to process large amounts of data, the data greediness of large databases, and the continuous distribution of data among third parties [13]. Even in the sectors of smart cities that the current infrastructure is able to support, there are issues of limited know-how and technical expertise. These challenges could be extended, as errors and omissions might compromise the entire scheme, leading to the leak of sensitive data. Regarding data distribution between third parties, the main source of concern could be the incompatibility between databases or software. Traditionally, the involved parties are liable for the storage and distribution of their own sensitive data. However, within smart cities, there is more than one party involved, and all have to be able to interact with each other. If even one of them cannot comply with the security principles, the whole network is vulnerable. This is further illustrated in the following example: In a smart healthcare environment, there is a hospital that does not comply with the encryption standards for the secure distribution of highly sensitive medical data. The data have to be sent to local pharmacies, which will be responsible for issuing the correct medication, depending on the prescriptions. Similarly, the data will be sent to the ministry of health to update the patients' histories. The transportation of unencrypted data holds major concerns in terms of confidentiality. As soon as the information is distributed in plain text (or using weak encryption), the data is susceptible to interception. As far as privacy is concerned, Ballesté et al. [14] analyzed the model of five dimensions (5D), which applies to smart cities. In other words, ICT experts are called to protect identity privacy, location privacy, query privacy, footprint privacy, and owner privacy. Researchers claim that as long as this model is followed, smart cities will be considered updated in terms of privacy.

To sum up, smart cities aim to address major global concerns, such as climate change, urbanization, limited resources, and high population growth [15]. However, there are various security challenges that need to be tackled. The following list mentions a few:

- The lack of technologies that will be able to process large volumes of data. As mentioned herein, the 3V model is the main pillar of the smart city model; however, it should never jeopardize security in its implementation.
- The IoT implementation will require a large concentration of services, applications, and connected nodes. All these elements might bring to light the heterogeneity of their functionality, which will eventually expose security vulnerabilities.
- The lack of predefined standards is an issue that is already a concern among ICT experts. As it stands, there is no overall security scheme that will be used as a guideline on how to capture, handle, process, and distribute data. Each party acts on their own judgement. Hence, the various parties are not streamlined on the way they handle security matters.

In the following chapter, we will look at blockchain technology, which aims to provide a solution to the manifold security issues. Blockchain became well known due to its interconnection with cryptocurrencies; however, we will only attempt to explain its mode of operation.

3 BLOCKCHAIN IN SMART CITIES

3.1 Blockchain

As mentioned in the introduction of this chapter, blockchain technology has become a point of reference as a potential solution to the emerging security problems that arise from the implementation of the IoT in smart cities. According to Nelson Rosario of Marshall Gerstein & Borun LLP, blockchain is defined as a "distributed ledger network using public-key cryptography to cryptographically sign transactions that are stored on a distributed ledger, with the ledger consisting of cryptographically linked blocks of transactions. The cryptographically linked blocks of transactions form what is known as a blockchain" [16]. To put it simply, blockchain can be seen as a spreadsheet that can be accessed by any computer in the network, and it tracks all the actions of these computers [17].

To understand what blockchain has to offer, it would be useful to see a simple card payment transaction and compare the scenario with the traditional way of payment. Let us think of a scenario in which user A wants to pay user B by card. Even though it seems like this is a direct interaction of A with B, in fact user A authorizes her bank to investigate by searching its database to determine whether A had sufficient funds to pay B. If this is true, the bank pays B with funds that are kept in the bank's database in order to close the transaction. The bank pays user B directly, therefore A pays user B indirectly. With blockchain technology, the funds of A are already distributed to all relevant parties in the form of an encrypted block that resides in the ledger. Upon the exchange of keys between the involved parties, the block that holds the information about A's funds is decrypted. Therefore, the role of the third party (in this case, the bank) becomes obsolete. There is a strong belief that the elimination of the third party in the process of the closing of a transaction will have, as an effect, the faster and less costly transaction with higher privacy [18].

Before the analysis of blockchain's applications, it would be beneficial to have an overview of the process. The basic steps include the following:

- A user is asking to process a transaction in the blockchain.
- The transaction is broadcast to the overall network.
- The transaction is confirmed by the use of well-known algorithms. In detail, one node is asked to solve a puzzle by using the unique header metadata. This process is called mining and is considered the most important part of the entire process for the implementation of blockchain.
- As soon as the node solves the puzzle, the solution has to be approved by the majority of the nodes that are connected in the network (consensus mechanism).
- The nodes that participated in the approval of the transaction receive their reward, which in this instance is a type of cryptocurrency.
- The processed transaction is incorporated in other existing transactions, which altogether form a block. The block is added to the blockchain. The newly added block is connected via the hash value of the previous block. Likewise, the new block will be connected with the next block that will be formed.
- The transaction is completed and all ledgers are updated with the new information.

The distinctive way of handling and recording data in the blockchain has instigated changes in the security sector. The interconnection of blocks and the fact that each transaction has to be approved by the majority of the existing nodes managed to solve major security issues that remained unaddressed until recently.

First, the implementation of blockchain eliminates the "single point of failure" vulnerability. This is due to the fact that information is not stored in a single ledger anymore. The prospective hacker has to alternate the entry in approximately 50% of the ledgers to complete an attack on a victim's bank account. As soon as all nodes have access to the altered information, any deviation from the original data will be detected immediately. In the traditional way of banking, simple access to the bank's database would be sufficient to complete the hack. Fig. 3 demonstrates the difference between the traditional way of keeping and distributing data as opposed to the blockchain way. In the former, there is a necessary dependence on the central database. Failure to access the database could create various operational issues. Conversely, in blockchain, each user holds a copy of the information.

Additionally, blockchain could provide solutions to the privacy of personal data. It is well known that end users' personal data are resold between companies. Many users are opposed to these practices, as they have concerns regarding the circumstances of distributing, and especially storing their data. The use of blockchain will permit the access of personal data only upon the owner's approval. The block that holds the information will only be decrypted as long the lawful owner and the third party agree to exchange decryption keys [19].

Apart from its application in privacy, blockchain will have a tremendous impact on the digital certification of individuals and organizations, as it will considerably speed up the transactions between two parties. In the smart city model, rapid data processing in the ocean of Big Data is paramount. In the traditional way of certification, the end user is obliged to seek help from an accredited third party to validate the originality of the document. The external help could be a notary, an auditor, or public authorities, among others. In the blockchain environment, all documents will be digitally signed and placed in the blockchain, where all approved parties will have access to them and will be able to exchange the documents necessary for a transaction without the need to get a third party to validate their authenticity [20]. The case of Estonia, which is considered a pioneer in its holistic approach to e-governance, is quite useful for understanding the digital signature—it will be explored later in this chapter.

As explained in the blockchain process, each transaction needs to be validated by the majority of the nodes that are connected in the network. In order to validate the transaction, there is a cryptographic puzzle that needs to be solved. This action is called "proof of work." This is followed by the consensus mechanism, which provides reliability and consistency of the specific transaction [21]. This mechanism is entirely different to the way we currently handle data: the user has no involvement in the way data are formed, let alone in the way the database is managed. As a result, there is no consistency in the data, and users are forced to trust the database manager regarding their authenticity and integrity.

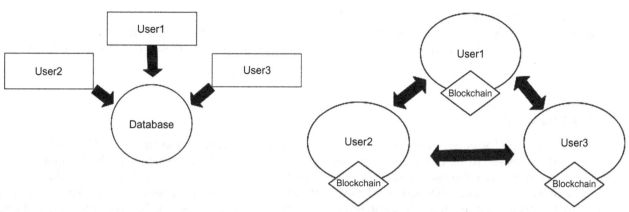

FIG. 3   Traditional database vs blockchain.

Probably the most drastic change that comes with blockchain is the ability to store and create smart contracts. Bitcoin was the first application to use the blockchain platform, and is considered the precursor to the success of all other platforms. Ethereum is one of those platforms, and Eth is the cryptocurrency that goes with it. Ethereum is purely based on the blockchain concept, and its main difference from bitcoin is that the latter has been created to register transactions and be used as a cryptocurrency [17]. Contrarily, Ethereum has the ability to handle smart contracts. Simply put, smart contracts are protocols of digital transactions, which are stored in the blockchain [22]. Smart contracts can be agreed upon between the involved parties without the need to be approved by a third one, such as a lawyer. As smart contracts are created directly (machine to machine), third parties become unnecessary.

3.2 Disadvantages

Blockchain technology has fueled hopes in the ICT community that it could provide a long-awaited solution to several ongoing security flaws. However, blockchain is not a panacea; even at its early stages, there are various disadvantages that have emerged, and this section attempts to showcase some of these.

The fact that blockchain technology is at its very early stages makes potential investors reluctant to implement it in their projects, which further affects the development of appropriate supporting infrastructure. Blockchain has not been tested under real economic conditions, hence it cannot be classified as a reliable solution yet [23]. Its use has been very sporadic, which makes industry leaders very skeptical about implementing it as a solution in their systems. Blockchain's momentum is building, although it mostly remains within academic circles for now.

Another major concern is the processing power required by the mining process. It has been estimated that a simple bitcoin transaction requires 5,000 times the processing power needed for a simple VISA card payment. This is due to the consensus mechanism, which requires the transaction to be validated by the majority of the participants (connected nodes). Miners work with application-specific integrated circuits (ASICs) used exclusively for this task. As a result, the overall cost should be calculated to account for the increasing energy consumption it requires. According to current estimations, by 2020, the electricity needed for bitcoin transactions will be equivalent to the electricity consumption in Denmark [24]. It is fair to say that there are various movements toward a solution to this problem. The Ethereum platform has integrated in its algorithm the concept of "Proof of Stake" (PoS), as opposed to the "Proof of Work" (PoW) that we have already seen in bitcoin. In the latter, miners compete against each other to validate the transaction as fast as they can. The miner that solves the puzzles first is allocated the block. In PoS, the Ethereum platform allocates the transaction by itself to the user according to their reserves in Eth (Ethereum's cryptocurrency) [25]. The main difference between the two concepts is that in PoS, the miners do not get a block reward, but only receive a transaction fee. For this reason, the miners of this type are called "forgers" [24]. The transition from PoW to PoS will dramatically reduce the time needed for the closure of one transaction. Following the PoW process, it is estimated that creation of one block takes 10 min. PoS aims to reduce the delay to 12 s [17]. Of course, this latency is still miles away from the desired time needed to make the distribution and access of information compliant with the precepts of smart cities.

Moreover, the "51% attack" increases the skepticism about blockchain technology. Satoshi Nakamoto explained that PoW makes it computationally impossible to compute the transaction as soon as the nodes that have the processing power in the network are honest [26]. The key point of this statement is the fact that the nodes ought to be honest. What could go wrong if an adversary manages to somehow control the majority of the nodes? The answer to this question, we will explain the concept of the "51% attack" risk. Fake information ceases to be fake when the majority of users agree and accept it. Similarly, when an attacker succeeds in altering data in the majority of the nodes, this information becomes accepted. However, it should be noted that this type of attack requires high volumes of computational power.

3.3 Use of Blockchain

Blockchain technology has been heavily criticized due to its connection with cryptocurrencies. However, there are plenty of initiatives related to its disengagement. The first signs of the implementation of the technology have appeared only recently, even though it has been more than 10 years since the appearance of blockchain. It was 2009 when the first cryptocurrency (bitcoin) to be based on the blockchain platform appeared. A few years later, blockchain tried to disconnect from the dependence on bitcoin, and managed to convince the ICT community that there is much more to it that needs to investigate [27]. It was estimated that within 2017, 15% of companies in the financial sector would have started using blockchain technology [28].

Transparency is the main issue at stake in the market, and blockchain is called to address this issue. The proposed way to store data gives the opportunity to derive helpful information directly from each part of the supply chain. Traditionally, consumers rely on the manufacturer to transmit accurate information regarding the product. For example, a company that trades meat is liable to inform the consumers about the origin of the meat, the storage conditions, and anything else that might be relevant to the product. The current situation involves strong elements of trust regarding the accuracy of the information. Just recently, we experienced the incidents of horse DNA found in beef. Blockchain will provide the opportunity to register the information on a product directly from its source. This information will be distributed directly to the relevant parties, thanks to its decentralized concept. Hence, the consumer will be able to have access to the information without prior scrutiny by third parties.

Another sector that seems to catch up with the current technologies is healthcare. There are plenty of applications in the overall environment of smart cities, and there has been a considerable interest in research on its implementation by making use of blockchain. Recently, we noticed the release of the Healthcoin platform, which claims to revolutionize the field by decentralizing medical data, by offering rewards with relevant services and products [29]. In particular, diabetics will be able to register their hemoglobin levels, which will correspond to an amount of awarded digital tokens. Afterward, they will be able to exchange the digital tokens with tax reduction and medical products relevant to diabetes. Needless to say, these examples demonstrate only the simple use of blockchain in this specific sector. In general, the decentralization of data aims to create an infrastructure that will provide not only balance between security and privacy, but also access to new services [30]. Identity management is a major challenge for the healthcare sector. Currently, all relevant stakeholders (doctors, patients, administration staff) are involved in an ongoing process of securing the identity of medical data. Consequently, there are delays in distribution, and reduced accessibility to medical data. Also, patients would expect to have more control over their own data, as opposed to what is available to third parties [31]. We have already indicated the need for increased transparency in data accessibility and a focus on the fact that users should have more control over their personal data. In the current situation, the trade and utilization of private data to and from third parties is a very lucrative market. Users are rarely aware that their data are used for irrelevant purposes to the ones initially agreed upon. By transferring personal data to the blockchain, the user will have full ownership over their data. Also, access to information will increase dramatically, as the patient in the healthcare application will be able to have direct access to the services of a different health institution: patient medical data will be available to hospitals and patients, and the latter will avoid the delays caused by the transfer of their medical data (sometimes even in hard copy!). The patient will simply have to give access to his or her medical records to whomever is deemed relevant. In Healthcoin, there are already developed platforms ready to provide solutions.

The financial sector has invested large amounts in the implementation of blockchain: it is estimated that within the past 3 years there has been an investment of 1.6 billion dollars, and 80% of the banks have started projects that are relevant to blockchain technology [32]. However, it is uncertain whether such a well-established and rigid sector will show a willingness to eventually embrace the new technology. As far as usage is concerned, it would be an omission not to mention the use of cryptocurrencies. Companies that accept payments in a decentralized manner are increasing by the day, and this is an area in which the financial sector will be naturally involved.

The practical implementations of blockchain are numerous, and it would be impossible to provide an exhaustive list of all areas here. Most importantly, the grand scheme of e-governance was purposefully omitted, as it will be investigated in depth in the next chapter.

4 E-GOVERNANCE

There has been a growing interest in the e-governance scheme in many countries, and especially in Europe, in an attempt to keep up with the new technology challenges. The United Nations 2016 EGDI Index, shown in Fig. 4, demonstrates the areas that offer e-governance services to their citizens.

According to this index, Europe is significantly ahead of the Americas and the world average. It is important to note that the index includes data only from countries that are members of the United Nations; however, it provides a suitable sample for drawing conclusions. Transparency and security are considered the main factors that instigated the local authorities to incorporate e-governance schemes in their agendas. The World Bank defined e-governance as the utilization of ICT to improve the efficiency, effectiveness, transparency, and accountability of a government. The authorities are moving their services online hoping to:

- Reduce costs
- Promote economic development
- Enhance transparency and accountability
- Improve service delivery
- Improve public administration
- Facilitate an e-society [33]

Toward achieving these goals, many countries invested in new technologies, educated core resources, and took some of their services online, even on a pilot basis. Estonia is considered a role model among the other countries, as it has successfully implemented an overall e-governance plan, as opposed to the other countries' sporadic initiatives. The Estonian head of ICT mentioned that in 2015, the entire project began as a startup, without any clear view of whether it was going to be successful, although they were convinced that it would be disruptive [34]. However, the enormous changes implied by such a statement go hand in hand with a certain amount of risk that needs to be considered before any steps are taken in this direction.

4.1 Blockchain in e-Governance

As already explained, the security issues that emerge from the extensive use of third-party solutions are a major concern. A thorough examination should be attempted in the areas of data ownership, data transparency, and access control [35]. The decentralized and distributed philosophy of blockchain is already implemented to provide solutions in e-governance. Essentially, blockchain will be used as the vehicle to guarantee the integrity of user data

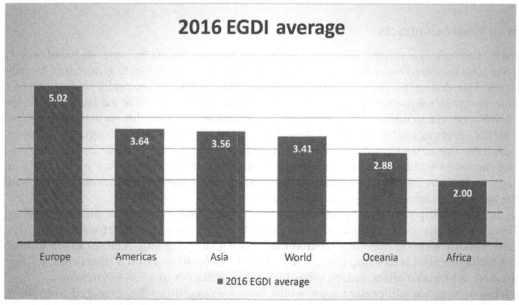

FIG. 4 EGDI index. *Source: United Nations.*

without the need to be validated by governmental institutions. For this reason, the first-time authentication of a user is an integral part of the process. As soon as the user is authenticated in person, they will be enabled to conduct online banking actions, including electronic fund transfers, to access international payment service providers, and digitally sign documents [36]. Meanwhile, the Dubai Land Department has already launched a platform based on blockchain technology that allows citizens to register all their real estate documents (sales agreements, ownership certificates, etc.) and perform payments without a physical presence requirement in any governmental building. As an outcome, customer service is accelerated, as all documents are available and certified, thanks to the distributed ledger [37].

In a similar, albeit more holistic, fashion, Estonia introduced the concept of e-residency. Before the launching of the e-governance scheme, in 2014, the Estonian government announced that any citizen, regardless of origin or location, could apply for an Estonian e-ID. This exercise was the precursor of e-governance, which was presented a few months later. According to the governmental website, the e-ID provided, among others [38]:

- Establishment of a company online
- Business banking accessibility and online payment services
- Full company ownership without the need of a local director
- E-signature and document authentication
- Secure document encryption
- Online tax declarations
- Online company operation

It is noteworthy that e-ID does not provide any EU rights, or the right to access countries in the EU as an Estonian citizen.

Some of the features of e-ID can address the issues of privacy and data security of the citizens. The integration of blockchain guarantees direct data access without the need of any further validation. In this way, the public sector, which traditionally was rigid and inflexible, managed to become innovative and ready to give answers to the new challenges of the society [39].

The bitcoin platform has increased the popularity of blockchain. However, it is not the only one. We have already mentioned Ethereum, which is considered its main rival. Gradually, more solutions have started emerging, each one claiming that they can deliver something new to the blockchain concept.

Monero is an open-source cryptocurrency. The creators claim that it is impossible to trace a token's owner. Naturally, the market's big players, such as IBM and Microsoft, created their own proprietary products. Specifically, Microsoft launched the Azure blockchain, which is based on the cloud service of the company. Likewise, IBM presented the IBM blockchain, which is using the existing IBM cloud platform. For further reading, Github provides an extensive list of each solution.

4.2 Security in Smart Contracts

It is expected that an entire governance mechanism—be it traditional or economic one—is based on a vast amount of agreements (contracts) between two or more parties. These contracts aim to facilitate governance by defining the various parameters and conditions to which all parties are required to comply. For example, we may have a simple agreement for a house rent with the use of a property agent. In this agreement, we have the landlord, the tenant, and the property agent, who acts as a facilitator. The agreement consists of terms and conditions that all parties need to comply with in order for the agreement to be considered lawful. The terms should be as thorough as possible to cover all the aspects of the deal. As soon as the agreement is signed, the property agent is responsible for notifying the local authorities and service providers (utilities service providers, etc.) about the change of tenancy so their data are up to date. All of these steps are the bare minimum for a simple transaction, where the landlord wants to make sure that he/she will receive the agreed rent amount at the end of the month.

To evaluate the security aspect of smart contracts, we first need to look into some of their technical aspects at their foundation. There are various coding languages that are used to deploy a smart contract, such as Solidity, Serpent, and LLL. At this time, Solidity seems to prevail as the dominant coding language [40]. A close examination of Solidity will reveal its heavy influence from JavaScript, C++, and Python. In order to work on a smart contract, we used a well-known IDE (Remix), which also offers, among other features, a debugger in a test environment.

In the following section, we will present some well-known vulnerabilities that emerged from the application of smart contracts. As the list is too long, we attempted to focus on vulnerabilities that have some effect in e-governance.

4.3 Reentrancy Vulnerability

Reentrancy vulnerability exposes a coding error that allows an adversary to execute a command multiple times before the update of the account of the victim. To clarify this, let us consider that a user A wants to send an amount (eth) to B, as agreed on a contract to meet its conditions. Then B is allowed to withdraw the amount from A's account. The bug is hidden in the sequence of the two main commands. The command *msg.sender.call.value* allows the repeat of the command because the balance of A's account (*userBalances[msg.sender]*) is updated only at the end. Hence, the attacker will be able to withdraw more eth, as the balance of A's account seems intact. Following is an example of this attack:

REENTRANCY VULNERABILITY

```
{
   throw;
 }
   balances[msg.sender] = 0;
function withdrawBalance() public {
   uint amountToWithdraw = userBalances[msg.sender];
   require(msg.sender.call.value(amountToWithdraw)()); // the code can be re-executed and deduct
the amount multiple times
userBalances[msg.sender] = 0;
}
```

Source: ethereum/wiki.

There are many approaches to fix this vulnerability. One approach would be to alter the sequence of commands, which will not allow the adversary to re-execute the withdrawal command.

REENTRANCY VULNERABILITY CORRECTED

```
function withdrawBalance() public {
   uint amountToWithdraw = userBalances[msg.sender];
   userBalances[msg.sender] = 0;
   require(msg.sender.call.value(amountToWithdraw)()); // The user's balance is already 0, thus the
command cannot be re-executed.
}
```

Source: ethereum/wiki.

The coder should substitute a line that indicates the user balance with the line that contains the command msg. sender.call.value. This will update the account balance of A as soon as the first command of withdrawal is executed. Hence, the account of B will be 0, which means that even if the command is repeated, there will be no amount to withdraw [41].

The reentrancy attack gained popularity in 2016, due to the Decentralized Autonomous Organization (DAO) hack. The DAO is an open-source computer program that runs on the Ethereum platform. The program allows users to code smart contracts associated with startups seeking crowdfunding [42]. As soon as the hacker detected the vulnerability, he/she managed to execute the withdrawal command repeatedly. The attack cost 50 million dollars in stolen cryptocurrency.

The specific attack shows the fragility of integrity, which is one of the basic pillars in security. Magazzeni et al. analyzed the counter measures needed to assure the safe functionality of smart contracts. They explain that the computer program should be doing only what it is intended to do. In other words, the contract should not allow any further execution, apart from the intended one. In the reentrancy example, the contract not only did what was it intended to do, but it also left a window for more. As soon as this window is exploited, the integrity of the contract is in doubt.

5 SMART CITY SECURITY MODEL

Smart cities are at our doorstep, and are going to play an important part of everyday life, in a variety of ways (Sklavos and Zaharakis) [43]. The growth is pervasive, with various aspects that need to be taken into consideration before they are considered a sustainable solution for the new era. The evolution from IoT to smart cities seems natural, although the collaboration of different disciplines and the demand of processing enormous volume of data raises many doubts regarding its success. The smart city networks are operating on heterogeneous devices and technologies [44]. Compatibility challenges are already a major security concern that still have to be remediated. In previous sections, we analyzed the various sectors that will be affected within the environment of a smart city, such as transportation, energy, and so forth. In this section, we present a hybrid model of a smart city from the angle of security. Although the features that make a smart city secure are multiple, we aim to focus only on those areas that are deemed crucial. Fig. 5 shows the basic elements of a secure smart city.

5.1 Data Management and Distribution

Blockchain has a prominent role to play in the fast-moving environment of smart cities. The IoT is approaching fast, and will be an integral part of the modern age. Blockchain and the IoT tend to unite forces to meet the high demands of smart cities, as well as to introduce new technologies and services. The new concept of Blockchain in IoT (BIoT) is becoming very popular in cities that have already started the practical implementation of a smart city environment.

The necessity of rapid access to real-time data has been expressed several times in this chapter. The introduction of BIoT will send technology in the right direction. The connected nodes will be able to access data directly from the sensors that are embedded in products and devices in a transparent and uninterrupted way [45]. Moreover, the combination of Blockchain and the IoT will give an extra boost to the efforts for trust, authentication, and standardization

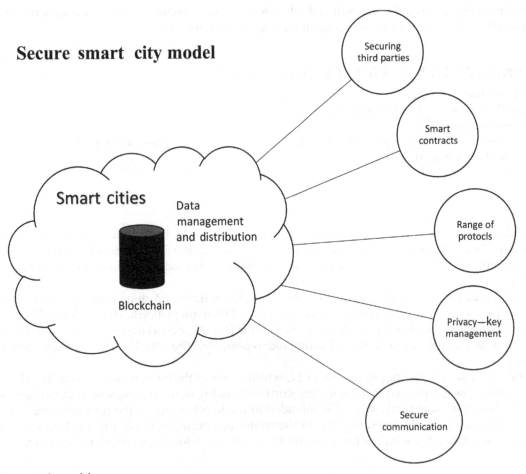

FIG. 5   Secure smart city model.

of various components in a smart city, and most importantly, for the capacity for peer-to-peer interaction without the need of the involvement of a third-party element [46].

5.2 Communication

In some functions of smart cities, privacy, integrity and anonymity are necessary. Blockchain should be able to provide solutions to these challenges, as they are paramount for essential services, such as e-voting. In the traditional way of e-voting, privacy, integrity, and anonymity are achieved through strong cryptography. However, there is a short period of vulnerability while the user decrypts the text in order to use it. During this short time gap, the information is in a plaintext format and is, therefore, vulnerable to interception. To avoid this risk, the calculations should be made without the need to decrypt the information.

On this matter, the Enigma protocol has been developed, which is based on blockchain, and uses homomorphic encryption. The protocol provides the opportunity for some information to remain decrypted, while allowing the user to perform calculations [47]. In this way, privacy and integrity are well protected. Homomorphic encryption is defined as the algorithm that allows the execution of calculations on encrypted fields. Eventually, the calculations produce an encrypted result, which, after being decrypted, remains the same, as if the calculation was made on plaintext directly [48].

This type of protocol could be applied in cases where the identification of the user is not paramount. For example, it could be used in [35]:

- Secure backend
- Blind e-voting where vote distribution is not required
- The IoT, where the source of the information is not necessary, for example, real-time data to drivers regarding a road accident
- Internal compartmentalization of large organizations against espionage or rogue employees
- Digital signature without any traces of the private key

5.3 Privacy—Key Management

Privacy should be an overall priority in smart cities. As it is a new concept for modern societies, privacy is a paramount element to establish smart cities in public opinion. The new technologies should be able to provide confidence to the users, who subsequently will adopt the services offered to them [49].

Key management will have a prominent role in securing privacy during the authentication process. Especially in the IoT era, lightweight cryptography schemes are necessary to reduce latency and resources. Recently, various lightweight cryptographic primitives have been introduced to substitute the conventional algorithms such as block ciphers, hash functions, and stream ciphers. The proliferation of the connected devices drives the urgency for more flexible solutions in the authentication of users. The performance advantages of lightweight ciphers provide smaller block and key sizes, as well as simpler key schedules [50]. Such schemes can be applied in various aspects of the IoT, apart from machine to machine authentication. Wireless networks could make use of the technology as energy consumption, overhead control, and reduced packet loss rate are key factors for performance enhancement [51].

5.4 Securing Third Parties

Smart cities will demand a plethora of solutions, technologies, and applications in order to meet the expectations of society. Service levels will have to improve, which will have a subsequent effect on the citizens' quality of life. Third-party vendors will be drawn in the game in order to meet the demands of the interconnected technologies. The ideal smart city model requires a strong accountability policy against the third parties that are going to be involved in the project. Strong contractual policies should be agreed upon to secure assets and datasets within the fast-moving environment of smart cities. On this note, the extensive use of open source solutions will have the opposite effect. Researcher Lisa Vaas set forth the example of the Heartbleed bug, which attacked the OpenSSL code. In this case, it is very hard to make accountable any stakeholder, hence other security requirements should be defined [52].

It is very important that all relevant parties have their responsibilities clarified well in advance. As a result, the duties and rights will be in line for the involved actors. The responsibilities should be defined by strong guidelines on maintenance of services, deployment of secure protocols, staff training, and testing provision for critical functions [53]. Moreover, the prioritization of data security through risk assessments and agreed incidence response plans will play a prominent role in smart cities [54]. The local authorities should be assured that there is a proactive plan in place with all security aspects agreed upon in advance in case of a security breach. This will provide peace of mind by establishing public confidence and strong supervision of the involved third parties.

5.5 Automation of Procedures—Smart Contracts

Smart contracts will disrupt the way of trading, exchanging services, and interacting between two parties. The ultimate aim of smart contracts will be to eliminate the need for a third-party element. The aim stands in decreasing the transaction time, resources, and effort. Using blockchain, two parties will be able to digitally sign a machine-readable contract. This move will remove from the process the services of third parties such as notaries, lawyers, and local authorities, as the information will be related to them directly. The omission of the third party makes the smart contract very attractive to consumers, as it will reduce the cost of each transaction (legal fees, commissions, etc.) [55]. A smart contract has the form of a code, and is a computerized transaction protocol suitable for achieving the correct execution of the terms of a contract [56]. The smart contract will be registered in the blockchain, and all relevant parties will have access to the terms and conditions at all times. It should be noted that smart contracts are not legal documents, as they are not covered by the contract law [55]. There are scholars who claim that smart contracts should have legal support during their creation, especially when these are referring to services that are under strict regulation [57].

Using smart contracts, the opportunities are unlimited. This is considered to be the main advantage of Ethereum over other platforms. Practically, it would be impossible to list all the application areas; to name a few, this model could find applications in crowdfunding, e-voting, digital signing of documents and e-auctions, among several others.

5.6 Protocols

Blockchain technology will be responsible for data storage, processing, and distribution, as its decentralized nature allows a more secure approach than the traditional way of data handling. Therefore, a new portfolio of protocols will be introduced for each function. Unfortunately, the one-size-fits-all concept does not suit this specific purpose. We have already examined the functionality of PoW and PoS. These two protocols seem to monopolize the interest of the blockchain community, as they are supported by bitcoin and Ethereum, respectively. However, in such a big smart urban setting, two protocols would not suffice. There are various other protocols that are currently used on the blockchain platform aiming to facilitate its more secure functionality.

In addition to the previously mentioned protocols, Proof of Activity (PoA) has been introduced. PoA combines the components from both PoS and PoW. The beginning of the procedure is similar to PoW, which means that potential miners are drawn into an arms race to solve a cryptographic quiz, which will allow them to claim the block. In contrast to the PoW protocol, the block will contain only the hash of the block header. Then, the PoS procedure comes into play. A group of stakeholders are asked to validate the transaction based on the number of coins they possess. This hybrid protocol promises an improved way of network topology that will need less energy to function. Also, there are lower transaction feeds involved, and incentives to the stakeholders to remain online [58].

We have already described the 51% vulnerability that affects mainly the PoW protocol. As the nodes can convert to adversaries, a more secure protocol should be used to eliminate the threat. For this purpose, an alternative consensus algorithm has been established. The protocol is called Proof of Vote (PoV) and is based on the bitcoin platform. The mechanism aims to "establish different security identity for network participants, so that the submission and verification of the blocks are decided by the agencies' voting in the league without the dependence on a third-party intermediary or uncontrollable public awareness" [59]. Compared with the main protocols that are in frequent use (PoW and PoS), PoV aims to provide a more controllable security and low delay during the time needed for the verification of a transaction.

6 CONCLUSIONS AND OUTLOOK

This chapter provides an overview of the technology of blockchain and how it can address the security challenges that we are facing during the transition toward the era of the IoT, and subsequently, to smart cities. At first, we examined the application of IoT in everyday life. It has already started making its appearance for industrial, as well as commercial, purposes. It is a standalone device that comprises the overall network, which means that various security issues are raised, depending on whether they are ready to comply with the new security standards. Gradually, we are transferring to the smart cities model. Their main aim is to make use of the advanced technology to gather mass volume of data that will be used for the improvement of our quality of life. We have stated the basic security issues that emerge from the lack of resources and the weakness to analyze the abundance of data within a realistic space of time.

Blockchain appears to be the chosen solution to provide answers to the IoT problems. We attempted a technical approach on how the technology works as opposed to the traditional way of storing and processing data. As in the case of IoT, we listed some of the areas in which blockchain could be applied, such as the financial sector, supply chains, and health care. The effect on the current way of living will be drastic, especially when it comes to the privacy and integrity of data. Moreover, the decentralized and publicly distributed approach of the data ledger will eliminate the current threat of the single point of failure. However, there are many aspects that need improvement in order to consider blockchain as a completely reliable solution. To name a few, there are questions raised regarding its ability to process data in an acceptable timeframe, which will comply with the increased demands of IoT. The latency on the creation of a block due to the consensus mechanism is a major drawback at this stage.

This chapter also presented the concept of e-governance through blockchain. E-governance is becoming very popular nowadays, and we experience its application in many countries, especially in Europe. Specifically, we analyzed the introduction of e-citizenship and e-ID in Estonia, and how this aims to change the dynamics between states and citizens. Smart contracts are a groundbreaking addition to the e-governance concept, and they are being served through the Ethereum platform. As in the case of the IoT and blockchain, smart contracts can be applied in many aspects of smart cities; however, there are already signs of vulnerability that expose them to threats. To this end, we proposed a hybrid model of a smart city that consisted of five basic elements that we deem essential to establish security and privacy.

To summarize, blockchain is a key element for data storage and distribution, which will be supported by strong blockchain protocols. Moreover, various lightweight cryptographic primitives should be applied to improve the levels of performance of the millions of interconnected nodes. As a further expansion of this study, the overall cost of the implementation of a secure smart city model could be analyzed. Sklavos and Souras [60] have produced a model of the cost categories that should be considered. The main elements included are the equipment and hardware, software, services, supplies, and personnel. Moreover, it is vital that third parties are secure, and operate in a strictly defined framework, which will make them accountable in case of a security breach. Smart contracts will assist in this effort by eliminating the need of third parties through their ability to establish a machine-readable contract. Finally, the proposed mode of smart cities should provide strong communication protocols to its citizens in order to boost confidence and secure their privacy.

APPENDIX

A.1 Smart Contract Proposal for Private Data Settlement in e-Governance

On many occasions, governmental authorities are not aware of the current status of their citizens, for example, when someone passes away. On such occasions, the authorities rely on next of kin or friends to inform them, and arrange all bureaucratic procedures that follow someone's death. For example, the next of kin should inform the registry office, the pension department (if applicable), social insurance services, deactivate their e-government credentials, and so forth. The procedure to inform all the relevant parties is a daunting task that requires too much time and resources. There are many occasions that some departments miss, neglect, or forget, without any information on the status of the citizen.

A.1.1 The Recommendation

The suggested smart contract aims to automate the procedure of updating all relevant parties about the death of a citizen. By making use of blockchain technology features, the created smart contract will inform all affected departments directly, without the need of personal involvement from whomever responsible; the public ledger of blockchain will be automatically updated. The advantages of this smart contract would be the following:

- Termination of benefits given by the state
- Deactivation of e-government credentials
- Initiation of procedures for status alternation in the public registry
- Settlement of any outstanding issues between state and individual

A.1.2 Procedure—Prerequisites

- The user is required to be registered on the e-government scheme with valid credentials
- Through the e-government portal, the user will be able to read the terms and conditions of the smart contract

— The user completes and digitally signs the certificate (certificate characteristics are explained in the next subsection)
— The certificate is accepted by the e-government portal
— The blockchain public ledger is updated and the contract can be retrieved by using the unique hash number
— When the account of the user remains inactive more than 6 months, the next of kin (3 individuals) are informed via email
— The next of kin are obliged to confirm the status of the citizen
— If the death of the citizen is confirmed, the smart contract is activated

A.1.3 Certificate

As discussed herein, the individual citizen should complete and sign a certificate that will form the terms and conditions of the smart contract. The certificate will have the following structure:

Field	Characteristic
User	*sig*
Officer ID	*sig*
E-governance ID	*sig*
Next of Kin 1	*sig*
Next of Kin 2	*sig*
Next of Kin 3	*sig*
Office issued	*location*
Creation	*timestamp*
Last modification	*timestamp*
Participation table	*timestamp/ring signatures*

References

[1] Roy, Siddiquee, Datta, Poddar, Ganguly, Bhattacharjee, Smart traffic & parking management using IoT, in: 2016 IEEE 7th Annual Information Technology, Electronics and Mobile Communication Conference (IEMCON), IEMCON, Vancouver, 2016, pp. 1–3.
[2] Sklavos, Zaharakis, Kameas, Kalapodi, Security & trusted devices in the context of internet of things (IoT), in: Euromicro Conference. Austria: Digital System Design, 2017.
[3] A.A. Shahzad, Y. Kim, A. Elgamoudi, Secure IoT platform for industrial control systems, in: 2017 International Conference on Platform Technology and Service (PlatCon), PlatCon, Busan, 2017, pp. 1–6.
[4] C. Bing, Cyberscoop, Retrieved from Cyberscoop: https://www.cyberscoop.com/hackable-iot-washing-machine-provides-channel-breaching-hospital/, 2017.
[5] FORTINET, Fortinet, Retrieved from Fortinet: https://www.fortinet.com/content/dam/fortinet/assets/white-papers/WP-IoT.pdf, 2017.
[6] N. Kshetri, Blockchain's Roles in Strengthening Cybersecurity and Protecting Privacy, Retrieved from Telecommunications Policy. http://www.sciencedirect.com/science/article/pii/S0308596117302483?via%3Dihub, 2017.
[7] Bhasin, Choudhury, Gupta, Kumar, Smart city implementation model based on IoT, in: 2017 International Conference on Big Data Analytics and Computational Intelligence (ICBDAC), ICBDAC, Chirala, 2017, pp. 211–216.
[8] T.E. Unit, The internet of things business index 2017, De Economist (2017).
[9] Jung, GreenBiz, Retrieved from IoT and Smart City Trends Boost Smart Waste Collection Market: https://www.greenbiz.com/article/iot-and-smart-city-trends-boost-smart-waste-collection-market, 2017.
[10] Pramanik, Laua, Demirkanb, Azadc, Smart health: big data enabled health paradigm within smart cities, Expert Syst. Appl. 87 (2017) 370–383.
[11] M.A. Amjad, Privacy analysis of smart city healthcare services, in: 2017 IEEE International Symposium on Multimedia, IEEE, 2017.
[12] D. Laney, 3-D Data Management: Controlling Data Volume, Velocity and Variety, MetaGroup, 2001.
[13] S. Ijaz, M. Ali Shah, A. Khan, M. Ahmed, Smart cities: a survey on security concerns, Int. J. Adv. Comput. Sci. Appl. (2016) 612–626.
[14] A.M. Ballesté, P. Pérez, A. Solanas, The pursuit of citizens' privacy: a privacy-aware Smart city is possible, IEEE Commun. Mag. 51 (6) (2013) 136–141.
[15] T. AlDairi, Cyber security attacks on smart cities and associated mobile technologies, in: The International Workshop on Smart Cities Systems Engineering, 2017.
[16] N.M. Rosario, The Emerging Blockchain Patent Landscape, 2017. Law360.
[17] G. Summers, Ethereum: Ethereum Investing, Programming, Mining, Blockchains, and Smart Contracts; Complete User's Guide for 2018, 2017.
[18] D. Schutzer, Financial Services Roundtable, Retrieved from Financial Services Roundtable: http://www.fsroundtable.org/cto-corner-what-is-a-blockchain-and-why-is-it-important/, 2016.
[19] N. Kshentri, Blockchain's roles in strengthening cybersecurity and protecting privacy, Telecommun. Policy 9 (2017) 22.
[20] M. Minelli, Harvard Business Review, Retrieved from Blockchain Will Help Us Prove Our Identities in a Digital World: https://hbr.org/2017/03/blockchain-will-help-us-prove-our-identities-in-a-digital-world, 2017.
[21] L. Xiaoqi, J. Peng, C. Ting, L. Xiapu, W. Qiaoyan, A survey on the security of blockchain systems, Futur. Gener. Comput. Syst. (2017), https://doi.org/10.1016/j.future.2017.08.020. in press.
[22] K. Minhaj, S. Khaled, IoT security: review, blockchain solutions, and open challenges, Futur. Gener. Comput. Syst. 82 (2017) 395–411.
[23] L. Nikhil, Dubai aims to be a city built on blockchain, Wall Street J. (2017).

[24] R. Ameer, Blockgeeks, Retrieved from Proof of Work vs Proof of Stake: Basic Mining Guide: https://blockgeeks.com/guides/proof-of-work-vs-proof-of-stake/, 2017.

[25] P. Fairley, The Ridiculous Amount of Energy It Takes to Run Bitcoin, Blockchain World, 2017.

[26] S. Nakamoto, Bitcoin.org, Retrieved from, https://bitcoin.org/bitcoin.pdf, 2008.

[27] V. Gupta, Harvard Business Review, Retrieved from, https://hbr.org/2017/02/a-brief-history-of-blockchain?referral=03759&cm_vc=rr_item_page.bottom, 2017.

[28] L. Shen, Fortune, Retrieved from, http://fortune.com/2016/09/28/blockchain-banks-2017/, 2016.

[29] R. Hanna, D. Auquier, Toumi, PHP115- Could Healthcoin Be A Revolution in Healthcare? Value in Health, 2017, p. A672.

[30] J.V. Dios, Medium, Retrieved from Why We're Building the Blockchain for Healthcare: https://blog.gem.co/why-were-building-the-blockchain-for-healthcare-bda5c09870aa, 2016.

[31] S. Manski, Building the blockchain world: technological commonwealth or just more of the same? in: The Future of Money and Further Applications of the Blockchain, 2017, pp. 511–522.

[32] J. McWaters, The future of financial infrastructure, in: World Economic Forum, Deloitte Consulting LLP, 2016.

[33] WorldBank. (n.d.). e-Gov Guideline. Retrieved from World Bank: http://siteresources.worldbank.org/INTEGOVERNMENT/Resources/e-Gov_guideline.pdf.

[34] J. Beumer, E-stonia – A Startup Country –(VPRO Documentary-2015), 2015 (Motion Picture).

[35] G. Zyskind, O. Nathan, A. Pentland, Decentralizing privacy: using blockchain to protect personal data, in: Security and Privacy Workshops (SPW), 2015, IEEE, San Jose, CA, USA, 2015.

[36] C. Sullivan, E. Burger, E-residency and blockchain, Comput. Law Secur. Rev. 33 (4) (2017) 470–481.

[37] T.W. Kwang, eGov Innovation, Retrieved from Dubai Land Department to conduct all transactions through blockchain: https://www.enterpriseinnovation.net/article/dubai-land-department-conduct-all-transactions-through-blockchain-106330370, 2017.

[38] Estonia, R. o. (n.d.). E-Residency. Retrieved from Republic of Estonia: https://e-resident.gov.ee/become-an-e-resident/.

[39] J. Millard, European strategies for e-governance to 2020 and beyond, in: Ojo, Adegboyega, Millard, Jeremy (Eds.), Government 3.0 – Next Generation Government Technology Infrastructure and Services, Springer, Cham, 2017, pp. 1–25.

[40] C. Frantz, M. Nowostawski, From institutions to code: towards automated generation of smart contracts, in: 2016 IEEE 1st Intternattiionall Workshops on Foundattiions and Applications off Sellff-Systtems, IEEE, 2016.

[41] Anonymous, Ethereum Contract Security Techniques and Tips, 2017. ethereum/wiki.

[42] D. Magazzeni, P. McBurney, W. Nash, Validation and verification of smart contracts: a research agenda, Computer 50 (2017) 57.

[43] N. Sklavos, I.D. Zaharakis, Cryptography and security in internet of things (IoTs): Models, schemes, and implementations, in: th IFIP International Conference on New Technologies, Mobility and Security (NTMS'16), IEEE, Larnaca, 2016.

[44] S. Chakrabarty, D. Engels, A secure IoT architecture for smart cities, in: 13th IEEE Annual Consumer Communications & Networking Conference, IEEE, 2016.

[45] SmartCity, Blockchain–Train of Innovative Thoughts Transforming Smart Cities, Retrieved from Smart City Press: https://www.smartcity.press/blockchain-implementations-in-smart-cities/, 2018.

[46] C. Review, Blockchain and IoT to Come Together as BIoT, Retrieved from CIO Review Team: https://www.cioreviewindia.com/news/blockchain-and-iot-to-come-together-as-biot-nid-4114-cid-135.html, 2017.

[47] D. Tiwari, MIT'S Enigma: Decentralized Cloud Platform with Guaranteed Privacy, Retrieved from Bitcoinist: http://bitcoinist.com/mit-enigma-decentralized-cloud-platform-guaranteed-privacy/, 2015.

[48] X. Yi, R. Paulet, E. Bertino, Homomorphic Encryption and Applications, Springer International Publishing, Cham, Switzerland, 2014.

[49] Bartoli, Soriano, Hernandez-Serrano, Dohler, Kountouris, Barthel, Security and privacy in your smart city, in: Barcelona Smart Cities Congress 2011, Barcelona, 2011.

[50] McKay, Bassham, Sönmez, Mouha, Report on Lightweight Cryptography, NIST, 2017.

[51] Qin, Jia, Yang, Wang, Ding, A lightweight authentication and key management scheme for wireless sensor networks, J. Sens. (2016) 9.

[52] L. Vaas, Establishing Security Guidelines for Smart City Projects, Retrieved from Hewlett Packard Enterprise, https://www.hpe.com/us/en/insights/articles/establishing-security-guidelines-for-smart-city-projects-1802.html, 2018.

[53] C. Levy-Bencheton, E. Darra, Cyber Security for Smart Cities, EU: ENISA, 2015.

[54] S. Durin, Building Smart City Security, Retrieved from Techcrunch: https://techcrunch.com/2015/09/12/building-smart-city-security/, 2015.

[55] M. Kõlvart, M. Poola, A. Rull, Smart contracts, in: M. Kõlvart, M. Poola, A. Rull (Eds.), The Future of Law and eTechnologies, Springer, Cham, 2016, pp. 133–147.

[56] A. Norta, Designing a Smart-Contract Application Layer for Transacting Decentralized Autonomous Organizations, Springer Nature Singapore Pte Ltd, 2017, p. 2017.

[57] F. Al Khalil, T. Butler, L. O'Brien, M. Ceci, Trust in smart contracts is a process, as well, in: FC 2017 Workshops 2017, International Financial Cryptography Association, Cork, 2017, pp. 510–519.

[58] I. Bentov, C. Lee, A. Mizrahi, Proof of Activity: Extending Bitcoin's Proof of Work via Proof of Stake, 2014.

[59] K. Li, H. Li, H. Hou, K. Li, Y. Chen, Proof of vote: a high-performance consensus protocol based on vote mechanism & consortium blockchain, in: 19th International Conference on High Performance Computing and Communications, IEEE, 2017, pp. 466–473.

[60] Sklavos, Souras, Economic models and approaches in information security for computer networks, Int. J. Netw. Secur. 2 (1) (2006) 14–20.

Further Reading

[61] i-scoop.eu, The Internet of Things (IoT)–Essential IoT Business Guide, Retrieved from i-sccop.eu: https://www.i-scoop.eu/internet-of-things-guide/#The_Internet_of_Things_in_an_infographic, 2017.

[62] A. Gruenheid, X. Luna Dong, D. Srivastava, Incremental record linkage, VLDB Endowment 7 (9) (2014) 697–708.

[63] A. Trafton, Research Reveals a Gender Gap in the Nation's Biology Labs, Retrieved from MIT news, http://news.mit.edu/2014/research-reveals-gender-gap-nations-biology-labs-0630, 2014.

4

Privacy-Aware Physical Layer Security Techniques for Smart Cities

Ravikant Saini and *Deepak Mishra*[†]

*Department of Electrical Engineering, Indian Institute of Technology Jammu, Jammu, India
[†]Department of Electrical Engineering (ISY), Linköping University, Linköping, Sweden

1 INTRODUCTION

The Internet of Things (IoT) was envisioned as a paradigm that removes the boundary between the physical and cyber worlds. It is a network of "things" that are an amalgamation of hardware and software to ensure connectivity and information exchange among each other. Thus, devices are connected through different access networks that are capable of collecting information and processing it to make decisions based on control parameters without any human intervention. The IoT consists of sensors, actuators, controllers, and communication networks. The interaction among the devices could range from simply turning home appliances on and off, to more sophisticated reporting on healthcare parameters and drug injections.

Because devices share information that may be critical to the overall operation of the IoT system, secrecy of information is an inherent challenge in the IoT. Security of communication is required at the uplink when sensors forward information to the controllers, as well as on the downlink where corrective measures are forwarded to actuators. Security issues should be investigated from the viewpoint of a passive eavesdropper just listening to the ongoing communication, and also from active eavesdroppers, which are the nodes present in the vicinity, but belonging to other untrusted vendors. Security in such an environment is a key challenge because of the constraints in system resources, such as the node's power and computational capability. Sensors and actuators are simple devices that may not be computationally strong. Thus, instead of cryptography, physical layer security (PLS) is a better solution, due to lower implementation costs and relatively low complexity.

In this chapter, we discuss how the conventional physical layer techniques can help in the revitalization of secure Smart Cities. After briefly introducing the needs of privacy-aware Smart Cities in Section 2, we present a brief overview highlighting the key features of physical layer techniques in Section 3. Building upon them, we present joint resource allocation schemes and green secure cooperative protocols for maximizing the achievable secure rate in Section 4. Thereafter, we respectively discuss in detail the role of a friendly jammer and a trusted relay in further secure enhancement in Sections 5 and 6. Last, after briefly presenting novel research directions in Section 7, we conclude the chapter with the key takeaways in Section 8.

2 PRIVACY-AWARE SMART CITIES

The IoT is not just a technology, but a finely woven network of technical solutions that provide smooth information and control flow from sensors to actuators. With smart sensors feeding critical information to controllers thorough heterogeneous networks that are computationally capable of processing bulk data and generating key decisions for real-time actuators present on the ground, the new paradigm offers smarter cities with advanced and adaptive facilities for the ever-increasing demands of the next generation.

2.1 Smart City Applications

Ideally, smart cities will include smart homes, smart health care, smart transport, smart girds, smart vehicles, and smart waste management, systems, among others. The smart home is a network of communicating devices that are capable of adjusting the aura and feel of the internal environment of the home. For example, after receiving a signal from your office controller, the house controller might activate the faucet for a warm bath, adjust AC to help you be more comfortable, turn on the TV and have it play your favorite show, and so forth. In a similar manner, smart health care would consist of a network of wearable sensors that record critical health parameters, and report any discrepancy therein to the concerned medical personnel, and might command the drug injectors to inject medicine.

Smart transportation is capable of optimizing the available resources so as to minimize travel duration, traffic jams, and traffic overloads by diverting and offloading the key congestion-prone routes. Smart grids are auto-tunable resources of energy that balance various sources of energy supplies to match the varying demands of Smart Cities based on space and time. The smart vehicle is a driverless vehicle that plans the journey ahead of time, anticipating the onroad traffic, and helping you enjoy your favorite video without being worried about the traffic and road. Smart waste management is a networked collection of dustbins, collectors, and disposal systems to help cities remain clean and tidy.

To summarize, the Smart City is the conceptualization of a utopian era in which machines/devices/things work together for the betterment of the personal and social life of each inhabitant, by adjusting its parameters to accommodate the varying demands of society in general, and the personal requirements of individuals.

2.2 Privacy and Security Issues

With this added infrastructure, Smart Cities have their own challenges, such as power consumption, monitoring, maintenance, and so forth. Most of the sensors are battery powered, which raises the concern of battery replacement, otherwise the whole system may topple down. Monitoring the key sensors and actuators may require human intervention, depending on their importance in the complete network. Maintenance is a big challenge that involves replacement of faulty devices, re-establishing any broken communication paths, and installing new hardware and/or software for further upgrading the infrastructure.

Along with all these infrastructure-related issues, open wireless communication between smart devices brings forth the challenge of securing key information, which is an important vulnerability. Smartness of devices relies on sending and receiving key information, which may be a sensory data or actuation control signal. Because this information can be intercepted by intruders, security of communication is a major challenge in IoT-based Smart Cities.

The repercussions of this security breach could lead to a loss of users' privacy due to availability of information from the sensors at home or on the road. Because all information regarding the daily routine of an individual is available, the scope of attacks may go beyond monetary losses to personalized attacks. For example, if the control signal to a drug injector could be manipulated, this could lead to the eventual death of an individual.

In contrast to targeting of the individual, there could be cases of hackers taking control of the whole infrastructure, which could create havoc, and put human lives at stake. Be it home, office, transportation, smart grid, or computation center, everything is remotely accessible at the cost of authentication. If somebody is able to break the security layer of authentication, he/she could move things as desired. Thus, the whole city, along with its inhabitants, is at risk of a virtual attack, planned by someone who is operating remotely.

3 OVERVIEW OF PHYSICAL LAYER SECURITY TECHNIQUES

Secure communication, in such an environment, is a key challenge because of the constraints of system resources, such as node's power and computational capability. Sensors and actuators are simple devices that may be battery powered, and may not be computationally strong. Thus, computation-based cryptography is not a feasible solution; instead, PLS is more promising, as it provides a relatively less complex solution to the secrecy problem.

3.1 Background

The key idea behind information theory-based PLS is to utilize the fading characteristics of the wireless channel to securely transmit a message from the source to the destination in the presence of an eavesdropper. PLS is based on the randomness of the channels. The secure rate is defined as the nonnegative difference between the rate of the intended user and the eavesdropper. Mathematically, a secure rate can be stated as:

$$R_s = [R_d - R_e]^+ \tag{1}$$

where $x^+ = \max\{0, x\}$, and R_d and R_e are, respectively, the rates of the desired destination and the eavesdropper.

Communication needs to be protected against the malicious intentions of an external eavesdropper. Security issues should be investigated from the viewpoint of a passive eavesdropper, who is just listening to the ongoing communication. Because these eavesdroppers are silent, their location and channel state information (CSI) cannot be estimated correctly. On the other hand, there could be active eavesdroppers that are active nodes present in the vicinity, but belonging to some other vendor. Because these are communicating nodes, their CSI can be estimated, and accordingly, their transmission strategy can be adapted. On the other hand, an example of an extreme scenario is that of untrusted users, which is a hostile situation, in which users have lost mutual trust and consider each other potential eavesdroppers. Thus, each user requests secure communication from the source, assuming all other users could be potential eavesdroppers.

3.2 Security Mechanisms Against External Eavesdroppers

An external eavesdropper is an entity external to the network, and interested in observing information being transmitted over the network. These may be nodes intentionally placed for eavesdropping, or may be nodes from other vendors, which are likely to eavesdrop on key information. In this scenario all users are trusted, and there is a passive eavesdropper who is interested in wiretapping the broadcast communication. Many system models have been considered with an external eavesdropper. There may be a single source-destination pair communication (cf. Fig. 1: EE_1), with single or multiple helper nodes (cf. Fig. 1: EE_2), and source to multiuser communication (cf. Fig. 2: EE_3) without helper and with helper nodes (cf. Fig. 2: EE_4).

3.2.1 Single Source-Destination Pair

Single source-destination pair communication (cf. Fig. 1: EE_1) in the presence of an eavesdropper has been studied extensively. Depending on the availability of perfect, imperfect, or partial CSI of the eavesdropper, the source may perform resource allocation optimally to maximize its sum secrecy rate against the eavesdropper. The source can utilize multiple antennas for improving the secrecy performance further. The author in [1] was the first to consider the security aspects in multiinput multioutput (MIMO) communication systems. He observed that, with proper utilization of space-time block coding techniques, the information hiding capabilities of the system are improved. The authors in [2] studied the utilization of artificial noise for secrecy performance improvement in two scenarios, one with a multiantenna transmitter, and the other with multiple helper nodes. The authors in [3] extended the concept of utilization of artificial noise to MIMO systems and developed secure capacity boundaries for MIMO systems. A parallel broadcast fading communication channel for sending a common message to both the destinations and one secret message to only one destination, was considered in [4], in which the authors derived the secrecy capacity regions, and the optimal power allocation, achieving the boundary of these regions.

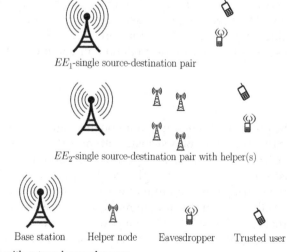

EE_1-single source-destination pair

EE_2-single source-destination pair with helper(s)

Base station   Helper node   Eavesdropper   Trusted user

FIG. 1 Single source-destination pair with external eavesdropper.

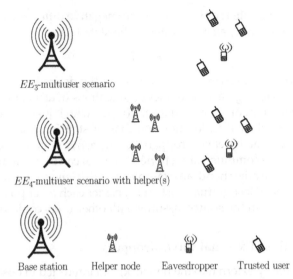

EE_3-multiuser scenario

EE_4-multiuser scenario with helper(s)

Base station   Helper node   Eavesdropper   Trusted user

FIG. 2   Multiple trusted users with external eavesdropper.

3.2.2 Single Source-Destination Pair With Trusted Helper Nodes

Further, external helper nodes can be introduced for improving the secrecy performance of the overall system. The helper node could be a jammer to degrade the channel of the eavesdropper, or a relay to improve the channel of the destination by providing communication diversity. Helper nodes in various modes of operation have been investigated (cf. Fig. 1: EE_2). The helper node could be a trusted/untrusted relay in single/multiple-antenna configurations. It can cooperate in any one of the cooperative schemes, such as decode and forward (DF), amplify and forward (AF), or cooperative jamming (CJ).

Assuming the helper node itself to be untrusted, the author in [5] considered the problem of deriving capacity theorems for secure communication from source to destination. The authors in [6] considered a DF relay-assisted secure communication, considering the availability of a direct path between the source and destination. The power allocation problem for secure rate maximization was considered under total system power constraints. In the same setup, Jindal and Bose [7] considered the subcarrier and power allocation problem with an AF relay. The problem of optimal relay selection from a pool of relays was considered by the authors in [8]. An optimal power allocation problem for a multi-hop cooperation communications system employing DF relays was recently considered in [9].

The helper node can be utilized as a friendly jammer, which can be utilized to send random data to degrade the capability of the eavesdropper. Extending the concept of artificial noise, the authors in [10] considered the possibility of sending a jamming signal from a helper node, which is independent of the message signal from the source. The optimal power allocation problem for a friendly jammer over OFDM channels was considered in [11]. Cooperation of relays was considered for two complementary problems, namely, sum rate maximization and sum power minimization under two modes of operation of relays, that is, DF relaying and cooperative jamming in [12]. Considering the possibility of utilizing some nodes for relaying and others for sending jamming signals, joint beamforming and a cooperative jamming strategy were considered in [13–15]. The authors in [16] considered the problem of deciding whether to relay or to jam in an AF relay-assisted single source-destination pair communication with an objective of ergodic secrecy rate maximization.

3.2.3 Multiuser Scenario

The authors in [17] considered the problem of sending a common message and independent confidential messages to each user in a multiuser broadcast communication system with an external eavesdropper (cf. Fig. 2: EE_3). The authors in [18] considered the problem of subcarrier and power allocation and artificial noise design for secure sum rate maximization with M trusted users and an external eavesdropper. In a similar multiuser setup, the authors in [19] considered the problem of maximizing the minimum of weighted sum secure rates of all the users in the presence of an eavesdropper. A resource allocation problem with multiple users was studied in [20], with boundaries on per-user tolerable secrecy outage probabilities, in which optimal power and subcarrier allocation policies were derived with the objective of maximizing the energy efficiency. In a DF relay-assisted multiuser secure communication system (cf. Fig. 2: EE_4), the average secrecy outage capacity maximization was studied in [21].

In general, there can be more than one external eavesdroppers in the system. These eavesdroppers may be either colluding or noncolluding eavesdroppers in nature. In case they are noncolluding, the user has to contend with the strongest among the eavesdroppers. In case there are colluding eavesdroppers, the secrecy problems become a bit more difficult, as the eavesdroppers can combine their respective observations to vandalize the secure communication.

3.3 Secure IoT With Untrusted Users

Untrusted users create a hostile scenario in which users do not even trust peers for secure communication. Such an environment is critical, and is imperative for secrecy analysis of a completely automatic system that covers all spans of human civilization. The key functionalities of a Smart City should be modeled on an untrusted user's system so that emergency services could be sustained even if some of the integral nodes of the communication network are themselves captured and misused by an external threat. An untrusted user scenario also helps in implementing the distributed and independent operation of the multiple heterogeneous energy-constrained low power wireless devices in the IoT.

Considering all other users as potential eavesdroppers, the source transmits secure data to the intended destination through optimal resource allocation. As it can be expected, a secure rate in this scenario is relatively lower, as the intended user has to contend all of the remaining users. The eavesdropper with the maximum rate is considered to be the equivalent eavesdropper. Thus, in order to achieve secure communication, the rate of the intended user should be greater than the rate of the equivalent eavesdropper.

3.3.1 Communication Without Helper Nodes

In the scenario with untrusted users (cf. Fig. 3), the authors in [22] studied the security rate regions for discrete memoryless interference and broadcast channels with two receivers, in an attempt to send confidential messages to respective receivers while keeping them secure from the others. The authors in [23] proposed to allocate a subcarrier to its best-gain user, and presented the optimal power allocation policy for a two-user OFDMA system. This scheme can be easily extended for a multiuser system model. The authors in [24] studied the subcarrier and power allocation for two classes of users. There are some secure users that have a fixed secure rate demand, and there are normal users that are served with best effort traffic.

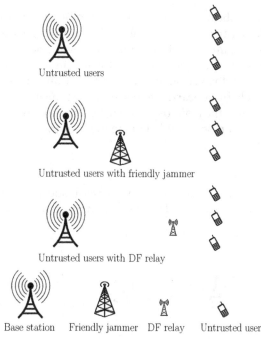

Untrusted users

Untrusted users with friendly jammer

Untrusted users with DF relay

Base station   Friendly jammer   DF relay   Untrusted user

FIG. 3 Various configurations investigated for implementing PLS techniques in a multiple untrusted users scenario.

3.3.2 Communication With Helper Nodes

In an external eavesdropper case, the intended user has to be stronger than the strongest among all eavesdroppers, while in the untrusted users case, intended user has to be the strongest among all the users. Thus, the untrusted users are part of a relatively constrained system, and secure rates are lower. In order to improve the secure rate, helper nodes could be used, as either a jammer or a relay. The utilization of these helper nodes can be justified only if there is sum secure rate improvement. However, this secure rate gain comes at the cost of power utilized by the helper node, and the complexity of optimal resource allocations performed for secrecy enhancement. The resource allocation problem for relay-assisted communication between multiple source-destination pairs with untrusted users was considered in [25].

4 JOINT OPTIMIZATION OF KEY RESOURCE ALLOCATION PARAMETERS IN PLS

To improve secrecy of the system through PLS, the key strategy is to increase the gap between the rate of the intended user and the eavesdropper. The rate depends on SNR, which in turn depends on the channel gain and power. Thus, *subcarrier allocation*, which identifies the user of a subcarrier, and *power allocation*, which decides how much power is to be allocated on the subcarrier, are some of the key controllers in resource allocation in secure communication. Utilizing the subcarrier and power resources optimally is referred as resource allocation. Next, we discuss the efficacy of resource allocation in the purview of a system with untrusted users.

In the downlink communication system, the base station (BS) is a main controller that sends key decisions to end point actuators for overall adaptation in the Smart City. In case BS wishes to use one or more of the nodes as helpers, then another interesting controller *mode selection* comes into the picture. In a simpler scenario, mode selection decides whether the helper node should be utilized or not. While in a complex scenario, mode selection identifies the mode in which the helper node should be utilized, that is, as a relay or a jammer. Optimal mode selection could be dependent on power allocation. Thus, optimal mode selection and power allocation could be interrelated. Refer to Fig. 4 for some of the key controllers in secure resource allocation.

4.1 Smart Resource Allocation Strategies

Resource allocation deals with sharing of the common system resources among users. In general, it includes subcarrier allocation, power allocation, mode selection, and subcarrier pairing (SCP).

4.1.1 Subcarrier Allocation

Subcarrier allocation, which divides subcarriers among the contending users, identifies the main user and also the corresponding eavesdropper on each subcarrier. Because subcarriers are independent in an OFDMA-based system, the subcarrier allocation problem can be decomposed at the subcarrier level, and can be completed in parallel. In secure communications, a subcarrier can be owned by the user with the maximum SNR over that subcarrier. For a system with background noise, SNR depends on the subcarrier gain and the transmit power over the subcarrier. The SNRs over a subcarrier are differentiated solely by subcarrier gains, because transmit power is the same for each user. Thus, the user with maximum subcarrier gains is the main user, and the user with next-best gain is the corresponding eavesdropper. This optimal subcarrier allocation strategy is independent of the power allocation, and can be completed independently before power allocation.

4.1.2 Power Allocation

After subcarrier allocation, the source-to-M user problem over each subcarrier is simplified to a source to two-user problem, in which the two users are the main user and the corresponding eavesdropper. Now, power allocation is to be

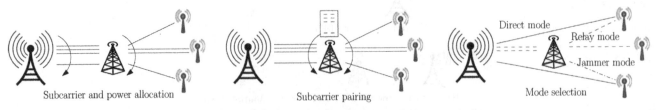

FIG. 4   Various resource allocation strategies for trusted relay-assisted secure cooperative communications.

completed, which decides optimal power on each subcarrier. Even though the subcarriers are independent, it is the power constraint that binds the system together, as the total power budget has to be shared among the subcarriers. The conventional water filling proposed for the nonsecure multicarrier communication system cannot be directly extended for secure communication systems as the secure rate definition involves channel gains of the main user as well as eavesdroppers. In case of a helper node, power allocation on the helper node depends on the mode of operation of the helper node.

4.1.3 Subcarrier Pairing

Subcarriers on the two hops of a relay-assisted secure communication system can be mapped independently. This strategy of mapping subcarriers is referred to as SCP. SCP results in an extra degree of freedom, which leads to secrecy performance improvement. This gain comes at the cost of the combinatorial aspect introduced by SCP. For an N subcarrier system, SCP introduces $N!$ combinations, out of which only one is optimal. The ordered pairing strategy proposed for nonsecure cooperative communication is not optimal for a secure communication system, as in secure systems, the channel gain of the eavesdropper also comes into the picture.

4.1.4 Mode Selection

This is an interesting, but not so obvious, observation on secrecy. Actually, a helper, whether in a relay mode or in a jammer mode, may help some of the subcarriers, but not all the subcarriers. Thus, identification of those subcarriers over which helper power should be utilized for relaying and over which jamming should be done is an important question. This identification task is more commonly referred to as "mode selection."

4.2 Optimal Cooperation Among the IoT Nodes

Even in an untrusted users scenario, there exists minimal cooperation among users. An intended user over a subcarrier may be equivalent to an eavesdropper on some other subcarrier. The source cannot penalize any user specifically, because all users are legitimate. Thus, it is just a matter of the role that a user plays on an individual subcarrier. Resource allocation distributes common resources in such a way that overall secrecy performance of the system is optimal through optimal cooperation among nodes.

With the addition of helper nodes, new channel gains come into the picture, which may help in improving the secrecy performance of the system. For example, even with a simplified scenario with just a main user and an eavesdropper, the relay mode introduces three channel gains (source to relay, and relay to each user), while the jammer mode introduces two channel gains (from the jammer to each user) over each subcarrier. These additional channel gains provide an additional degree of freedom. Next, we discuss the utilization of this additional degree of freedom, which is achieved through the usage of a helper node.

4.2.1 Helper Node as a Jammer

While using a helper as a jammer, the intention is to decrease the SNR of the eavesdropper. However, in an untrusted multiuser scenario, the jammer has to use caution, as a user who is an eavesdropper on some subcarrier may be an intended user on some other subcarrier. Thus, utilizing jammer power on each subcarrier is an important decision that has to be taken on by each subcarrier. Jammer is supposed to send an independent jamming signal, which will effect both the intended user, as well as the eavesdropper. Thus, secrecy enhancement can be achieved if the jammer affects eavesdropper channel more harshly compared with the channel of the intended user.

4.2.2 Helper Node as a Relay

A relay node provides coverage enhancement and/or diversity. In case the source is not able to reach users directly, relays are used to provide coverage enhancement. On the other hand, even if a direct link from the source to users is available, a relay may be utilized to improve the secrecy performance. In this case, a relay provides additional diversity by offering an alternate path of information transfer to users. The operation protocol of the relay could be AF, DF, randomize and forward (RF), and so forth. Regardless of direct link availability, there could be individual or sum power budget constraints on the system. Other system scenarios could include a pool of relays, relays with multiple antennas, or trusted or untrusted relays.

An IoT-based secure communication system has to be investigated for optimization of these key controllers. Through optimal utilization of all the resources, the secrecy performance of the IoT system can be optimized.

5 SMART-FRIENDLY JAMMING FOR SECRECY ENHANCEMENT

To determine the efficacy of a friendly jammer in improving the secrecy performance of a system with untrusted users, we should consider the downlink of an OFDMA system with a single source $\mathcal{S}$ (BS), a friendly jammer $\mathcal{J}$, and M untrusted mobile users $\mathcal{U}_m$ (MUs) [26]. The jammer is capable of collecting CSI from the users in the uplink. In the downlink, the jammer can send a jamming signal on each subcarrier, which is unknown to users.

Joint resource allocation, including subcarrier allocation and optimal power allocation at the source, as well as the jammer, has been considered. Thus, optimization is a combinatorial problem involving binary and real variables. Observing the complexity of the joint resource allocation involving subcarrier allocation at the source as well as the jammer, and then power allocation at the source and the jammer, the problem is divided in parts. Initially, the system assumes that the jammer is not present at all. Obtaining subcarrier allocation at the source improves secure rate conditions through jammer power utilization. This helps in deciding the subcarriers over which jammer power should be utilized. Over those subcarriers where jammer power is to used, there is an optimal jammer power that should be utilized for maximizing the secure rate. Finally, a joint power allocation (JPA) strategy based on alternate optimization and primary decomposition is developed, which solves the power allocation optimally.

It is assumed that the source has perfect CSI of source-to-MU and jammer-to-MU channel pairs for all the MUs. Let $h_{i,n}$ and $g_{i,n}$ denote the channel coefficients to the ith user from the source and the jammer, respectively, over subcarrier n as shown in Fig. 5. Let P_{s_n} and P_{j_n} be source and jammer power over subcarrier n. The secure rate that is achieved by user m on the nth subcarrier is given as [23, 24]:

$$
\begin{aligned}
R_{s_{m,n}} &= \{R_{m,n} - R_{e,n}\}^+ \\
&= \left[\log_2\left(1 + \frac{P_{s_n}|h_{m,n}|^2}{\sigma^2 + \pi_{j_n} P_{j_n}|g_{m,n}|^2}\right) - \max_{o \in \{1,2,\dots,M\}\setminus m} \log_2\left(1 + \frac{P_{s_n}|h_{o,n}|^2}{\sigma^2 + \pi_{j_n} P_{j_n}|g_{o,n}|^2}\right) \right]^+
\end{aligned}
\tag{2}
$$

where σ^2 is the AWGN noise variance, $\pi_{j_n} \in \{0,1\}$ is a binary variable indicating the absence or presence of jammer power on subcarrier n, o is one of the potential eavesdroppers, and e is the equivalent eavesdropper.

5.1 Joint Source and Jammer Resource Allocation Problem

The joint source and jammer resource optimization problem for weighted sum secure rate maximization can be stated as:

$$
\begin{aligned}
\mathcal{P}_1 : \underset{P_{s_n}, P_{j_n}, \pi_{m,n}, \pi_{j_n}}{\text{maximize}} \quad & \sum_{m=1}^{M}\sum_{n=1}^{N} w_m \pi_{m,n} R_{s_{m,n}} \\
\text{subject to} \quad & \\
C_{1,1} : \sum_{n=1}^{N} P_{s_n} \le P_S, \quad & C_{1,2} : \sum_{n=1}^{N} P_{j_n} \le P_J, \quad C_{1,3} : \pi_{j_n} \in \{0,1\} \ \forall \ n, \\
C_{1,4} : \pi_{m,n} \in \{0,1\} \ \forall \ m,n, \quad & C_{1,5} : \sum_{m=1}^{M} \pi_{m,n} \le 1 \ \forall \ n, \quad C_{1,6} : P_{s_n} \ge 0, P_{j_n} \ge 0 \ \forall \ n
\end{aligned}
\tag{3}
$$

where $\pi_{m,n}$ is the binary allocation variable indicating whether subcarrier n is allocated to user m or not, w_m is the priority weight imposed by higher layers to prioritize user m, and P_S and P_J are source and jammer power budgets, respectively. There are four variables per subcarrier in the optimization problem described in Eq. (3): two binary indicator variables π_{j_n} and $\pi_{m,n}$, and two continuous power variables P_{s_n} and P_{j_n}.

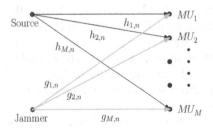

FIG. 5 Broadcast secure OFDMA communication system with untrusted users and a friendly jammer.

The problem has nonlinear, nonconvex objective function, and combinatorial aspects due to binary variables. Because the problem belongs to the class of NP-hard problems and there is no polynomial time optimal solution possible [27, 28], the problem is handled by breaking it in parts to find a near optimal solution. For this, subcarrier allocation at the source is performed without considering the presence of a jammer. Then those subcarriers over which a jammer can improve the secure rate are determined, and finally, optimal JPA is performed.

5.1.1 Subcarrier Allocation at the Source

If a jammer is absent, $\pi_{j_n} = 0 \ \forall \ n$, and the secure rate definition in Eq. (2) changes to:

$$R_{s_{m,n}}\big|_{\pi_{j_n}=0} = \left[\log_2 \left(1 + \frac{P_{s_n}|h_{m,n}|^2}{\sigma^2} \right) - \max_{o \in \{1,2,\dots,M\} \setminus m} \log_2 \left(1 + \frac{P_{s_n}|h_{o,n}|^2}{\sigma^2} \right) \right]^+ \tag{4}$$

Observing Eq. (4), it is noted that in order to have a positive secure rate over subcarrier n, $|h_{m,n}|$ should be the maximum channel gain, that is, $|h_{m,n}| > \max_{o \in \{1,2,\dots,M\} \setminus m} |h_{o,n}|$ irrespective of P_{s_n}. Thus, the subcarrier allocation policy can be stated as:

$$\pi_{m,n} = \begin{cases} 1 & \text{if } |h_{m,n}| = \max_{i \in \{1,2,\dots,M\}} |h_{i,n}| \\ 0 & \text{otherwise} \end{cases} \tag{5}$$

5.1.2 Subcarrier Allocation at the Jammer, and Jammer Power Boundaries

Because the jammer affects all the users and reduces the SNR of each user, it appears counterintuitive that the secure rate could be improved though jammer power. But if the effect on the eavesdropper is compared with the main user, then there is a gain in the secure rate. In order to give a simple proof of concept, consider a simple OFDMA system with four nodes: source, jammer, and two users, m and e. Let subcarrier n be given to user m, and e is the corresponding eavesdropper. The possibility of secure rate improvement over subcarrier n is described by the following proposition.

Proposition 1. *The secure rate over a subcarrier n owned by user m, that is, $|h_{m,n}| > |h_{e,n}|$ can be improved with the help of jammer power if $|g_{e,n}| > |g_{m,n}|$ and the source and jammer powers P_{s_n} and P_{j_n} are constrained as:*

$$P_{s_n} > P_{s_n}^{th_i} \triangleq \begin{cases} \dfrac{\sigma^2 \left(|g_{m,n}|^2 |h_{m,n}|^2 - |g_{e,n}|^2 |h_{e,n}|^2 \right)}{\left(|g_{e,n}|^2 - |g_{m,n}|^2 \right) |h_{m,n}|^2 |h_{e,n}|^2}, & \text{if } \dfrac{|g_{m,n}||h_{m,n}|}{|g_{e,n}||h_{e,n}|} > 1 \\ 0, & \text{otherwise} \end{cases} \tag{6}$$

$$\text{and} \quad P_{j_n} < P_{j_n}^{th_i} \triangleq \dfrac{P_{s_n} \alpha_n + \sigma^2 \beta_n}{|g_{m,n}|^2 |g_{e,n}|^2 \left(|h_{m,n}|^2 - |h_{e,n}|^2 \right)}$$

where $\alpha_n = \left(|g_{e,n}|^2 - |g_{m,n}|^2 \right) |h_{m,n}|^2 |h_{e,n}|^2$ and $\beta_n = \left(|g_{e,n}|^2 |h_{e,n}|^2 - |g_{m,n}|^2 |h_{m,n}|^2 \right)$.

In the constrained domain described by the channel conditions and power constraints, the secure rate of user m over n is a quasiconcave function of jammer power P_{j_n} such that there exists an optimal jammer power $P_{j_n}^o$ achieving the maximum secure rate over that subcarrier.

Based on the channel conditions described by Proposition 1, a prospective set of subcarriers is created over which the secure rate can be improved by jammer power. The resulting subcarrier allocation policy indicating whether to use jammer power over a subcarrier, is given as:

$$\pi_{j_n} = \begin{cases} 1 & \text{if } |g_{e,n}| > |g_{m,n}| \\ 0 & \text{otherwise.} \end{cases} \tag{7}$$

5.1.3 Joint Optimization of Source and Jammer Power

Based on the decision on utilization of jammer power over a subcarrier using the result of Proposition 1, all subcarriers are divided in two sets: $\{\mathcal{J}_0\}$—over which jammer power cannot be used, and $\{\mathcal{J}_1\}$—over which jammer power can be used for secure rate improvement. On the subcarriers of set $\{\mathcal{J}_0\}$ only source power allocation has to be done, while on the subcarriers of set $\{\mathcal{J}_1\}$ joint source and jammer power allocation have to be done. Let the SNRs of the user m, without jammer power and with jammer power over subcarrier n, be denoted as $\gamma_{m,\,n}$ and $\gamma_{m,\,n}'$, respectively, that is, $\gamma_{m,n} = \frac{P_{s_n}|h_{m,n}|^2}{\sigma^2}$; $\gamma_{m,n}' = \frac{P_{s_n}|h_{m,n}|^2}{\sigma^2 + P_{j_n}|g_{m,n}|^2}$. The joint source and jammer power allocation problem can be expressed as:

$$\mathcal{P}_2: \quad \underset{P_{s_x}, P_{s_y}, P_{j_y}}{\text{maximize}} \left\{ \sum_{x \in \mathcal{J}_0} w_x' \left[\log_2(1 + \gamma_{m,x}) - \log_2(1 + \gamma_{e,x}) \right] \right.$$

$$\left. + \sum_{y \in \mathcal{J}_1} w_y' \left[\log_2(1 + \gamma_{m,y}') - \log_2(1 + \gamma_{e,y}') \right] \right\} \tag{8}$$

subject to

$$C_{2,1}: \sum_{x \in \mathcal{J}_0} P_{s_x} + \sum_{y \in \mathcal{J}_1} P_{s_y} \leq P_S, \quad C_{2,2}: \sum_{y \in \mathcal{J}_1} P_{j_y} \leq P_J, \quad C_{2,3}: P_{j_y} > P_{j_y}^l \;\; \forall \;\; y \in \mathcal{J}_1,$$

$$C_{2,4}: P_{j_y} < P_{j_y}^u \;\; \forall \;\; y \in \mathcal{J}_1, \quad C_{2,5}: P_{s_x} \geq 0, P_{s_y} \geq 0 \;\; \forall \;\; x \in \mathcal{J}_0, y \in \mathcal{J}_1$$

where w_n' is priority weight mapped on each subcarrier n based on main user m on the nth subcarrier.

The source power is a common resource between the subcarriers of the set $\{\mathcal{J}_0\}$ and $\{\mathcal{J}_1\}$, while the jammer power is exclusively for the subcarriers of set $\{\mathcal{J}_1\}$ only. Power allocation problems over the complimentary sets of subcarriers are coupled through the source power, as indicated in the complicating constraint $C_{2,\,1}$, and are dependent on optimal source power sharing between the two sets of subcarriers. Thus, *primal decomposition* (PD) can be used to solve the optimization problem (8). The problem can be solved by dividing it into one master problem (an outer loop that shares the source power budget) and two subproblems (an inner loop, that solves the power allocations over complimentary sets) [29]. In the first subproblem source power has to be allocated over set $\{\mathcal{J}_0\}$, and in the second subproblem, source and jammer power has to be allocated jointly over set $\{\mathcal{J}_1\}$.

5.2 Numerical Results and Discussion

Performance of the downlink of an OFDMA system with $N = 64$ subcarriers is obtained through MATLAB simulations. All subcarriers are assumed to have quasistatic Rayleigh fading. Path loss exponent = 3 is considered to model the effect of large-scale fading. The source is located at the origin. All untrusted users are randomly located inside a unity square in the first quadrant. AWGN noise variance is assumed to be $\sigma^2 = 1$. EPA is equal power allocation, while OSPWJ is optimal source power allocation without a jammer. JPASO is a suboptimal version of joint optimization JPA, which provides a less complex solution though at the cost of some performance degradation [30].

The secure rate and fairness performance of the proposed JPA scheme with respect to source power is presented in Fig. 6 at two jammer powers, $P_{J1}/\sigma^2 = 0$ dB and $P_{J2}/\sigma^2 = 6$ dB. "Asymp opt" indicates the performance of the

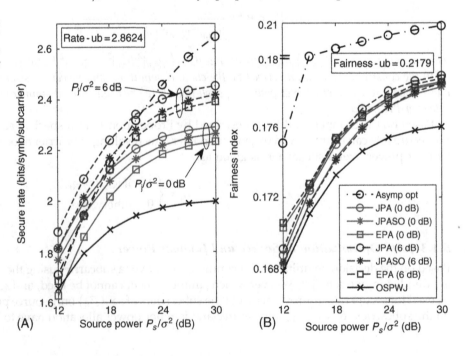

FIG. 6 Secure rate (A) and fairness (B) performance versus source power at $P_{J1}/\sigma^2 = 0$ dB and $P_{J2}/\sigma^2 = 6$ dB. *Rate-ub*, rate upper boundary; *Fairness-ub*, fairness upper boundary.

asymptotically optimal scheme that has been plotted to observe the effectiveness of the proposed scheme in reaching an optimal solution with $(P_S \to \infty)$. The system's upper boundaries on secure rate and fairness have been indicated in text boxes in the respective subfigures.

As observed from Fig. 6A, the secure rate is increasing with jammer power. However, the secure rate does not increase infinitely with jammer power, and even with infinite jammer power, the secure rate's upper boundary is "Asymp opt." Further, with infinite source power and infinite jammer power, the secure rate's upper boundary is "Rate-ub."

6 TRUSTED RELAY-ASSISTED SECURITY IMPROVEMENT OF UNTRUSTED USERS

Depending on the mode of operation, a helper node can be used as an amplify and forward, or decode and forward, relay. Further, depending on whether a direct link from the source to destination is available or not, the resource allocation problem changes. If a direct link is not available, the source has no other option but to use relay, whereas if a direct link is available, the source can either use the direct mode or the relay mode. Thus, optimal mode selection comes into the picture.

6.1 Secure DF Relaying Without Direct Link Availability

To investigate security among IoT nodes operating over orthogonal frequencies, here we revisit a recent investigation [31] on the downlink of a secure OFDMA-based cooperative communication system with a single source $\mathcal{S}$, a trusted DF relay $\mathcal{R}$, and multiple untrusted users (cf. Fig. 7). Let the channel coefficients between the source to the relay on the nth subcarrier be denoted as $h_{R,\,n}$. No direct connectivity is assumed between source $\mathcal{S}$ and users $\mathcal{U}_m$. Let the channel coefficient from the relay to the ith user be denoted as $f_{i,\,n}$. All channel links are assumed to follow quasistatic Rayleigh fading. The source is assumed to have perfect CSI for all the channel links. All system nodes are assumed to have a single antenna and operate in half-duplex mode.

Let R_{sr_n} and R_{rm_n}, respectively, denote the rates of the source to the relay, and the relay to the mth user link over subcarrier n. Rate $R_{m,\,n}$ of user m over subcarrier n, in conventional DF relay-assisted cooperative communication, is given as:

$$R_{m,n} = \frac{1}{2} \min \left\{ R_{sr_n}, R_{rm_n} \right\} \tag{9}$$

Using Eq. (9), the secure rate definition can be simplified as

$$R_{s_{m,n}} = \frac{1}{2} \left\{ \min \left(R_{sr_n}, R_{rm_n} \right) - R_{re_n} \right\}^+ \tag{10}$$

6.1.1 Sum Rate Maximization

Let P_{s_n} and P_{r_n}, respectively, denote the source and the relay power over subcarrier n. The sum secure rate maximization problem can be described as follows:

$$\mathcal{P}_3: \quad \underset{P_{s_n}, P_{r_n}, \pi_{m,n}}{\text{maximize}} \left[R_S = \sum_{m=1}^{M} \sum_{n=1}^{N} \pi_{m,n} R_{s_{m,n}} \right]$$

subject to

$$C_{3,1}: \sum_{m=1}^{M} \pi_{m,n} \leq 1 \ \forall \ n, \ C_{3,2}: \pi_{m,n} \in \{0,1\} \ \forall \ m,n, \ C_{3,3}: \sum_{n=1}^{N} P_{s_n} \leq P_S, \tag{11}$$

$$C_{3,4}: \sum_{n=1}^{N} P_{r_n} \leq P_R, \ C_{3,5}: P_{s_n} \geq 0, P_{r_n} \geq 0 \ \forall \ n.$$

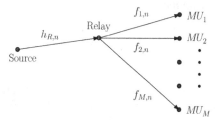

FIG. 7 DF relay-assisted cooperative secure OFDMA communication system with untrusted users.

where $\pi_{m,n}$ is a binary subcarrier allocation variable indicating whether subcarrier n is allocated to user m or not. For each subcarrier n, there are three variables: two power variables P_{s_n} and P_{r_n} are real, and the subcarrier allocation variable $\pi_{m,n}$ is binary. The problem $\mathcal{P}_3$, which has a nonlinear, nonconvex objective function, is a mixed-integer, nonlinear problem belonging to the class of NP-hard. In order to tackle the problem, it is solved in parts. First, the subcarrier allocation policy is found, and then the optimal power allocation is determined.

6.1.1.1 Subcarrier Allocation

The feasibility of achieving a positive secure rate by a user m over a subcarrier n is given by the following proposition.

Proposition 2. *In DF relay-assisted secure communication with untrusted users, a positive secure rate over a subcarrier n can be achieved if and only if: (i) the subcarrier is allocated to user having maximum channel gain on that subcarrier, and (ii) the source to relay link is stronger compared with the relay to eavesdropper link over that subcarrier.*

First condition results in the subcarrier allocation policy at the relay

$$\pi_{m,n} = \begin{cases} 1 & \text{if } |f_{m,n}| > \max_{o \in \{1,2,\dots M\}\setminus m} |f_{o,n}| \\ 0 & \text{otherwise} \end{cases} \tag{12}$$

The second condition $R_{re_n} < R_{sr_n}$, simplified as $P_{r_n}|f_{e,n}|^2/\sigma^2 < P_{s_n}|h_{R,n}|^2/\sigma^2$, results in a power optimization constraint.

Following the observations of Proposition 2, the secure rate definition can be rewritten as

$$R_{s_{m,n}} = \frac{1}{2}\left[\log_2\left(\frac{1 + \min\left(\dfrac{P_{s_n}|h_{R,n}|^2}{\sigma^2}, \dfrac{P_{r_n}|f_{m,n}|^2}{\sigma^2}\right)}{1 + \dfrac{P_{r_n}|f_{e,n}|^2}{\sigma^2}}\right)\right] \tag{13}$$

6.1.1.2 Power Allocation

The optimal subcarrier allocation policy takes care of the first condition $R_{re_n} < R_{rm_n}$, and the second condition $R_{re_n} < R_{sr_n}$ is imposed as a power optimization constraint. The equivalent power optimization problem can be expressed as

$$\mathcal{P}_4: \quad \underset{P_{s_n}, P_{r_n}, t_n}{\text{maximize}} \left[\hat{R}_S(t_n, P_n^r) \triangleq \sum_{n=1}^{N}\frac{1}{2}\left\{\log_2\left(\frac{1+t_n}{1+\dfrac{P_{r_n}|f_{e,n}|^2}{\sigma^2}}\right)\right\}\right]$$

subject to

$$C_{4,1}: t_n \leq \frac{P_{s_n}|h_{R,n}|^2}{\sigma^2} \quad \forall\ n \tag{14}$$

$$C_{4,2}: t_n \leq \frac{P_{r_n}|f_{m,n}|^2}{\sigma^2} \quad \forall\ n$$

$$C_{4,3}, C_{4,4}, C_{4,5} \text{ as } C_{3,3}, C_{3,4}, C_{3,5} \text{ in Eq.(11)}$$

$$C_{4,6}: \frac{P_{r_n}|f_{e,n}|^2}{\sigma^2} \leq \frac{P_{s_n}|h_{R,n}|^2}{\sigma^2} \quad \forall\ n$$

The objective of the problem is proved to be a pseudolinear function. The problem $\mathcal{P}_4$ belongs to the class of generalized convex problems that can be solved optimally by solving KKT conditions. Theorem 1 defines the optimal power allocation for the problem $\mathcal{P}_4$ [32].

Theorem 1. *To achieve the maximum secure rate over a subcarrier in a DF relay-assisted secure communication, the source and relay powers should be related in such a way that*

$$P_{s_n}|h_{R,n}|^2 = P_{r_n}|f_{m,n}|^2 \tag{15}$$

6.1.2 Sum Power Minimization

In this section, the sum power minimization problem subject to a secure rate guarantee is discussed. In order to achieve fair resource allocation, a minimum support secure rate requirement R_{ssr} for each user is considered. This fairness consideration leads to a more complex problem, because there are M rate constraints to be satisfied by the allocation scheme instead of one.

In order to achieve a positive secure rate over a subcarrier, the subcarrier allocation has to be done based on the ideology of allocating a subcarrier to its best-gain user (Eq. 12). If a user is unable to get even a single subcarrier, then such a user cannot be considered for power allocation. Further, the secure rate over each subcarrier is bounded; thus, if a user cannot achieve the rate requirement R_{ssr} then that user is also taken out of the power allocation framework. Let U^a be the set of active users who can achieve the secure rate guarantee. Let B_m denote the set of best subcarriers allocated to user m. The sum power optimization problem can be stated as

$$\mathcal{P}_5: \quad \underset{P_{s_n}, P_{r_n}}{\text{minimize}} \sum_{m \in U^a} \sum_{n \in B_m} (P_{s_n} + P_{r_n})$$

subject to

$$C_{5,1}: \sum_{n \in B_m} R_{s_{m,n}} \geq R_{ssr} \ \forall \ m \in U^a$$

$$C_{5,2}: P_{s_n}, P_{r_n} \geq 0 \ \forall \ n \in B_m, \ \forall \ m \in U^a$$

(16)

Because all the subcarriers are independent, the user rate constraints described by $C_{5,1}$ can be satisfied in parallel. It means that the complete problem can be decomposed at the user-level, which can be solved in parallel. The overall system power requirement is obtained as the summation of all the parallel solutions.

6.1.3 Results and Discussion

Numerical results for a DF relay-assisted secure communication are presented in this section. The downlink of an OFDMA system with $N = 64$ subcarriers and $M = 8$ users is considered. The source and the relay are located at $(0, 0)$ and $(0, 1)$, respectively. All untrusted users are assumed to be located randomly inside a unit square, centered at $(2, 0)$. A "uniform" scheme performs equal power allocation.

The variation of the sum secure rate R_S^* (or $\hat{R}_S^*$) with the source power budget P_S is presented in Fig. 8A. The performance is observed at various values of the relay power budget P_R. As observed, optimal power allocation leads to performance gain in the secure rate; however, there are diminishing returns.

The sum power required per user to achieve the minimum support secure rate R_{ssr} is plotted in Fig. 8. It is observed that the power requirement increases exponentially with R_{ssr}. The results have been plotted for various values of numbers of users M. Note that the sum power required per user for a fixed value of R_{ssr} increases with M. At higher values of M, there are effectively fewer subcarriers per user, which causes the power requirement to increase. Because of the efficient utilization of resources, optimal SCP results in less power being required.

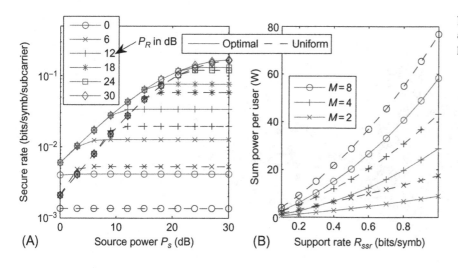

FIG. 8 Secure rate versus source power (A), and sum power per user versus minimum support rate (B) performance.

6.2 Secure DF Relaying Under Direct Link Availability

In this section, the problem of resource allocation assuming the availability of a direct link from source to users is discussed [33]. In such a scenario, the most important challenge is to decide whether to utilize a relay over a subcarrier. This is referred to as mode selection.

Let the rate achieved by user $\mathcal{U}_m$ over subcarrier n in DC and RC mode be denoted as $R_n^m|_{DC}$ and $R_n^m|_{RC}$, respectively. In order to achieve the maximum rate, the effective rate R_n^m is given by

$$R_n^m = \max\left\{ R_n^m|_{DC}, R_n^m|_{RC} \right\}. \tag{17}$$

Let us assume that R_n^{sm}, R_n^{sr}, and R_n^{srm}, respectively, denote the rates of $\mathcal{U}_m$ for $\mathcal{S}-\mathcal{U}_m$, $\mathcal{S}-\mathcal{R}$, and $\mathcal{S}-\mathcal{R}-\mathcal{U}_m$ links over subcarrier n. R_n^{srm} is the rate of $\mathcal{U}_m$ after using maximum ratio combining (MRC) over the signals from $\mathcal{S}$ and $\mathcal{R}$. The rates of $\mathcal{U}_m$ in DC and RC modes are:

$$R_n^m|_{DC} = R_n^{sm}; \quad R_n^m|_{RC} = (1/2)\min\left\{ R_n^{sr}, R_n^{srm} \right\} \tag{18}$$

$\frac{1}{2}$ in $R_n^m|_{RC}$ arises due to the half duplex protocol. Thus, $R_n^m = \frac{1}{2}\max\left\{ 2R_n^{sm}, \min\left\{ R_n^{sr}, R_n^{srm} \right\} \right\}$. Simplifying the rate definition, boundary conditions on channel gains, and relay and source powers are performed as follows:

$$R_n^m = \begin{cases} \dfrac{1}{2} R_n^{sr} & \text{if } \gamma_n^{sr} \geq \gamma_n^{sm} a_n^m, P_n^r \geq \max\{P_{n_l}^{rm}, P_n^s \Delta_n^m\} \\[2mm] \dfrac{1}{2} R_n^{srm} & \text{if } \gamma_n^{sr} \geq \gamma_n^{sm} a_n^m, P_n^s \Delta_n^m \geq P_n^r \geq P_{n_l}^{rm} \\[2mm] R_n^{sm} & \text{otherwise} \end{cases} \tag{19}$$

where $\Delta_n^m \triangleq \frac{\gamma_n^{sr} - \gamma_n^{sm}}{\gamma_n^{rm}}$. Using this simplified definition, the secure rate positivity condition in RC mode is obtained as follows:

Proposition 3. $\mathcal{U}_m$ can achieve a positive secure rate over a subcarrier n in RC mode if: (i) $\gamma_n^{sr} > \max\{\gamma_n^{so} a_n^o\}$, (ii) $P_n^r > \max\{P_{n_l}^{ro}\}$, (iii) $P_n^r \leq P_n^s \Delta_n^m$, and (iv) $\Delta_n^m = \min\{\Delta_n^o\} \ \forall \ o \in \{1, 2, \dots M\}$.

In case a subcarrier can be used on both the DC and RC mode, conditions of achieving a more secure rate in RC mode compared with DC mode are obtained. After simplifying these conditions, it is observed that there are some subcarriers that are exclusively in DC mode, some subcarriers exclusively in RC mode, and some that can be in both modes of operation, and can switch between the two modes, depending on source power allocation. Finally, observing that optimal mode selection depends on power allocation, an asymptotically optimal mode selection policy and a suboptimal mode policy are proposed which are independent of power allocation.

Assuming the source and the relay to be located at $(0, 0.5)$ and $(0, -0.5)$, respectively, locations of users with varying degree of RC mode subcarriers has been plotted in Fig. 9. This figure shows the utility regions of a DF relay by identifying the user locations that benefit from the presence of the relay. Observe that the utility regions are not circular due to the availability of a direct link from the source.

FIG. 9   Relay utility regions.

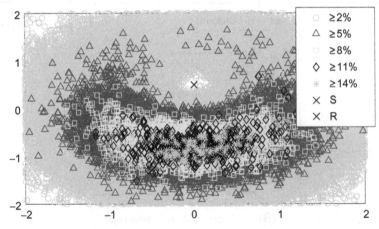

6.3 Secure Amplify and Forward Relaying

An AF relay has been considered to assist secure communication to untrusted users from a source in the absence of a direct link. In an AF relay-assisted communication system, the rate of user $\mathcal{U}_m$ over subcarrier n, R_n^m is given as [7]:

$$R_n^m = \frac{1}{2}\log_2\left\{1 + \frac{P_n^s\gamma_n^{sr}P_n^r\gamma_n^{rm}}{\sigma^2\left(\sigma^2 + P_n^s\gamma_n^{sr} + P_n^r\gamma_n^{rm}\right)}\right\} \tag{20}$$

The secure rate positivity condition $R_n^m > R_n^e$ leads to optimal subcarrier allocation at the relay. The subcarrier allocation in this case is similar to that of the DF relay scenario without a direct link, that is, allocation of a subcarrier to the user with maximum channel gain over that subcarrier. Once subcarrier allocation is done, optimal power allocation should be done at the source, as well as relay, jointly. The nature of secure rate $R_{s_n}^m$ with power allocations P_n^s and P_n^r is described by the following proposition.

Proposition 4. *The secure rate $R_{s_n}^m$ of user $\mathcal{U}_m$ over a subcarrier* n *in an AF relay-assisted secure communication system is a concave function of P_n^s, and a pseudoconcave function [32] of P_n^r, achieving a unique maxima.*

Observing that the secure rate is a concave-increasing function of source power P_n^s, the source power budget will be fully utilized. Because there is an optimal relay power P_n^r, the relay power budget may or may not be fully utilized. The JPA is proved to be a generalized convex problem. The optimal power allocation at the source and relay can be obtained by solving the KKT conditions.

7 NOVEL PROPOSALS AND FUTURE RESEARCH DIRECTIONS

The IoT, being a network of multiple interconnected devices that are either collecting, processing, or receiving information based on the different layers of system architecture they are placed in, is prone to severe security concerns. The limited computational complexity and battery-constrained energy resources further exacerbate the severity of this security concern. Also, it is worth noting that the privacy issues arise at all layers of the IoT architecture; namely, the perception layer, network layer, and application layer [34]. Maintaining the key aspects of security such as confidentiality, integrity, availability, and trust requires thorough investigation based on the severity of the impact of the attack, which largely depends on the criticality of information.

In this section, we present some recent developments that have stemmed from the preceding observations that need further research and investigation to reach to their best possible utility.

7.1 Specific Attack Mechanisms for IoT Systems

From the systems perspective, security requirements can be categorized as confidentiality, integrity, and availability. Confidentiality ensures that the information flow has not been intercepted by an eavesdropper. Integrity means that the content has not been tampered with during the information flow from the sender to the receiver by an unauthorized entity. Availability is to ensure smooth function of the system such that it does not get flooded by spurious traffic by an attacker.

Based on the layer of operation, these security requirements could be breached by an invader through various forms of attack [34]. At the perception layer, which collects the data from the group of sensors, the invader could try to change the collected data and destroy the devices. At the network layer, the invader could break the communication link by making the devices unavailable. The application layer is close to human interaction; and thus susceptible to software attacks such as phishing and malware attacks.

So, we note that layer-specific protocols are needed to address the intricacies of the security demands at different layers that need to fight against very diverse kinds of attacks.

7.2 Novel Security Proposals

Because the research on PLS is still in its initial years, it would require a great deal of research to find novel strategies and solutions for making PLS secure IoT systems a reality. Following are some of the novel strategies developed to address this.

7.2.1 Optimal Localization of Helper Node(s)

After observing the significance of helper nodes in improving the secrecy performance of a communication system, the next concern is the optimal location of a helper node for a group of untrusted users. Assuming the group of users to be contained inside a conceptual bounded region, the optimal relay location problem is then simplified to a one-dimensional search problem. However, the original problem, with all its practical conditions, is a two-dimensional search. Optimal relay locations have to be investigated, assuming either the ergodic secrecy rate, or the outage capacity as a performance metric. Further, finding an optimal number of helper nodes (i.e., their density) for an underlying secrecy throughput requirement, is an interesting problem from the viewpoint of network planners.

7.2.2 Subcarrier Pairing

SCP has been shown to help in improving the spectral and/or energy efficiency of the system [35]. It has been proved that for sum rate maximization, the channel gains should be the same on all the subcarriers. However, channel gains are discrete quantities, and equal channel gains are not possible. Thus, effective channel gains, that is, the end-to-end channel gains from the source to the user, should vary only minimally. In this purview, optimal SCP can be utilized to match channel gains in such a way that the variance of the effective channel gains is minimized. Utilization of SCP in connection with a relay selection problem where there is a pool of relays is a very interesting research challenge, as there may be a possibility of choosing relays in such a way that the effective channel gains have minimum variance.

7.3 Future Research Directions

In this section, some threads for open research directions from the perspective of utilizing PLS for an IoT system are discussed.

7.3.1 Building-Up Mutual Trust

Coming up reaching to a common trust platform where devices from various vendors could share their data reliably with each other is a major focus area before the idea of the IoT can become to a reality. Investigation into the impact of false information injection by a malicious node is required, as it could lead to manipulation of the behavior of the system. Similarly, ensuring identity verification is a key challenge, as impersonation could lead to information leakage. Because information sensors and actuators are low power devices with limited computation capabilities, investigation into the kind of attacks that can be performed at these two extreme ends of the whole infrastructure is one of the key challenges. Ensuring secrecy performance subject to outage constraints is a more practical problem compared with simple instantaneous sum rate maximization studies.

7.3.2 Implementing Security Under Channel Estimation Errors

Implementation of availability of CSI, or even the channel distribution information (CDI) of eavesdroppers, requires power, computation, and bandwidth, which are already constrained resources in the IoT. Thus, a thorough study on optimal sharing is required. Even then, most of the eavesdroppers are passive, and difficult to detect. Assuming uniform distribution of eavesdroppers according to the Poisson point process may not be practical, as density of IoT devices may vary from location to location, for example, density in a high-rise building is greater than that of a parking lot. Thus, practical scenarios could be quite challenging in mathematical analysis as the security performance is strongly influenced by the channel estimation errors. Further, assuming multiple eavesdroppers are independent can help in initial studies, but the scenario of multiple colluding eavesdroppers is a very real potential scenario, which could make privacy a tough challenge.

7.3.3 Utilizing Energy Harvesting Technology for Secrecy Enhancement

Harvesting energy from the ambient or dedicated radio frequency signals has emerged as a potential candidate to help in the realization of perpetually operating IoT networks [36]. Utilizing neighboring nodes as relays or jammers has already been an interesting area of research. Using ambient or jamming/interference signals for energy harvesting, or using the harvested energy for jamming to improve the secrecy performance, requires further investigation [37]. As discussed in [38] and Section 4.2, the efficient utilization of the harvested energy involves optimal decision making regarding the most cooperative mode. Further, the possibility of placing data collectors among sensory nodes subject to secrecy performance requirements is an interesting challenge that is open to the research community.

7.3.4 Securing Next Generation Networks Exploiting the Massive Antenna Array Applications

The proposals and optimization designs outlined in this chapter for single-antenna communications can be extended to address the challenges and demands of efficiently securing multiple-antenna systems. In particular, apart from the resource allocation strategies outlined in Section 4, we need to design the optimal precoder and decoder (also called beamforming weights) to maximize the performance in secure multiantenna communication networks [39]. The security of multiple-antenna systems is vary critical due to their wide adoption in fifth-generation wireless networks for jointly enhancing spectral and energy efficiency, while providing uniform service to a large number of users. Also, this setup is more hostile, as we have to tackle multiantenna eavesdropping, or jamming, or both. So, novel green joint cooperative optimization schemes should be investigated.

7.3.5 Physical Layer Security Test Bed: A Proof of Concept

It would definitely be an interesting challenge transform these the theoretical concepts into a practical reality. A test bed implementing secure communication systems with untrusted users would help in validating the proposed resource allocation strategies, and help fine-tune them, as per the requirements. Here the adaptability and reconfigurability of the commercially available software defined radio kits can be utilized to model the operation of the helper nodes (friendly jammer or trusted relay) for validating the strategies proposed for secure IoT, or in general, privacy-aware Smart Cities.

8 CONCLUSION

Because IoT is a network of communicating devices, secrecy of information is a crucial concern. In this purview, this chapter describes key secrecy challenges, and the gravity of their effects on the overall performance of IoT-based Smart Cities. After giving a brief background and a literature survey on PLS, the key controllers of the resource allocation and their joint optimization strategies are discussed in detail. In order to further improve the secrecy performance of an IoT network with untrusted users, green optimized protocols for the efficient utilization of the helper nodes, available as jammers or relays, has been presented. Key analytical insights have been outlined to address the practical challenges in creating secure, low-power IoT devices in Smart Cities. Elaborating on the current ideas and proposals, the chapter closes by highlighting novel research directions that need to be pursued, along with the issues that need to be resolved in the future for fully achieving the goal of privacy-aware Smart Cities.

References

[1] A.O. Hero, Secure space-time communication, IEEE Trans. Inf. Theory 49 (12) (2003) 3235–3249.

[2] R. Negi, S. Goel, Secret communication using artificial noise, Proc. IEEE VTC-Fall, vol. 3, 2005, pp. 1906–1910. Dallas, TX.

[3] A. Khisti, G. Wornell, A. Wiesel, Y. Eldar, On the Gaussian MIMO wiretap channel, in: Proc. IEEE ISIT, 2007, pp. 2471–2475. Nice, France.

[4] Y. Liang, H.V. Poor, S. Shamai, Secure communication over fading channels, IEEE Trans. Inf. Theory 54 (6) (2008) 2470–2492.

[5] Y. Oohama, Capacity theorems for relay channels with confidential messages, Proc. IEEE ISIT, 2007, pp. 926–930. Nice, France.

[6] C. Jeong, I.-M. Kim, Optimal power allocation for secure multicarrier relay systems, IEEE Trans. Signal Process. 59 (11) (2011) 5428–5442.

[7] A. Jindal, R. Bose, Resource allocation for secure multicarrier AF relay system under total power constraint, IEEE Commun. Lett. 19 (2) (2015) 231–234.

[8] Y. Zou, X. Wang, W. Shen, Optimal relay selection for physical-layer security in cooperative wireless networks, IEEE J. Sel. Areas Commun. 31 (10) (2013) 2099–2111.

[9] J.H. Lee, Optimal power allocation for physical layer security in multi-hop DF relay networks, IEEE Trans. Wirel. Commun. 15 (1) (2016) 28–38.

[10] X. Tang, R. Liu, P. Spasojevic, H.V. Poor, Interference assisted secret communication, IEEE Trans. Inf. Theory 57 (5) (2011) 3153–3167.

[11] M. Ara, H. Reboredo, F. Renna, M.R.D. Rodrigues, Power allocation strategies for OFDM Gaussian wiretap channels with a friendly jammer, in: Proc. IEEE ICC, 2013, pp. 3413–3417. Budapest, Hungry.

[12] J. Li, A.P. Petropulu, S. Weber, On cooperative relaying schemes for wireless physical layer security, IEEE Trans. Signal Process. 59 (10) (2011) 4985–4997.

[13] H.M. Wang, M. Luo, X.G. Xia, Q. Yin, Joint cooperative beamforming and jamming to secure AF relay systems with individual power constraint and no eavesdropper's CSI, IEEE Signal Process. Lett. 20 (1) (2013) 39–42.

[14] H.M. Wang, M. Luo, Q. Yin, X.G. Xia, Hybrid cooperative beamforming and jamming for physical-layer security of two-way relay networks, IEEE Trans. Inf. Forensics Secur. 8 (12) (2013) 2007–2020.

[15] H.M. Wang, F. Liu, M. Yang, Joint cooperative beamforming, jamming, and power allocation to secure AF relay systems, IEEE Trans. Veh. Technol. 64 (10) (2015) 4893–4898.

[16] H. Deng, H.M. Wang, W. Guo, W. Wang, Secrecy transmission with a helper: to relay or to jam, IEEE Trans. Inf. Forensics Secur. 10 (2) (2015) 293–307.

[17] A. Khisti, A. Tchamkerten, G.W. Wornell, Secure broadcasting over fading channels, IEEE Trans. Inf. Theory 54 (6) (2008) 2453–2469.

[18] H. Qin, X. Chen, X. Zhong, F. He, M. Zhao, J. Wang, Joint power allocation and artificial noise design for multiuser wiretap OFDM channels, in: Proc. IEEE ICC, 2013, pp. 2193–2198. Budapest, Hungry.

[19] S. Karachontzitis, S. Timotheou, I. Krikidis, K. Berberidis, Security-aware max-min resource allocation in multiuser OFDMA downlink, IEEE Trans. Inf. Forensics Secur. 10 (3) (2015) 529–542.

[20] D.W.K. Ng, E.S. Lo, R. Schober, Energy-efficient resource allocation for secure OFDMA systems, IEEE Trans. Veh. Technol. 61 (6) (2012) 2572–2585.

[21] D.W.K. Ng, E.S. Lo, R. Schober, Secure resource allocation and scheduling for OFDMA decode-and-forward relay networks, IEEE Trans. Wirel. Commun. 10 (10) (2011) 3528–3540.

[22] R. Liu, I. Maric, P. Spasojevic, R.D. Yates, Discrete memoryless interference and broadcast channels with confidential messages: secrecy rate regions, IEEE Trans. Inf. Theory 54 (6) (2008) 2493–2507.

[23] E.A. Jorswieck, A. Wolf, Resource allocation for the wire-tap multi-carrier broadcast channel, in: Proc. ICT, 2008. Saint-Petersburg, Russia.

[24] X. Wang, M. Tao, J. Mo, Y. Xu, Power and subcarrier allocation for physical-layer security in OFDMA-based broadband wireless networks, IEEE Trans. Inf. Forensics Secur. 6 (3) (2011) 693–702.

[25] Z. Ho, E. Jorswieck, S. Engelmann, Information leakage neutralization for the multi-antenna non-regenerative relay-assisted multi-carrier interference channel, IEEE J. Sel. Areas Commun. 31 (9) (2013) 1672–1686.

[26] R. Saini, A. Jindal, S. De, Jammer-assisted resource allocation in secure OFDMA with untrusted users, IEEE Trans. Inf. Forensics Secur. 11 (5) (2016) 1055–1070.

[27] D. Yuan, J. Joung, C.K. Ho, S. Sun, On tractability aspects of optimal resource allocation in OFDMA systems, IEEE Trans. Veh. Technol. 62 (2) (2013) 863–873.

[28] Y.-F. Liu, Y.-H. Dai, On the complexity of joint subcarrier and power allocation for multi-user OFDMA systems, IEEE Trans. Signal Process. 62 (3) (2014) 583–596.

[29] S. Boyd, L. Xiao, A. Mutapcic, J. Mattingley, Notes on decomposition methods, 2008. http://see.stanford.edu/materials/lsocoee364b/08-decomposition_notes.pdf (Accessed August 2014).

[30] R. Saini, A. Jindal, S. De, Jammer assisted sum rate and fairness improvement in secure OFDMA, Proc. IEEE ICC, 2015, pp. 7263–7268.

[31] R. Saini, D. Mishra, S. De, OFDMA-based DF secure cooperative communication with untrusted users, IEEE Commun. Lett. 20 (4) (2016) 716–719.

[32] M.S. Bazaraa, H.D. Sherali, C.M. Shetty, Nonlinear Programming: Theory and Applications, John Wiley & Sons, New York, NY, 2006.

[33] R. Saini, D. Mishra, S. De, Utility regions for DF relay in OFDMA-based secure communication with untrusted users, IEEE Commun. Lett. 21 (11) (2017) 2512–2515.

[34] J. Lin, W. Yu, N. Zhang, X. Yang, H. Zhang, W. Zhao, A survey on Internet of Things: architecture, enabling technologies, security and privacy, and applications, IEEE Internet Things J. 4 (5) (2017) 1125–1142.

[35] R. Saini, D. Mishra, S. De, Novel subcarrier pairing strategy for DF relayed secure OFDMA with untrusted users, in: Proc. IEEE GLOBECOM Workshops, 2017, pp. 1–6. Singapore.

[36] D. Mishra, S. De, Energy harvesting and sustainable M2M communication in 5G mobile technologies, in: Internet of Things (IoT) in 5G Mobile Technologies, Springer-Verlag Handbook, 2016, pp. 99–125.

[37] H. Xing, K.K. Wong, Z. Chu, A. Nallanathan, To harvest and jam: a paradigm of self-sustaining friendly jammers for secure AF relaying, IEEE Trans. Signal Process. 63 (24) (2015) 6616–6631.

[38] D. Mishra, S. De, D. Krishnaswamy, Dilemma at RF energy harvesting relay: downlink energy relaying or uplink information transfer? IEEE Trans. Wirel. Commun. 16 (8) (2017) 4939–4955.

[39] A. Yazdan, J. Park, S. Park, T.A. Khan, R.W. Heath, Energy-efficient massive MIMO: wireless-powered communication, multiuser MIMO with hybrid precoding, and cloud radio access network with variable-resolution ADCs, IEEE Microw. Mag. 18 (5) (2017) 18–30.

5

Crowdsensing and Privacy in Smart City Applications

Raj Gaire*, Ratan K. Ghosh[†], Jongkil Kim[‡], Alexander Krumpholz*,
Rajiv Ranjan[§], R.K. Shyamasundar[¶], and Surya Nepal[‖]

*CSIRO Data61, Canberra, ACT, Australia
[†]Department of Computer Science and Engineering, Indian Institute of Technology (IIT) Kanpur, Kanpur, India
[‡]School of Computing and Information Technology, University of Wollongong, Wollongong, NSW, Australia
[§]School of Computing, Urban Sciences Building, Newcastle University, Newcastle upon Tyne, United Kingdom
[¶]Department of Computer Science and Engineering, Indian Institute of Technology (IIT) Bombay, Mumbai, India
[‖]CSIRO Data61, Epping, NSW, Australia

1 INTRODUCTION

Smart cities are intelligent cities. Smartness of economy, people, governance, mobility, environment, and living are the defining characteristics of smart cities [1]. Intelligence in a smart city is built upon measuring phenomena, or *things*, of interest, and using them for making smart decisions. Measuring things using sensors has been considered as the key aspect of a smart city [2]. Today, sensors can measure a wide variety of phenomena. Moreover, because the size of these sensors has become smaller, they have now been embedded in many household and personal devices, including, but not limited to, smartphones, vehicles, televisions, and gaming devices. These sensors can be used collectively for community-based *crowdsourcing* of the collection of measurements, a.k.a, *mobile crowdsensing* [3]. Because crowdsensing involves people and their private devices, privacy and security are the *prima facia* concerns. Although the terms "mobile crowdsensing" and "crowdsensing" are often used interchangeably, in our opinion, the term "mobile crowdsensing" covers only a subset of the broader term "crowdsensing." In this chapter, first, we will attempt to define crowdsensing as a broader term for crowdsourced sensing. Second, we will discuss privacy issues, concerns, and considerations in crowdsensing applications. Third, we will present two case studies to illustrate privacy issues in smart city crowdsensing and approaches to address those issues. Finally, we will discuss and draw conclusions.

2 DEFINING CROWDSENSING

In this section, we will discuss the terminologies used in the sensing domain to help establish a general definition of crowdsensing.

2.1 Sensing

The Webster online dictionary defines sensing as *becoming aware of something via the senses*.[1] This is a generic definition. Note that this definition does not differentiate among different types of senses. Indeed, sensing can be

[1] See http://www.webster-dictionary.org/definition/sensing.

performed by not only the sensory organs of humans or animals, but also different types of sensors, including electronic sensors.

In the computer science community, the W3C SSN ontology [4] defines sensing as a process that provides an estimated value of a phenomenon. This definition shows the realization that measuring a phenomenon often involves measurement errors. Therefore, a measurement value should be treated as an estimation, rather than an absolute value. Again, this definition does not differentiate whether the sensing is performed by an electronic device or a nonelectronic object, including human.

2.2 Sensors and Sensing

The W3C SSN ontology [4] also defines sensors as things that perform sensing by transforming an incoming stimulus into a digital representation. The low cost of electronic sensors has made them the technology of choice for estimating the value of a phenomenon. These sensors are already used in modern cities for various purposes. For example, sensors are used to measure weather conditions such as temperature, relative humidity, and wind direction/velocity. These measurements are used to forecast the fire danger ratings of bushfires in Australia [5], as well as to assess and plan for fire-fighting activities during bushfires, as discussed later in Section 4.

Smartphones have become ubiquitous in our everyday lives. The sensors embedded in smartphones can also observe several phenomena. In addition to the sensors in smartphones, people are now at the forefront of sensing and transforming the observations into electronic data. In other words, people are working as social sensors [6]. These observations gathered from social sensors can be used to generate different types of intelligence. For example, people often use social media platforms such as Twitter to publish disaster-related observations. Such data has already been used for early detection of disasters [7], as well as for situational awareness during disaster events [8].

Arguably, humans can sense many phenomena for which sensors might be either unavailable or only available at a very high cost. For example, people can assess nonphysical phenomena such as feelings, moods, tastes, and smell. Furthermore, for some phenomena, the same sensor reading might have different meanings for different people. For example, the same temperature could be considered comfortable to some people, while not so comfortable to others. Therefore, it is important to consider both electronics as well as nonelectronics sensing when developing applications for smart cities.

2.3 Crowdsensing in Smart Cities

In the case of a smart city, sensing is not limited to a single phenomena. Rather, it has to cover different phenomena at different locations across the city. Owning the infrastructure to collect measurements about these phenomena may at times be very expensive, and at other times, almost impossible. Therefore, community-based crowdsourced sensing, or crowdsensing in short, can play an important role in collecting information in smart cities.

We noticed that the terms "crowdsensing" and "mobile crowdsensing" have often been used interchangeably, and we disagree with such uses, for the following reasons. The specialized term "mobile crowdsensing" was coined by Ganti et al. [3] to refer to crowd-based sensing using electronic sensors embedded in personal mobile devices. Guo et al. [9] extended this concept of mobile crowdsensing to mobile crowd sensing and computing (MCSC). Formally, MCSC is defined as *a new sensing paradigm that empowers ordinary citizens to contribute data sensed or generated from their mobile devices and aggregates and fuses the data in the cloud for crowd intelligence extraction and human-centric service delivery*. This definition includes data sensed by sensors, as well as that contributed by users through mobile devices. Even though the definition of MCSC tries to broaden the notion of mobile crowdsensing, using this definition as a definition of the broader term "crowdsensing" is still not appropriate.

Firstly, mobility is a major component of the mobile crowdsensing and MCSC definitions. However, in many cases, personal sensing devices might not be mobile at all. For example, homes are often installed with security camera devices at fixed locations that have already been used to sense criminal activities in modern cities. Similarly, many homes in modern cities have been installed with solar panels for electricity generation that are capable of monitoring the generation and use of electricity in these homes. These devices are not mobile, yet this information about electricity generation and use, combined with weather forecasting, could be used to predict the electricity demand of a smart city. We have previously studied the use of locally installed weather stations in farms for welfare assessment of the animals in the farms [10]. Similar to farms, people in smart cities could install their own miniature weather stations in their backyards to collect and share more precise weather condition data around their homes. In all of the preceding scenarios, sensors are not attached to any mobile devices. They are not mobile either. Yet, they contribute to the intelligence of a smart city.

And secondly, electronic sensors are the primary components of the preceding definition of mobile crowdsensing. However, many of the phenomena of interest need subjective assessment by humans. For example, people constantly sense their environment (e.g., comfort, happiness) and share the information in social media such as Facebook and Twitter using mobile and nonmobile devices. In a city, people might identify a peculiar smell around a certain location, or a peculiar taste in the water in their homes. They would notify authorities, and might also post messages on social media about these issues. Crowd-based sensing mechanisms are already embedded in modern cities as a key component of the postmarket surveillance of medicine for discovery of side effects [11]. In all these examples, the information can be useful to authorities to identify problems, develop an appropriate solution quickly, and potentially save lives. These nonmobile data that are sensed and shared by the crowd, not necessarily using mobile phones, would not be considered crowdsensed data if judged by the narrow definition of mobile sensing. Therefore, a more general definition is required.

2.4 Defining Crowdsensing

We define crowdsensing as *an inverse form of crowdsourcing [12] in which a vast number of independently owned entities (in other words, crowd including but not limited to people) knowingly (e.g., participatory) or unknowingly (e.g., opportunistically) as well as directly (e.g., by typing) or indirectly (e.g., through computer/mobile applications) sense and share the estimation of a phenomena that can be opportunistically used for decision making.* Unlike in crowdsourcing, the crowd is not asked to contribute data to solve a given problem. Rather, the crowd senses and shares data, which is used opportunistically to make evidence-based, and hence smart, decisions. The Internet of Things (IoT), specialized applications, including predictive applications, mobile phone apps, and Internet-based applications, as well as generic social media applications can be considered the enablers of crowdsensing. Considering this broader definition, the enablers of crowdsensing are more useful when developing a smart city application, as discussed in later sections.

3 PRIVACY IN CROWDSENSING

Privacy is a fundamental human need. As highlighted by O'Hara [13], a person may feel comfortable knowing that some personal information is known by friends, other information is known by their banker, and yet other information is known by their doctor. However, the person may not feel comfortable if any of the three know all the facts about him/her. This is because the collection of information about an individual allows extraction of knowledge about the individual's habits, beliefs, and health; and therefore may create an unfair disadvantage for the individual [14–16]. Furthermore, knowledge of personal facts may lead to inflicting personal harm, as well as illegal activities, such as identity theft, blackmailing, and burglaries committed against the person. Therefore, considering privacy, specifically in crowdsensing applications, is very important [17].

According to Martinez-Balleste et al. [18], there are five types of citizen's privacy: identity privacy, query privacy, location privacy, footprint privacy, and owner privacy. The *identity privacy* describes the problem that users can be identified when they communicate with smart city components. For example, an application installed in a smartphone could not only contribute to crowdsensing, but also share the person's personal information. Identity privacy is not limited to the identify of the individual contributing to crowdsensing. Sometimes, the information contributed by a person may contain the private details of other people. For example, a nonsocial media user can be profiled using information shared about the person from other users [19]. Similarly, multimedia data may contain images of other people, revealing their privacy [20]. The *query privacy* relates to the queries asked by users. By analyzing the query, the user could be identified [21]. The *location privacy* covers the information about the position of users at given times. Devices such as modern mobile phones can gather GPS-based position information like longitude and latitude, revealing spatiotemporal preferences of their users. Someone querying for a location-based service, for example, a nearby restaurant, can expose its location. From location data and timestamps, a person's demographic information, home and work addresses, commute routes, and other habits can be derived [22–24]. The *footprint privacy* is about the risks involved with the combination of little pieces of information that are left in a system. For example, when using a web browser to access a web page, the cookie left on a device is a footprint of the web page that can reveal an individual's preferences. Finally, the *owner privacy* addresses the problem of querying data about the owner of the data contributed by a user. For example, the citizen may contribute to the electricity use of their home, which could be used to infer potentially business-sensitive information about the electricity providers.

The Aadhaar case study presented in Section 5 will illustrate how a system that can potentially bring smartness to an entire country may inflict some of the aforementioned privacy issues. Legal instruments are necessary to protect citizen privacy, as well as to deter any misuse of people's private data.

3.1 Privacy Laws in Australia

In Australia, the Privacy Act 1988[2] regulates the handling of personal information about individuals. It defines personal information as the *information or an opinion, whether true or not, and whether recorded in a material form or not, about an identified individual, or an individual who is reasonably identifiable.* According to this definition, privacy is not only related to an individual's personal information, such as name, date of birth, address, and so forth, but also related to any commentary or opinion about the person. The Privacy Act includes 13 Australian Privacy Principles (APP)[3] that are applicable to APP entities, including most Australian Government agencies and businesses. In addition, the Australian Information Commissioner can make or approve legally binding and nonbinding guidelines and rules.

Modern technologies make the collection and storage of data, the extraction of information, and the discovery of knowledge fast. On one hand, it makes new applications such as smart cities feasible. But on the other hand, it can lead to erosion of privacy for the individuals [25]. Specifically in the case of crowdsensing applications, the private information about an individual could be collected or inferred leading to personal, social, and legal consequences. Therefore, smart cities must consider the privacy-related obligations and implications of their applications.

3.2 Privacy Obligations

Using crowdsourced data carries the risk of illegally accessing, storing, sharing, and potentially revealing private or confidential information about people. If not considered carefully, the information that should be protected may be released to the public, not only causing damage to reputations, but also leading to legal infringements. Following are some privacy-related obligations for an entity collecting crowdsensed data.

3.2.1 Security of Personal Information

An entity holding personal information is required to take all reasonable steps to protect the information from misuse, interference, and loss, as well as from unauthorized access, modification, and disclosure. The technologies related to privacy and security improve over time. As such, the steps taken in the past as reasonable measures may not be reasonable in today's context. Therefore, APP entities should regularly assess their approaches in regard to the security of personal information.

3.2.2 Compliance Implications

An APP entity is required to take reasonable steps in terms of implementation practices, procedures, and systems to ensure compliance with the APP. The APP entities should regularly assess their privacy compliance practices and procedures.

3.2.3 Privacy Policy

The APP privacy policy states that an APP entity must clearly express and keep its privacy policy about the management of personal information up-to-date. As such, the privacy policy might need to be reviewed to include the provision of usage, storage, sharing, and publication of crowdsensed data in the policy.

3.2.4 Use or Disclosure

An APP entity may collect personal information about an individual for a specific purpose. Such information must not be used or disclosed for a different purpose without the individual's consent. In case of exceptional circumstances outlined in the APP, the APP entity must take reasonable steps to ensure that the information is de-identified before disclosure.

Smart cities need to collect data from a plethora of sensors, transport the data over the network to servers in the cloud for storage and processing, and use the data to make decisions about the city's infrastructure and services in a smarter way. Although the use of crowdsensed data may not be an issue when developing smart city applications, this system involves several risks for the city and its citizens.

---

[2] See https://www.legislation.gov.au/Series/C2004A03712.

[3] See https://www.oaic.gov.au/individuals/privacy-fact-sheets/general/privacy-fact-sheet-17-australian-privacy-principles.

3.3 Privacy and Security Risks

Due to the involvement of personal information, crowdsensing can inflict three types of risks: (1) risk to crowdsensing participant devices, (2) risk to the owners of the devices, and (3) risk to the crowdsensing data storage and processing servers. First, the participating devices bear security risks, as these devices could be attacked to enable leakage of sensitive information. For example, [26] identified security vulnerabilities of the Philips Hue Smart Light Bulb that could be used to attack these devices. In addition, the crowdsensing network could be spoofed to collect personal information. Second, the risk may not be limited to devices. It could be extended to the owners of the devices. Malicious or semihonest entities in a crowdsensing application could access personal information and use the information to cause harm to the user [27, 28]. For example, the surveillance systems installed at homes could be used to spy on others or the owner itself [29]. Similarly, crowdsensing applications are vulnerable to the Sybil attack [30], leading to harmful activities against individuals. Finally, the smart city application server infrastructure bears the risk of being attacked, as it contains a lot of data about citizens. Hence, storage and publication of data, both directly or accidentally, can have several privacy-related implications.

3.4 Privacy Implications

Following are some privacy-related implications associated with collection and release of data from smart city servers.

3.4.1 Privacy Infringement

A business may collect and hold personal information about private citizens when serving them using a crowdsensing-based smart city application. As an APP entity, the business is legally obliged to uphold the privacy law and protect the information. Publication of data publicly poses the risk of releasing private information, if not considered carefully.

3.4.2 Publication of That Is Data Against the Law

Publication of data is sometimes prohibited by law due to its sensitivity, or when it infringes on someone's rights or freedoms. For example, publishing the detailed map of a military site might be prohibited by law. Yet, when Strava published the heatmap of Fitbit users,[4] it could be used to identify sensitive military locations and their supply routes,[5] publication of which could be deemed against the law.

3.4.3 Trade Secret Protection Infringement

In today's globalization era, businesses closely interact with each other, sharing necessary information. As such, a business entity may hold information that is sensitive to its business partners and might be considered as trade secrets. For example, a business might use IoT devices to monitor and manage operations of another business. If used in a crowdsensing application, this data could expose the trade secrets of the business involved.

3.4.4 Mosaic Effect

Anonymization is one of the approaches used in privacy protected sharing of data. Even when the data is anonymized and released publicly, the de-identified data could be combined with other datasets to infer the identity of individuals. This approach of inferring information by using data from multiple sources, also known as the mosaic effect, is of a particular concern. Even after removing personal data before publishing, data from locations with small populations may still reveal individual identities by implication. For example, O'Hara [13] explained how anonymization of a subset of data by Google Street View led to identification of the beliefs and opinions of anonymized entities, and made them the subjects of vandalism.[6]

---

[4] See https://labs.strava.com/heatmap/.

[5] See http://www.abc.net.au/news/science/2018-01-29/strava-heat-map-shows-military-bases-and-supply-routes/9369490.

[6] See http://www.bbc.com/news/technology-11827862.

3.5 Privacy Protection Mechanisms in Crowdsensing

Crowdsensing applications usually have access to either direct personal information or spatiotemporal data that can be used to indirectly infer the personal information. Several privacy protection mechanisms have been proposed focusing on both direct and indirect access to personal information. In crowdsensing applications, a single mechanism might not be enough to ensure protection of private information of the participants. A combination of these mechanisms can be useful [31], as discussed in the case studies provided in later sections.

3.5.1 Avoidance

The best way to protect people's private information is not to collect or store it in the first place. For example, as discussed in Section 5, if a business needs to authenticate an individual using a third-party application, then neither the business nor the third-party application should store the information related to the individual's authentication.

3.5.2 Cryptography

Cryptographic techniques are used to ensure secrecy and integrity of data in the presence of an adversary. Based on the security needs and the threats involved, various cryptographic methods such as *symmetric key cryptography* or *public key cryptography* can be used during transportation and storage of the data. In addition, a *homomorphic encryption* allows various computations to take place on encrypted data without requiring the data to be decrypted for processing. From the privacy perspective, these techniques are useful to protect personal information from being leaked during transportation and from storage servers [31].

3.5.3 Anonymity and Pseudonyms

When contributing to crowdsensing, the user's identity and location need to be protected. Anonymization of users or using pseudonyms can help achieve the protection. Specifically, the data attributes that are related to user identification can be removed to achieve anonymity. Similarly, to hide the real identity of users from the cloud infrastructure, trusted third-party-based pseudonymizers can be used to map the users to pseudonyms [18], as well as to separate the location from the data [24]. Furthermore, methods such as *spatial cloaking*, for example, by using *k-anonymity* to improve anonymity by grouping users of relative proximity to each other, or by replacing their position with the location of a close point of interest, thus a cohort of users share the same location information [24, 32]. Finally, *data aggregation* approaches are used in crowdsensing applications to provide summarized data instead of the raw data (e.g., monitoring traffic), thereby removing identifiable information from the data [33–35].

3.5.4 Data Obfuscation

Even when the private information of an individual is removed, accurate values of the remaining attributes of the record could still be used to identify the individual [36]. Data obfuscation can help achieve the user's privacy by transforming private data, for example, time or location, in such a way that the adversary cannot infer this data from other data [32, 36, 37]. For example, a numerical data could be transformed by applying a linear function on the original data to obtain a perturbed data. Similarly, the original data of a record could be swapped among all the other records to create obfuscation. In another approach, random noise could be added to the original data to obtain perturbed data. *Differential privacy* is an obfuscation method in which a randomized function is applied to the original dataset such that the removal of a single record does not significantly alter the likelihood of an output [38]. It helps protect the privacy of records in a database by adding some randomness to the data [23, 33, 39, 40].

3.5.5 Access Control Mechanisms

In some crowdsensing applications, the private data about the citizen could be collected and stored for legitimate reasons, for example, counter-terrorism, or providing efficient services to citizens [41]. Even when the data is encrypted before storing, the data could still be accessible to all the individuals who have access to the storage systems. This opens the possibility of an insider attack, as discussed in Section 5. Protecting privacy in such cases requires proper information flow models such as the Bell-LaPadula model [42, 43], the Lattice model [44], and the Readers-Writers Flow Model (RWFM) [45] to protect the user's information.

4 CASE STUDY: PRIVACY IN CROWDSENSING FOR DISASTER MANAGEMENT

A disaster can come in many forms, causing loss of lives and severely affecting the economy [46]. The United Nations International Strategy for Disaster Reduction (UN/ISDR) [47] defines disaster as a serious disruption of the functioning of a community or a society, at any scale, frequency, or onset, due to hazardous events leading to the impact of humans, materials, and economic and environmental losses. The source of disaster can be natural, anthropogenic, or both. Natural disasters are associated with natural processes and phenomena, such as hurricanes, tsunamis, and earthquakes; while anthropogenic disasters are predominantly induced by human activities, for example, civil wars.

According to the Emergency Events Database (EM-DAT) figures [48], a total of 346 natural disaster events occurred globally in 2015 alone. These events caused 22,773 casualties, leaving 98.6 million people affected. The economic cost of these events was a massive US$66.5 billion. Therefore, considering disaster management as a part of developing smart cities is very important.

Information is crucial before, during, and after the event of a disaster. Information and communication technologies (ICTs) have already been used to support disaster risk management activities [49]. For example, computer modeling is used to forecast natural disasters, including the probability of the occurrence of flood and fire, and the path of a hurricane. During the disaster event, timely acquisition and processing of data and extraction of accurate information plays a crucial role in providing situational awareness that helps carry out an appropriate disaster response. Because the people who are in the disaster area, including those affected by the disaster, accurately know the situation on the ground, they can be the primary source of data. As such, crowdsensing the situational awareness during a disaster is a perfectly sensible approach.

We developed a prototype of the situational awareness system using the crowdsensed data from sensors, specialized applications including mobile/web applications, and social media. Fig. 1 demonstrates different crowdsensors required to assess and manage the situation in a natural disaster situation. In order to understand our approach of crowdsensing in disaster management, let us first consider a disaster scenario.

4.1 A Motivating Disaster Scenario

In Australia, the Crisis Coordination Center (CCC) is responsible for large-scale disaster management. The CCC is a round-the-clock all-hazards management facility that provides security, counter-terrorism, and the monitoring and reporting of natural disasters and other emergencies. The CCC has policies and procedures in place for the actions to be undertaken during disaster events. Part of its remit is the analysis of data from multiple sources, in other words, data fusion, to understand the scope and the impact of a disaster event.

Imagine that the weather forecast in a certain area predicts heavy rainfall that can possibly cause flooding in the area. After receiving information from the Bureau of Meteorology, an Australian Government Agency responsible

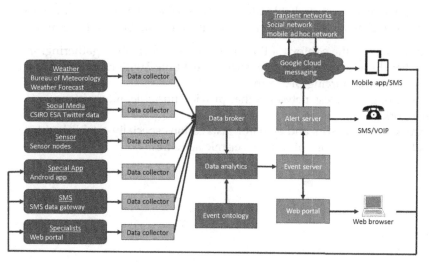

FIG. 1 A system architecture for disaster management.

for monitoring weather, climate, and water,[7] the CCC creates a transient social network to provide targeted information to the people in the area. Telstra, a telecommunication provider, provides a list of landline phone numbers installed in the area. Similarly, all the mobile service providers provide a list of mobile phones that are roaming around in the area. This information is used to contact people in the area and encourage them to use the mobile app, and register their phones to receive emergency situation information and enable ad hoc networking when necessary. Besides the mobile app, hotlines and SMS services are provided for people to contact emergency services. John has followed the instructions and is emergency ready.

As expected, severe flooding has just occurred. John and other people are now providing information to CCC about the situation around them. John is diabetic and has just fainted. The app installed in John's phone is sending an alert to his doctor about his deteriorating blood sugar levels. The doctor has informed the authorities, who are now on their way to help him. People are in touch with their families and friends using social media such as Twitter and Facebook, providing information about their situations. The flood has also caused electricity outages in some areas, while the telecommunications network is affected in another area. Being connected to a transient network over an ad hoc network of mobile phones, people in those outage areas are still connected to the rest of the world. Finally, sensors that are monitoring weather, water quality, air quality, and so forth are providing crucial information that can affect the health and well-being of people living in the area.

At CCC, data is being processed to gather intelligence about the ground situation. The data is coming from sensors installed in various locations; pictures about the situations that are posted on social media; and the needs at different locations that are posted in the CCC application by the ground volunteers. The information is helping them to make crucial decisions.

4.2 Crowdsensing in Disasters

In the preceding scenario, CCC is a specialized entity whose goal is to mitigate the effect of a disaster. It needs to sense the *situational awareness* as the phenomena of interest. CCC does not own any infrastructure in the disaster zone. Therefore, it needs to *sense* the situational awareness from sources that are owned, typically, by other entities, including but not limited to the general public. Hence, it is an exemplary use case of crowdsensing.

Crowdsensing the situational awareness can be achieved by using three types of data sources: (1) sensors, (2) specialized applications, and (3) social networks. In the preceding disaster scenario, a rain precipitation sensor installed at BOM weather stations, as well as at homes of individuals, can provide information about the amount of precipitation. BOM also uses the data to forecast weather patterns of coming days and generate warnings. This information can be used to predict the level of flooding in an area, and plan for disaster mitigation and recovery. People can use specialized applications such as the triple zero app[8] to alert emergency services about emergency needs. Use of SMS in emergency situations is common in many countries. Similarly, social networks can sometimes be turned into specialized applications in disaster situations. For example, Facebook can be converted to a crisis response app in case of emergencies.[9] Similarly, Twitter can be used to detect a disaster, as well as assess ground-level information about the situation.[10] In all these examples, the situational awareness is opportunistically sensed by using data generated by several independent entities.

In situations arising out of disaster management; unstable, unreliable ad hoc channels could become the only means of communication and information gathering. The characteristics of such communication can be listed as follows:

- The nature of the disaster-related communication, in the context of the smart city, is information gathering.
- Information at ground zero is generated either through crowd sensing, such as real-time Twitter, or submission of information by mobile digital volunteers to a crowdsourcing platform.
- Mostly the information flow is carried out through wireless networks that provide unstable, intermittent connectivity, and through open public networks.
- The other major sources of information are wireless sensors and actuator installations specially established for detecting events, such as mudslides, floods, storms, fire, or volcanic or seismic activities.

---

[7] See http://www.bom.gov.au/.

[8] See http://emergencyapp.triplezero.gov.au/.

[9] See https://www.facebook.com/about/crisisresponse/.

[10] See https://esa.csiro.au/.

Thus the network paths have to overcome a whole range of network interoperability and connectivity issues. In disaster situations, we specifically explored the uses of delay-tolerant networks to create transient social networks [50]. We further assessed the privacy aspects in disaster management, particularly when using such applications, as discussed next.

4.3 Privacy in Disaster Management

Leaving the technical problems such as connectivity and internetwork operability aside, the privacy issues in information gathering and use are minimal. In this case, there are two possible approaches to data gathering: (i) information is shared voluntarily by the user of the device, (ii) or it is gathered involuntarily from embedded device sensors. In both cases, location information and other individual details are important, and may still be embedded inside the collected data. Such information may involuntarily leak the user's privacy as it may provide enough information about the movement of the user. Even digital volunteers may expect anonymization of information they would share through the first approach.

In our approach, we considered security and privacy in both mobile phone apps and sensor-based IoT systems. A Sybil attack is a possible attack in a smartphone-based disaster management application [30]. The Sybil attack is an attack wherein a reputation system is subverted by forging identities in peer-to-peer networks. The lack of identity in such networks enables the bots and malicious entities to simulate fake GPS reports to influence social navigation systems. The Sybil attack is more critical in a disaster situation where people are willing to help the distressed person. The vulnerability could be misused to compromise people's safety. For example, the malicious user can simulate a fake disaster alarm to motivate a good Samaritan to come for help in a lonely place and cause harm. The attacker can also divert the attention of rescue teams from a real disaster. Using appropriate cryptography combined with an appropriate access control model could help disseminate information while protecting privacy in a crowdsensing application.

People try to do their best to communicate with others when they are in a distressed situation. In this situation, one challenge is to disseminate information while controlling the access to the information. Proper information flow models such as the Bell-LaPadula model [42, 43], the Lattice model [44], and the RWFM [45] can be used to protect the user's information. Combined with proper access control mechanisms, those information flow models can be used to guarantee that the information flow follows the required privacy rules and does not leak any critical information to the adversary. For example, in RWFM, the sender can control the readers of a message by specifying their names in the readers list.

Another hard challenge in this situation is to enable end-to-end security and privacy in processing big data streams emitted by geographically distributed mobile phones and sensors. We have investigated and proposed a number of techniques (refer to [51–55] for details). Applications in risk-critical domains such as disaster management need near-real-time stream data processing in large-scale sensor networks. We introduced a data stream manager (DSM) to perform security verification just before the stream processing engine. DSM works by removing the modified data packets and supplying only original data back to the steam-processing engine for evaluation. Furthermore, we proposed a dynamic key-length-based security framework (DLSeF) based on a shared key derived from synchronized prime numbers; the key is dynamically updated at short intervals to thwart potential attacks [52]. DLSeF has been designed based on symmetric key cryptography and dynamic key length to provide more efficient security verification of big sensing data streams. Furthermore, to secure big sensing data streams, we have also proposed a Selective Encryption (SEEN) method that satisfies the desired multiple levels of confidentiality and data integrity [54].

In this way, we ensured that the data is encrypted when flowing across the mobile ad hoc network, and when stored in a database, while the read-write flow model is used to ensure access to the data is controlled appropriately.

5 CASE STUDY: CITIZEN PRIVACY IN AADHAAR

An entity is responsible for maintaining security of private information of the users of its infrastructure and services. These responsibilities are broadly defined in law, as discussed in Section 3, specifically in Section 3.1 in the Australian context. Governments are the entities who often need to uniquely identify their citizens in order to efficiently and seamlessly provide necessary services. For example, the US Government issues social security numbers (SSN)[11]

[11] See https://www.ssa.gov/ssnumber/.

to provide and monitor social securities to its residents. The SSN of an individual is considered sensitive and secret. The Australian Government requires individuals to obtain a tax file number (TFN)[12] for tax purposes, a medicare card for medical benefits, and a centerlink number for social services.[13] An attempt at building an identity platform for the United Kingdom was dropped at the intervention of its Parliament.[14]

Recently, the Government of India developed an identity platform called Aadhaar.[15] Aadhaar is a biometrics-based identity database and authentication system. Because today's mobile phones and personal devices are capable of collecting the biometric information of their users, they could be used to connect to Aadhaar to ascertain the users' identities for crowdsensing applications in smart cities. As such, it offers an excellent case study, and shows the need for an integrated working of technologies, processes, and the law to realize the needed privacy along with the bearers of trust.

5.1 About Aadhaar

The government has set up an exclusive agency called the Unique Identification Authority of India (UIDAI) to build an identity platform called Aadhaar for people residing in India, including noncitizens. Aadhaar has a huge central database that includes demographic and biometrics information of over 1.2 billion individuals. It has a significant amount of person-centric information, including multiple biometrics such as photographs, finger prints, and images of irises from which a person can be uniquely identified. One of the main reasons for creating Aadhaar as a huge Social Identification System (SIS) was to prevent massive leakages and large-scale fraudulent transactions in the implementation of the targeted delivery of subsidies for the poor.

The government intends to use this platform not only to provide and monitor the delivery of social services, but also to use it as an identity verification system for a wide range of purposes. It already provides an authentication service to Authentication User Agencies (AUAs) such as civil supplies, insurance companies, and banks to affirm the identities of individuals based on their biometrics and Aadhaar number. A top-level view of the Aadhaar operating ecosystem [56] is provided in Fig. 2.

UIDAI claims that its implementation of the SIS system ensures that AUAs cannot infringe on the user's privacy. It dismisses any scope of massive-scale surveillance as being alleged by the rights activists. In its defense, UIDAI technology support groups reveal its technology stack as having multiple layers of autonomous entities. There is a Central IDentities Repository (CIDR) that provides identity service, enrolment packets, authentication logs, a variety of meta data, as well as transactional logs. Identification service requests are channeled through Authentication Service

FIG. 2   A top-level view of the Aadhaar operation ecosystem.

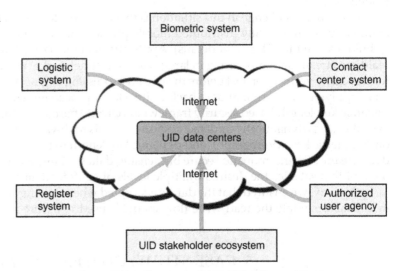

[12] See https://www.ato.gov.au/Individuals/Tax-file-number/.

[13] See https://www.humanservices.gov.au/.

[14] See https://www.gov.uk/identitycards.

[15] See https://uidai.gov.in/en.

Agencies (ASAs) working as intermediaries or third-party verification agencies, between CIDR and AUA. ASAs must have prior registrations in order to avail CIDR services.

Note that several apps, including the ones by government agencies, have been built on the Aadhaar platform, and are in wide use. One can gauge the possibilities of privacy leaks and compromises on personal information through them. Before we delve into the privacy issues with Aadhaar, let us present the necessary background information first.

5.2 Authentication and Authorization

In 2007, the OECD developed a recommendation on electronic authentication for its member countries [57]. India has a working relationship with OECD as a nonmember country. According to the recommendation, authentication is *"A function for establishing the validity and assurance of a claimed identity of a user, device, or other entity in an information or communications system.* One of the principles advocated in the OECD guidelines for authentication/authorization is, *Do not include authorization (which is a separate but a related process that refers to verifying the person's or organization's authority to conduct specified transactions). Typically, decisions concerning authorization are the purview of the relying party (i.e., the entity or person that is relying on the identity assertion to make the authorization decision)."*

As Aadhaar has a huge central biometric database being used for authentication (or identification), it is necessary to look at the issues of security/privacy in such a context.

5.3 Biometrics and Privacy

5.3.1 Biometrics Are Not Secret

While biometrics such as fingerprints, iris scans, and facial images are *private*, they are not *secret*. We leave a copy of our fingerprints on almost everything we touch. A modern smartphone is capable of taking high-resolution pictures of our faces from which the iris biometrics can be extracted. Thus, unless we spend our life wearing gloves and shades, there is no hope that our biometrics can be kept secret. Just as our names are not secret, our biometrics are available to the people we encounter in our daily lives. Arguably, our names could be treated as being more secret than our biometrics.

Technically, anyone can create a database of biometrics of people in public. However, such a possibility can be discarded for the following reasons. First, unlike one's name, other people have no use for one's biometrics in normal daily life, and hence, people do not pay attention to them. For this reason, people may mistakenly believe that their biometrics are secret. Second, although people's biometrics are publicly available, there is no public database from which biometrics can be freely downloaded. Such a database would be deemed illegal in many countries.

5.3.2 Biometrics Matching

Biometric matching techniques give probabilistic, not deterministic, answers. In other words, the biometrics scanner scores a match on a scale of 0%–100%. It cannot give a straightforward *yes* or *no* answer. In Aadhaar, the UIDAI technical support group claims [41] that the False Positive Identification Rate of biometrics matching is as low as 0.0025% for every 1:N searches. UIDAI has the capacity to scale up to one million enrolments per day. Therefore, in the full scale enrolment process, just about 25 false positive matches may need to be manually judged. At this rate, the false positives will not create major problems, even if the gallery continuously keeps on growing.

Because *biometric* information is *at most private and never a secret*, using biometrics for authentication has a few issues, which are discussed as follows.

5.4 Biometrics and Authentication

The current size of the Aadhaar biometrics gallery is more than 1.2 billion records. When using biometrics together with other attributes, such as Aadhaar number or name, the chances of getting both of them matched together are still very low, at a 0.0025% false positive rate. In other words, it is comparable to using *username* and *password* for authentication, where the username is a unique identity and the password is associated with the username, but is secret. If the biometrics alone are used, then this scenario will be similar to using a password alone for authentication/authorization, and even the password is not secret, as explained previously. Moreover, if the authority of authentication is given to a scanner/server connected to UIDIA, then each biometrics scan will produce more than 30,000 matches; and hence, this process will fail to adequately authenticate an individual. In addition, if an individual can obtain the Aadhaar number of any of the 30,000 other individuals whose biometrics identities are similar to his or her own biometrics identities, then the individual can flawlessly acquire the other individual's identity, and be able to access services, including social, as well as financial services. Even if an individual's biometrics do not match another individual's biometrics, the individual can still break the authentication system by cloning the other individual's identity, as demonstrated by the BAIDU Security Lab.[16] Finally, the UIDAI base automatic authentication system could potentially lead to *Denial of Service*, as all the records need to be compared for each record search. Thus, leaving authority of authentication/identity to electronic devices, and putting the server at risk.

5.5 Privacy Pitfalls of Authentication

According to Schneider [58], textbook material from a yet-to-be-published book on Cybersecurity by Prof. Fred Schneider, a leading security expert from Cornell University who has championed several cybersecurity guidelines in the United States, authentication, when undertaken injudiciously, can lead to privacy violations for the following reasons.

First, in authenticating somebody, you learn their identity, and thus, you also learn an associated set of attributes, some of which could be considered personal information. Thus, authentication could lead to the revelation of personal information.

Second, a threat to privacy arises when authentication is used to validate participants in some action. It is possible that participation is deemed private (e.g., certain medical purchases or medical procedures); thus the side effect of authentication is to associate personal information with an identity. This problem is compounded when the same identifier is used to authenticate an individual in connection to multiple actions, leading to the capabilities of third parties to be able to connect seemingly unrelated actions with a single individual, and then make inferences about associated additional attributes of that individual.

Third, in a sense, requirement of authentication implicitly institutes a form of authorization. Thus, the prospect of undergoing authentication inhibits people from engaging in activities they fear could be misconstrued, deemed inappropriate, or lead to retribution. The concern here is not that there is an erosion of basic freedoms when authentication is required, but that this erosion is inadvertent. The concern is that the policy—*not side effects of a system's construction*—should be what dictates who may engage in what activities, and authorization—*not authentication*—mechanisms should be what implements such policy.

Finally, an authentication system collects, and possibly stores, information for subsequent use. *Note that information collected without consent should never be allowed to be abused (that includes linking, etc.).*

Consequently, widespread deployment of authentication mechanisms increases plausible privacy violations in three ways: (i) personal information could be abused by the agency collecting it, (ii) stored personal information could be stolen, and (iii) having personal information further increases the risk of inference by linking shared identities or other shared attributes.

5.6 Authentication Guidelines

Some of the broad guidelines that exist in the context of instituting e-authentications, including crowdsensing, are described in following sections [58].

5.6.1 Seek Consent

The entity performing authentication should seek consent from the users about what information will be stored and what will be revealed to the authenticating entities. In this way, the people become aware that they are relinquishing some control over the confidentiality of personal information to that identity.

5.6.2 Select Minimal Identity

The authentication should be performed only against the identities that embody the smallest set of attributes needed for the task. This reduces unnecessary exposure of privacy-related attributes to the system.

---

[16] See http://sgcsc.sg/doc/Camp2/WS-06.pdf.

5.6.3 Limit Storage

The information about authenticated identities should not be saved unless there is a clear need. Moreover, the information should be deleted once it is no longer needed. It reduces the chances that the saved identity information can subsequently be re-targeted for uses not implied by the consent of the user that allowed its collection.

5.6.4 Avoid Linking

A single, shared attribute allows linking the identities that contain this attribute, and that could violate privacy by revealing the attributes comprising one identity to those who learn the other identity. Thus, it is important to eschew including the same unique attribute (e.g., identifier) in different identities.

Now, let us turn to UIDAI claims regarding Aadhaar.

5.7 Issues of Privacy Leaks With Aadhaar

Looking at the issues of biometric databases, as well the guidelines for avoiding privacy violations discussed herein, it is obvious that preventing privacy violations in cyberspace for the largest database of biometrics in the world will be a significant challenge.

5.7.1 User Expectation

People provide their biometrics for a variety of purposes, including visas for foreign countries. Therefore, the main question here is, *Is Aadhaar at least as safe as those systems?*

Two important characteristic differences from Aadhaar operation in the context of visa issuance are:

1. The biometric database is exclusively used for the purpose of issuance of visas with limited storage, as highlighted herein, against the passport cum visa number of the individual.
2. The authority of authentication is with the immigration officer, and not the database server.

Thus, one expects a trusted process that involves minimal invasion of privacy with consent.

5.7.2 Insider Attacks

As highlighted already, privacy characterization is dependent on the law of the land. Keeping this in mind, there has been an important case (among many cases) currently at the Supreme Court of India for adjudication about the UIDAI claims and the counter claims made by the activists spearheading the assurance of privacy-preserving implementation.[17] This will have a long-standing bearing on the interpretation of privacy law in the context of technology. The basic premise in all of the privacy issues mentioned herein mainly stems from insider attacks.

From a user perspective, an insider attack on privacy issues can be classified as:

1. Protection of privacy against registration authority.
2. Protection of privacy against access network operators.
3. Protection of privacy against attacks using a set of correlated queries by a set of colluding agencies.

In the context of the first type of insider attack, in January 2018, a leak of Aadhaar numbers was reported by a journalist who paid just Rs. 500 (equivalent to ≈US$8) to access personal data from an enrolment center. Even though this event may look insignificant, there are possible dire consequences from such incidents. Specifically, the Aadhaar system has a false positive rate of 0.0025% for a biometric match. Arguably, for each individual in the database, there are possibly 30,000 individuals whose biometrics identities match with the individual in a database of 1.2 billion individuals. Consequently, if one can collude with the insiders to obtain the Aadhaar number of someone else whose biometric profiles matches with one's own biometric profile, he will be able to use the obtained identity for various purposes, including financial gains or even criminal activities.

Although one can argue that the processes can be strengthened to avoid such possibilities, it clearly demonstrates that a group of colluding insiders can compromise a surveillance system and breach both privacy and security.

In the contexts of other two types of attacks, these insider attacks are technical in nature. Particularly, the attack of type 3 appears to be technically extremely difficult. Fortunately, creating such attacks needs an active and cohesive collaboration across agencies, which is difficult to accomplish and prone to leakage. A multiauthority strong

---

[17] Supreme Court has upheld constitutional validity but struck down some provision of Aadhaar Act.

attribute-based encryption framework [59, 60] could possibly alleviate these problems. The kernel level support for role-based decryption rights [61–63] could also enhance the trustworthiness of data.

5.8 Security of Aadhaar

The CEO of UIDAI on March 22, 2018 presented to the Supreme Court of India the physical security details of 2048 bit RSA encryption,[18] security reviews conducted, and so forth (refer blog [65] for the technical points presented by the CEO of Aadhaar). In biometric databases of the magnitude of Aadhaar, it is important to ensure that long-term keys do not compromise past session keys. It would be nice if properties such as *forward secrecy (FS)* were implemented in Aadhaar. FS protects past sessions against future compromises of secret keys or passwords. A perfect FS assures that the compromises of long-term keys in the communication protocols do not compromise the past session keys. Whether or not this property is satisfied in the process provided by Aadhaar [66] needs a thorough analysis.

As highlighted herein, in the context of Aadhaar, the same database is used for a variety of purposes, and hence, linking of several authentications exist on the same identifier. Thus, it is not easy to prove that there is no violation of privacy. Even the claim of *no storage* by Aadhaar needs careful analysis in the context of using profiles to track identities, as revealed in the infamous leakage on Facebook. The experiment [67] shows the privacy leakage from a wide spectrum of angles.

As per the UIDAI website, Aadhaar can be used both for identity (one can download e-Aadhaar on one's smartphone that will serve as an identity), as well as for authentication. Thus, the process has to make clear the relationship of the biometric usage for accessing the database.

5.9 Issues in Anonymization and Virtual IDs

Recently, UIDAI announced the use of virtual IDs (creatable by the user) for authentication, rather than the person's Aadhaar number. While it appeals generally, one needs to be clear about the possibilities of compromise[19] of ones' Aadhaar number; virtual numbers still look risky (one needs to answer the question of whether the Aadhaar number is a private or a secret number—if it is used as an identity, certainly it cannot be a secret number). Note that biometric access control is used in a controlled environments such as accessing server rooms, airport gates, and so forth, and not in public environments, as the biometric can be cloned as highlighted already.

In general, privacy concerns in crowdsensing arise from the requirements of the disclosure of personal information such as IMEI numbers of mobile devices, SIM IDs, phone numbers, IP addresses, locations, cell tracking, and other subscriber-related information. From such information, one can easily extract the home or the office address of the person. Therefore, anonymization[20] of data appears to be the only way to encourage an individual to share *the* data. However, complete anonymization could create the problem of malicious individuals sharing spurious and concocted data. So, there is a need to balance between two conflicting requirements; the anonymization and the trustworthiness of data, in order to establish an effective privacy-preserving crowdsensing mechanism for surveillance/smartness.

Typically, servers managed by a trusted third party (like it is done in authenticating credit card transactions, DNS, etc.) are made available for gathering data through crowdsensing. Alternatively, an individual can upload videos or images on a specified third-party server. This server removes all traces of tracking information (e.g., personal IDs, phone numbers, GPS data, car license numbers) before sending event-related data to the security surveillance and control system. The server itself should be accessible only through multiple layers of strong cryptographic frameworks. Most crowdsensing systems incorporate the reputations of participants tailored to specific surveillance systems [68–71]. IncogniSense [71] frameworks propose the use of two basic features: (i) using multiple virtual IDs with dynamic or periodic changes, and (ii) mapping exact reputation values to a range, where a range is mapped to a reputation group. Mapping a reputation to a range, and the use of a dynamic virtual ID completely masks the ID of individual participants. However, this adds extra overhead in the management of crowdsensed data, either in terms of complex algorithms (for dynamic assignment of pseudo-names) or in terms of maintaining redundancy on participant information [72].

---

[18] For an assessment of 2048 encryption, refer to [64].

[19] The era of social networks has seen a rise in profiling, compounded with privacy breaches, such as the recent (March 2018) Facebook data breach.

[20] Recently, Facebook Inc., admitted that data on as many as 87 million people, most of them in the United States, may have been improperly shared with the research firm Cambridge Analytica. The challenge is to understand how effective the anonymization is, and how much profiling can it withstand. As in the case of authentication, it may inhibit people from sharing data (even under anonymization) and engaging in activities that they fear could be misconstrued or exploitable.

6 CONCLUSION

In the age of digital technologies, where a personal phone is capable of collecting, storing, and transmitting personal data, even without the person's conscious knowledge, privacy issues have become highly complicated and extremely important. Particularly, in the case of crowdsensing, where an individual's smartphone and other personal devices embedded with modern sensors are involved in collecting and transmitting information, privacy becomes a real issue.

In this chapter, we explored crowdsensing in smart city applications and its privacy implications. First, we presented various definitions related to the term "crowdsensing." We demonstrated that the current definition of mobile crowdsensing that is used interchangeably with crowdsensing is not appropriate, because crowdsensing could be done by using nonmobile sensors, as well as by using people as social sensors. Second, we explored various aspects of privacy, including legal definitions, obligations to crowdsensing service providers, risks, implications, and possible solutions. Third, we presented two case studies relevant to crowdsensing. In the first case study, we demonstrated how crowdsensing can be used in disaster management. Although the privacy concerns during a disaster event could be considered minimal, the fact that the data collected during the disaster can remain available long after the event is a real concern. As such, the privacy issues in this case study are managed by using cryptography and appropriate access control mechanisms. In the second case study, we discussed how citizens' information can be collected by the governments, and how the citizen's private data can be prone to privacy risks. We discussed the possibility that the authorities could compromise a system to access peoples' personal information. In all these cases, there is no single solution that can solve all the privacy problems in these crowdsensing applications. However, a combination of possible solutions can be used to achieve the maximum possible protection of the private information.

On one hand, people contributing to crowdsensing applications to make their cities smarter need to easily and clearly understand how their private data are going to be used. Therefore, further research is required to make the understanding of privacy issues easier and more controllable. On the other hand, the entities working with crowdsensing data containing people's private information need to have adequate knowledge of their privacy obligations, the implications, and the appropriate protection mechanisms. As the attempt to use crowdsensing data for making smart decisions in smart cities will continue, ongoing research will be required to identify and address privacy issues in those applications.

ACKNOWLEDGMENTS

This research is funded by the Australia India Strategic Grant AISRF-08140 and DST/INT/Aus/P-61/2013 dated 05/05/2014.

References

[1] R. Giffinger, C. Fertner, H. Kramar, R. Kalasek, N. Pichler-Milanović, E. Meijers, Smart Cities—Ranking of European Medium-Sized Cities, Vienna University of Technology, 2007. http://www.smart-cities.eu/download/smart_cities_final_report.pdf.

[2] A. Caragliu, C. Del Bo, P. Nijkamp, Smart cities in Europe, J. Urban Technol. 18 (2) (2011) 65–82.

[3] R. Ganti, F. Ye, H. Lei, Mobile crowdsensing: current state and future challenges, IEEE Commun. Mag. 49 (11) (2011) 32–39.

[4] L. Lefort, C. Henson, K. Taylor, P. Barnaghi, M. Compton, O. Corcho, R. Garcia-Castro, J. Graybeal, A. Herzog, K. Janowicz, et al., Semantic sensor network XG final report, W3C Incubator Group Report 28, 2011.

[5] I.R. Noble, A.M. Gill, G.A.V. Bary, McArthur's fire-danger meters expressed as equations, Aust. Ecol. 5 (2) (1980) 201–203.

[6] H. Roitman, J. Mamou, S. Mehta, A. Satt, L.V. Subramaniam, Harnessing the Crowds for Smart City Sensing, ACM, New York, NY, 2012.

[7] R. Power, B. Robinson, D. Ratcliffe, Finding fires with Twitter, in: Australasian Language Technology Association Workshop, vol. 80, 2013, pp. 80–89.

[8] J. Yin, A. Lampert, M. Cameron, B. Robinson, R. Power, Using social media to enhance emergency situation awareness, IEEE Intell. Syst. 6 (2012) 52–59.

[9] B. Guo, Z. Wang, Z. Yu, Y. Wang, N.Y. Yen, R. Huang, X. Zhou, Mobile crowd sensing and computing: the review of an emerging human-powered sensing paradigm, ACM Comput. Surv. 48 (1) (2015) 7.

[10] K. Taylor, C. Griffith, L. Lefort, R. Gaire, M. Compton, T. Wark, D. Lamb, G. Falzon, M. Trotter, Farming the web of things, IEEE Intell. Syst. 28 (6) (2013) 12–19.

[11] S. Karimi, C. Wang, A. Metke-Jimenez, R. Gaire, C. Paris, Text and data mining techniques in adverse drug reaction detection, ACM Comput. Surv. 47 (4) (2015) 56.

[12] D.C. Brabham, Crowdsourcing as a model for problem solving, Convergence 14 (1) (2008) 75–90.

[13] K. O'Hara, Transparent government, not transparent citizens: a report on privacy and transparency for the Cabinet Office, 2011.

[14] J.E. Cohen, What privacy is for, Harv. Law Rev. 126 2013.

[15] D.J. Solove, Why privacy matters even if you have 'nothing to hide', The Chronicle of Higher Education, 2011.

[16] T.J. Magi, Fourteen reasons privacy matters: a multidisciplinary review of scholarly literature, Libr. Q. 81 (2) (2011) 187–209.

[17] L. Cilliers, S. Flowerday, Information security in a public safety, participatory crowdsourcing smart city project, in: 2014 World Congress on Internet Security (WorldCIS), IEEE, 2014, pp. 36–41.

[18] A. Martinez-Balleste, P.A. Perez-Martinez, A. Solanas, The pursuit of citizens' privacy: a privacy-aware smart city is possible, IEEE Commun. Mag. 51 (6) (2013) 136–141.

[19] D. Garcia, Leaking privacy and shadow profiles in online social networks, Sci. Adv. 3 (8) (2017) e1701172.

[20] Y. Li, Y.-S. Jeong, B.-S. Shin, J.H. Park, Crowdsensing multimedia data: security and privacy issues, IEEE Multimedia 24 (4) (2017) 58–66.

[21] R. Jones, R. Kumar, B. Pang, A. Tomkins, I know what you did last summer: query logs and user privacy, in: Proceedings of the Sixteenth ACM Conference on Conference on Information and Knowledge Management, ACM, 2007, pp. 909–914.

[22] H. Li, H. Zhu, S. Du, X. Liang, X. Shen, Privacy leakage of location sharing in mobile social networks: attacks and defense. IEEE Trans. Dependable Secure Comput. (2016). https://doi.org/10.1109/TDSC.2016.2604383.

[23] P. Joglekar, V. Kulkarni, Privacy issues in urban computing using mobile crowdsensing, Int. J. Comput. Appl. 168 (3) (2017) 23–26.

[24] H. To, C. Shahabi, Location privacy in spatial crowdsourcing, 2017.

[25] M. Enserink, The end of privacy, Science 347 (6221) (2015) 490–491.

[26] E. Ronen, A. Shamir, A.-O. Weingarten, C. O'Flynn, IoT goes nuclear: creating a ZigBee chain reaction, in: 2017 IEEE Symposium on Security and Privacy (SP). IEEE, 2017, pp. 195–212.

[27] L. Pournajaf, L. Xiong, D.A. Garcia-Ulloa, V. Sunderam, A survey on privacy in mobile crowd sensing task management, Mathematics and Computer Science, Emory University, 2014. Technical Report TR-2014-002.

[28] L. Pournajaf, D.A. Garcia-Ulloa, L. Xiong, V. Sunderam, Participant privacy in mobile crowd sensing task management: a survey of methods and challenges, ACM SIGMOD Rec. 44 (4) (2016) 23–34.

[29] K. Zhang, J. Ni, K. Yang, X. Liang, J. Ren, X.S. Shen, Security and privacy in smart city applications: challenges and solutions, IEEE Commun. Mag. 55 (1) (2017) 122–129.

[30] M.B. Sinai, N. Partush, S. Yadid, E. Yahav, Exploiting social navigation, arXiv preprint arXiv:1410.01512014.

[31] S. Blasco, J. Bustos-Jiménez, G. Font, A. Hevia, M.G. Prato, A three-layer approach for protecting smart-citizens privacy in crowdsensing projects, in: SCCC, 2015, pp. 1–5.

[32] I.J. Vergara-Laurens, L.G. Jaimes, M.A. Labrador, Privacy-preserving mechanisms for crowdsensing: survey and research challenges, IEEE Internet Things J. 4 (4) (2017) 855–869.

[33] M. Huai, L. Huang, Y.-E. Sun, W. Yang, Efficient privacy-preserving aggregation for mobile crowdsensing, in: BDCloud, 2015, pp. 275–280.

[34] M. Zhang, L. Yang, X. Gong, J. Zhang, Privacy-preserving crowdsensing—privacy valuation, network effect, and profit maximization, in: GLOBECOM, 2016, pp. 1–6.

[35] I. Vakilinia, J. Xin, M. Li, L. Guo, Privacy-preserving data aggregation over incomplete data for crowdsensing, in: GLOBECOM, 2016, pp. 1–6.

[36] D.E. Bakken, R. Rarameswaran, D.M. Blough, A.A. Franz, T.J. Palmer, Data obfuscation: anonymity and desensitization of usable data sets, IEEE Secur. Priv. 2 (6) (2004) 34–41.

[37] L. Huning, J. Bauer, N. Aschenbruck, A privacy preserving mobile crowdsensing architecture for a smart farming application, in: CrowdSenSys, 2017, pp. 62–67.

[38] C. Dwork, Differential privacy: a survey of results, in: International Conference on Theory and Applications of Models of Computation, Springer, 2008, pp. 1–19.

[39] L. Wang, D. Zhang, D. Yang, B.Y. Lim, X. Ma, Differential location privacy for sparse mobile crowdsensing, in: ICDM, 2016, pp. 1257–1262.

[40] Y. Sei, A. Ohsuga, Differential private data collection and analysis based on randomized multiple dummies for untrusted mobile crowdsensing, IEEE Trans. Inf. Forensics Secur. 12 (4) (2016) 926–939.

[41] UIDAI counters criticism over 'false positives', Biom. Technol. Today 2011 (4) (2011) 3.

[42] D.E. Bell, L.J. La Padula, Secure computer system: unified exposition and multics interpretation, MITRE Corp, Bedford, MA, 1976. Technical Report.

[43] M.A. Bishop, Introduction to Computer Security, Pearson Education, Inc., Boston, MA, 2005

[44] D.E. Denning, A lattice model of secure information flow, Commun. ACM 19 (5) (1976) 236–243.

[45] N.V.N. Kumar, R.K. Shyamasundar, Realizing purpose-based privacy policies succinctly via information-flow labels, in: 2014 IEEE Fourth International Conference on Big Data and Cloud Computing (BdCloud), 2014, pp. 753–760.

[46] H.E. Miller, K.J. Engemann, R.R. Yager, Disaster planning and management, Commun. IIMA 6 (2) (2006) 25–36.

[47] UNISDR, Terminology, (2017). http://www.unisdr.org/we/inform/terminology.

[48] Centre for Research on the Epidemiology of Disasters (CRED), 2015 Disasters in Numbers, 2016.

[49] Asian Disaster Preparedness Center, Module 9: ICT for disaster risk management, 2011.

[50] A. Bhatnagar, A. Kumar, R.K. Ghosh, R.K. Shyamasundar, A framework of community inspired distributed message dissemination and emergency alert response system over smart phones, in: 2016 8th International Conference on Communication Systems and Networks (COMSNETS), 2016, pp. 1–8.

[51] D. Puthal, S. Nepal, R. Ranjan, J. Chen, DPBSV—an efficient and secure scheme for big sensing data stream, in: Internet of Things. IoT Infrastructures. IoT360 2015. Lecture Notes of the Institute for Computer Sciences, Social Informatics and Telecommunications Engineering, 2015, pp. 246–253.

[52] D. Puthal, S. Nepal, R. Ranjan, J. Chen, et al., A dynamic key length based approach for real-time security verification of big sensing data stream, in: J. Wang (Ed.), Web Information Systems Engineering—WISE 2015, Lecture Notes in Computer Science, vol. 9419, Springer, 2015, pp. 93–108.

[53] N.V.N. Kumar, R.K. Shyamasundar, An end-to-end privacy preserving design of a map-reduce framework, in: 2016 IEEE 18th International Conference on High Performance Computing and Communications; IEEE 14th International Conference on Smart City; IEEE 2nd International Conference on Data Science and Systems (HPCC/SmartCity/DSS), 2016, pp. 1469–1476.

[54] D. Puthal, X. Wu, S. Nepal, R. Ranjan, J. Chen, SEEN: a selective encryption method to ensure confidentiality for big sensing data streams, IEEE Trans. Big Data (2017). https://doi.org/10.1109/tbdata.2017.2702172.

[55] D. Puthal, S. Nepal, R. Ranjan, J. Chen, A synchronized shared key generation method for maintaining end-to-end security of big data streams, in: Web Information Systems Engineering—WISE 2015, 2017.

[56] F. Zelazny, The evolution of India's UID program, vol. 168, Center for Global Development, 2012.

[57] OECD, OECD recommendation on electronic authentication and OECD guidance for electronic authentication., OECD, 2007. Technical Report.

[58] F. Schneider, Authentication for people, (2009). https://www.cs.cornell.edu/fbs/publications/chptr.AuthPeople.pdf.

[59] M. Chase, S.S.M. Chow, Improving privacy and security in multi-authority attribute-based encryption, in: Proceedings of the 16th ACM Conference on Computer and Communications Security, CCS '09, 2009.

[60] M. Li, S. Yu, Y. Zheng, K. Ren, W. Lou, Scalable and secure sharing of personal health records in cloud computing using attribute-based encryption, IEEE Trans. Parallel Distrib. Syst. 24 (1) (2013) 131–143.

[61] D.R. Kuhn, Implementation of role-based access control in multi-level secure systems, 2000, US Patent 6,023,765.

[62] R. Sandhu, D. Ferraiolo, R. Kuhn, et al., The NIST model for role-based access control: towards a unified standard, in: ACM Workshop on Role-Based Access Control, vol. 2000, 2000, pp. 1–11.

[63] E. Bertino, P.A. Bonatti, E. Ferrari, TRBAC: a temporal role-based access control model, ACM Trans. Inf. Syst. Secur. 4 (3) (2001) 191–233.

[64] M. Nemec, M. Sys, P. Svenda, D. Klinec, A. Matyas, The return of Coppersmith's attack: practical factorization of widely used RSA moduli, in: IEEE CCS 2017, 2017, pp. 1631–1648.

[65] S. Vombatkere, Data protection with concrete walls and uncrackable encryption, March 24, 2018, https://countercurrents.org/2018/03/24/data-protection-with-concrete-walls-and-uncrackable-encryption/.

[66] Aadhaar, Aadhaar authentication API specification—version 2.0 (revision 1), 2018, https://uidai.gov.in/images/FrontPageUpdates/aadhaar_authentication_api_2_0.pdf (accessed 8 May 2018).

[67] V.T. Patil, R.K. Shyamasundar, Undoing of privacy policies on Facebook, in: G. Livraga, S. Zhu (Eds.), 31th IFIP Annual Conference on Data and Applications Security and Privacy (DBSEC), Data and Applications Security and Privacy XXXI, vol. LNCS-10359, Springer International Publishing, Philadelphia, PA, 2017, pp. 239–255.

[68] A. Dua, N. Bulusu, W.-C. Feng, W. Hu, Towards trustworthy participatory sensing, in: Proceedings of the 4th USENIX Conference on Hot Topics in Security, HotSec'09, 2009, p. 8.

[69] K.L. Huang, S.S.K. Kanhere, W. Hu, Are you contributing trustworthy data?: The case for a reputation system in participatory sensing, in: Proceedings of the 13th ACM International Conference on Modeling, Analysis, and Simulation of Wireless and Mobile Systems, ACM, 2010, pp. 14–22.

[70] K.L. Huang, S.S. Kan, W. Hu, A privacy-preserving reputation system for participatory sensing, in: 2012 IEEE 37th Conference on Local Computer Networks (LCN), IEEE, 0122, pp. 10–18.

[71] D. Christin, C. Roßkopf, M. Hollick, L.A. Martucci, S.S. Kanhere, IncogniSense: an anonymity-preserving reputation framework for participatory sensing applications, Pervasive Mob. Comput. 9 (3) (2013) 353–371.

[72] D. He, S. Chan, M. Guizani, User privacy and data trustworthiness in mobile crowd sensing, IEEE Wirel. Commun. 22 (1) (2015) 28–34.

6

Privacy Preservation in Smart Cities

Youyang Qu, Mohammad Reza Nosouhi, Lei Cui, and Shui Yu

School of IT, Deakin University, Geelong, Australia

1 INTRODUCTION

The Smart City is no longer just a concept. A growing number of governments have started developing their own smart projects, and some intelligent applications have been used in practice, such as smart car parking, smart utility management, smart healthcare service, smart communication, and smart homes. Predictably, in the near future, people will live in a city embedded with billions of smart devices, connected through heterogeneous networks and systems. Personal data of users are sensed, collected, stored, and spread anytime, which can be further analyzed by service providers and third parties to improve the quality of services. Moreover, governments can utilize large amounts of data to perfect future city plans and improve related strategies.

Although these smart applications have brought tangible benefits to modern society, privacy issues have become worthy of attention in Smart Cities. For example, consumers may release their location information when using location-based services (LBS), such as the smart car parking system and navigation tools. Consumption information from smart meters can be used to infer appliance usage states and user behavior [1]. In addition, data over-collection and knowledge over-mining by service providers may reveal sensitive information that individuals are unwilling to share [2]. According to new research by TRSUTe [3], around 60% of US Internet users understand that smart devices can collect their personal data, and nearly 90% of Internet users hope to have the ability to control the data being collected by various devices. Therefore, it is of great importance to take effective measures to avoid privacy violations.

During the past decades, many privacy protection mechanisms (e.g., cryptography, biometrics, anonymity) have been applied in different application fields. However, compared with the Web era, the Internet of Things (IoT) is more vulnerable to privacy violations, and it is unrealistic to use them directly under the Smart City scenario for following reasons. First, the computational power of most sensors and devices is limited, which means that developing light-weight protection algorithms becomes an inevitable trend. Second, compared with traditional applications, the characteristics of smart systems (scalability, heterogeneity, mobility, etc.) lead to more strict requirements for guaranteeing the effectiveness of privacy protection. Third, smarter attackers and new developed malware can even bypass the current attack prevention mechanisms. Last but not least, we should be aware that the construction of nontechnical necessities, such as related strategies in terms of governance, education, and policies, is also at a quite early stage.

Accordingly, we aim at providing an extensive overview of existing privacy issues and up-to-date privacy protection strategies in Smart Cities. We also try to identify some potential research opportunities for readers who are interested in this promising and practical field.

2 PRIVACY CONCERNS AND ATTACKS IN SMART CITIES

Almost every aspect of personal privacy is potentially at stake in a Smart City [4]; personal sensitive information such as location, identity, habits, and social interactions will be breached if not well protected. In order to give readers a better understanding of privacy issues in the Smart City environment, in the following, we review significant problems that have been found or studied from the perspective of different smart applications.

2.1 Privacy Concerns in Smart Cities

2.1.1 Smart Mobility

Smart mobility is of significant importance to modern cities, as it is designed to improve the safety of road traffic and the efficiency of transportation [5]. Related applications include road traffic adjustment, navigation, road surface condition sensing, and so on. However, the large volume of trajectory data may be analyzed to infer locations and mobility patterns of a user. Even worse, the trajectory information can be exposed to criminal activities. Take car-hailing applications for example, where each trip record will be stored. If this information is not well protected, taxi drivers or attackers may have a complete view of a user's location and tracks.

2.1.2 Smart Home

Smart homes are always equipped with numerous sensors and Internet-connected devices, which means that the information about offline activities of users may be captured and transmitted outside of the home. The device manufacturers and Internet service providers can access the sensitive data, such as security codes, child behaviors, sleeping patterns, and so forth. Although some transport layer encryption methods have been applied to prevent attackers from eavesdropping on sensitive in-home information, it was proved that users' privacy can still be attacked by using metadata from devices in smart homes [6].

2.1.3 Smart Grid

Smart metering infrastructure is an important component of smart grids, which enable distributed system operators to record real-time power consumption periodically and optimize services for residents. However, the ability to monitor power flows also raises concerns about privacy, because it can expose the private life of residents (e.g., living habits, working hours, and whether the residents are away from their home) [7]. If the data is stolen by attackers or illegally used by untrusted system operators, the privacy of customers might be compromised. Therefore, how to protect a residence's sensitive information has become a hot research topic.

2.1.4 Smart Healthcare

It has been predicted that in the following decades, the way of healthcare services provided will be transformed from hospital-centered to home-centered by 2030 [8]. With the development of this IoT-based healthcare application, privacy breaches have become one of the major threats. It is common knowledge that health-related data is a personal asset that needs to be controlled by patients, rather than being scattered in different healthcare systems [9]. Unfortunately, privacy protection in smart healthcare systems remains a bottleneck [10]. The main reason is that sharing of healthcare data is the prerequisite to ensure the quality of healthcare services.

2.1.5 Smart Cards

Smart cards are widely used in smart systems, such as logging of healthcare services and transactions, processing transit passengers, and for marketing purposes. However, sensitive data, including identity, trajectories, and behavior patterns about cardholders could be collected and stored by smart cards. If the card is stolen by untrusted entities, personal data may be directly disclosed. In addition, it could be repurposed by service providers for tracking, profiling, and advertising [4].

2.2 Up-to-Date Attacks

In this section, we focus on the most severe existing attacks, including background knowledge attacks, collusion attacks, Sybil attacks, eavesdropping attacks, spam attacks, likability attacks, inside curious attacks, outside forgery attacks, and identity attacks. The current attacks have seriously impacted Smart Cities and caused degraded service quality [11].

2.2.1 Background Knowledge Attack

A background knowledge attack is one of the most popular attacks to breach an individual's privacy. Adversaries hold prior beliefs about specific people in Smart Cities, which are also referred to as background knowledge. Based on this, adversaries can launch an attack that includes a combination of techniques. The attack results are always regarded as a postbelief. If a postbelief contains more sensitive information than a prior belief, we know the attack has been successfully conducted [12]. The difficulty in defending against a background knowledge attack is that it is not easy to model the prior beliefs of adversaries. Therefore, it is hard to measure adversaries and attacks quantitatively.

2.2.2 Collusion Attack

Collusion attacks are widely used in multiple party scenarios. Multiple adversaries can collude with each other to gain more sensitive information about a certain person of event [13]. Adversaries usually hold different prior beliefs, which provides an incentive to carry out a collusion attack [14]. Therefore, the key point in defending against a collusion attack is that the privacy-level in a system should be kept uniform to make sure the adversaries have no incentive to launch this attack.

2.2.3 Sybil Attack

The sybil attack is usually launched within the scenario of a reputation-involved system. During the attack process, an adversary generates a large amount of pseudo names, and further gains maximum influence [15]. Based on the influence, the adversary can mislead the other people in the system or even fool the central authority. Privacy leaks happen during the attack. Whether the attack can be successfully launched is decided by the cost of fake identities and establishing a trust mechanism between the central authority and the identities.

2.2.4 Eavesdropping Attack

In the case of an eavesdropping attack, adversaries usually eavesdrop on the information communication and transmission process by means of modern hacking technologies, including the Internet, electromagnetic waves, and so on. This type of attack is launched by unauthorized real-time interception of private communication [16]. Therefore, it is important to secure the communication to prevent privacy leakage.

2.2.5 Spam Attack

Spam attacks have been researched because email came into existence. In common cases, an adversary tries to send emails to recipients whose email addresses are obtained in advance. Compared with commercial advertising, spam attacks can cause harm. By launching spam attack, adversaries can disrupt data filtering at first, and further spy on the storage space. A proposed system named "LENS" can address spam attacks and prevent their transmission by means of gate keepers [17].

2.2.6 Linkability Attack

Linkability attacks are becoming more and more popular in this Big Data era. As in a Smart City, people can have various identities in the system corresponding to different interests, communities, organizations, and so on. Therefore, a certain individual may share different kinds of sensitive information with different identities [18]. As technologies of machine learning (ML) and data fusion become more and more mature, it is easy for adversaries to link sensitive data from various sources and finally launch this attack.

2.2.7 Inside Curious Attack

The inside curious attack is also known as the man-in-middle attack. In this case, adversaries can manipulate other people in the system. The inside curious attack is widely applicable in Diffie-Hellman-based key exchange schemes. The goal of this attack is to compromise availability, confidentiality, and integrity. Based on an inside curious attack, adversaries can also launch a collusion attack to upgrade the attack performance.

2.2.8 Outside Forgery Attack

In an outside forgery attack, misleading messages are generated with fake information, so that adversaries can initiate other plotting attacks, such as the location-tracking attack. There are five phases for a forgery attack, in which we use vehicular social networks as an example.

First, the victim node and the adversary node establish a link with location information. Second, the adversary node creates a malicious payload for the victim node. Third, the victim node sends a request to a social spot s_1 for cookies. Fourth, s_1 gives the email address of the victim node to the adversary node. Last, the social spots reset the certificates. In this way, an outside forgery attack is performed and the privacy of victim nodes will be compromised [11].

2.2.9 Discussion on Attacks

The preceding attacks are the most severe attacks in systems with sensitive information. However, attacks are always launched in a combination. For example, background knowledge attack would be launched with a collusion attack. Thus, privacy preservation focuses on overall protections rather than solving one single attack, which is quite critical. Therefore, new methods and frameworks against attacks are urgently needed.

In addition, there are a lot of other kinds of attacks that will cause privacy leakage in certain situations, for example, global external attacks, impersonation attacks, successive-response attacks, profile attacks, location attacks, and so on. Interested readers can refer to Ferrag et al. [11] for more details.

3 CURRENT PRIVACY PROTECTION METHODS

Privacy protection has become one of the biggest problems in our data-driven society. Many related studies have been completed in the past two decades. Clustering-based methods are first applied in privacy protection domains [19–21]. Differential privacy, due to its rigorous privacy guarantee, has attracted increasing attention and applications. In this section, we focus on the domain of the Smart City, and try to provide an extensive review of developed protection technologies, which are summarized from the perspective of different disciplines.

3.1 Cryptography

Cryptographic algorithms are the most frequently used privacy protection method in the IoT domain. Many cryptographic tools have been applied in practice. Unfortunately, traditional encryption mechanisms with overly computational complexity cannot meet the new requirements for smart applications, especially for those systems that consist of many resource-constraint devices [22]. Consequently, how to develop lightweight yet effective encryption algorithms is of significant practical value.

Homomorphic encryption (HE), as a method of performing calculations on encrypted information, has received increasing attention in recent years. The key function of it is to protect sensitive information from being exposed when performing computations on encrypted data. For example, Abdallah et al. [23] developed a lightweight HE-based privacy protection data aggregation method for smart grids that can avoid involving the smart meter when aggregate readings are performed. Another work by Talpur et al. [24] proposed an IoT network architecture based on HE technology for healthcare monitoring systems. Despite the great potential of HE methods, computational expense may restrict the application of this method.

Zero-knowledge proof is another cryptographic method that allows one party to prove something to other parties, without conveying additional information. For application in the Smart City domain, Dousti et al. [25] developed an authentication protocol for smart cards through zero-knowledge proofs.

3.2 Biometrics

In IoT-based applications, biological features (e.g., voices, irises, fingerprints, faces, and even brainwaves) are widely used in access control and authentication systems, which is a direct way to make sensitive data of customers unavailable to illegal users. Specifically, it has two key steps. At the beginning, the biometric information is stored in a database. For the second step, the corresponding biometric features are sampled again and compared with previous stored datasets for authentication. Biometric methods can provide stronger protection in comparison with traditional password-based methods. There is a serious concern that the biological data itself is sensitive. If these bio-based methods are not appropriately used, the identity characteristics of users could be compromised [26]. To solve this problem, Wang et al. [27] developed privacy-preserving biometric schemes to make it difficult for adversaries to infer biometric identities.

3.3 Differential Privacy

Differential privacy [28]: The randomized mechanism A with domain H is ϵ-differential private if for all and for all adjacent $x, y \in H$ (i.e., $||x - y|| \leq 1$) we have

$$\Pr[A(x) \in S \leq \exp(\epsilon) \Pr[A(x) \in S, \tag{1}$$

where ϵ is the privacy level that is a positive value and denotes the level of privacy guarantees such that a smaller value represents stricter privacy requirements. In other words, for a smaller ϵ, the mechanism makes any adjacent data more indistinguishable. The reason is that for a small value of ε, with almost same probability, the published $A(x)$ and $A(y)$ are placed in the same region S. However, for a large ϵ, this probability is much higher for $A(x)$ than $A(y)$, which makes them more distinguishable.

Therefore, mechanism A can address privacy concerns that individuals might have about the release of their private information. Note that differential privacy is a definition, not an algorithm [29]. In other words, we can have many differentially private algorithms for a privacy scenario and a given ϵ. One of the most popular mechanisms developed based on differential privacy frameworks is the Laplace mechanism, in which Laplace-distributed noise is added to users' private data to make it ϵ-differential private.

Laplace mechanism [29]: Given the private data $x \in H$, the Laplace mechanism is defined as

$$A_L(x,\epsilon) = x + N,\qquad(2)$$

where N is Laplace-distributed noise with a scale parameter $1/\epsilon$ and zero mean, that is,

$$N \ Lap\left(0, \frac{1}{\epsilon}\right).\qquad(3)$$

The probability density function for N is:

$$f_N(n) = \frac{\epsilon}{2}\exp(-\epsilon|n|),\qquad(4)$$

where ϵ denotes the privacy level required by the user.

The Laplace distribution is a symmetric version of the exponential distribution. According to its probability density function, with high probability, the Laplace mechanism generates much stronger noise for small values of privacy levels and vice versa [29].

It can be easily shown that the Laplace mechanism preserves ϵ-differential privacy [29]. In other words, if A_L is a Laplace mechanism, then the randomized response $A_L(x, \epsilon)$ is ϵ-differential private.

3.4 Blockchain

The blockchain technique has been widely applied to protect privacy in the IoT domain in recent years. A survey done by Christidis et al. [30] indicates its realizability and significant value in the IoT ecosystem. A key characteristic of blockchain is that it is decentralized, enabling applications to operate in a distributed way. For example, Yue et al. [9] developed a novel healthcare system architecture based on blockchain, which makes it possible for patients to share personal healthcare data while protecting their data privacy. To mitigate the privacy issues in smart vehicles, Dorri et al. [31] propose a blockchain-based architecture to guarantee the security of vehicular ecosystems and protect the privacy of end users. Another recent work by Kosba et al. [32] proposed a powerful privacy protection smart contracts system based on the blockchain model. In addition, there are many novel blockchain-based protection technologies developed for other smart applications. However, it still has great potential in this field. We need to take steps to make the best use of this technology to cope with privacy problems in Smart Cities.

3.5 Game Theory

Game theory is widely known as a powerful mathematical tool. It has been applied to solve many privacy problems successfully in recent years. The fact that game theory relies on distributed, timely action, and proven mathematics is the main reason behind its popularity [33]. One application is to cooperate and improve classic privacy protection algorithms. For example, Liu et al. [34] adopted Bayesian game techniques to develop a dummy-based k-anonymity method for preserving location privacy of users. More relevant to Smart Cities, Yassine et al. [35] have used the concept of differential privacy to limit information leakage, and relied on game theory to model the privacy tradeoffs in smart grids. We believe that with the rapid evolution of the everything-connected Smart City, game-theoretic approaches will play a significant role in solving new security and privacy issues that have developed in this smart era.

3.6 Machine Learning and Data Mining

In this field, the popular ML technologies are mainly applied to do analysis, prediction, permission control, and achieve the goal of personalization. For example, Wijesekera et al. [36] designed a machine-learned model to predict privacy preferences of mobile users when using smart applications. To protect personal sensitive data in smart devices, Rodriguez et al. [37] developed a method through unsupervised and supervised train models that can prevent personal data from being sent to any distrusted entities in the cloud. However, both of these methods have a common problem, which is the need for further studies to overcome the drawbacks. The subjective responses (training dataset) from participants differ from the real situation in a smart environment. Another advantage of the ML-based method is that it can reduce the burden on the user configuring permission settings in applications.

In Smart Cities, data mining (DM) technologies have been widely used by service providers and governments to improve the quality of services. However, the over-collection of personal data collected by smart devices around users also brings significant privacy concerns. Sensitive knowledge, such as social styles, behavior patterns, and even religious beliefs, can be mined by untrusting parties. Therefore, privacy-preserving data mining (PPDM) technologies have received increasing attention in recent years [38].

3.7 Nontechnological Strategies

Nontechnological countermeasures are indispensable complements for existing technical solutions, such as the introduction of related regulations, policies, and education programs [39]. Developed policies mainly include guidelines for access, for accounting of disclosures, amendment requests, verification, privacy notices, antiretaliation, and so forth. As entities that play significant roles in Smart City, governments have a responsibility to enforce sophisticated regulations to protect data and the framework of smart systems. At the same time, clear laws and punishments should be made to deter attackers. Furthermore, related professional training is also an important way to solve the problem of personal data disclosure. For example, it enables designers of smart applications to develop services with powerful privacy controls. In addition, education can also contribute a lot to helping users gain enough protecting knowledge in the Smart City environment [40]. It was reported that customers are likely to ignore privacy concerns for the benefits and convenience of smart services [41].

3.8 Social Link Privacy Protection

In terms of privacy protection, we believe social link privacy is also very important, in addition to traditional identity privacy. Adversaries can mine a lot more sensitive information if they can access an individual's social links. Therefore, in this section, we move on to current privacy protection schemes dealing with social links.

3.8.1 Machine Learning-Based Social Link Privacy

With the fast development of ML and DM, more and more advanced technologies have been introduced to enhance the discovery of social links. In [42], the authors first tried to use ML-based methods to discover social links, and then shed light on how to design defense schemes to better protect against ML-based attacks.

The proposed social link discovery scheme has three phases. In the first phase, a random walk method is employed to generate random walk traces. The method is on the user-location bipartite graph, while the traces denote neighbors of each person inside the system. In the next phase, the authors use the generated random walk traces as a training set and import them into a learning model to extract features. The mobility features of each individual are mapped into a continuous vector space. In the last phase, we further measure the similarity between two individuals based on the mobility features, and predict the social link between them in an unsupervised setting.

$G = (U, L, E)$ denotes the graph where U represents a set of individuals, while E represents the edges between U and L. We use t_w and l_w to be walk times and walk length, respectively. In addition, we employ v_{cur}, v_{cur}^{nb}, and v_{cur}^w to stand for current node, neighbor nodes, and the corresponding weights between them. Built upon this, we demonstrate the random walk generation algorithm, as described in Algorithm 1.

In the rest of this work, the authors leverage hiding, replacement, and generalization methods to defend the proposed social link discovery model. Extensive evaluation results show that hiding and replacement offer superior performance over generalization. Furthermore, although both hiding and replacement can achieve a satisfying trade-off between privacy and data utility, they are prominent in different aspects. Hiding can achieve higher-data utility, while replacement can provide better privacy protection.

3.8.2 Recommendation-Based Social Link Privacy

Smart Cities can also make recommendations based on social links, for example, friend recommendations, interest recommendations, and so forth. In this case, privacy leakage also becomes a big problem, for the recommendation can reveal social links, which is unacceptable in Smart Cities.

In [43], the authors proposed a privacy-preserving friend recommendation scheme based on trust. Similar to daily life, social relationships in Smart Cities are shared by each individual's attributes, for example, friends, relatives, and colleagues. This indicates that recommendations based on attributes may lead to fine granularity of social links.

ALGORITHM 1 RANDOM WALK GENERATION

Require: A preobtained location bipartite graph $G = (U, L, E)$;
Ensure: Random Walk Traces ω;

1: $\omega \leftarrow [\ ]$;
2: **while** $u \in U$ **do**
3:   **while** $i \leq t_w$ **do**
4:     $\Omega \leftarrow [u]$;
5:     $v_{cur} \leftarrow u$;
6:     **while** $j \leq l_w$ **do**
7:       $v_{cur}^{nb}, v_{cur}^{w} \leftarrow \text{GetNb}(v_{cur}, G)$;
8:       extract v_{cur}'s neighbors v_{cur}^{nb} and the corresponding weights v_{cur}^{w};
9:       $v_{next} \leftarrow \text{Sampling}(v_{cur}^{nb}, v_{cur}^{w})$;
10:      append v_{next} to ω;
11:      $v_{cur} \leftarrow v_{next}$;
12:     **end while**
13:     append ω to Ω;
14:   **end while**
15: **end while**

Therefore, this work allows individuals to submit their attributes to match friends and establish social relationships using a multihop trust chain.

The design objectives are both trust-based recommendation and privacy preservation. For trust-based recommendations, they establish the multihop chain based on a 1-hop trust social relationship between pairwise individuals. In the case of privacy preservation, three types of privacy are considered, including social coordinate privacy, identity and network address privacy, and trust-level privacy.

Moreover, four types of adversaries are taken into consideration. The first type of adversary tries to obtain an individual's identity privacy, and social link privacy, and release the sensitive information to the public. The second type of adversary accesses the location information (including IP or Mac address) and tracks them during the recommendation process. The third type of adversary has the ability to launch an impersonation attack on honest individuals, and further deviate the recommendation process. The fourth type of adversary leverages faking their own social features and relationships, and misleads the system to make inaccurate or even incorrect recommendations.

The system first defines some social features, such as vectors, in order to measure the social link. Then a modified KNN algorithm is employed to do the social link clustering. This will decide whether two individuals can be friends. At last, a cryptography-based method is introduced to achieve a trust-based privacy-preserving friend recommendation (Algorithm 2).

ALGORITHM 2 TRUST-BASED PRIVACY PRESERVING FRIEND RECOMMENDATION

Require: Two individuals u_1, u_2;
Ensure: Recommendation without privacy leakage;

1: Trust-level establishment;
2: Social features extraction as vectors;
3: **while** Input a new individual **do**
4:   Calculate distance between individuals based on vectors;
5:   Use KNN algorithm to cluster;
6:   **if** Distance $\leq$ social distance **then**
7:     Use cryptography-based method to perform recommendation;
8:   **end if**
9: **end while**

ALGORITHM 3 ICA-RST LABEL GENERATION ALGORITHM

Require: Users, links, attribute set, labels of unknown users;

Ensure: Updated label;

1: Learn classifier C utilizing only attributes;

2: **for** Each user **do**

3:   Predict the labels of the unknown users utilizing C;

4: **end for**

5: **for** All t **do**

6:   Store the known labels and the predicted labels;

7:   **for** Each user **do**

8:     Calculate link features utilizing known labels and the predicted labels;

9:   **end for**

10:   Learn new classifier C_n utilizing all of the attributes and labels;

11:   **for** Each user **do**

12:     Repredict the unknown labels utilizing C_n;

13:   **end for**

14: **end for**

15: Return updated label.

3.8.3 Data Sanitization-Based Social Link Privacy

Improper data release in Smart Cities could severely breach the privacy of individuals. Among all the privacy issues, the social link privacy is inherently important. It is possible for adversaries to predict sensitive information by postprocessing, for example, DM, ML, collusion, and so forth. Therefore, it is necessary to sanitize sensitive data before publishing.

In [44], the authors conduct research on defending sensitive information inference attacks by collective data sanitization. In this work, they first propose an inference attack in which adversaries utilize a group of nonsensitive attributes and social links to obtain more sensitive information from the victims. Moreover, they develop a collective data sanitization method to manipulate the nonsensitive attributes and social links between individuals. The core idea is to sanitize social links and make best use of various data-manipulating methods.

In terms of the proposed inference attack, the authors first establish a rough attribute set based on indiscernibility relations, attribute dependency, and reduction. Second, they leverage this attribute set to generate the decision rules. The last step is to perform prediction based on social links. The prediction is quite challenging because individual labels are partially missing. One of the most fundamental ideas is that we predict a group label roughly, and then update the predicted outputs in an iterative way.

The label generation algorithm is named "ICA-RST." The details are in Algorithm 3.

4 LOCATION PRIVACY IN SMART CITIES

One some of the most applicable data collected from individuals or visitors in a Smart City is GPS data. Real-time access to an individual's location data enables us to have more efficient systems for public transport, real-time smart traffic management, and many other location-aware services in our Smart City. Developments in smart phone technology make it possible to easily gather individuals' location data because they carry smartphones that have been equipped with embedded GPS units. Moreover, in a Smart City, GPS data are collected from vehicles as well. For example, in Singapore, the government has recently planned a project to install GPS On-Board Units in all cars, which communicate with a satellite system to monitor the real-time location of each vehicle, along with its speed and direction. The gathered information will be used for determining how much drivers should pay for using freeways, busy roads, and parking spots.

However, the big issue is how to preserve the location privacy of individuals and visitors in a Smart City because local governments and companies might sell users private location data to third parties for commercial benefits. People will not collaborate with new Smart City services if they have concerns about their privacy. Therefore, privacy must be considered in Smart City strategies, otherwise they will not be welcomed by people. Particularly, location privacy has always had a specific importance for users, because if it is violated, other private information about individuals, such as health conditions and political tendencies can be inferred. Even if users' names or ID are hidden, or pseudonyms are used, it has been shown that other private data about users may be obtained by analyzing their position data only [26, 45].

In this chapter, we discuss the location privacy issue in two parts. First, we review LBS in Smart Cities, which can cause many location privacy challenges. In addition, a brief review on the current location privacy protection methods for these services is presented. Second, we present a concise definition of differential privacy, and review the location privacy methods and techniques that work based on the differential privacy framework.

4.1 Location-Based Services in Smart Cities

LBS are some of the most popular and useful location-aware services offered in Smart Cities. Location-based service providers (LSP) use individuals' location data to provide their requested information, such as the nearest ATM, restaurant, or retail store. These location data have three dimensions: personal, spatial, and temporal, indicating a user's location at a specific time.

Different methods have been proposed to protect location privacy of LBS users [45, 46]. These methods can be categorized in different ways. In [4], they have been categorized as spatial anonymization, obfuscation, and private retrieval methods. However, in [47] they have been classified from a different point of view as dummy-based, K-anonymity, differential privacy, and cryptography-based methods. Regardless of how we classify them, they all have a common goal: to protect a user's location privacy while ensuring that the user benefits from advantages of the service.

Each of the aforementioned methods has its own strengths and weaknesses. But among them, dummy-based methods have drawn the attention of researchers due to their unique features [46–49]. In these techniques, users send fake location data (dummies) to the service provider along with their real location. This makes the user's real location hidden among dummies; therefore, it is hard for the adversary to infer the real locations. After receiving a request, the service provider replies to users by offering the data related to all the locations requested by a user (real and dummies). Each user extracts the data that is related to his/her real location and discards the others. The most important advantage of dummy-based methods is that they do not rely on a trusted third-party anonymizer. Moreover, users do not need to encrypt the requests. Thus, there is no need to share a key between the LSP and users.

There have been other research efforts based on the K-anonymity technique to protect location privacy of LBS users [49–52]. These methods work based on a trusted third-party server, which is called an anonymizer, between users and the service provider. The anonymizer receives service requests from users and generalizes their location into a larger region (cloaking region) such that it covers the locations of other users, as well as the location of the requesting user. Therefore, the anonymizer hides the real location of a user among other locations. Although these methods reduce the communication cost between users and anonymizers, they might degrade QoS when there are not enough users (at least users) near the requesting user. In these cases, the anonymizer has to increase the radius of cloaking regions to find enough users. Thus, greater service latencies occur due to the increased processing times. To address this issue, research has been done in [51, 52] to improve QoS for the mentioned circumstances. Researchers have proposed a technique to minimize the area of cloaking regions using footprint-historical locations of other users.

There are some other location privacy protection methods that work based on the differential privacy framework [53, 54] and cryptography [55, 56]. Moreover, several dummy-based schemes [45–47, 57] have been proposed for location privacy protection. As we mentioned before, in dummy-based methods, users submit their location data, including noise (some fake location data or dummies) to the service provider directly. Therefore, a trusted anonymizer is no longer needed to hide real locations among other location data, and submit user's requests. In [45, 57], two dummy generation algorithms have been presented, moving in a neighborhood and moving in a limited neighborhood. In these algorithms, the first set of dummy locations is chosen randomly, but the next dummies are generated in a neighborhood of the previous position of the dummies. Moreover, to reduce the communications overhead caused by sending dummies, a cost reduction technique was proposed in [45]. However, generating dummies at random or through a fixed rule cannot provide flexible location privacy for users. Hence, in [46], a Privacy-Area Aware scheme is proposed based on a flexible dummy generation algorithm in which dummies are generated according to either a virtual grid or circle. This technique offers configurable and controllable dummy generation by which it is possible to control the user's location privacy. However, a disadvantage of this method is that it doesn't consider the nature of the region. For example, some dummies may be generated in places in which a user is unlikely to be (e.g., in a river). To address this problem, in [58] a Dummy-Location Selection method has been proposed to prevent the adversary from using side knowledge such as a region map. This is done by carefully selecting dummies based on the entropy metric.

However, in [47, 59] it has been shown that when the aforementioned dummy-based methods are used by users to generate dummy locations, the adversary can identify some dummies with a minimum correct ratio of 58%. This can be done by analyzing the spatiotemporal correlation between neighboring location sets. Therefore, Spatiotemporal Correlation-Aware privacy protection schemes have been proposed in [47, 59], in which correlated dummies are filtered out and only uncorrelated dummies are sent to LSP.

Other research has recently been conducted on the location privacy of geo-social networks (GeoSNs) users in [60–62]. GeoSNs are a variety of social networks by which users can find their favorite events, persons, or groups in a specific region in the city. Moreover, they can identify popular places by comparing how many people have already checked-in at different places. This is done by utilizing users' location data that has been shared by them in that region. In fact, GeoSNs combine location recommendation services (such that services offered by LBS) with the social network functionality [62]. In other words, they can be viewed as location-based social networks that connect people in a specific region based on their interests.

In [62], GeoSNs were classified into three categories according to the services they offer: content-centric, check-in based, and tracking-based. In addition, the main privacy issues that threaten users' location privacy were identified. The authors of [63] have studied techniques to sanitize users' location data before publishing them as location recommendations in GeoSNs. These techniques work based on differential privacy frameworks. Furthermore, to improve the accuracy of location recommendations, they have identified some effective factors that improve data accuracy regarding the privacy protection and data utility trade-off. In [61] a location-privacy-aware framework is offered to publish reviews for local business service systems. The proposed framework publishes reviews based on utility to achieve two main goals, maximizing the amount of public reviews that users share, and having the maximum number of businesses that obey the proposed public principle.

4.2 Location Privacy Protection Based on Differential Privacy

Differential privacy [28] is a privacy-preserving framework that enables data analyzing bodies to promise privacy guarantees to individuals who share their personal information. In fact, differentially private mechanisms can make users' private data available for data analysis, without needing data clean rooms, data usage agreements, or data protection plans [29]. More precisely, a differentially private mechanism that publishes users' private data provides a form of indistinguishability between every two adjacent databases. Here, "adjacent" means that they differ only in a single record. However, as you see later, we will extend the concept of "adjacency" to the location domain.

In this chapter, we consider the set of private data $H \subseteq R^2$ because our goal is to protect users' location data, which is assumed as $L = \{latitude, longitude\}$, where $L = \{latitude, longitude \in R\}$ are GPS coordinates in the ranges $[-90, 90]$ and $[-180, 180]$, respectively. Moreover, the adjacency relation defined in the standard differential privacy should be customized, because we need a mechanism for publishing location data that guarantees that every two adjacent locations are indistinguishable to some extent. For this reason, in the following, we customize the adjacency relation defined in standard differential privacy in order to use a differential privacy framework in the location domain.

Definition 1. (Adjacency Relation)

Locations L and L' are considered adjacent if the distance between them is less than a predefined value D, that is

$$\|L - L'\| \leq D. \tag{5}$$

Using Definition 1 we customize the standard definition of differential privacy to our needs. For this reason, we present the concept of location privacy in Definition 1.

Definition 2. ((D, ϵ)-Location Privacy)

Suppose $L \in R^2$ is an user's private location and $L' \in R^2$ is adjacent to L (i.e., $\|L - L'\| \leq D$). Mechanism $A: R^2 \rightarrow R^2$ is (D, ϵ)-location private if for any we have

$$\ln \left(\frac{\Pr[A(L) \in S]}{\Pr[A(L') \in S]} \right) \leq \epsilon. \tag{6}$$

Intuitively, if an adversary wants to infer L, the distinguishability between L and any adjacent location L' that he or she selects is limited by ϵ. In other words, all adjacent locations L' have an equal chance to be placed in the region where $A(L)$ is located. Therefore, the level of distinguishability is determined by the privacy-level ϵ.

A few location privacy protection mechanisms have been proposed based on differential privacy. A perturbation technique based on differential privacy was introduced in [64] to achieve geo-indistinguishability for protecting the exact location of a user. This technique adds random Laplace-distributed noise to users' locations in order to sanitize their location before publishing. In [65] a differentially private hierarchical location sanitization (DPHLS) approach has been proposed for location privacy protection in large-scale user trajectories.

The approach provides a personalized hierarchical mechanism that protects a user's location privacy by hiding his or her location in a dataset that includes a subset of all possible locations that he or she might visit in a region. By doing this, the level of location randomization is reduced, hence, the amount of noise required for satisfying differential privacy conditions is minimized.

5 FUTURE RESEARCH DIRECTIONS AND PERSPECTIVES

From what has been presented, numerous protection strategies have been developed. However, considering the complicated environment of Smart Cities, there are still many challenges that need effective solutions. One main difficulty is the availability of protection mechanisms. For example, some well-developed algorithms cannot be directly used, because of the limit on computation power of smart devices. In addition, the mobility of smart devices and dynamic of IoT networks have note been fully considered, which makes it hard to guarantee the accuracy and time-effectiveness of preserving algorithms. Another problem is the limited ability of users to control their personal data. They are unable to know if untrusted service providers will analyze their data to mine more sensitive information. Furthermore, offenders and malware are becoming smarter than before; sometimes they can even weaken the protection algorithms. According to these problems, we provide the following items as future directions in this field.

5.1 Data Minimization

Data minimization is a direct way to limit privacy leakage. Intuitively, the less data there is to collect, store, and share by smart devices, the easier it is for users to protect their personal information. Another level of meaning in "data minimization" is to limit the knowledge discovery. For example, if the objective of a service is to recommend an exercise routine, it should be restricted to infer locations of users without the explicit permission of customers. Therefore, developing novel PPDM technologies or hiding sensitive mining results are worth studying.

5.2 Personalized Protection

Common privacy-related studies assume that protection levels remain constant throughout the life of privacy protection mechanisms, which results in an uniform preserving standard. However, privacy concerns and protection requirements of users are essentially personalized in the real world, especially for those customized services. Providing the same level of protection for each user may not be fair. In addition, assuming attackers have the same background knowledge may have an adverse impact on the data utility and the quality of services. Therefore, it is important to develop personalized methods to preserve privacy and maintain a good level of data utility while enjoying these smart applications.

5.3 Privacy by Design

"Privacy by design" is a positive strategy to cope with privacy problems in Smart City, which mainly has the following principles: proactive action instead of a remedial protection strategy after privacy violations; privacy embedded into the design; full functionality with full privacy protection, respect of the privacy of users, protecting privacy during the whole lifecycle of data, and so forth. Recently, there have been some efforts that combine this principle to design new systems [66]. However, Perera et al. [2] argue that most current "privacy-by-design" frameworks are unavailable to provide specific guidance that enables engineers to design IoT applications.

5.4 The Trade-Off Between Privacy and Data Utility

It is impossible to maximize both data utility and privacy protection in different methods. The utility-privacy trade-off is still an open challenge in the privacy protection domain. Due to the resource-constrained, dynamic, and mobility characteristics of IoT-based systems, this problem is considerably reinforced and it has been regarded as an important factor need to be taken into consideration before developing novel mechanisms. Based on this, how to pursue higher-data utility and benefits from smart services while guaranteeing acceptable privacy needs further studies.

5.5 Transparency and Self-Control

When developing smart applications, sufficient transparency of personal data should be considered, because customers are able to be clear about the states of their data (e.g., what kinds of data is stored, whom it will be shared with, and how the data is protected). In this way, if their privacy is at risk, it could be evaluated. Self-control means data owners have the ability to control and determine data granularity, protection methods, data acquisition, data retention periods, and so on. Smart services should provide various choices for users according to their preferences [2].

6 SUMMARY

In this chapter, we first talk about current privacy concerns and attacks and the rationale behind them. Second, we demonstrate existing privacy protection schemes in Smart Cities. Third, two separate chapters are leveraged to discuss social link privacy and location privacy, respectively. Fourth, we illustrate some promising research directions based on our analysis. This chapter aims at shedding light on future privacy preservation in Smart Cities.

References

[1] J. Fan, Q. Li, G. Cao, Privacy disclosure through smart meters: reactive power based attack and defense, in: 2017 47th Annual IEEE/IFIP International Conference on Dependable Systems and Networks (DSN), IEEE, 2017, pp. 13–24.
[2] C. Perera, C. McCormick, A.K. Bandara, B.A. Price, B. Nuseibeh, Privacy-by-design framework for assessing Internet of Things applications and platforms, in: Proceedings of the 6th International Conference on the Internet of Things, ACM, 2016, pp. 83–92.
[3] T. Blog, Internet of Things Industry Brings Data Explosion, but Growth Could be Impacted by Consumer Privacy Concerns, (2014) Retrieved May, 13, 2015.
[4] D. Eckhoff, I. Wagner, Privacy in the Smart City—applications, technologies, challenges and solutions, IEEE Commun. Surv. Tutorials 20 (2017) 489–516.
[5] Z. Ning, F. Xia, N. Ullah, X. Kong, X. Hu, Vehicular social networks: enabling smart mobility, IEEE Commun. Mag. 55 (5) (2017) 16–55.
[6] N. Apthorpe, D. Reisman, S. Sundaresan, A. Narayanan, N. Feamster, Spying on the Smart Home: Privacy Attacks and Defenses on Encrypted IoT Traffic, 2017. arXiv preprint arXiv:1708.05044.
[7] S. Finster, I. Baumgart, Privacy-aware smart metering: a survey, IEEE Commun. Surv. Tutorials. 16 (3) (2014) 1732–1745.
[8] C.E. Koop, R. Mosher, L. Kun, J. Geiling, E. Grigg, S. Long, C. Macedonia, R.C. Merrell, R. Satava, J.M. Rosen, Future delivery of health care: cybercare, IEEE Eng. Med. Biol. Mag. 27 (6) (2008) 29–38.
[9] X. Yue, H. Wang, D. Jin, M. Li, W. Jiang, Healthcare data gateways: found healthcare intelligence on blockchain with novel privacy risk control, J. Med. Syst. 40 (10) (2016) 218.
[10] T. Gong, H. Huang, P. Li, K. Zhang, H. Jiang, A medical healthcare system for privacy protection based on IoT, in: 2015 Seventh International Symposium on Parallel Architectures, Algorithms and Programming (PAAP), IEEE, 2015, pp. 217–222.
[11] M.A. Ferrag, L.A. Maglaras, A. Ahmim, Privacy-preserving schemes for ad hoc social networks: a survey, IEEE Commun. Surv. Tutorials. 19 (4) (2017) 3015–3045.
[12] D. Riboni, L. Pareschi, C. Bettini, JS-reduce: defending your data from sequential background knowledge attacks, IEEE Trans. Dependable Secure Comput. 9 (3) (2012) 387–400.
[13] M. Rezvani, A. Ignjatovic, E. Bertino, S. Jha, Secure data aggregation technique for wireless sensor networks in the presence of collusion attacks, IEEE Trans. Dependable Secure Comput. 12 (1) (2015) 98–110.
[14] F. Koufogiannis, G.J. Pappas, Diffusing private data over networks, IEEE Trans. Control Netw. Syst. 5 (2016) 1027–1037.
[15] D. Quercia, S. Hailes, Sybil attacks against mobile users: friends and foes to the rescue, in: 29th IEEE International Conference on Computer Communications, Joint Conference of the IEEE Computer and Communications Societies, March 15–19, 2010, San Diego, CA, USA (INFOCOM 2010), 2010, pp. 336–340.
[16] B. Ying, D. Makrakis, H.T. Mouftah, Privacy preserving broadcast message authentication protocol for VANETs, J. Netw. Comput. Appl. 36 (5) (2013) 1352–1364.
[17] S. Hameed, X. Fu, P. Hui, N.R. Sastry, LENS: leveraging social networking and trust to prevent spam transmission, in: Proceedings of the 19th Annual IEEE International Conference on Network Protocols, ICNP 2011, Vancouver, BC, Canada, October 17–20, 2011, pp. 13–18.
[18] R. Yu, J. Kang, X. Huang, S. Xie, Y. Zhang, S. Gjessing, MixGroup: accumulative pseudonym exchanging for location privacy enhancement in vehicular social networks, IEEE Trans. Dependable Secure Comput. 13 (1) (2016) 93–105.
[19] Y. Qu, S. Yu, L. Gao, J. Niu, Big Data set privacy preserving through sensitive attribute-based grouping, in: 2017 IEEE International Conference on Communications (ICC), IEEE, 2017, pp. 1–6.
[20] Y. Qu, S. Yu, L. Gao, S. Peng, Y. Xiang, L. Xiao, FuzzyDP: Fuzzy-based Big Data publishing against inquiry attacks, in: 2017 IEEE Conference on Computer Communications Workshops (INFOCOM WKSHPS), IEEE, 2017, pp. 7–12.

[21] Y. Qu, J. Xu, S. Yu, Privacy preserving in Big Data sets through multiple shuffle, in: Proceedings of the Australasian Computer Science Week Multiconference, ACM, 2017, p. 72.

[22] Q. Jing, A.V. Vasilakos, J. Wan, J. Lu, D. Qiu, Security of the Internet of Things: perspectives and challenges, Wirel. Netw.20 (8) (2014) 2481–2501.

[23] A. Abdallah, X. Shen, A lightweight lattice-based homomorphic privacy-preserving data aggregation scheme for Smart Grid, IEEE Trans. Smart Grid9 (2016) 396–405.

[24] M.S.H. Talpur, M.Z.A. Bhuiyan, G. Wang, Shared-node IoT network architecture with ubiquitous homomorphic encryption for healthcare monitoring, Int. J. Embed. Syst. 7 (1) (2014) 43–54.

[25] M.S. Dousti, R. Jalili, An efficient statistical zero-knowledge authentication protocol for smart cards, Int. J. Comput. Math. 93 (3) (2016) 453–481.

[26] S. Yu, Big privacy: challenges and opportunities of privacy study in the age of Big Data, IEEE Access. 4 (2016) 2751–2763.

[27] Y. Wang, J. Wan, J. Guo, Y.-M. Cheung, P.C. Yuen, Inference-based similarity search in randomized montgomery domains for privacy-preserving biometric identification, IEEE Trans. Pattern Anal. Mach. Intell. 40 (2017) 1611–1624.

[28] C. Dwork, Differential privacy, in: Automata, Languages and Programming, 33rd International Colloquium, ICALP 2006, Venice, Italy, July 10–14, 2006, Proceedings, Part II, 2006, pp. 1–12.

[29] C. Dwork, A. Roth, The algorithmic foundations of differential privacy, Found. Trends Theor. Comput. Sci. 9 (3–4) (2014) 211–407.

[30] K. Christidis, M. Devetsikiotis, Blockchains and smart contracts for the Internet of Things, IEEE Access. 4 (2016) 2292–2303.

[31] A. Dorri, M. Steger, S.S. Kanhere, R. Jurdak, Blockchain: a distributed solution to automotive security and privacy, IEEE Commun. Mag. 55 (12) (2017) 119–125.

[32] A. Kosba, A. Miller, E. Shi, Z. Wen, C. Papamanthou, Hawk: the blockchain model of cryptography and privacy-preserving smart contracts, in: 2016 IEEE Symposium on Security and Privacy (SP), IEEE, 2016, pp. 839–858.

[33] C.T. Do, N.H. Tran, C. Hong, C.A. Kamhoua, K.A. Kwiat, E. Blasch, S. Ren, N. Pissinou, S.S. Iyengar, Game theory for cyber security and privacy, ACM Comput. Surv. (CSUR)50 (2) (2017) 30.

[34] X. Liu, K. Liu, L. Guo, X. Li, Y. Fang, A game-theoretic approach for achieving k-anonymity in location based services, in: INFOCOM, 2013 Proceedings IEEE, 2013, pp. 2985–2993.

[35] A. Yassine, A.A.N. Shirehjini, S. Shirmohammadi, Smart meters Big Data: game theoretic model for fair data sharing in deregulated smart grids, IEEE Access3 (2015) 2743–2754.

[36] P. Wijesekera, A. Baokar, L. Tsai, J. Reardon, S. Egelman, D. Wagner, K. Beznosov, The feasibility of dynamically granted permissions: aligning mobile privacy with user preferences, in: 2017 IEEE Symposium on Security and Privacy (SP), IEEE, 2017, pp. 1077–1093.

[37] S.S. Rodrıguez, L. Wang, J.R. Zhao, R. Mortier, H. Haddadi, Personal model training under privacy constraints, CoRR, abs/1703.00380 40 (2017) 24–38.

[38] K. Xing, C. Hu, J. Yu, X. Cheng, F. Zhang, Mutual privacy preserving k-means clustering in social participatory sensing, IEEE Trans. Ind. Inf. 13 (4) (2017) 2066–2076.

[39] R. Kitchin, Getting smarter about smart cities: improving data privacy and data security, Department of the Taoiseach on behalf of the Government Data Forum, 2016.

[40] W. Hurst, N. Shone, A. El Rhalibi, A. Happe, B. Kotze, B. Duncan, Advancing the micro-CI testbed for IoT cyber-security research and education, Think Mind(2017) 129–134.

[41] N. Aleisa, K. Renaud, Yes, I know this IoT device might invade my privacy, but I love it anyway! A study of Saudi Arabian perceptions, in: Proceedings of the 2nd International Conference on Internet of Things, Big Data and Security, IoTBDS 2017, Porto, Portugal, April 24–26, 2017, pp. 198–205.

[42] M. Backes, M. Humbert, J. Pang, Y. Zhang, walk2friends: inferring social links from mobility profiles, in: Proceedings of the 2017 ACM SIGSAC Conference on Computer and Communications Security, CCS 2017, Dallas, TX, USA, October 30 to November 3, 2017, pp. 1943–1957.

[43] L. Guo, C. Zhang, Y. Fang, A trust-based privacy-preserving friend recommendation scheme for online social networks, IEEE Trans. Dependable Secure Comput. 12 (4) (2015) 413–427.

[44] Z. Cai, Z. He, X. Guan, Y. Li, Collective data-sanitization for preventing sensitive information inference attacks in social networks, IEEE Trans. Dependable Secure Comput. 15 (2016) 577–590.

[45] H. Kido, Y. Yanagisawa, T. Satoh, An anonymous communication technique using dummies for location-based services, in: Proceedings of the International Conference on Pervasive Services 2005, ICPS '05, Santorini, Greece, July 11–14, 2005, pp. 88–97.

[46] H. Lu, C.S. Jensen, M.L. Yiu, PAD: privacy-area aware, dummy-based location privacy in mobile services, in: Seventh ACM International Workshop on Data Engineering for Wireless and Mobile Access, Mobide 2008, June 13, 2008, Vancouver, British Columbia, Canada, Proceedings, 2008, pp. 16–23.

[47] H. Liu, X. Li, H. Li, J. Ma, X. Ma, Spatiotemporal correlation-aware dummy-based privacy protection scheme for location-based services, in: 2017 IEEE Conference on Computer Communications, INFOCOM 2017, Atlanta, GA, USA, May 1–4, 2017, pp. 1–9.

[48] M.L. Yiu, C.S. Jensen, J. Møller, H. Lu, Design and analysis of a ranking approach to private location-based services, ACM Trans. Database Syst. 36 (2) (2011) 10:1–10:42.

[49] C. Chow, M.F. Mokbel, X. Liu, A peer-to-peer spatial cloaking algorithm for anonymous location-based service, in: 14th ACM International Symposium on Geographic Information Systems, ACM-GIS 2006, November 10–11, 2006, Arlington, Virginia, USA, Proceedings, 2006, pp. 171–178.

[50] P. Kalnis, G. Ghinita, K. Mouratidis, D. Papadias, Preventing location-based identity inference in anonymous spatial queries, IEEE Trans. Knowl. Data Eng. 19 (12) (2007) 1719–1733.

[51] Y. Wang, D. Xu, X. He, C. Zhang, F. Li, B. Xu, L2P2: location-aware location privacy protection for location-based services, in: Proceedings of the IEEE INFOCOM 2012, Orlando, FL, USA, March 25–30, 2012, pp. 1996–2004.

[52] X. Li, E. Wang, W. Yang, J. Ma, DALP: a demand-aware location privacy protection scheme in continuous location-based services, Concurr. Comput. Pract. Exper. 28 (4) (2016) 1219–1236.

[53] Y. Xiao, L. Xiong, Protecting locations with differential privacy under temporal correlations, in: Proceedings of the 22nd ACM SIGSAC Conference on Computer and Communications Security, Denver, CO, USA, October 12–16, 2015, pp. 1298–1309.

[54] M.E. Andrés, N.E. Bordenabe, K. Chatzikokolakis, C. Palamidessi, Geo-indistinguishability: differential privacy for location-based systems, in: 2013 ACM SIGSAC Conference on Computer and Communications Security, CCS'13, Berlin, Germany, November 4–8, 2013, pp. 901–914.

[55] R. Schlegel, C. Chow, Q. Huang, D.S. Wong, User-defined privacy grid system for continuous location-based services, IEEE Trans. Mob. Comput. 14 (10) (2015) 2158–2172.

[56] A. Khoshgozaran, C. Shahabi, Blind evaluation of nearest neighbor queries using space transformation to preserve location privacy, in: Advances in Spatial and Temporal Databases, 10th International Symposium, SSTD 2007, Boston, MA, USA, July 16–18, 2007, Proceedings, 2007, pp. 239–257.

[57] H. Kido, Y. Yanagisawa, T. Satoh, Protection of location privacy using dummies for location-based services, in: Proceedings of the 21st International Conference on Data Engineering Workshops, ICDE 2005, April 5–8, 2005, Tokyo, Japan, 2005, p. 1248.

[58] B. Niu, Q. Li, X. Zhu, G. Cao, H. Li, Achieving k-anonymity in privacy-aware location-based services, in: 2014 IEEE Conference on Computer Communications, INFOCOM 2014, Toronto, Canada, April 27 to May 2, 2014, pp. 754–762.

[59] M.R. Nosouhi, V.V.H. Pham, S. Yu, Y. Xiang, M. Warren, A hybrid location privacy protection scheme in Big Data environment, in: 2017 IEEE Global Communications Conference, GLOBECOM 2017, Singapore, December 4–8, 2017, pp. 1–6.

[60] A.I. Abdelmoty, F. Alrayes, Towards understanding location privacy awareness on geo-social networks, ISPRS Int. J. Geoinf. 6 (4) (2017) 109.

[61] X. Zheng, Z. Cai, J. Li, H. Gao, Location-privacy-aware review publication mechanism for local business service systems, in: 2017 IEEE Conference on Computer Communications, INFOCOM 2017, Atlanta, GA, USA, May 1–4, 2017, pp. 1–9.

[62] C.R. Vicente, D. Freni, C. Bettini, C.S. Jensen, Location-related privacy in geo-social networks, IEEE Internet Comput. 15 (3) (2011) 20–27.

[63] J. Zhang, G. Ghinita, C. Chow, Differentially private location recommendations in geosocial networks, in: IEEE 15th International Conference on Mobile Data Management, MDM 2014, Brisbane, Australia, Vol. 1, July 14–18, 2014, pp. 59–68.

[64] M.E. Andrés, N.E. Bordenabe, K. Chatzikokolakis, C. Palamidessi, Geo-indistinguishability: differential privacy for location-based systems, in: 2013 ACM SIGSAC Conference on Computer and Communications Security, CCS'13, Berlin, Germany, November 4–8, 2013, pp. 901–914.

[65] S. Wang, R.O. Sinnott, S. Nepal, Protecting the location privacy of mobile social media users, in: 2016 IEEE International Conference on Big Data, BigData 2016, Washington, DC, USA, December 5–8, 2016, pp. 1143–1150.

[66] D. Preuveneers, W. Joosen, Privacy-enabled remote health monitoring applications for resource constrained wearable devices, in: Proceedings of the 31st Annual ACM Symposium on Applied Computing, ACM, 2016, pp. 119–124.

7

Privacy and Security Aspects of E-Government in Smart Cities

Longzhi Yang, Noe Elisa, and Neil Eliot

Department of Computer and Information Sciences, Northumbria University, Newcastle Upon Tyne, United Kingdom

1 INTRODUCTION

Initiatives for Smart Cities and their enabling technologies started several years ago. For example, the UK Government committed to fund a £24 million project in 2014 in Glasgow to develop city management systems, and at the same time provided £3 million of funding to London, Bristol, and Peterborough for smart projects [1]. Around the same time there was also £73 million of funding made available to projects specifically looking at capturing and analyzing data. Research councils also made available £95 million of funding to support smart projects, which included the development of smart devices. More recently the government has pledged a commitment to support the provision of a country-wide communications infrastructure (including high-speed broadband connectivity) through its "digital communications infrastructure strategy" [2]. All of these developments and initiatives have led to an increase in the use of information and communication technologies (ICT) and a proliferation of Internet of Things (IoT) devices from domestic appliances through to sensor networks.

Smart Cities are now a reality. Smart City initiatives, such as the those outlined herein, are part of a globally driven change by governments to manage the integration of computer systems and urbanization [3]. These same initiatives will eventually drive global economic growth and improve the individual's quality of life. The United Nations Population Fund indicated that about 3.3 billion (54% of the world population) lived in urban areas in 2014. This number will increase to about 5 billion (about 66%) by 2030 [4]. This dramatic growth in urban populations will generate a significant increase in the number of interconnected devices, and subsequently, electronic government (e-government) will be needed to be at the center of Smart Cities' expansion. Smart Cities present new economic opportunities to governments, but with technological developments there will be security and privacy threats. Smart Cities will require large-scale networks to accommodate these diverse devices. All cities are managed by government authorities, and they will be responsible for delivering e-government services with strict governance policies.

Indeed, e-government is an integral part of a Smart City, and an "enabler" within the Smart City domain. The International Telecommunication Union defines Smart Cities as: "A smart sustainable city is an innovative city that uses ICTs and other means to improve quality of life, efficiency of urban operation and services, and competitiveness, while ensuring that it meets the needs of present and future generations with respect to economic, social, environmental as well as cultural aspects" [5]. The technologies that make up a Smart City include smart meters, IoT devices, IoT sensors, networked Information Technology (IT) services, telecommunications, wired and wireless infrastructure technologies, software, and so forth. E-government is defined as the utilization of ICT to deliver public services to individuals and other government stakeholders transparently, effectively, and efficiently through the World Wide Web [6]. Therefore, e-government is the counterpart of conventional government in the context of Smart Cities, compared with its counterpart of conventional cities.

The common objective of Smart Cities and e-government is to improve the quality of an individual's life by providing quality e-services. When discussing Smart Cities it is hard not to mention e-government as an enabler of all the services offered by the Smart Cities. For example, a Smart City with healthcare functionality helps individuals live healthy lives by providing easy access to medical facilities. Connected devices in Smart Cities can assist public health professionals through the integration of medical systems and patient data records that are usually managed by e-government [7]. Common challenges for both Smart Cities and e-government include security and privacy, among others. These challenges have attracted increasingly more research efforts, and various effective measures have been proposed in the literature in an effort to address such challenges.

Almost every country now provides online services using some form of e-government portal [8], this is predominantly via websites and mobile applications. Good examples are the UK's government portal (https://www.gov.uk/) and the Singapore Government's eCitizen portal (https://www.ecitizen.gov.sg/). Both provide government services and information to individuals. The challenges that e-government services encounter are no different than any other major IT-based system. The usual "Big Three" of Confidentiality, Integrity, and Accessibility (CIA), as defined by ISC^2 [9] as part of Certified Information Systems Security Professional (CISSP) Course [10], must be considered. This can be an issue in some areas of the world, particularly in developing countries [11, 12] where ICT resources are limited.

This chapter investigates the issues associated with e-government systems and Smart Cities, and provides countermeasure suggestions for possible vulnerabilities. The rest of this chapter is organized as follows. Section 2 covers the definitions of e-government and Smart Cities. Section 3 discusses cybersecurity issues in e-government systems and Smart Cities, and highlights the technologies and solutions that can be used to combat them. Section 4 details privacy issues and solutions in e-government and Smart Cities. Section 5 proposes a framework of a decentralized, secure, and privacy-preserving e-government system using blockchain technology and Artificial Intelligence (AI) advances. Finally, Section 6 summarizes and highlights the future of Smart Cities and the challenges they face.

2 E-GOVERNMENT IN SMART CITIES

A Smart City usually accommodates multiple organizations, each of which has their own information governance in place. From the definition of e-government and Smart Cities, as introduced in the last section, a Smart City includes e-government and uses ICT to deliver services to the community. Added to this urbanization is an inevitable result of modern society. If there are no plans to accommodate these developments, an issue can arise through the development of disparate systems that cannot be integrated. The solution is to provide guidance and support to enable cities to develop in a coordinated and innovative manner [13], allowing organizations to realize the power of new and smart technologies. Smart governance is a product of e-government that offers efficient e-participation, e-services, and public administration, making it one of the most essential components of a Smart City's development.

E-government is driving the future of Smart Cities. This is due, in part, to its goal of supporting global adoption and widening participation. Smart Cities are the atomic nodes of future globally connected "smart" systems. These systems include the smart global super grid [14], global supply chain [15], global high-speed communications, and more in an effort to support globally optimized human activities and to maximize social gains. The successful implementation of super global optimization systems is supported by the rapid development of ICT, especially super high-speed information networks, cloud computing, AI and machine learning, IoT, and Big Data technologies. This multidisciplinary effort will combine the advances of individual disciplines and amplify the summation of benefits from all involved disciplines.

A Smart City is not limited to the use of technology alone; rather, it involves other determinants of sustainability and urban growth, including human capital [16], education, social capital, and environmental issues [17]. A Government is responsible for the administration and management of a Smart City by collaborating with different stakeholders to achieve better and sustainable Smart City developments that reduce the costs of service provision and allow better management of a city's resources [18, 19]. The key components of a Smart City are illustrated in Fig. 1. These include smart energy, smart buildings, smart mobility, smart technology, smart infrastructure, smart government, smart education, smart citizens, and smart security (physical and soft). Zhang et al. [20] and Al-Hader et al. [21] identify these components by highlighting the benefits they provide to individuals. Smart Cities may utilize different combinations of these components, depending on the cities' needs [22].

Fundamentally, e-governance incorporated into e-government systems supports Smart Cities by making administrative tasks efficient and transparent while providing enhanced information and service delivery to individuals and businesses, improving public information and resource management. A good example of urban governance exists in the *Amsterdam Smart City* project [23]. The project is a partnership of 11 businesses, authorities, and research institutions with the aim of developing the Amsterdam Metropolitan Area into a Smart City with good standards of living, excellent working environment, efficiency mobility, accessible public services, and open data.

Local government policies play an important role in the implementation of Smart Cities' governance. Local authorities are informed by a number of policies from different governing bodies or departments that may be poorly

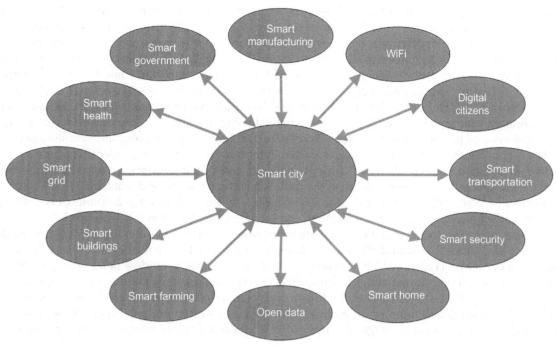

FIG. 1 Components of a Smart City.

coordinated, fragmented, conflicting, or overlapping. The lack of rigor in these policies restricts or hampers the implementation of Smart City infrastructures [13]. The success of a Smart City therefore rests upon a set of strong, consistent policies being propagated from the highest level of Government, down to local government departments [24].

Three types of policy integration are summarized by Van Winden for a successful innovation integration: sectoral, horizontal, and vertical [25]. Sectoral integration is the coordination of sector-based policies, such as transport policy, spatial planning, housing policy, and so forth. Sectoral integration is relevant to urban "areas" although it is very difficult to realize in practice. Horizontal integration focuses on the alignment of policies between authorities in a metropolitan area. This type of policy integration is vital for the expansion of cities where economic units are governed by multiple authorities. This may lead to conflicting competition. Vertical integration concerns the coordination between the different layers of government, typically national, regional, and local.

Local authorities must follow the appropriate policies that bring benefits to the urbanization process in implementing Smart Cities, although the majority of Smart City research focuses on technological innovation and future exploitation of Smart City initiatives [13]. This is consistent with the study carried out by Meijer et al. [26] who conclude that the focus of Smart City governance implementation is not about the technical issues; but rather, institutional change and acknowledging the political nature of appealing visions of sociotechnical governance.

3 SECURITY OF E-GOVERNMENT

E-government systems are designed to provide online service to individuals, businesses, and government departments [27]. Government to Citizens (G2C) disseminates information to individuals, such as driver license renewal, application of birth/death/marriage certificates, online payment of income tax, and so forth. Government to Business (G2B) exchanges information between government and businesses such as policies, rules and regulation, online application of business permits, and so forth. Government to Government (G2G) offers transactions between government departments such as central/national and local councils. G2G also deals with international information flow between governments.

Although the adoption of e-government systems by cities to provide efficient and effective services over the Internet, security and privacy threats remain a major concern. Some of the major threats are identity theft and privacy violations [28]. Many members of the public are not ready to engage with electronic public services due to a lack of trust, which is identified by Palanisamy et al. as a significant barrier to the adoption of e-government systems [29]. If e-government systems are not well secured, cyber-attacks are inevitable. The most common cyber-attacks are Denial of Service (DoS) attacks, unauthorized network access, theft of personal information, online financial fraud, website defacement, application layer attacks such as cross site scripting (XSS), and penetration attacking [28].

Alshehri and Drew argue that privacy and security must be protected to increase users trust while interacting with e-government services [30]. As technologies advance, the number of attacks increase as cyber criminals come up with new attack methods. The risks and challenges associated with the introduction of ICT into the infrastructure of a city and government are mainly due to poor security in WiFi networks that give access to e-services. Cybersecurity specialists need to develop tools and methods that can produce self-healing systems that react to attacks and defend themselves autonomously. This type of technology can be achieved using machine learning and AI techniques [31].

E-government systems perform three basic operations: data transfer, data processing, and data storage [32]. Privacy may be violated in any of these operations. A user's personal information, such as their identity, medical records, and other sensitive information, could be disclosed through metadata analysis. If an attacker can compromise the security of the Smart City and access the information, then the confidentiality, integrity, and availability (CIA), which are the core components of CISSP, will be in jeopardy due to connected devices storing large amounts of sensitive personal information, that is, photocopier hard drives, printers and scanners, mobile phones, and so forth.

As new devices are connected to Smart Cities, there is a greater chance of a vulnerable devices being added that may open up an attack space that would allow access to existing devices. Due to the nature of these devices security and privacy are a concern. "Traditional" cyber-security solutions may not provide a defense [33]. Cyber criminals are coming up with new sophisticated attack techniques every day, making it difficult to predict the kind of attacks e-government systems will be subjected to in the future. This is more of a concern with the introduction of devices that have the ability to establish communication links without a user's intervention. Cyber-attacks can take several forms, some may causes system damage, disruption to a communication infrastructure, or extract sensitive information.

3.1 Dimensions of Security in E-Government

The dimensions of e-government security include technical, organizational, scientific, legal, economic, and informational issues [34]. These areas are usually addressed through security mechanisms, careful system design, and policy measures [12]. Security mechanisms are developed to detect, prevent, and recover from a security attack. This usually involves many approaches, including cryptography firewalls, and operating system security. System design involves the deployment and configuration of hardware, software, and data recovery (backups) to maintain a smooth operation of e-government systems. Policies (which include audits) are implemented by the management and authorities by setting up procedures for planning, testing, certification, monitoring, auditing, and accrediting e-government systems. Different models, known as e-government maturity models (eGMMs), guide and benchmark e-government development from the perspective of management. For example, a comprehensive e-government information security maturity model was proposed by Karokola et al. in order to guide the inclusion of security in e-government systems by government policy makers [35].

According to Jimenez et al., security measures can be implemented at the physical, technical, or management levels [36]. Physical security includes safeguarding e-government network equipment, data, information, and other valuable assets from being destroyed by operation mistakes, natural disaster, computer crime, or any other attempt that can cause physical destruction of assets, loss of information, or interruption of the system operations. Technical security is achieved by using computer network products such as firewalls, Intrusion Detection Systems (IDS), Intrusion Prevention Systems (IPS), secure routers, and switches as shown in Fig. 2 to secure e-government systems against many cyber-attacks.

These devices are configured to filter network traffic into and out of e-government systems (routers and firewalls), and also to identify any signs of suspicious activity (IDS). This is an area where AI could be used. Management security measures focus on the setting up of policies, regulations, and legal protection for the purpose of easing the integration of e-government management and technology while guaranteeing the security of e-government systems. Among these security measures, firewalls, IDS, IPS, encryption, and secure networks are the most common security measures that have been implemented to secure e-government agencies against cyber threats [36]. IDSs are passive in nature and only identify potential problems; while IPSs are dynamic in nature, and reconfigure a network based on identified activity.

New technologies, such as blockchains and advances in AI, are being incorporated into networking and IT, and therefore affecting e-government systems and Smart Cities. For example, AI has been applied to intrusion detection using various Artificial Immune Systems and Fuzzy Inference Systems [37–40]. Meng et al. proposed that, using blockchain technology, it would allow a collaborative intrusion detection architecture to be produced [41]. This IDS

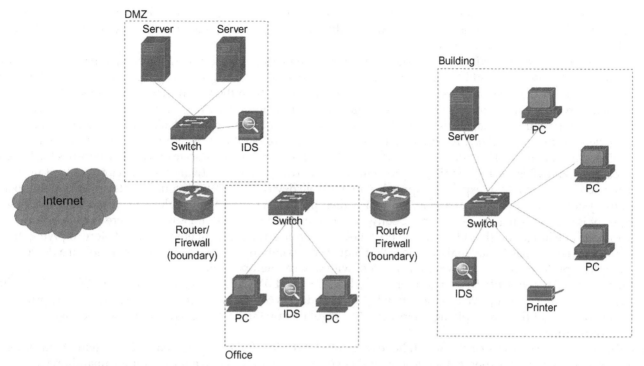

FIG. 2 E-government technical security measures.

framework would have the ability to detect attacks such as DoS by allowing various decentralized IDS nodes to exchange data and information with each other. Each IDS node monitors and records network events and exchanges it with the rest of the nodes to determine any sign of anomaly associated with the traffic. This distributed architecture is not a new idea, as it is already used in honeynets [42]. The difference would be that the end-point nodes in a honeynet are deployed using client/server architecture, where the blockchain would exchange information in a peer-to-peer architecture.

3.2 Technologies for Secure E-Government Systems

E-government systems need to built around CIA. Many modern technologies, and underpinning theoretical break-throughs in AI, telecommunication, cryptography, and authentication have been used in implementing the confidentiality and integrity components of e-government systems. These technologies are summarized as follows:

1. *Blockchain*: According to Dorri et al. blockchain technology has the potential to solve many of the security issues in Smart Cities [43]. Blockchain is a peer-to-peer distributed database (ledger). Blockchain maintains a list of continuously growing records called blocks that are linked and secured using public key cryptography [44]. Blockchain was originally developed for cryptocurrency as its underlying technology; however, it can be used in any system that does not require an intermediary. The blockchain consensus algorithms make sure that no one node verifies a block without agreement from other nodes. In order to break the blockchain security, an attacker would need to hack the majority of the peers in the network at the same time. This makes such an attack difficult [43]. Blockchain technology has been investigated as a potential decentralized security application for health care, higher education institutions, smart homes, and IoT [44–48].
2. *Artificial intelligence and machine learning*: Machine learning algorithms have been used for the identification of abnormal network traffic, for example, intrusion/threat detection [31, 49–53], DoS [54], and email phishing [55]. These detection methods are usually developed by training machine learning algorithms using datasets that include both normal and adversarial activities that describe the patterns of behavior for both normal users and attackers. The algorithms are then applied to test datasets that are not part of the original training data, to verify the ability of the algorithm and identify normal and adversarial activity. This is similar to the identification of phishing or spam emails using the bag of words (BoG) approach [55]. The BoG relies on a set of keywords (or in Machine Learning (ML) terms "features") that are used to distinguish between normal and spam emails. The BoG is usually

constructed from historic emails (normal and spam). According to Huang et al., existing intrusion detection solutions using machine learning cannot eliminate adversaries completely, therefore, the development and use of hybrid systems may be more appropriate [56].

3. *Biometric security and surveillance*: Biometric security is a suitable solution to use in smart governance to combat illegal entry to resources and identity theft. Biometric authentication uses traits to identify individuals. Biometric authentication is the recommended solution for sensitive data by both the US and UK Governments [57, 58]. Biometric security can be grouped into physiological and behavioral biometrics. Physiological biometrics cover fingerprints, face, iris, retina, and so forth. Behavioral biometrics cover voice, gait, signature, and so forth.

4. *Patching security vulnerabilities*: As vulnerabilities and exploits are identified by security specialists, they are cataloged in a database. They are then ranked based upon threat severity on a scale of 0 to 10, where 0 is the lowest threat level and 10 is the highest [59]. A problem can arise when system software on devices is not kept up to date and a vulnerability or exploit is exposed. A exploitable device in a network could create an entry point to an entire system. If the device is part of a Smart City, then the Smart City is vulnerable. The only solution to these types of issues is for regular or automatic software updates to be carried out. However, there is a caveat on automatic patching. You should always test patches in an offline development environment before applying them to a live system. A patch may make changes that require intervention, or may change the operation of a device, for example, a protocol version change may interfere with device interoperability.

5. *Deep packet inspection (DPI)*: DPI is a technique used by IDS's and IPS's to analyze network traffic. DPI analyzes the payload component of a packet to identify what type of data is being transferred on a network. This is usually carried out in real time by applying "signatures" or regular expressions to the payload for well-known protocols [60].

6. *Enhanced connected device security*: Smartphones are popular devices for accessing Smart City systems. Smartphone manufacturers employ strong authentication and encryption schemes to make it difficult for unauthorized users to access the data stored on these devices (encryption), or to access (passwords and biometrics) the functionality of the device. Biometric authentication, such as fingerprint readers, are common on most medium- to high-end smartphones. Another entry point for a cyber-attack is via nefarious smartphone applications. Smartphone operating systems are secured, in part, by an approvals process. Before an application is allowed onto an official app store, it is checked by the OS manufacturer. However, this process is not always successful, as illustrated by the banking app vulnerability found in 2017 [61].

7. *Mutual authentication and nonrepudiation*: All Smart City devices connected to e-government systems must be authenticated before transmitting data to ensure security. If mutual authentication is performed properly, devices can only accept connections and commands from authorized systems. This is achieved by making sure that devices are authenticated and data is encrypted before being transmitted over a Smart City network. To reduce the possibility of the encryption being compromised, public/private key encryption should be used. This service should be provided by a third party to provide nonrepudiation and an assurance that keys are genuine. These types of services can be provided by companies such as Verisign or Thwate.

Cyber-attacks and information breaches cannot be eliminated entirely, despite the advancement of available technologies. As well as the technological issues that must be addressed, the public must also be educated to keep their data secure and safe through information security awareness programs such as https://www.getsafeonline.org/, http://www.safetynetkids.org.uk, and https://staysafeonline.org/.

3.3 Security Challenges

As the user base and deployment of smart technologies increases, e-government agencies face the challenges of maintaining security. The next generation of e-government systems will be required to integrate with services such as geospatial information, regulatory publications, and public deliberation data, which enhances the experience and the innovation of applications [62]. Threats to e-government will also be more complex, targeting the client end points, the communications infrastructure, and the back end servers [63]. The implementation and development of Smart City systems are therefore challenging from both the technical and the user perspective [20]. The main challenges are summarized as follows:

- *Physical connectivity*: The physical distribution of a Smart City's infrastructure and the diverse devices that are connected can introduce an attack surface. Due to the distributed nature of a Smart City and multiple stakeholders having access to the core infrastructure, devices can be added in environments that do not have sufficient physical security enabling attackers to gain access, this may compromise the security of the entire infrastructure, even though parts of the infrastructure are well managed and controlled.

- *WiFi security*: WiFi devices with default passwords or/and unencrypted connections increase the threat landscape in a Smart City. There is also the issue of compromised WiFi encryption technologies such as WEP [64], and more recently, the WPA2 KRACK vulnerability (CVE-2017-13077 to CVE-2017-13082, CVE-2017-13084, CVE-2017-13086 to CVE-2017-13088) both allowing access to supposedly secured networks. These types of vulnerabilities are often detected by attackers during a "war drive."
- *Hardware security*: This is usually caused by the built-in security of devices not being considered [65]. An example of this would be a switch that is not properly configured or has the default password giving access to the network layer of a Smart City. This vulnerability can also be introduced with the weak encryption in IoT devices due to their low computational power, for example, a device only supporting SSHv1 [66]. Lack of IoT device standardization can also introduce an attack vector allowing the introduction of fake data for the purpose of rendering a system unusable.
- *Bandwidth consumption*: As large numbers of sensors, systems, and users engage with a Smart City, bandwidth requirements will increase; therefore, an important consideration in building a Smart City is the physical deployment of services and creating a flexible environment that is capable of supporting high levels of traffic. This could be achieved through the introduction of traffic management such as multiprotocol label switching and geo-load balancing, for example, using split horizons in a domain name system [67].
- *Application risks*: Software products with security vulnerabilities (software design and bugs) impose a big risk in Smart Cities. Applications that are used by different organizations to access corporate data may contain security weaknesses.
- *Smart vehicles*: In a Smart City where devices are all interconnected, you can consider a vehicle as an end-point device. If the vehicles relay positional information and other telemetry data to a central point, it is possible to identify optimum traffic routing to speed up transit times. This could be achieved by altering traffic light timings or diverting specific vehicles onto specific routes based on a criterion. Cybersecurity is a concern in this area in terms of maintaining an efficient flow of traffic. There is also the issue of self-driving smart cars that would need to be connected to the Smart City infrastructure and the consequences of compromising a vehicle's navigation and control [68]. Some self-driving cars use Ethernet protocols that require network aggregation (broadcast), which adds a level of complexity and vulnerabilities to the network.

Once the attack surface of an environment, in this case a Smart City, is known, it is important to develop security metrics for measuring the effectiveness and efficiency of the security and privacy measures that are required to deal with different kinds of threats [69]. Some of the common security threat types and the countermeasures in e-government systems and Smart Cities are summarized in Table 1 [65].

The developed security metric should not only focus on the current state of an e-government system, but also be future-proof. This will provide the fundamental evidence for policy makers and authorities in efficient governing of Smart Cities for security and safety.

4 PRIVACY PRESERVING FOR E-GOVERNMENT

The "Big Three" CIA, as discussed in Section 1, are the cornerstones of security requirements, and increasing one of them invariably weakens the others; this is also true with e-government systems. The growing volume of digital interactions between consumers has caused concerns [48, 70]. Privacy concerns are identified as a key challenge to policy, regulation, and legislation in the 21st century [71]. E-government systems collect a lot of confidential information about individuals, products, and financial transactions. If information of this type is compromised, it will lead to the loss of faith in e-government and Smart Cities and what they are trying to offer [72, 73].

One major concern with respect to government systems is the capturing and use of personal and sensitive information, and there are fears that the information could be used to monitor the public, which is considered by many as an invasion of their privacy [70]. There are also fears that the information could be obtained by cyber criminals. These concerns are well founded as there are a number of well documented cases where information has been leaked. In 2015, the US Government suffered a massive cyber-attack exposing sensitive information of around 21.5 million people, including employees and their family members [74]. The attack resulted in the exposure of social security numbers, fingerprints, credit card information, addresses, health and financial records, and other private information. As well as coordinated attacks on the US Government systems, there are also cases in the United States where local

TABLE 1   Security Threats and Countermeasures in E-Government Systems and Smart Cities [65]

Serial No.	Attack	Countermeasure(s)
1	Identity theft	Awareness training, risk assessment, insider threat analysis, and secure WiFi networks are commonly used for safe handling of confidential information and personal data
2	DoS	DoS is a result of flooding attacks trying to make the system unavailable by generating more data than the system can handle. Different techniques exist to mitigate jamming attacks, for example, intrusion detection and prevention techniques (Radiflow, Snort)
3	Malware	Malicious software attacks can be prevented by using antivirus software and keeping software up to date in the Smart City
4	IOT node security	Trust management techniques are often used to ensure trustworthiness of nodes and communication to ensure security and privacy of IoT sensors
5	Attacks on IOT devices	The keys to countering such attacks are lightweight cryptographic solutions, such as TinySA, and making use of IoT forensics (DigiCert IoT PKI Solutions, and Symantec solutions)
6	RFI conflict collision	RFID anticollision techniques such as spread spectrum can be used to resolve this issue
7	Side channel attack	Can be prevented by using time-stamps and signing the packets with an algorithm, such as Elliptic Curve Digital Signature Algorithm
8	Eavesdropping and traffic analysis	Encryption and cryptographic solutions are strong enough and can counter these attacks
9	GPS spoofing	Technical countermeasures include using military precise positioning system signals instead of civic standard positioning system signals
10	Replay attacks	To counter replay attacks, a system can keep a cache of exchanged messages and compare new messages with previously received messages
11	Man-in-the-middle attack	Prevention techniques such as cryptographic techniques can be efficient for this type of attack
12	Data modification	Public key infrastructure (PKI) can be used to counter such attacks

RFI (usually seen as RFID), Radio Frequency Identification; *RFID,* Radio Frequency Identification.

e-government sites had individual's names, social security numbers, property tax records, and other private information accessible without requiring login credentials [75].

It is the responsibility of a government to ensure an individual's information is secured and the users' privacy is preserved during data collection, processing, storage, and exchange. Therefore, the e-government infrastructure and all the devices connected to the infrastructures need to be protected with appropriate measures. Extensive study has been dedicated to the security of network infrastructure that an e-government system would adopt, which leads to an e-government system with better privacy-preserving. In addition, IoT devices can be susceptible to leaking information during information collection, transmission, and processing [20], and must be covered by the same level of protection. The type of data an IoT device may hold could be personal identity, location, health data, and lifestyle.

4.1 Privacy Preserving Through Security Measures

Security, privacy, and interoperability are the key elements to build trust among users in e-government systems, and it is of vital importance to protect an individual's privacy to build trust in e-government initiatives and development [76]. According to a study conducted by Moen et al., a large number of e-government websites have no privacy policy [77]. Privacy can be promoted by setting up guidelines, procedures, compliance programs, and training and awareness.

The e-government systems could improve security by introducing transport layer security and using a secure socket layer (TLS/SSL) certificates that implement a PKI [72]. PKI requires that users maintain their software to ensure the latest TLS/SSL certificates are being used. PKI's use a trusted third party, a certification authority (CA) to offer certificates to the user's devices. If CA is compromised, it may lead to privacy and security problems [78]. Setfanova et al. propose that biometric security should be incorporated in e-government portals using either fingerprints, irises, or facial recognition for authentication [79]. However, biometric technology can be expensive and difficult to implement.

An authentication framework known as the Greek Authentication Framework [80] can ensure security and privacy of e-government users by applying different registration and authentication procedures using a single central public portal interfaced with ministerial departments (service providers [SPs]). The framework consists of two parts: the identity provider (IdP) and the SP. This is the same process that is used with Shibboleth authentication, which is extensively employed in higher education and research in the United Kingdom [81]. Users have to register with an IdP at a central portal that is then used to access services from an SP. Because all users are administered by a single central portal, it must be configured in such a way as to not present a possible single point of failure. This framework uses PKI to ensure confidentiality, but having a single authentication center limits the integrity and availability of data in case it is compromised.

Incorporating blockchain technology in the Smart City devices will ensure privacy and security between devices, users, and smart systems [48]. The Secure Framework for Future Smart City was developed using multicloud and cloud federation services and validated using the cloud analytic tool [82]. Multicloud and federated cloud were used in order to prevent data loss and allow interoperability between diverse IoT devices in the Smart City. Using Zero-Knowledge Protocol based on Elliptic Curve Discrete Logarithm Problem, a security protocol was developed and integrated with the framework. Elliptic curve cryptography provides strong security using short keys that have a low resource requirement compared with other algorithms such as SHA256.

4.2 Privacy-Preserving Challenges

More than 80% of e-government sites have been found to have common web server-based vulnerabilities such as cross site scripting and Structured Query Language (SQL) injection [77]. The Open Web Application Security Project [83] identified that any organization connected to the Internet is vulnerable to threats affecting confidentiality, integrity, availability, authenticity, and accountability. Therefore, any security design must address these requirements in its design. The main challenges regarding privacy concerns arising in e-government systems, as a result of integration with Smart Cities, include:

- *Data privacy and protection concerns*: Personal private information can be gathered in the Smart City without the user's consent. Data privacy can be affected by surveillance, aggregation, extended use, and data leakage. As such, stronger protection of the privacy of a user's information must be provided [70]. An individual's data should not be leaked, extended, or used for a purpose that it was not meant for during collection and processing; in the United Kingdom, this is covered by the Data Protection Act [84].
- *More connections mean less privacy*: A Smart City generally consists of many integrated systems, but each system holds its own dataset relating to the functional aspects of that system. A problem arises when this data becomes metadata through its aggregation. This aggregation could allow the "behavior" of an individual to be tracked; for example, tracking the position of an individual over time based on bank card transactions.
- *Real-time mass surveillance*: Authorities often employ surveillance systems within a Smart City. With the introduction of technologies such as facial recognition, the video feeds could be used to identify and track an individual. Although this information is collected from the public infrastructure, it may expose confidential details about an individual. For example, if a person attending a cancer clinic for tests is identified from a video feed, and this fact is recorded by Smart City surveillance technology, when the individual applies for an insurance policy, they could be rejected based on having attended the clinic. The individual's right to privacy has been violated.
- *Smart City systems interoperability*: Interoperability of systems means data is translated and transferred through an infrastructure, which will introduce potential vulnerabilities in the Smart City infrastructure. This situation is expected to increase significantly [85].

The authorities must make sure that information collected from and about an individual is kept, stored, processed, and transferred confidentially. Some organizations already use financial activity as a measure of consumer activity to influence the development of new products (i.e., spending habits). It is the responsibility of local authorities to make sure that no data remains open so as to preserve a user's privacy and maintain trust.

5 A SECURE AND PRIVACY-PRESERVING E-GOVERNMENT FRAMEWORK

An e-government framework must ensure security and privacy, which can be achieved by utilizing blockchain and AI techniques. The framework proposed here is illustrated in Fig. 3. The main data links shown are for individuals interacting with the Smart City services, Business to Business communications (B2B), Business to Government

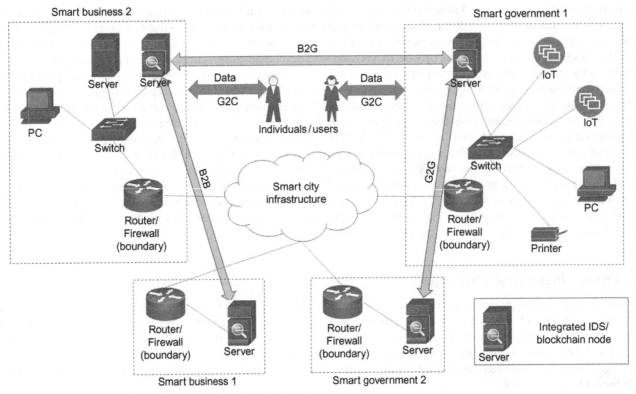

FIG. 3 The proposed e-government security and privacy framework.

communications (B2G), G2G communications, and G2C communications. Data entry to the system is via the consumers (individuals) of those systems and other automated data capture facilities, such as the IoT devices (as shown in Smart Government 1). The framework is distributed on a peer-to-peer model with intersystems communications between each peer using blockchain and IDS technologies to provide cross system privacy. Machine learning is proposed to implement a dynamic "immune system" at each node that is able to discriminate between malicious and normal activities. This model uses blockchain and intrusion detection as complementary technologies; blockchain ensures privacy, security, and trust; while intrusion detection helps detect anomalies during blockchain transactions [41].

The framework consists of four logical layers as shown in Fig. 4. The first layer is the data storage layer (*database layer*), this is where the data capturing through direct user input and automated IoT devices is stored. This layer is a distributed layer where only specific sets of data are stored relating to each system. This data is stored in two specific sets; data that requires authentication to be accessed (permissioned) and public data (permissionless). The second layer is the *security and privacy layer* that protects the transactions between end users and intersystem data transfer though the use of IDSs. The third layer is the Smart City communications infrastructure (*communications layer*), and consists of

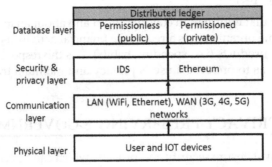

FIG. 4 The layers on the security and privacy framework.

many communications architectures such as Ethernet, serial, WiFi, and so forth. The fourth layer (*physical*) is the data capture component of the system, which consists of direct user data entry or automated data capture via IoT devices.

The framework as shown in Fig. 3 is able to:

- detect intrusion and prevent the network from attacks such as DoS, malware, and so forth;
- maintain anonymity and encryption to ensure information privacy (which is provided by blockchain technology);
- scale to permit users and known government organizations to join the network;
- generate IDs and blockchain addresses for individuals, IoT devices, sensors, and other e-government affiliates; and
- allow IDs and the blockchain addresses for e-government users and devices to access records from any peer node.

The distributed ledger can be implemented via Ethereum [86]. Ethereum is an open software platform based on blockchain technology with the tools to build decentralized applications. A smart contract protocol running on the Ethereum platform can be used to simulate real contracts, such as tax and insurance payments, employment contracts, utility bill payment, and so forth [87]. The contract functionality provided by Ethereum is an alternative to storing an individual's sensitive records. It reduces third-party costs in traditional transactions and guarantees security and reliability. Blockchain transactions constitute an atomic change in a record state in a system. Each transaction attempts to be validated by all nodes and must be confirmed by the majority of the nodes before the transactions are accepted on the chain.

When an end-point data capture entity (individual or IoT device) registers with the Smart City, an ID for the endpoint is issued and a blockchain address is created containing a public and private key. Using their IDs and the blockchain addresses, an end-point entity can create, delete, and update their records from any node. Every transaction is authenticated and added to the ledger. The ledger, being a distributed architecture, broadcasts the request across the network for validation. A ledger record includes the following information:

- entity ID;
- the record identifier (e.g., name); and
- the record value.

The validation process of a transaction requires a consensus from the majority of the network nodes. All nodes in the network contain a copy of the record. A distributed consensus protocol validates the chronological validity of the change request. The Ethereum particularly uses the proof of work (PoW) consensus algorithm. To calculate the PoW, a cryptographic hash function such as SHA 256 (secure hash algorithm-256 bits) is used to generate a hash value for each new block [88]. For a block to be validated and accepted by the rest of the peers, the hash must be a value less than the current target. After validation, the new block is chained into the end of the blockchain and the new state of the blockchain is broadcasted to the network. This process does incur a propagation delay which can be up to 15 seconds when using Ethereum [89].

The IDS should be implemented at two levels, first, at the perimeter boundaries of each network, and second, within the Smart City nodes. This is to address any network traffic and transaction-based malicious attacks. The failure of validation for all traffic and transactions will lead to one of two consequences: (1) the transactions being dropped and reported, (2) the corresponding IPS being blocked if one is used. An IDS is usually implemented as a set of trained classifiers that automatically detect malicious network traffic. The blockchain usually does not have the functionality to validate traffic, and in this case, an IDS/IPS is essential.

Modern IDS/IPS systems are often implemented using general classifiers developed by the machine learning communities with the support of known attacks using labeled datasets such as the intrusion dataset KDD99 [90], malware datasets from NETRESEC [91], and application layer DDoS datasets [92]. These datasets were captured in a real network environment using common network monitoring tools; consequently, they are usually of high dimensions that correspond to the general network traffic metrics such as packet flags, size, host and network address, and port numbers. Note that there are noisy and redundant dimensions that will adversely affect the performance of IDS/IPS. Therefore, feature selection approaches are often used for reprocessing [93–95].

The IDS/IPS systems can be evaluated in the field using open source tools. Many of the most common tools can be found in the Kali Linux [96], which is specifically designed for cybersecurity testing, for example, nmap for network reconnaissance via port scanning. Port scanning is used for malicious purposes to search for potentially vulnerable machines on a network. The nmap tool can be used to carry out several types of scans, such as ping scans, and can be tailored through parameters to run in different modes/speeds to try and circumvent detection. These tests should all be carried out as part of a penetration test.

6 CONCLUSIONS

As more and more sensitive information goes online, more care needs to be taken in how it is transmitted, stored, and processed. Smart Cities and e-government are driving up the amount of data being gathered and shared, and are a contributing factor to the increase. Cyber criminals are constantly developing more sophisticated hacking techniques every day. This chapter has discussed the current situation, and available technologies and difficulties in implementing e-government in the context of Smart Cities from the perspective of security, and privacy. Based on the investigation, a general decentralized e-government framework is proposed in this chapter, and blockchain and AI technologies are suggested as the appropriate building blocks in implementing such a system. Blockchain technology ensures the privacy, security, and integrity of sensitive information; while AI powers the development of intrusion detection and prevention systems. Going forward, further investigation is required to explore the employment of other AI technologies in supporting the development of a secure, privacy-preserving e-government system, such as automated registration services. Also, systematic validation and evaluation of the proposed system is required before a deployment takes place; which is work that remains to be done.

References

[1] K. Rush, Digital Glasgow Roadmap 2014, 2014. https://www.glasgow.gov.uk/CHttpHandler.ashx?id=18230&p=0. Accessed 1 April 2018.

[2] K. Rush, The digital communications infrastructure strategy, 2014. https://www.gov.uk/government/publications/the-digital-communications-infrastructure-strategy/the-digital-communications-infrastructure-strategy. Accessed 1 April 2018.

[3] A. Ojo, E. Curry, T. Janowski, Designing next generation smart city initiatives-harnessing findings and lessons from a study of ten smart city programs 182, 2014, 43–67.

[4] UNFPA, Urbanization, 2016. Available from: https://www.unfpa.org/urbanization/ (Accessed 26 January 2018).

[5] ITU, Focus group on smart sustainable cities, 2015. https://www.itu.int/en/ITU-T/focusgroups/ssc/Pages/default.aspx. Accessed 3 April 2018.

[6] K. Layne, J. Lee, Developing fully functional e-government: a four stage model, Gov. Inf. Q. 18 (2) 2001, 122–136.

[7] R. Khatoun, S. Zeadally, Cybersecurity and privacy solutions in smart cities, IEEE Commun. Mag. 55 (3) 2017, 51–59.

[8] Peña-López, I., et al., UN e-Government Survey, 2014. E-Government for the Future We Want, UNPAN, 2014, https://publicadministration.un.org/egovkb/en-us/reports/un-e-government-survey-2014.

[9] Inc ISC2, Cybersecurity and IT security certifications and training, 2018. https://www.isc2.org/. Accessed 3 April 2018.

[10] S. Hernandez, Official (ISC) 2 Guide to the CISSP CBK, Auerbach Publications, USA, 2012.

[11] E. Noe, Usability, accessibility and web security assessment of e-government websites in Tanzania, Int. J. Comput. Appl. 164 (5) 2017, 42–48.

[12] W.C. Barker, E-government security issues and measures, 2005. Tech. Rep.

[13] T. Nam, T.A. Pardo, Smart city as urban innovation: focusing on management, policy, and context, in: Proceedings of the 5th International Conference on Theory and Practice of Electronic Governance, ACM, 2011, pp. 185–194.

[14] J.W. Feltes, B.D. Gemmell, D. Retzmann, From smart grid to super grid: solutions with HVDC and FACTS for grid access of renewable energy sources, in: 2011 IEEE Power and Energy Society General Meeting, 2011, pp. 1–6.

[15] Chartered Institute of Procurement and Supply, Global Supply Chains, 2018. https://www.cips.org/en-GB/knowledge/procurement-topics-and-skills/srm-and-sc-management/global-supply-chains/. Accessed 10 April 2018.

[16] M. Blaug, The empirical status of human capital theory: a slightly jaundiced survey, J. Econ. Lit. 14 (3) 1976, 827–855.

[17] A. Caragliu, C. Del Bo, P. Nijkamp, Smart cities in Europe, J. Urban Technol. 18 (2) 2011, 65–82.

[18] R. Giffinger, H. Gudrun, Smart cities ranking: an effective instrument for the positioning of the cities? ACE 4 (12) 2010, 7–26.

[19] A. Zanella, N. Bui, A. Castellani, L. Vangelista, M. Zorzi, Internet of Things for smart cities, IEEE Internet Things J. 1 (1) 2014, 22–32.

[20] K. Zhang, J. Ni, K. Yang, X. Liang, J. Ren, X.S. Shen, Security and privacy in smart city applications: challenges and solutions, IEEE Commun. Mag. 55 (1) 2017, 122–129.

[21] M. Al-Hader, A. Rodzi, A.R. Sharif, N. Ahmad, Smart city components architecture, in: International Conference on Computational Intelligence, Modelling and Simulation, 2009 (CSSim'09), IEEE, 2009, pp. 93–97.

[22] S.P. Mohanty, U. Choppali, E. Kougianos, Everything you wanted to know about smart cities: the Internet of Things is the backbone, IEEE Consum. Electron. Mag. 5 (3) 2016, 60–70.

[23] Amsterdam Smart City, 2018. https://amsterdamsmartcity.com/. Accessed 10 April 2018.

[24] B. Johnson, Cities, systems of innovation and economic development, Innovation 10 (2–3) 2008, 146–155.

[25] W. Van Winden, Urban governance in the knowledge-based economy: challenges for different city types, Innovation 10 (2–3) 2008, 197–210.

[26] A. Meijer, M.P.R. Bolívar, Governing the smart city: a review of the literature on smart urban governance, Int. Rev. Adm. Sci. 82 (2) 2016, 392–408.

[27] L. Carter, F. Bélanger, The utilization of e-government services: citizen trust, innovation and acceptance factors, Inf. Syst. J. 15 (1) 2005, 5–25.

[28] F. Bélanger, L. Carter, Trust and risk in e-government adoption, J. Strateg. Inf. Syst. 17 (2) 2008, 165–176.

[29] R. Palanisamy, B. Mukerji, Security and privacy issues in e-government, in: E-Government Service Maturity and Development: Cultural, Organizational and Technological Perspectives, IGI Global, 2012, pp. 236–248.

[30] M. Alshehri, S. Drew, E-government fundamentals, in: IADIS International Conference ICT, Society and Human Beings, 2010.

[31] J. Li, L. Yang, Y. Qu, G. Sexton, An extended Takagi-Sugeno-Kang inference system (TSK+) with fuzzy interpolation and its rule base generation, Soft Comput. 2017, https://doi.org/10.1007/s00500-017-2925-8.

[32] A. Arroub, B. Zahi, E. Sabir, M. Sadik, A literature review on Smart Cities: paradigms, opportunities and open problems, in: 2016 International Conference on Wireless Networks and Mobile Communications (WINCOM), IEEE, 2016, pp. 180–186.

[33] A.S. Elmaghraby, M.M. Losavio, Cyber security challenges in Smart Cities: safety, security and privacy, J. Adv. Res. 5 (4) 2014, 491–497.

[34] N.R. Al-Rodhan, The Five Dimensions of Global Security: Proposal for a Multi-Sum Security Principle, LIT Verlag, Münster, 2007.

[35] G. Karokola, S. Kowalski, L. Yngstrom, Secure e-government services: towards a framework for integrating it security services into e-government maturity models, in: Information Security South Africa (ISSA), 2011, IEEE, 2011, pp. 1–9.

[36] C.E. Jiménez, F. Falcone, J. Feng, H. Puyosa, A. Solanas, F. González, E-government: security threats, e-Government 11 2012, 21.

[37] L. Yang, Z. Zuo, F. Chao, Y. Qu, Fuzzy interpolation systems and applications, in: S. Ramakrishnan (Ed.), Modern Fuzzy Control Systems and Its Applications, InTech, Rijeka, 2017. chap. 3.

[38] L. Yang, Q. Shen, Closed form fuzzy interpolation, Fuzzy Sets Syst. 225 2013, 1–22.

[39] L. Yang, F. Chao, Q. Shen, Generalized adaptive fuzzy rule interpolation, IEEE Trans. Fuzzy Syst. 25 (4) 2017, 839–853.

[40] M. Stampar, K. Fertalj, Artificial intelligence in network intrusion detection, in: 2015 38th International Convention on Information and Communication Technology, Electronics and Microelectronics (MIPRO), IEEE, 2015, pp. 1318–1323.

[41] W. Meng, E.W. Tischhauser, Q. Wang, Y. Wang, J. Han, When intrusion detection meets blockchain technology: a review, IEEE Access 6 2018, 10179–10188.

[42] L. Spitzner, The honeynet project: trapping the hackers, IEEE Secur. Priv. 99 (2), 2003, 15–23.

[43] A. Dorri, S.S. Kanhere, R. Jurdak, P. Gauravaram, Blockchain for IoT security and privacy: the case study of a smart home, 2017 IEEE International Conference on Pervasive Computing and Communications Workshops (PerCom Workshops), IEEE, 2017, pp. 618–623.

[44] K. Christidis, M. Devetsikiotis, Blockchains and smart contracts for the Internet of Things, IEEE Access 4 2016, 2292–2303.

[45] A. Dubovitskaya, Z. Xu, S. Ryu, M. Schumacher, F. Wang, Secure and trustable electronic medical records sharing using blockchain, ArXiv preprint arXiv:1709.06528 2017.

[46] M. Turkanović, M. Hölbl, K. Košič, M. Heričko, A. Kamišalić, EduCTX: a blockchain-based higher education credit platform, IEEE Access 6 2018, 5112–5127.

[47] S. Huh, S. Cho, S. Kim, Managing IoT devices using blockchain platform, in: 2017 19th International Conference on Advanced Communication Technology (ICACT), IEEE, 2017, pp. 464–467.

[48] K. Biswas, V. Muthukkumarasamy, Securing smart cities using blockchain technology, in: 2016 IEEE 18th International Conference on High Performance Computing and Communications; IEEE 14th International Conference on Smart City; IEEE 2nd International Conference on Data Science and Systems (HPCC/SmartCity/DSS), IEEE, 2016, pp. 1392–1393.

[49] N. Naik, P. Jenkins, B. Kerby, J. Sloane, L. Yang, Fuzzy logic aided intelligent threat detection in Cisco adaptive security appliance 5500 series firewalls, in: 2018 IEEE International Conference on Fuzzy Systems (FUZZ-IEEE), IEEE, 2018.

[50] N. Naik, P. Jenkins, R. Cooke, L. Yang, A fuzzy technique for detecting and inhibiting fingerprinting attack in low interaction honeypot, in: 2018 IEEE International Conference on Fuzzy Systems (FUZZ-IEEE), IEEE, 2018.

[51] N. Elisa, L. Yang, N. Naik, Dendritic cell algorithm with optimised parameters using genetic algorithm, in: 2018 IEEE Congress on Evolutionary Computation (IEEE CEC 2018), IEEE, 2018.

[52] J. Li, Y. Qu, F. Chao, H.P.H. Shum, E.S.L. Ho, L. Yang, Machine learning algorithms for network intrusion detection, in: L.F. Sikos (Ed.), AI in Cybersecurity, Springer, New York, NY, 2018.

[53] L. Yang, J. Li, G. Fehringer, P. Barraclough, G. Sexton, Y. Cao, Intrusion detection system by fuzzy interpolation, in: 2017 IEEE International Conference on Fuzzy Systems (FUZZ-IEEE), 2017, pp. 1–6.

[54] J. Li, L. Yang, X. Fu, F. Chao, Y. Qu, Dynamic QoS solution for enterprise networks using TSK fuzzy interpolation, in: 2017 IEEE International Conference on Fuzzy Systems (FUZZ-IEEE), 2017, pp. 1–6.

[55] I. Fette, N. Sadeh, A. Tomasic, Learning to detect phishing emails, in: Proceedings of the 16th International Conference on World Wide Web, ACM, New York, NY, USA, 2007, pp. 649–656.

[56] L. Huang, A.D. Joseph, B. Nelson, B.I. Rubinstein, J. Tygar, Adversarial machine learning, in: Proceedings of the 4th ACM Workshop on Security and Artificial Intelligence, ACM, 2011, pp. 43–58.

[57] NIST, Biometrics—NIST, 2017. https://www.nist.gov/programs-projects/biometrics. Accessed 12 April 2018.

[58] NCSC, End User Devices: Authentication Policy NCSC Site, 2016. https://www.ncsc.gov.uk/guidance/end-user-devices-authentication-policy. Accessed 12 April 2018.

[59] S. Özkan, CVE security vulnerability database, 2018. https://www.cvedetails.com/. Accessed 12 April 2018.

[60] S. Kumar, S. Dharmapurikar, F. Yu, P. Crowley, J. Turner, Algorithms to accelerate multiple regular expressions matching for deep packet inspection, SIGCOMM Comput. Commun. Rev. 36 (4) 2006, 339–350.

[61] H. Bodkin, Flaw discovered in banking app leaving millions vulnerable to hack, 2017. https://www.telegraph.co.uk/science/2017/12/06/flaw-discovered-banking-apps-leaving-millions-vulnerable-hack/. Accessed 12 April 2018.

[62] V. Tountopoulos, I. Giannakoudaki, K. Giannakakis, L. Korres, L. Kallipolitis, Supporting security and trust in complex e-government services, in: Secure and Trustworthy Service Composition, Springer, 2014, pp. 219–233.

[63] C. Mazumdar, A.K. Kaushik, P. Banerjee, On information security issues in e-governance: developing country views, CSDMS J 2009.

[64] S.V. Reddy, K.S. Ramani, K. Rijutha, S.M. Ali, C.P. Reddy, Wireless hacking—a WiFi hack by cracking WEP, 2010 2nd International Conference on Education Technology and Computer, vol. 1, 2010. pp. V1-189–V1-193.

[65] A. Gharaibeh, M.A. Salahuddin, S.J. Hussini, A. Khreishah, I. Khalil, M. Guizani, A. Al-Fuqaha, Smart cities: a survey on data management, security, and enabling technologies, IEEE Commun. Surv. Tutorials 19 (4) 2017, 2456–2501.

[66] M.I.T.R.E. Corporation, CVE-2001-1473: The SSH-1 protocol allows remote servers to conduct man-in-the-middle attacks, 2017. https://www.cvedetails.com/cve/cve-2001-1473. Accessed 13 April 2018.

[67] R.P.S. Pierre, Distributed denial of service congestion recovery using split horizon DNS, 2011. US Patent 7,987,255.

[68] Z.A. Baig, P. Szewczyk, C. Valli, P. Rabadia, P. Hannay, M. Chernyshev, M. Johnstone, P. Kerai, A. Ibrahim, K. Sansurooah, et al., Future challenges for smart cities: cyber-security and digital forensics, Digit. Investig. 22 2017, 3–13.

[69] M.H. Zu'bi, H.H. Al-Onizat, E-government and security requirements for information systems and privacy, J. Manag. Res. 4 (4) 2012, 367–375.

[70] L. Van Zoonen, Privacy concerns in smart cities, Gov. Inf. Q. 33 (3) 2016, 472–480.

[71] S. Prentice, G. Dewnarain, The future of the Internet: fundamental trends, scenarios and implications to heed, Gartner 2012. http://www.gartner.com/technology/core/products/research/topics/emergingTrendsTechnologies.jsp.

[72] C. Lambrinoudakis, S. Gritzalis, F. Dridi, G. Pernul, Security requirements for e-government services: a methodological approach for developing a common PKI-based security policy, Comput. Commun. 26 (16) 2003, 1873–1883.

[73] T.J. Perez, Municipal e-government security: what is the greatest challenge? in: 2015 48th Hawaii International Conference on System Sciences (HICSS), IEEE, 2015, pp. 2263–2271.

[74] E-government sounds great until the first hack. Available from: https://www.bloomberg.com/view/articles/2017-11-21/e-government-sounds-great-until-the-first-hack/ (Accessed 13 January 2018).

[75] J.J. Zhao, S.Y. Zhao, Opportunities and threats: a security assessment of state e-government websites, Gov. Inf. Q. 27 (1) 2010, 49–56.

[76] M.I. Manda, J. Backhouse, Addressing trust, security and privacy concerns in e-government integration, interoperability and information sharing through policy: a case of South Africa, in: CONF-IRM, 2016, p. 67.

[77] V. Moen, A.N. Klingsheim, K.I.F. Simonsen, K.J. Hole, Vulnerabilities in e-governments, Int. J. Electron. Secur. Digit. Forensics 1 (1) 2007, 89–100.

[78] C. Ellison, B. Schneier, Ten risks of PKI: what you're not being told about public key infrastructure, Comput. Secur. J. 16 (1) 2000, 1–7.

[79] M. Stefanova, S. Stefanov, O. Asenov, Identity protection accessing e-government through the biometric authentication methods, in: 2012 6th IEEE International Conference on Intelligent Systems (IS), IEEE, 2012, pp. 403–408.

[80] D. Prokopios, G. Dimitris, G. Stefanos, L. Costas, L. Mitrou, Towards an enhanced authentication framework for e-government services: the Greek case, Trust Secur. 2009, 189–196.

[81] JISC, UK Federation Information Centre, 2017. https://www.ukfederation.org.uk/. Accessed 12 April 2018.

[82] H. Djigal, F. Jun, J. Lu, Secure framework for future smart city, in: 2017 IEEE 4th International Conference on Cyber Security and Cloud Computing (CSCloud), IEEE, 2017, pp. 76–83.

[83] D. Wichers, Owasp top-10 2013, OWASP Foundation, February 2013.

[84] legislation.gov.uk, Data protection act 2015, 2015. http://www.legislation.gov.uk/ukpga/1998/29/contents. Accessed 12 April 2018.

[85] A. Bartoli, J. Hernandez-Serrano, M. Soriano, M. Dohler, A. Kountouris, D. Barthel, On the Ineffectiveness of Today's Privacy Regulations for Secure Smart City Networks, Smart Cities Council, Washington, DC, 2012.

[86] G. Wood, Ethereum: a secure decentralised generalised transaction ledger, Ethereum Project Yellow Paper 151 2014, 1–32.

[87] A. Kosba, A. Miller, E. Shi, Z. Wen, C. Papamanthou, Hawk: the blockchain model of cryptography and privacy-preserving smart contracts, in: 2016 IEEE Symposium on Security and Privacy (SP), IEEE, 2016, pp. 839–858.

[88] Z. Zheng, S. Xie, H. Dai, X. Chen, H. Wang, An overview of blockchain technology: architecture, consensus, and future trends, in: 2017 IEEE International Congress on Big Data (BigData Congress), IEEE, 2017, pp. 557–564.

[89] I. Weber, V. Gramoli, A. Ponomarev, M. Staples, R. Holz, A.B. Tran, P. Rimba, On availability for blockchain-based systems, in: 2017 IEEE 36th Symposium on Reliable Distributed Systems (SRDS), IEEE, 2017, pp. 64–73.

[90] KDD Cup 1999 Data. Available from: http://kdd.ics.uci.edu/databases/kddcup99/kddcup99.html/ (Accessed 13 February 2018).

[91] Network Forensics and Network Security Monitoring. Available from: http://www.netresec.com/ (Accessed 13 December 2017).

[92] R. Fontugne, P. Borgnat, P. Abry, K. Fukuda, Mawilab: combining diverse anomaly detectors for automated anomaly labeling and performance benchmarking, in: Proceedings of the 6th International Conference, ACM, 2010, p. 8.

[93] Y. Qu, Y. Rong, A. Deng, L. Yang, Associated multi-label fuzzy-rough feature selection, in: 2017 Joint 17th World Congress of International Fuzzy Systems Association and 9th International Conference on Soft Computing and Intelligent Systems (IFSA-SCIS), 2017, pp. 1–6.

[94] Q. Guo, Y. Qu, A. Deng, L. Yang, A new fuzzy-rough feature selection algorithm for mammographic risk analysis, in: 2016 12th International Conference on Natural Computation, Fuzzy Systems and Knowledge Discovery (ICNC-FSKD), 2016, pp. 934–939.

[95] Q. Sun, Y. Qu, A. Deng, L. Yang, Fuzzy-rough feature selection based on α-partition differentiation entropy, in: The 13th International Conference on Natural Computation, Fuzzy Systems and Knowledge Discovery, 2017.

[96] Offensive Security, Kali Linux | Penetration Testing and Ethical Hacking Linux Distribution, 2108. Available from: https://www.kali.org/ (Accessed 13 December 2017).

8

Big Data in Cybersecurity for Smart City Applications

Ronald Doku and Danda B. Rawat

Cybersecurity and Wireless Networking Innovation (CWiNs) Lab, Department of Electrical Engineering and Computer Science, Howard University, Washington, DC, United States

1 INTRODUCTION

Smart Cities are starting to become popular. City officials are now investing in technological improvements for their cities despite the reluctance of central governments, who value secure, stable situations over the uncertainties and vulnerabilities that innovations of a Smart City may bring. The ultimate goal of a Smart City is to improve the lives of its citizens. With that being said, a Smart City may differ from city to city. The criteria for determining what sort of smart infrastructure a city may focus on depends on the needs of its inhabitants. For example, some cities may require more smart transportation infrastructure than others, and thus, that specific Smart City may focus more on improving its transportation system. The growth of Big Data (see Fig. 1) and development of Internet of Thing (IoT) technologies have been central in the practicality of Smart City inventiveness [1]. Data collection and analysis is key for all of these to happen. Smart Cities are usually built on wireless networks, a wide range of sensors, radio frequency, and more recently, 5G has been researched for its use in Smart Cities. All these are sources of heterogeneous data that require the use of Big Data analytics to gain insights from the data they generate (see Fig. 2). These devices working together make up the IoTs in Smart Cities.

Issues associated with Smart Cities can boil down to Information and Communication Technology (ICT), IoT, and Big Data challenges. This chapter discusses Big Data in cybersecurity issues for different Smart City applications (see Fig. 3). Big Data can be described as facts collected about reality. These facts can be generated from sensors that can be embedded in any physical object surrounding us. The idea behind this is, the more facts we gather about things around us, the more we can improve lives by using this information to better understand our surroundings. These sensors are communicating with each other more frequently than usual. The side effect to this, however, is that, the more automated things get, the more vulnerable we become. These devices need to be online mostly, producing information and transmitting information among each other and to servers. This brings various security issues as accessing the Internet is akin to opening Pandora's box. In addition, the amount of data being generated is enormous, and they are so many different forms. This has created a scenario where our ability to collect data overwhelms our capacity to protect it. Laney [2] came up with the term the three V's, which he associated with Big Data. These terms were volume, velocity, and variety. Volume represents the fact that the data being generated is enormous, velocity represents the fact that data is being generated at an alarming rate, and variety represents the fact that the data being generated comes in all types of forms. The very attributes that define Big Data are the same elements that make it vulnerable. The plot further thickens as most of this data is saved on cloud storage systems that are supposed to be secure and be trustworthy. However, major companies can take advantage of this collected data to learn more about users to predict buying and behavior patterns. This can be seen as a major privacy issue. Furthermore, these cloud systems are not immune to security attacks and sensitive data leakages, as can be seen in various high profile companies' data breaches. The fact is, more data is about to be generated. We are about to enter the age of the IoTs and the Smart City, and it has been predicted that in a few years, there will be billions of devices connected. However, technologies repurposed for the IoTs were not intended for secure communications, leaving networks and data vulnerable.

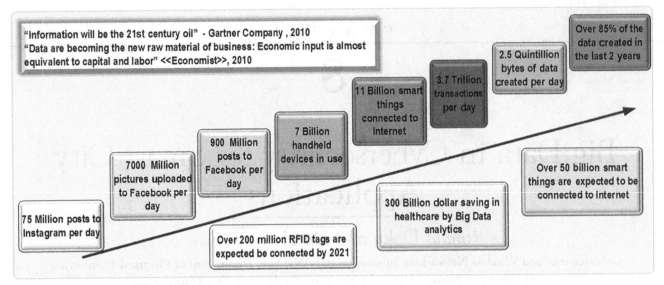

FIG. 1   Big Data is growing constantly.

FIG. 2   Big Data and analytics advantages for different applications.

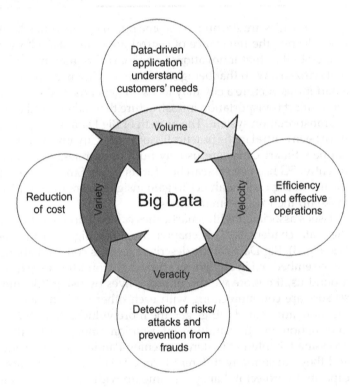

The IoTs will raise security issues because it is being developed rapidly, and there are significant challenges involved in securing it that still need to be addressed. Also, the data needed for use in Smart Cities needs to be accurate, and this has presented the perfect opportunity for cyber criminals to attack. Attackers now focus on altering the data in Smart City applications to mislead the users or applications, which is an attack called data sabotage. This attack deals with the integrity aspect of the Confidentiality, Integrity and Availability (CIA) triad of cybersecurity. This chapter discusses the data integrity and confidentiality issues associated with Smart City applications in the following sections. This chapter also presents a brief review on some of the recent related research on Big Data-enabled Smart City security.

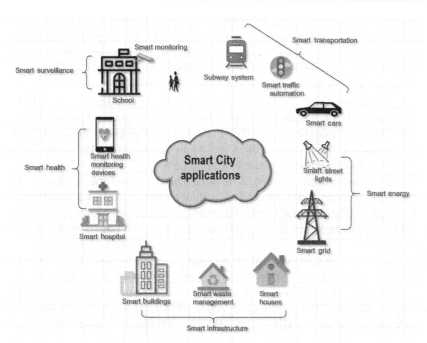

FIG. 3 Smart City applications.

2 BRIEF REVIEW ON BIG DATA-ENABLED CYBERSECURITY IN THE SMART CITY

Big Data has been used for different purposes as shown in Fig. 2. All Smart City applications require robust data gathering and analytics to make informed decisions and to provide secure and privacy aware services. Smart City applications need different methods for securing Smart City data from malicious attacks or cyber criminals [3]. Smart Cities are expected to offer an opportunity to facilitate development, employment, wealth, education, and better social welfare via an amalgamation of careful planning, allied communities, a learned populace, and clever technology. Through creation of Smart Cities, huge data is generated by smart devices and applications, but the gathering of this huge data may pose security hazards that, when unattended, may lead to data abuse or cybercrimes. Also, while examining multipurpose management of Smart City applications using cloud-based platforms, wireless smart-sensors (including noninvasive) promote sharing of information dynamically, thereby facilitating novel user-friendly and secure services for a compatible interface between human beings and the environment [4]. Note that the cyber threats and criminality ought not to deter technological progress, and the capacity to utilize ICT for constructive purposes. Cloud-based computing platforms could facilitate the real-time monitoring and global view for Smart City applications. Existing cloud architectures may not be suitable for all Smart City applications, so we may need to fine tune the cloud architecture to suit the needs and to allow integration of numerous business intelligence platforms for business analytics and integration of data. There are several challenges such as complexity, hyperconnectivity, industrialized hacking, and boundary loss that complicate the engineering predicament of cyberspace in Smart Cities [5]. Smart Cities will be major components in driving a nation's wealth and novelty, as well as the world's economy, and thus Smart City applications must provide optimal safety, security, and resilience. To make Smart Cities smarter and better, agencies need well-educated cybersecurity engineers to join them with needed skill sets to come up with techniques for offering cyber defense solutions to combat advanced cyberattacks.

Smart Cities should also consider both business operation and technical perceptions while evaluating threats and enhancing data security and privacy [6]. As noted, Smart Cities bring in data with affluent information that facilitates clear visibility in the operation of different Smart City applications; however, the adversaries could misuse the data to take advantage of it. Before deploying any Smart City applications, careful examination of cyber threats through modeling and risk evaluations should be carried out by data gathering, processing, and analyzing [7]. It is recommended that the Smart City needs a proper examination of data and its validity, and in-depth examination of the processes involved in information collection for any applications and their operations. Wang et al. [8] discussed a three-layer system of management in support of Smart City mobility by focusing on bus transit. Layer 1 included the application of new Big Data methods for calculation of the travel time of the bus, and demands of passengers, effectively and economically. In Layer 2, the system is comprised of the bus delay causal relationship and the passage transport pattern's network analysis as the two key components of analysis. Layer 3 offers decision support in an interactive visualization setting. It is noted that urbanization in developing nations has led to escalated demand for efficient public transit regardless of inadequate resources, hence the significance of the three-layer system of management in enabling urban planners to assess the effect of their policies and come up with effective solutions.

Barshir and Gill [9] have presented an IoT Big Data Analytics (IBDA) model as a technology solution for Big Data management with an aim of analyzing real-time data obtained from IoT sensors situated within smart buildings. The IBDA framework runs on top of the existing Big Data analytics setting, which makes the model compatible with traditional and emerging Smart City applications, including "IoT-enabled Big Data Analytics for smart buildings" and airplane systems for monitoring the levels of oxygen inside airplanes. Tang et al. [10] have presented a data intensive analysis for Smart City application that collects data from different types of sensors. The proposed model deals with the issues of geodistribution's natural occurrences using a computing model to facilitate latency-sensitive monitoring, location-awareness, and intelligent control. This model utilizes a smart pipeline system of monitoring founded on fiber optic sensors in identifying events capable of threatening the safety of the pipeline. This approach has the potential for practical use in Smart City applications in the future.

Shukla et al. [11] have presented an application of Big Data analytics in establishing a smart transportation system for making data-driven decisions in transportation systems. The deployment of ICT and IoT-enabled applications is a key factor in the establishment of Smart City projects globally. This has resulted in smart transit systems with vast levels of real-time data required to be transmitted, collected, interpreted, analyzed, and stored. The technologies have been associated with the increased efficient application of smart transit systems, which are usually considered economical and socially effectual.

Puthal et al. [12] have presented a Selective Encryption (SEEN) technique in securing big sensing data streams that suits the preferred manifold levels of data integrity and confidentiality. The proposed technique is based on two main concepts: a seamless key refreshment procedure that does not disrupt the encryption or decryption of the data stream; and common shared keys that are usually started and updated by Data Server Manager (DSM) without the need for retransmission. This approach also ensures the privacy of the gathered data through prevention of private information from falling into the hands of the wrong individuals. Another approach offered in Shao et al. [13] provides intelligent processing and application resolution to big surveillance video data based on the occurrence of identification and transmission of information from front-end smart cameras. Video surveillance systems remain a central part of the security and safety of contemporary cities, due to the fact that smart cameras are able to monitor and prealarm abnormal events or behaviors. The proposed framework provides services to constantly prealarm events that pose security risks, to considerably minimize storage capacity of the recorded video in addition to extensively accelerating the process of retrieving the evidence. The application of secure multimedia Big Data in the trust-assisted sensor cloud (TASC) is another aspect of Smart Cities [14]. This approach helps to examine and identify the key issues affecting the achievement of secure multimedia Big Data in TASC. This was achieved by coming up with two forms of TASC: TASC-M (TASC with manifold trust value thresholds) and TASC-S (TASC with one trust value threshold). Zaman et al. [15] have presented a smart neighborhood application with the intent of maintaining an inventive economy in the present era of Big Data.

Hassanein and Oteafy [16] have studied the challenges of big sensed data in the IoT systems. Typically, IoT systems are intrinsically created on data acquired from heterogeneous sources. With the endeavors of collecting more data for improved analytics, a considerable number of IoT systems are initiating key challenges, such as burdening the networking infrastructure with data velocity and sheer volume produced by IoT systems. Also, Big Data is starting to advance into the power industry. Smart grid data is different from other types of Big Data [17], and decisions should be made in real time to avoid power outage. When smart grid companies, as part of the Smart City, require their users to pay bills online, that involves private information of the consumers. In smart grid systems, smart home appliances could leak the lifestyle of the neighbors, which then brings up privacy issues for the neighbors. Similarly, Qiu et al. [18] have studied the heterogeneous IoTs (Het-IoT) by considering four different layers in Het-IoT comprised of networking, cloud computing, sensing, and applications. Het-IoT could help to change people's comprehension of basic computer science values, among other scientific values in Smart City environments.

3 SMART HEALTHCARE SYSTEMS IN SMART CITIES

There are problems with our healthcare system. The cost is rising, the quality of service leaves much to be desired, and the access to timely care still needs to be improved. The population demographics have changed as well.

Millennials are now taking over from the baby boomers. Millennials want things delivered to them, and they seem to be responding well to the idea of having healthcare services brought to them. A smart healthcare system could achieve this by delivering health care to the people without them having to step in a hospital for frequent check ups. This could also ensure the possibility of people handling emergency situations by themselves [19]. This can be accomplished by having doctors, patients, and health insurers share vital information when needed (Fig. 4). A smarter health system would also entail an interconnected healthcare network where health professionals will have updated information about a patient's health records instantaneously. A connected health system would allow doctors to collaborate on diagnosis and treatment plans no matter where they are. This would ensure that, patients receive better quality service. Another advantage of a having a smart healthcare system is the ability to save time and costs, thereby causing medical professionals to shift their attention to focusing on other areas, such as the prevention of disease in a community. Advanced Big Data analytics models can be used to monitor the health of citizens and monitor disease outbreaks. An anomaly detection system that tracks the health of people based on data from the smart health cloud could be a useful tool in the early detection and prevention of disease outbreak. Also, insights derived from Big Data analytics is helping researchers discover new drugs and therapies using fast, reliable supercomputers to test different drug candidates to see what works and what does not. Another example of smart healthcare systems is the ability of a car to be able to call an ambulance faster than a phone in case of a car accident. Devices will be able to automatically deliver important and often life-saving data to hospitals. An ambulance can gather critical information before arriving at the hospital. All these will be able to happen by finding a way to connect many different applications and technologies in one coherent network. An example of a component of the smart health system is a Wireless Body Area Network, which monitors the vitals of an individual remotely. This technology can help monitor an individual's heart rate, body temperature, electrocardiography, and blood pressure, which can all be done in real time. We have now understood that for a smart healthcare system to work effectively, a lot of data has to be generated. There will be vast amounts of data flowing from every imaginable source in healthcare systems. The next section discusses how best to secure this generated data from cyberattacks.

3.1 Securing Smart Healthcare Data

Ensuring the security of sensitive data such as health records is a confidentiality issue. Confidentiality issues could arise in situations where an individual may have mental issues or a sexually transmitted disease that he/she would not want anyone to know about. Data masking, encryption, and access control are the main techniques used for protection and privacy of health data. A lot of research has been done in these areas [20–34]. Other approaches to ensure privacy protection would be taking into account a person's societal importance. The stakes become higher when the individual

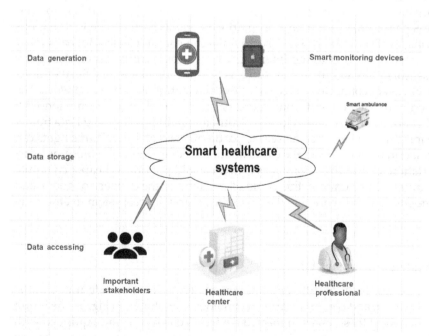

FIG. 4   Typical block diagram of a smart e-health application in a Smart City.

is a known public figure, and thereby susceptible to frequent attacks. This may need to be taken into consideration when transferring personal data on a smart health system. We can classify data based on a person's societal importance and by determining the sensitivity levels of the data [35]. A ranking algorithm can be used to determine attributes within the data that are the most sensitive and require more security because protecting everything securely in the cloud is a difficult task [36, 37]. Further ways of protecting data in a smart health environment are the use of steganography and image cryptography to hide health-related information [38]. Also, for the storing of data on a smart health device, the first data that the user accesses is dummy/decoy data. The dummy data would have similar characteristics to that of the user's data, but with the important attributes being tweaked a little. The decoy/dummy are always retrieved at the beginning, until the system can confirm the identity of the user [39]. The combination of the flexibility of attribute-based encryption and the efficiency of symmetric encryption can be used to secure this data [26]. The encrypted MongoDB approach can be used [40], which utilizes a homomorphic asymmetric cryptosystem that can be used for the encryption of user data and in achieving privacy protection in relational database systems at health centers and on mobile devices. A privacy-preserving dot product has also been used in data mining for a long time as it helps in curbing statistical analysis attacks. It is now being used in Big Data for its anonymous private profile matching, which can be used in mobile healthcare Big Data [41]. Lately, blockchain technology has been emerging as one of the alternatives for providing privacy and security for healthcare data. The bottom line here is that no single approach can provide both security and privacy for health care in the Smart City environment [42].

4 SMART TRANSPORTATION SYSTEMS IN SMART CITIES

The continuous existence and growth of human beings has always been dependent on the transit of people and goods and services from one place to another. Transportation has been driving the society forward. Smart phones began the trend of humans interacting with smart devices, and this has now seen a tremendous growth in other areas, with smart transportation being one. People are now trying to find new ways of transporting goods. The world is becoming more organized and global, and transportation infrastructure is needed to play a vital role in this growth for successful advancement. There is a growing demand for people, goods, and services to be moved around the globe from one place to another. Sensors are now being installed in traffic lights at intersections across various cities. The goal of these sensors is to render real-time monitoring of traffic volume, and have the ability to adjust the timing on traffic lights accordingly. This is done to manage congestion. Information gathered in the form of Big Data can help reduce emissions and bring down pollution when thoroughly analyzed. Sensors found on the roads could measure traffic density and types at different times during the day, as well as the emissions caused by vehicles and the traffic jam caused by different parameters. This data will then be transmitted to the cloud. The traffic monitoring department could use collected data for managing traffic congestion and traffic jams in a real-time manner. This could help to avert traffic jams by directing other vehicles to less packed roads. In terms of smart cars, modern cars come with various distinct electronic units for computing, storing, and communications. These units can communicate with each other over the vehicle's intranet. Vehicles are also able to connect to the Internet, which poses security issues. Also, new vehicles can be attacked easily because the sensors placed in them may serve as possible attack vectors. Furthermore, in an intelligent transportation system, each and every connected car is part of the transportation systems network. The sensors within the cars exchange information with each other. Connected cars can also exchange information with roadside equipment and traffic facilities. All information is sent to a cloud platform for analysis using a Big Data framework, which then turns the data into useful information before being sent to parties in need of them. Traffic lights can also be adjusted accordingly based on information retrieved from the cloud about traffic situations. Mobility, as a service, is seen as the next big thing in transportation. One of the advantages is that it could provide a cheaper commute compared with the regular method of commuting. Furthermore, this could also extend to the delivery of goods and services. Trucks and drones could be become smarter and work together with the Smart City ecosystem to efficiently deliver goods and services [43].

4.1 Securing Smart Transportation Systems in Smart Cities

Transportation systems are becoming connected with its different components (vehicles, roadside units, traffic lights, pedestrian, etc.) and smarter with information and communication technologies, as shown in Fig. 5. The future of transportation systems lies in the data generated by these smart connected devices. Vehicles are now equipped with computer vision systems, various kinds of sensors and cameras. Vehicles communicate with each other by sharing

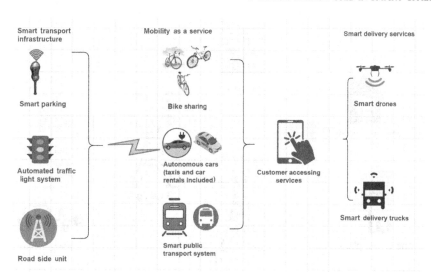

FIG. 5 Components of a smart transportation system.

real-time information about instances on the road such as construction sites, road conditions, and so forth. where data integrity is very crucial. Specifically, data integrity is the main security issue associated with the security of smart transportation. Modified data in autonomous driving vehicles may cause accidents. Like confidentiality, integrity is an important aspect of the CIA triad. It deals with the trustworthiness of data. Trustworthiness can be determined when the origin of the data is known, and the tracking of any modification that has been made. Thus, we first have to confirm the authenticity of the source of the data. Data provenance is a key aspect of the determining data integrity. However, the issue arises when we have to deal with data integrity in real time, as most smart transportation networks do. A good research topic involves addressing data integrity issues in real time. This is because most smart transportation components need to make decisions on the fly. This is a stream processing (processing in real time) issue that comes along with all the data being generated. This data could also use a batch processing approach where the data will be stored and analyzed later. An architecture that merges both batch and stream processing [44] can address the issue of batch and stream processing of data. However, stream and batch processing of data at the same time is difficult because the system cannot recognize data based on their types, which tends to pose veracity issues. To remedy this, a Lambda architecture was proposed. This Lambda architecture approach has the capability to join both batch and stream processing, which is viewed as the next Big Data processing computing system scheme because it merges results from both pipelines. Furthermore, Intrusion Detection Systems in vehicular networks are also an important research area that uses Big Data analytics and machine learning to achieve this.

5 SMART ENERGY GRID IN SMART CITIES

The electric grid has been around for ages. The demand for use of electricity before was less because most homes were as a few light bulbs and a television were the ones that consume electricity owned by most homes. However, times have changed and homes now have a lot of electronic devices. Our traditional grid has continued to be the same, thus there is the need for a change to delivering electricity. The smart grid needs to offer efficiency, reliability, and on-demand supply using bidirectional communications. The smart grid uses two-way communications where electricity and information can be exchanged between utility services and its customers. It is a developing network of communications, controls, computers, automation, and new technologies and tools working together to make the grid more efficient, more reliable, more secure, and greener. The smart grid enables newer technologies to be integrated, such as wind and solar energy production and plug-in electric vehicle charging, as shown in Fig. 6. The smart grid will replace the aging infrastructure of today's grid and utilities and can better communicate with us to help manage our electricity needs. The smart home communicates with the grid and enables consumers to manage their electricity usage by measuring a home's electricity consumption more frequently through a smart meter. Utilities can provide their customers with much better information to manage their electricity bills within a home area network. Furthermore, there are lots of streetlights in cities all over the world. Lighting consumes about 15% of the world's electricity and streetlights are responsible for more than half of a city's energy bill. Cities face budget issues and are also under public

FIG. 6 Different components of a Smart Grid system.

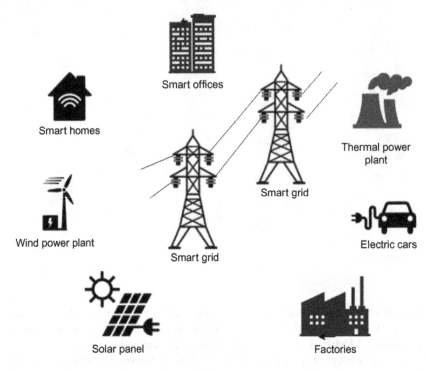

pressure to reduce their carbon footprint. Energy-efficient lighting can play an important role in helping cities address their energy needs. A smart lighting network can monitor and dim streetlights to match traffic flow or program them to turn on and off according to the time of day. The network infrastructure for smart lighting can also support a variety of other applications such as intelligent traffic lighting system. All of these systems will generate data. The capability of Big Data is being brought to the electric grid. The goal is to make these things work in a way that is more convenient with reduced costs and improves the quality of life of people. The insights generated from the Big Data of a smart grid can help cities achieve this. The challenges before us are just as much about data and communication as they are about energy consumption.

5.1 Securing Smart Energy

Smart energy would require both the confidentiality aspects and integrity aspects of the CIA triad for cybersecurity. Big Data is making its way through the power industry. The smart grid has unique characteristics peculiar to it [17, 45] that could take advantage of Big Data analytics. However, Big Data in smart grids has its own security issues as well. Energy grid companies also provide online payments to customers, which means smart grid data involves a user's sensitive information as well. This requires Big Data confidentiality techniques on the data generated [20–34]. The smart grid needs different architecture to provide security and privacy to strengthen the traditional ways of protecting smart grid data. The integrity of the data in a smart grid is one of the vital undertaking parameters. False data injection attacks on meters could lead to blackouts [46]. Artificial intelligence is used to identify compromised meters by being able to predict the expected measurements. Rawat and Bajracharya [47] and Anwar et al. [48] use anomaly detection techniques to identify the abnormal patterns in network power flows in real time to detect attacks.

6 SUMMARY

This chapter has presented different applications that are an integral part of the Smart City that could take advantage of Big Data analytics for security. It has also presented some of the important components of a Smart City, the Big Data it generates, and how that can be used to protect the Smart City applications and ecosystem. Smart City applications, such as smart health care, smart transportation, and smart grids, should ensure security and privacy of their users and data by complying with the CIA security triad. This chapter has listed some of the challenges each application could face and how different approaches can be used to solve those challenges.

References

[1] S.M. Wu, T.-C. Chen, Y.J. Wu, M. Lytras, Smart Cities in Taiwan: a perspective on Big Data applications, Sustainability 10 (1) (2018) 106.

[2] D. Laney, 3D data management: controlling data volume, velocity and variety, META Group Res. Note 6 (70) (2001) 1–6.

[3] S. Harris, Securing big data in our future intelligent cities, in: Proc. of the IET Conference on Future Intelligent Cities, 2014, pp. 8–4.

[4] M. Giacobbe, M. Coco, A. Puliafito, M. Scarpa, A cloud-based access control solution for advanced multi-purpose management in Smart City scenario, in: 2014 International Conference on Smart Computing Workshops (SMARTCOMP Workshops), IEEE, 2014, pp. 35–40.

[5] M.S. John-Green, T. Watson, Safety and Security of the Smart City—when our infrastructure goes online, in: 9th IET International Conference on System Safety and Cyber Security, 2014pp. 1–6. https://doi.org/10.1049/cp.2014.0981.

[6] P. Wang, A. Ali, W. Kelly, Data security and threat modeling for smart city infrastructure, in: 2015 International Conference on Cyber Security of Smart Cities, Industrial Control System and Communications (SSIC), IEEE, 2015, pp. 1–6.

[7] P.A. Pena, D. Sarkar, P. Maheshwari, A Big-Data centric framework for smart systems in the world of Internet of everything, in: 2015 International Conference on Computational Science and Computational Intelligence (CSCI), IEEE, 2015, pp. 306–311.

[8] Y. Wang, S. Ram, F. Currim, E. Dantas, L.A. Sabóia, A Big Data approach for smart transportation management on bus network, in: 2016 IEEE International Smart Cities Conference (ISC2), IEEE, 2016, pp. 1–6.

[9] M.R. Bashir, A.Q. Gill, Towards an IoT Big Data analytics framework: smart buildings systems, in: 2016 IEEE 18th International Conference on High Performance Computing and Communications; IEEE 14th International Conference on Smart City; IEEE 2nd International Conference on Data Science and Systems (HPCC/SmartCity/DSS), IEEE, 2016, pp. 1325–1332.

[10] B. Tang, Z. Chen, G. Hefferman, S. Pei, T. Wei, H. He, Q. Yang, Incorporating intelligence in fog computing for Big Data analysis in smart cities, IEEE Trans. Ind. Inf. 13 (5) (2017) 2140–2150.

[11] S. Shukla, K. Balachandran, V. Sumitha, A framework for smart transportation using Big Data, in: International Conference on ICT in Business Industry & Government (ICTBIG), IEEE, 2016, pp. 1–3.

[12] D. Puthal, X. Wu, S. Nepal, R. Ranjan, J. Chen, SEEN: a selective encryption method to ensure confidentiality for big sensing data streams, IEEE Trans. Big Data (2017)https://doi.org/10.1109/TBDATA.2017.2702172.

[13] Z. Shao, J. Cai, Z. Wang, Smart monitoring cameras driven intelligent processing to big surveillance video data, IEEE Trans. Big Data 4 (1) (2018) 105–116.

[14] C. Zhu, L. Shu, V.C. Leung, S. Guo, Y. Zhang, L.T. Yang, Secure multimedia Big Data in trust-assisted sensor-cloud for smart city, IEEE Commun. Mag. 55 (12) (2017) 24–30.

[15] H.B. Zaman, A. Ahmad, N.A. Hamid, A.K. Sin, A. Hussain, M. Hannan, H.M. Saad, Integrated smart neighborhood framework and application to sustain an innovative digital economy in the 4IR and Big Data era, in: 2017 3rd International Conference on Science in Information Technology (ICSITech), IEEE, 2017, pp. 7–12.

[16] H.S. Hassanein, S.M. Oteafy, Big sensed data challenges in the Internet of Things, in: 2017 13th International Conference on Distributed Computing in Sensor Systems (DCOSS), IEEE, 2017, p. 207, 208.

[17] J. Zhao, Y. Wang, Y. Xia, Analysis of information security of electric power Big Data and its countermeasures, in: 2016 12th International Conference on Computational Intelligence and Security (CIS), IEEE, 2016, pp. 243–248.

[18] T. Qiu, N. Chen, K. Li, M. Atiquzzaman, W. Zhao, How can heterogeneous Internet of Things build our future: a survey, IEEE Commun. Surv. Tutorials 20 (3) (2018) 2011–2027.

[19] S.P. Mohanty, U. Choppali, E. Kougianos, Everything you wanted to know about smart cities: the Internet of Things is the backbone, IEEE Consum. Electron. Mag. 5 (3) (2016) 60–70.

[20] J. Kepner, V. Gadepally, P. Michaleas, N. Schear, M. Varia, A. Yerukhimovich, R.K. Cunningham, Computing on masked data: a high performance method for improving Big Data veracity, in: 2014 IEEE High Performance Extreme Computing Conference (HPEC), IEEE, 2014, pp. 1–6.

[21] D. Wang, B. Guo, Y. Shen, S.-J. Cheng, Y.-H. Lin, A faster fully homomorphic encryption scheme in Big Data, in: 2017 IEEE 2nd International Conference on Big Data Analysis (ICBDA), IEEE, 2017, pp. 345–349.

[22] B. Cui, B. Zhang, K. Wang, A data masking scheme for sensitive Big Data based on format-preserving encryption, in: 2017 IEEE International Conference on Computational Science and Engineering (CSE) and Embedded and Ubiquitous Computing (EUC), vol. 1, IEEE, 2017, pp. 518–524.

[23] T.B. Patil, G.K. Patnaik, A.T. Bhole, Big Data privacy using fully homomorphic non-deterministic encryption, in: 2017 IEEE 7th International Advance Computing Conference (IACC), IEEE, 2017, pp. 138–143.

[24] M. Li, S. Yu, K. Ren, W. Lou, Securing personal health records in cloud computing: patient-centric and fine-grained data access control in multi-owner settings, in: SecureComm, vol. 10, Springer, 2010, pp. 89–106.

[25] T. Yang, P. Shen, X. Tian, C. Chen, A fine-grained access control scheme for Big Data based on classification attributes, in: 2017 IEEE 37th International Conference on Distributed Computing Systems Workshops (ICDCSW), IEEE, 2017, pp. 238–245.

[26] S. Pérez, J.L. Hernández-Ramos, D. Pedone, D. Rotondi, L. Straniero, A.F. Skarmeta, A digital envelope approach using attribute-based encryption for secure data exchange in IoT scenarios, in: Global Internet of Things Summit (GIoTS), IEEE, 2017, pp. 1–6.

[27] A. Al-Mamun, K. Salah, S. Al-Maadeed, T.R. Sheltami, BigCrypt for Big Data encryption, in: 2017 Fourth International Conference on Software Defined Systems (SDS), IEEE, 2017, pp. 93–99.

[28] X. Dong, R. Li, H. He, W. Zhou, Z. Xue, H. Wu, Secure sensitive data sharing on a Big Data platform, Tsinghua Sci. Technol. 20 (1) (2015) 72–80.

[29] A. Sharma, D. Sharma, Big Data protection via neural and quantum cryptography, in: 2016 3rd International Conference on Computing for Sustainable Global Development (INDIACom), IEEE, 2016, pp. 3701–3704.

[30] C. Zhao, J. Liu, Novel group key transfer protocol for Big Data security, in: 2015 IEEE Advanced Information Technology, Electronic and Automation Control Conference (IAEAC), IEEE, 2015, pp. 161–165.

[31] S. Almuhammadi, A. Amro, Double-hashing operation mode for encryption, in: 2017 IEEE 7th Annual Computing and Communication Workshop and Conference (CCWC), IEEE, 2017, pp. 1–7.

[32] A. Kulkarni, C. Shea, H. Homayoun, T. Mohsenin, Less: Big Data sketching and encryption on low power platform, in: Proceedings of the Conference on Design, Automation & Test in Europe, European Design and Automation Association, 2017, pp. 1635–1638.

[33] A. Al-Shomrani, F. Fathy, K. Jambi, Policy enforcement for Big Data security, in: 2017 2nd International Conference on Anti-Cyber Crimes (ICACC), IEEE, 2017, pp. 70–74.

[34] A. Soceanu, M. Vasylenko, A. Egner, T. Muntean, Managing the privacy and security of eHealth data, in: 2015 20th International Conference on Control Systems and Computer Science (CSCS), IEEE, 2015, pp. 439–446.

[35] M.R. Islam, M. Habiba, M.I.I. Kashem, A framework for providing security to personal healthcare records, in: 2017 International Conference on Networking, Systems and Security (NSysS), IEEE, 2017, pp. 168–173.

[36] R. Achana, R.S. Hegadi, T. Manjunath, A novel data security framework using E-MOD for Big Data, in: 2015 IEEE International WIE Conference on Electrical and Computer Engineering (WIECON-ECE), IEEE, 2015, pp. 546–551.

[37] S.-H. Kim, N.-U. Kim, T.-M. Chung, Attribute relationship evaluation methodology for Big Data security, in: 2013 International Conference on IT Convergence and Security (ICITCS), IEEE, 2013, pp. 1–4.

[38] A. Unal, Security in Big Data of medical records, in: 2014 Conference on IT in Business, Industry and Government (CSIBIG), IEEE, 2014, pp. 1–2.

[39] H.A. Al-Hamid, S.M.M. Rahman, M.S. Hossain, A. Almogren, A. Alamri, A security model for preserving the privacy of medical Big Data in a healthcare cloud using a fog computing facility with pairing-based cryptography, IEEE Access 5 (2017) 22313–22328.

[40] G. Xu, Y. Ren, H. Li, D. Liu, Y. Dai, K. Yang, CryptMDB: a practical encrypted MongoDB over Big Data, in: 2017 IEEE International Conference on Communications (ICC), IEEE, 2017, pp. 1–6.

[41] C. Hu, Y. Huo, Efficient privacy-preserving dot-product computation for mobile Big Data, IET Commun. 11 (5) (2016) 704–712.

[42] X. Yue, H. Wang, D. Jin, M. Li, W. Jiang, Healthcare data gateways: found healthcare intelligence on blockchain with novel privacy risk control, J. Med. Syst. 40 (10) (2016) 218.

[43] D.B. Rawat, C. Bajracharya, Vehicular Cyber Physical Systems: Adaptive Connectivity and Security, Springer, New York, NY, 2017.

[44] H.H. Huang, H. Liu, Big Data machine learning and graph analytics: current state and future challenges, in: 2014 IEEE International Conference on Big Data (Big Data), IEEE, 2014, pp. 16–17.

[45] J. Hu, A.V. Vasilakos, Energy Big Data analytics and security: challenges and opportunities, IEEE Trans. Smart Grid 7 (5) (2016) 2423–2436.

[46] K. Khanna, B.K. Panigrahi, A. Joshi, AI-based approach to identify compromised meters in data integrity attacks on smart grid, IET Gener. Transm. Distrib. 12 (5) (2017) 1052–1066.

[47] D.B. Rawat, C. Bajracharya, Detection of false data injection attacks in smart grid communication systems, IEEE Signal Process. Lett. 22 (10) (2015) 1652–1656.

[48] A. Anwar, A.N. Mahmood, Z. Tari, Ensuring data integrity of OPF module and energy database by detecting changes in power flow patterns in smart grids, IEEE Trans. Ind. Inf. 13 (6) (2017) 3299–3311.

9

Free Public Wi-Fi Security in a Smart City Context—An End User Perspective

C. Louw and B. Von Solms
University of Johannesburg, Johannesburg, South Africa

1 INTRODUCTION TO WI-FI—AN END USER'S PERSPECTIVE

With migration and growing population numbers placing increasing pressure on urban settlements to deliver improved services, harvesting the power that information and communication technologies (ICTs) have to offer to optimize not only various service delivery processes, but also the urban dweller's participation therein [1], becomes an obvious choice. At the same time, the United Nations Special Rapporteur report in 2011 referred to access to the Internet as an essential part of freedom of expression, and in 2016, the United Nations Human Rights Council released a nonbinding resolution condemning international disruption of Internet access by governments [2].

In this context, many jurisdictions have recognized Internet access as a basic human right, resulting in Internet access gradually becoming a necessary utility on par with that of running water and electricity. Naturally, the inclusion of this resource becomes vital in current and future smart city developments, with certain municipalities already having acknowledged that improving citizens' access to online information and services, and engaging them in policy and decision-making, enhance local democracy [3].

Furthermore, as participatory action and engagement of urban dwellers plays an important role in the success of smart city initiatives and the smart city model as a whole [1], free, public Wi-Fi is a viable option that may be employed to advance this endeavor. Smart city Wi-Fi can not only act as a gateway to Internet connectivity, but arguably also grant urban dwellers a voice that can be heard as smart city development and optimization efforts progress, thereby improving the quality of life for all.

Various types of end users may form part of this urban dweller collective, each benefitting from smart city Wi-Fi offerings in a unique way. Freelancers, for example, have been offered new ways to do their work, often using different Wi-Fi locales for different phases of their work [4]. Furthermore, Wi-Fi locales may offer entrepreneurs opportunities for co-working, which further contributes to the development of informal interaction, social support, collaboration, innovation, and eventual job creation [4].

As urban areas are typically more densely populated than rural areas, urban smartphone users may find that some parts of the broadband network can become congested at peak load, resulting in delayed and slow service [5]. As a result, Wi-Fi offloading has become increasingly popular among mobile network providers in which the offloading of data traffic to Wi-Fi networks alleviates the load on mobile networks [6]. In certain cases, up to 30% of mobile traffic could potentially be offloaded to already deployed smart city Wi-Fi infrastructure, possibly resulting in better quality of service for urban smartphone users, an increase in clients for providers [7], and a reduction of the possible over-investment in broadband peak-load capacity [5]. Smart city Wi-Fi offerings may also enhance a smart city's attractiveness to an international audience thereby contributing to its stature as a smart tourism destination of choice [8].

From this discussion it becomes clear that when information and services are offered online, the number of potential outcomes the Internet has to offer increases [9]. When looking at smart cities specifically, this creates new potential for engaging local communities [5] of both a permanent (residents) and temporary (visitors, tourists, etc.) nature. Smart city Wi-Fi offerings may thus be to the advantage of numerous benefactors, including the smart city itself.

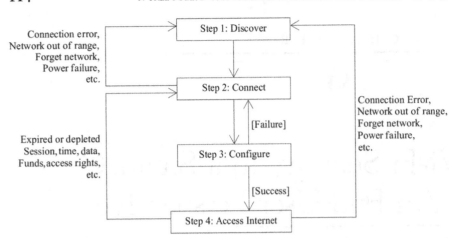

FIG. 1   User journey of connecting to a generic Wi-Fi network (by the authors).

While various stakeholders (discussed in more detail in Section 3.1) may be responsible for the initiation and eventual provisioning of Wi-Fi in an urban environment, it is still the responsibility of the end user to actively connect to, configure, and make use of the resource with their own Wi-Fi enabled device(s). In order to gain a better understanding of the steps involved in this process and to ensure that the reader may follow along in subsequent discussions of this chapter, Fig. 1 illustrates the typical user journey involved in connecting to a generic Wi-Fi network with a Wi-Fi enabled device.

The process of connecting to a particular (available) Wi-Fi network commences in step 1 by activating the Wi-Fi scanning or discovery functionality of a Wi-Fi-enabled device, such as a smartphone, for example. This typically allows the device to discover available networks within its vicinity, thereby producing a list of active Wi-Fi networks that may be connected to. Any user can thus wirelessly access the network from anywhere in range of the wireless access point (WAP), also known as the Wi-Fi hotspot. Users may thus have to adjust themselves and their devices to ensure that they are within the range of their desired hotspot, with ranges varying from one device to another.

By identifying the desired Wi-Fi network name (also known as the network's service set identifier or SSID) from a list of available networks, an end user manually selects the network they wish to connect to (for a first-time connection). In the event of an error (such as failure to obtain an Internet Protocol (IP) address (for further details see Forshaw [10])) occurring, steps 1 and 2 are repeated until a connection can be established.

Once a connection is established with the desired network, step 3 involves configuring the connection. In certain cases, configuration may be done automatically between devices while in other cases, end users may be required to manually configure a connection themselves (discussed in more detail in Section 4). Once configuration is successful, the user is connected to the Internet and may start making use of the resource until their access is revoked or they are disconnected from the network.

In the event of a configuration failure, however, the user may remain connected to the network, although Internet access (step 4) is not granted until successful configuration (step 3) takes place.

In certain instances, Wi-Fi networks that had previously been discovered by an end user's device, and successfully configured and connected to, may be stored and remembered. This allows the device to automatically reconnect to the network if it becomes available again, however, from a security perspective, this may render a device vulnerable and exposed to possible outsider attacks (as will be discussed in Section 2).

While numerous additional steps may be introduced to the process of connecting to a Wi-Fi network, the 4 steps consisting of discovery, connection, configuration, and Internet access, broadly summarize a user's journey through almost any Wi-Fi connection process.

Despite the relatively simplistic nature of this process from an end user's perspective, numerous opportunities for exploitation, thereby exposing or intercepting valuable end user data, are possible. This is a cause for concern as such behavior may undermine the advancement of smart city initiatives at large. This subsequently forms the topic of discussion in the next section.

2 TYPICAL WI-FI ATTACKS/VULNERABILITIES: AN OVERVIEW

With a better understanding of the typical process involved in connecting to a Wi-Fi network from an end user's perspective, we now proceed by identifying a subset of Wi-Fi attacks and vulnerabilities that may possibly be exploited by cybercriminals during a user's Wi-Fi journey. As previously mentioned, security becomes a prominent concern as far as smart city Wi-Fi is concerned, as these facilities may not only attract the attention of the end user, but also that of the abuser (cybercriminal). As such, end users may be negatively affected by making use of smart city Wi-Fi that, in essence, has the prime purpose of being uplifting, supportive, informative, and empowering.

As numerous different kinds of attacks may occur during numerous different phases of an end user's Wi-Fi journey, various opportunities exist for cybercriminals to exploit the process. We introduce the reader to some of the most basic, yet common, types of outsider attacks including the likes of sniffing, evil twin attacks, and rogue networks/honeypots, while also discussing unintentional insider mistakes that may render the network vulnerable, such as the introduction of rogue access points and mishandled security setups.

Initial preventative measures and remedial recommendations are suggested from both the end user and smart city Wi-Fi management perspectives, also pointing out why the introduction of appropriate documents and policies is important before a smart city Wi-Fi service is made available.

2.1 Typical Wi-Fi Attacks and Vulnerabilities

With numerous Wi-Fi hotspots being required to create a sufficiently comprehensive coverage area within an urban settlement, numerous potential points of weakness are subsequently also introduced. Due to the public nature of these hotspots, they present ideal candidates for exploitation by outside (ab)users, although mistakes made by inside service provisioning/management may possibly also render parts of the network vulnerable. It is thus important to understand the typical attacks and vulnerabilities that can be introduced from both these perspectives in order to minimize, or ideally, mitigate them.

2.1.1 Outsider Attacks

2.1.1.1 Packet Analyzing/Sniffing

Packet analyzers, sometimes also referred to as packet sniffers, allow the capturing or monitoring of network traffic through the installation of custom software on a device. Generally, a device's network connection ignores traffic that is not addressed to it, but by making use of sniffing software, the device can pick up everything that is being transmitted over the network. Although this technique may be used in a non-malicious way from a maintenance, monitoring, and troubleshooting perspective [11], it may also be abused to inspect data packets and extract valuable information such as passwords, IP addresses, and so forth. This, in turn, may result in the launching of more sophisticated types of attacks including:

- *Spoofing Attacks*: A spoofing attack occurs when a packet sniffer impersonates another device or user on a network. This is typically done in order to launch attacks against network hosts, steal data, spread malware, or bypass access controls that have been put in place [12]. Furthermore, several different types of spoofing attacks may be utilized in this endeavor, including IP address spoofing attacks, Address Resolution Protocol (ARP) spoofing attacks, and Domain Name System (DNS) server spoofing attacks.
- *Session Sidejacking*: A session sidejacking attack allows packet sniffers to steal session cookies or variables, thereby ultimately hijacking a user's session (on a particular social network for example) and impersonating them.
- *Man-in-the-Middle Attack*: A man-in-the-middle attack, often abbreviated as MITM, MitM, MiM, or MIM, allows a packet sniffer to redirect all traffic between two parties communicating over the same network, without the end parties being aware of it [13]. This ultimately allows the cybercriminal to insert themselves into a conversation between these two parties, impersonating both parties, and gaining access to information that the two parties were trying to send to each other. The information may simply be intercepted and sent along to the intended recipient, or the information may be intercepted and modified, and the modified information may then be sent along.

In general, packet analyzing/sniffing is difficult to detect, which mostly means that in practice, it is rarely done or even attempted [14]. This subsequently makes public Wi-Fi hotspots an ideal target for this kind of attack, with sniffing tools such as Wireshark (https://www.wireshark.org/) being readily available to the general public for download.

2.1.1.2 Evil Twins

Evil twins are carefully designed and implemented to look and act exactly like a legitimate Wi-Fi network and/or known AP. This is due to cybercriminals being able to create a clone of a particular AP that is possibly already known and trusted by end users and their devices, resulting in an identical replica. When end users make the decision to connect via this AP, however, they're actually connecting to the evil twin, which then proceeds to send user information to the cybercriminal instead [15].

2.1.1.3 Rogue Networks/Honeypots

Rogue networks, or honeypots, typically masquerade as a legitimate AP and entice end users with the appeal of open, free Internet access requiring no password or other configuration (thereby bypassing step 3 in Fig. 1). Drawn by the appeal of instant, free Internet access, users may be more inclined to join this particular network and, unknowingly, have their data sniffed (as discussed in Section 2.1.1.1) by the cybercriminals that have intentionally set up this trap.

2.1.2 Insider Mistakes/Vulnerabilities

2.1.2.1 Rogue Access Points

Rogue APs are additional access points that have been installed on a pre-existing network. These APs generally come in the form of wireless routers, installed by well-meaning employees who intend to expand a network's reach, thereby granting more users access to the particular Wi-Fi network [15]. Often, however, these routers may not be configured properly, which results in them being easy to break into, even though the network itself might be secure.

Rogue APs have been used in several attacks, such as packet sniffing and man-in-the-middle attacks (as discussed in Section 2.1.1.1), with these vulnerabilities becoming a serious security threat to users in public and enterprise networks. Moreover, it is easy to install malicious APs using mobile devices and networks, with existing solutions not effectively detecting these rogue APs, thereby introducing potential additional points of vulnerability [16].

2.1.2.2 Mishandled Wi-Fi Security Setups

With numerous technical advancements being made relating to network and device security, user error often still is identified as one of the most common threats [15]. As such, when making use of a public Wi-Fi network, end users cannot operate under the assumption that employees who have set up the network have taken every step necessary to ensure data protection. Often times, employees are the ones responsible for choosing to just leave default usernames and passwords on a Wi-Fi router, subsequently making the network incredibly easy to access [15].

A study conducted by Zafft and Agu [17] further found that on average, 45 percent of Wi-Fis at the city-level, in eighteen cities within the United States, were unsecure. These unsecure Wi-Fi networks were identified as those that do not use Wired Equivalent Privacy (WEP), Wi-Fi Protected Access II (WPA2), or any (802.11) Wi-Fi security standard. As such, these networks, and subsequently the end users, are laid bare to various kinds of attacks due to negligible end user setup procedures that cannot provide even basic security.

2.2 Remedial/Preventative Recommendations

With our discussions in Sections 2.1.1 and 2.1.2 on public Wi-Fi security concerns having been approached from both an outsider and insider perspective, it is equally important to point out ways in which such attacks or vulnerabilities may be mitigated from both these perspectives.

2.2.1 End User Wi-Fi Security Advice

By making sure that the most recent device software has been installed on their device, end users ensure that they receive the most recent security updates and patches to first protect their device that they wish to connect to public Wi-Fi, as well as its operating system (OS).

Additionally, end users may install antivirus software on their device, many of which not only have a free version available, but also Wi-Fi network security shields. Additional software installations that may offer further protection also include a firewall and a Virtual Private Network (VPN).

By confirming a free Wi-Fi network's name (SSID) with the expected provider, instances of connecting to the wrong network (evil twin or rogue network) may be avoided. In the event of a website being accessed while making use of free Wi-Fi, end users should ensure that a secure browsing session is set up, indicated by "https" in the uniform resource locator (URL) of the website.

In general, end users should also minimize the number of sensitive transactions that they perform while connected to public Wi-Fi. Lastly, in the event of Wi-Fi not actively being used on a device, end users should take care to deactivate the Wi-Fi scanning operation on their device. This may eliminate the device automatically connecting to an evil twin or rogue network while the end user is unaware of it.

2.2.2 Provider/Management Wi-Fi Security Advice

Similar to that of the end user, Wi-Fi provisioning or management entities should first ensure that the most recent device software has been installed across relevant network components to receive the latest security updates and patches.

Default or easy to guess values (such as user names and passwords) should also be changed when configuring Wi-Fi routers, while secure protocols should be used to ensure that data is encrypted before being transmitted across the network. Examples of possible secure protocols that may be implemented include Hyper Text Transfer Protocol Secure (HTTPS) (see Forshaw [10] and Oppliger [18]), Secure File Transfer Protocol (SFTP) (see Long et al. [19]), and Secure Shell (SSH) (see Oppliger [20]).

In the event of an unsecure protocol being used, Wi-Fi providers may still protect the network and data that it transmits by using encryption software prior to initiating the transmission of data. As such, VPN (Virtual Private Network) (see Lewis [21]), VNC (Virtual Network Computing) Protocol (see Roebuck [22]), and RDP (Remote Desktop Protocol) (see Forshaw [10]) may be used to provide encrypted, remote computing. Although Feil [23] found that mutually authenticated, encrypted VPN tunnels are acceptably secure for most networks, migrating to next-generation solutions, when available, is paramount. Ensuring that up to date software and protocols are used at all times is thus key.

As it currently stands, most routers come with the ability to enable one of numerous wireless encryption standards which include: Wired Equivalent Privacy (WEP), Wi-Fi Protected Access (WPA), or Wi-Fi Protected Access 2 (WPA2). These may then be used in conjunction with a Pre-shared Key (PSK) and/or Temporal Key Integrity Protocol (TKIP) configuration. The following list presents these Wi-Fi protocols and configurations in the order of most secure to least secure [24]:

1. WPA2 Enterprise (802.1x Radius)
2. WPA2-PSK + AES
3. WPA-PSK + AES or WPA-PSK + TKIP
4. WPA + TKIP
5. WEP
6. Open Network (no security)

While choosing the most secure configuration option is ideal, it may not always be possible, and depends greatly on the deployment environment and infrastructure capabilities. An effort should, however, be made to provide the most secure router configuration possible.

In addition to using secure protocols and encrypting data, optimizing a network structure by implementing switch technology rather than hub technology may introduce an additional level of security [25]. A switch typically transmits a message that it receives only to its intended recipient on a network whereas a hub transmits the messages it receives across the entire network. Switches are subsequently inherently more secure than hubs, and therefore recommended.

Regularly sniffing networks using wireless sniffer software may also assist with gaining an overview of a network from the perspective of an attacker. This may advance the discovery of not only sniffing attack vulnerabilities, but also active sniffing attacks that are still in progress [25]. Additionally, by ensuring that no rogue access points are present on the network, the introduction of additional weak points may be minimized.

Finally, due to the public nature and potential high volume usage of smart city Wi-Fi, complete threat or vulnerability detection and prevention may never be achieved. Similarly, the chosen threats/vulnerabilities and advice given in this section are by no means exhaustive and do not provide a guarantee on ensuring the safety of any Wi-Fi network. As such, the focus should not be on determining if an attack will happen, but rather, when an attack will happen, and designing response mechanisms accordingly.

The implementation and integration of an end user information security portal may thus prove to be a complementary asset to smart city Wi-Fi in this regard.

2.3 End User Information Security Portal Development

The rapid evolution of technology combined with the advancements in vulnerability exploitation techniques demand a new way of approaching the problem of ensuring information security in smart cities. With end users being a common component in any smart city, this may provide an opportunity to approach the problem from a fresh perspective, that is, from the perspective of the end user.

To assist in this endeavor, there is a need for an efficient, centralized and rapid communication mechanism to identify and warn end users of possible threats so that they may take action accordingly. By implementing and integrating an information security portal with the end user Wi-Fi journey, important information pertaining to possible network vulnerabilities may be communicated directly to end users as they make use of the service.

Additionally, pertinent information relating to Wi-Fi usage, training, awareness, and so forth may also be provided through such a portal, thereby possibly minimizing cybercrime incidences from an end user perspective. A focus should thus be on delivering a well-designed electronic participation tool/services to complement smart city Wi-Fi provisioning, taking into account citizens' needs, thereby engaging them in public affairs such as information security [3].

In the event where the deliverance of such a portal is not possible, social networks may seem a viable alternative option to be used to reach and engage a large audience. Historically, however, the openness of these platforms has instilled doubt on whether relevant discussion brokering is capable of successfully reaching all core stakeholders [26]. As a result, by implementing a user portal, relevant information may be communicated specifically to active and continuously engaging stakeholders that make use of a particular Wi-Fi network. User portals may thus become a core part of the Wi-Fi configuration and user authentication (step 3 in Fig. 1) or usage (step 4 in Fig. 1) phases, thereby seamlessly blending in with the overall user experience.

Despite the contribution that the introduction of such a user portal may have, however, the overreaching discussion in this section points out that mistakes, and subsequently also vulnerability, in public Wi-Fi networks may be introduced from both the end user and designated Wi-Fi provider's perspectives. In the event of losses being suffered by end users while making use of the Wi-Fi provisioned by the smart city specifically, the end user may blame the smart city for their loss and as a result, they may feel that the smart city needs to be held liable for the damages.

As such, the importance of ensuring the inclusion of appropriate documents and policies (such as terms and conditions, a disclaimer, privacy statement, etc.) in the delivery of smart city Wi-Fi comes under scrutiny next.

3 SERVICE DELIVERY DOCUMENTS AND POLICIES

According to Kletz [27], if a task is completed once a year it never becomes routine, and mistakes of forgetfulness are less likely. This observation is very much applicable in the context of making use of smart city Wi-Fi as end users may become so accustomed to the procedure involved when connecting to this resource, they may miss some of the smaller details that could indicate a possible security breach, even if they are well aware of the impeding dangers and how to identify them. By letting the operation become almost automatic, it is not monitored by the conscious mind and, if for any reason the normal pattern is interrupted, a step may be left out, a warning missed, or the task performed wrong [27].

Similarly, end users that do not have any experience with Wi-Fi, smartphones, or any other piece of technology that may be used to access the Internet, may remain blissfully unaware of possible security breaches and lurking dangers, thereby inadvertently exposing themselves and their data to cybercriminals. As free Wi-Fi provisioning by smart cities may be the only means of connecting to the Internet for many of these end users, a certain level of trust in the service is not only given, but also expected, by default. Furthermore, by shifting the delivery of numerous core smart city services to an online context, inexperienced users are, to a certain extent, forced to adopt the use of this technology to assure the delivery of daily necessities. They may indirectly thus be forced to make a mistake.

In both the case of an experienced and inexperienced end user, there is thus an inherent risk of suffering a loss by making use of smart city Wi-Fi. In the event of such a loss being of great consequence, end users may hold the smart city responsible, subsequently seeking compensation. This may become an expensive exercise for both smart cities and end users alike, ultimately proving to be detrimental to the smart city concept as a whole. Liability in the event of loss is a topic that should thus be carefully considered before public Wi-Fi is made available to end users in general.

When, once again, looking at smart cities specifically, this task may become slightly more complex as numerous stakeholders, including industry partners, may be responsible for the provisioning of Wi-Fi. Nevertheless, the investment risk in building such an extensive infrastructure is high, due to uncertainties in service revenues and the major capital investment needed to achieve the critical mass of Wi-Fi hotspots and their combined overall footprint [28]. As such, incurring losses from any of the two stakeholders' perspective could prove to be catastrophic.

It is important to therefore understand which stakeholders may typically be involved in the creation of such Wi-Fi infrastructure, also considering viable alternatives, consequences, and response mechanisms that should be put in place.

3.1 Smart City Wi-Fi Provisioning

Smart city Wi-Fi opens up opportunities not only for smart cities to engage with end users, but possibly also for corporate or industry sponsors to engage with or advertise to the same end users. This may prove to be beneficial to all parties involved, although from a business perspective, it may be seen as granting monopoly to a certain service provider or sponsor. Problems with competition policy may thus arise in this instance and such cases have already been recorded in North America and Europe in particular [29]. Awarding contracts to third parties in provisioning Wi-Fi to a smart city should thus be managed in a transparent and fair manner to avoid any controversy or negative connotations being associated with the service.

Numerous combinations of industry partners may be used by smart cities to assist in the endeavor of providing Wi-Fi at various dedicated locations. Drawing on community expertise, open-source software, and non-hierarchical organizational strategies, community wireless networks (CWN) may also be used to engage volunteers or sponsors in building networks for public Internet access and community media [5]. Naturally, a return on investment is expected in such a case [30], and as a result, numerous Wi-Fi revenue models, depending on the sponsoring entity, are summarized in Table 1.

While operators may benefit from free Wi-Fi offerings by incurring additional sales beyond that of the initial free bundle that is offered, venue owners may benefit by attracting patrons with the convenience of free Wi-Fi, while also retaining visitors for longer periods of time as they make use of the Wi-Fi on offer at the premises [30].

Advertisers are offered an opportunity to directly interact with end users within a certain geographic location, while analytics users may obtain valuable statistical data that may be used in further market research. Lastly, city councils, municipalities, and governments are offered an opportunity to enhance the attractiveness of a particular venue, city, province, or country by strategically integrating the delivery of free Wi-Fi [30].

While sponsors may intend smart city Wi-Fi networks to be used for the greater good, end users may feel that the smart city or participating sponsor of the Wi-Fi should be held liable, in the case of them suffering a loss while making use of the service. Moreover, in the event of an end user suffering tremendous loss while making use of smart city Wi-Fi, a sponsoring entity may choose to withdraw from the Wi-Fi delivery initiative in the interest of self-preservation and, once again, this may be to the detriment of a smart city initiative as a whole.

As the prevention of such incidences from a technical point of view may prove to be an impossible task from both a smart city and end user's perspective (as discussed in Section 2), the introduction of appropriate documents and policies becomes a key component in defining responsibility (or non-responsibility) in the event of loss incurred while making use of a smart city Wi-Fi service.

While the requirements of each smart city may differ based on the sponsor of the Wi-Fi, the main documents or policies that should be considered for inclusion in any free Wi-Fi service include:

1. Terms and conditions
2. Acceptable use policy
3. Privacy policy

TABLE 1   Wi-Fi Sponsor and Revenue Model

Sponsor	Value obtained
Operator	Offers an initial free data bundle (per venue) to encourage end users to buy additional premium data when the free bundle runs out. This business model depends on a certain conversion ratio being achieved.
Venue owner	The owner of a small venue, such as a café or restaurant sponsors Wi-Fi to attract or retain patrons for prolonged periods of time. The Wi-Fi is seen as part of the value offered to the end user (for example, in a hotel or at a conference center). The venue may be large (a shopping mall, public beach or tourist precinct), and be co-sponsored by a group of commercial interests.
Advertiser	An advertiser pays the operator to interact with end users who, as a targeted audience, do not pay for access.
Analytics user	A company pays for legitimate access to end user information, derived from sponsored Wi-Fi access systems. These systems can build sophisticated customer information and aggregate trends, based on variables, such as customer Internet use behavior, and location usage information.
Government	A city council, municipality, or local, provincial, or national government can sponsor Wi-Fi to promote socio-political or economic objectives at the level of a venue, city, province, or country.

From C. Geerdts, A. Gillwald, E. Calandro, C. Chair, M. Moyo, B. Rademan, Developing Smart Public Wi-Fi in South Africa. (2016). Available from: https://www.researchictafrica.net/ publications/Other_publications/2016_Public_Wi-Fi_Policy_Paper_-_Developing_Smart_Public_Wi-Fi_in_South_Africa.pdf (Accessed 4 February 2018).

Of course, not all documents are required, and the combination of required documents will depend on a smart city's (and the appropriate sponsors involved) approach in delivering free Wi-Fi. Overall, however, the chosen connectivity conditions and policies should be geared toward promoting the right of all citizens to access the Internet, regardless of their ability to pay for the service [31]. Furthermore, free and unrestricted access without any sacrifices to ensuring privacy should be the guiding principles in such a policy implementation.

Ensuring that end users accept the required policies before making use of the provisioned Wi-Fi is strongly advisable. This can be done during the configuration phase (step 3 in Fig. 1) by making use of two main techniques:

1. *Inferred Policy Acceptance*: By automatically implying "by making use of this service you agree to the following…" end users indirectly accept the documents and policies as set out by the sponsor, as soon as they start making use of the Wi-Fi.
2. *Explicit Policy Acceptance*: By explicitly requiring the end user to indicate their acceptance of documents and policies before making use of a Wi-Fi service, for example, by clicking on a text box that states "I hereby accept the following …", their active participation is ensured. As such, more control is granted to the sponsor, as users who do not explicitly accept the documents and policies are not granted access to the Internet. They may therefore be successfully logged in and connected to the network (step 2 in Fig. 1), but as mentioned in Section 1, this may not necessarily mean that they may make use of the Internet (step 4 in Fig. 1).

Ensuring the multi-language provisioning of required documents and policies may become a contentious issue in this case, as end users ultimately need to understand what they are agreeing to. With smart cities being a place of residence for numerous international inhabitants, it should be kept in mind that a smart city's tourism appeal may possibly draw an even wider, linguistically diverse tourist audience as a smart tourism destination [8]. Careful consideration should thus be given to the supported languages of translation for documents and policies, taking into account this international appeal.

Foreign language support, specifically for Chinese, English, French, German, Japanese, and Spanish has been identified on some of the world's leading official destination websites [32]. The same approach may be taken when implementing a smart city destination's Wi-Fi portals that subsequently provide end users with the documents and policies that require their acceptance. While translation may require additional skills and expertise from a development or translation team, instant translate approaches provided by website plug-ins (such as the Google Translate website plug-in, for example) may offer a faster, though often less accurate, alternative to communicating with a global audience [32].

In the next section we elaborate more on how document and policy acceptance can be incorporated with user authentication techniques, while also examining the approaches taken by two leading international smart cities.

4 USER AUTHENTICATION

A major concern with free Wi-Fi is that it presents challenges for authenticating user identities as any user can wirelessly access the network from anywhere in range of the WAP or hotspot. Unlike private organizations that try to restrict access to their Wi-Fi and network infrastructure by means of authentication and access control mechanisms that are carefully maintained and monitored by dedicated teams, whether local or remote, the aim of smart city Wi-Fi hotspots is to create an inclusive environment for all end users to make use of the resource. As such, free access forms the basis of the service.

In the event of an end user suffering a loss while making use of the provisioned Wi-Fi, appropriate documents and policies should be put in place to limit the liability of the provider, as discussed in the previous section. Having end users agree to and accept the necessary documents and policies before making use of a Wi-Fi service is thus vital.

Keeping track of which users do, in fact, accept these documents and policies may become a challenging task in environments where masses of users are making use of a network. In such cases, keeping track of individual device IP or media access control (MAC) addresses (for further details see Forshaw [10]) may not be a viable option, due to the sheer volume of users and quick turnaround time. Instead, user authentication procedures based on unique user identifiers may prove to be more suitable.

Typically, such authentication occurs during the configuration phase (step 3) of the user Wi-Fi journey as depicted in Fig. 1. The configuration phase thus plays an important role in the process of connecting to the Internet and, as mentioned previously, being connected to a particular Wi-Fi network does not necessarily mean that a user has been granted access to the Internet.

During this configuration phase, a variety of methods may be implemented to either grant or deny end users access to the Internet, in addition to ensuring that they have accepted the appropriate documents and policies, as discussed in the previous section. Of course, the choice may be made to not authenticate users, thereby skipping configuration (step 3 in Fig. 1) entirely and simply allowing direct access to the Internet. Although this approach may be seen as convenient from both the end user and smart city's perspectives, it does not instil any sense of accountability or traceability pertaining to an end user's online behavior.

Additionally, appropriate documents and policies would need to be made available separately, possibly resulting in end users not being aware of the risk associated with their choice to make use of a particular smart city Wi-Fi. Moreover, identifying which party should accept responsibility in the case of loss may become an exponentially more complex task, once again, to the detriment of the smart city concept as a whole.

In order to avoid such a situation from arising, choosing to authenticate users during the configuration phase may alleviate some of the pressure on the smart city. Simple acceptance of documents and policies, signing up using unique identifiers or signing in using third party service credentials are approaches that may typically be utilized in a dashboard fashion, to assist in this endeavor. Each of these approaches is discussed in more detail next.

4.1 End User Authentication Techniques

4.1.1 Simple Acceptance

With a simple acceptance user authentication method, end users who connect to a Wi-Fi are automatically redirected to an authentication page. The role of this authentication page is to allow end users to implicitly or explicitly accept the documents and policies as stipulated by the service provider, after which, if accepted, their Internet session may then begin. In the event of Wi-Fi being sponsored by a third party (as discussed in Section 3.1), this page may also be used to expose end users to advertisements of the sponsors in order to start their browsing session or redirect end users to the website of the sponsor just as their session commences.

Session variables may be implemented to keep track of a user's browsing session and inform them in the event of this having exceeded a certain time or data allowance. Keeping track of individual device IP addresses and MAC addresses is paramount, although IP and MAC spoofing techniques may be used, thereby rendering this an exercise in futility.

4.1.2 Sign-up Using a Unique Identifier

In order to track end users individually and create a sense of responsibility, certain service providers may require end users to sign up before being granted access to the Internet. This process entails registering with a unique identifier, typically an email address or telephone number, and creating unique sign-in credentials to the Wi-Fi network. After registration has been successfully completed, the same credentials are then used to log in to make use of the Internet.

As discussed in Section 3.1, the data that is captured during the sign-up process may further be used by Wi-Fi sponsors for various purposes, including pursuing increased sales figures, targeted advertising, data analysis, and so forth. In certain parts of the world, however, transparency of personal data processing is a basic privacy principle, and a right that is acknowledged by data protection legislations [33]. The implications of processing personally identifiable user information during sign up should thus be anticipated within the constructs of local laws, such as the EU general data protection regulation (see www.eugdpr.org), for example. The jurisdiction and applicability of such laws should also be clearly stipulated in the appropriate documents and policies (as discussed in Section 3.1) to avoid any confusion that may arise across local and international jurisdictions.

Finally, the implementation of an end user sign-up procedure may simplify the task of keeping track of a session by associating usage limits (volume/time) to a dedicated user profile. Of course, one of the ways in which this approach may be circumvented by end users is by creating multiple accounts, each linked to a separate email address.

4.1.3 Sign-in Using Third-Party Service Credentials

Very often, end users already have existing online credentials that may be used to log in to other third-party services, such as email or social networks. By allowing end users to reuse their credentials of already existing, uniquely identifiable user accounts, the process in accessing Wi-Fi resources may be greatly simplified through the integration of third-party Application Programming Interfaces (APIs). Of course, the additional documents and policies required to make use of these services should be included and accepted by end users.

This approach combines the convenience of not having to sign up for the service from an end user's perspective, yet assures a certain level of user accountability from a management perspective. This provides a best of both worlds

TABLE 2   Free Wi-Fi User Authentication Techniques Advantages and Disadvantages

	Advantages	Disadvantages
Simple Acceptance	+ Fast	− Difficult to track individual users
Sign up using Unique Identifier	+ User accountability	− Slow − Data processing laws applicable
Sign in using Third-Party Service Credentials	+ User accountability + Relatively fast	− Third-party documents and policies applicable − Excludes certain users

approach, although on the other hand, it may exclude those users who do not have existing third-party accounts from accessing a vital resource. As such, combining a third-party sign in service option with a fall-back or default sign-up option, using a unique identifier for example, a more inclusive and accessible service may be created.

4.1.4 Analysis of User Authentication Techniques

As each of the aforementioned user authentication techniques comes with their own advantages and disadvantages, Table 2 provides a summary of these for quick reference.

While simple acceptance may provide end users fast access to the Internet, it does make monitoring individual behavior more challenging. By requiring end users to sign up by making use of a unique identifier, a sense of user accountability is established, although the sign-up process may be slow, and additional data processing laws are applicable to personally identifiable information. Lastly, by allowing users to sign in using third-party service credentials, user accountability is established, while also offering a relatively fast sign-in procedure. Third-party service documents and policies do become important to take into consideration, although making use of only this approach may result in the exclusion of certain users who do not have existing credentials. As such, a combination of approaches may also be used to create a more inclusive and accessible environment.

This may, however, become a cumbersome task from a managerial point of view and instead, harvesting the power that a cloud solution has to offer through Wi-Fi as a service (WaaS) may prove to be a viable alternative to consider. Regardless of the chosen implementation technique, unique identifiers and authentication create a sense of accountability and traceability among end users—a core aspect that should form part of any smart city initiative.

With a better understanding of the possible approaches that may be used with user authentication, we now identify which approaches have been taken by two international smart cities including Barcelona in Spain, and Geneva in Switzerland.

4.2 Exemplary Smart City Wi-Fi User Authentication

4.2.1 Barcelona

The city council of Barcelona, located in Catalonia, Spain, offers free Wi-Fi (as surveyed in September 2017) to visitors by requesting their email address, place of residence, and explicit acceptance of the Terms and Conditions of Use (as is visible in Fig. 2).

An option is provided to view the Terms and Conditions of Use before acceptance, with explicit acceptance being a prerequisite to make use of the service. A confirmation email is sent to the email address that the end user uses for signing up, after which they may start making use of the service.

A multi-language service delivery approach is taken, which ensures that the service is available in English, while the option to upgrade to premium services by making use of an industry partner (KubiWireless) or roaming service provider partner is also on offer.

4.2.2 Geneva

The city of Geneva, located in the canton of Geneva, Switzerland, offers free Wi-Fi (as surveyed in July 2017) by requesting end users to register with a mobile telephone number, as is visible in Fig. 3.

A confirmation code (or one-time pin) is sent via Short Message Service (SMS) to the specified number, after which a user is expected to reproduce the code (thereby verifying their number) in order to complete configuration. Once activated, this code is valid for 6 months of usage, and by choosing to log in, an end user automatically accepts the General Terms and Conditions.

FIG. 2   Barcelona City Council's free Wi-Fi configuration page on a smartphone (September 2017) (by the authors).

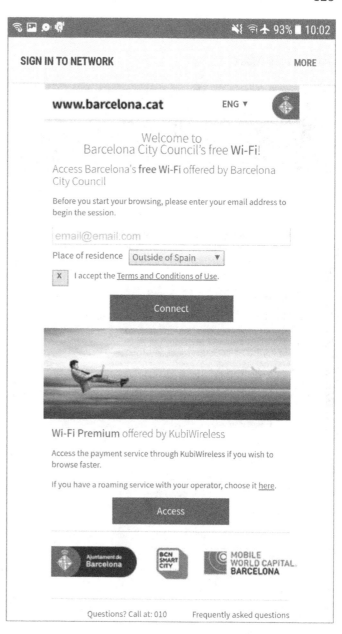

A multi-language approach has been chosen that includes English, German, French, and Italian. While the city of Geneva makes the free Wi-Fi facilities available, an industry partner (Monzoon Networks AG) is responsible for actual service provisioning.

4.2.3 Smart City Wi-Fi Comparative Analysis and Discussion

While both Barcelona and Geneva offer urban dwellers the opportunity to connect to the Internet through publically provisioned Wi-Fi networks, certain similarities, yet subtle differences, exist between the configuration approaches chosen, as visible in Table 3.

While Barcelona opted for requesting an email as a unique end user identifier, Geneva opted for a mobile telephone number instead. Mobile telephone numbers do, however, create a certain level of exclusion for foreign visitors (tourists) that are not in possession of a local SIM card, whereas email is borderless.

In the case of Barcelona, policy acceptance has explicitly been requested, while Geneva implicitly implies acceptance of policies once a user logs in. Multilingual support is offered in both cases, while industry sponsors are also involved (although in different capacities) in both cases.

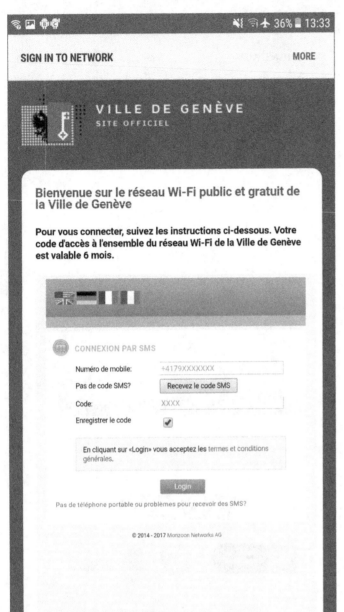

FIG. 3   City of Geneva free Wi-Fi configuration page on a smartphone (July 2017) (by the authors).

TABLE 3   Barcelona and Geneva: Free Wi-Fi Configuration and User Authentication Approaches

	Barcelona	Geneva
Access Method Identifier	Email	Mobile Telephone Number
Policy Acceptance	Explicit	Inferred
Language Support	Multi	Multi
Industry Sponsor Involved	Yes	Yes

By following the examples of these two smart cities, unique identifiers, policy acceptance, multilingual support, and industry involvement may be considered for inclusion in both existing and prospective smart city Wi-Fi delivery undertakings. The requirements may, of course, be adapted based on the individual need of each smart city.

5 FUTURE RESEARCH DIRECTIONS AND PERSPECTIVES

While this chapter has focused on incorporating elements from both theory and practice, limited examples of smart cities (Barcelona and Geneva) and their chosen Wi-Fi configuration and user authentication approaches are presented. By expanding the work to incorporate findings from additional smart cities, a more comprehensive study may be compiled to identify trends on a global scale.

6 CONCLUSION

For many years, Wi-Fi, or IEEE802.11 wireless LANs were considered an interesting technology, but not for mainstream implementation or usage [34]. Not too long after the introduction of this technology, however, business and home users started realizing the practical benefits, and recently also, smart cities.

A typical smart city may consist of various categories of end users, such as citizens, government agencies, industry partners, tourists, and so forth, with each end user having their own set of requirements for smart city applications, services, and the accepted quality of service [35]. While participatory action and engagement of urban dwellers plays an important role in the success of smart city initiatives and the smart city model as a whole [1], free, public Wi-Fi is a viable option that may be employed to advance this endeavor, and subsequently, improve the quality of life for all.

The introduction of such new solutions is necessary, not only to improve the quality of daily life with innovative, efficient protocols, but also in terms of security and reliability. Security and reliability are core components of any public Wi-Fi network and being able to ensure privacy will be a vital prerequisite to consumer acceptance [36]. Furthermore, smart city networks may start to infiltrate numerous private homes thereby "violating" the most intimate spaces of urban dwellers—if end users classify this as unsecure, the smart city vision could most certainly collapse irreparably [37].

In response to these observations, in this chapter we have examined the current state of play relating to the security of smart city initiatives by employing a bottom-up approach, that is, approaching the problem from the perspective of the end user (urban dwellers). As these users may become more reliant on smart city Wi-Fi for various aspects of everyday life, it is worth noting that these hotspots may not only attract the attention of the end user, but also that of the abuser (cybercriminal). As such, end users may be exposed to numerous types of threats when making use of these public Wi-Fi networks, with various phases of their user journey being susceptible to attacks. While packet analyzing/sniffing, evil twins, and rogue networks/honeypots are typically launched by outsiders, various insider mistakes and vulnerabilities may also be introduced to an otherwise secure network, including rogue access points and mishandled Wi-Fi security setups.

Various preventative measures may be put in place from both the perspectives of an end user and smart city, although the safest network is still no network at all [34]. As this is not a feasible choice for smart cities, the focus should rather be on when, and not if, an attack, vulnerability, or mistake will occur, while plans should be put in place to respond accordingly.

Despite the perceived dangers that making use of unsecure Wi-Fi may present from a security and privacy point of view, end users have been found very likely to misjudge risky situations, and would still make use of smart city Wi-Fi under circumstances where the risks taken are not consistent with maximizing utility [38]. By introducing an end user information security portal or dashboard, however, training and awareness content may be communicated directly to end users while seamlessly blending in with the Wi-Fi user journey. This may enhance user awareness and approach the problem of ensuring information security from a fresh perspective, that is, from the perspective of the end user.

As many stakeholders including operators, venue owners, advertisers, analytics users, and government, to mention only a few, may be involved in the provisioning of smart city Wi-Fi, appropriate documents and policies should also be incorporated and accepted by end users before making use of the service, in order to protect the interests of all parties involved. Privacy protection should be imposed by law with clear and rigorous policies adapted to the smart city context to ensure future growth and adoption of the technology [37].

In order to instil a sense of accountability and traceability, end user authentication may further be employed by means of simple acceptance, signing up with a unique identifier or signing in using existing third-party credentials. Through either implicit or explicit document or policy acceptance techniques, it may be ensured that end users have agreed to the appropriate policies during the configuration phase, before starting to make use of the service.

While various different approaches have been employed by the cities of Barcelona and Geneva, both cities have provided end users with a configuration dashboard to assist with setting up their connection. By expanding the content provided on these dashboards, smart cities may ensure that proper security training and awareness content reaches all end users of the service, in a language of their choice.

Despite the potential increased user awareness, training, and engagement that may result, vulnerabilities, exploitation, mistakes, and misuse will inevitably still occur. There is thus a risk that technology can do more harm than good. Additionally, technology can easily become an excuse for end users to adopt a careless consumerism behavior, arguing that technology will eventually solve all problems [39], including that of security. Smart cities should thus ensure that they are in a position to respond accordingly.

As it currently stands, there is no model smart city that can provide a development roadmap or blueprint for others to follow and as such, each smart city will, to a certain extent, rely on end user feedback and engagement to facilitate successful future growth. By adopting a user-centric view, this chapter has focused on numerous aspects that should be taken into consideration when granting end users a voice through the deliverance of smart city Wi-Fi, ultimately contributing to collectively overcoming smart city growing pains, more securely.

References

[1] T. Yigitcanlar, Smart cities: an effective urban development and management model? Aust. Plann. 52 (1) (2015) 27–34, https://doi.org/10.1080/07293682.2015.1019752.

[2] P. Jougleux, Is EU copyright law a danger to online freedom of expression? in: S. Katsikas, V. Zorkadis (Eds.), E-Democracy – Privacy-Preserving, Secure, Intelligent E-Government Services. e-Democracy 2017. Communications in Computer and Information Science, vol. 792, Springer, Cham, 2017, https://doi.org/10.1007/978-3-319-71117-1_9.

[3] C. Costopoulou, F. Ntalianis, M. Ntaliani, S. Karetsos, E. Gkoutzioupa, e-Participation provision and demand analysis for greek municipalities. in: S. Katsikas, V. Zorkadis (Eds.), E-Democracy – Privacy-Preserving, Secure, Intelligent E-Government Services. e-Democracy 2017. Communications in Computer and Information Science, vol. 792, Springer, Cham, 2017, https://doi.org/10.1007/978-3-319-71117-1_1.

[4] L. Forlano, WiFi geographies: when code meets place. Geogr. Inf. Soc. 25 (5) (2009) 344–352, https://doi.org/10.1080/01972240903213076.

[5] A. Powell, WiFi publics producing community and technology. Int. J. Inf. Commun. Soc. 11 (2008) 1068–1088, https://doi.org/10.1080/13691180802258746.

[6] M. Seufert, T. Griepentrog, V. Burger, T. Hoßfeld, A simple WiFi hotspot model for cities. IEEE Commun. Lett. 20 (2) (2016) 384–387, https://doi.org/10.1109/LCOMM.2015.2509074.

[7] V.F.S. Mota, D.F. Macedo, Y. Ghamri-Doudane, J.M.S. Nogueira, On the feasibility of WiFi offloading in urban areas: the Paris case study, 2013 IFIP Wireless Days (WD), Valencia, 2013, 2013, pp. 1–6, https://doi.org/10.1109/WD.2013.6686530.

[8] K. Boes, D. Buhalis, A. Inversini, Conceptualising smart tourism destination dimensions. in: I. Tussyadiah, A. Inversini (Eds.), Information and Communication Technologies in Tourism 2015, Springer, Cham, 2015, https://doi.org/10.1007/978-3-319-14343-9_29.

[9] A.J.A.M. Van Deursen, E.J. Helsper, The third-level digital divide: who benefits most from being online? in: L. Robinson, S.R. Cotten, J. Schulz, T. M. Hale, A. Williams (Eds.), Communication and Information Technologies Annual (Studies in Media and Communications), Vol. 10, Emerald Group Publishing Limited, Bingley, UK, 2015, pp. 29–52.

[10] J. Forshaw, Attacking Network Protocols: A Hacker's Guide to Capture, Analysis, and Exploitation, No Starch Press, San Francisco, CA, 2018.

[11] S. Phang, H. Lee, H. Lim, Design and implementation of V6SNIFF: An efficient IPv6 packet sniffer, Proceedings of the 2008 Third International Conference on Convergence and Hybrid Information Technology – Volume 02 (ICCIT '08), Vol. 2, IEEE Computer Society, Washington, DC, USA, 2008, pp. 44–49, https://doi.org/10.1109/ICCIT.2008.279.

[12] N. Du Paul, Spoofing Attack: IP, DNS & ARP, Available from: https://www.veracode.com/security/spoofing-attack, 2017. Accessed 4 February 2018.

[13] J. Belenguer, C.T. Calafate, A low-cost embedded IDS to monitor and prevent man-in-the-middle attacks on wired LAN environments, Proceedings of the the International Conference on Emerging Security Information, Systems, and Technologies (SECUREWARE '07), IEEE Computer Society, Washington, DC, USA, 2007, pp. 122–127.

[14] Colasoft, Packet Sniffing, Available from: http://www.colasoft.com/resources/packet_sniffing.php, 2018. Accessed 4 February 2018.

[15] M. Jones, 10 Public Wi-Fi Security Threats You Need to Know, Available from: https://www.safervpn.com/blog/10-public-wi-fi-security-threats/, 2017. Accessed 4 February 2018.

[16] I. Kim, J. Seo, T. Shon, J. Moon, A novel approach to detection of mobile rogue access points. Secur. Commun. Netw. 7 (10) (2014) 1510–1516, https://doi.org/10.1002/sec.756.

[17] A. Zafft, E. Agu, Malicious WiFi networks: a first look, 37th Annual IEEE Conference on Local Computer Networks - Workshops, Clearwater, FL, 2012, pp. 1038–1043, https://doi.org/10.1109/LCNW.2012.6424041.

[18] R. Oppliger, SSL and TLS: Theory and Practice, second ed., Artech House, Boston, 2016.

[19] J. Long, M. Lui, M. Gray, A. Chan, Pro Spring Integration, Apress, New York, 2011.

[20] R. Oppliger, Internet and Intranet Security, Artech House, Boston, 2002.

[21] M. Lewis, Comparing, Designing, and Deploying VPNs, Cisco Press, Indianapolis, Ind, 2006.

[22] K. Roebuck, Virtual Network Computing (VNC): High-Impact Strategies – What You Need to Know: Definitions, Adoptions, Impact, Benefits, Maturity, Vendors, Tebbo, London, 2011.

[23] H. Feil, 802.11 wireless network policy recommendation for usage within unclassified government networks, in: Proceedings of the 2003 IEEE Conference on Military Communications – Volume II (MILCOM'03), Vol. II, IEEE Computer Society, Washington, DC, USA, 2003, pp. 832–838.

[24] J. Fitzpatrick, The Difference Between WEP, WPA, and WPA2 Wi-Fi Passwords, Available from: https://www.howtogeek.com/167783/htg-explains-the-difference-between-wep-wpa-and-wpa2-wireless-encryption-and-why-it-matters/, 2016. Accessed 1 April 2018.

[25] Veracode, Appsec Knowledge Base – Packet Analyzer, Available from: https://www.veracode.com/security/packet-analyzer, 2017. Accessed 4 February 2018.

[26] A. Karamanou, E. Panopoulou, V. Cipan, D. Čengija, D. Jelić, E. Tambouris, K. Tarabanis, Fostering active participation of young people in democratic life: a case study using the #ask dashboard, in: S. Katsikas, V. Zorkadis (Eds.), E-Democracy – Privacy-Preserving, Secure, Intelligent E-Government Services. e-Democracy 2017. Communications in Computer and Information Science, 792 Springer, Cham, 2017.

[27] T.A. Kletz, The man in the middle—some accidents caused by simple mistakes. Ind. Manag. Data Syst. 82 (3/4) (1982) 11–13, https://doi.org/10.1108/eb057237.

[28] P. Vidales, A. Manecke, M. Solarski, Metropolitan public WiFi access based on broadband sharing, 2009 Mexican International Conference on Computer Science, Mexico City, 2009, pp. 146–151, https://doi.org/10.1109/ENC.2009.22.

[29] J. Potts, Economics of public WiFi, Aust. J. Telecommun. Digit. Econ. 2 (1) (2014) 20. Published by Telecommunications Association Inc., ABN 34 732 327 053, https://doi.org/10.18080/ajtde.v2n1.20.

[30] C. Geerdts, A. Gillwald, E. Calandro, C. Chair, M. Moyo, B. Rademan, Developing Smart Public Wi-Fi in South Africa, 2016, Available from: https://www.researchictafrica.net/publications/Other_publications/2016_Public_Wi-Fi_Policy_Paper_-_Developing_Smart_Public_Wi-Fi_in_South_Africa.pdf (Accessed 4 February 2018).

[31] C.L.C. Penteado, P.R.E. De Souza, I. Fortunato, S.A. Da Silveira, Connectivity public policy in the network society: the case of "WiFi Livre SP". in: L. Robinson, J. Schulz, H.S. Dunn (Eds.), Communication and Information Technologies Annual (Studies in Media and Communications), vol. 12, Emerald Group Publishing Limited, Bingley, UK, 2016, pp. 299–314, https://doi.org/10.1108/S2050-206020160000012018.

[32] C. Louw, Good, better, best practise – a comparative analysis of official destination websites, Afr. J. Hosp, Tour. Leis. 6 (3) (2017) 26. http://hdl.handle.net/10210/259378.

[33] P. Murmann, S. Fischer-Hübner, Tools for achieving usable ex post transparency: a survey. IEEE Access 5 (2017) 22965–22991, https://doi.org/10.1109/ACCESS.2017.2765539.

[34] J. Edney, W.A. Arbaugh, Real 802.11 Security: Wi-Fi Protected Access and 802.11i, Addison-Wesley Longman Publishing Co., Inc., Boston, MA, USA, 2003.

[35] A. Gharaibeh, M.A. Salahuddin, S.J. Hussini, A. Khreishah, I. Khalil, M. Guizani, A. Al-Fuqaha, Smart cities: a survey on data management, security and enabling technologies. IEEE Commun. Surv. Tutorials 19 (2017) 2456–2501, https://doi.org/10.1109/COMST.2017.2736886.

[36] A. Bartoli, M. Soriano, J. Hernandez-Serrano, M. Dohler, A. Kountouris, D. Barthel, Security and privacy in your smart city, Proceedings of Barcelona Smart Cities Congress 2011, 29–2 December 2011, Barcelona (Spain), 2011.

[37] A. Bartoli, J. Hernandez-Serrano, M. Soriano, M. Dohler, A. Kountouris, D. Barthel, On the ineffectiveness of today's privacy regulations for secure smart city networks, Proceedings of third IEEE International Conference on Smart Grid Commuications, Tainan City Taiwan, 5–8 November 2012, 2012.

[38] N. Sombatruang, M.A. Sasse, M. Baddeley, Why do people use unsecure public wi-fi?: an investigation of behaviour and factors driving decisions, Proceedings of the 6th Workshop on Socio-Technical Aspects in Security and Trust (STAST'16), ACM, New York, NY, USA, 2016, pp. 61–72, https://doi.org/10.1145/3046055.3046058.

[39] S. Uffer, R. Moyser, Towards Cognitive Cities: Advances in Cognitive Computing and its Application to the Governance of Large Urban Systems. vol. 33, Springer International Publishing, Switzerland, 2016, https://doi.org/10.1007/978-3-319-33798-2.

10

Techniques for Privacy Preserving Data Publication in the Cloud for Smart City Applications

Yousra Abdul Alsahib S. Aldeen[*,†] *and Mazleena Salleh*[†]

*Department of Computer Science, College of Science for Women, University of Baghdad, Baghdad, Iraq
[†]Faculty of Computing, University Technology Malaysia, Skudai, Malaysia

1 OVERVIEW

A smart city is a coherent concept to integrate multiple information and communication technologies (ICT) solutions in a secure way to manage the city's possessions, especially the urban areas, using ubiquitous computing technologies to improve the quality of life of people [1]. The advantages of information and computing technologies (ICT) in a smart city are enormous, such as security devices, smart energy meters, home life, and smart appliances for health. These advantages offer unmatched conveniences and quality of life [2]. Smart city technologies can be considered a fusion of information systems and social systems, which are organized for the management of numerous city infrastructures such as waste, traffic, sewage, electricity, water quality, air pollution monitoring, and fire and crime resources; preserving renewable resources and organizing city policies and programs for city planners [3]. In spite of the enormous advantages of smart cities, serious issues such as reliability, stability, and privacy can be assured if they are careful in the design and development of smart city schemes [1]. Privacy is a serious issue that has to be classified discreetly. Nobody wants their daily activities or personal habits tracked. Because personal devices are pervasive, location privacy becomes especially significant.

An important information source for research and analysis is the data from different organizations. Usually, this sensitive or private data information includes medical data, census data, voter registration data, social network data, and customer services data. Hiding the sensitive information of individuals is a major concern of cloud service providers in data publishing [4]. Fig. 1 demonstrates the three domains of privacy preservation of the stored data, which include the user domain, cloud domain, and recipient domain. In common practice, any user or organization shares the stored data records to the cloud service provider. Service providers further publish these datasets to any research center (viz. medical research). For example, hospitals serve as the data owners, and medical research centers act as data recipients. The cloud domain facilitates the hardware and software infrastructures to the service provider for supplying the shared medical records as outsourced storage [5].

Before outsourcing the data to the cloud for publication, data privacy (sensitive information of individuals) must be protected and well-preserved. This is resolved using data anonymization techniques such as K-anonymity, (α, k)-anonymity, and L-diversity. The data providers implement various privacy requirements while releasing their original data to the cloud, which often poses a challenge. Despite the development of numerous potential data anonymization techniques for dispersed databases, their independent efficient implementation remains far from being achieved. Thus, a combined or individually anonymized database is required by data analysts or users.

This chapter discusses a heuristic anonymization technique for privacy-preserving data publication in the cloud for smart cities. The proposed technique is significant for anonymous data protection that already exists in servers as individual databases, where all local anonymized datasets are inserted through the secure algorithm. The proposed

FIG. 1 Various domains of the stored data privacy preservation.

FIG. 2 Conceptualization of privacy preserving data publication.

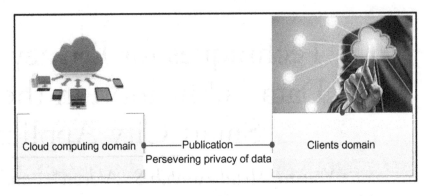

technique combines the privacy models (L-diversity, K-anonymity and (α, k)-anonymity). To start with, the heuristic K-anonymity technique has been proposed to protect the published datasets. Then, a heuristic L-diversity is integrated with an heuristic (α, k)-anonymity technique to facilitate published datasets in the cloud environment. Experimental procedures have been applied to bank datasets, and the results illustrate that the proposed technique has outperformed the existing techniques. Fig. 2 illustrates the conceptual framework of this chapter. The two domains are the client's domain and the cloud's domain. The privacy of clients should be preserved while publishing their datasets. Therefore, an effective technique is needed for preserving the privacy of clients.

2 HEURISTIC ANONYMIZATION CONSIDERATIONS

The smart city has a large number of applications, extending from smart card services for easy authentication and payment, to smart mobility applications that improve traffic efficiency and reduce CO_2 emissions, to smart resource management of water or electricity. The efficiency of these and other smart city applications heavily depend on data gathering, interconnectivity, and extensiveness [6].

The number and complexity of smart city technologies, the assailants, and applications make it difficult to keep track of privacy risks for people. Mostly, the application itself does not pose a risk, but the route an application uses impacts the underlying technologies. For example, cashless payment procedures for public transportation do not constitute a privacy risk, but can be performed in a privacy-attacking track, such as using smart cards that identify private information [7]. Based on the complexity of the smart city scenery, the implementation of privacy protection is complicated, especially with the variety of applications, technologies, involved parties, privacy threats, and existing protection techniques. It is necessary to understand these aspects and their interconnection to able the engineers, investors, and researchers to design a privacy-friendly smart city. Table 1 shows a comparison between the weakness and strength of client privacy preservation in the smart city environment based on the types of privacy.

Privacy preservation for published data in CC requires an intensive study to identify privacy needs, as well as to define the obstacles to the proposed technique. The following paragraphs describe the parameters required to execute the heuristic anonymization technique. Several types of research has explained the necessary considerations for the proposed heuristic anonymization technique. These include:

Anonymization model: There are different types of privacy models proposed for preserving privacy of data, such as K-anonymity, L-diversity, and (α, k)-anonymity. K-anonymity maintains the data authenticity [13], where the values of quasi-identifier (QI) attributes (age, zip, gender) in each tuple in the table are matched to at least $(K-1)$ tuples as shown in Fig. 3. But K-anonymity [14] suffers from homogeneity, where the QI group encloses several tuples with the same sensitive attributes (SA). This leads to a violation of the privacy of data.

Thus, the L-diversity model is used for maintaining the minimum K group size, with varieties of sensitive attributes. Conversely, the drawback of this particular diversity model is that it considers the setting of parameters in L-diversity

TABLE 1 Illustrate a Comparison Between the Weakness and Strength of the Client Privacy Preservation in the Smart City Environment

Privacy types	Strength of the client privacy preservation	Weakness of the client privacy preservation
Privacy of location	It is usually defined as the safeguard of spatio-temporal information [8]	Breach location privacy can discover a person's workplace and home. Moreover, it allows inferences about other types of privacy, for example, purchase patterns, health, or personal habits [3]. Furthermore, co-location information permits inferences about a person's social life [8]
Privacy of state of body & mind	It includes the state of body and mind involved in a person's bodily characteristics, such as genomes, biometrics, their health, emotions, mental states, thoughts, and opinions [9]	A breach of the privacy of the state of body and mind can lead to discrimination by employers and insurance companies [9]
Privacy of social life	It is a person's social life, including the contents of social interactions, for example, what was said in a conversation or posted on a social media site. Moreover, metadata about interactions, such as who a person reacts with, when, and for how long [10]	A breach of social privacy permits inferences about other kinds of privacy, such as interactions with a particular hospital, which can disclose information about a person's health [10]
Privacy of behavior & action	It includes a person's habits, hobbies, activities, and purchase styles while shopping online or when using credit cards; details may be shared with shops [11]	Taking advantage of this information for other purposes, such as aimed advertisements, can establish a violation of privacy. Frequently, this information allows far-reaching inferences to be made about the client's life, and consequently, other types of privacy [11]
Privacy of media	It includes privacy of video, images, audio, and any individual data about a person [12]	Redistributing or creating client-related media without their approval constitutes a privacy breach [12]

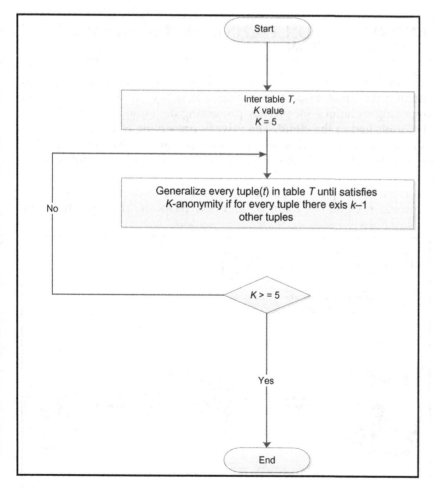

FIG. 3 *K*-anonymity model.

model as unsuitable. To overcome this limitation, the (α, k)-anonymity model is introduced. This model, being highly sensitive, provides improved protection through constraining the frequency of the anonymity values group, and a smaller amount than specified in parameter α. It evades the condition, where occurrences of given superficial information are too high, and enhance the diversity of SA. The hospital data sheet (medical record) is one such example, where patients being treated for HIV, for example, may consider their medical treatment to include sensitive data and need privacy.

Conversely, for common diseases such as fever, flu, and so forth, data protection is not necessary. To handle these situations, the best solution is the (α, k)-anonymous model, where only pertinent and sensitive property values are important and need protection. Although the (α, k)-anonymous model is robust, it protects only the sensitive attributes of the highest level sensitive property values. It does not follow the process of other levels, such as the sensitivity of the same property value. For that, the (α, L)-diversification K-anonymity model is the best for combining models such as L-diversity (α, k)-anonymity, and K-anonymity model. The (α, L)-diversification K-anonymity model is considered an enhancement to K-anonymity.

Entropy: Entropy is a vital measure in information theory. The amount of uncertainty involved in the value of a random variable or the outcome of a random process is quantified by entropy. For example, outcome identification of a fair coin flip (with two equally likely outcomes) provides less information (lower entropy) than specifying the outcome from a roll of a die (with six equally likely outcomes). Mutual information, channel capacity, error exponents, and relative entropy are some other important measures in information theory [15].

Privacy: It is the ability of an individual or group to protect themselves, or information about themselves, thereby expressing themselves selectively. Presently, data privacy in the cloud system is one the major concerns. Consequently, the privacy preservation technique should be able to preserve the privacy for published data to meet the new data and users requirements [5].

Information loss: The notion of information loss is used to quantify the amount of information that is lost due to K-anonymization [16].

3 PROPOSED HEURISTIC ANONYMIZATION TECHNIQUE FOR PRIVACY PRESERVATION

In this technique, the (α, L)-diversification K-anonymity model is adopted as the enhancement of K-anonymity. The concept of this model is based on combining the three models, including L-diversity (α, k)-anonymity, and K-anonymity. The aim of the heuristic anonymizing technique for privacy preserving data mining in the cloud is to ensure strong confidentiality for data to be published in the cloud. The privacy preserving techniques for data publishing are categorized into theoretical and heuristic types. This research proposed an heuristic technique [7]. Although numerous heuristic techniques are introduced to guarantee strong privacy preservation, a unified algorithm is far from being developed.

Fig. 4 depicts an overview of privacy preserving techniques for published data in the cloud environment. It is composed of three domains, which are data provider, cloud environment, and data recipient. The data should be

FIG. 4 Overview of proposed privacy preserving techniques for published data.

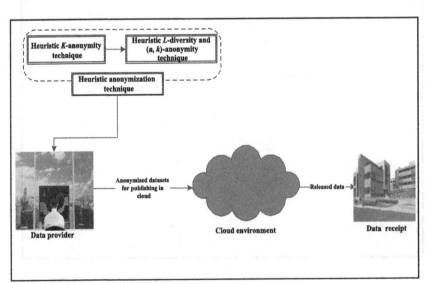

anonymized before publishing in cloud computing by the data provider. Data recipient like any research centre can access and utilize the published data in the cloud. The proposed technique in this study is heuristic anonymization which is composed of two parts. The first part explains the heuristic K-anonymity technique and the second part explains heuristic L-diversity and (α, k)-anonymity technique to overcome the limitations of the heuristic K-anonymity technique.

3.1 Heuristic K-Anonymity Technique

The aim of this technique is to anonymize QI attributes to prevent reaching sensitive attributes. The main screen of code writing based on Visual Studio Microsoft for heuristic K-anonymity technique is shown in Fig. 5. Figs. 6 and 7 illustrate how to import the bank data that is used in this study. Based on the proposed technique, this data will be anonymized. By applying the generalization operation the process of anonymization on imported data is achieved as illustrated in Fig. 8.

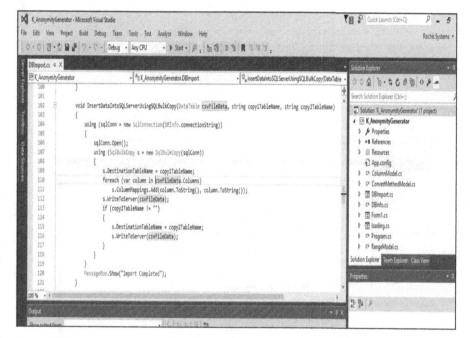

FIG. 5 Main screen of code writing based on Visual Studio Microsoft for heuristic K-anonymity technique.

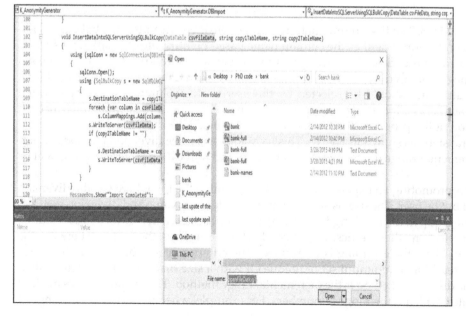

FIG. 6 Importing bank data.

FIG. 7   Determines success of importing the bank data.

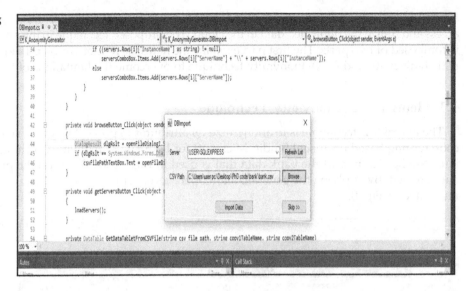

FIG. 8   Process of anonymization.

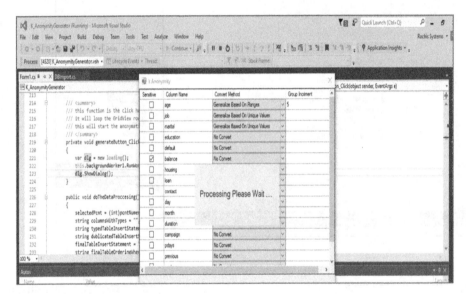

There are four columns, as shown in Fig. 8. The first column determines the sensitive attributes (the balance is chosen as sensitive in this study). The second column defines the column name based on attributes of bank data such as age, job, and marital status. The third column defines the convert method (diversion method). One of the diversion methods that is capable of performing K-anonymity for the suitable attribute should be chosen in this column. A suitable mode for corresponding attributes should be selected by the user in this column. For example, when the attribute is a set of numbers, such as age, as appeared in the second column of Fig. 8, the incremental range method should be chosen then. After execution of the program, the bank data is anonymized, as shown in Fig. 9.

This technique is achieved in several steps as shown in Fig. 10. This technique has three diversion methods of performing K-anonymity, including incremental range, incremental suppression, and unification. These methods will be discussed later.

The technique generally starts from promoting an expert in the data to determine the QI, where QI, the diversion method, and K values are determined by the user. The user is able to determine the QI, K value and diversion method. The K value denotes the length of the K group in the resulting K-anonymized data, as shown in Fig. 10. In this research, K values are changed to examine their effect on other metrics, as discussed in Section 4. Thus, the trade-off between the privacy and utility of data is achieved. Next, the grouping is performed. The criterion of stopping the technique is based on confirming the condition of reaching a minimum set of unique QI with a size that is equal to or more than the K value. The first mechanism of the diversion method is the incremental range method. The purpose of this method is to perform K-anonymity for attributes, which is the range of numbers. For example, when the attribute is a range of

Age	Job	Marital	Education	Default	Balance	Housing	Loan	Contact	Day	Month	Duration	Campaign	pdays	Previous	poutcome	y
50–100	Student-management	Married	Primary-tertiary	No	2143	Yes	No	Unknown	5	May	261	1	−1	0	Unknown	No
0–50	Housemaid-technician	Single	Unknown-secondary	No	29	Yes	No	Unknown	5	May	151	1	−1	0	Unknown	No
0–50	Entrepreneur-services	Married	Unknown-secondary	No	2	Yes	Yes	Unknown	5	May	76	1	−1	0	Unknown	No
0–50	Unknown-blue-collar	Married	Unknown-secondary	No	1506	Yes	No	Unknown	5	May	92	1	−1	0	Unknown	No
0–50	Unknown-blue-collar	Single	Unknown-secondary	No	1	No	No	Unknown	5	May	198	1	−1	0	Unknown	No
0–50	Student-management	Married	Primary-tertiary	No	231	Yes	No	Unknown	5	May	139	1	−1	0	Unknown	No
0–50	Student-management	Single	Primary-tertiary	No	447	Yes	Yes	Unknown	5	May	217	1	−1	0	Unknown	No
0–50	Entrepreneur-services	Divorced	Primary-tertiary	Yes	2	Yes	No	Unknown	5	May	380	1	−1	0	Unknown	No
50–100	Self-employed-retired	Married	Primary-tertiary	No	121	Yes	No	Unknown	5	May	50	1	−1	0	Unknown	No
0–50	Housemaid-technician	Single	Unknown-secondary	No	593	Yes	No	Unknown	5	May	55	1	−1	0	Unknown	No
0–50	Unemployed-admin.	Divorced	Unknown-secondary	No	270	Yes	No	Unknown	5	May	222	1	−1	0	Unknown	No
0–50	Unemployed-admin.	Single	Unknown-secondary	No	390	Yes	No	Unknown	5	May	137	1	−1	0	Unknown	No
50–100	Housemaid-technician	Married	Unknown-secondary	No	6	Yes	No	Unknown	5	May	517	1	−1	0	Unknown	No
50–100	Housemaid-technician	Married	Unknown-secondary	No	71	Yes	No	Unknown	5	May	71	1	−1	0	Unknown	No
50–100	Entrepreneur-services	Married	Unknown-secondary	No	162	Yes	No	Unknown	5	May	174	1	−1	0	Unknown	No
50–100	Self-employed-retired	Married	Primary-tertiary	No	229	Yes	No	Unknown	5	May	353	1	−1	0	Unknown	No
0–50	Unemployed-admin.	Single	Unknown-secondary	No	13	Yes	No	Unknown	5	May	98	1	−1	0	Unknown	No
50–100	Unknown-blue-collar	Married	Primary-tertiary	No	52	Yes	No	Unknown	5	May	38	1	−1	0	Unknown	No

FIG. 9   Anonymized bank data.

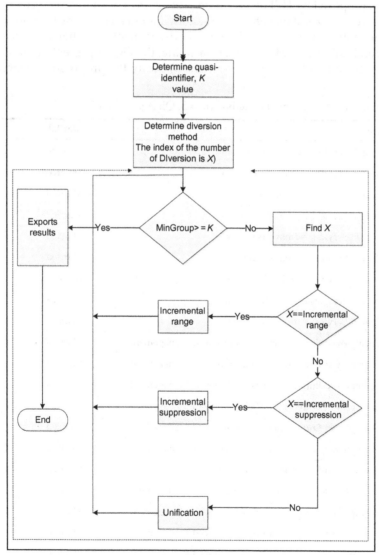

FIG. 10   Flowchart of heuristic K-anonymity technique.

numbers (set of numbers) such as age, date, and time; then the user may select an incremental range. For that, the user must select a suitable mode with corresponding attributes. Consequently, the user provides the value of the increment for combining records with a sub-range in the age attribute. For example, if a user provided 5 as range incremental, then the technique could be used to start generalizing by combining the sub-range 20–24 into one group, then 25–29 into another group, and so on.

The second mechanism of the diversion method is the incremental suppression method. It is performed by incrementally replacing the characters "*". Thus, different values are included in one group once they are matched with each other. This diversion can be used with ZipCode. The third mechanism of the diversion method is the unification, which simply combines more than one of the distinct values of the attributes. This is similar to combining different cities in the attribute address under the name of the state that includes them. Two resulting groups are shown in Table 2. Variable X in the flowchart indicates the index of the number of diversions that are performed on the attribute.

In Fig. 10, the QI, X (the index of the number of diversion method) and K value are determined. If X is an incremental range, then an incremental range method is chosen. In this method, the attribute is a range of numbers (set of numbers) such as age, date, time, and so forth. The user might select an incremental range, and provide the value of each increment to combine the records with respect to a sub-range in the age attribute. For X to be incremental suppression, then this method is applied by performing it incrementally to replacing the characters of the attribute to "*". Consequently, once two values or more match each other, they are included in one group, and the diversion is used with ZipCode. Otherwise, the unification method is applied. This operation is iterative until the desired K value is reached. Fig. 11 represents the pseudo code of the heuristic K-anonymity steps.

The technique has been proposed by [17] based on only theoretical K-anonymity. The theoretical K-anonymity is shown in Fig. 3, while this study is based on enhanced K-anonymity in an heuristic technique, as shown in Fig. 10. The proposed heuristic K-anonymity is achieved by three methods, as mentioned herein, which are (incremental range, incremental suppression, and unification). For further clarifying, the Fig. 11 presented the steps of the proposed technique. The steps shown in green (light gray in print versions) clarify the proposed enhanced K-anonymity.

TABLE 2   Two Groups Resulting From Applying the Method ($K = 5$, QI: Age and Job)

	Age	Job	Marital	Education	Balance
1	90–105	Retired-Services-Admin.-Technician	Divorced	Secondary	1
2	90–105	Retired-Services-Admin.-Technician	Divorced	Primary	712
3	90–105	Retired-Services-Admin.-Technician	Married	Unknown	775
4	90–105	Retired-Services-Admin.-Technician	Married	Unknown	775
5	90–105	Retired-Services-Admin.-Technician	Married	Unknown	775
6	90–105	Retired-Services-Admin.-Technician	Married	Unknown	775
7	90–105	Retired-Services-Admin.-Technician	Divorced	Secondary	1234
8	90–105	Retired-Services-Admin.-Technician	Divorced	Primary	2282
9	90–105	Retired-Services-Admin.-Technician	Married	Secondary	0
1	75–90	Unemployed-Entrepreneur-Self-Employed-Management	Married	Unknown	4984
2	75–90	Unemployed-Entrepreneur-Self-Employed-Management	Married	Unknown	1780
3	75–90	Unemployed-Entrepreneur-Self-Employed-Management	Married	Unknown	4984
4	75–90	Unemployed-Entrepreneur-Self-Employed-Management	Married	Unknown	4984
5	75–90	Unemployed-Entrepreneur-Self-Employed-Management	Married	Unknown	1780
6	75–90	Unemployed-Entrepreneur-Self-Employed-Management	Married	Tertiary	5619
7	75–90	Unemployed-Entrepreneur-Self-Employed-Management	Married	Unknown	1780
8	75–90	Unemployed-Entrepreneur-Self-Employed-Management	Married	Unknown	1780
9	75–90	Unemployed-Entrepreneur-Self-Employed-Management	Married	Primary	6483
10	75–90	Unemployed-Entrepreneur-Self-Employed-Management	Married	Tertiary	0
11	75–90	Unemployed-Entrepreneur-Self-Employed-Management	Married	Secondary	0

```
1.        INPUT : Quasi_Identifiers, Diversion _Method, K
2.        OUTPUT: K_Anonymized_Table
3.        Main
4.                WHILE(MinGroup<K)
5.                    X=Find_Index_of_Min (Diversion _Level[])
6.                        IF(Diversion _Method(x)==INCREMENTAL_RANGE)
7.                        Incremental_Range(x);
8.            ELSEIF(Diversion _Method(x)==INCREMENTAL_SUPPRESSION)
9.                Incremental_Suppression(x);
10.         ELSEIF(Diversion _Method(x)==UNIFICATION)
11.             Unfication(x);
12.         End While
13.         Diversion _Level[x]++;
14.     END
```

FIG. 11   Algorithm representing the pseudo code for heuristic *K*-anonymity technique.

3.2 Heuristic (*L*-Diversity) and (*α, k*)-Anonymity Technique

K-anonymity is extended using an *L*-diversity and (*α, k*)-anonymity method to maintain a limit of maximum frequency of distance (sensitive) values in the critical attributes. Fig. 12 shows a new value of *K* that is enabled once the *K*-groups are generated.

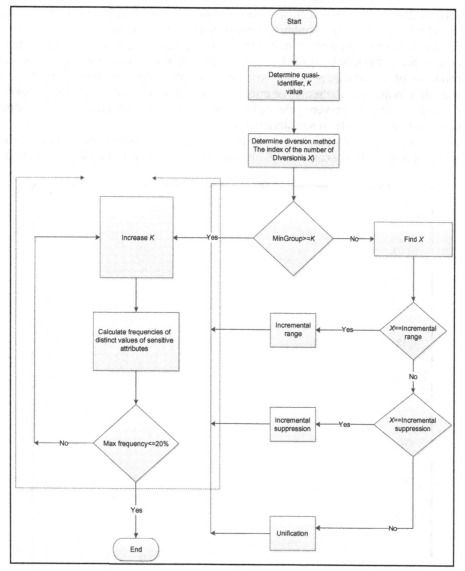

FIG. 12   Flowchart of heuristic (*L*-diversity) and (*α, k*)-anonymity technique.

```
1.        INPUT : Quasi_Identifiers, Diversion _Method, K
2.        OUTPUT: K_Anonymized_Table
3.        Main
4.        K_Anonymity(K);
5.        While(Max_Freq()<0.2)
6.            K++;
7.            K_Anonymity(K);
8.            Export_Table
9.        End
```

FIG. 13   Pseudo-code for heuristic (*L*-diversity) and (α, *k*)-anonymity.

To overcome the weakness of *K*-anonymity, such as the QI group having several tuples with same sensitive attributes value, one needs to achieve *L*-diversity with (α, *k*)-anonymity methods. Furthermore, *K* is increased to enhance the diversity in the data until the achieved maximum frequency is <20%. This percentage is selected based on the natural of data as tuneable parameter. In other words, to decrease the frequency of sensitive attributes, this percentage is selected heuristically.

Fig. 13 represents the steps of pseudo code of heuristic (*L*-diversity) and (α, *k*)-anonymity. Meanwhile, the frequencies are calculated for distinct values of sensitive attributes. If they meet the condition (less 20%), the loop is ended, else it is continued to increase *K* until the condition is met. This percentage is based on nature of dataset. It is considered as a tunable parameter as mentioned herein. The percentage chosen is heuristic.

The frequencies of distinct values of sensitive attributes are measured with respect to *L*-diversity with (α, *k*)-anonymity techniques by increasing *K* to maintain a limit of maximum frequency of distance values in the sensitive attributes. Fig. 14 demonstrates the frequency of distinct values with respect to increased *K*. This demonstrates spreading of the critical values among the whole equivalent group. It is observed that there is less possibility of privacy violation when the frequencies of critical values are decreased in every equivalent group of tuples. For example, if a record has a critical value of high frequency, the sensitive information for the particular individual can be breached easily. There is diversity on critical values to prevent privacy breaches. This histogram illustrates the reduction in frequency value of tuples and increase of diversity in sensitive values.

The technique has been proposed by [17] based on only theoretical *K*-anonymity without combining with other privacy metrics. The proposed technique combines *K*-anonymity with *L*-diversity and (α, *k*)-anonymity by decreasing

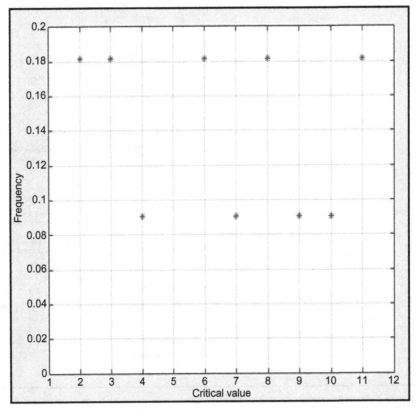

FIG. 14   Histogram of distinct values of sensitive attributes.

the frequencies of sensitive attributes and divesting the sensitive attributes as shown in Fig. 12. For further clarifying, the Fig. 13 presented the steps of the proposed technique. The steps shown in green (light gray in print versions) clarify the proposed technique.

4 EXPERIMENTAL RESULTS AND EVALUATION

The experimental results demonstrate that the present heuristic anonymization technique can prevent privacy breaches in published datasets in the cloud environment. By taking advantage of K-anonymity, L-diversity, and (α, k)-anonymity, the unified technique overcomes the weakness of each model. For the first experiment, the value of K is taken as 20. Every group possesses many tuples, and the range is increased to 25. This produced strong privacy at the cost of enhanced information loss. Therefore, it is essential to reduce the K value. In the second experiment, the K value is chosen to be 10. The information loss is still increased as outlined. Then, the value of K is changed to 5, and this time, the information loss is reduced within a lower range as shown in Table 2.

Table 2 lists the result after applying the heuristic K-anonymity technique. As shown in Table 2, two groups result from using the proposed technique where the K value is 5. The QI attributes that were generalized are (age and job). The first group has nine tuples. This means that every tuple in this group has matched with the other eight tuples in the same group, so it is hard to distinguish every tuple. The second group has eleven tuples that are indistinguishable. The difference in the number of anonymized tuples in every group is based on the condition Mingroup $\geq K$, as shown in Fig. 10.

Table 3 lists the result after applying the heuristic (L-diversity) and (α, k)-anonymity technique. It is clear that the equivalent group contains at least L acceptable values of sensitivity attributes, which has 6053, 643, 1411, 1483, 397, 499, 2235, 0, 1381, 2140, and 5944 balances. This signifies the presence of diversity in sensitive attributes with diminished frequency values. For example, in the first sensitive value (6053), the frequency is reduced with increasing K value, similarly for other sensitive attributes. Furthermore, the group size is found to increase with the decrease in frequency values of sensitive attributes. Small group sizes revealed the higher frequency. These frequencies are reduced by increasing the group size to avoid threats.

The efficiency and effectiveness of the heuristic anonymization technique is compared with the recent state-of-the-art technique [17]. The performance evaluation of the heuristic anonymization technique is carried out using UTD Anonymization ToolBox software, where entropy and execution time are calculated as privacy measures that are reflected in Eq. (1) to Eq. (6).

Let A^p (spec) mean the anonymity before performing spec. A^c represents the anonymity after performing spec. Privacy loss caused by spec is calculated by

$$PL = A^P - A^c \tag{1}$$

Bottom up generalization (BUG):

$$ILPG = IL\left(gen\right)/\left(PG\left(gen\right)+1\right) \tag{2}$$

$$\sum_{IL = c \in child(p)} \left(R_c/R_p\right)I(R_c) - I(R_P) \tag{3}$$

$$PG = A^{p(gen)} - A^{c(gen)} \tag{4}$$

i. *Entropy*: It is a measure of unpredictability of information content. The evaluation is made by estimating the entropy measure of each of them using the expression [18]:

$$Entropy(E) = -\sum_{a \in A} p(E, a) \log P(E, a) \tag{5}$$

where A is the set of attributes domain, and $p(E,a)$ is the fraction of records in E with values a.

ii. *Execution time*: the execution time is computed via the following formulae (http://www.avr-tutorials.com/):

$$ET = T \times C \tag{6}$$

where period $(T) = 1/$Frequency (f), the total number of cycle (C) to execute the piece of code given.

Entropy Evaluation: The UTD Anonymization Tool Box is used to compare the results of the heuristic anonymization technique with K-anonymity and original data, as shown in Fig. 15. The evaluation is made by estimating the entropy measure of each of them using Eq. (5). Fig. 15 displays that the K-anonymity reduced the entropy level of the data by

TABLE 3   Results of Heuristic (L-Diversity) and (α, k)-Anonymity Technique

Age	Job	Marital	Education	Balance
75–100	Unknown-Student-Housemaid-Unemployed-Entrepreneur-Blue-Collar	Divorced-Single-Married	Unknown-Primary-Tertiary-Secondary	6053
75–100	Unknown-Student-Housemaid-Unemployed-Entrepreneur-Blue-Collar	Divorced-Single-Married	Unknown-Primary-Tertiary-Secondary	6053
75–100	Unknown-Student-Housemaid-Unemployed-Entrepreneur-Blue-Collar	Divorced-Single-Married	Unknown-Primary-Tertiary-Secondary	643
75–100	Unknown-Student-Housemaid-Unemployed-Entrepreneur-Blue-Collar	Divorced-Single-Married	Unknown-Primary-Tertiary-Secondary	1411
75–100	Unknown-Student-Housemaid-Unemployed-Entrepreneur-Blue-Collar	Divorced-Single-Married	Unknown-Primary-Tertiary-Secondary	1411
75–100	Unknown-Student-Housemaid-Unemployed-Entrepreneur-Blue-Collar	Divorced-Single-Married	Unknown-Primary-Tertiary-Secondary	1483
75–100	Unknown-Student-Housemaid-Unemployed-Entrepreneur-Blue-Collar	Divorced-Single-Married	Unknown-Primary-Tertiary-Secondary	397
75–100	Unknown-Student-Housemaid-Unemployed-Entrepreneur-Blue-Collar	Divorced-Single-Married	Unknown-Primary-Tertiary-Secondary	397
75–100	Unknown-Student-Housemaid-Unemployed-Entrepreneur-Blue-Collar	Divorced-Single-Married	Unknown-Primary-Tertiary-Secondary	499
75–100	Unknown-Student-Housemaid-Unemployed-Entrepreneur-Blue-Collar	Divorced-Single-Married	Unknown-Primary-Tertiary-Secondary	2235
75–100	Unknown-Student-Housemaid-Unemployed-Entrepreneur-Blue-Collar	Divorced-Single-Married	Unknown-Primary-Tertiary-Secondary	0
75–100	Unknown-Student-Housemaid-Unemployed-Entrepreneur-Blue-Collar	Divorced-Single-Married	Unknown-Primary-Tertiary-Secondary	0
75–100	Unknown-Student-Housemaid-Unemployed-Entrepreneur-Blue-Collar	Divorced-Single-Married	Unknown-Primary-Tertiary-Secondary	499
75–100	Unknown-Student-Housemaid-Unemployed-Entrepreneur-Blue-Collar	Divorced-Single-Married	Unknown-Primary-Tertiary-Secondary	1381
75–100	Unknown-Student-Housemaid-Unemployed-Entrepreneur-Blue-Collar	Divorced-Single-Married	Unknown-Primary-Tertiary-Secondary	1381
75–100	Unknown-Student-Housemaid-Unemployed-Entrepreneur-Blue-Collar	Divorced-Single-Married	Unknown-Primary-Tertiary-Secondary	1381
75–100	Unknown-Student-Housemaid-Unemployed-Entrepreneur-Blue-Collar	Divorced-Single-Married	Unknown-Primary-Tertiary-Secondary	2140
75–100	Unknown-Student-Housemaid-Unemployed-Entrepreneur-Blue-Collar	Divorced-Single-Married	Unknown-Primary-Tertiary-Secondary	0
75–100	Unknown-Student-Housemaid-Unemployed-Entrepreneur-Blue-Collar	Divorced-Single-Married	Unknown-Primary-Tertiary-Secondary	5944
75–100	Unknown-Student-Housemaid-Unemployed-Entrepreneur-Blue-Collar	Divorced-Single-Married	Unknown-Primary-Tertiary-Secondary	2140
75–100	Unknown-Student-Housemaid-Unemployed-Entrepreneur-Blue-Collar	Divorced-Single-Married	Unknown-Primary-Tertiary-Secondary	0

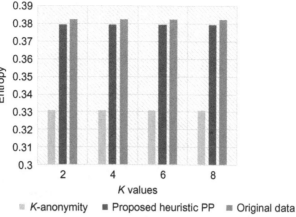

FIG. 15 Comparison of entropy measure for *K*-anonymity and heuristic anonymization technique.

13.5% from 0.3823 to 0.3308. However, by implementing the heuristic anonymization technique on the same dataset, the entropy revealed a reduction of 0.75% only, which is much lower compared with the *K*-anonymity technique (13%). This clearly indicates the outperformance of the heuristic anonymization technique in preserving the entropy of the data with a small percentage of difference from the original data. It is important to note that the entropy measure depends on the data. Moreover, the entropy measure of the heuristic anonymization technique is observed to be too close to the entropy measure of the original data. This signifies that the entropy measure for the heuristic anonymization technique is superior to the entropy measure of *K*-anonymity. In addition, the entropy is discerned to be insensitive to the value of *K*. This can be interpreted with the large amount of data with respect to small ranges of values of *K*.

Privacy Measure: Privacy is complementary of entropy. The privacy measure of the heuristic anonymization technique is evaluated using the UTD Anonymization Tool Box. The privacy is observed to decrease with the increase of information contents. Privacy measures for *K*-anonymity and heuristic anonymization techniques are compared in Fig. 16. The privacy level is found to be enhanced in the presence of *K*-anonymity. Thus, it is established that the heuristic anonymization possesses more utility than the normal *K*-anonymity. Owing to this attribute, the heuristic anonymization technique protects privacy without increasing information loss, where the preserved privacy level is >65%. Moreover, the percentage remains the same even with the increase of information, and the preserving entropy of the original data does not exceed 10%. Indeed, it is a good performance indicator of the heuristic technique.

Execution Time: The computational complexity of both *K*-anonymity and the heuristic anonymization technique are evaluated in terms of their execution time, as illustrated in Fig. 17. It is evident that the heuristic anonymization technique required less execution time than *K*-anonymity. The embedment of other models such as *L*-diversity and (α, *k*)-anonymity in the heuristic anonymization technique ensure strong privacy without affecting execution time.

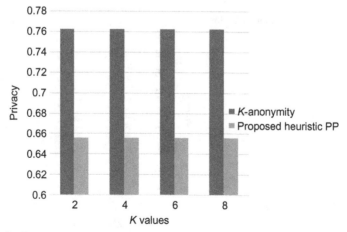

FIG. 16 Comparison of privacy for *K*-anonymity and heuristic anonymization technique.

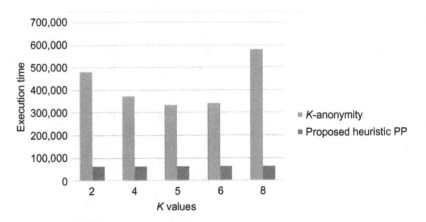

FIG. 17   Execution time for *K*-anonymity and heuristic anonymization technique.

5 DISCUSSION OF VALIDATION

This chapter has focused on preserving privacy for data publishing in the cloud for smart cities. The heuristic anonymization technique has been evaluated and compared with [17]. Zhang et al. have proposed a theoretical approach. The UTD Anonymization Tool Box is used to compare the results of the heuristic anonymization technique with [17]. Fig. 18 clearly shows that the heuristic anonymization technique achieves more information preservation (higher entropy values) than the benchmark technique [17]. With *K* ranging from 4 to 8, the heuristic anonymization technique is capable of sustaining the entropy level to be >0.37, while in [17] the anonymiztion has resulted in an entropy level close to 0.35. This means that the heuristic anonymization technique has improved over the benchmarked technique by 7.38%.

Fig. 19 displays a comparison of privacy between the heuristic anonymization technique and [17]. The heuristic anonymization technique revealed a more stable privacy level than [17], despite the change of values of *K*.

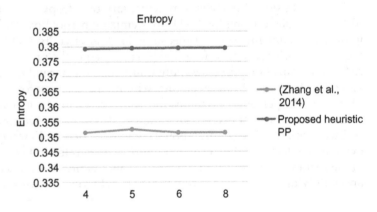

FIG. 18   Comparison of entropy measure for heuristic anonymization technique and Zhang et al.

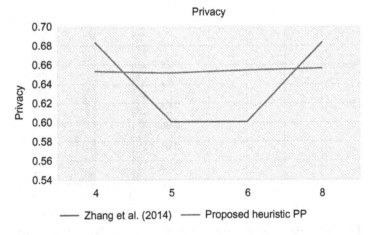

FIG. 19   Comparison of privacy for heuristic anonymization technique and Zhang et al.

For $K = 5, 6$ the privacy of [17] has declined from 0.68 to 0.60, while in heuristic anonymization, the technique is capable of preserving the same level of privacy without any reduction. Thus, the experimental results validated that the heuristic anonymization technique significantly improved the performance of [17] over existing techniques, regardless of the K-anonymity parameter.

6 SUMMARY

The concept of smart cities is complex and attractive. Diverse concepts, applications, and technologies interact to include every aspect of the digital life. However, the high level of interconnectivity adds to the body of privacy issues. Merging numerous data sources from different data holders, devices, technologies, and applications can develop service quality and availability, but also grows the risk for privacy violations through correlation. The innovation and novelty in the smart city do not originally lie in the applications, but in the use of underlying technologies that enable them. One of the technologies that is used in the smart city is CC. This chapter provides the basic concept of the anonymization model, and demonstrates that the synergy of different privacy preserving models can provide a strong privacy balance with the information utilization. The detailed correlation between cloud computing and privacy preserving of published data is exemplified. With the materialization of CC technologies, various organizations have attempted to leverage the Internet-based paradigm. The main aim is to optimize the utility of computing resources in a flexible and scalable manner.

Despite the increased use of cloud-based platforms in diverse business areas, the privacy and security requirements have prevented their adoption in the healthcare and related areas for smart cities. Actually, the privacy concerns (data utilization requirements) of different data providers (consumers) are quite different. Over the years, numerous techniques have been developed to ensure the privacy of sensitive data publication in the cloud environment. Yet, no precise and efficient solution for privacy has been achieved. To surmount these limitations, this chapter proposed a data privacy preserving technique useful for cloud publishing for smart cities. To achieve high-quality generalization, an anonymization technique is developed by unifying techniques such as heuristic K-anonymity, heuristic L-diversity, and (α, k)-anonymity. The need of a hybrid solution via the innovative integration of different privacy protection models is justified. The experimental results obtained using the proposed anonymization technique revealed enhanced privacy protection, and offered the obligatory data for research analysis. In recent years, the importance of data sharing for various applications has been well understood. However, publishing data into CC for smart cities raises serious concerns about revealing the private information of individuals. To protect the privacy of individuals, datasets should be anonymized before being released to CC. Current studies have revealed that simply removing explicit identifiers, for example, name and social security number (SSN), from the dataset, is insufficient to preserve privacy. This is because of (QI) attributes, which can jointly identify individuals uniquely.

Thus, the identity of individuals, as well as their sensitive information, can be easily violated if the published data is joined with any external dataset. However, the majority of the research, such as [19, 20, 17, 21–23] could not reach the optimal solution. These techniques are based on theoretical anonymization and use only K-anonymity to anonymize datasets. As mentioned earlier, K-anonymity suffers from a homogeneity problem, which needs to be improved.

These techniques have failed to suggest a unique technique by combining K-anonymity with other privacy metrics. Consequently, the performance of the privacy and utility of datasets has been affected. So, the clients of the cloud are not sure about attainment of strong techniques with minimal information loss. Fig. 20 shows the diagram of privacy-preserving techniques for published data.

The technique based on heuristic anonymization will be beneficial if exploited to combine and integrate with privacy metrics, resulting in a unique technique. The current techniques based on heuristic anonymization have proposed a method to solve privacy issue [24–28].

All of these proposed approaches, techniques, and frameworks are based on other PPDM methods, or on combining the anonymization method with other PPDM methods such as data distortion, data swapping, and so forth. Hence, this will affect the performance in respect to privacy failure, the capacity to determine the original user data from the modified one, loss of information, and estimation of the data accuracy loss; which is computationally very expensive. Although a few researchers have focused on the trade-off between privacy and utility of data [25–27], they have failed to achieve unique techniques for privacy preservation.

The sheer volume of technologies and systems make the creation of a privacy-friendly smart city overwhelming. However, we think that there are guidelines and research directions that can be tracked to meaningfully increase the level of privacy in future smart cities. In this chapter, we also discussed some of the research directions that have not yet been very closely examined in the case of smart cities, as follows.

FIG. 20 Privacy persevering techniques for published data in CC.

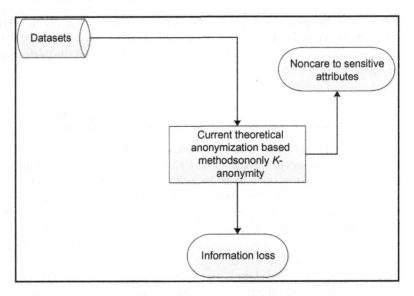

Combined or Compassable Privacy Technologies: Certainly, smart cities combine so many technological components that it is not easy to achieve privacy. Instead, we claim that the interactions between technologies and data have to be considered to design combined privacy technologies [2]. This is especially significant because many smart cities start with separated solutions that are integrated gradually. One way to simplify combined privacy protection is to concentrate on the interfaces between various systems, on their level of interconnectivity, and most importantly, on the data exchanged.

Reward and Implementation: Combined privacy techniques and privacy architectures are aimed at integrating separated privacy protection mechanisms into more common, or even holistic, solutions. This integration is complex in smart cities, not only by a large number of subsystems, but also by a large number of investors. Different investors should work together on an operational level to perform combined privacy techniques in cooperation with privacy architecture. However, this cooperation can involve severe privacy risks because it may permit investors to combine data from several sources. To alleviate these risks and understand the full possibility of privacy-friendly smart cities, cities need to set incentives that encourage privacy-friendly cooperation and present ways to impose privacy.

References

[1] L. van Zoonen, Privacy concerns in smart cities, Gov. Inf. Q. 33 (3) (2016) 472–480.
[2] A.S. Elmaghraby, M.M. Losavio, Cyber security challenges in smart cities: safety, security and privacy, J. Adv. Res. 5 (4) (2014) 491–497.
[3] A. Giannakoulias, Cloud computing security: protecting cloud-based smart city applications, J. Smart Cities 2 (1) (2016) 66–77.
[4] M. Prakash, G. Singaravel, An approach for prevention of privacy breach and information leakage in sensitive data mining, Comput. Electr. Eng. (2015) 1–7.
[5] J.J. Yang, J.Q. Li, Y. Niu, A hybrid solution for privacy preserving medical data sharing in the cloud environment, Futur. Gener. Comput. Syst. 43–44 (2014) 74–86.
[6] D. Eckhoff, I. Wagner, Privacy in the smart city – application, technologies, challenges and solutions, IEEE Commun. Surv. Tutorials (2017) 1–28.
[7] A. Rial, G. Danezis, M. Kohlweiss, Privacy-preserving smart metering revisited, Int. J. Inf. Secur. 17 (1) (2018).
[8] S. Warren, L. Brandeis, The right to privacy, Harv. Law Rev. 4 (5) (1890) 193–220.
[9] D.J. Solove, A taxonomy of privacy, Univ. Pa. Law Rev. 154 (3) (2006) 477.
[10] S. Gutwirth, R. Leenes, P. De Hert, Y. Poullet, European Data Protection: Coming of Age, Springer, The Netherlands, 2013, pp. 1–440.
[11] A. Pfitzmann, M. Hansen, A terminology for talking about privacy by data minimization: anonymity, Unlinkability, Undetectability, Unobservability, Pseudonymity, and identity Management, Tech. Univ. Dresden, 2010, pp. 1–98.
[12] H. Nissenbaum, Privacy as contextual integrity, Wash. L. Rev. (2004) 101–139.
[13] X. Zhu, T. Chen, Computer, informatics, Cybern. Appl. 107 (2012) 915–923.
[14] Hamza, Attacks on anonymization-based privacy-preserving: a survey for data mining and data publishing, J. Inf. Secur. 2013 (2013) 101–112.
[15] S. Dedeo, Information Theory for Intelligent People, 2012, pp. 1–7.
[16] J.L. Lin, M.C. Wei, C.W. Li, K.C. Hsieh, in: A hybrid method for k-anonymization, Proceedings of the 3rd IEEE Asia-Pacific Services Computing Conference, APSCC 2008, 2008, pp. 385–390.
[17] X. Zhang, C. Liu, S. Nepal, C. Yang, W. Dou, J. Chen, A hybrid approach for scalable sub-tree anonymization over big data using MapReduce on cloud, J. Comput. Syst. Sci. 80 (5) (2014) 1008–1020.

[18] X. Zhang, C. Liu, C. Yang, W. Dou, J. Chen, Combining Top-Down and Bottom-Up: Scalable Sub-Tree Anonymization over Big Data using MapReduce on Cloud, 2013.

[19] X. Ding, Q. Yu, J. Li, J. Liu, H. Jin, Distributed anonymization for multiple data providers in a cloud system, in: Lecture Notes in Computer Science (including Subseries Lecture Notes in Artificial Intelligence and Lecture Notes in Bioinformatics), vol. 7825, 2013, , pp. 346–360.

[20] B.B. Patil, A.J. Patankar, in: Multidimensional k-anonymity for protecting privacy using nearest neighborhood strategy, 2013 IEEE International Conference on Computational Intelligence and Computing Research, IEEE ICCIC 2013, 2013. p. IEEE Podhigai; IEEE Signal Processing, Computation.

[21] C. Tai, P.S. Yu, M. Chem, in: Privacy preserving frequent pattern mining on multi-cloud environment, 2013 International Symposium on Biometrics and Security Technologies, July, 2013, , pp. 235–240.

[22] K. Doka, D. Tsoumakos, N. Koziris, in: KANIS: Preserving k-anonymity over distributed data, Proceedings of 5th International Workshop on Pers. Access, Profile Manag. Context Aware Databases (PersDB 2011), September 2, 2011, Seattle, WA, USA, 2011.

[23] A. Monreale, D. Pedreschi, R.G. Pensa, F. Pinelli, Anonymity preserving sequential pattern mining, Artif. Intell. Law 22 (2) (2014) 141–173.

[24] A.E. Cicek, M.E. Nergiz, Y. Saygin, Ensuring location diversity in privacy-preserving spatio-temporal data publishing, VLDB J. 23 (4) (2014) 609–625.

[25] H. Tian, W. Zhang, in: Privacy-preserving data publishing based on utility specification, Proc. Soc. 2013, 2013, , pp. 114–121.

[26] R.H. Khokhar, R. Chen, B.C.M. Fung, S.M. Lui, Quantifying the costs and benefits of privacy-preserving health data publishing, J. Biomed. Inform. 50 (2014) 107–121.

[27] X. He, D. Li, Y. Hao, H. Chen, Utility-Friendly Heterogenous Generalization in Privacy Preserving Data Publishing, No. 818, 2014, pp. 186–194.

[28] G. Zhang, Y. Yang, J. Chen, A historical probability based noise generation strategy for privacy protection in cloud computing, J. Comput. Syst. Sci. 78 (5) (2012) 1374–1381.

11

Security in Smart Cyber-Physical Systems: A Case Study on Smart Grids and Smart Cars

Sandeep Nair Narayanan*, Kush Khanna[†], Bijaya Ketan Panigrahi[†], and Anupam Joshi*

*University of Maryland Baltimore County, Baltimore, MD, United States
[†]Indian Institute of Technology Delhi, New Delhi, India

1 INTRODUCTION

Across the globe, cities are expanding in size and infrastructure. The idea of Smart Cities plays a vital role in offering higher efficiency, comfort, awareness, and convenience to end users. Harrison et al. [1] describe the Smart City as an instrumented, interconnected, and intelligent city. They instrument different sectors of smart infrastructure, such as smart energy, smart transportation, smart governance, smart healthcare, smart buildings, and so forth to capture real-world data and interconnect them to share this data among different services. The shared data is then used to make intelligent operational decisions using complex analytics and provide better facilities to end users. Smart Cyber-Physical Systems (CPSs) are essential components of all smart infrastructure. According to the National Science Foundation (NSF),[1] "Cyber-physical systems integrate sensing, computation, control and networking into physical objects and infrastructure, connecting them to the Internet and each other." Smart cars and smart grids are two CPS domains that have demonstrated tremendous growth over the past few decades. However, the capabilities of these CPSs to influence critical infrastructure make them a lucrative target for hackers. Some of the attacks even have a direct impact on the economy of a nation. For example, consider the attack on the Ukrainian smart grids [2]. It left a whole city without heat and electricity in the cold of December for many hours. Similarly in the domain of smart cars, although they are capable of providing efficient transportation and fewer accidents, the potential attacks against them are alarming. The famous Jeep Hack of 2016, in which the researchers manipulated a moving unaltered vehicle on the road, resulted in Chrysler recalling 1.4 million[2] vehicles. Hence, there is an urgent requirement to secure these individual Smart City components. In this chapter, we delve into the general architecture and security of smart grids and smart cars.

Electrical energy is considered the most efficient form of energy for generation, transmission, and energy conversion. The traditional power grid is getting smarter with large-scale automation and integration of new smart components capable of quick decision making, thereby improving the reliability of the entire system. The futuristic "smart grid" is a cyber-physical power system of interconnected smart metering infrastructure that enables autonomous and resilient operation. Due to technological advances, many consumer-centric facilities such as demand-side management, advanced metering infrastructure, dynamic pricing, and incentives have evolved for serving the consumer in a better and more reliable way. The huge amount of data collected from smart meters across the cities will result in better management of resources, ultimately lowering the cost for consumers.

---

[1] See https://www.nsf.gov/news/special_reports/cyber-physical/.

[2] See https://www.wired.com/2015/07/jeep-hack-chrysler-recalls-1-4m-vehicles-bug-fix/.

Another CPS that acquired smart decision-making capability is cars. They developed from being just mechanical devices into machines that can drive autonomously. They can provide safe, efficient, and fast transportation in Smart Cities. Driver-assisted features, such as antilock braking systems (ABS), adaptive cruise control, and blind spot warning systems, are becoming the de facto in many newer cars. For example, the latest version of the Accord from Honda Motor Company has the *Honda Sensing*[3] (Honda's package of smart features such as the Collision Mitigation Braking System, Road Departure Mitigation System, Adaptive Cruise Control, and Lane Keeping Assist System) feature as a default, even for its base version. Current cutting-edge research in this domain focuses on autonomous driving in which a car can navigate you from one location to another without direct human intervention. Waymo[4] (an Alphabet company), Uber,[5] GM motors,[6] Tesla,[7] and so forth are some the automotive giants who are innovating in this area. Waymo's fleet of autonomous cars has already driven more than 4 million[8] combined miles on normal roads.

When the smart features of CPSs were upgraded, they were connected to the cloud environment over the Internet, either directly or indirectly. The lack of connectivity was acting as a security feature in disguise until it became defunct. Moreover, power grids and automobiles existed for a long period, and evolved over the past century. The design considerations for some of the legacy systems were efficiency and speed with lower priority to security features such as authentication and authorization. For example, the Controller Area Network (CAN) bus used in many cars is a simple broadcast bus and messages on it are considered authenticated. An attacker who can sneak a crafted message on this bus can perform many malicious activities. Supporting such legacy devices makes their security complicated and opens many interesting research avenues.

This chapter explores the general architecture of smart grids and smart cars as smart CPSs in Section 2. Sections 3 and 4 then delve into the security in smart grids and smart cars by discussing specific attacks and countermeasures proposed to identify those attacks. Finally, this chapter is concluded in Section 5 by presenting the future outlook on the cybersecurity issues in smart systems, and discussing recommendations.

2 GENERAL SMART CYBER-PHYSICAL SYSTEM ARCHITECTURE

As described in Section 1, smart CPSs are essential components of a Smart City. Each system should be instrumented and interconnected to build it. In this section, we describe the architecture of two such instrumented smart CPSs, smart grids (Section 2.1) and smart cars (Section 2.2).

2.1 Smart Cyber-Physical System: Smart Grids

The union of Information Technology (IT) and Operational Technology (OT) has resulted in higher reliability, efficiency, better services, and ease of use for customers and utilities in every domain. In the recent past, the electrical energy sector is witnessing extensive modernization owing to the convergence of cyber and physical technologies. The main objective of the power system is to generate and transmit electrical energy from the power plants to the consumers reliably and efficiently. A cyber-physical power system can be considered a conventional power grid with integrated communication technologies enabling cyber and physical connections between various power system components. An overview of the electrical power system with a review of state-of-the-art communication technology is presented in later sections.

2.1.1 Electric Power system

The conventional power system can be broadly divided into three core domains: generation, transmission, and distribution. The generating units (power plants) are generally located in remote areas far from the end consumers. To transmit electrical power efficiently, the voltage level at the generation site is stepped up using power transformers. The generation site is also equipped with generation remote terminal units (RTUs), integrated electronic

---

[3] See https://automobiles.honda.com/safety.

[4] See https://waymo.com/.

[5] See https://www.uber.com/.

[6] See https://www.gm.com/.

[7] See https://www.tesla.com/.

[8] See https://waymo.com/ontheroad/.

devices (IEDs), current and voltage transformers (CTs/PTs), relays, and circuit breakers (CBs) for protection and control of critical generating units. The transmission system transmits high-voltage electrical power to the distribution system, which further distributes electrical energy to the consumers (industries, commercial buildings, hospitals, and households) as shown in Fig. 1. The transmission system is equipped with phasor measurement units (PMUs), RTUs, and IEDs to measure voltage and current for the operation, and to monitor power systems. In the smart grid environment, the measured data from various RTUs, PMUs, and IEDs are received by data concentrating units installed at the substations, and are further transmitted to a control center. The operation of conventional power systems with the integration of communication technology is more transparent as the latter has enabled wide area situational awareness of power system components available at the control center.

2.1.1.1 Power System Operation and Control

Supervisory control and data acquisition (SCADA) systems receive metered data for monitoring the operation of a power system. Based on the measurements received from the SCADA system, a state estimator (SE) is used to obtain an accurate snapshot of the power system in real-time [3]. Power system stability and security studies rely heavily on the estimated states. To ensure the accuracy of the estimated states, an SE generally uses redundant measurements that will filter out noises and telemetry errors [4]. Estimation of voltages at each bus (node) of the power system is the prime objective of an SE. The measurements required for the correct estimation of $V\angle\theta$ (complex voltage) at each bus are real and reactive power injections at buses; real and reactive power flows in the transmission lines; and voltage measurements at generator buses.

For N bus power system, the total number of states to be estimated is $2N - 1$; that is, $N - 1$ angles (one angle is considered as the reference angle) and N voltage magnitudes.

The state vector is given as,

$$x = [\theta_2, \theta_3, ..., \theta_N, V_1, V_2, ..., V_N].$$

(1)

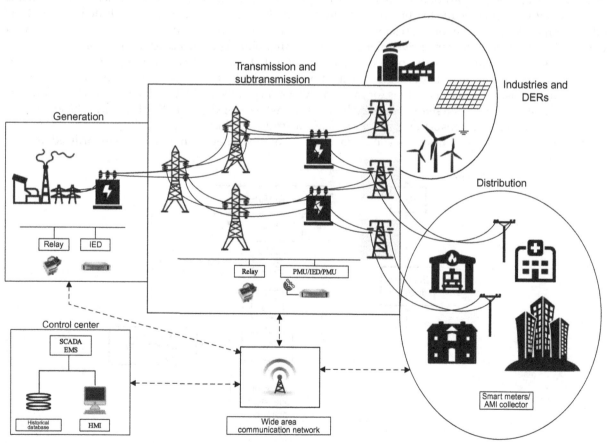

FIG. 1 Complete smart grid schematic.

Once the power system states are estimated, the security and contingency analysis is carried out for the power system's estimated snapshot. The EMS is responsible for unit commitment, economic load dispatch, automatic generation control, and many other critical functions of the power grid. Fig. 2 highlights the importance of SE in the operation and control of power systems.

2.1.1.2 Communication Technology

To transfer information from RTUs, IEDs, and relays to substations; from substations to regional and central load dispatch centers; from market operators to independent system operators (ISOs); and in a smart grid environment, from end consumers to utilities and vice versa, the smart cyber-physical power system uses varied communication technologies. Dedicated cables, optical fiber communication, wireless communication, and power line carriers are some of the communication technologies used in the smart grid. For substation automation (SA), the IEC 61850 Standard enhances the interoperability of devices from different vendors. In addition, IEC 61850 supports high-speed communication of generic object oriented substation event (GOOSE) messages for sending trip commands from relays to CBs, as shown in Fig. 3. IEC 61850 also supports sampled values to send measured voltage and current values from the measurement devices to the merger units. Manufacturing message specification is used to communicate device status and control commands to and from IEDs.

Deployment of PMUs increases the situational awareness of large-scale power systems. PMUs are capable of sampling data at 60–240 Hz. The sampled data is time stamped and synchronized using global positioning systems (GPS). The data from the PMU is transmitted to the phasor data concentrator (PDC) using a standard IEEE C37.118 protocol. PDC further communicates over the Ethernet and local area network of the substation or control center to the SA/SCADA/EMS system. PMUs facilitate voltage and current measurements with a common reference (as data is time stamped), which results in accurate state estimation (SE) and enhances the observability of the power system.

2.2 Smart Cyber-Physical System: Smart Cars

Smart cars are an integral part of new Smart Cities. Apart from providing human convenience, they can alleviate traffic issues, reduce accidents due to human error, provide intelligent and time-bound goods delivery, and so forth. A modern car has a large number of smart subsystems (Fig. 4) and they make a lot of intelligent decisions every second. Some example subsystems are ABS, driver alertness monitoring, blind spot detection, and so forth.

Automobiles as just moving parts, pulleys, and mechanical devices solely controlled by human drivers are antiquated. Advancements in microprocessor technologies resulted in the addition of electronic control units (ECUs) for making fast and smart decisions for many activities. Typically, an ECU will be connected to different sensors (e.g., acceleration sensor, rain sensor, ambient light sensor, wheel speed sensor, RPM sensor, vehicle speed sensor, oxygen sensor, temperature sensor) and actuators (e.g., instrument clusters, spark plugs, airbag inflators) using cables. Even though all automobiles have similar facilities, as of now, they do not have a standardized architecture.

FIG. 2   SCADA/EMS operation flow.

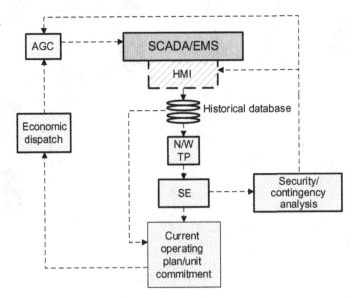

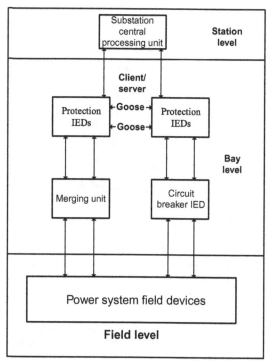

FIG. 3 SA communication architecture (IEC 61850).

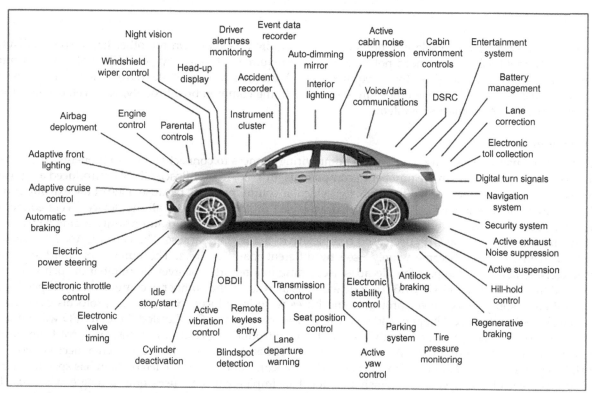

FIG. 4 Modern car subsystems. *(Courtesy: Clemson Vehicular Electronics Laboratory.)*

Different manufacturers such as Honda, Toyota, BMW, Benz, Kia, and General Motors use different types of equipment, internal wiring architecture, and protocols. However, in general, we can see that all of them use one or more buses inside, and most of the subsystems and sensors are connected to them as shown in Fig. 5. A subsystem needs to meet specific constraints according to the task it is assigned to. For example, ABS needs to meet strict time

FIG. 5   General vehicle architecture.

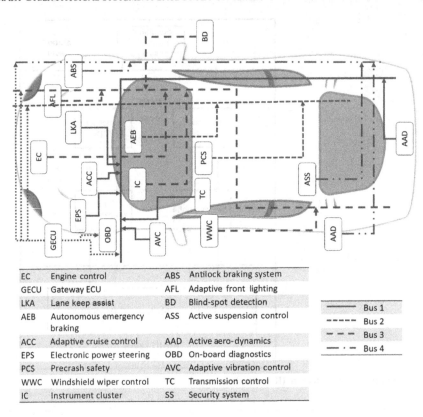

EC	Engine control	ABS	Antilock braking system
GECU	Gateway ECU	AFL	Adaptive front lighting
LKA	Lane keep assist	BD	Blind-spot detection
AEB	Autonomous emergency braking	ASS	Active suspension control
ACC	Adaptive cruise control	AAD	Active aero-dynamics
EPS	Electronic power steering	OBD	On-board diagnostics
PCS	Precrash safety	AVC	Adaptive vibration control
WWC	Windshield wiper control	TC	Transmission control
IC	Instrument cluster	SS	Security system

——— Bus 1
- - - - - Bus 2
— — — Bus 3
— · — Bus 4

requirements. Otherwise, the vehicle will not stop at the required location. On the other hand, some subsystems, such as entertainment subsystems, need not meet the time requirement, but they need high-volume data transfer. Different buses are chosen based on these requirements. Attributed to lack of standardization, some sensors are directly connected to the ECU, while others are connected to the common bus. Broadly, each vehicle has at least a common bus and different smart subsystems.

2.2.1 Common Bus

Earlier vehicle manufacturers used a point-to-point wiring harness to connect all the components, and it became complicated due to an increase in the number of components. In 1986, Robert Bosch GMBH introduced a lightweight and low-cost serial bus protocol called the CAN for vehicular communication, because none of the existing protocols had the required characteristics. CAN was a broadcast-based protocol in which all the devices were connected to the same bus, and all devices saw all network communications. Error correction and priority maintenance were its important characteristics, along with decreased complexity in the wiring harness. The newer CAN 2.0 specification was published in 1992, and became widely used by different manufacturers. The number of smart systems has increased considerably over the past few decades. According to a report,[9] the average number of such systems in a car increased from 24 in 2002 to 70 in 2013. To cope with this increase in the number of components and speed requirements of different subsystems, newer protocols and buses were introduced. Some of the protocols over the CAN bus are the ISO-TP protocol, CANopen, and so forth. A newer version of CAN called the CAN-FD was introduced in 2011, which offered flexible data rates. Other protocols introduced include the PWM protocol from Ford, the Keyword protocol (KWP2000), the VPW protocol used in GM and Chrysler, the local interconnect network (LIN) protocol,[10] the media oriented system transport (MOST) protocol,[11] and so forth. Each of them has specific characteristics. For example, LIN is a very inexpensive protocol to implement, and uses only a single wire bus. But it supports only up to 20 kbps. On the other hand, a version of the MOST protocol supports up to 150 Mbps, with the associated complexity of implementation. Another high-speed bus with a communication speed of up to 10 Mbps

---

[9] See http://cvrr.ucsd.edu/ece156/AutomotiveSensors-Review-IEEESensors2008.pdf.

[10] See https://vector.com/vi_lin_spec_download_en.html.

[11] See https://www.mostcooperation.com/publications/specifications-organizational-procedures/request-download/mostspecificationpdf/.

is FlexRay.[12] Due to diminishing support and increasing cost, newer vehicles are moving toward a newer protocol, automotive Ethernet.[13] As of now, a common practice seen among manufacturers is to use different protocols and buses for different subsystems. Typically, MOST or FlexRay are used for high-end systems, CAN is used for mid-range systems, and LIN is used for low-cost devices.

2.2.2 Smart Subsystems

More and more driver-assisted technologies are becoming the de facto in a modern car. Some of the driver-assisted technologies available in a car include ABS, cruise control, lane-assist, power brakes, power steering, central locking systems, and so forth. Technology is now taking the next step to move toward autonomous control in which the subsystems will take over driving as a whole. Broadly, we classify these subsystems into three categories.

1. *Indicative smart subsystems*: Indicative systems identify certain states of the vehicle using their sensory inputs just to alert the driver. The smart blind-spot detection system is an example-indicative system that detects objects in a car's blind spot (the region around the vehicle that is not visible to the driver using rear view mirrors) and alerts the user. It uses sensory inputs such as radar and ultrasonic, and vehicle speed sensors to detect an alien object's presence. On detection, depending on the system, it alerts the user using a display, sound, or haptic warning in the steering wheel or seats. Other examples of indicative systems include lane departure warnings, tire pressure monitoring, and so forth.
2. *Reactive smart subsystems*: Reactive smart systems, on the other hand, take necessary actions to avoid potentially dangerous incidents. A very common example of such a system is an adaptive cruise control system that automatically adjusts the speed of a vehicle for the live road traffic. It uses a headway radar or lidar to detect traffic in front, and utilizes vehicle speed sensors, accelerator pedal position, and brake pedal position to identify the action to be taken for maintaining a safe distance on the road. It will then actuate the throttle or brakes to adjust the speed of the vehicle automatically when the vehicle is in a cruise mode. Other example subsystems include adaptive front lighting, parking systems, auto dimming mirrors, ABSs, airbag deployment, and so forth.
3. *Predictive smart subsystems*: In predictive smart systems, after identifying specific states of the vehicle, they anticipate certain actions from the driver. Instead of directly affecting the state of the car using actuators, they get the vehicle ready for such actions. A typical example of such a system is collision warning with brake support from Ford. In the event of an obstacle ahead and a potential collision, the system not only warns the user about the condition, it precharges the braking systems. This action will help to apply a full application of the brakes with a simple touch on the brake pedal, hence avoiding an imminent collision. The precrash safety feature found in some automobiles is another example for such systems.

3 SECURITY IN SMART CYBER-PHYSICAL SYSTEMS: SMART GRIDS

Cyber threats have now expanded from just targeting computers and smartphones to hacking power grids. In the recent past, many attacks on power grids have been reported.

1. *The attack on the Ukrainian power grid*: On December 23, 2015, a cyberattack on the Ukrainian power grid resulted in a power outage to approximately 225,000 customers. The attackers used spear phishing to gain access to the business networks. Using virtual private networks, the adversary entered the ICS network. Further, the attackers used existing remote access tools for issuing the critical commands directly from the remote station, mimicking an HMI operator. The attackers opened various CBs, which resulted in a system-wide collapse. The illegal entry into the utility's SCADA and control center caused these attacks. The attack also forced the system operators to move to manual mode to prevent further escalation. This attack exposed the vulnerabilities in the existing infrastructure. It is thus learned that an adversary can use spear phishing to install malware in a smart power grid network and use it to launch attacks. The Electricity Information Sharing and Analysis Center (E-ISAC) recommends various countermeasures to prevent attacks such as the one on the Ukraine in the future [2].
2. *Attacks on PMUs*: PMUs are deployed in many remote locations to capture phasors accurately and more frequently compared with traditional SCADA devices for wide area measurement, protection, and control. As the PMUs are time stamped using GPS signals, the measurements are vulnerable to data and GPS spoofing. An

---

[12] See https://svn.ipd.kit.edu/nlrp/public/FlexRay/FlexRayProtocolSpecificationVersion3.0.1.pdf.

[13] See http://www.opensig.org/about/specifications/.

adversary can cause an erroneous GPS clock offset of the PMU receiver, resulting in false time stamp calculation [5]. The error in time stamp calculation by the PMU can adversely affect the stability of the power system. It is also observed that the errors can even cause the tripping of generators and transmission lines.

It is also worth noting that an adversary need not intrude into the actual PMU device, he/she just needs to modify the timing signal received by the PMU device. The resulting measurements with incorrect timestamps will be communicated to the system operator, resulting in a false estimation of states. It will affect the voltage stability, fault location, and detection in transmission lines [6].

3. *Attacks on state estimation*: Reliable and secure operation of electrical grid banks rely on the precise estimation of the power system's operating state [4]. The integrity of SE depends on the precision of the measurement sensors. The dependence of the SCADA/EMS on the communication technology makes SE susceptible to data integrity attacks. Because SE is the crux of the entire power system operation and control, malicious data injection attacks in the measurement sensors can have catastrophic consequences.

False data injection attacks (FDIAs) can be random or targeted. FDIAs compromise both the confidentiality and integrity of the information obtained from smart meters. In a random-attack scenario, the attacker injects malicious data into random measurement sensors with a goal of making the SE erroneous. The random attacks can still be detected by the control center, but rather imperfectly due to the presence of measurement noise [7]. However, in targeted FDIAs, the goal is to inject predetermined errors in some specific state variables [8]. Such attacks, if injected stealthily on certain specific measurement sensors, are undetectable for the system operator as they bypass the bad data detection (BDD), even without meter noise.

A simple FDIA can be launched by injecting significant errors into the measurements. The errors should be just enough to cause changes in the system state, but also small enough to bypass BDD. The attack can be formulated as

$$J(\hat{x}_{bad}) = \sum_{i=1}^{m} (z_i - h(\hat{x}) + a_i)^2 / \sigma_i^2 \leq \tau. \tag{2}$$

Here a_i is the malicious error injected in the sensor z_i, $h(\hat{x})$ is the measurement function, $\hat{x}$ is the estimated state vector, and τ is the threshold for BDD.

If we assume that the adversary has acquired the network and topology information, a stealthy attack can be launched bypassing BDD [4], that is, $\| z - H\hat{x} \| \leq \tau$, if the attack vector, $a = Hc$, shown as follows:

$$\begin{aligned} \| (z+a) - H(\hat{x}+c) \| &= \| z - H\hat{x} + a - Hc \| \\ &= \| z - H\hat{x} \| \leq \tau. \end{aligned} \tag{3}$$

Here, H is measurement Jacobian. An adversary can launch an attack on any state variable, or multiple states, by making sure that the attack vector a satisfies Eq. (3). Even with limited network information or access to limited smart meters, the FDIAs can be launched [9].

FDIAs also impact the real-time power market where SE is used to determine real-time locational marginal prices [10, 11]. Furthermore, coordinated FDIAs with physical attacks can also be launched that are capable of causing system-wide disruptions. The adversary with access to network topology can craft a load redistribution attack, thereby forcing the system operator to change the generator dispatch schedule, which can cause uneconomic operation of power systems, transmission line overloading [12], load shedding [13], and in the worst case, cascaded tripping of power system components [14].

3.1 Countermeasures

For protecting smart grids against cyberattacks, a smart security infrastructure is required. Smart security includes security of both OT and IT. Encryption, digital signature, and authentication codes can be embedded in the information security layer to ensure confidentiality, integrity, and availability of information to both the sender and receiver. IT infrastructure includes servers and routers. Protocols and servers must be secured to maintain secure communication between PMUs, RTUs, IEDs, and the control center. It will also help to avoid malicious code injection and Denial of Service (DoS) attacks. Countermeasures for FDIAs can be categorized as *detection-based defense* and *protection-based defense*.

3.1.1 Protection of Critical Devices

The electrical power grid is a huge network of transmission lines, generation plants, and substations. The complex interconnectivity, which continues to grow and expand, has thousands of metering devices located miles apart for continuous monitoring to control power system events in real time. The cost of securing all the metering devices can be massive. To minimize the cost of protection, it is necessary to identify and protect critical components to secure power system operations. Graph theoretical approaches are applied to identify critical metering devices [15, 16]. Metering devices can also be identified and protected by considering the interaction between the attacker and defender. The optimization problem can be modeled for minimizing the number of smart meters protected such that none of the states can be attacked [17].

3.1.2 Moving Target Defense

The moving target defense (MTD) can also be applied to deceive adversaries in real time. The topology of the network can be dynamically changed without affecting generator and load dispatch, which will minimize the risks of data integrity attacks. The system operator randomly uses multiple sets of measurements for estimating the states, as shown in Fig. 6. The attacker, unaware of measurement sets used by the control center, fails to launch the attacks [18].

The operator can dynamically change network parameters to detect FDIAs. Distribution FACTS (D-FACTS) devices can be used to slightly modify the line reactances. The integrity of measurements can be validated if a proportional change is observed in the measurements [19].

3.2 Detection of FDIAs

Analyzing smart meter/sensor data along with corresponding power system events helps in detecting FDIAs. The measurement pattern is usually observed and compared with the previous data to detect measurement anomalies. FDIAs may be random or targeted. For the random attack, contrasting patterns in measurements compared with historical measurements could easily separate attack measurement samples from true measurements. However, if the attacked measurements follow the same pattern, a measurement variation-based approach is used for detecting anomalies [20]. The measurement variation-based approach uses real-time and historical measurement variations to calculate relative entropy. For each sample, the relative entropy is compared with a predefined threshold for detecting FDIAs. To further improve detection efficiency, transformation techniques are used on the measurement variations before calculating relative entropy [21].

3.2.1 Data-Driven Approach

With more and more automation incorporated at the OT level, a huge amount of data is available at the control center. This data can be used to detect abnormal behavior in these smart CPSs. SCADA receives data from sensors and metering devices that is used for Wide Area Monitoring, Protection and Control (WAMPAC), and is also stored in the historical database. Machine learning approaches can be used for short-term forecasting of power system states to detect anomalies in real time [22]. The approach is effective against detecting measurement anomalies that could cause significant operational impacts.

An artificial neural network is a network designed to replicate the human brain to perform complex tasks. A properly trained neural network can solve complex real-world problems, such as forecasting and estimation. A basic neural network consists of weights, bias, adders, and an activation function. Out of various neural network designs, feed-forward (FF), along with back propagation (BP), is the most popular architecture among researchers. An

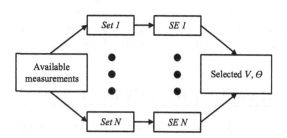

FIG. 6   Simple MTD strategy.

FIG. 7   An artificial neural network for load predictors.

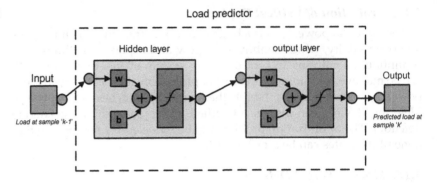

FIG. 8   Schematic for a data-driven approach to detect/identify FDIAs.

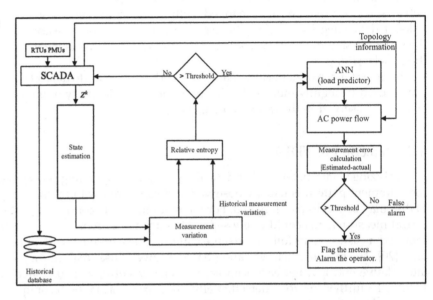

FFBP neural network [23] is used for estimating the load based on the loading condition of the preceding sample, as shown in Fig. 7. In the training phase, the neural network maps input-output for a given process. In this learning phase, the weights are optimized such that the error in the output is minimized. Once the training is complete, the network is tested with new inputs, and it is expected to have an accurate output.

For large power systems (with thousands of buses), the forecasting load for each sample can burden the SE process, which runs at 2-minute intervals. Therefore, the relative entropy-based detection strategy [21] can be used to raise an alarm in the event of attack detection. For the sample that is flagged as malicious, the load predictor strategy can be used for identifying compromised sensors [23]. The inputs to the load predictor are weather details (temperature, humidity, pressure, due point) for the present and previous sample, and demand at the previous sample. The output of the load predictor is the predicted demand for the present sample (the one flagged attacked during detection). The measurements for the predicted load are compared with actual measurements available from SCADA. The error is compared with a predefined threshold to identify the corrupted sensors. The complete schematic for the data-driven approach is shown in Fig. 8.

Once the attacked sensors are identified, the system operator can either replace the meters, use a different set of measurements, or discard the measurements, provided that the power system remains observable. The system operator can also use the pseudo-measurements to estimate the states and maintain observability. Moreover, strict measures can also be taken to ensure security once the sensors are identified.

4 SECURITY IN SMART CYBER-PHYSICAL SYSTEMS: SMART CARS

An unwanted aftereffect of automobiles becoming autonomous or semiautonomous is the potential for attackers to confuse or hack it. Researchers and hackers enlist various attacks that are possible on automobiles. We categorize these attacks under three different labels, which are described as follows.

1. *Direct physical access attacks*: In such attacks, the attacker will have complete access to the vehicle, and he or she can modify the software and hardware in it at his or her will. A potential attacker can be your mechanic or a car wash person. Hoppe et al. [24, 25] demonstrated many such attack scenarios. In the first attack scenario, an arbitrary code added to ECU resulted in a 0-day attack in which the car windows opened when its speed exceeded 200 kmph (kilometers per hour). In another attack, they demonstrated how airbag control systems can be removed from a car and could be masked using injected code. Other demonstrations include attacks on gateway ECUs and warning lights. Research from Koscher et al. [26] evaluated a car and performed extensive lab and on-road tests to demonstrate various attacks. On-road tests were performed at a decommissioned airport runway with a lot of safety precautions. Researchers manually introduced packets into the vehicular system to perform the attacks. Among the different attacks performed, some could be manually over-ridden, while others could not be. It is not very surprising that many of the attacks can be done on a running car also. Attacks demonstrated include frequent activation of lock relays and windshield wipers, trunk popping, permanent horn activation, disabling window and key lock relays, temporary RPM increase, idle RPM increase, prevention of braking, uneven engagement of car brakes, falsified speedometer readings, radio volume increase, car alarm honking, engine killing, and so forth. Some of the performed attacks are innocuous, but if used with a malicious intent, they can cause loss of reputation and trust. For example, if the car engine stops suddenly, the reliability aspect will be badly affected.

2. *Indirect physical access attacks*: In indirect physical access, the attacker cannot modify the hardware, but can introduce alien devices, such as CD, USB, and on-board diagnostic (OBD) devices. Devices that are connected to the OBD port of a vehicle with advanced external connectivity are a new trend in automobiles. The OBD port, being connected to the external CAN bus, can fetch various information about the car, including error codes. Most of these tools provide intelligent information about the car, and are connected to the Internet/cloud. Some of the popular devices include Automatic,[14] Progressive Snapshot,[15] Ford Reference VI,[16] Verizon Hum,[17] and so forth and a wide range of corresponding mobile phone applications. Miller and Valasek [27] demonstrated various attacks possible on cars using this OBD port. An OBD port is mandated by federal law in all cars in the United States, which has been in effect since 1996. It is generally used for monitoring emissions statistics by motor vehicle departments, checking the health of a car by mechanics, and so forth. They use ECOM cables to communicate with the CAN bus of two vehicles, the Ford Escape and Toyota Prius, and used tools, such as ECOMCat to read and write to the bus. Their research started with simple attacks such as displaying false data on the dashboard, and simple DoS attacks by overwhelming the bus. Eventually, they showed more advanced attacks such as disabling brakes, applying brakes, killing the engine, and so forth by introducing crafted packets to the CAN bus.

3. *External attacks*: In such attacks, attackers will make use of the external open interfaces or software vulnerabilities on an unaltered/factory condition vehicle. Researchers Miller and Valasek [28] famously hacked into an unaltered Jeep vehicle and controlled it remotely. The attack reportedly resulted in a 1.4 million vehicle recall by Chrysler. The Jeep is an advanced connected vehicle that has mobile connectivity built in using the Sprint network in the United States. Researchers reverse engineered and found that the D-Bus service (a software bus for interprocess communication and remote procedure calls) is running on the port 6667, and can be accessed anonymously. It will also allow anyone to run arbitrary code on the vehicle's head unit. Interestingly, they discovered that vulnerable vehicles can be found by just scanning the port 6667 on IP addresses starting with 21.0.0.0/8 and 25.0.0.0/8. The initial steps in the exploit chain include target identification (the IP address of the vehicle by scanning for port 6667) and exploitation of the OMAP chip in the head unit using D-Bus service. To control non-CAN features such as the radio, only these steps are necessary. However, in order to get control of the vehicle, the attacker can modify the v850 microcontroller firmware. Once done, the hacker is in a position to introduce arbitrary CAN messages to the vehicle, and hence can remotely control the vehicle. Despite fail-safe practices such as shutting down the system in case of irregularity, the attackers were able to perform malicious activities, such as killing the engine while running, locking and unlocking the car, activating the blinkers and windshield wipers, partially controlling the steering wheel (exploiting parking assist features, but only at low speeds), and so forth. Several other reports claim a crypto attack [29] on the keyless entry feature on cars from popular makers, including Volkswagen, Skoda, Volvo, and so forth.

---

[14] See https://www.automatic.com/.

[15] See https://www.progressive.com/auto/discounts/snapshot/.

[16] See https://shop.openxcplatform.com/ford-reference-vi.html.

[17] See https://www.hum.com/productstext.

4.1 Countermeasures

One of the core problems with the vehicular architecture is the presence of comparatively primitive bus technology, lacking cutting-edge security features, with far more sophisticated subsystems running on top. For example, the CAN bus is a broadcast-based bus in which all connected devices can see all the traffic, and there is no in-built concept of authentication or authorization. Any message on the wire is authenticated by default. This enables an attacker to introduce well-formed packets on to the wire to perform malicious activities. Research enlists two categories of techniques to secure the environment, which are described in the following sections.

4.1.1 Attack Prevention Techniques

The first approach is to prevent the attacks from happening. According to Wolfe et al. [30], a combination of hardware protection techniques, software protection techniques, and secure communication are required to achieve this. Newer protocols (varying in capabilities, speed, implementation overhead, and so forth) and the modification of existing protocols are proposed with this intent. LCAP [31] (Lightweight CAN Authentication Protocol) is one such protocol, with minimum overhead, that is a modification to the existing CAN network. The technique is based on a preshared key and magic number exchanged between the sender and receiver. At the beginning of a drive cycle, all devices perform an initial setup, and will have a session key, HMAC key, and a channel initial magic number, which are used for subsequent message transmissions. For data exchange, the sender will append the magic number to the message and encrypt it using a session key. The receiver will authenticate the message using the magic number after decrypting it. However, this protocol will have the overhead for cryptographic calculations.

CANAuth [32] is another proposed protocol that is backward compatible. This protocol also depends on a preshared key stored in a tamper-proof location with each of the entities. A session key will be generated using the preshared key and it will be used for authenticating messages. In CANAuth, considering the hard constraints on time and message length, the authentication data is transmitted out of band using the CAN+ [33] protocol. Each authentication message will have a 32-bit counter value to prevent replay attacks and an 80-bit signature with this protocol.

LiBrA-CAN [34] is another proposed protocol to prevent attacks that uses CAN-FD[18] (a newer CAN protocol with flexible data rates). LiBrA-CAN presents two new paradigms, namely, key splitting and MAC mixing for message authentication. The protocol can be used in a master oriented flavor (a node with higher computational capabilities is used for authentication), which includes centralized, cumulative, and load balanced authentication schemes, or distributed flavor, which includes two-stage authentication and multimaster authentication schemes. In comparison with other protocols, they have efficient forgery detection using MAC mixing and lesser authentication delays.

Apart from protocol-specific drawbacks such as time constraints, the requirement of preshared keys and higher computational power are some disadvantages of such techniques. Another major drawback for this class of techniques is that we can only protect future vehicles, not the present ones on the road. Moreover, the automotive domain is a huge industry, and it requires a long time to change. Koscher et al. [26] describe these stringent "operational and economic realities" in the automotive industry and explain the importance of a detection strategy for automobiles.

4.1.2 Attack Detection and Mitigation

The second strategy to make the automotive domain safe is attack detection and mitigation. Different companies have come up with automotive intrusion detection systems. Panasonic Corporation is developing an intrusion detection and prevention system[19] (IDPS) that combines host intrusion detection technology (which combines behavioral information), in-vehicle device-type intrusion detection technology (it monitors and detects unauthorized commands in the in-vehicle network, both CAN-based and Ethernet-based), and cloud-type vehicle intrusion detection technology (detects intrusion by analyzing logs collected from different vehicles using machine learning). Karamba Security[20] is another company that develops tools such as *Karamba Carwall* (it generates policies based on factory settings and embeds them into ECUs to continuously validate actions at runtime) and *Karamba SafeCAN* (it authenticates and hardens in-car network communications, helping ECUs to ignore commands from invalid ECUs or physical hacks). Escrypt[21] is yet another company that develops an IDPS for vehicles. Their products, *CycurIDS* and *CycurGUARD*, analyze data from multiple vehicles and detect potential intrusions. We can classify the basic research in this domain into two subcategories based on whether the technique uses a semantic understanding of the underlying data.

---

[18] See https://can-newsletter.org/assets/files/ttmedia/raw/e5740b7b5781b8960f55efcc2b93edf8.pdf.

[19] See http://itsworldcongress2017.org/wp-content/uploads/2017/11/kishikawa_20171025.pdf.

[20] See https://karambasecurity.com/products.

[21] See https://www.escrypt.com/en/solutions-overview.

4.1.2.1 Statistics-Oriented Techniques

Research enlists different techniques for attack detection and mitigation. One such research direction is by applying machine learning techniques on raw CAN messages without considering the semantics of the messages.

Muter et al. [35] proposed an entropy-based approach for anomaly detection in vehicles. In this technique, various information theoretic measures are used to calculate entropy. Entropy, in general, measures "how much coincidence" of a given dataset, or it represents the abstract representation of randomness. However, due to restricted vehicular network specifications, the amount of randomness (or entropy) is low. Hence, in their approach, they consider an adaptation of the existing entropy-based intrusion detection techniques. To calculate entropy, they use three levels of data abstraction. Binary-level data abstraction consists of raw ones and zeros. At this level, either a bitwise classifier (which considers each bit as an event) or x-bitwise classifier (a combination of x bits is considered as an event) can be used. The next level of abstraction is the signal level, in which an event is generated for every signal value of the CAN message. The assumption is that there are only fixed messages in a vehicular network unlike a general protocol such as TCP or UDP. The final level of abstraction is the protocol level. CAN defines 12 fields for data frames in the base format. The classifier in this level generates an event for every field in the CAN message. The entropy (Eq. 4) and relative entropy (Eq. 5) are calculated using standard information theoretic techniques. Their technique was put against simulated attack scenarios such as *increased frequency*, *message flooding*, and so forth, and showed that most attack scenarios caused variations in the calculated entropy, and could be utilized for detecting anomalies.

$$H(X) = \sum_{x \in C_X} P(x) \log \frac{1}{P(x)}$$

where

$\quad C_x$: Set of classes for dataset X,

$\quad P(x)$: Probability of x in X.

(4)

$$RelEnt(p/q) = \sum_{x \in C_X} p(x) \log \frac{p(x)}{q(x)}$$

where

$\quad C_x$: Set of classes for dataset X,

$\quad p(x), q(x)$: Probability distribution over $x \in C_x$.

(5)

Taylor et al.[36] use long short-term memory (LSTM) to detect anomalies. LSTM is used to learn long-term dependencies in sequences of data. In their research, they considered each bit on the CAN message as a feature for the LSTM and trained the network. Logically, once trained, the network will be able to predict the next CAN message, given a previous sequence of CAN messages. In this technique, they trained a separate LSTM network for each CAN message. For detecting an anomaly, a scalar anomaly score is required. To generate this score, they use the binary loss function, which is defined as

$$L\left(\hat{b}_k, bk\right) = -\left(b_k \log\left(\hat{b}_k + \epsilon\right) + (1 - b_k) \log\left(1 - \hat{b}_k + \epsilon\right)\right)$$

where

$\quad b_k$: kth bit in the Message at step i,

$\quad \hat{b}_k$: kth bit's predicted value by the network,

$\quad \epsilon$: a fixed value that caps the maximum loss.

(6)

The loss function will have a low value for incorrect and middling predictions and very high value for confident and incorrect predictions. The final anomaly score is calculated by combining the bit losses over the entire sequence using various strategies such as *maximum bit loss* (maximum of all bit losses over the entire sequence), *maximum word loss* (maximum in average bit loss over all words), *window max* (maximum in average bit loss over words in a window), *log window max* (log mean of average bit loss over words in a window), *sequence mean* (mean bit loss over the complete sequence), and so forth. To detect anomalies, an empirically found threshold will be used on the calculated scalar value.

In other parallel research, Kang et al. [37, 38] used deep neural networks (DNNs) directly on the bit stream. The motivation behind using a DNN is its ability to model nonlinear relationships. In their training phase, features representing the statistical behavior of the CAN packet are extracted. For feature extraction efficiency, they use each bit in the DATA field (64 bits) of a CAN packet as features. To reduce the dimension, they propose splitting the DATA field into mode information and value information depending on the CAN message ID and avoid using unwanted bits from training. Now using these extracted features, they train a deep neural network with the input layer's size as the number of extracted features, and the output layer with two neurons. In between, the network will have a fixed number of neurons. The two output neurons represent an attack packet and a normal packet, respectively. That is, if the first neuron is activated, it signifies that it is an attack packet, and if the other neuron is activated, it signifies a normal packet. In comparison with an FF network, they were able to get a better performance on their evaluation with data generated using open car test-bed and network experiments (OCTANE) [39].

4.1.2.2 Semantics-Oriented Techniques

All the preceding techniques consider a CAN packet as a flow of structured bit streams of messages. In semantics-oriented techniques, the semantics of the messages are considered. It implies that each CAN message is first interpreted as a state of the automobile, or action performed on it.

Narayanan et al. [40] hypothesize that the flow of packets in a car is not just a flow of independent messages, but they form the state of that vehicle. As a result, we can extract the sequence of observations from this bit stream. For example, $O = O_1, O_2, O_3, ..., O_t, ..., O_n$ can be a sequence of n observations extracted from a car, where O_t is the observation at time t. Each observation $O_t \in O$ is a vector $O_t = \langle v_{t,1}, v_{t,2}, v_{t,3}, ..., v_{t,i}, ..., v_{t,m} \rangle$, where $v_{t,i}$ represents the value of a sensor/ECU i at time t. For example, consider only two sensors (the speed sensor and door sensor), and the following sequence of observations from O_1 to O_6 under three different conditions.

Normal Sequence	Abnormal Sequence$_1$	Abnormal Sequence$_2$
$O_1 \leftarrow \langle v_{1,1}=0, v_{1,2}=Closed \rangle$	$O_1 \leftarrow \langle v_{1,1}=20, v_{1,2}=Closed \rangle$	$O_1 \leftarrow \langle v_{1,1}=20, v_{1,2}=Closed \rangle$
$O_2 \leftarrow \langle v_{2,1}=0, v_{2,2}=Open \rangle$	$O_2 \leftarrow \langle v_{2,1}=22, v_{2,2}=Closed \rangle$	$O_2 \leftarrow \langle v_{2,1}=22, v_{2,2}=Closed \rangle$
$O_3 \leftarrow \langle v_{3,1}=0, v_{3,2}=Closed \rangle$	$O_3 \leftarrow \langle v_{3,1}=25, v_{3,2}=Open \rangle$	$O_3 \leftarrow \langle v_{3,1}=25, v_{3,2}=Closed \rangle$
$O_4 \leftarrow \langle v_{4,1}=2, v_{4,2}=Closed \rangle$	$O_4 \leftarrow \langle v_{4,1}=28, v_{4,2}=Open \rangle$	$O_4 \leftarrow \langle v_{4,1}=85, v_{4,2}=Closed \rangle$
$O_5 \leftarrow \langle v_{5,1}=5, v_{5,2}=Closed \rangle$	$O_5 \leftarrow \langle v_{5,1}=30, v_{5,2}=Closed \rangle$	$O_5 \leftarrow \langle v_{5,1}=28, v_{5,2}=Closed \rangle$
$O_6 \leftarrow \langle v_{6,1}=7, v_{6,2}=Closed \rangle$	$O_6 \leftarrow \langle v_{6,1}=34, v_{6,2}=Closed \rangle$	$O_6 \leftarrow \langle v_{6,1}=25, v_{6,2}=Closed \rangle$

The first column under *Normal Sequence* represents a normal scenario of events in which a passenger enters the car while the speed remains 0. However, consider the sequence of observations under *Abnormal Sequence$_1$*. While the speed is increasing from 20 to 34, a door is reported as open, which is against general logic. If the sensor values are taken separately, they look normal, but taking them together makes it look abnormal. Yet another example is given under the sequence *Abnormal Sequence$_2$* in which the speed is showing a sudden spike from $25 \rightarrow 85$ and then $85 \rightarrow 28$ which is very abnormal in itself.

Hidden Markov models [41] (HMM) are used to find the posterior probability of a sequence. In this technique, an HMM model is trained from the normal sequence of observations extracted from the CAN bit stream. During the anomaly detection phase, the incoming bit stream is first converted to a sequence of observations. Using a window size (representing the number of observations need to be considered at one go), the posterior probability of the sequence is determined. An empirically determined threshold is then used to detect anomalous windows of observations. In the evaluation of the system, different single sensor and multisensor anomalous scenarios were easily detected.

```
HASCOMPONENT (VEHICLE, ENVIRONMENTLIGHTSENSOR) ^ HASCOMPONENT (VEHICLE,
    VEHICLESPEEDSENSOR) ^ HASCOMPONENT (VEHICLE, HEADLIGHT) ^
    HASSTATEVALUE (ENVIRONMENTLIGHTSENSOR, "LOW") ^ HASSTATEVALUE
    (HEADLIGHT, "OFF") ^ HASSTATEVALUE (VEHICLESPEED, "HIGH") ==>
    HASSTATEVALUE (CURRENTVEHICLESTATE, "ANOMALOUS NO LIGHT")}
```

In another work, Narayanan et al. [42] used semantic web technologies to detect various attacks. They used logical reasoning over a knowledge base and current sensor values to extract context from data. Their proposed architecture has two components, a cross-component inferencing engine and a local context detection (LCD) layer. The cross-component inferencing engine internally uses an ontology to represent the domain knowledge. The ontology is an extended version of IOT-lite ontology with new attributes, such as *senseAttribute* and *hasStateValue*. It is then populated with domain-specific instances and domain-specific rules (specified using SWRL [43]). The LCD layer extracts valid messages from the bit stream and further processes them to generate local contexts. Some examples of local context include *highSpeed*, *normalSpeed*, *suddenAcceleration*, and so forth. Technically, any machine learning technique could be deployed to generate local contexts. Now a reasoner will reason over these local contexts to detect anomalous situations. Domain experts can also write rules on top of this ontology using SWRL. An example SWRL rule that suggests driving without headlights while lighting conditions are poor is presented herein. The main challenge in this technique is to aggregate all the domain knowledge rules, and this research proposes to develop a rule mining engine from available normal data.

5 CONCLUSION AND FUTURE DIRECTIONS

Smart CPSs are essential components of Smart Cities, and their secure operation is critical to maintaining integrity and trustworthiness of the entire infrastructure. Section 2 described the architecture of two such smart CPSs. We can find many similarities between these domains.

- Both CPSs have a large number of sensors connected to the network. In a smart car, the interconnection network is within the car, while the interconnection network of smart grids spans across a much larger landscape.
- Both CPSs take smart decisions after complex calculations on real-world data collected from these sensors.
- Another similarity in both the domains is the constraints they had while developing the system. In both smart cars and smart grids, the need for supporting legacy systems is vital. Otherwise, it will be a substantial financial burden to replace all existing infrastructure. In smart grids, replacing the entire existing infrastructure with more advanced and secure infrastructure is nearly impossible because of this. Similarly in smart cars, to change the ECUs and different ECU components in a car, the century-old automotive industry might need to disrupt its assembly line and subcomponent manufacturers (and bear the associated cost).
- Due to the presence of constraints in their architecture, the system designers did not implement robust, cryptographically secure protocols for their communication. Attackers utilized this as a vulnerability point. For example, because most cars use less secure broadcast buses internally, any message on the CAN is directly authenticated and authorized. The system cannot differentiate between a message from an attacker and a message from a legitimate ECU. Similarly, in the smart grid domain, smart meters at home can act as an entry point for the adversary to trace back to the control center and inject malicious code to manipulate the operation at his or her will.
- Often classic cybersecurity techniques (the same as any other cyber domains) are utilized to access the CPS network. For example, in the Ukrainian power grid attack, the attackers used spear phishing and stealing valid credentials to gain access to the network. Similarly, in the Jeep hack of 2016, researchers used an open Dbus service to gain initial access to the car's internal network.
- A full-scale attack on CPSs can cause financial damage, reputation loss, and large-scale service disruptions. The financial implications of recalling 1.4 million vehicles after the Jeep hack was reported, and large-scale power outages caused by the Ukrainian smart grid hack are authentic testimonies for this.
- Secure protocols and control units are solutions in both these domains. However, the requirement to support legacy systems makes detection strategies vital in both domains. Even after complete migrations to newer and more secure protocols, detection strategies will remain significant, because a determined attacker is always out there trying to find ways to get into the system.

Researchers demonstrated various attacks on these CPS domains, which are detailed in Sections 3 and 4. Many of the current countermeasures proposed to defend attacks in both these domains use a data-driven approach. However, these techniques either consider values from different streams separately, or do not consider the semantics of the system, and overlook certain stealthy attacks. If domain semantics are avoided, a determined attacker can utilize this to find ways past their detection. For example, to evade the detection of fault data injection, a skilled attacker injects errors only in small magnitudes, which will not raise alarm. To see the effect of ignoring the interrelationship between sensors, consider the scenario in which the speed of a car is increasing gradually. This is not an abnormal scenario until there is an obstruction in front of it. Similarly, in the smart grid domain, a fault in a transmission line will cause transience in voltages and currents, but line overloading will exist only when there is more consumption of power in the nearby buses.

Future research on these domains will stem from the fact that they share many characteristics, problems, and scenarios. A study on the adaptability of techniques applicable in one domain to another is an interesting avenue to explore. Another path to consider is the development of a human-like learning and monitoring system. It is clear that the attacker's intention is always to disrupt the normal behavior of the system (in both smart grids and smart cars). For example, in the Ukrainian smart grid attack, the attackers went on to open the CBs for multiple substations together, and in the Jeep hack, hackers killed the engine of a moving car. These situations are improbable in a normal environment, and could be easily detected by a human monitoring the system. In the case of humans, we interpret context from all the measurements and analyze the situation. We can also learn from previous experiences. Holistically, a more robust risk assessment model, and techniques that can learn and adapt on their own are required to protect the individual ecosystems and infrastructure. Exploring more advanced machine learning techniques such as convolutional neural networks and adversarial networks, can develop such systems. Such techniques can also provide common domain-independent learning systems that can automatically extract context from different sensor data and detect attacks.

References

[1] C. Harrison, B. Eckman, R. Hamilton, P. Hartswick, J. Kalagnanam, J. Paraszczak, P. Williams, Foundations for smarter cities, IBM J. Res. Dev. 54 (4) 2010 1–16.
[2] Defense Use Case, Analysis of the Cyber Attack on the Ukrainian Power Grid, Electricity Information Sharing and Analysis Center (E-ISAC), 2016.
[3] F.C. Schweppe, Power system static-state estimation, Part I, II, III, IEEE Trans. Power App. Syst. 89 (1) 1970 120–135.
[4] A. Abur, A. Gomez-Exposito, Power System State Estimation: Theory and Implementation, CRC Press, 2004.
[5] X. Jiang, J. Zhang, B.J. Harding, J.J. Makela, A.D. Domı, et al., Spoofing GPS receiver clock offset of phasor measurement units, IEEE Trans. Power Syst. 28 (3) 2013 3253–3262.
[6] Z. Zhang, S. Gong, A.D. Dimitrovski, H. Li, Time synchronization attack in smart grid: impact and analysis, IEEE Trans. Smart Grid 4 (1) 2013 87–98.
[7] O. Kosut, L. Jia, R.J. Thomas, L. Tong, Malicious data attacks on the smart grid, IEEE Trans. Smart Grid 2 (4) 2011 645–658.
[8] Y. Liu, P. Ning, M.K. Reiter, False data injection attacks against state estimation in electric power grids, ACM Trans. Inf. Syst. Secur. 14 (1) (2011) 13.
[9] X. Liu, Z. Li, Local load redistribution attacks in power systems with incomplete network information, IEEE Trans. Smart Grid 5 (4) 2014 1665–1676.
[10] A.L. Ott, Experience with PJM market operation, system design, and implementation, IEEE Trans. Power Syst. 18 (2) 2003 528–534.
[11] T. Zheng, E. Litvinov, Ex post pricing in the co-optimized energy and reserve market, IEEE Trans. Power Syst. 21 (4) 2006 1528–1538.
[12] X. Liu, Z. Li, Trilevel modeling of cyber attacks on transmission lines, IEEE Trans. Smart Grid (99) 2015. https://doi.org/10.1109/TSG.2015.2475701.
[13] Y. Yuan, Z. Li, K. Ren, Quantitative analysis of load redistribution attacks in power systems, IEEE Trans. Parallel Distrib. Syst. 23 (9) 2012 1731–1738.
[14] K. Khanna, B.K. Panigrahi, A. Joshi, Bi-level modelling of false data injection attacks on security constrained optimal power flow, IET Gener. Transm. Distrib. 11 (14) 2017 3586–3593.
[15] R.B. Bobba, K.M. Rogers, Q. Wang, H. Khurana, K. Nahrstedt, T.J. Overbye, Detecting false data injection attacks on DC state estimation, in: Preprints of the First Workshop on Secure Control Systems, CPSWEEK, 2010, 2010. vol.
[16] S. Bi, Y.J. Zhang, Defending mechanisms against false-data injection attacks in the power system state estimation, in: 2011 IEEE GLOBECOM Workshops (GC Wkshps), IEEE, 2011, pp. 1162–1167.
[17] R. Deng, G. Xiao, R. Lu, Defending against false data injection attacks on power system state estimation, IEEE Trans. Ind. Inf. 13 (1) 2017 198–207.
[18] Y. Yao, Z. Li, MTD-inspired state estimation based on random measurements selection, in: 2016 North American Power Symposium (NAPS), IEEE, 2016, pp. 1–6.
[19] K.R. Davis, K.L. Morrow, R. Bobba, E. Heine, Power flow cyber attacks and perturbation-based defense, in: 2012 IEEE Third International Conference on Smart Grid Communications (SmartGridComm)2012, pp. 342–347.
[20] G. Chaojun, P. Jirutitijaroen, M. Motani, Detecting false data injection attacks in AC state estimation, IEEE Trans. Smart Grid 6 (5) 2015 2476–2483.
[21] S.K. Singh, K. Khanna, R. Bose, B.K. Panigrahi, A. Joshi, Joint-transformation-based detection of false data injection attacks in smart grid, IEEE Trans. Ind. Inf. 14 (1) 2018 89–97.
[22] A. Ashok, M. Govindarasu, V. Ajjarapu, Online detection of stealthy false data injection attacks in power system state estimation, IEEE Trans. Smart Grid (99) 2017, https://doi.org/10.1109/TSG.2016.2596298.
[23] K. Khanna, B.K. Panigrahi, A. Joshi, AI-based approach to identify compromised meters in data integrity attacks on smart grid, IET Gener. Transm. Distrib. 12 (5) 2018 1052–1066.
[24] T. Hoppe, J. Dittman, Sniffing/replay attacks on CAN buses: a simulated attack on the electric window lift classified using an adapted CERT taxonomy, in: Proceedings of the 2nd Workshop on Embedded Systems Security (WESS), 2007, pp. 1–6.

[25] T. Hoppe, S. Kiltz, J. Dittmann, Security threats to automotive CAN networks-practical examples and selected short-term countermeasures, in: Computer Safety, Reliability, and Security, Springer, 2008, pp. 235–248.

[26] K. Koscher, A. Czeskis, F. Roesner, S. Patel, T. Kohno, S. Checkoway, D. McCoy, B. Kantor, D. Anderson, H. Shacham, et al., Experimental security analysis of a modern automobile, in: 2010 IEEE Symposium on Security and Privacy (SP), IEEE, 2010, pp. 447–462.

[27] C. Miller, C. Valasek, Adventures in automotive networks and control units, in: DEF CON 21 Hacking Conference, Las Vegas, NV, 2013.

[28] C. Miller, C. Valasek, Remote exploitation of an unaltered passenger vehicle, Tech. Rep., Blackhat, 2015.

[29] D. Storm, Hack to steal cars with keyless ignition: Volkswagen spent 2 years hiding flaw. Available from: http://www.computerworld.com/article/2971826/cybercrime-hacking/hack-to-steal-cars-with-keyless-ignition-volkswagen-spent-2-years-hiding-flaw.html.

[30] M. Wolf, A. Weimerskirch, T. Wollinger, State of the art: embedding security in vehicles, EURASIP J. Embed. Syst. 2007 (1) 2007 074706.

[31] A. Hazem, H.A. Fahmy, LCAP-A lightweight CAN authentication protocol for securing in-vehicle networks, in: 10th ESCAR Embedded Security in Cars Conference, Berlin, Germany, 6, 2012. vol.

[32] A. Van Herrewege, D. Singelee, I. Verbauwhede, CANAuth—a simple, backward compatible broadcast authentication protocol for CAN bus, in: ECRYPT Workshop on Lightweight Cryptography, 2011.

[33] T. Ziermann, S. Wildermann, J. Teich, CAN+: a new backward-compatible Controller Area Network (CAN) protocol with up to 16× higher data rates, in: Proceedings of the Conference on Design, Automation and Test in Europe, European Design and Automation Association, 2009, pp. 1088–1093.

[34] B. Groza, S. Murvay, A. Van Herrewege, I. Verbauwhede, LiBrA-CAN: lightweight broadcast authentication for controller area networks, ACM Trans. Embed. Comput. Syst. 16 (3) 2017 90.

[35] M. Müter, N. Asaj, Entropy-based anomaly detection for in-vehicle networks, in: 2011 IEEE Intelligent Vehicles Symposium (IV), IEEE, 2011, pp. 1110–1115.

[36] A. Taylor, S. Leblanc, N. Japkowicz, Anomaly detection in automobile control network data with long short-term memory networks, in: 2016 IEEE International Conference on Data Science and Advanced Analytics (DSAA), IEEE, 2016, pp. 130–139.

[37] M.-J. Kang, J.-W. Kang, A novel intrusion detection method using deep neural network for in-vehicle network security, in: 2016 IEEE 83rd Vehicular Technology Conference (VTC Spring), IEEE, 2016, pp. 1–5.

[38] M.-J. Kang, J.-W. Kang, Intrusion detection system using deep neural network for in-vehicle network security, PLoS ONE 11 (6) 2016 e0155781.

[39] C.E. Everett, D. McCoy, OCTANE (Open Car Testbed and Network Experiments): bringing cyber-physical security research to researchers and students, in: CSET, 2013.

[40] S.N. Narayanan, S. Mittal, A. Joshi, OBDSecureAlert: an anomaly detection system for vehicles. in: 2016 IEEE International Conference on Smart Computing (SMARTCOMP), 2016, pp. 1–6, https://doi.org/10.1109/SMARTCOMP.2016.7501710.

[41] L. Rabiner, B. Juang, An introduction to hidden Markov models, IEEE ASSP Mag. 3 (1) 1986 4–16.

[42] S. Nair, S. Mittal, A. Joshi, Using semantic technologies to mine vehicular context for security, in: 37th IEEE Sarnoff Symposium, 2016.

[43] I. Horrocks, P.F. Patel-Schneider, H. Boley, S. Tabet, B. Grosof, M. Dean, et al., SWRL: a semantic web rule language combining OWL and RuleML, W3C Member Submission 21 2004 79.

12

Priority-Based and Privacy-Preserving Electric Vehicle Dynamic Charging System With Divisible E-Payment

Mahmoud Nabil*, Muhammad Bima*, Ahmad Alsharif*, Willaim Johnson*, Surya Gunukula*, Mohamed Mahmoud*, and Mohamed Abdallah†

*Department of Electrical and Computer Engineering, Tennessee Tech University, Cookeville, TN, United States
†College of Science and Engineering, Hamad bin Khalifa University, Doha, Qatar

1 INTRODUCTION

Electric vehicles (EVs) have become increasingly popular due to zero CO_2 emissions and their promotion of renewable resource energy generators. Instead of relying on gasoline for energy, they can just be plugged in and have their batteries charged. One of the challenges facing the wide acceptance of EVs is that it takes a lot of time to recharge batteries, and less time, in comparison, to discharge. This, therefore, requires that EVs will frequently be charged as drivers use them [1]. Dynamic charging is a technology that is proposed to ameliorate this situation. It enables moving EVs to charge wirelessly from stationed charging pads (CP) [2]. The EV, therefore, does not need to stop and wait in order to get charged. It gets charged as it goes over the CPs.

Before charging, the EV needs to communicate with various system entities that include a bank, a charging service provider (CSP), roadside units (RSUs), and CPs. However, these communications raise privacy and security concerns that should be thoroughly investigated to ensure the proper functionality of the system. In this chapter, we present a scheme that provides integrated, secure, and privacy-preserving authentication, prioritization, and payment for dynamic charging. First, the EV should communicate with the bank to purchase divisible e-coins that will be used when the EV needs to charge. Hence, a secure, efficient, and flexible payment mechanism should be employed to facilitate the payment and spending of e-coins so that each EV can adjust the value of the e-coin according to the charging amount. Moreover, EV drivers should be able to purchase the e-coins anonymously to preserve their location privacy. An efficient divisible payment scheme is proposed in [3] that allows the user to purchase divisible e-coins of value 2^n from the bank, then the user can spend anonymously adjustable e-coin values at different merchants. Divisible e-coins are a requirement for the flexibility of the dynamic charging system, where the EVs can adjust the e-coin value according to the amount of the energy required. In our scheme, we integrated the payment scheme proposed in [3] with our authentication and priority determination to allow EV to purchase and spend divisible e-coins efficiently. Moreover, we modified the verifications needed by the payment scheme to prevent false accusation attacks of double-spending, which can happen when a legitimate EV spends an e-coin at a malicious CSP. This CSP can pass the e-coin to another EV that can also spend the e-coin at a different CSP. Therefore, when both CSPs deposit their e-coins at the bank, the legitimate EV is detected as a double-spender. Our modifications prevent this scenario from happening in the system.

After the EV purchases an e-coins, it communicates with the CSP by sending a charging request that includes the amount of needed energy, whereas the CSP needs to check if it has enough energy to service the set of requests it receives at a given instance in time. In the event that the available energy cannot serve all requests, prioritization becomes necessary. EVs are serviced based on a set of predefined criteria, and the necessity of the demands [4, 5]. For example, ambulances and police vehicles should be given high priority. In our scheme, a priority policy is determined by each charging station, and a multiauthority, attribute-based encryption (ABE) scheme is used to ensure the security and privacy of the policy [6].

Moreover, the charging process requires exchanging messages between EV, RSUs, and CPs to charge authorized EVs, but this can be used to identify EV, hence, the location privacy of the EV driver can be breached. Because these messages are transmitted via wireless communications, it is imperative that the data are secured against any eavesdropper. In order to address these issues, an efficient hierarchical authentication scheme that is based on symmetric-key cryptography is used. The scheme allows the EV to first authenticate with the CSP and receive secret keys, called tokens, that are shared with the RSUs. After using these tokens to authenticate to the RSUs, the EV receives another secret token that is shared with a number of CPs under each RSU control to further authenticate with the CPs for the charging process.

Designing an efficient, privacy-preserving, and secure scheme that integrates authentication, prioritization, and payment for dynamic charging systems is a challenging task. It is necessary for the dynamic charging system to efficiently authenticate the EVs that need to charge. Also, the payment process should be efficient and flexible. In summary, for the dynamic charging system to be fully functional, EVs need to be able to communicate securely and anonymously with several entities. The CSP, on the other hand, should be able to discern authorized EVs and allow them to authenticate to RSUs and CPs to charge. Activities such as bill payment should be performed seamlessly while preserving the privacy of the EV drivers. Unlike existing schemes for dynamic charging systems [4, 7] that do not provide an integrated solution for the dynamic charging system, in this chapter, an efficient and secure privacy-preserving scheme for dynamic charging of EVs is presented that provides an integrated solution for anonymous authentication, prioritization, and payment. The main three components of our scheme are summarized as follows.

- *Multiauthority attribute-based prioritization.* The CSP is able to securely prioritize charging requests based on the attributes of the EV received from different authorities. During this prioritization, the attributes values of EVs are kept confidential from the CSP. It only knows that a given EV fulfills a given attribute requirement, but does not know the exact attribute set the EV possesses. In addition, this secure prioritization prevents any malicious EV from claiming a false priority level.
- *E-payment.* An efficient, flexible, and anonymous e-payment scheme with divisible e-coins is used for billing in the proposed dynamic charging system. The scheme allows the EV to spend a prepurchased e-coin at the charging station anonymously and efficiently. Furthermore, the value of the e-coin can be adjusted according to the amount of charge that the EV gets.
- *Efficient hierarchical authentication.* A lightweight and scalable authentication scheme based on symmetric-key cryptography is presented to enable fast authentication between the EV and CSP. The scheme allows the EV to get secret tokens from CSPs that are shared with the RSUs. These tokens allow mutual authentication between the EV and RSU. Similarly, the EV receives secret tokens from the RSU that are shared with the CPs it controls to allow authentication between the EV and CPs.

The remainder of this chapter is organized as follows. A review of existing literature is presented in Section 2. Preliminaries are presented in Section 3. The proposed scheme is explained in Section 4. Security analysis and performance evaluation of the proposed scheme are presented in Sections 5 and 6, respectively. Finally, conclusions are drawn in Section 7.

2 LITERATURE REVIEW

This section discusses the related literature in the area of priority-based, privacy-preserving dynamic charging systems. The discussion in this section is divided into three parts that focus on the main aspects of the chapter, namely: authentication, payment, and prioritization.

2.1 Anonymous Authentication Schemes for Electric Vehicle Charging

Several authentication schemes have been proposed for EV communication [1, 2, 8, 9]. In [8], a scheme, called Lynx was developed to perform real-time reporting of EV information, such as the trip start time, state of charge, and so forth. anonymously to the utility company. A token is generated by EV, which it uses to create secret keys shared with the utility using the Diffie-Hellman protocol. In addition, Lynx uses a partially blind signature scheme to ensure the anonymity of users. The scheme also encourages EV participation by giving anonymous reward receipts created by the utility.

Portune+ [9] proposes an authentication scheme in a dynamic charging system that relies on symmetric-key cryptography. The scheme allows the EVs to anonymously authenticate to the CPs while their location privacy is being maintained. Because the EV will be moving over multiple CPs as it charges, billing is implemented in such a way that the total amount is computed only after the charging session is complete. Also, CPs are required to forward authentication credentials to subsequent CPs, so the EV does not have to authenticate frequently. However, the key distribution process is inefficient, as the utility needs to forward all pseudonyms and corresponding keys to all CPs. CPs also need to have a large storage space to store these data, thereby leading to significant storage and communication overhead.

In [2], a fast authentication scheme is proposed for EV charging. The scheme uses a Just Fast Keying [10] approach to initiate the charging session with each RSU, which serves as an intermediary between the EV and the utility. To enable a fast response and eliminate the need for the EV to frequently authenticate as it travels between RSUs, EV credentials are forwarded from one RSU to another. The scheme, however, is susceptible to a replay attack, does not consider the privacy of EVs, and also does not consider payment.

An authentication scheme was proposed in [1] to expedite the authentication between EV and CPs. The scheme consists of two main parts: direct and indirect authentication. In the direct authentication, the EV and CP authenticate with each other directly. After that, the CP forwards the authentication request to the utility for the authentication of drivers. Elgamal encryption over an elliptic curve is used for storing cryptographic keys in a revocation list. EVs have their credentials stored in a tamper-proof module, and are activated for usage by the registered motor authority (MA). These keys are updated at specific intervals by the same authority. For revocation of keys, a number of registered revocation authorities have to cooperate, using credentials from MA to identify the EV associated with a key. A large number of CPs, and the frequency of communication with the utility can lead to a communication bottleneck at the CSP.

2.2 E-Payment Schemes

In line with maintaining anonymity while charging, it is imperative that the payment scheme preserves the privacy of EV drivers. An e-cash system can provide anonymity to EV drivers. However, the lingering problem of double spending in e-cash system still persists. This problem is defined as the act of spending a given denomination of cash more than once, that is, after it has been initially spent. Empowered by the anonymity that e-cash provides, malicious EV drivers involved in double spending will go unpunished unless something is done to impose accountability. This section discusses some of the e-cash schemes that have been presented in the literature to address the aforementioned issues.

In [11], Camenisch et al. proposed an efficient offline anonymous e-cash scheme, where a user can withdraw a wallet containing 2^l e-coins, where coins could be spent without being linked together. This scheme utilizes storage space efficiently and does not require a third party to trace e-coins. The anonymous identity of users is rescinded if it carries out double spending, thereby all spending of these e-coins can be traced by using the technique of verifiable encryption during the withdrawal protocol.

A bandwidth efficient offline anonymous e-cash scheme is proposed in [12]. This scheme provides traceable e-coins so that double-spent e-coins can be linked to the identity of users without the need for a trusted third party. The major difference from previous works is that any party can trace the e-coins of the same user once this user double spends. Whenever a user double spends an e-coin, the bank can detect the identity of the user given two payment transcripts from the same e-coin. Subsequently, all later spending by the same user is identified by the merchant during the payment protocol.

Baldimsti et al. propose a transferable e-cash scheme that enables users to transfer e-coins not just to merchants, but among other users, before depositing the e-coins in the bank [13]. The scheme enables fully anonymous transferable e-cash and does not need a trusted third party. A malleable signature [14] is used to enable the secure and anonymous transfer of e-coins. The scheme also enforces the anonymity of users as long as they do not double spend. The serial number of the e-coin is changed when it is transferred to another user. If two e-coins C and C' have the same serial number, but different double-spending tags when the DS and DS' are deposited, it means one of the users double spent the e-coin. Banks can use the two double spent tags to reveal the identity of the user who double spent the e-coin. Some payment schemes use a TPM to achieve security [15, 16].

For the application of EV charging, few payment schemes have been developed [16, 17]. Zhao et al. propose an anonymous payment scheme for EV charging in [15]. The idea is that EVs are authenticated anonymously using anonymous credentials sent to the CSP by the trusted platform module (TPM). This module is assumed to be trusted and cannot be compromised so that it can prevent malicious attacks. Based on this premise, an anonymity revocation mechanism was not considered in the scheme, because EV cannot perform any illegal activity. At the time of charging, the TPM presents the credential and some attributes of the vehicle to the CSP server. TPM authenticates EV to the CSP server using direct anonymous attestation. After that the server performs necessary price checks for billing of EV and updates the credentials of EVs with a new balance if the charge request is granted.

In [16], a secure and privacy-preserving payment system for EVs using the Camenisch-Lysyanskaya (CL) signature and TPM technique was proposed. The CL signature is used to preserve the privacy of EV drivers while they schedule charging service for EVs. A punishment mechanism is also enforced for drivers who make reservations but do not show up. In the event of a car's theft or loss, the EV driver can cooperate with a trusted authority (TA) to find it. EV is required to prove to the CSP that it has enough to cover the bills using a range-proof technique. This scheme also supports dynamic pricing, where pricing is based on charging time, location, or attributes of the user.

In [17], an offline payment scheme for EV charging is proposed. In the scheme, users need to register with a contracted supplier (CS). The CS serves as an intermediary between the EV and the CSP. When the EV receives charging services from any CSP, it authenticates itself using a pseudonym it received from the CS. Any billing for the charge goes to the CS, which will in turn bill EV.

In [18], a divisible cash scheme based on a binary tree was presented, in which a user can withdraw e-coins of monetary value and spend any value between 2^0 and 2^l anonymously while offline from the bank, and without e-coins being linked in multiple transactions. This scheme enables users to withdraw and spend multiple e-coins efficiently. Using the binary tree approach, a serial number S is generated for each node to detect double spending. Each node is assigned a tag key, which is equal to the concatenation of two children tag keys. The root tag key and the identity of the user are signed by the bank when the user makes a withdrawal. While spending, a security tag T is generated by the spender. The spender, then, has to prove that S and T are well formed using a zero-knowledge proof [19–22] without revealing any personal identity information.

Our proposed scheme is primarily based on Canard et al. [3], which provides a flexible and efficient means of e-coin spending. The scheme uses a public global tree structure to construct all the e-coins in the system. The tree is constructed by the bank, thereby eliminating the need for users to prove that the tree is well formed, unlike in the case of [18]. When a user purchases an e-coin, he or she gets a certificate on a random secret x. This secret value defines all the serial numbers associated with the purchased e-coin that can be generated using that public tree. To spend a node from the tree, a user computes an e-coin value (g_s, t_s) for that node by using the public parameters of that node along with the user's secret. The user has to prove to the CSP that (g_s, t_s) is well formed. During the deposit process, the CSP submits (g_s, t_s) given by the user to the bank. Given (g_s, t_s), the bank can compute all the serial numbers related to that node and check for double spending by comparing it with previously deposited e-coin serial numbers. If a duplicate serial number is found, it indicates the presence of double spending. The user stays anonymous until it he or she commits a double-spending offense. We modified the verifications needed by the payment scheme to prevent a false accusation attack of double-spending results from a collusion between a malicious CSP and a malicious EV to bypass e-coins spent by a legitimate EV. This helps to prevent the possibility of an EV wrongfully spending an e-coin it does not own.

2.3 Electric Vehicle Charging Priority Determination

Due to the limitation in generated power in the power grid, it is not feasible to provide charge for all EVs at all times. The solution to this is to prioritize the allocation of power to vehicles based on available power and pending demand. Various techniques have been proposed in the literature to coordinate charging among EVs [23]. In order for the coordination authority to perform this function, some data about the EVs need to be provided, and this calls for concern as it relates to privacy and security of personal data. A number of research papers have been published on privacy preservation of users personal data while coordinating their EV charge schedules [4, 7, 24].

In [24], an indirect charge coordination scheme was proposed, which requires scheduling of optimal charging stops for EVs as they travel on the road. It uses the A^* search algorithm to estimate the best path for stop locations for the EV while traveling. EV is given the responsibility of selecting preferred locations, while the algorithm does the selection based on the current state of the charge of the vehicle, as well as the charging facility. The objective of the scheme is to minimize the overall travel by considering the wait time. The scheme is termed, indirect coordination, because it considers the battery's state of charge in the coordination. The scheme was shown to perform well under varying traffic conditions. However, the billing and privacy of EV users were not considered in the scheme.

A privacy-preserving EV-charging coordination scheme is presented in [7]. In this scheme, each electric storage unit (ESU) sends an encrypted charging request to an aggregator. This request includes the identity of the ESU, the state of the battery, the charging demand, and the time to complete the charge. For anonymity purposes, the aggregator shuffles the identities of all ESUs with their charging requests and forwards these requests to the charging coordinator. The charging coordinator executes a modified version of the knapsack algorithm in order to schedule the charging based on their priorities, taking into consideration the charging capacity constraints. In addition, the authors proposed adding noise to each ESU request (i.e., state of the battery, and time to charge) to prevent linking requests sent from one ESU.

Charge coordination involves assigning a charge to EVs based on a set priority. However, the approach in the papers discussed heretofore is different from our specific application. We, therefore, consider using preassigned attributes for EVs to determine the priority for a charging request. Similar to our proposal, in [4], an attribute-based prioritization scheme for EV charging is proposed. The scheme uses the EV attributes to determine the type of charging service it should receive. Two services are considered: quality guaranteed service (QGS) and best effort service (BES). In QGS, an EV gets a guarantee of its requested charge while in BES, it gets charged based on remaining energy available at charge station after serving QGS. However, the scheme was developed for a plug-in charging scenario, and considers only two levels of priority. Our scheme considers multiple levels of priority and multiple authorities.

3 PRELIMINARIES AND SYSTEM MODELS

3.1 Network Model

As illustrated in Fig. 1, the considered dynamic charging system consists of charging stations, EVs (users), banks, attribute authorities (AA), and an offline TA. Each charging station has a CSPs server, RSUs, and CPs. The RSUs are access points that are deployed across the charging section on the road that can be extended to several miles. The CPs are the elements that provide charging to EVs. The considered system has multiple AAs, such as government agencies, police departments, healthcare departments, veterans services, and so forth. Each AA is responsible for distributing a set of secret keys used to identify the assigned attributes to an entity. The charging station can also act as an AA to assign attributes to users for different memberships such as regular, premium, and so forth.

The communication between entities with the bank can be done using the Internet. EVs communicate with RSUs and CPs using dedicated short-range communication technology [25]. Between the EV and CSP, a wireless communication scheme, such as 4G, could be used.

Each EV maintains an account with the bank and uses this account to purchase anonymous coins to pay for charging. The EV is authenticated when it has shown evidence of being capable of making payment. CPs need to authenticate EVs before switching on to charge them.

3.2 Adversary and Threat Model

We consider a strong adversary model, assuming that all entities are not fully trusted except the TA. The bank and CSP are considered honest-but-curious. They aim is to learn the locations of EV drivers but not to disrupt the proper operation of the scheme. External attackers may eavesdrop on the communication to infer sensitive information about users for payment. EVs and CSPs can launch collusion attacks to falsely accuse legitimate EVs of double spending. The EVs may attack the system by charging without making proper payments or impersonating other EVs while purchasing a charge, thereby using their account. Malicious EVs may claim attributes they do not have in order to receive an undeserved higher priority for charging.

3.3 Cryptographic Hash Function

A cryptographic hash function (H) maps data of an arbitrary size to a fixed data size (i.e., $H : \{0,1\}^* \rightarrow \{0,1\}^n$). The fixed data size is known as a hash value. Hash functions are typically used for achieving data integrity. Some examples of hash functions being used in many applications include SHA-1 [26, 27]. The security properties of a cryptographic hash function are as follows:

1. *Preimage resistance.* Given a message m, it is very easy to compute its hash $h = H(m)$, but given hash value h. it is infeasible to compute the message m, that is, the hash function is one way.

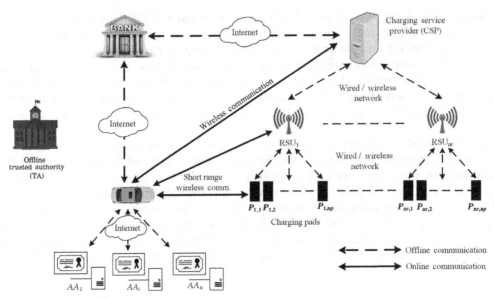

FIG. 1   The considered network model.

2. *Second preimage resistance.* Given an input m_1 it is infeasible to find a different m_2 such that $H(m_1) = H(m_2)$.
3. *Collision resistance.* It is infeasible to find any two different messages m_1 and m_2 such that $H(m_1) = H(m_2)$. If such a pair of messages is found, this is called a cryptographic hash collision.

3.4 Attribute-Based Encryption

ABE is a public key encryption scheme that allows access control over encrypted data by assigning secret keys to the attributes of each user. The user is, therefore, only able to decrypt a ciphertext if he or she has the associated attributes. To implement ABE, access structure and linear secret-sharing schemes are used [6].

3.4.1 Access Structures

Let U be the set of all attributes in the system. An access structure A on U is a collection of nonempty sets of attributes. The sets of attributes that can satisfy the access structure A are called the authorized sets, and the sets that are not in A are called the unauthorized sets. Additionally, an access structure is called monotone if attributes in sets $\forall B, C \in A$ and $B \subseteq C$, and $C \in A$.

3.4.2 Linear Secret-Sharing Schemes

Linear secret sharing is a method of distributing a shared secret among a set of entities such that any subset can reconstruct the secret using its shares. The concept of linear secret sharing can be summarized as follows.

Let p be a prime number and U the attribute universe. A secret-sharing scheme ($\mathcal{S}$) with secrets taken from the field Z_p^* is linear over Z_p^* if:

1. The shares of a secret $z \in Z_p^*$ for each attribute form a vector over Z_p.
2. For each access policy A on U, there exists a matrix $A \in Z_p^{l \times n}$, called the share-generating matrix with l rows and n columns, and a function δ that labels the rows of A with attributes from U, that is, $\delta: [l] \to U$.

According to [28], a secret-sharing scheme should satisfy the reconstruction requirement and the security requirement, which means an authorized set of attributes can reconstruct the secret and any unauthorized set of attributes cannot reveal any partial information about the secret. There exist some constants $\{c_i\}_{i \in I}$ in Z_p such that for any valid shares $\{\lambda_i = (Av)_i\}_{i \in I}$ of a secret z according to $\mathcal{S}$, it is true that: $\sum_{i \in I} c_i \lambda_i = z$, or equivalently $\sum_{i \in I} c_i A_i = (1, 0, \ldots, 0)$, where A_i is the ith row of A. Note that if the access policy is encoded as a monotonic Boolean formula over attributes, there is a generic algorithm that generates the corresponding access policy in polynomial time [28, 29].

3.5 Bilinear Pairing

Bilinear pairings map two elements from two cryptographic groups to a third group. Let G_1 and G_2 be both cyclic multiplicative groups of prime order p. Let g be a generator of G_1 and g' be a generator of G_2. e is a bilinear pairing function that maps an element from G_1 and an element from G_2 to an element in G_T, that is, $e(g, g') \rightarrow G_T$. The pairing can be symmetric if the input elements of the pairing are from the same group, that is, $G_1 = G_2$, whereas it is called asymmetric if the input elements are from two different groups (i.e., $G_1 \neq G_2$). A bilinear pairing function e has the following properties:

1. *Bilinearity*: For all $u \in G_1$, $v \in G_2$, and $a, b \in Z_q^*$, we have $e(u^a, v^b) = e(u, v)^{ab}$.
2. *Nondegenerate*: There exists $g \in G_1$ and $g' \in G_1$ such that $e(g, g') \neq 1$. In other words, the mapping cannot be the trivial map that sends every pair of elements in $G_1 \times G_2$ to the identity in G_T.
3. *Computable*: There is an efficient algorithm to compute $e(g, g')$.
4. *Admissible*: A pairing is admissible if the mapping is also nondegenerate and computable.

3.6 Zero-Knowledge Proof

A zero-knowledge proof, also known as a proof of knowledge, is a two-party protocol that runs between a prover and a verifier in which the verifier can be convinced of the validity of an assertion submitted by the prover. Proofs of knowledge have two properties:

1. *Completeness*: Given an honest prover and an honest verifier, if the assertion is true, the verifier should be convinced of the assertion's validity.
2. *Soundness*: If a dishonest prover P can, with nonnegligible probability, successfully execute the protocol with the verifier V, then there exists an expected polynomial time algorithm M that can be used to extract from this prover knowledge, which with overwhelming probability allows successful subsequent protocol executions.

A proof of knowledge is called a zero-knowledge proof if it does not allow the verifier to learn any information about the assertion itself, other than the one bit that represents either true or false.

The Schnorr protocol [30] is an example of proof of knowledge as described in Fig. 2. In this protocol, the prover has knowledge of a secret value x, and the public generator $g \in Z_q$. He or she computes and publishes $y = g^x$. To prove that he has knowledge of the secret value x, the prover first commits to a random value $r \in_R Z_q$ by computing and sending $t = g^r$. In the second round, the verifier sends a challenge c to the prover. Finally, the prover computes and sends the response $s = r + cx \pmod{q}$, and the verifier is able to verify its knowledge of the value x by computing $t' = g^s y^{-c}$ and comparing it to the previously received value t.

In the payment, the Fiat-Shamir heuristic will be used to compute noninteractive proofs as described in [30]. Different from the Schnorr protocol, the challenge c is generated by the hash function $c = hash(g, t, m)$, of the concatenation of the witness g and t, and the message m.

3.7 Blind-LRSW Signature

A blind signature is a form of digital signature in which the content of a message is masked (blinded) before it is signed by the signer. Similar to a digital signature, a valid blind signature can also be verified by anyone who receives

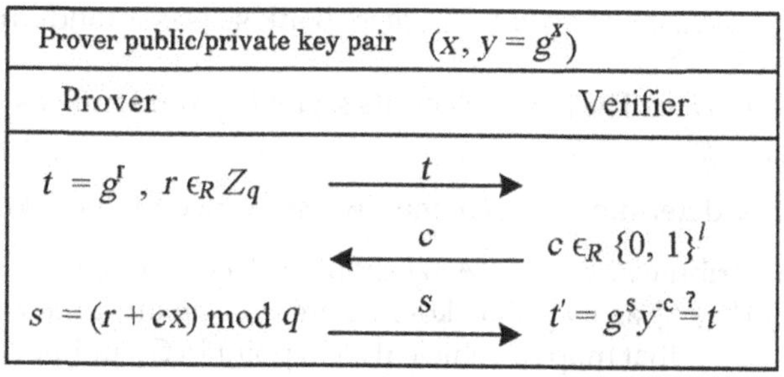

Prover public/private key pair $(x, y = g^x)$	
Prover	**Verifier**
$t = g^r$, $r \in_R Z_q$ $\xrightarrow{\quad t \quad}$	
$\xleftarrow{\quad c \quad}$	$c \in_R \{0, 1\}^l$
$s = (r + cx) \bmod q$ $\xrightarrow{\quad s \quad}$	$t' = g^s y^{-c} \stackrel{?}{=} t$

FIG. 2 The Schnorr protocol.

the signature on the original (unblinded) message, and the signer cannot deny signing the message. Blind signatures are used to verify the authenticity of a message, and are generally used in privacy-related applications, where the signer and the message owner are different parties.

The Blind-LRSW (B-LRSW) signature [31] is an example of blind signature scheme that is based on CL signatures [32], where the signature is done on a commitment of some secret. The B-LRSW signature scheme has three phases: (1) *Key Generation (KeyGen)*, (2) *Sign*, and (3) *Verify*. We briefly describe the construction.

1. *Keygen*: Set secret key $sk = (\alpha, \beta) \leftarrow Z_p^*$ and public key $pk = (u_1, u_2) \leftarrow (g^\alpha, g^\beta)$ where $g \in G_1$.
2. *Sign* (sk, g^m): Given g^m as input instead of the actual message $m \in Z_p^*$ (m is known only to user), the signer selects a random $r \leftarrow Z_p^*$ and returns $\sigma = (Z_1, Z_2, Z_3, Z_4) = (g^r, g^{r\beta}, g^{r(\alpha + m \cdot \alpha\beta)}, g^{r\beta m})$, where $g \in G_1$.
3. *Verify* (pk, m, σ): Accept the signature only if $Z_4 = Z_2^m$, $e(Z_1, u_2) = e(Z_2, g)$ and $e(Z_3, g) = e(Z_1 \cdot Z_4, u_1)$.

An interesting feature of this scheme is that any signature $\sigma = (Z_1, Z_2, Z_3, Z_4)$ on a message m can be randomized by selecting a random $t \leftarrow Z_p^*$ and computing $\sigma' = (Z_1^t, Z_2^t, Z_3^t, Z_4^t)$, which is still a valid signature on m. The interesting point is that, given (σ, σ') but not m, it is hard to decide whether these signatures were issued on the same message or not under the external Diffie-Hellman (XDH) assumption. This property can be used to prevent linking messages sent from the same user to preserve privacy.

4 PROPOSED SYSTEM

4.1 Overview

An overview of the proposed scheme is presented in the flow chart given in Fig. 3. After initializing the system, the EV can purchase divisible e-coins from the bank, and when the EV needs to charge, it should send a request to the CSP. The CSP checks if the available energy supply can serve all the charging requests. If the available energy is enough, then there is no need to run the prioritization scheme, and all EVs can charge. Otherwise, the prioritization scheme is run, and the highly prioritized requests are served without exceeding the available energy supply. Then, each EV pays for charging by sending an e-coin to the CSP. The CSP should first verify the validity of the e-coin, and then send secret tokens to the EV to use them to authenticate to the RSUs. After authentication with RSUs, each RSU sends another secret token to the EV to authenticate to CPs. The CPs only charge the EVs that can authenticate correctly. Finally, the CSP can deposit the e-coins in the bank. The details of the proposed scheme are explained in the following sections. All notations used are declared on Table 1.

4.2 Initialization

An offline TA chooses bilinear groups G_1 and G_T of prime order p with generators g and g_t, respectively. In addition, a symmetric pairing $e : (G_1 \times G_1 \rightarrow G_T)$ is constructed by the TA. The public parameters of the system are $GP = (p, G_1, G_T, g, g_t, e)$, CSP selects a random secret key $msk \xleftarrow{R} Z_p^*$ and computes the public key as $mpk = g^{msk}$. In addition, each EV selects a random secret key $usk \xleftarrow{R} Z_p^*$ and computes the public key as $upk = g^{usk}$. All entities need to have certificates from a certificate authority for their public keys.

The bank performs two actions during initialization. It generates two sets of keys and constructs a public e-coin tree that is associated with the e-coins that are to be used for payment as explained in Section 4.3.

For key generation, the following two sets of keys should be generated by the bank.

1. *Public/private key pair for authentication and signing messages:*Bank selects a random secret key $bsk \xleftarrow{R} Z_p^*$ and then computes its public key as $bpk = g^{bsk}$.
2. *Public/private key pair for creating e-coins:*The bank selects its secret key randomly as $sk = (\alpha, \beta) \xleftarrow{R} Z_p^*$ and computes its public key as $pk = (u_1, u_2) = (g^\alpha, g^\beta)$.

In order to initialize the priority determination scheme, two steps need to be taken.

1. *Attribute authority setup*: Each attribute authority (AA_θ) should select two random keys $(\alpha_\theta, y_\theta) \xleftarrow{R} Z_p^*$ as secret keys. Then, it publishes $PK = \{e(g,g)^{\alpha_\theta}, g^{y_\theta}\}$ as its public key, where θ is the attribute authority identifier. In addition, public hash function $H : \{0,1\}^* \rightarrow G_1$ that maps a vehicle ID to a point in G_1, public hash function $F : \{0,1\}^* \rightarrow G_1$ that maps an attribute $u \in U$ to G_1, and a function T that maps an attribute $u \in U$ to AA_θ.

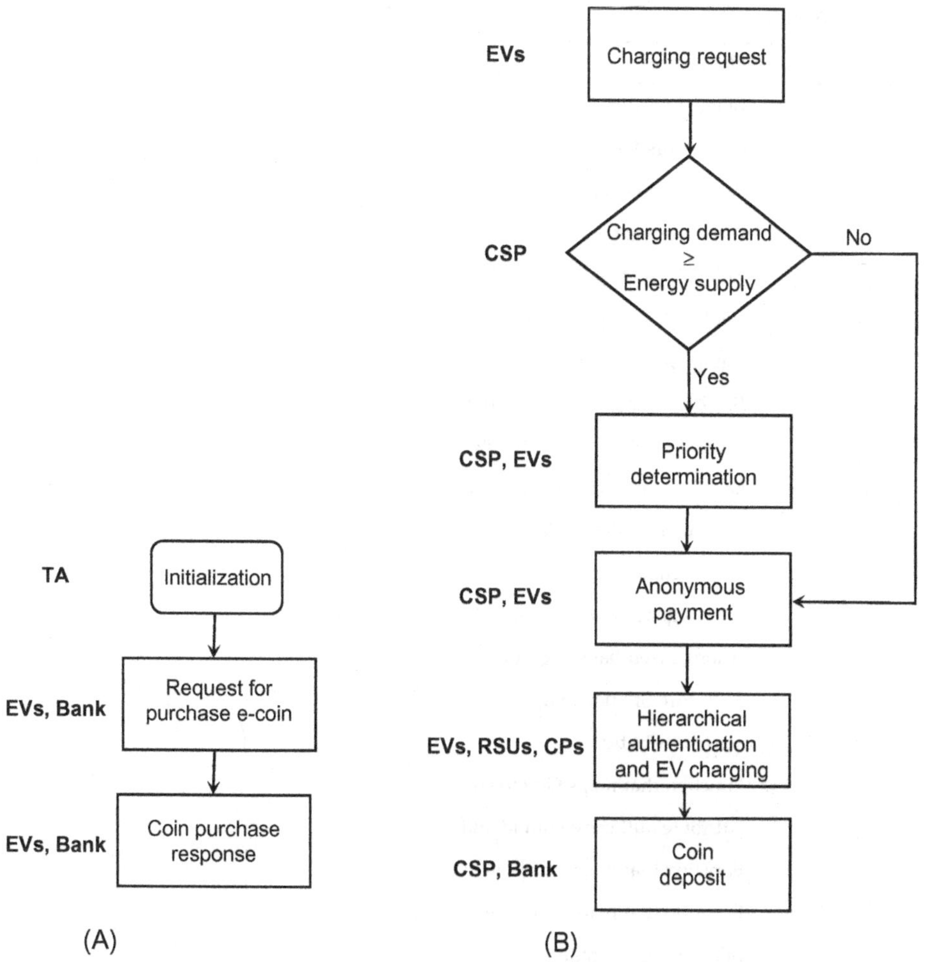

FIG. 3 Overview of proposed scheme. (A) Purchase of e-coin. (B) EV charging procedure.

2. *Attribute secret key generation*: Each EV gets a key for each assigned attribute by the attribute authority computed using $GID, \theta, u \in U, (\alpha_\theta, y_\theta)$ and the global parameters GP. The authority first chooses a random $t \xleftarrow{R} Z_p^*$ and outputs to the user the secret key as:

$$SK_{GID,u} = \{K_{GID,u} = g^{\alpha_\theta} H(GID)^{y_\theta} F(u)^t, K'_{GID,u} = g^t\}. \tag{1}$$

4.3 Purchase of E-Coins

As discussed in [3], the bank creates and broadcasts a public e-coin tree T that has n levels, where the maximum e-coin value of this tree is 2^n.

As shown in Fig. 4A, each internal node s is associated with an element $g_s \in G_1$ and each leaf f in the tree is associated with an element $\chi_f \in G_T$. This approach to build the e-coin tree makes the payment divisible where the user can spend one e-coin of value 2^n or less. Along with these elements, the public parameters of the tree also contain, for each leaf f and any node s on the path to f from root, an element $g_{s \to f} \in G_1$ such that $e(g_s, g_{s \to f}) = \chi_f$. Note that any leaf value represents a serial number associated with any internal nodes on its path to the root. This serial number is used to detect any double-spending action in the system. Users use the public values of nodes at the time of spending to create an e-coin. As shown in Fig. 4B, the public e-coin tree enables the user to spend a divisible e-coin value by selecting a node from the tree and use it for payment. Spending any internal node from the tree by the user also means that the user spent the subtree's leaves (serial numbers) of this node.

Let S_n be the set of all nodes in the tree and F_n be the set of leaves. For any node s, $s \in S_n$, the set $F_n(s)$ is the set of leaves in the subtree of that particular node.

TABLE 1   Table of Notation

Notation	Description
$G_1 G_T$	Bilinear groups
$g, \bar{g}$	Generators for G_1
$g_s \in G_1$	Associated generator for e-coins
$g_t \in G_T$	Associated generators for CSP challenge message
mpk, msk	Public/private pair for the CSP
upk, usk	Public/private pair for the EV
bpk, bsk	Public/private pair for the bank
$u1, u2$	Bank key for generating e-coins
α, β	Secret key of bank to generate e-coins
$\alpha_\theta, \beta_\theta$	Secret key of attribute authority
GID	Unique user global identifier
Sig	DSA signature
σ_B	Bank signature on the coin
σ'_B	Anonymized bank signature
π	Signature of knowledge
U	Set of attributes
H	Function that maps GID to G_1
AA_θ	Attribute authority with identifier θ
F	Function that maps attribute U to G_1
T	Function that maps attribute U to U_θ
e	Bilinear pairing map
n_r, n_p, n	Number of RSU, charge pad, and EV, respectively
d	Number of attributes
l	Number of nodes in the payment tree

FIG. 4   Payment public tree. (A) Public e-coin tree; (B) example of four-level public e-coin tree.

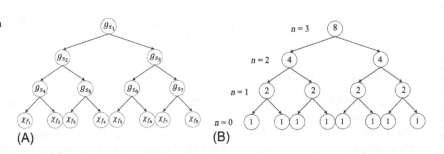

- For each node $s \in S_n$, r_s is randomly selected from Z_p^* such that $g_s = g^{r_s}$.
- For each leaf $f \in F_n$, the bank selects l_f randomly from Z_p^*.
- For each leaf $f \in F_n$, and each node $s \in S_n$ on the path of f to the root of the tree, the bank calculates $g_{s \to f} = g^{l_f / r_s}$.

The random value r_s is kept secret by the bank, while l_f, $\forall f \in F_n$, is not needed anymore and can be discarded after creating the tree and all the other values are public. The secret r_s will be used later by the bank to identify the double spender at the time of double spending. Users and merchants (charging stations) need to know only the system public parameters. The $g_{s \to f}$ is only used by the bank for calculating the serial numbers of the spent e-coins, so that it can detect

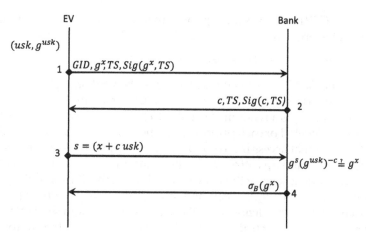

FIG. 5   E-coin purchase.

any double-spending action. The bank should decide the number and the depth of the public trees. The reason for having different public trees is for adding flexibility to the payment system.

To purchase e-coins, an EV should contact the bank directly using its real identity so that the amount of purchase can be deducted from its bank account. First, the EV should select a random secret $x \xleftarrow{R} Z_p^*$. Then the EV should get the bank's signature on which x, this signature will implicitly define all the serial numbers associated with this e-coin as χ_f^x for each leaf f. In order to spend a node s of height l in the tree, the EV computes $t_s = g_s^x$ and proves to CSP that it is well formed by using the signature of the bank on x. Given t_s at the time of deposit, the bank can compute all the serial numbers related to that spent node using $g_{s \to f}$ and can find the double spender, if the e-coin was double spent.

The exchanged messages between EV and the bank during coin purchase are given in Fig. 5. These are further outlined as follows:

- The EV computes a random number $x \xleftarrow{R} Z_p$ then sends its real identity GID, g^x and its signature $Sig(g^x, TS)$ to the bank, where TS is the time stamp. Using Schorr's protocol, CSPs challenge the EV with c, and the EV has to prove the knowledge of x to the bank, as given in messages 2 and 3 in Fig. 5.
- The bank signs g^x and sends e-coins to EV if the submitted proof is valid and g^x has not been used before, where

$$\sigma_B = (Z_1, Z_2, Z_3, Z_4) = (g^r, g^{r\beta}, g^{r(\alpha + x\alpha\beta)}, g^{r\beta x}). \tag{2}$$

This signature proves that the e-coin has been issued by the bank.

- EV verifies the received e-coins as follows.
  $Z_4 \overset{?}{=} Z_2^x$, $e(Z_1, u_2) \overset{?}{=} e(Z_2, g)$, and $e(Z_3, g) \overset{?}{=} e(Z_1.Z_4, u_1)$

4.4 Proposed Scheme Modes of Operation

In our scheme, two modes of operations are supported by the CSP; namely, the priority mode and regular mode. In the priority mode, the CSP does not have enough energy supply to satisfy the current charging demand of the EVs. Therefore, it prioritizes the requests and charges the high-priority requests without exceeding the total energy supply. Within the same priority level, the requests are served in order of first-come-first-charge (FCFC). Multiauthority ABE is used to protect the priority determination process [6]. In regular mode, the CSP has enough energy supply to satisfy all the incoming charging requests. The next sections explain the protocols used in each operation mode.

4.4.1 Priority Mode of the Proposed Scheme

During this mode, the CSP should first determine the EV's charging priorities by challenging them using multi-authority ABE. The idea is that the CSP sends encrypted messages using multiauthority ABE. Then, only the EVs having a given priority level should have the secret keys needed to decrypt the challenge message. Then, each EV should send a proof of decrypting the message to gain a relevant priority level. Finally, the CSP charges the highest priority requests without exceeding the energy supply and uses an FCFC procedure for EVs that have the same priority level. The detailed steps involved in determining the priority level are outlined as follows:

1. *Challenge of CSP*: Sending the challenge from the CSP to the EVs is the first step in the process of priority determination. Initially, the CSP creates its own priority policy of different priority levels by using the attributes taken from multiple

attribute authorities. Then, the CSP broadcasts these priority policies along with the corresponding challenges (ABEs) and the maximum amount of energy an EV can charge. The format of the challenge is

$$challenge_p = CT_p, TS, Sig(CT_p, TS), \tag{3}$$

where TS is the timestamp and $Sig(CT_p, TS)$ is the signature of the CSP on ciphertext CT_p.

In order to compute the ciphertext of a priority policy, the CSP encrypts different messages $g_t^{r_p}$, for different priority levels, where $g_t \in G_T$, $r_p \xleftarrow{R} Z_p^*$ is a random element selected by CSP for each priority level p and $\{1 \le p \le \mathcal{N}\}$, and $\mathcal{N}$ is the number of priority levels. For each priority level, the CSP creates an access policy (A, δ) with $A \in \{Z_p^*\}^{l*n}$, where l is the number of rows in that access matrix and δ is the function that maps rows of the access matrix to the attributes. ρ is another function that maps attributes to its authorities $\rho: [l] \to U_\theta$ as $\{\rho(\cdot): T(\delta(\cdot))\}$. To encrypt the message $g_t^{r_p}$, the CSP needs the public keys of the relevant attribute authorities, and the public parameters. The CSP first creates two random vectors $v = (z, v_2, ..., v_n)^T$ and $w = (0, w_2, ..., w_n)^T$, where $\{z, v_2, ..., v_n, w_2, ..., w_n\}$ are elements randomly selected from Z_p^*. We denote λ_x as the share of the random secret z corresponding to row x, that is, $\lambda_x = (A_x \cdot v)$ and w_x denotes the share of 0, that is, $w_x = (A_x \cdot w)$, where A_x is the xth row of access matrix A. Then, the CSP chooses a random element $t_x \xleftarrow{R} Z_p^*$ for each row and computes the ciphertext CT_p as:

$$\begin{aligned}
C_0 &= g_t^{r_p} \cdot e(g, g)^z; \\
\{C_{1,x} &= e(g, g)^{\lambda_x} e(g, g)^{\alpha_{\rho(x)} t_x}; \\
C_{2,x} &= g^{-t_x}; \\
C_{3,x} &= g^{y_{\rho(x)} t_x} g^{w_x}; \\
C_{4,x} &= F(\delta(x))^{t_x}\}_{x \in [l]}.
\end{aligned}$$

By the same method, the CSP creates different ciphertexts with different policies for each priority level and then broadcasts the challenges of the different priority levels.

2. *Response of EV.* In order to get a prioritized charging service, each EV needs to check the priority policies and determine whether its attributes can satisfy a priority level and then decrypt the corresponding ciphertext to prove its priority level to the CSP, as given in Fig. 6. Each EV uses its secret key to decrypt the corresponding ciphertext and compute a session key using the decrypted message $g_t^{r_p}$. Then, the EV encrypts the decrypted message using the session key as a proof for having the related priority level.

The EV takes the policy (A, δ), and the corresponding ciphertext (CT) and uses its secret keys $(K_{GID,u}, K'_{GID,u})$ for a subset of rows A_x of satisfied attributes in the access matrix, then for each row x, EV computes:

$$C_{1,x} \cdot e(K_{GID,\delta(x)}, C_{2,x}) \cdot e(H(GID), C_{3,x}) \cdot e(K'_{GID,\delta(x)}, C_{4,x}) = e(g, g)^{\lambda_x} \cdot e(H(GID), g)^{w_x}$$

Then, it calculates the constants $c_x \in Z_p$ such that $\Sigma_x c_x A_x = (1, 0, ..., 0)$ and computes:

$$\Pi_x (e(g, g)^{\lambda_x} \cdot e(H(GID), g)^{w_x})^{c_x} = e(g, g)^z.$$

This is true because $\lambda_x = (A_x \cdot v)$ and $w_x = (A_x \cdot w)$, where $\langle(1, 0, ..., 0) \cdot v\rangle = z$ and $\langle(1, 0, ..., 0) \cdot w\rangle = 0$. The message can be decrypted as $g_t^{r_p} = C_0/e(g, g)^z$. EV uses the received message $g_t^{r_p}$ to compute a session key with the CSP as $k = g_t^{r_i \cdot r_p}$, where $r_i \in Z_p^*$ is the random number selected by EV_i. EV sends $H_k(g_t^{r_p}), g_t^{r_i}$ to the CSP, which will be used by the CSP to establish the session key. $H_k(g_t^{r_p})$ is used as a proof by the EV that it correctly decrypted the attribute-based encrypted challenge. In addition, the EV should send the amount of energy it needs to charge.

FIG. 6   Exchanges messages in priority mode of our scheme.

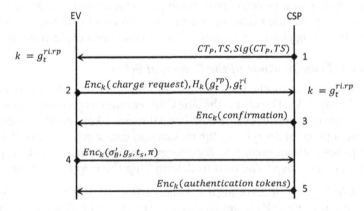

3. *Payment.* After the EV gets a confirmation on its charge request from the CSP, the EV should send the encryption of anonymous e-coin (g_s, t_s), the anonymized bank signature $\sigma'_B = (Z^t_1, Z^t_2, Z^t_3, Z^t_4)$ where $t \leftarrow Z^*_p$, and its own signature π to CSP as shown in Fig. 6, where $\pi = C^x$ is the signature of the EV and $C = \text{H}(\sigma'_B, t_s, g_s, ID_{CSP}, TS)$. The CSP verifies the signatures as follows.

To verify the bank's signature to make sure the coin is issued by the bank, the following two verifications are required. The first verification is

$$e(Z'_1, u_2) \stackrel{?}{=} e(Z'_2, g). \qquad (4)$$

The verification proof is as follows.

$$\begin{aligned} e(Z'_1, u_2) &= e(g^{tr}, g^\beta) \\ &= e(g^{tr\beta}, g) \\ &= e(Z'_2, g). \end{aligned}$$

The second verification is

$$e(Z'_3, g) \stackrel{?}{=} e(Z'_1 \cdot Z'_4, u_1). \qquad (5)$$

The verification proof is as follows.

$$\begin{aligned} e(Z'_3, g) &= e(g^{tr(\alpha + x\alpha\beta)}, g) \\ &= e(g^{tr}g^{tx\beta}, g^\alpha) \\ &= e(Z'_1 \cdot Z'_4, u_1). \end{aligned}$$

Then, the CSP should verify the EV's signature, by performing the following two verifications. The first verification is

$$e(Z'_2, t_s) \stackrel{?}{=} e(Z'_4, g_s). \qquad (6)$$

The verification proof is as follows.

$$\begin{aligned} e(Z'_2, t_s) &= e(g^{tr\beta}, g^x_s) \\ &= e(g^{tr\beta x}, g_s) \\ &= e(Z'_4, g_s). \end{aligned}$$

The second verification is

$$e(\pi, g_s) \stackrel{?}{=} e(C, t_s). \qquad (7)$$

The verification proof is as follows

$$\begin{aligned} e(\pi, g_s) &= e(C^x, g_s) \\ &= e(C, t_s). \end{aligned}$$

Finally, the CSP sends authentication tokens to EV after it verifies the tendered credentials. These tokens will allow the EV to authenticate to the RSUs and to obtain secret tokens to authenticate CPs to be charged.

4.4.2 Regular Mode of the Proposed Scheme

The exchanged messages in the regular mode of our scheme are illustrated in Fig. 7. First, the EV should send a charging request to the CSP, which should reply with a response message. In these two messages, the EV and CSP should mutually authenticate each other and establish a session key. Finally, the EV should pay to receive tokens that should be used for authentication to the RSUs.

1. *EV charge request.* The EV decides the amount of energy, to purchase and sends a request to CSP containing the tree node g_s and the corresponding e-coin $t_s = g^x_s$ for payment.
2. *CSP response.* After the CSP receives the request it should select $r \stackrel{R}{\leftarrow} Z^*_p$ and establish a session key as $k = g^{x \cdot r}_s$, and responds with $g^r_s, H_k(g^x_s, g^r_s), Sig(H_k(g^x_s, g^r_s))$, where Sig is the CSP signature on $H_k(g^x_s, g^r_s)$. All exchanged messages between the EV and CSP should be encrypted by the session key k.

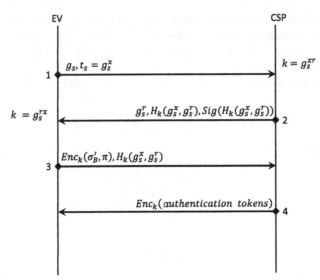

FIG. 7   Exchanged messages in the regular mode of our scheme.

3. *EV payment.* The EV verifies the signature of the CSP on the message and computes a session key $k = g_s^{rx}$. In addition, the EV should send the anonymized bank signature σ'_B and its own signature π encrypted to the CSP for payment clearance. The CSP sends the authentication tokens to EV after it verifies the e-coin, as explained in Section 4.4.1.

4.5 Hierarchical Authentication

The CSP shares a group secret key with all RSUs under its control. The CSP selects two random seeds (γ_{n,n_r} and $\mu_{1,1}$), encrypts them using the group key, and broadcasts them to RSUs. Each RSU uses the seeds to compute the secret shared tokens matrices as illustrated in Fig. 8A and B.

The group secret key is hashed iteratively along with the received token (γ_{n,n_r} and $\mu_{1,1}$) to generate $\{\gamma_{n-1,n_r}, \gamma_{n-2,n_r}, \dots, \gamma_{1,n_r}\}$ and $\{\mu_{2,1}, \mu_{3,1}, \dots, \mu_{n,1}\}$. Each RSU only needs to store one column from the matrix in the figures, but it is still required to iteratively compute tokens until it arrives at its assigned column. However, the CSP needs to compute the whole matrices because it will be interacting with all EVs. Because of the complexity of computing all keys, it is best generated at night, or at times when traffic is very low. After computing its two sets of tokens, each RSU should compute the shared keys with the EVs by XORing corresponding two elements in the matrices, as indicated in Fig. 9.

On the other hand, when an EV_i authenticates itself to the CSP, it receives two seed tokens ($\mu_{i,1}$ and γ_{i,n_r}) to compute the shared keys with the RSUs by hashing the two tokens and XORing each two elements, as illustrated in Fig. 10. Each EV can only compute one row in the matrix. The same technique used to share keys between RSUs and EVs is employed between EVs and CPs under the control of a given RSU. However, only one token set is used, unlike in the case of the CSP-RSU. Each RSU shares a group key with its CPs, which is used to compute shared secret tokens. The RSU selects a random seed (Ω_{n,n_p}), encrypts it using the group key, and then broadcasts it to the CPs. Each CP computes the secret shared keys, similar to the procedure used between the CSP and RSU. For each RSU, the token set generated can only be used to serve n EVs.

EV_i uses the received tokens from the CSP to authenticate itself at RSU_j and subsequently at CPs; two tokens from CSP and one token from RSU_j. For CP authentication, EV_i will first receive a token from RSU_j after authenticating with it. This token can only be used for authentication with CPs under the control of the issuing RSU_j. The scheme can limit the number of CPs, an EV can receive charge from, as illustrated in Fig. 11. For example, if an EV needs to charge from the CPs under the 5th RSU to the CPs under the 10th RSU, the CSP should send it the tokens $\mu_{i,5}$ and $\gamma_{i,10}$. As illustrated in the figure, the EV can compute the keys only for these RSUs. The EV cannot calculate other keys because hash functions are one way.

The authentication takes place in a hierarchical structure. First, at the CSP, as discussed earlier; then at the RSU_j and finally at the CPs. A *challenge/response* authentication technique is used to enable entities to prove knowledge of the secret keys. When RSU_j needs to authenticate an EV_i, it sends a challenge packet containing a random number, r_i. EV_i then responds with an authentication code, as shown in Eq. (8).

$$\text{Authentication code} = H(\gamma_{i,j} \oplus \mu_{i,j} \| r_i). \tag{8}$$

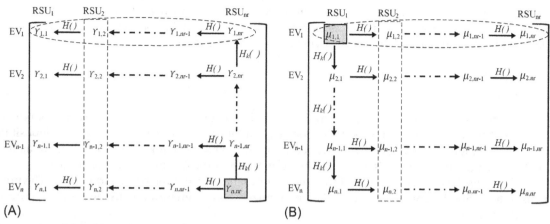

FIG. 8 Computation of shared keys. (A) Using the seed γ_{n,n_r} to compute a set of tokens; (B) using the seed $\mu_{1,1}$ to compute a set of tokens.

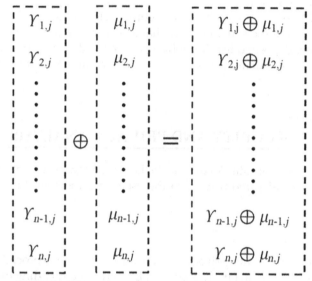

FIG. 9 Computation of shared keys with CSP by RSU$_i$.

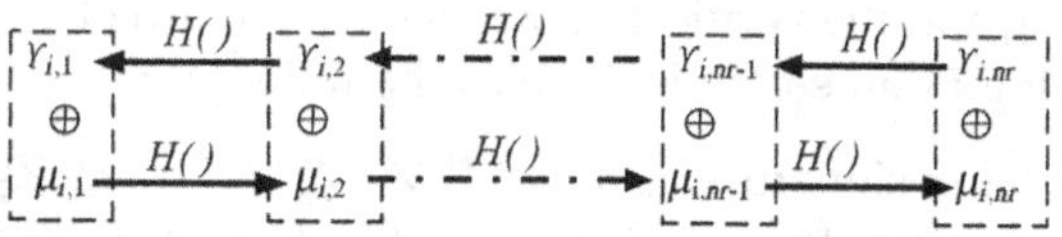

FIG. 10 Computation of shared keys with RSUs by EV$_i$.

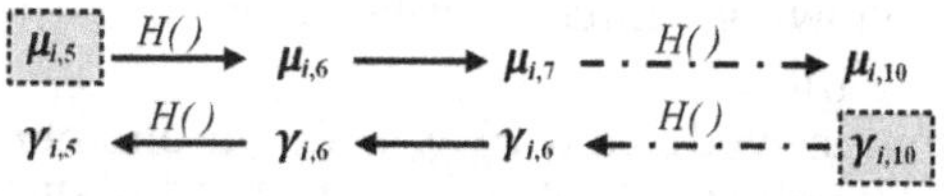

FIG. 11 Charging from the pads of 5th RSU to the pads of 10th RSU.

After verifying the received code, the RSU sends a confirmation code to the EV (see Eq. 9, where the key $\gamma_{i,j} \oplus \mu_{i,j}$ is used to encrypt the packet). It also sends an encryption of the token the EV needs to compute the shared keys with CPs.

$$\text{Confirmation code} = H(\gamma_{j,*} \oplus \mu_{j,*} \| r_i \| 1). \tag{9}$$

EV_i decrypts the received message from RSU and computes the shared keys with the CPs. A *challenge/response* technique, similar to the one between EV_i and RSU, is used to authenticate EV_i with the CPs. Once the authentication process completes and EV_i is authenticated, the CP switches on to charge the EV_i.

4.6 Coin Deposit

In order to update its bank account, the CSP should deposit the e-coins in the bank with the corresponding evidence submitted by EVs. This deposit does not need to be done right after each EV charges. But CSP can deposit the e-coins collected in 1 day (or a few days) all at once. After receiving the coins, the bank should verify them against double spending first before updating the CSP's account. The verification of the e-coins is done as follows.

Verification of coin authenticity. This verifies if the coin was purchased from the bank and is valid. The public key of the bank is used to verify the coin's signature (the anonymized bank signature) as follows $e(Z'_1, u_2) =^? e(Z'_2, g)$ and $e(Z'_3, g) =^? e(Z'_1 \cdot Z'_4, \hat{u}_1)$.

Verify EV's purchase approval. The bank should verify that the EV approved the purchase as follows: $e(Z'_2, t_s) =^? e(Z'_4, g_s)$ and $e(\pi, t_s) =^? e(C, g_s)$.

If it fails, it means a CSP tried to attack the system by impersonating an EV, and therefore gets punished.

Double-spending detection. This verification aims to ensure that an e-coin (g_s, t_s) has not been double spent. During the coin deposit, the bank should use $g_{s \rightarrow f}$ for each f in the subtree below node s and compute each leaf serial number as $e(t_s, g_{s \rightarrow f}) = \chi_f^x$. Then it searches if these serial numbers have been previously deposited. If not, all serial numbers have to be saved by the bank in a deposited list. If double spending is detected, the bank uses the secret r_s that was used to construct the public tree to calculate $t_s^{r_s} = (g^{x/r_s})^{r_s} = g^x$, which can be used to identify the user that launched the attack.

5 SECURITY AND PRIVACY ANALYSIS

In this section, we examine the possible attacks that can be launched against our proposed scheme. We also explain how our scheme can protect the security and privacy of the users, and their sensitive data.

5.1 Payment Attacks

In this section we discuss the security and privacy aspects for the payment procedure used by the EVs.

False accusation. Malicious CSP may try to falsely accuse an EV of double spending by bypassing the e-coin spent by a legitimate EV to another EV. This kind of attack can take place when two CSPs try to deposit the same e-coin at the bank. This attack can be prevented in our proposed scheme by using the signature of knowledge π. We modified the verifications needed by the payment scheme proposed in [3] to prevent this kind of attack. To make the explanations clear, we briefly discuss the spending and the verification needed by Canard et al. [3], then we explain how the attack can be done. In [3], the user spending of an e-coin is done as the following.

1. User computes the anonymized bank signature as $\sigma'_B = (Z'_1, Z'_2, Z'_3, Z'_4) = (Z_1^t, Z_2^t, Z_3^t, Z_4^t)$ where $t \leftarrow Z_p^*$.
2. User selects a random $k \leftarrow Z_p^*$ and computes $k_1 = g_s^k$, $k_2 = Z_2^k$, $C = H(\sigma'_B, t_s, k_1, k_2, info)$, and $\lambda = k + Cx$.
3. Finally, the user sends $(\sigma'_B, g_s, t_s, C, \lambda)$ to the merchant.

The merchant should compute the following values for verifications, $l_1 = g_s^{\lambda} t_s^{-C}$, $l_2 = Z_2'^{\lambda} Z_4'^{-C}$, and $C' = H(\sigma'_B, t_s, l_1, l_2, info)$. Then, the following three verifications are needed by the merchant. $C =^? C'$, $e(Z_1, u_2) =^? e(Z_2, g)$, and $e(Z_3, g) =^? e(Z_1 \cdot Z_4, u_1)$.

A malicious merchant can forward the received e-coin $(\sigma'_B, g_s, t_s, C, \lambda)$ to another malicious user who can simply modify the proof (C, λ) and replace C with $\tilde{C}$, and λ with $\lambda \tilde{C}/C$, where $\tilde{C} \leftarrow Z_p^*$. Then, malicious user can spend the modified e-coin $(\sigma'_B, g_s, t_s, \tilde{C}, \lambda \tilde{C}/C)$ at any other merchant without being detected. (Note the linearity of the equation of $\lambda = k + Cx$.) Finally, the legitimate user can be detected as double spender by the bank. This scenario is completely eliminated in our system by the two verifications in Eqs. (6), (7), where the EV generates a signature of knowledge on $H(\sigma'_B, t_s, g_s, ID_{CSP}, TS)$, which is signed using the secret value x at the time of spending. This can prove to the CSP and the bank that someone who knows the secret value x has generated that signature. By this way, we have prevented any entity from falsely accusing an honest EV of double spending.

Double spending. When a CSP submits a signed e-coin to the bank for deposit, the bank can easily detect whether the e-coin was double spent by comparing the serial numbers of the given e-coin and the serial numbers of previously spent e-coins. If the bank finds the same serial number twice, that means the EV has double spent the e-coin and the bank can find the identity of, and punish the double spender.

Forging e-coins. In order to forge e-coins, the attacker should either be able to compute a valid signature of the bank, or it should compute the secret value (x) of any user using the communication of EV with the bank or CSP. It is impossible to compute the private key of the bank and it is also impossible to calculate the secret value (x) even if the attacker knows g_s^x and g_s of a user based on the Discrete Logarithm Problem.

Purchasing e-coins without payment. When an EV purchases e-coins, it has to use its real identity so that the bank can make sure that the EV has enough money to pay for the e-coins. A malicious EV cannot impersonate other EVs to obtain e-coins without payment because the malicious EV has to compute a valid signature to authenticate itself. Also, if an attacker eavesdrops on the communications between the bank and an EV, he or she cannot compose the e-coin without knowing the secret value x that is used to create e-coin g_s^x.

Charging more than the payment. As explained earlier, the CSP can charge EVs partially by allowing them to charge from only a fixed number of CPs by giving the EV seed tokens to compute keys shared with some set of RSUs. As shown in Fig. 11, although the EV can compute $\gamma_{i,4}$, it cannot compute $\mu_{i,4}$ to compute an extra key. Similarly, although the EV can compute $\mu_{i,11}$, it cannot compute $\gamma_{i,11}$ for an extra key. The EVs cannot compute more keys to charge from more CPs because hash chains are one way. In addition, given one set of tokens, our key generation technique does not allow the EVs to derive other tokens because they do not know the group key used to compute the keyed hash values.

E-coins unlinkability. Every time an EV spends an owned e-coin, it generates an anonymized and valid bank signature σ'_B. Given the pair of bank signatures (σ_B, σ'_B), it is hard to decide whether these signatures were issued on the same e-coin or not under the external Diffie-Hellman (XDH) assumption.

5.2 Priority Determination Attacks

In this section, we discuss the security and privacy aspects of the priority determination scheme between CSP and EV.

Fine-grained access control. The CSP broadcast the access policies for each priority level and generate the challenge for EVs during priority mode. The policy may have attributes created by different authorities, and support both "AND" and "OR" relations among the attributes [6]. The EV can respond correctly to the CSP challenge if, and only if, the EV's attributes satisfy the priority level access policy. Thus, the fine-grained access control is achieved by the proposed scheme.

Attributes complement. In the priority determination, EVs cannot collude to attack the system by using their attributes together in order to satisfy the priority policy created by the CSP. This attack cannot be possible if none of the colluded EVs can alone satisfy the priority policy using their own attributes. This is because the part of the secret key $K'_{GID,u} = g^t$ is unique for each user, which prevents the users from colluding in order to satisfy a policy. During decryption, the random secret t selected by an authority can only be canceled by its corresponding part of the secret key $K_{GID,u} = g^{\alpha_\theta} H(GID)^{y_\theta} F(u)^t$ and cannot be canceled by using secrets of any other users.

Messages confidentiality. The external attackers can eavesdrop on the wireless communication in the network and capture the transmitted data and try to infer sensitive information about the user's identity, attributes, and locations. The communication between EVs and CSPs uses an authentication-based symmetric-key establishment mechanism in which a random symmetric session key is established between these two entities after performing authentication. This symmetric key between the CSP and EV is used to encrypt the exchanged messages, and thus the external attackers cannot infer any useful information if the encryption scheme is secure and the secret keys are not known to the attackers.

5.3 Authentication Attacks

In our scheme, signatures are used to mutually authenticate EVs to the bank and the CSP. Keyed hashes are used to authenticate EVs to RSUs and CPs. Also, if an EV can calculate the correct key shared with the CSP, this is a proof that the EV is the one that created the g_s^x of the e-coin because the computation of the key needs the secret x.

Identity anonymity. In the proposed scheme, EVs use anonymous e-coins for payment and authentication. The e-coins cannot be linked to the EV that bought them due to using a blind signature. To elaborate, the real identity of an EV is used only once during the purchase of e-coins, which is necessary to clear the payment. However, when an e-coin is sent by a CSP for the double-spending check, the bank cannot link it to an honest EV to preserve users' privacy unless the user double-spends. As a result, our scheme provides full anonymity, and the CSP cannot link an EV to its real identity. The bank can only reveal the identity of the EV if, and only if, the user double-spends the e-coin.

Coins and charging requests unlinkability. If different e-coins and charging requests are sent from the same EV at different occasions, neither the bank nor the CSP can link them and know that they are sent from the same EV. This is because e-coins use one-time random numbers (x) that are not linkable, and can make the e-coins different. The attackers may even collude to compromise the privacy of a legitimate user and to expose the location of the EV. The attackers can be any combination of eavesdroppers, EVs, CSPs, and even the bank. For example, to compromise the privacy of an EV, a CSP colludes with the bank and tries to link the messages exchanged during withdrawal and spending, but it is impossible to link σ_B created during withdrawal and σ'_B created during spending, even though those two values are created using the same secret value x.

Keys reuse attack. Attackers may try to reuse old keys shared with RSUs and CPs to charge more than once for only one payment. This is not possible in our scheme because the RSUs and CPs delete the keys from the list of valid keys once they are used. Also, the CSP and the RSUs should make sure that the seed tokens used to calculate the keys are not reused.

Man-in-the-middle attack. In our scheme, the Diffie-Hellman technique is used to enable EVs to establish shared session keys with CSPs. The man-in-the-middle attack is not possible because the CSP signs its share of the Diffie-Hellman session key and the EV's share g^x, which is signed by the bank, and it is not feasible to forge these signatures.

6 PERFORMANCE ANALYSIS

In this section, we evaluate the performance of the proposed scheme in terms of computation and the communication overhead. These metrics measure the real-time computation burden and the size of exchanged packets in our scheme.

6.1 Computation Overhead

The computation overhead measures the time needed to compute the packets or perform validation operations on the received packets. In order to evaluate the computation overhead of our scheme, the Python charm cryptographic library [33] is used. In our evaluation, an Intel Core i7-4765T 2.00 GHz and 8 GB RAM machine are used. For symmetric pairing, we used a supersingular elliptic curve with the symmetric Type 1 of size 512 bits (SS512 curve) [34]. All cryptographic operations were run 1000 times, and average measurements are reported in Table 2.

Table 3 gives the required time to set up various entities in our scheme during initialization. Each EV needs one exponentiation in G_1 for public/private pair key generation. The bank performs five exponentiations in G_1 for public key generation, in addition to $(2^l - 1)$ asymmetric pairing and exponentiation in G_1 to create a public e-coin tree with l nodes for regular e-coins. Each attribute authority needs one pairing, one exponentiation in G_1, and one exponentiation in G_T for public key generation. In addition, for each attribute key, four exponentiations in G_1, two hash operations to G_1, and two multiplication operations in G_1 are required. CSP performs one exponentiation in G_1 for public key generation, in addition to $2 \times (n - 1) \times (n_r - 1)$ hashing operations to create two set of tokens shared with the RSUs. Each RSU needs, at most, $2 \times (n - 1) \times (n_r - 1)$ hash operations to create two sets of tokens shared with the CSP. To create shared tokens between each CP and its RSU, each CP has to perform $n - 1$ keyed hashes, and at most $n_p - 1$ unkeyed hashes, which takes at most, $(n - 1) \times (n_p - 1)$ hashing operations.

Table 4 gives the computation overhead of various entities in the system during message exchange. During the e-coin purchase, four messages are exchanged between the EV and the bank, as shown in Fig. 5. Each EV performs the following computation: for message (1) one exponentiation in G_1 and one signature; for message (2) one signature verification; for message (3) point addition, which is assumed to be negligible; for message (4) one e-coin signature verification, which has three asymmetric pairings and one multiplication in G_1. The total computations done by the EV can be formulated as $3T_1 + T_2 + T_5 + T_{10} + T_{11}$. On the other hand, the bank performs the following computations: for message (1) one signature verification; for message (2) one signature; for message (3) two exponentiations and one multiplication in G_1; for message (4) one e-coin signature, which has four exponentiations in G_1. The total computations done by the bank can be formulated as $6T_2 + T_5 + T_{10} + T_{11}$.

During regular service, four messages are exchanged between the EV and the CSP, as shown in Fig. 7. Each EV performs the following computations: for message (1) one exponentiation in G_1; for message (2) one exponentiation

TABLE 2 Computational Overhead for Cryptographic Operations

	Operation	Time
T_1	Pairing $e(g_1, g_1)$	1.34 ms
T_2	$g^a \in \mathbb{G}_1$	2.03 ms
T_3	$g^a \in \mathbb{G}_T$	9.56 μs
T_4	$H: \{0,1\}^* \rightarrow \mathbb{G}_1$	0.065 ms
T_5	$g_1 \times g_2 \in \mathbb{G}_1$	5.13 μs
T_6	$g_1 \times g_2 \in \mathbb{G}_T$	1.68 μs
T_7	HMAC or SHA1	3.6 μs
T_8	AES encryption	29.49 μs
T_9	AES decryption	12.85 μs
T_{10}	DSA Sig	6.91 ms
T_{11}	DSA Sig Verify	7.2 ms

TABLE 3 Setup Times of Various Entities

Entities		Computation	Time (ms)
EV	Public/private key generation	T_2	2.03
Bank	Public/private key generation	$3T_2$	6.09
	Building tree	$(2^l - 1) \times (T_2 + T_1)$	$(2^l - 1) \times 3.37$
Attribute authority	Public/private key generation	$T_1 + T_2 + T_3$	3.38
	Attribute generation	$4T_2 + 2T_4 + 2T_5$	8.25
CSP	Public/private key generation and shared keys generation	$T_2 + 2 \times (n-1) \times (n_r - 1) \times T_7$	$2.03 + 0.007 \times (n-1) \times (n_r - 1)$
RSU	Shared keys generation	$2 \times (n-1) \times (n_r - 1) \times T_7$	$0.007 \times (n-1) \times (n_r - 1)$
Charging pad	Shared keys generation	$(n-1) \times (n_p - 1) \times T_7$	$0.003 \times (n-1) \times (n_p - 1)$

TABLE 4 Computation Overhead

		Computation	Time (ms)
Authentication to bank	EV	$3T_{1+T_2+T_5+T_{10}+T_{11}}$	20.16
	Bank	$6T_{2+T_5+T_{10}+T_{11}}$	26.29
Regular authentication to CSP	EV	$7T_{2+2T_7+T_8+T_9+T_{11}}$	21.45
	CSP	$8T_{1+2T_2+T_5+T_7+T_8+T_9+T_{10}}$	27.74
Prioritized authentication to CSP	EV	$3dT_1 + 6T_2 + (d+2)T_3 + (3d+1)T_6 + 2T_7 + 2T_8 + 2T_9 + T_{11}$	4.03d+19.49
	CSP	$(2d+9)T_1 + 4dT_2 + (2d+2)T_3 + dT_4$ $+ (d+1)T_5 + (d+1)T_6 + T_7 + 2T_8 + 2T_9 + T_{10}$	10.9d+19.08
Authentication to RSU	EV	$2T_{7+T_9}$	0.02
	RSU	$2T_{7+T_9}$	0.03
Authentication to CP	EV	$2T_7$	0.007
	CP	$2T_7$	0.007

in G_1, one keyed hash for verification, and one signature verification; for message (3) four exponentiations in G_1 for bank signature anonymization, one hash operation and one exponentiation in G_1 for generation of π, and one AES symmetric-key encryption; for message (4) one AES symmetric-key decryption. The total computations done by the EV can be formulated as $7T_2 + 2T_7 + T_8 + T_9 + T_{11}$. On the other hand, the CSP performs the following computations: for message (1) one exponentiation in G_1; for message (2) one exponentiation in G_1, one keyed hash for verification, and one signature; for message (3) eight asymmetric pairing operations and one multiplication in G_1 for verification of bank signature, and one AES symmetric-key decryption; for message (4) one AES symmetric-key encryption. The total computations done by the CSP can be formulated as $8T_1 + 2T_2 + T_5 + T_7 + T_8 + T_9 + T_{10}$.

During prioritized service, five messages are exchanged between the EV and the CSP, as shown in Fig. 6. Each EV performs the following computations: for message (1) the EV decrypts the attribute-based encrypted challenge by computing $3d$ symmetric pairing, $3d + 1$ multiplication in G_T, and $d + 1$ exponentiation in G_T, in addition to one signature verification; for message (2) one exponentiation in G_T, one keyed hash, and one AES symmetric encryption; for message (4) one exponentiation in G_1 for t_s, one hash operation and one exponentiation in G_1 for π, four exponentiations in G_1 for bank signature anonymization, and finally one AES symmetric encryption; for messages (3) and (5) two AES symmetric-key decryptions. The total computations done by the EV can be formulated as $3dT_1 + 6T_2 + (d + 2)T_3 + (3d + 1)T_6 + 2T_7 + 2T_8 + 2T_9 + T_{11}$. On the other hand, the CSP performs the following computations: for message (1) the CSP encrypts a challenge by computing $2d + 1$ symmetric pairing operations, $2d + 1$ exponentiation in G_T, $d + 1$ multiplication in G_T, $4d$ exponentiation in G_1, d hash to G_1, and d product in G_1, in addition to one signature; for message (2) one exponentiation in G_T, one keyed hash for verification, and one AES symmetric decryption; for message (3) one AES symmetric encryption; for message (4) eight asymmetric pairing operations and one multiplication in G_1 for verification of bank signature, and one AES symmetric-key decryption. The total computations done by the CSP can be formulated as $(2d + 9)T_1 + 4dT_2 + (2d + 2)T_3 + dT_4 + (d + 1)T_5 + (d + 1)T_6 + T_7 + 2T_8 + 2T_9 + T_{10}$.

For EV authentication with the RSU, it needs two hashing operations, one XOR operation, and one AES decryption to authenticate itself to each RSU. The XOR operations are ignored because they are infinitesimally small. The total computations done by the EV can be formulated as $2T_7 + T_9$. On the other hand, the RSU needs to perform one symmetric encryption and two hashing operations to authenticate each EV. The total computations done by the RSU can be formulated as $2T_7 + T_9$.

For EV authentication with CP, it needs two hashing operations and one XOR operation. The total computations done by the EV can be formulated as $2T_7$. On the other hand, each CP needs two hashing operations to authenticate each EV. The total computations done by the RSU can be formulated as $2T_7$.

6.2 Communication Overhead

The communication overhead is measured by the number of bytes in every communication message sent. Table 5 gives the communication overhead of various entities in the system during message exchange. During the e-coin purchase, four messages are exchanged between the EV and the bank, as shown in Fig. 5. The EV sends the following

TABLE 5   Communication Overhead

		Communication (bytes)
Authentication to bank	EV	328
	Bank	260
Regular authentication to CSP	EV	320
	CSP	252
	EV	660
Prioritized authentication to CSP	CSP	$256d + 236$
Authentication to RSU	EV	20
	RSU	40
Authentication to CP	EV	20
	CP	40

messages: message (1) requires 4 bytes for GID, 4 bytes for TS, 64 bytes for g^x, and 128 bytes for σ_U; message (3) requires 64 bytes for s. The total packet size sent by the EV is 328 bytes. On the other hand, the bank sends the following messages: message (2) requires 4 bytes for TS, 64 bytes for c, and 128 bytes for $\sigma_B(c\|TS)$; message (4) is four group points of 64 bytes each. The total packet size sent by the bank is 260 bytes.

During regular service, four messages are exchanged between the EV and the CSP, as shown in Fig. 7. The EV sends the following messages: message (1) requires two group points of total size of 128 bytes, and message (3) requires five group points encrypted with AES with a total size of 320 bytes, and 20 bytes for the HMAC. The total packet size sent by the EV is 468 bytes. On the other hand, the CSP sends the following messages: message (2), which requires 64 bytes for one group point, 20 bytes for HMAC, and 128 bytes for signature; message (4) requires 40 bytes for authentication tokens. The total packet size sent by the CSP is 252 bytes.

During prioritized service, three messages are exchanged between the EV and the CSP, as shown in Fig. 6. The EV sends message (2), which contains 10 group points of 640 bytes, and 20 bytes for the HMAC, so the total size is 660 bytes. On the other hand, the CSP sends message (2), which contains an ABE challenge of size $(4d + 1) \times 64$ bytes, 4 bytes for the TS, and 128 signature; for message (3) it requires 40 bytes for authentication tokens. The total packet size sent by the CSP is $256d + 236$ bytes.

For EV authentication with RSU, the EV receives 40 bytes for the challenge and the confirmation and sends 20 bytes for the authentication code. The same packets size is sent for the authentication with the CP.

7 CONCLUSIONS AND FUTURE WORK

In this chapter, we presented an integrated and secure scheme that offers anonymous authentication, prioritization, and payment for dynamic charging systems. The scheme allows EVs to purchase divisible e-coins from the bank that can later be used for the recharge of EV batteries. In addition, the scheme allows the CSPs to offer prioritized service to EVs based on the charging demand and its energy supply. Prioritization is performed using multiauthority ABE to authenticate EVs that needs to charge. Moreover, an efficient hierarchical authentication scheme that is based on symmetric-key cryptography is used to authenticate EVs to RSUs and CPs. Our extensive privacy and security analysis have demonstrated that our scheme is secure against different attacks, and can achieve required privacy features. Also, our measurements have demonstrated that the computational and communication overhead of the proposed scheme are acceptable.

In the future, this work can be extended by investigating a blockchain-based payment system for the EV-charging station transactions. The payment system will consider the physical routes taken by the EV to mitigate the scalability problems of the blockchain, which can help in achieving faster verification of the charging request transaction. For example, the EV can initially provide the route to the blockchain, which can help in achieving faster verification of the charging request transaction. We also plan to introduce prediction techniques in our system to assess and estimate the traffic patterns on the basis of time and location. This helps the dynamic charging system to allocate the best charging station in the travel route of an EV. To achieve this, we can also introduce an entity (or a company) that is independent from all the charging stations that receives the encrypted charging requests that include the EVs' travel routes, amount of charge required, its desired power ratings, the arrival time, and so forth. The company can then use the EV's requests to understand the distribution of the requests, and then it should use this information to determine the best routes that can satisfy all the EV's requests while providing the requested/acceptable amount of charging. In this technique, we need to use the concept of computation over encrypted data to protect the privacy of EV drivers while providing the best charging service to the EVs. This extension aims to achieve fairness in the charging distribution and prioritization, and to accomplish high driver satisfaction.

ACKNOWLEDGMENTS

This research work is financially supported by the Natural Sciences Foundation of the United States, under grant numbers 1619250, 1618549, and 1560434. In addition, parts of this work, specifically Sections 4.3, 4.4.1, 4.4.2, and 4.6 were made possible by NPRP grant number NPRP 9-055-2-022 from the Qatar National Research Fund (a member of the Qatar Foundation). The statements made herein are solely the responsibility of the authors.

References

[1] R. Hussain, D. Kim, M. Nogueira, J. Son, A. Tokuta, H. Oh, A new privacy-aware mutual authentication mechanism for charging-on-the-move in online electric vehicles, in: Proceedings of the 11th International Conference on Mobile Ad-hoc and Sensor Networks (MSN), IEEE, 2015, pp. 108–115.

[2] H. Li, G. Dán, K. Nahrstedt, Proactive key dissemination-based fast authentication for in-motion inductive EV charging, in: Proceedings of the International Conference on Communications (ICC), IEEE, 2015, pp. 795–801.

[3] S. Canard, D. Pointcheval, O. Sanders, J. Traoré, Divisible e-cash made practical, in: Proceedings of the International Workshop on Public Key Cryptography (IACR), Springer, 2015, pp. 77–100.

[4] M. He, K. Zhang, X.S. Shen, PMQC: a privacy-preserving multi-quality charging scheme in V2G network, in: Proceedings of the Global Communications Conference (GLOBECOM), IEEE, 2014, pp. 675–680.

[5] S. Sahoo, D.R. Pullaguram, S. Mishra, A consensus priority algorithm based V2G charging framework for frequency response, in: Proceedings of the 7th Power India International Conference (PIICON), IEEE, 2016.

[6] Y. Rouselakis, B. Waters, Efficient statically-secure large-universe multi-authority attribute-based encryption, in: Proceedings of the International Conference on Financial Cryptography and Data Security, Springer, 2015, pp. 315–332.

[7] A. Sherif, M. Ismail, M. Pazos-Revilla, M. Mahmoud, K. Akkaya, E. Serpedin, K. Qaraqe, Privacy preserving power charging coordination scheme in the smart grid, in: Transportation and Power Grid in Smart Cities: Communication Networks and Services, John Wiley, UK, 2018.

[8] H. Li, G. Dán, K. Nahrstedt, Lynx: authenticated anonymous real-time reporting of electric vehicle information, in: Proceedings of the International Smart Grid Communications (SmartGridComm), IEEE, 2015, pp. 599–604.

[9] H. Li, G. Dán, K. Nahrstedt, Portunes+: privacy-preserving fast authentication for dynamic electric vehicle charging, IEEE Trans. Smart Grid 8 (5) (2017) 2305–2313.

[10] W. Aiello, S.M. Bellovin, M. Blaze, R. Canetti, J. Ioannidis, A.D. Keromytis, O. Reingold, Just fast keying, ACM Trans. Inf. Syst. Secur. 7 (2) (2004) 242–273.

[11] J. Camenisch, S. Hohenberger, A. Lysyanskaya, Compact e-cash, in: Eurocrypt, 3494 Springer, 2005, pp. 302–321 vol.

[12] M.H. Au, S.S. Chow, W. Susilo, Short e-cash, in: Proceedings of the International Conference on Cryptology in India, Springer, 2005, pp. 332–346.

[13] F. Baldimtsi, M. Chase, G. Fuchsbauer, M. Kohlweiss, Anonymous transferable e-cash, in: Public Key Cryptography, 2015, pp. 101–124.

[14] M. Chase, M. Kohlweiss, A. Lysyanskaya, S. Meiklejohn, Malleable signatures: new definitions and delegatable anonymous credentials, in: Proceedings of the 27th Computer Security Foundations Symposium (CSF), IEEE, 2014, pp. 199–213.

[15] T. Zhao, C. Chen, L. Wei, M. Yu, An anonymous payment system to protect the privacy of electric vehicles, in: Proceedings of the Sixth International Conference on Wireless Communications and Signal Processing (WCSP), IEEE, 2014, pp. 1–6.

[16] T. Zhao, C. Zhang, L. Wei, Y. Zhang, A secure and privacy-preserving payment system for electric vehicles, in: Proceedings of the International Conference on Communications (ICC), IEEE, 2015, pp. 7280–7285.

[17] M.A. Mustafa, N. Zhang, G. Kalogridis, Z. Fan, Roaming electric vehicle charging and billing: an anonymous multi-user protocol, in: Proceedings of the International Conference on Smart Grid Communications (SmartGridComm), IEEE, 2014, pp. 939–945.

[18] S. Canard, A. Gouget, Divisible e-cash systems can be truly anonymous, in: Eurocrypt, 4515, Springer, 2007, pp. 482–497 vol.

[19] J. Camenisch, M. Michels, Proving in zero-knowledge that a number is the product of two safe primes, in: Proceedings of the International Conference on the Theory and Applications of Cryptographic Techniques, Springer, 1999, pp. 107–122.

[20] D. Chaum, T.P. Pedersen, Transferred cash grows in size, in: Workshop on the Theory and Application of Cryptographic Techniques, Springer, 1992, pp. 390–407.

[21] M. Girault, G. Poupard, J. Stern, On the fly authentication and signature schemes based on groups of unknown order, J. Cryptol. 19 (4) (2006) 463–487.

[22] C.-P. Schnorr, Efficient identification and signatures for smart cards, in: Proceedings of the International Conference on the Theory and Application of Cryptology, Springer, 1989, pp. 239–252.

[23] S. Deilami, A.S. Masoum, P.S. Moses, M.A. Masoum, Real-time coordination of plug-in electric vehicle charging in smart grids to minimize power losses and improve voltage profile, IEEE Trans. Smart Grid 2 (3) (2011) 456–467.

[24] V. del Razo, H.-A. Jacobsen, Smart charging schedules for highway travel with electric vehicles, IEEE Trans. Transp. Electrific. 2 (2) (2016) 160–173.

[25] M. Raya, A. Aziz, J.-P. Hubaux, Efficient secure aggregation in VANETs, in: Proceedings of the 3rd International Workshop on Vehicular Ad Hoc Networks—VANET, ACM Press, 2006.

[26] J.E. Silva, An Overview of Cryptographic Hash Functions and Their Uses, GIAC Security Essentials Practical Version 1.4b Option 1, January 15, 2003

[27] P. Gauravaram, Cryptographic Hash Functions: Cryptanalysis, Design and Applications (Ph.D. thesis), Queensland University of Technology, 2007.

[28] A. Beimel, Secure Schemes for Secret Sharing and Key Distribution, Technion-Israel Institute of Technology, Faculty of Computer Science, Israel, 1996.

[29] A. Lewko, B. Waters, Decentralizing attribute-based encryption, in: Proceedings of the Annual International Conference on the Theory and Applications of Cryptographic Techniques, Springer, 2011, pp. 568–588.

[30] S. Goldwasser, Y. Kalai, On the (in)security of the Fiat-Shamir paradigm, in: Proceedings of the 44th Annual Symposium on Foundations of Computer Science, IEEE, 2003.

[31] L. Chen, P. Morrissey, N.P. Smart, DAA: fixing the pairing based protocols, IACR Cryptol. ePrint Arch. 2009 (2009) 198.

[32] J. Camenisch, A. Lysyanskaya, Signature schemes and anonymous credentials from bilinear maps, in: Annual International Cryptology Conference, Springer, 2004, pp. 56–72.

[33] J.A. Akinyele, C. Garman, I. Miers, M.W. Pagano, M. Rushanan, M. Green, A.D. Rubin, Charm: a framework for rapidly prototyping cryptosystems, J. Cryptogr. Eng. 3 (2) (2013) 111–128.

[34] S.E.C.G. SEC, 2: Recommended Elliptic Curve Domain Parameters, Standards for Efficient Cryptography Group, Certicom Corp, 2000.

13

Secure IoT Structural Design for Smart Homes

Aniruddha Bhattacharjya, Xiaofeng Zhong, Jing Wang, and Xing Li

Beijing National Research Center for Information Science and Technology, Department of Electronic Engineering, Tsinghua University, Beijing, China

1 SMART HOME SECURITY

1.1 Introduction

Smart cities are large systems with numerous complexities. These cities are composed of distributed and uninterrupted systems that are comprised of and use mission-critical data. The major problem is that the data must be *secured end-to-end*. Smart cities that include the *Power Internet of Things (PIoT)* and *smart home* are currently entirely IoT-enabled. Based on the IoT and day-by-day operations, these security phenomena will increase. The security of smart cities is totally reliant on the security of the underlying IoT protocols, and *these protocols already have considerable vulnerabilities*. A sample secure IoT structural design for smart cities can be comprised of *trusted SDN regulators, an incorporated registry*, a key management system, and black networks. The security services provided through this architecture extend beyond the basic security provided by IoT protocols. We all know that smart home applications of all variations are emerging in the market. We know that Cisco VNI has forecasted that Internet-of-Things (IoT) connections will rise by 43% each year. We are about to see worldwide smart home applications in 2018 reach 2 billion.

The *Philips Hue Connected bulb* offers the user the ability to operate the lighting system in the home wirelessly. This bulb is comprised of an Ethernet-supported bridge that receives directives from the user's app and communicates these directives to the bulbs by use of the ZigBee-Light link protocol. In this study, by use of HTTP commands, the data are exchanged among the app and the bridge. *However, the communications are not encrypted*. Therefore, an eavesdropper could easily deduce the actions that the user conducts on the bulb. Additionally, even though the device executes access control, such as the way it maintains a list of users, this list is similar to a legitimate user's list. Therefore, it can be taken out by any attacker, who can later masquerade as a legitimate user. As a result, the attacker can get full control over that bulb. When the security measures and practice are being implemented, there are extreme changes between devices based on specific factors, such as the manufacturer, the device's abilities, and the mode of operation. Thus, one good solution can be use of the *software defined networking (SDN)* to execute and establish dynamic security rules that can proceed depending on the context, such as the time of day. It is believed that this kind of method can enhance the present security resolutions applied by device builders, and can furthermore offer privacy abilities that may not be supported by the builder.

Another example is the Belkin WeMo motion sensor and switch kit. Using WiFi, it can be connected to the Internet and permit the user to manage the power socket for any electrical home appliances. The home appliances range from desk lamps and coffee machines to room heaters. One large problem is that we can effortlessly attack this device first by steering an SSDP discovery to obtain the IP address of the WeMo devices along with the ports that they are listening through. Additionally, this SSDP discovery can be used to learn the SOAP commands, along with their arguments, which these devices support. After this step, the most dangerous issue is that the attacker can empower remote access on the device only by registering as an authentic user. The attackers stage this attack by sending a suitable SOAP-formatted POST command. Therefore, as a consequence, this approach offers the attacker the remote right of access to the device from any place in the world, which is highly dangerous.

The Nest smoke alarm is also a daily life application in the smart home. The Nest smoke alarm directs information consisting of reports and alerts (if needed) to the user's mobile app. Thus, the Nest smoke alarm offers the user peace of mind about the safety of their house. This alarm does not depend on the user's location. The Nest smoke alarm is fitted with sensors that are able to discover motion and light. This can also detect if any user is in that room, or if he/she has turned on/off the lights. Therefore, these abilities also directly raise a privacy issue, because the user may have a feeling that they are being watched and tracked inside their own home. The biggest advantage of this Nest smoke alarm is that every bit of data that is exchanged with the Nest smoke alarm is totally encrypted, thereby resulting in eavesdroppers being unable to read the communications data.

Another exciting smart application in smart homes is the Withings Smart Baby Monitor, which is fit with an IP camera. This application is highly exciting and empowers us to monitor our baby at our house through an app on our mobile phone. We can capture and analyze all Wi-Fi packets to/from the baby monitor. The data are exchanged in plain text. However, to have the right to use the camera, a user must gain a one-time access token from the server. Nonetheless, this application is vulnerable to the *"man-in-the-middle" attack*. Here, the victim's app can be permitted to validate itself to the server and attain the session ID. However, by the use of ARP poisoning, they can hijack the connection. This method allows the attacker to substitute the source IP address with his own IP address to get full rights to use the camera feed.

Another good application is the Withings Smart Body Analyzer. It is a scale that can also measure the BMI, heart rate, and body fat. Wi-Fi can connect it to the Internet. Additionally, it can work by use of a Bluetooth pairing with the Withings Health Mate App. However, the most dangerous problem is that the user's personal information (for example, their name, weight, height, age, and gender) is sent unencrypted in plain text over the Wi-Fi channel. Another dangerous issue is that the scales transmit their MAC address and a secret key. If we can capture the Bluetooth packets, the MAC address and a secret key together can be used to produce an MD5 digest, which can be further used by the server for authentication purposes. However, the most dangerous problem is that by capturing this information, anybody can restructure the digest, which can empower them to masquerade as the device that is totally unknown to the server.

Therefore, as a whole, these smart home appliances have security pitfalls that need a secure architecture. In this chapter, we propose generic architecture for smart cities, which is applicable to all smart home appliances.

1.2 X.805 Standard

For smart homes or any extended appliances, we can use the X.805 standard with a range of options, such as optical networks that are wire lined and wireless. The X.805 standard uses three security layers. These layers are the application layer, the services layer, and the infrastructure layer. Additionally, it projects the three security planes of the end user, control, and management. The planes depend on the performed initiates over the network. The X.805 standard projected eight security dimensions to address the general system vulnerabilities. General system vulnerabilities include data integrity, privacy, authentication, data confidentiality communication security, availability, access control, and non-reputation. Fig. 1 depicts the complete architecture of the X.805 standard, which is largely comprised of the security layers of the X.805 standard. These security layers are already working with diverse communication systems, such as the IP-based network, Wi-Fi, or ATM. We can apply this X.805 standard to a range of options, such as optical networks, wire lined, and wireless. Additionally, it can be applicable to several kinds of networks, such as governmental networks, datacenter networks, enterprise networks, and service provider networks. Our major problems are destruction, corruption, removal, disclosure, and interruption of the data or the network's resources. The X.805 standard can be a good application as a *security mechanism* to be used with explicit DTLS and IPSec protocols for an IoTs constrained network that is running CoAP. In reality, we can consider different CoAP interactions. For example, it may be machine-to-machine, or may be a client/server tactic. The CoAP server, in some instances, can perform as a gateway proxy for relaying the HTTP client's demand to have the right to use a resource on a CoAP server. For this scenario, the CoAP proxy actually performs the operation for translating or mapping among the CoAP and the HTTP, and vice versa. One point to mention is that the CoAP network can be a closed network, which does not spread out to the Internet. Therefore, the CoAP traffic will be on the inside, and only be bi-directional among CoAP clients and CoAP server(s). In addition, the CoAP network can be extended with proper integration into the traditional Internet with the support of the 6LowPAN and CoAP/HTTP mapping procedures. In this environment, traversing traffic will be straightforward because the CoAP denotes a subset of the HTTP protocol in its own architectural design. Nevertheless, security is still a big concern, and requires the focus to be on the CoAP projection using either the DTLS or IPSec to give protection to the CoAP interactions. *Therefore, applying an X.805 threat model can be an excellent resolution.*

1.3 Secure IoT Structural Design for Smart Cities

Smart cities are large systems with lots of complexities, with distributed and uninterrupted systems that are comprised of and use mission-critical data. The major problem is that the data must be secured end-to-end. Smart cities are

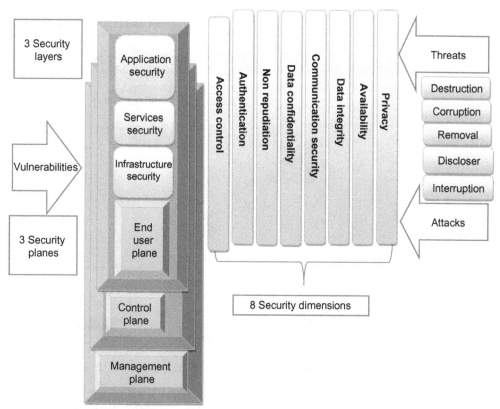

FIG. 1 Architecture of the X.805 standard.

currently totally IoT-enabled based on the IoT, and these phenomena will increase day by day. Nonetheless, their security is totally reliant on the security of the underlying IoT protocols, and these protocols are already significantly vulnerable. A sample secure IoT structural design for smart cities is comprised of trusted SDN regulators, an incorporated registry, a key management system, and black networks. The security services provided through this architecture extend beyond the basic security provided by IoT protocols. Fig. 2 depicts the *basic constituents of a secure IoT structural design for smart cities*. These basic constituents are comprised of black networks, trusted SDN regulators, an incorporated registry, and a key management system. We all know that the smart city IoT networks work with heterogeneous technologies across numerous device types. These security building blocks empower the secure communications and authentication required for all of these heterogeneous technologies. The IoT node has resource constraints that result in it not being able to provide security that is embedded inside all IoT nodes. There can be *four essential building blocks* of a secure IoT architecture for a smart city. They are as follows:

- Black networks for offering data authentication, data confidentiality, the integration of data and data privacy;
- A trusted third party (TTP) as a regulator for efficient and unidentified routing through IoT nodes that can become passive up to 90% of the time;
- An incorporated registry for a database of such devices as sensors, gateways, nodes, and their attributes; and
- Key management for an external key management system for IoT networks.

As shown in Fig. 2, the black networks are networks that are responsible for securing all data, including the metadata, which accompany each frame or packet in an IoT protocol. One of the highlights is that this kind of network encrypts the payload and the meta-data inside IoT protocol link layer communications. Likewise, the meta-data are self-sufficiently able to get security in the network layer. There are several encryption options, such as using Grain128a or AES in various modes (the EAX or OFB modes). By use of a shared secret, the resultant compatible frame permits the intended receiver to receive the message in the approved manner and decode the message. This type of network is highly useful in defending both passive and active attacks. It is able to offer privacy, integrity, and confidentiality in IoT networks due to the authenticated and secured communications. This kind of secure communication is applicable to both the link layer and the network layer. One issue is that encrypting the header produces routing issues for IoT nodes, especially those that are in the passive mode most of the time.

The sample components of a secure IoT structural design for smart cities with their offered security services are shown in Table 1.

FIG. 2   Basic components of a secure IoT structural
design for smart cities.

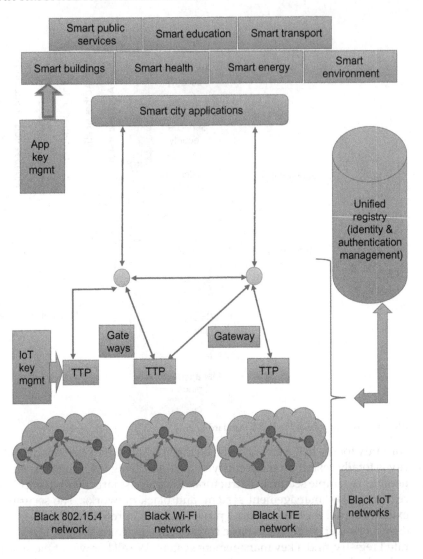

TABLE 1   Sample Components of a Secure IoT Structural Design for Smart Cities With Their Offered Security Services

IoT-based smart city security	
Security component	**Security services**
Black networks	Confidentiality, integrity, privacy
Trusted SDN regulator	Secure routing (black packets). Availability
United registry	Identity management, node authentication, authorization, accounting, availability and mobility
Key management	External key management

In the structural design in Fig. 2, the trusted SDN (software-defined networking) regulators control and coordinate the flow of communications between and among IoT nodes and the left part of the network's framework. The SDN is a networking paradigm that helps to separate the control flow from the data packet flow. This SDN controller is a very effective resolution for the routing issues, which we have seen in the privacy protective IoT black networks.

For consolidating the heterogeneous technologies and addressing the schemes and devices that form the IoT networks for a smart city, the incorporated registry is used. The idea can be extended to a visiting incorporated registry for IoT nodes, which is only mobile and cross networks. In a smart city environment, we have numerous wireless technologies, such as Wi-Fi and LTE, and we have numerous protocols, such as Bluetooth Low Energy, 6LoWPAN,

Wireless HART, and ZigBee. We have numerous addressing schemes, such as RFID addressing, Bluetooth 48-bit addressing, E.164 addressing, and IPv6 128-bit addressing. These identities, as a prerequisite, incorporate an attribute set for accounting, authentication, authorization, and identity management. Additionally, we need the translations among wireless technologies, protocols, and addressing schemes, which are obligatory. The incorporated registry simplifies the conversion.

Another issue is that in the resource-constrained IoT, the nodes do the communication in a very secure way by using a shared key. To get more simplicity and resource efficiency, we should use symmetric keys. Key management addresses such issues as key generations, the storage of keys, and key management for communications with keys with proper security. In the environment of a distributed mobile system, key distribution is a serious issue for symmetric keys. One good solution is the use of a hierarchical key management system. This concurrently allows for an efficient key distribution and for the secure use of the symmetric keys to be used by authorized devices. Therefore, in a nutshell, an independent hierarchical key management and distribution system for each layer of the communication protocol will definitely be a good solution. Therefore, as in the smart city environment, we have numerous protocols, access technologies, functions, and several types of nodes. Thus, it is obligatory to have a secure key management system for the purpose of using keys, changing keys, distributing keys, storing keys, revoking keys, and generating keys.

2 POWER INTERNET OF THINGS (PIoT)

2.1 Power Internet of Things (PIoT)—Introduction

Currently, the power Internet of Things (PIoT) is a common term in the environment of the fast expansion of smart grids, and increasing integration of the Internet of Things (IoT) technologies within the grid is occurring. Some of the examples of this integration are improved metering systems, the smart substations, electric vehicle systems, and so forth. Therefore, a power grid supported by IoT is called the *Power Internet of Things (PIoT)*. The communication technology, information technology, and sensing technology in the physical power grid are totally interdependent. They actually form a complex binary network that is denoted as the *cyber-physical power grid (CPPG)*. In PIoT, for acquiring the parameters of the smart grid related to all the facets of the operational standing of the state of the environments and the device's status in the smart grid, sensing technologies are being used. Sensing technology is used with lots of transformations, and this is made possible by numerous sensors used for several purposes, such as for an electrical signal or for acquiring a range of physical and chemical parameters. In addition, sensing technology can be used for biological information recognition, transformation, and addressing those parameters. Some problems can occur in some environments, and the sensors can work in an unverified area. Therefore, in this scenario, off-course network communications are totally open and can be observed. In addition, a sensor node is also very easy to capture, modify, or damage. Thus, our point is that the Power Internet of Things (PIoT) is mainly significant for ensuring the *data's integrity, accuracy, and privacy*.

2.2 Security Framework and Attacks

In general, a security framework that is designed for the PIoT can be comprised of three layers, including the *perception layer, the network layer, and the application layer*. In this study, we can consider a three-dimensional configuration with active defense tactics that will offer a comprehensive shield. One approach can be a *binary network denoted as the cyber-physical network* with prevention and control policies to stop the system disaster risk, but with a proper balance of the minimum costs. Another approach can be the *generalized power system (GPS) joined with electric power systems (EPS), the information and communication systems (ICS), and the monitoring and control system (MCS)*. However, the ICS and MCS have many weaknesses, flaws, and failures. In addition, recently, we have seen that the GPS has faced the Stuxnet attack in Iran. Another approach can be a *security structure for wireless communications in a smart distribution grid (SDG)*, which is comprised of the *smart tracking firewall* for addressing the matter of the intrusion detection and response measures for the SDG in the operational environment of the smart grid. In the smart grid, all vehicles, switches, towers, meters, transformers, circuits, and other electrical tools constitute an interconnected network, which in reality works in combination with the Internet of Things technologies to form the Power Internet of Things (PIoT). In the PIoT, the electrical equipment with the increased processing unit of the standardized intelligence information work as the nodes in the network. Another highlight is that by using the standardized protocols, it is realized that the exchange and sharing of the information can also be done. Additionally, another advantage is that by combining the building and upwarding systems, the PIoT upgraded the present system from the departmental level, along with the business level, to the enterprise-class applications to ensure parity with the modern era's needs.

The Power Internet of Things (PIoT) faced some thought-provoking *security concerns and a diversity of attacks at every level of the network*. The reason for these thought-provoking security concerns and a diversity of attacks are the special environments, related factors, and applications. Some of the security concerns are as follows.

(1) *Physical Attack*

Physical attacks mainly consist of electronic jamming and physical detention. Thus, the adversary can effortlessly access the right of entry or tamper with the tools, protocols, and applications for eavesdropping or interrupting the network's information.

(2) *DoS Attack and Hello Flood Attack*

In general, the DoS attack occupies the communication channel for the purpose of the proliferation of the possibility of collision aiming at blocking the channel. Additionally, adversaries can also start DoS attacks to continue in the communication state, and it can cause the sensor junction point to consume increasingly more energy. Therefore, as an outcome, it can stop the whole network.

(3) *False Routing Attack*

In this type of attack, by the use of deception, alterations, and the re-transmission of routing information, attackers make routing loops, invite or reject network traffic, and spread out or shorten the routing path. Additionally, with this attack, they can do fake messaging, partition the network, and increase the end-to-end delay.

(4) *Selective Forward Attack*

In this type of attack, a node obtains or does not obtain a packet for forwarding. Therefore, this attack creates the situation in which the packet cannot go to the right destination.

(5) *Sinkhole Attack and Wormholes Attack*

These attacks are highly dangerous. These kinds of attacks will create a scenario where it can show that the system is satisfactory, trustworthy, and efficient, and it attracts around nodes to select it as the point in the routing path. Due to the inherent mode of communication for sensor networks, all packets are directed to the same end point. As a result, it is mostly susceptible to these attacks.

(6) *Sybil Attack*

In the scenario of this attack, a single node has several capabilities in the network. Therefore, this node is a good choice for being a node in the routing path. After that step, it is combined with other types of attacks. Then, it is used in combination with others to attack the objective.

(7) *Cross-layer Attacks*

The cross-layer interference attack approaches are for encrypted wireless network communications. The core idea of this technique is that in the link layer, the channel conditions are detected by the sensing modules, and begin recording at the beginning of the transmission of the packet's transmission interval. Additionally, another highlight is that the interference module is accountable for the attack.

Therefore, for such applications as the expansion of the web application model, the expansion of network technology, and the in-depth use of the Internet of Things technology, numerous technical developments have been adopted, along with an increasing number of security dangers. Therefore it is important to protect the substation automation, relay shielding and safety devices, power plant control automation, electricity market, electricity user information acquisition, grid dispatching automation, power load control, smart electricity, and other fields. The PIoT security framework should be dependent on the exploration of the information security risk and the information security laws and regulations of the concerned country, and the power industry of that concerned country. Several attacks can be undertaken, such as the service disruption of the PIoT, mischievous penetration attacks, and unlawful operation with intelligent terminals. Sometimes business data may be altered or lost. *Therefore, a good resolution to battle these attacks can be a security framework with the four levels of physical security, network security, platform security, and application security.*

A PIoT policy with *"dual-network, dual-partition protection" with an added level of protection and multi-layered defense* can safeguard the grid's information security. For the security of information, we can isolate the network within and outside the network. Additionally, we can form three levels of defense from all facets. These levels encompass the *data and its management, the host, the border, the network, and the application*. As a result, we can attain good levels of protection. Therefore, in this way, in this kind of environment, we can use the system's proof of identity and the risk valuation of the electric power information system. Additionally, we can consider the valuation of the system's security

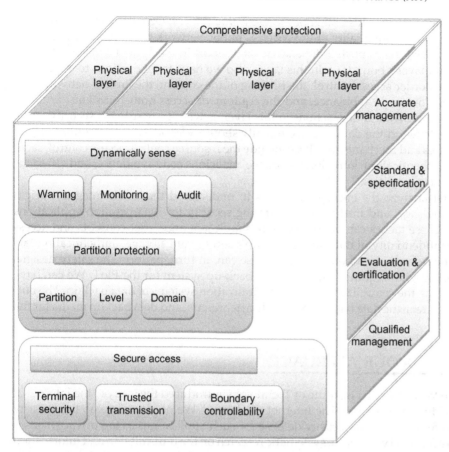

FIG. 3 Sample active defense approach system.

classification and the security levels in compliance with the defined security rules. One sample *active defense approach system* is depicted in Fig. 3.

For offering security in the PIoT, the concerned grid can implement a partition policy, a dual network policy, and a dual computer policy. This policy is easy to understand, and it actually implements dissimilar protections for several operation systems. Another issue is that we have to safeguard the access security due to numerous wireless devices accessing the smart grid. We should have mechanisms for the terminal's security, the operation channel's security, and the border's security for the purpose of defending the information security inside and outside the concerned network. It also should offer us services, such as being "leak-proof, tamper-proof, and anti-control." We have to use the IoT technology to understand the complete dynamic of the PIoT. For example, the dynamic observations should be on the security status of the terminal equipment, the information networks, and the information systems.

Therefore, all these steps have to be included in a set of perfect security measures. Now let's discuss the layer-wise security actions.

2.3 Security Attacks' Counter-Actions, Layer-Wise

First, let's discuss the perception layer security actions to be taken by the intelligent terminals and devices. Mainly we need to implement the following actions in this layer:

- local action authentication,
- login limitation,
- terminal network address restriction,
- proof of identity check for the user of the access device, and
- access restriction of resources by control necessities.

We also should employ the *intelligent terminal security module* for the storage of operation-critical data (e.g., identification information). Additionally, this secure module can be used for the local security aimed at the data protection. In addition, the devices without the security modules should also take actions to defend the authentication information (e.g., the ciphertext to stop unauthorized reading).

The next layer is the *network layer*; therefore, let us discuss the actions in this layer. In the network layer, because we have a wireless public network, information security risks exist. Thus, the key intelligent terminal should not use this technology to act as the telecommunications network. It's obligatory to use *end-to-end cryptographic* tactics for defending the data's freshness and the integrity and confidentiality of the wireless public network transmissions. Additionally, depending on the situation, we may need to establish independent safety tools in the system's master station's boundary and the communication network layer's boundary. In this layer, also we have to take actions to implement the security audit and security tactics, the border access control, the filtering of the content, the limited network connection, the intrusion avoidance, the malicious code avoidance, and the equipment access authentication.

Another layer is the *application layer*, and we should take actions in this layer as well. To ensure the security of the implementation system, the operating system and the database, we initially should *select and set the security tactics of systems* to understand the security structures and mechanisms. These include the resource control, access control, security audit, residual information defense, authentication, intrusion avoidance, malicious code avoidance, and others, as the level of information security protection necessities.

At the application level, we must first analyze the encryption tactics to understand the data's integrity, origin authentication, confidentiality defense, message, and freshness. For offering security for the operation applications software, we can apply many methods. These tactics can be the software's fault tolerance, user consents and access control, residual information defense, confidentiality of data storage, completion of data storage, authentication tactics, non-repudiation, management of the resources, and other facets. These can, in turn, perform the safety designs and the application security audits. Another vital requirement is the data back-up system for the PIoT. We can have two combinations of the data backup system, the centralization and decentralization systems of data backup. The outcome of these mechanisms is that we have a realistic data backup policy, disaster rescue, and data backup media for the purpose of safekeeping.

3 OUR APPROACH

In 1999, the Auto-ID Laboratory at the Massachusetts Institute of Technology introduced the idea of "the Internet of Things." Next, in 2005, we had the "ITU Internet Reports: The Internet of Things." We need to develop the security structural design of the IoT in order to offer information security defense for such applications as tag privacy, sensor data security, and data transmissions. We need very in-depth, systematic research on the transmission and information security of the core network, which depends on the IoT or networking industry security of the IoT. We have seen that recent works simply add safety methods in each layer. However, this is not at all sufficient. We have seen that, depending on the privacy homomorphism, the computational insufficiency of traditional algorithms is enhanced to protect users' personal privacy and security. This concept is one of the milestone ideas. However, the homomorphism technology presently is not sufficiently as mature as is required. At present, the homomorphism algorithm is capable of offering complete integer operations. Nonetheless, currently, this algorithm is comprehensive to the real region, and security is a large issue. Another disadvantage is that notably few homomorphism properties are held by the privacy homomorphism. Therefore, we need more developed homomorphism, which can be extensively used in the IoT. We have worked on the *multilayer Hybrid RSA-based solution for personal messaging for more efficiency and strong security and privacy*, as shown in Fig. 4. Our Hybrid RSA scheme now works for human messaging. The later stage of this hybrid RSA cipher can be used for the Internet of Everything (IoE) and the Internet of Things (IoT) for end-to-end encryption with high efficiency and high security with authentication and privacy protection.

We run our scheme for 2 min and we have recorded the CPU usage with the JVM plus the application usage, as shown in Fig. 5. It only occupied 5% of the CPU (Application +JVM) throughout the two minutes of continuous messaging between two peers.

FIG. 4   Our hybrid RSA scheme.

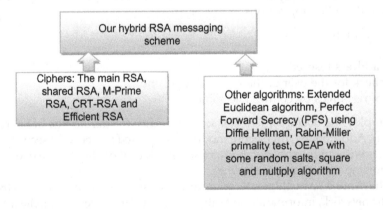

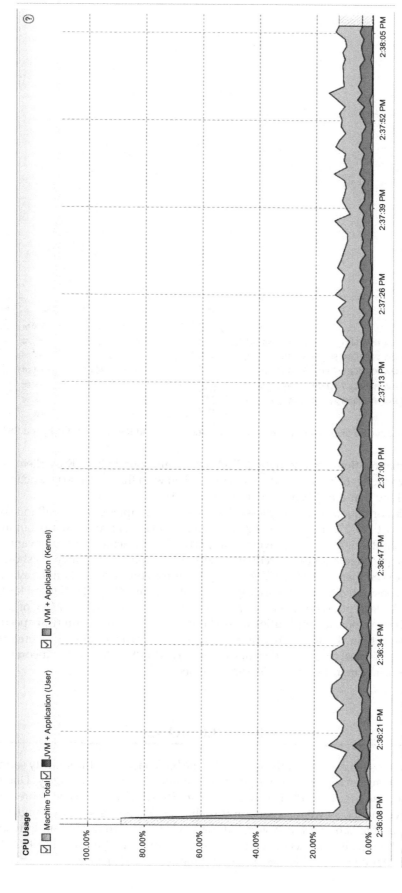

FIG. 5 CPU usage with the JVM plus the application usage of the hybrid RSA-based personal messaging scheme.

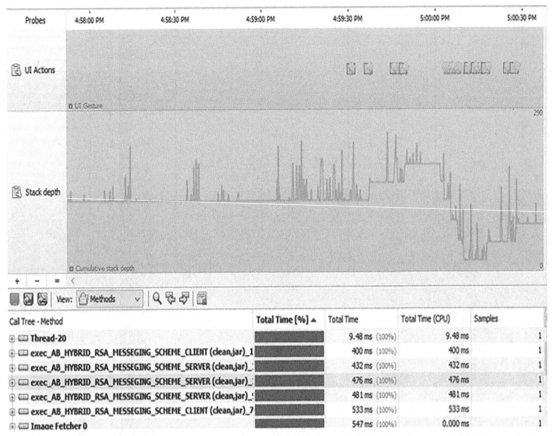

FIG. 6   Testing execution and initiation time for one hybrid RSA server and one hybrid RSA client of the hybrid RSA messaging scheme.

The execution and initiation time for one hybrid RSA server and one hybrid RSA client is significantly less at 400 ms to 533 ms, as shown in Fig. 6. It has shown us the time taken with the user interface action and the stack depth. Therefore, these results show that our scheme is very lightweight.

Our scheme in the 2 min continuous personal messaging scenarios occupies only 0.5 GiB to 1.0 Gib of memory, with the JVM CPU usage at almost 1%–2%, as shown in Fig. 7. Therefore, in a real-time scenario, our messaging scheme has shown that it is also very lightweight. This lightweight property of our scheme is very relevant to our daily lives. We have further analyzed the package-wise time occupancy with the memory occupancy, as shown in Fig. 8.

After that step, we have seen that our Hybrid RSA decryption is 8.84 times faster than the available RSA variants, as shown in Fig. 9. We have considered the main RSA, Mpower RSA, Mprime RSA, Rebalanced RSA, Rprime RSA, Batch RSA, and our Hybrid RSA Decryption (where for our calculation, we have used $b=4$ (no. of messages), $k=3$ (no. of primes), and $s=160$ in the appropriate applications), as shown in Fig. 9. The theoretical speed of our Hybrid RSA Decryption is 9 times faster than the RSA with 1024 bit keys, as shown in Table 2. Therefore, from Table 2 and Fig. 9, we can see that we get almost the same efficiency for our Hybrid RSA Decryption theoretically, and in real-time testing, it's much more efficient than the available RSA schemes.

4 CONCLUSIONS

The generic security actions to be taken for the IoT denote the basic facility of the security services that comprise its availability, authentication, authorization, non-repudiation, confidentiality, and integrity. Due to the security structural design of the IoT and smart cities, PIoT is still growing. Thus, the best way to represent the security needs can be through a reference model, as we discussed in this chapter. Therefore, it is well-understood that any single structural design will be problematic for the system. All researchers, governments, and industries are dedicated to evolving and regulating the identity and security mechanisms for the IoT's building blocks. We already know that researchers are forming better cryptographic algorithms and modes for IoT devices. We also know that some studies

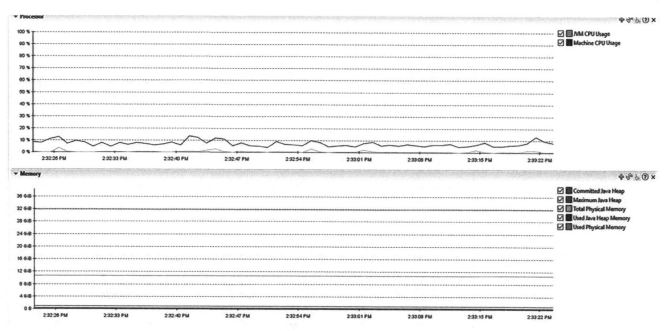

FIG. 7   Processor usage with memory occupancy for one hybrid RSA server and one hybrid RSA client of the hybrid RSA messaging scheme.

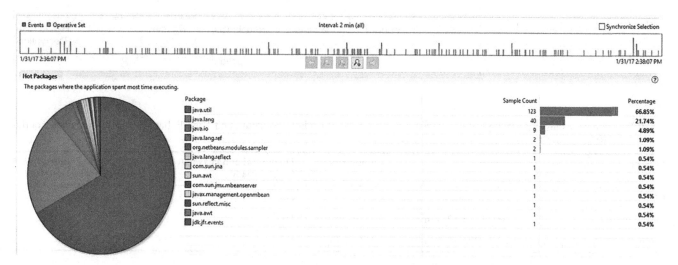

FIG. 8   Package-wise time occupancy with memory occupancy for one hybrid RSA server and one hybrid RSA client of the hybrid RSA messaging scheme.

on *lightweight dedicated hash functions* are occurring. Everybody in this area is trying to establish a new *cryptographic hash algorithm* that is able to transform a variable-length message into a short, digestible message. The Internet Engineering Task Force intends to apply Internet standards to the IoT. We have seen that many researchers have tweaked the IPsec protocol to establish the network-layer security between the Internet hosts and constrained devices. However, some issues are still difficult to resolve. We all know that the IPsec requires a shared password for the encryption and decryption of all incoming and outgoing messages. Nonetheless, the big issue is that if these passwords are static, then it can be compromised after thousands of messages. For resolving this issue, the IKE (Internet Key Exchange) and IKEv2 protocols were formed. These protocols have promised protected communications among two devices and are capable of generating new shared passwords by use of circling derivative tactics. We can use the Datagram Transport Layer Security (DTLS) to protect UDP packets (even over IPsec). Additionally, the hybrid cipher can be a good choice. Our Hybrid RSA scheme now works for human messaging. In later stages, this Hybrid RSA cipher can be used for the

FIG. 9 Cost estimation comparisons of the variants of the RSA and our hybrid RSA decryption scheme.

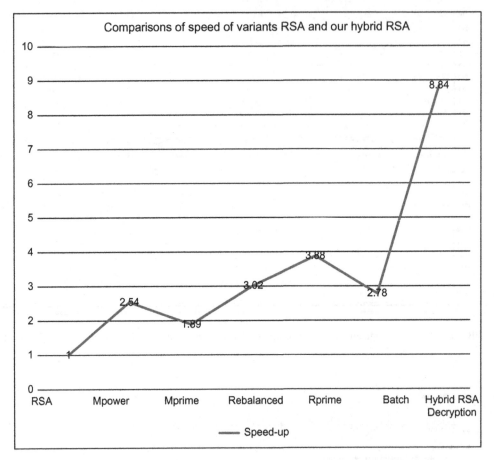

TABLE 2 Comparisons of the Complexity of the Decryptions, Theoretical Enhancements, and Their Enhancements in the Practice of the RSA, CRT-RSA, and Our Hybrid RSA Decryption

Variant	Speed	Complexity	Theoretical enhancement for $n = 1024$ bit	Approximated enhancement in practice for $n = 1024$ bit
RSA	$3n^3 + n^2 + o(n^2)$	$O(n^3)$	1.0	1.0
RSA with CRT	$3n^3/4 + 7n^2/2 + o(n^2)$	$2 \cdot O((n/2)^3)$	4.0	4.0
Our hybrid RSA decryption	$n^3/3 + 19n^2/3 + o(n^2)$	$r \cdot O((n/r)^3)$	r^2	9.0

Internet of Everything (IoE) and Internet of Things (IoT) for end-to-end encryption with high efficiency and high security with authentication and privacy protection.

In general, forthcoming studies on the security concerns of the Internet of Things would mostly focus on the resulting characteristics, such as the following: the open security system, the individual privacy protection mode, the terminal security function, the related laws for the security of the Internet of Things, and so forth. It is a necessity that the security of the Internet of Things is more than a technical problem, which also preconditions a series of policies, laws, and regulations, and a perfect security management system for mutual collocation.

ACKNOWLEDGMENTS

This work is supported by the National Natural Science Foundation of China (No. 61631013) and Key Laboratory of Universal Wireless Communications (Beijing University of Posts and Telecommunications), Ministry of Education, P.R.China (No.KFKT- 2014101).

Further Reading

[1] M. Dell'Amico, M.S.I.G. Serme, A.S. de Oliveira, Y. Roudier, Hipolds: a hierarchical security policy language for distributed systems, Inf. Secur. Tech. Rep. 17 (3) (2013) 81–92.

[2] I. Bagci, S. Raza, T. Chung, U. Roedig, T. Voigt, in: Combined secure storage and communication for the internet of things, 2013 IEEE International Conference on Sensing, Communications and Networking, SECON 2013, New Orleans, LA, United States, 2013, pp. 523–631.

[3] C.H. Liu, B. Yang, T. Liu, Efficient naming, addressing and profile services in internet-of-things sensory environments, Ad Hoc Netw. 18 (2013) 85–101.

[4] A. Jara, V. Kafle, A. Skarmeta, Secure and scalable mobility management scheme for the internet of things integration in the future internet architecture, Int. J. Ad Hoc Ubiquitous Comput. 13 (3–4) (2013) 228–242.

[5] S. Li, P. Gong, Q. Yang, M. Li, J. Kong, P. Li, in: A secure handshake scheme for mobile-hierarchy city intelligent transportation system, International Conference on Ubiquitous and Future Networks, ICUFN, Da Nang, 2013, pp. 190–191.

[6] K.C. Kang, Z.-B. Pang, C.C. Wang, Security and privacy mechanism for health internet of things, J. Chin. Univ. Posts Telecommun. 20 (Suppl 2) (2013) 64–68.

[7] F. Goncalves, J. Macedo, M. Nicolau, A. Santos, in: Security architecture for mobile e-health applications in medication control, 2013 21st International Conference on Software, Telecommunications and Computer Networks, SoftCOM 2013, Primosten, 2013, pp. 1–8.

[8] J. An, X. Gui, W. Zhang, J. Jiang, J. Yang, Research on social relations cognitive model of mobile nodes in internet of things, J. Netw. Comput. Appl. 36 (2) (2013) 799–810.

[9] P. Kasinathan, G. Costamagna, H. Khaleel, C. Pastrone, M. Spirito, Demo: An ids Framework for Internet of Things Empowered, 6lowpan, Berlin, Germany, 2013, pp. 1337–1339.

[10] Z. Shelby, B. Frank, D. Sturek, in: Constrained application protocol (CoAP), Internet-Draft (Work in Progress Draft-ietf-corecoap-018), Sensinode, SkyFoundry, Pacific Gas and Electric, 2013.

[11] Bell Labs, "The Bell Labs" Security Framework: Making the Case for End-to-End Wi-Fi Security, http://www.webtorials.com/main/resource/papers/lucent/paper90/wireless3.pdf. Accessed 14 October 2013.

[12] BETaaS Consortium, D1.4.2 – TaaS Reference Model, http://www.betaas.eu/docs/deliverables/BETaaS%20-%20D1.4.2%20-%20TaaS%20Reference%20Model%20v1.0.pdf, 2013. Accessed 11 March 2014.

[13] IoT@Work Consortium, D1.2 – Final framework architecture specification, https://www.iot-at-work.eu/data/D1.3IoT@WorkArchitecturefinalv1.0-submitted.pdf, 2013. Accessed 20 July 2014.

[14] M. Abomhara, G.M. Koien, Security and privacy in the internet of things: Current status and open issues, in: Privacy and Security in Mobile Systems (PRISMS), IEEE, 2014, pp. 1–8.

[15] A.W. Atamli, A. Martin, Threat-based security analysis for the internet of things, in: Secure Internet of Things (SIoT), IEEE, 2014, pp. 35–43.

[16] BETaaS Consortium, BETaaS Building the Environment for the Things as a Service D2. 2.2 – Specification of the extended capabilities of the platform, 2014, pp. 1–61.

[17] IoT-A Consortium, Iot-A Unified Requirements, http://www.iot-a.eu/public/requirements/. Accessed 31 January 2014.

[18] L. Gao, X. Bai, A unified perspective on the factors influencing consumer acceptance of internet of things technology, Asia Pac. J. Mark. Logist. 26 (2) (2014) 211–231.

[19] V. Gazis, C.G. Cordero, E. Vasilomanolakis, P. Kikiras, A. Wiesmaier, in: Security perspectives for collaborative data acquisition in the internet of things, International Conference on Safety and Security in Internet of Things, Springer, 2014.

[20] IoT-A Consortium, IoT-A–Internet of Things Architecture, http://www.iot-a.eu. Accessed 27 January 2014.

[21] O. Logvinov, B. Kraemer, C. Adams, J. Heiles, G. Stuebing, M.L. Nielsen, B. Mancuso, Standard for an Architectural Framework for the Internet of Things (IoT) IEEE P2413 Webinar Panelists, 2014, pp. 1–12.

[22] A. Zanella, N. Bui, A.P. Castellani, L. Vangelista, M. Zorzi, Internet of things for smart cities, IEEE Internet Things J. 1 (2014) 22–32.

[23] L.A. Grieco, M.B. Alaya, T. Monteil, K.K. Drira, in: Architecting information centric ETSI-M2M systems, 2014 IEEE International Conference on Pervasive Computing and Communication Workshops (PERCOM WORKSHOPS), 24–28 March, 2014.

[24] J. Anderson, L. Rainie, The Internet of Things will Thrive by 2025, PewResearch Internet Project, http://www.pewinternet.org/2014/05/14/internet-of-things/, 2014.

[25] Z. Yan, P. Zhang, A.V. Vasilakos, A survey on trust management for internet of things, J. Netw. Comput. Appl. 42 (2014) 120–134.

[26] G. Piro, G. Boggia, L.A. Grieco, in: A standard compliant security framework for ieee 802.15.4 networks, Proceedings of IEEE World Forum on Internet of Things (WF-IoT), Seoul, South Korea, 2014, pp. 27–30.

[27] J.-Y. Lee, W.-C. Lin, Y.-H. Huang, in: A lightweight authentication protocol for internet of things, 2014 International Symposium on Next-Generation Electronics, ISNE 2014, Kwei-Shan, 2014, pp. 1–2.

[28] M. Turkanovic, B. Brumen, M. Hlbl, A novel user authentication and key agreement scheme for heterogeneous ad hoc wireless sensor networks, based on the internet of things notion, Ad Hoc Netw. 20 (2014) 96–112.

[29] N. Ye, Y. Zhu, R.-C.B. Wang, R. Malekian, Q.-M. Lin, An efficient authentication and access control scheme for perception layer of internet of things, Appl. Math. Inf. Sci. 8 (4) (2014) 1617–1624.

[30] A. Cherkaoui, L. Bossuet, L. Seitz, G. Selander, R. Borgaonkar, in: New paradigms for access control in constrained environments, 2014 9th International Symposium on Reconfigurable and Communication-Centric Systems-on-Chip (ReCoSoC), Montpellier, 2014, pp. 1–4.

[31] S. Sicari, A. Rizzardi, C. Cappiello, A. Coen-Porisini, in: A NFP model for internet of things applications, Proceedins of IEEE WiMob, Larnaca, Cyprus, 2014, pp. 164–171.

[32] X. Wang, J. Zhang, E. Schooler, M. Ion, in: Performance evaluation of attribute-based encryption: toward data privacy in the IoT, 2014 IEEE International Conference on Communications, ICC 2014, Sydney, NSW, 2014, pp. 725–730.

[33] J. Su, D. Cao, B. Zhao, X. Wang, I. You, ePASS: an expressive attribute-based signature scheme with privacy and an unforgeability guarantee for the internet of things, Futur. Gener. Comput. Syst. 33 (2014) 11–18.

[34] L.B. Peng, W.B. Ru-chuan, S. Xiao-yu, C. Long, Privacy protection based on key-changed mutual authentication protocol in internet of things, Commun. Comput. Inf. Sci. 418 (CCIS) (2014) 345–355.

[35] A. Ukil, S. Bandyopadhyay, A. Pal, in: Iot-privacy: to be private or not to be private, Proceedings of IEEE INFOCOM, Toronto, ON, 2014, pp. 123–124.

[36] S. Sicari, C. Cappiello, F.D. Pellegrini, D. Miorandi, A. Coen-Porisini, A security-and quality-aware system architecture for internet of things, Inf. Syst. Front. 18 (2014) 665–677.

[37] G.D. Tormo, F.G. Marmol, G.M. Perez, Dynamic and flexible selection of a reputation mechanism for heterogeneous environments, Futur. Gener. Comput. Syst. 49 (2014) 113–124.

[38] L. Gu, J. Wang, B.B. Sun, Trust management mechanism for internet of things, China Commun. 11 (2) (2014) 148–156.

[39] Y.-B. Liu, X.-H. Gong, Y.-F. Feng, Trust system based on node behavior detection in internet of things, Tongxin Xuebao/J. Commun. 35 (5) (2014) 8–15.

[40] J. Singh, J. Bacon, D. Eyers, in: Policy enforcement within emerging distributed, event-based systems, DEBS 2014 – Proceedings of the 8th ACM International Conference on Distributed Event-Based Systems, 2014, pp. 246–255.

[41] R. Neisse, G. Steri, G. Baldini, in: Enforcement of security policy rules for the internet of things, Proceedings of IEEE WiMob, Larnaca, Cyprus, 2014, pp. 120–127.

[42] A. Gòmez-Goiri, P. Orduna, J. Diego, D.L. de Ipina, Otsopack: lightweight semantic framework for interoperable ambient intelligence applicationus, Comput. Hum. Behav. 30 (2014) 460–467.

[43] G. Colistra, V. Pilloni, L. Atzori, The problem of task allocation in the internet of things and the consensus-based approach, Comput. Netw. 73 (2014) 98–111.

[44] Y. Wang, M. Qiao, H. Tang, H. Pei, Middleware development method for internet of things, Liaoning Gongcheng Jishu Daxue Xuebao (Ziran Kexue Ban)/J, Liaoning Tech. Univ. (Nat. Sci. Ed.) 33 (5) (2014) 675–678.

[45] H. Ferreira, R. De Sousa Jr, F. De Deus, E. Canedo, in: Proposal of a secure, deployable and transparent middleware for internet of things, Iberian Conference on Information Systems and Technologies, CISTI, Barcelona, 2014, pp. 1–4.

[46] B. Niu, X. Zhu, H. Chi, H. Li, Privacy and authentication protocol for mobile rfid systems, Wirel. Pers. Commun. 77 (3) (2014) 1713–1731.

[47] Y.-S. Jeong, J. Lee, J.-B. Lee, J.-J. Jung, J. Park, An efficient and secure m-ips scheme of mobile devices for human-centric computing, J. Appl. Math. 2014 (2014) 1–8.

[48] J. Geng, X. Xiong, Research on mobile information access based on internet of things, Appl. Mech. Mater. 539 (2014) 460–463.

[49] S. Kubler, K. Frmling, A. Buda, A standardized approach to deal with firewall and mobility policies in the IoT, Pervasive Mob. Comput. 20 (2014) 100–114.

[50] C. Perera, P. Jayaraman, A. Zaslavsky, D. Georgakopoulos, P. Christen, in: Mosden: An internet of things middleware for resource constrained mobile devices, Proceedings of the Annual Hawaii International Conference on System Sciences, Washington, DC, USA, 2014, pp. 1053–1062.

[51] J. Montavont, D. Roth, T. Nol, Mobile {IPv6} in internet of things: analysis, experimentations and optimizations, Ad Hoc Netw. 14 (2014) 15–25.

[52] D. Rosario, Z. Zhao, A. Santos, T. Braun, E. Cerqueira, A beaconless opportunistic routing based on a cross-layer approach for efficient video dissemination in mobile multimedia IoT applications, Comput. Commun. 45 (2014) 21–31.

[53] J.P. Espada, V.G. Daz, R.G. Crespo, O.S. Martnez, B.P. G-Bustelo, J.M.C. Lovelle, Using extended web technologies to develop bluetooth multi-platform mobile applications for interact with smart things, Inf. Fusion 21 (2014) 30–41.

[54] T.-M. Gronli, P. Pourghomi, G. Ghinea, Towards NFC payments using a lightweight architecture for the web of things, Computing 97 (2014) 985–999.

[55] J. Daubert, A. Wiesmaier, P. Kikiras, in: A view on privacy & trust in iot, In IOT/CPS-Security Workshop, IEEE International Conference on Communications, ICC 2015, London, GB, 8–12 June, 2015, IEEE, 2015.

[56] A.-R. Sadeghi, C. Wachsmann, M. Waidner, in: Security and privacy challenges in industrial internet of things, Annual Design Automation Conference, ACM, 2015, p. 54.

[57] S. Sicari, A. Rizzardi, L.A. Grieco, A. Coen-Porisini, Security, privacy and trust in internet of things: the road ahead, Comput. Netw. 76 (2015) 146–164.

[58] Z.-k. Zhang, M. Cheng, Y. Cho, S. Shieh, in: Emerging security threats and countermeasures in IoT, ACM Symposium on Information, Computer and Communications Security, ACM, 2015, pp. 1–6.

[59] A. Bhattacharjya, X. Zhong, J. Wang, in: Strong, efficient and reliable personal messaging peer to peer architecture based on Hybrid RSA, Proceedings of The International Conference on Internet of Things and Cloud Computing (ICC 2016) ISBN 978-1-4503-4063-2/16/03, March 22nd to 23rd 2016, in The Møller Centre-CHURCHILL COLLEGE, Cambridge, United Kingdom. EI Accession number: 20162702561683, 2016.

[60] A. Bhattacharjya, X. Zhong, J. Wang, An end to end users two way authenticated double encrypted messaging scheme based on hybrid RSA for the future internet architectures, Int. J. Inf. Comput. Secur. 10 (2018) 63–79. EI Accession number: 20180604772681.

[61] A. Bhattacharjya, X. Zhong, J. Wang, L. Xing, On mapping of address and port using translation (MAP-T), Int, J. Inf. Comput. Secur. (2019), https://doi.org/10.1504/ijics.2018.10008372.http://www.inderscience.com/info/ingeneral/forthcoming.php?jcode=ijics.

[62] A. Bhattacharjya, X. Zhong, J. Wang, HYBRID RSA based highly efficient, reliable and strong personal Full Mesh Networked messaging scheme, Int. J. Inform. Comput. Secur. 10 (4) (2018) 418–436.

[63] A. Bhattacharjya, X. Zhong, J. Wang, X. Li, Security challenges and concerns of internet of things (IoT), in: S. Guo, D. Zeng (Eds.), Cyber-Physical Systems: Architecture, Security and Application, EAI/Springer Innovations in Communication and Computing, Springer, Cham, 2019.

[64] A. Bhattacharjya, X. Zhong, J. Wang, L. Xing, Present scenarios of IoT projects with security aspects focused, in: Digital Twin Technologies and Smart Cities, Internet of Things (IoT), in press, CiteScore 0.88, https://www.scopus.com/sourceid/21100826426?origin=resultslist.

[65] A. Bhattacharjya, X. Zhong, J. Wang, L. Xing, CoAP—application layer connection-less lightweight protocol for the Internet of Things (IoT) and CoAP -IPSEC Security with DTLS Supporting CoAP, in: Digital Twin Technologies and Smart Cities, Internet of Things (IoT), in press, CiteScore 0.88, https://www.scopus.com/sourceid/21100826426?origin=resultslist.

[66] A. Bhattacharjya, X. Zhong, J. Wang, L. Xing, Secure Hybrid RSA (SHRSA) based multilayered authenticated, efficient and End to End secure 6-layered personal messaging communication protocol, in: Digital Twin Technologies and Smart Cities, Internet of Things (IoT), in press, CiteScore 0.88, https://www.scopus.com/sourceid/21100826426?origin=resultslist.

[67] oneM2M, http://www.onem2m.org/.

[68] BUTLER Project, http://www.iot-butler.eu.

[69] HYDRA Project, http://www.hydramiddleware.eu/.

[70] Usable Trust in the Internet of Things, http://www.utrustit.eu/.

[71] iCORE Project, http://www.iot-icore.eu.

[72] HACMS Project, http://www.defenseone.com/technology.

[73] National Science Foundation Project, http://www.nsf.gov.

[74] Roseline Project, https://sites.google.com/site/roselineproject/.

[75] XIA-NP Project, http://www.cs.cmu.edu/xia/.

[76] NDN-NP Project, http://named-data.net/.

[77] NEBULA Project, http://nebula-fia.org/.

[78] MobilityFirst-NP Project, http://mobilityfirst.winlab.rutgers.edu/.

[79] FIRE EU-China Project, http://www.euchina-fire.eu/.

[80] FIRE EU-Korea Project, http://eukorea-fire.eu/.

[81] EU-Japan Project, http://www.eurojapan-ict.org/.

[82] Extensible Markup Language (XML), Available from: http://www.w3.org/XML/.

[83] "Routing Over Low power and Lossy networks" ROLL Working Group, Available at: http://datatracker.ietf.org/wg/roll/.

[84] Constrained RESTful Environments (CoRE) Working Group, Available at: https://datatracker.ietf.org/wg/core/charter/.

[85] European FP7 IoT@Work project, http://iot-at-work.eu.

[86] M. Gudgin, M. Hadley, N. Mendelsohn, J.-J. Moreau, H. Nielsen, A. Karmarkar, Y. Lafon, "Simple Object Access Protocol (SOAP)". Version 1.2 Part 1: Messaging Framework, W3C, 2001.

14

Outlier Discrimination and Correction in Intelligent Transportation Systems

Junqin Huang, Linghe Kong, and Guihai Chen
Shanghai Jiao Tong University, Shanghai, China

1 INTRODUCTION

The rapid growth of vehicles brings the problem of traffic congestion. Shanghai, New York, and Paris, for example, which are the largest cities in the world, suffer from constant traffic congestion. It is essential for drivers to check the traffic conditions before going out via navigation applications such as AMAP, Google Maps, Baidu Map, and so forth.

Traditionally, these navigation applications have provided traffic conditions by collecting location data from users or in-vehicle sensing devices in real time. Due to its openness, malicious users could upload fake data to the data center intentionally, which would make navigation applications provide misleading traffic information. As a result, the transportation system falls into chaos. On the other hand, hardware heterogeneity and failure [1] may cause bias or missing information in collected location data.

In Fig. 1, a snapshot of the road network in downtown Chengdu, which we research in this chapter, is shown. We collect traffic condition data of these roads from AMAP [2] every 5 min for 24 h. Fig. 2 shows the missing ratio of traffic condition data. By statistics, 42% of the total data are missing. The large missing ratio and potential faulty values increase the misleading traffic information. It is significant to discriminate the outliers to guarantee an efficient transportation system, which motivates us to propose a novel method to address it.

Lots of work has been contributed to this field, such as Yoon et al. [3] utilize traffic patterns on a specific road segment to estimate traffic conditions, which needs large datasets in identifying traffic conditions, and each road, which is analyzed independently, is not suitable for the real-time environment (e.g., navigation applications). Li et al. [4] propose a compressive sensing-based method to estimate missing values in urban traffic sensing; however, this method does not take faulty data into consideration, which may lead to reconstruction deviation. Cheng et al. [5] propose a DECO framework to improve data quality for crowd-sensing applications. They believe users who have a good reputation will not upload faulty data, which is impractical, too. In summary, although some algorithms and methods are proposed to address such problems, few of them are practical in real life.

In this chapter, we propose an outlier discrimination and correction (ODC) method to discriminate faulty data and reconstruct missing data in traffic condition datasets. Through simulations conducted on traffic condition datasets from AMAP, we observe that ODC can produce only about a 6 km/h reconstruction error, even with a missing data ratio $\beta = 50\%$ and faulty data ratio $\alpha = 30\%$.

Our contributions can be summarized as follows:

- We propose the ODC method, which is applied to outlier detection and missing data reconstruction in the field of traffic information. It only uses single dimension information, that is, the average speed for analysis, so it takes very little time and is suitable for real time applications.
- We mine temporal stability and spatial correlation features from traffic condition datasets, and utilize these hidden structures to improve performance of compressive sensing.
- We evaluate ODC based on real urban traffic condition datasets, demonstrating that it produces low reconstruction errors, even when the missing ratio is 50% and the faulty ratio is 30% in traffic condition datasets.

FIG. 1   Road network of Chengdu downtown region.

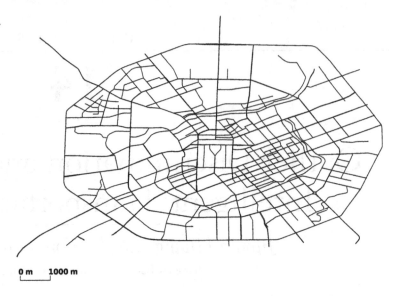

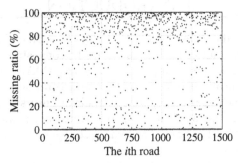

FIG. 2   Missing ratio of traffic condition data from AMAP.

The rest of this chapter is organized as follows. In Section 2, we formulate the problem. In Section 3, we analyze the hidden structures in traffic condition datasets. The compressive sensing-based method, ODC, is proposed in Section 4. In Section 5, we evaluate the ODC method through real urban traffic traces. We introduce related work in Section 6 and conclude this chapter in Section 7.

2 PROBLEM FORMULATION

The better traffic conditions are, the higher the driving speed allowed, so we adopt the mean velocity of roads as the metric for quantifying traffic conditions in this chapter. As shown in Fig. 1, the road network consists of n roads (different directions of the same road are considered different roads). The sensing period includes t time slots. Each road updates its mean velocity once per time slot by calculating real-time changes of location data from users. $x(i, j)$ denotes the mean velocity of road i at time slot j, where $i = 1, 2, ..., n$ and $j = 1, 2, ..., t$.

Definition 1. Traffic Condition Matrix (TCM) describes the mean velocity of road i in time slot j. TCM is defined by $X = (x(i, j))_{n \times t}$.

Each line of X represents a time series of mean velocity of one road. And every data point is valid, that is, no missing or faulty data points.

Definition 2. Direct Sensory Matrix (DSM) is an $n \times t$ matrix, which contains mean velocity calculated through raw data, where we may find missing or faulty data points. DSM is denoted by S, defined as follows:

$$S(i, j) = (s(i, j))_{n \times t} = \begin{cases} 0 & \text{if } x(i, j) \text{ is missing} \\ x(i, j) + \xi & \text{otherwise} \end{cases} \tag{1}$$

Data error is denoted by ξ, $s(i, j)$ is considered a faulty data point if $|\xi| > \eta$, where η is a predefined threshold, otherwise as a normal one.

Definition 3. Faulty Matrix (FM) is an $n \times t$ matrix, denoted by F, set $F(i,j)$ to 1 if $s(i,j)$ is faulty, defined as:

$$F(i,j) = \begin{cases} 1 & \text{if } s(i,j) \text{ is faulty} \\ 0 & \text{otherwise} \end{cases} \tag{2}$$

Definition 4. Existence Matrix (EM) is denoted by E, represents if $x(i,j)$ is collected in S, defined as:

$$E(i,j) = (\varepsilon(i,j))_{n \times t} = \begin{cases} 0 & \text{if } x(i,j) \text{ is not in } S \\ 1 & \text{otherwise} \end{cases} \tag{3}$$

Definition 5. Faulty Data Detection Matrix (FDM) is an $n \times t$ matrix, denoted by D, marks out the faulty data detected through the ODC method, defined similar to F.

Definition 6. Reconstruct Matrix (RM) is generated by interpolating the missing or faulty values in DSM to approximate to TCM. RM is defined by $\hat{X} = (\hat{x}(i,j))_{n \times t}$.

Definition 7. Binary Index Matrix (BIM) combines E and D, marks out trusted data, that is, not missing or faulty data. BIM is denoted by B, defined as:

$$B = (b(i,j))_{n \times t} = E \cap \overline{D} \tag{4}$$

The first problem is to detect faulty data in S, formulated as:

Problem 1 (Faulty Data Detection in Direct Sensory Matrix (FDSM)).

Given S and E, the FDSM problem is to find D, the expectation of D is as close to F as possible. That is,

$$\begin{aligned} &\text{Objective}: \min \|D - F\|_F \\ &\text{Subject to}: S, E \end{aligned} \tag{5}$$

where $\|\cdot\|_F$ is the Frobenius norm used to measure the difference between D and F. That is, $\|D - F\|_F = \sqrt{\sum_{i,j}(D(i,j) - F(i,j))^2}$.

The second problem is to reconstruct the real traffic condition (TCM) based on the sensory data (DSM).

Problem 2 (Traffic Condition Reconstruction in Road Networks (TCRN)).

Given S and B, the TCRN problem is to find the optimal $\hat{X}$ that approximates X as closely as possible, that is,

$$\begin{aligned} &\text{Objective}: \min \|X - \hat{X}\|_F \\ &\text{Subject to}: S, B \end{aligned} \tag{6}$$

3 TRAFFIC CONDITION DATA MINING

We gather the real-time traffic condition data from AMAP [2], which is available on the Internet. The dataset collects the mean velocity of roads in the Chengdu downtown region, covering a period of 24 h on November 25, 2017. It contains 1487 roads and 288 time slots, with slot intervals of 5 min. However, we cannot utilize the raw data from AMAP because of the existence of missing and faulty data, which will lead to the lack of ground truth. To generate TCM, we perform preprocessing and select complete subsets from raw data. The selected subset contains 617 roads $\times$ 288 slots.

3.1 Discovery Over Low Rank Structure

The mean velocity of different roads over different times are not independent, there are structures. We reveal the inherent structure with the singular value decomposition (SVD), which is a kind of factorization of a matrix. SVD is usually used for creating a low rank matrix approximation. The matrix $(x(i,j))_{n \times t}$ can be decomposed as:

$$X = U\Sigma V^T = \sum_{i=1}^{\min(n,t)} \sigma_i u_i v_i^T \tag{7}$$

where U is an $n \times n$ unitary matrix (i.e., $UU^T = U^TU = I$), V^T is the transpose of an $t \times t$ unitary matrix, Σ is an $n \times t$ diagonal matrix with the singular value σ_i of X on the main diagonal, where $\sigma_i \geq \sigma_{i+1}$, $i = 1, 2, \ldots, \min(n,t)$.

The matrix is low rank if $r \ll \min(n,t)$, r is equal to nonzero singular values. σ_i represents the ith largest singular value of X, which means X can be approximately denoted by top r singular values.

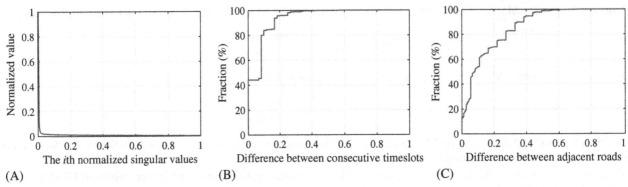

FIG. 3   Traffic condition hidden structures mining from the complete subset. (A) Low rank feature; (B) temporal stability feature; (C) spatial correlation feature.

$$\sum_{i=1}^{r}\sigma_i \approx \sum_{i=1}^{\min(n,t)}\sigma_i \tag{8}$$

In Fig. 3A, we illustrate the distribution of singular values in TCM. The X-axis denotes the ith largest singular value, and the Y-axis presents the values of ith singular value, and both of them are normalized. This figure shows that the top 50% singular values contribute the most energy in traffic condition data. This means that TCM has low rank structures, which is the prerequisite for using compressive sensing.

3.2 Temporal Stability Feature

The mean velocity of a road changes stably between adjacent timeslots in general when the interval is not too large. On the basis of this observation, we analyze the traffic condition data in the time dimension to reveal temporal features. We measure the temporal stability of road i at timeslot j by calculating the difference between adjacent timeslots as

$$\triangle x(i,j) = |x(i,j) - x(i,j-1)| \tag{9}$$

The CDF of $\triangle x(i,j)$ is plotted in Fig. 3B. The X-axis denotes difference between adjacent timeslots (normalized), and the Y-axis presents the cumulative probability of $\triangle x(i,j)$. We can observe that above 40% $\triangle x(i,j)$ in TCM are 0, and above 95% $\triangle x(i,j)$ are less than 0.2. This indicates that temporal stability exists in TCM. On the basis of this observation, we can improve the compressive sensing by adding a temporal feature dimension.

3.3 Spatial Correlation Feature

From the road network in Fig. 1, we can observe that there are many adjacent roads, and the mean velocity between adjacent roads is usually similar. Hence, we can consider the difference from the space dimension.

In traffic condition datasets from AMAP, roads are characterized through polylines, which consist of several latitude and longitude coordinates. Thus, we can utilize these latitude and longitude coordinates to find out if two roads are adjacent. To illustrate it in mathematical form, the adjacent roads matrix (ARM) is defined as follows:

$$H(a,b) = \begin{cases} 1 & \text{if } a \text{ and } b \text{ are adjacent} \\ 0 & \text{otherwise} \end{cases} \tag{10}$$

where $a = 1, 2, \ldots, n$ and $b = 1, 2, \ldots, n$. ARM is an $n \times n$ matrix, denoted by H, which presents the spatial correlation of any two roads.

We measure the spatial correlation of road i at timeslot j by calculating the difference in mean velocity between road i and the average of its all adjacent roads. $\theta x(i,j)$ is calculated as:

$$\theta x(i,j) = \left| x(i,j) - \frac{H(i,:)X(:,j)}{\sum H(i,:)} \right| \tag{11}$$

where $H(i,:)$ is the ith row of H, $X(:,j)$ is the jth column of X. $H(i,:)X(:,j)$ presents the sum values of all adjacent roads of road i at timeslot j. $\sum H(i,:)$ presents the number of adjacent roads of road i.

The CDF of $\theta x(i,j)$ is plotted in Fig. 3C. The X-axis depicts the normalized difference in mean velocity between road i and the average of its all adjacent roads. The Y-axis presents the cumulative possibility. This figure shows that above 80% $\theta x(i,j)$ are smaller than 0.3 and almost all of $\theta x(i,j)$ are smaller than 0.5. This observation indicates that TCM also has a spatial correlation feature, which means we can improve compressive sensing from a spatial dimension.

4 ODC METHOD BASED ON COMPRESSIVE SENSING

Based on the preceding observations, we propose and detail the ODC method in this section.

4.1 Overview

The ODC method is proposed to discriminate faulty data and correct them in traffic condition datasets. Thus the ODC method consists of two main procedures, which are discrimination and correction. The ODC method is based on compressive sensing technology, which is effective for reconstruct missing data in structured or redundancy datasets. However, the result of reconstruction is not so effective when there is massive faulty data in dataset, that is, faulty data can cause a large deviation during the reconstruction procedure. Therefore, we need to discover faulty data before correcting to mitigate reconstruction deviation.

Fig. 4 shows the program flow chart of the ODC method. We take Direct Sensory Matrix S, Existence Matrix E, ARM H, λ_1, λ_2, λ_3, rank bound r, and iteration times $maxIter$ as inputs and Reconstruct Matrix $\hat{X}$, and Faulty Data Detection Matrix D as outputs. D is set to all ones at the beginning of the procedure because the ODC method aims to find more faulty data. There are three main functions in the ODC method, which are $FaultyDataDetection()$, $ASD()$, and $updateFDM()$. The task of $FaultyDataDetection()$ is to discriminate faulty data by utilizing its temporal-spatial correlation, as we discuss in Sections 3.2 and 3.3, and mark faulty data points in D. Then ODC combines E and D, and marks out trusted data points in B. B is taken as an input of $ASD()$, which is to reconstruct missing data in the dataset (faulty or missing data are both taken as missing data in $ASD()$). The output of $ASD()$ is Reconstruct Matrix $\hat{X}$, $updateFDM()$ compares $\hat{X}$ and S to update the Faulty Data Detection Matrix D. The ODC method repeats this process until D is not

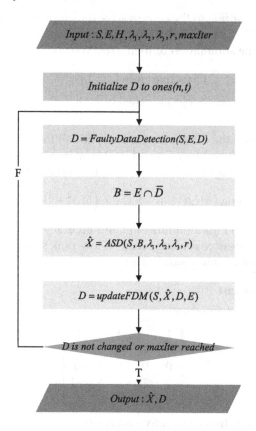

FIG. 4 ODC method flow chart.

changed after updating or iteration times have reached *maxIter*. We will detail these three functions, *FaultyDataDetection()*, *ASD()*, and *updateFDM()*, in the rest of this section, that is, the Optimization of Compressive Sensing and Faulty Data Detection Approach Based on the Temporal Stability Feature.

4.2 Optimization of Compressive Sensing

Compressive sensing is known as an effective technique to reconstruct missing data for sparse matrices. The main idea of compressive sensing is that datasets in the real world often contain structures or redundancy, which we have revealed in Section 3.1 for traffic condition datasets. Thus, we utilize compressive sensing to compute an estimate of traffic condition matrix $\hat{X}$ that approximates the real traffic condition matrix X.

Because of the low rank feature of X, we can approximately represent X by its r largest singular values. According to Eqs. (7), (8), we can approximately represent X as

$$\hat{X} = \sum_{i=1}^{r} \sigma_i u_i v_i^T \tag{12}$$

Actually, $\hat{X}$ is the best r-rank approximation that minimizes the Frobenius norm between X and $\hat{X}$.

However, it is impossible to directly find the $\hat{X}$, because we do not know X and the proper rank. Thus, we can alternatively solve the following rank minimization problem:

$$\text{Objective}: \min\left(rank\left(\hat{X}\right)\right)$$
$$\text{Subject to}: \hat{X} \circ B = S \tag{13}$$

where $\circ$ refers to the Hadamard product ($\hat{X} \circ B = S$ means $\hat{X}(i,j)B(i,j) = S(i,j)$).

However, it is difficult to solve this minimization problem because it is nonconvex. To address this difficulty, we make use of the SVD-like factorization of $\hat{X}$:

$$\hat{X} = U\Sigma V = LR^T \tag{14}$$

where $L = U\Sigma^{1/2}$ and $R = V\Sigma^{1/2}$. According to the compressive sensing theory, if the restricted isometry property [6] holds, minimizing the nuclear form [7–9] can perform rank minimization exactly for a low rank matrix, that is, we just find matrix L and R that minimize the summation of their Frobenius norms as:

$$\text{Objective}: \min\left(\|L\|_F^2 + \|R\|_F^2\right)$$
$$\text{Subject to}: (LR^T) \circ B = S \tag{15}$$

In practice, L and R that strictly satisfy the constraint are likely to fail for two reasons. First, there are noises in the sensory data that may lead to the over-fit problem. Second, TCM can be a low rank matrix, although it may not exactly be low ranking. Thus, we use the Lagrange multiplier to relax the constraint:

$$\min\left(\|(LR^T) \circ B - S\|_F^2 + \lambda_1\left(\|L\|_F^2 + \|R\|_F^2\right)\right) \tag{16}$$

where λ_1 controls the trade-off between rank minimization and accuracy fitness.

Although the performance of compressive sensing relies on low rank structure, it can also be improved by taking temporal stability and spatial correlation into consideration.

4.2.1 Temporal Stability Improvement

The temporal constraint matrix $\mathbb{T}$ is defined as:

$$\mathbb{T} = \begin{bmatrix} 1 & -1 & 0 & \cdots & 0 \\ 0 & 1 & -1 & \ddots & \vdots \\ 0 & 0 & 1 & \ddots & 0 \\ \vdots & \vdots & \ddots & \ddots & -1 \\ -1 & 0 & 0 & \cdots & 1 \end{bmatrix}_{t \times t} \tag{17}$$

which describes the difference between two consecutive timeslots.

$LR^T\mathbb{T}$ captures temporal stability of the traffic condition dataset, which we have revealed in Section 3.2. Hence, we can introduce the temporal constraint $\left\|LR^T\mathbb{T}\right\|_F^2$ into Eq. (16) to filter more noises and errors.

4.2.2 Spatial Correlation Improvement

The spatial constraint matrix is denoted by $\mathbb{H}$, which outlines the difference between adjacent roads at the same timeslot; its definition is similar to $\mathbb{H}$ in [10].

$\mathbb{H}$ indeed is a transformation of the ARM H: (1) The central diagonal of $\mathbb{H}$ is given by $\mathbb{H}(i,i)=(-\sum H(i,:))$, where $H(i,:)$ means the ith row in H. Other elements in $\mathbb{H}$ are the same as H. (2) Normalize rows of $\mathbb{H}$ and we get the final $\mathbb{H}$ transformed from H. For example, if there is an ARM H:

$$H=\begin{bmatrix}0 & 0 & 1\\ 1 & 0 & 1\\ 1 & 0 & 0\end{bmatrix} \tag{18}$$

after the preceding steps of transformation, the spatial constraint matrix is:

$$\mathbb{H}=\begin{bmatrix}1 & 0 & -1\\ \frac{1}{2} & 1 & \frac{1}{2}\\ -1 & 0 & 1\end{bmatrix} \tag{19}$$

It is obvious that $\mathbb{H}LR^T$ represents the difference between road i and the average value of its adjacent roads. Similar to $LR^T\mathbb{T}$, $\mathbb{H}LR^T$ captures spatial correlation of the traffic condition dataset, which has been mined in Section 3.3. We can also introduce the spatial constraint $\left\|\mathbb{H}LR^T\right\|_F^2$ into Eq. (16) to help make a more accurate estimation of LR^T.

Hence, after exploiting the temporal-spatial stability features in the traffic condition dataset, we optimize the compressive sensing approach by developing Eq. (16) as:

$$\min\left(\left\|\left(LR^T\right)\circ B-S\right\|_F^2+\lambda_1\left(\|L\|_F^2+\|R\|_F^2\right)+\lambda_2\left\|\mathbb{H}LR^T\right\|_F^2+\lambda_3\left\|LR^T\mathbb{T}\right\|_F^2\right) \tag{20}$$

where λ_2 and λ_3 are used as the scaling of $\left\|\mathbb{H}LR^T\right\|_F^2$ and $\left\|LR^T\mathbb{T}\right\|_F^2$.

4.2.3 Optimized Compressive Sensing Algorithm

The target of the optimized compressive sensing algorithm is to find L and R that minimize Eq. (20). We define the objective function as

$$f(L,R)=\left\|\left(LR^T\right)\circ B-S\right\|_F^2+\lambda_1\left(\|L\|_F^2+\|R\|_F^2\right)+\lambda_2\left\|\mathbb{H}LR^T\right\|_F^2+\lambda_3\left\|LR^T\mathbb{T}\right\|_F^2 \tag{21}$$

It is obvious that $f(L,R)$ is nonconvex. However, if we fix L or R, the function on the other variables is convex. Thus, we utilize the alternating steepest descent (ASD) algorithm [11, 12] to do the minimization, which is commonly used in the low rank matrix completion. The pseudo code of ASD is shown in Algorithm 1, Σ_r means the first r columns of Σ.

The main idea of ASD is to apply the steepest gradient descent to $f(L,R)$ with respect to L and R. First, L and R are randomly initialized. Then we fix L and update R by using a single step of simple line search along the gradient descent direction. And next, we fix R and update L using a similar approach. This process is repeated until convergence (we consider it is convergent when the change of the function value is less than a threshold).

To detail the line search along the gradient descent directions, we denote

$$f(L,R)=f_1(L,R)+f_2(L,R)+f_3(L,R)+f_4(L,R) \tag{22}$$

where

$$f_1(L,R)=\left\|\left(LR^T\right)\circ B-S\right\|_F^2$$
$$f_2(L,R)=\lambda_1\left(\|L\|_F^2+\|R\|_F^2\right)$$
$$f_3(L,R)=\lambda_2\left\|\mathbb{H}LR^T\right\|_F^2$$
$$f_4(L,R)=\lambda_3\left\|LR^T\mathbb{T}\right\|_F^2$$

The gradient descent directions are

$$\nabla_l=\nabla_l^1+\nabla_l^2+\nabla_l^3+\nabla_l^4$$
$$\nabla_r=\nabla_r^1+\nabla_r^2+\nabla_r^3+\nabla_r^4 \tag{23}$$

ALGORITHM 1

ALTERNATING STEEPEST DESCENT: ASD()

Require: Direct Sensory Matrix S, Binary Index Matrix
B, $\mathbb{H}$, $\mathbb{T}$, λ_1, λ_2, λ_3, rank bound r

Ensure: Reconstruct Matrix $\hat{X}$

1: $[n,t] \leftarrow size(S)$;
2: $S' \leftarrow S$;
3: **for** $S'(i,j)$ in S' **do**
4: **if** $B(i,j)=0$ **then**
5: $S'(i,j) \leftarrow$ average of two nearest values;
6: **end if**
7: **end for**
8: $[U,\Sigma,V] \leftarrow SVD(S')$;
9: $L \leftarrow U \cdot \Sigma_r^{1/2}$;
10: $R \leftarrow V \cdot \Sigma_r^{1/2}$;
11: **repeat**
12: $\beta_1 \leftarrow f(L,R)$;
13: Calculate ∇_l and ∇_r according to Eq. (25);
14: $\alpha_l \leftarrow$ arg $\min_t f(L-\alpha\nabla_l,R)$;
15: $\alpha_r \leftarrow$ arg $\min_t f(L,R-\alpha\nabla_r)$;
16: $L \leftarrow L-\alpha_l\nabla_l$;
17: $R \leftarrow R-\alpha_r\nabla_r$;
18: **until** $\frac{\beta_2-\beta_1}{\beta_1} <$ threshold;
19: $\hat{X} \leftarrow L \cdot R^T$;
20: **return** $\hat{X}$;

where

$$\nabla_l^1 = 2\left((LR^T)\circ B - S\right)R$$
$$\nabla_l^2 = 2\lambda_1 L$$
$$\nabla_l^3 = 2\lambda_2 \mathbb{H}^T\mathbb{H}LR^T R$$
$$\nabla_l^4 = 2\lambda_3 LR^T \mathbb{T}\mathbb{T}^T R$$
$$\nabla_r^1 = 2\left((RL^T)\circ B^T - S^T\right)L$$
$$\nabla_r^2 = 2\lambda_1 R$$
$$\nabla_r^3 = 2\lambda_2 RL^T \mathbb{H}^T\mathbb{H}L$$
$$\nabla_r^4 = 2\lambda_3 \mathbb{T}\mathbb{T}^T RL^T L$$

The steepest descent along L and R are selected to minimize the updated value of $f(L,R)$ along the direction ∇_l and ∇_r, respectively. We denote α_l and α_r as the steepest descent stepsize along the gradient descent directions. Thus, the values of L and R are updated as:

$$L = L - \alpha_l\nabla_l$$
$$R = R - \alpha_r\nabla_r \tag{24}$$

α_l and α_r are selected to minimize the value of $f(L,R)$ along the direction ∇_l and ∇_r, that is,

$$\alpha_l = \text{arg} \min_t f(L-\alpha\nabla_l,R)$$
$$\alpha_r = \text{arg} \min_t f(L,R-\alpha\nabla_r) \tag{25}$$

We differentiate the f and set it to zero, then we can solve α_l and α_r.

However, considering $f(L,R)$ is nonconvex, ASD may converge to a local optimal point. To mitigate this, we initialize the value of L and R by: (1) Let $S' = S$ and the missing data points in S' are replaced with the average value of two nearest existing values. (2) Use SVD to decompose the S' and compute the L and R. In this way, we can get the optimized L and R with closer starting points to the optimal one, which mitigates the local optimal problem.

4.3 Faulty Data Detection Approach Based on the Temporal Stability Feature

The Faulty Data Detection Approach is based on the temporal stability of the traffic condition dataset. In Fig. 3B, we can observe that the traffic condition dataset has good temporal stability features (difference between consecutive timeslots of >95% data are <20%). Thus, we can utilize this feature to discriminate faulty data before reconstruction and make D closer to F at the start point.

ALGORITHM 2

$FAULTYDATADETECTION()$

Require: Direct Sensory Matrix S, Existence Matrix E, Faulty Data Detection Matrix D

   Ensure: Faulty Data Detection Matrix D

1:    $[n,t] \leftarrow size(S)$;
2:    $T = S\mathbb{T}$;
3: **for** $i \leftarrow 1$ **to** n **do**
4: **for** $j \leftarrow 1$ **to** t **do**
5: **if** $E(i,j) = 0$ **or** $D(i,j) = 0$ **then**
6: **continue** ;
7: **end if**
8:    $el \leftarrow new\ Array()$;
9: **for** $k \leftarrow j - \lfloor window/2 \rfloor$ **to** $j + \lfloor window/2 \rfloor$ **do**
10: **if** $k \neq j$ **and** $E(i,j) \neq 0$ **and** $D(i,j) \neq 0$ **then**
11:    $el \leftarrow [el, T(i,k)]$;
12: **end if**
13: **end for**
14:    $ratio = \max(el) - \min(el)$;
15: $m = mean(el)$;
16: **if** $|T(i,k) - m| < ratio/2$ **then**
17:    $D(i,j) \leftarrow 0$;
18: **end if**
19: **end for**
20: **end for**
21: **return** D;

The difference between consecutive timeslots is formulated in Eq. (9). Thus we can introduce matrix T to store the difference between the consecutive timeslots in each road, which is calculated as $T = X\mathbb{T}$, where $\mathbb{T}$ is defined in Eq. (17), $T(i, j)$ represents the difference between $X(i, j - 1)$ and $X(i, j)$.

The pseudo code of the Faulty Data Detection Approach is shown in Algorithm 2. The main idea of the faulty data detection method is to calculate the average value of the difference between consecutive timeslots in ith road, and compare it with $T(i, j)$, if the difference between them is less than the dynamic threshold, $X(i, j)$ is considered normal data. The threshold is determined by the largest variation range in each road. But considering that change gradients differ at different times of a day, we further refine the 288 timeslots into several segments with $window$ width so that we can make the threshold more precisely. So we calculate the $ratio$ as Algorithm 2 in each loop, and compare $T(i, j)$ with the average value of points in the range of the window to judge whether $X(i, j)$ is normal data or not. D is initialized as all ones for the first time its executed, this may cause some normal data to be misjudged. Nevertheless, the aim of D is to mark out faulty data as much as possible, and this also ensures the convergence of the ODC method.

Other than detecting faulty data before reconstruction, we need to update D according to estimated $\hat{X}$ after that. We need a $n \times t$ matrix to record the difference between X and $\hat{X}$, which is defined as:

$$\delta_{n \times t} = |X - \hat{X}| \tag{26}$$

If $\delta(i, j)$ is less than lower threshold $thres_l$ and $D(i, j)$ is 1, we set it to 0. If $\delta(i, j)$ is larger than the upper threshold $thres_u$ and $D(i, j)$ is 0, we set it to 1. $thres_l$ and $thres_u$ depend on the tolerance of data deviation. No operation will be done if $X(i, j)$ is a missing data point (i.e., $E(i, j)$ is 0). The pseudo code of $updateFDM()$ is shown in Algorithm 3.

ALGORITHM 3

$UPDATEFDM()$

Require: Direct Sensory Matrix S, Existence Matrix E, Faulty Data Detection Matrix D, Reconstructed Matrix $\hat{X}$

   Ensure: Faulty Data Detection Matrix D

1: **for** $i \leftarrow 1$ **to** n **do**
2: **for** $i \leftarrow 1$ **to** t **do**
3: **if** $E(i,j) = 0$ **then**
4: **continue** ;
5: **end if**
6: **if** $\delta < thres_l$ **and** $D(i,j) = 1$ **then**
7:    $D(i,j) = 0$;
8: **end if**
9: **if** $\delta > thres_u$ **and** $D(i,j) = 0$ **then**
10:    $D(i,j) = 1$;
11: **end if**
12: **end for**
13: **end for**
14: **return** D;

5 PERFORMANCE EVALUATION

5.1 Evaluation Settings

Dataset for evaluation is the same as Section 3. We select a complete subset that contains 617 roads × 288 slots, with slot intervals of 5 min.

Generation of missing and faulty data: For the generation of missing data, we rely on the generation of Existence Matrix E. We set E to all ones first, then select a fraction of elements randomly in E and set them to zeros with the control of missing ratio (β) predefined. The generation of faulty data is done in a similar way. We set Faulty Data Matrix F to all zeros at first, and then select a fraction of elements to ones with the control of faulty ratio (α). Besides that we add a random bias ξ to corresponding elements in X, which are marked as faulty data. Thus, we can get the Direct Sensory Matrix S as:

$$S(i,j) = X(i,j)E(i,j) + \xi_{i,j} \cdot F(i,j) \tag{27}$$

where $\xi_{i,j}$ means the random value of bias here.

Evaluation criteria: The performance of ODC will be analyzed in faulty data discrimination and missing data reconstruction. For faulty data discrimination, we evaluate the performance through *Precision*, *Recall*, and *Accuracy*, which are defined as:

$$Precision = \frac{TP}{TP+FP}, \quad Recall = \frac{TP}{TP+FN}, \quad Accuracy = \frac{TP+TN}{TP+FP+TN+FN} \tag{28}$$

where TP, FP, TN, and FN are:

- True Positive: considered faulty data, and indeed, is faulty data
- False Positive: considered faulty data, but indeed, is normal data
- True Negative: considered normal data, and indeed, is normal data
- False Negative: considered normal data, but indeed, is faulty data

For missing data reconstruction, we evaluate the performance through ER, which represents the average values of reconstruction errors in missing and faulty data, which is defined as:

$$ER = \frac{\displaystyle\sum_{where\ B(i,j)=0} \left| X(i,j) - \hat{X}(i,j) \right|}{\displaystyle\sum_{where\ B(i,j)=0} 1} \tag{29}$$

To verify the effectiveness of the ODC method, we select another two methods when evaluating the performance in faulty data discrimination for comparison:

- ODC-without-HT: ODC method without temporal-spatial improvement.
- FDD: The faulty data detection method that is proposed in Section 4.3.

And another three methods when evaluating missing data reconstruction:

- ODC-without-HT: ODC method without temporal-spatial improvement.
- ASD: Compressive sensing algorithm applied in ODC, which is used for reconstructing missing data.
- ASD-without-HT: This is similar to ASD, the difference is that they are not improved by temporal-spatial features.

5.2 Performance Analysis: Faulty Data Discrimination

In this section, we evaluate the performance in faulty data discrimination. We conduct three experiments in this evaluation, where missing data ratio $\beta = 10\%$, 30%, and 50%, respectively, and faulty data ratio α varies from 10% to 50% in each experiment. The result of evaluation is shown in Fig. 5.

We observe that the performance of ODC-like methods in precision is better than FDD, and the gap between ODC and ODC-without-HT is not large. Comparing with Fig. 5A–C, we can observe that precision reaches the maximum value when the faulty data ratio $\alpha = 30\%$, and precision decreases with the growth of missing data ratio β on the whole. Because of the intervals of traffic information from the AMAP update is a bit long (i.e., 5 min), the variation range of

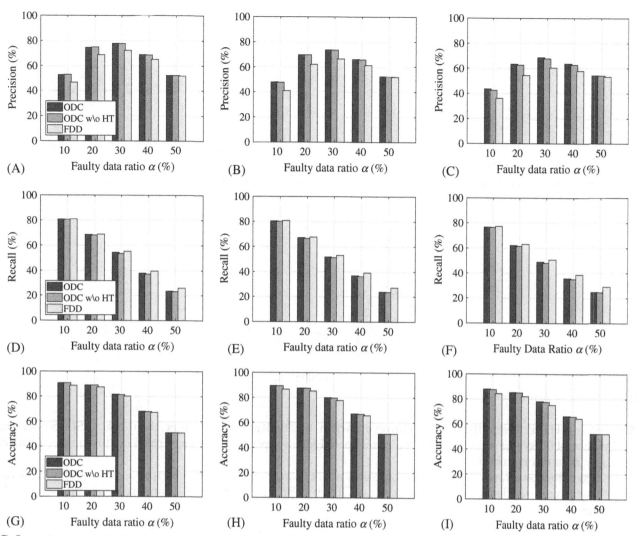

FIG. 5   Performance analysis in faulty data discrimination. (A) Missing data ratio $\beta = 10\%$; (B) missing data ratio $\beta = 30\%$; (C) missing data ratio $\beta = 50\%$; (D) missing data ratio $\beta = 10\%$; (E) missing data ratio $\beta = 30\%$; (F) missing data ratio $\beta = 50\%$; (G) missing data ratio $\beta = 10\%$; (H) missing data ratio $\beta = 30\%$; (I) missing data ratio $\beta = 50\%$.

mean velocity cannot be well defined, which leads to discriminating faulty data with difficulty. But it is clear that ODC-like methods do help to improve faulty data discrimination.

The recall of three methods decrease with the growth of the faulty data ratio, and the gap among them is not large. In terms of accuracy, we can observe that ODC-like methods outperform the FDD method. The accuracy of ODC-like methods is above 80% when faulty ratio $\alpha \leq 30\%$ and missing ratio $\beta \leq 30\%$, even when missing ratio is 50%, there remains nearly 80% accuracy in ODC-like methods.

In summary, the differences of reconstruction in ODC-like methods do not influence the performance of faulty data discrimination much, and ODC-like methods outperform FDD method in terms of precision and accuracy on the whole.

5.3 Performance Analysis: Missing Data Reconstruction

In this section, we evaluate the performance in missing data reconstruction. The experiments are conducted when missing data ratio $\beta = 10\%$, 30%, and 50%, and faulty data ratio α varies from 10% to 50% in each experiment. The result is shown in Fig. 6. It is obvious that the ODC method outperforms another three methods.

In Fig. 6, we can observe that when the faulty ratio is small (i.e., $\alpha = 10\%$), the performance of ODC and ODC-without-HT are almost the same. And the gap of the reconstruction error between ODC and ODC-without-HT increase with the growth of the faulty data ratio. We notice that when the faulty ratio $\leq 20\%$, the performance of

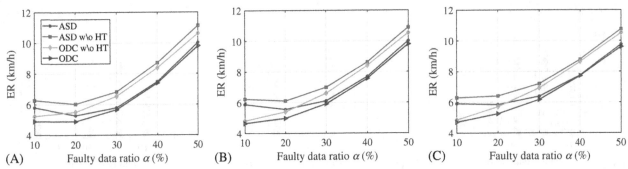

FIG. 6	Performance analysis in missing data reconstruction. (A) Missing data ratio $\beta = 10\%$; (B) missing data ratio $\beta = 30\%$; (C) missing data ratio $\beta = 50\%$.

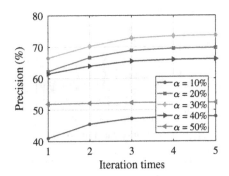

FIG. 7	Convergence rate of ODC when $\beta = 30\%$.

ODC-without-HT is better than ASD. However, when the faulty ratio is larger than 20%, ASD outperforms ODC-without-HT. We can conclude that temporal-spatial features play an important role in improving performance of missing data reconstruction.

The reconstruction error of the ODC method is only about 6 km/h, even when faulty ratio $\alpha = 30\%$ and missing ratio $\beta = 50\%$, which can be tolerated. The performance of ODC is improved by about 15% compared with ASD-without-HT on average.

5.4 Convergence of ODC

We analyze the convergence rate of ODC at last. Fig. 7 shows that when missing ratio $\beta = 30\%$, faulty ratio varies from 10% to 50%, the precision will be convergent within five times of iterations. We can notice that the first three iterations contribute to nearly all improvement, and later iterations contribute to little improvement. Thus we can conclude that the convergence of ODC is good.

6 RELATED WORK

The rapid growth in the number of motor vehicles causes heavy traffic jams, drivers are now mostly dependent on navigation applications before going out. But missing data and faulty data are common in data from sensors [10, 13, 14]. There is a great deal of research in this area.

SEER [15] figure out the redundancy of traffic datasets and utilize multichannel singular spectrum analysis to recover missing data. However, SEER does not take faulty data into consideration. The traditional outlier detection technique [16, 17] can be an alternative method for faulty data detection, but this technique cannot tolerate a high rate of missing data. Yoon et al. [3] estimate traffic conditions through traces of vehicles in each road segment, which needs large amounts of data to build a road segment model. And each road segment can only be analyzed independently, which is not suitable for real-time applications. Cheng et al. [5] propose the DECO model, and utilize compressive sensing techniques to reconstruct missing data, and detect faulty data based on users' reputations. They believe that users who have a good reputation will not upload faulty data, which may not necessarily be true.

Although some methods and algorithms have been proposed, few of them can effectively exploit the hidden structures in traffic condition datasets. The compressive sensing [18, 19] technique can tolerate a high rate of missing data, and is good for recovering missing data in a low rank matrix. However, a compressive sensing technique cannot be directly applied to traffic condition datasets because of the existence of faulty data, which may lead to reconstruction deviation [20]. Thus, we need to discriminate faulty data before recovering missing data.

7 CONCLUSION

In this chapter, we proposed an ODC method to discriminate misleading information and correct missing data in intelligent transportation systems. First, we uncovered the common problem that misleading and missing information exists in traffic condition datasets. Then we mined the hidden structures in traffic condition datasets, such as the low rank feature, and temporal-spatial correlation. On the basis of these observations, we have designed an outlier detection method to discriminate faulty data. And then we utilized temporal-spatial features to improve performance in missing data reconstruction based on a compressive sensing technique. Extensive evaluations are conducted using real urban traffic datasets, which demonstrates that ODC can produce only about a 6 km/h reconstruction error, even when the missing ratio is 50% and the faulty ratio is 30%.

In this work, we only utilize a single dimension of traffic conditions (i.e., the mean velocity of roads), which brings limited improvement. In the future, we can mine more dimensions of traffic conditions by using raw GPS data collected from vehicles, such as the number of vehicles on each road, and the headway directions. Also, we can utilize some information from map data such as lanes of roads, road speed limitations, locations of traffic lights, and so forth, which can help us improve performance in discrimination and correction.

References

[1] S. Nikolic, V. Penca, M. Segedinac, Semantic web based architecture for managing hardware heterogeneity in wireless sensor network, in: International Conference on Web Intelligence, Mining and Semantics, WIMS 2011, Sogndal, Norway, May, 2011, pp. 1–9.

[2] AMAP, Traffic condition data collected from AMAP. Available from: http://lbs.amap.com/api/webservice/guide/api/trafficstatus/ (Accessed 15 January 2018).

[3] J. Yoon, B. Noble, M. Liu, Surface street traffic estimation, in: International Conference on Mobile Systems, Applications and Services, 2007, pp. 220–232.

[4] Z. Li, Y. Zhu, H. Zhu, M. Li, Compressive sensing approach to urban traffic sensing, in: International Conference on Distributed Computing Systems, 2011, pp. 889–898.

[5] L. Cheng, J. Niu, L. Kong, C. Luo, Y. Gu, W. He, S.K. Das, Compressive sensing based data quality improvement for crowd-sensing applications, J. Netw. Comput. Appl. 77 (2016) 123–134.

[6] E.J. Candes, The restricted isometry property and its implications for compressed sensing, C. R. Math. 346 (9–10) (2008) 589–592.

[7] E.J. Candes, B. Recht, Exact matrix completion via convex optimization, Found. Comput. Math. 9 (6) (2008) 717.

[8] B. Recht, W. Xu, B. Hassibi, Necessary and sufficient conditions for success of the nuclear norm heuristic for rank minimization, IEEE Conf. Decis. Control 16 (5) (2008) 3065–3070.

[9] B. Recht, M. Fazel, P.A. Parrilo, Guaranteed minimum-rank solutions of linear matrix equations via nuclear norm minimization, SIAM Rev. 52 (3) (2007) 471–501.

[10] L. Kong, M. Xia, X.Y. Liu, M.Y. Wu, X. Liu, Data loss and reconstruction in sensor networks, in: INFOCOM, 2013 Proceedings IEEE, 2013, pp. 1654–1662.

[11] J. Tanner, K. Wei, Low rank matrix completion by alternating steepest descent methods, Appl. Comput. Harmon. Anal. 40 (2) (2016) 417–429.

[12] F. Wu, D. Liu, Z. Wu, Y. Zhang, G. Chen, Cost-efficient indoor white space exploration through compressive sensing, IEEE/ACM Trans. Netw. (99) (2017) 1–17.

[13] M. Balazinska, A. Deshpande, M.J. Franklin, P.B. Gibbons, J. Gray, M. Hansen, M. Liebhold, S. Nath, A. Szalay, V. Tao, Data management in the worldwide sensor web, IEEE Pervasive Comput. 6 (2) (2007) 30–40.

[14] H. Kurasawa, H. Sato, A. Yamamoto, H. Kawasaki, M. Nakamura, Y. Fujii, H. Matsumura, Missing sensor value estimation method for participatory sensing environment, in: IEEE International Conference on Pervasive Computing and Communications, 2014, pp. 103–111.

[15] H. Zhu, Y. Zhu, M. Li, L.M. Ni, SEER: metropolitan-scale traffic perception based on lossy sensory data, in: INFOCOM, 2009, pp. 217–225.

[16] A.J. Fox, Outliers in time series, J. R. Stat. Soc. 34 (3) (1972) 350–363.

[17] V. Hodge, J. Austin, A survey of outlier detection methodologies, Artif. Intell. Rev. 22 (2) (2004) 85–126.

[18] D.L. Donoho, Compressed sensing, IEEE Trans. Inf. Theory 52 (4) (2006) 1289–1306.

[19] E.J. Candes, T. Tao, Near-optimal signal recovery from random projections: universal encoding strategies? IEEE Trans. Inf. Theory 52 (12) (2006) 5406–5425.

[20] E.J. Candes, Y. Plan, Matrix completion with noise, Proc. IEEE 98 (6) (2009) 925–936.

Secure Data Dissemination for Smart Transportation Systems

Zouina Doukha' and Iman Loumachi
USTHB University, Algiers, Algeria

1 INTRODUCTION

The beginning of the 21st century witnessed an extraordinary revolution in computer networks. This is especially the case for emerging wireless technologies that aim to extend communication capabilities to environments where their presence can create new kinds of networks, such as cellular networks, Mobile ad hoc NETworks (MANETs), Wireless Sensor Networks (WSNs), Wireless Mesh Networks (WMN), and so forth. Vehicular Ad Hoc NETworks (VANETs), one promising form of this extension, support road infrastructure that becomes a geographical space hosting moving vehicles that can exchange data in order to widen the drivers' visibility of their environment for a safe, beneficial, and enjoyable travel experience. VANETs have several distinguishing characteristics. The high mobility is likely to engender network partitions that cause connectivity losses. The movement of vehicles is relatively predictable because it is constrained by roads, signposts, and obstacles such as buildings. Architecturally, each vehicle is equipped with a wireless device known as an On-Board Unit that allows it to communicate with other vehicles, as well as with roadside units (RSUs), which can be used as access points to provide a connection to a backbone network that offers several services, such as traffic management and Internet access. Embedded devices provide vehicles with high calculating, memorizing, and sensing capabilities in addition to an unlimited energy source, which the vehicles' batteries guarantee. This is a noteworthy advantage for VANETs, compared with other wireless networks, such as MANETs and WSNs. However, many challenges must be considered when designing a dissemination protocol, such as a heterogeneous environment, network partitioning, scalability, and packet loss due to signal distortions.

In fact, several technologies, such as cellular, Bluetooth, and Ultra-Wide Band can be envisioned for VANETs. However, Dedicated Short Range Communications/Wireless Access in Vehicular Environments (DSRC/WAVE) is the preferred technology for VANETs due to its suitability and low device costs. Recently, the rise of cloud computing technology enabled its integration with vehicular technology for its capability of storage, data processing, and mainly its reliable and efficient data accessing [1]. Integrating cloud computing with vehicular networks appears to be imperative to propel VANET applications and provide innovative services to improve the safety, security, and efficiency of transport systems. To realize these ambitious applications, the key technique of dissemination is used to propagate pertinent information where broadcast communication is widely used to cover all interested parties. The literature abounds with work on dissemination. Additionally, the real deployment of VANET is mostly supported by the trustworthiness of disseminated data. In fact, false information sent by malicious node could result in drastic consequences on traffic quality and drivers/passengers' lives. In the following sections, we present the main orientations considered by researchers. The aim of this chapter is to present a comprehensive survey of message dissemination techniques for safety applications in the VANET. We classify proposed protocols based on their applications and strategies, and we review each class of protocols with respect to its strengths and weaknesses. Then, we emphasize the security issue regarding dissemination. The rest of the chapter is organized as follows. Section 2 presents dissemination protocols, classifies them, and highlights their contributions and weaknesses. Section 3 addresses the security issue for VANET dissemination. Section 4 discusses challenges that still need to be addressed, and makes some concluding remarks.

2 DISSEMINATION PROTOCOLS

According to their significance for human life, safety applications can be of two types: life-critical safety and announcement safety. The first type is related to a dangerous event, such as an accident or abnormal driving, that happened or may happen on the road. The goal of dissemination in this case is to prevent accidents or to avoid exacerbating them if they have already occurred. The second class is concerned with providing general information about traffic conditions, such as jams, work zones, and bad weather. The goal of dissemination in this class is to improve traffic flow. In the literature, proposed protocols for safety dissemination can be grouped into three main classes, as shown in Fig. 1 and described in Table 1.

2.1 Centralized Scheme

Centralized schemes can be useful for announcing general information about traffic, including bad weather, work zones, and hazards. It is also used for accident avoidance in intersections and road segments containing certain conditions that might lead to an accident. Examples of such conditions include speeding drivers, drivers who run red lights or stop signs, pedestrians, work zones, and so forth. In these scenarios, V2I safety can be enhanced through connectivity that enables the exchange of information between vehicles and infrastructure and between infrastructure components. Based on the available information, various operations, such as statistics and traffic regulation, may also help to enhance road conditions. According to this scheme, vehicles pass their information to the RSU. The backbone network processes the collected information from the RSUs, which ensures the high availability of pertinent information that can be requested by passing vehicles in turn. In this context, the authors of [2] proposed a V2I scheme to estimate the density of vehicles based on the number of beacons received by RSUs. They consider that the complexity of the roadmap topology influences the accuracy of the results. However, the short connection time between vehicles and RSUs and overload of RSUs located near dense roads lead to delayed services and a high request drop rate. In view of that, a cooperative load balancing (CLB) technique among the RSUs is proposed in [3], in which a loaded RSU transfers requests to other RSUs based on a number of criteria, such as the request delay tolerance, the current load of the destined RSU, and the direction of the requester vehicle. In [4], an enhanced technique is proposed (ECLB) in which requests are prioritized based on their remaining delay tolerance. The authors in [5] addressed the geocast problem in

FIG. 1 Classification of dissemination protocols for safety application.

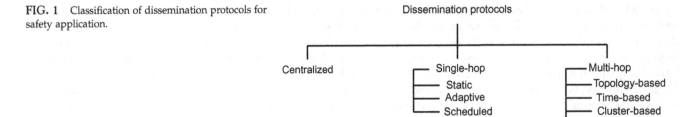

TABLE 1 Data Dissemination Protocols

Class	Goal	Type	Delay
Centralized	General information	Announcement	Tolerant
	Hello	Announcement	Real time
	Accident avoidance	Life-critical	Real time
Single-hop	Neighborhood discovery	Announcement	Real time
	Traffic management	Announcement	Tolerant
	Accident avoidance	Life-critical	Real time
Multihop	Emergency	Life-critical	Real time
	Critical information	Life-critical	Real time

VANETs. Given a piece of message, they modeled the region of interest as a quadtree. Then, they used an election approach to select the optimal RSU to forward the message to the destination area. In order to minimize the RSU response delay and bandwidth consumption, network coding may be useful [6] for broadcasting many data items in one packet by encoding requested data items. Recently, novel architectures have been proposed, including the integration of many existing technologies such as long-term evolution technology (LTE) advanced, the growing 5G, and cloud computing. Following this trend, the authors of [7] proposed a new Cloud-assisted Message Downlink Dissemination Scheme (CMDS). In this scheme, the cloud continuously collects massive traffic flow information. The safety messages in the cloud server are first transmitted to the suitable mobile gateways, which are buses equipped with both cellular and VANET interfaces. Then, those gateways deliver the message to nearby vehicles by V2V communication.

2.2 Single-Hop Dissemination Protocols

Single-hop dissemination is used to collect information about surroundings. It is also useful in cooperative tasks such as V2V density estimation and accident avoidance based on periodic broadcasts. As it is shown in Fig. 1, single-hop dissemination schemes can be classified into three main approaches namely: static period, adaptive, and scheduled. Table 2 provides qualitative analysis of these protocols based on different parameters.

2.2.1 Static Period-Based Protocols

These protocols are mainly information centric. The proposed protocols exchange positional information and statuses to estimate the state of road traffic and gain local knowledge about neighboring areas. An example of these protocols is [8] where the authors proposed node density estimation based on V2V periodic exchange of beacons. They consider the received signal strength as an indicator of a number of transmitting nodes. To estimate the level of road congestion level, the authors in [9] proposed a mechanism based on fuzzy logic. They used the traffic density information and the vehicle's speed as inputs in the fuzzy system and provided the traffic congestion as output. The main drawback of using beacons as a source of information is the inaccuracy on the collected information in the case of a long period and significant consumption of channel bandwidth in the case of a short period. In [10], the authors designed an experiment to measure the amount of stress on the medium when piggybacking application data onto scheduled beacons and compared it with the situation in which application data is forwarded independently. They argue that piggybacking application data onto beacons leads to a lower busy time on the medium in comparison with the separate spread of data, where the nodes have to access the medium separately. However, in case of urgent event, the transmission will be delayed until the next scheduled beacon.

TABLE 2   Qualitative Analysis of Single-Hop Dissemination Protocols

Protocol	Simulator	Environment	Propagation Model	Goal	Metric
Static period protocols					
[8]	Matlab	Highway, urban	Stochastic model	Density estimation	Number of simultaneously transmitting nodes, average of received power
[9]	iTETRIS	Highway, bidirectional	Cheng highway	Congestion detection	Congestion detection probability, congestion estimation error, traffic jam length estimation error
[10]	Analysis + MIXIM	A road (12 km)	Log-normal	Forwarding via beacons	Delay, packet reception probability
Adaptive protocols					
[13]	JIST/SWANs	TIGER database	Two-ray ground and shadow fading models	Cooperative awareness	Beacon load, awareness probability
[14]	$GEMV^2$	Google Map	Geometry-based	Cooperative awareness	Neighbor awareness, channel busy ratio
[15]	Analysis + ADTF	Intersections	Not provided	Collision prediction	Probability of the occurrence of a collision
Scheduled transmission-based protocols					
[16]	Veins	Highway, unidirectional	TwoRayGround	Cooperative awareness	Channel load, percentage awareness, reception ratio

2.2.2 Adaptive Protocols

Static period-based protocols do not consider the communication load in the network, which can drastically vary over time, leading to packet loss due to collisions and degradation of the network performance [11]. Many protocols have been proposed in the literature trying to find the best compromise between beacon rate and accuracy [12, 13]. The purpose of the adaptive approach is to adjust the communication parameters such as beacon rate and transmission power according to collected information about the environment, as the authors of [14] did. They aim to improve cooperative awareness taking into account the specific environment, such as intersections, highways, and suburban roads, and application requirements in terms of bandwidth utilization. To adjust the transmit power, the authors use Path Loss Exponent estimation based on a neighbor's transmit power. Furthermore, they use the channel busy ratio and the current beacon rate as an input and derive the next beacon rate. To avoid traffic hazards, the authors of [15] proposed an approach to situation analysis at intersections based on object-oriented Bayesian networks that deduct collision probability from the perceived environment through communication.

2.2.3 Scheduled Transmission-Based Protocols

In [16], the authors proposed to schedule the transmission of periodic messages according to vehicles' geographical position. Their aim is to avoid collisions by serializing transmissions instead of contending them. This approach may be more beneficial if it is combined with an adaptive approach.

2.3 Multihop Dissemination Protocols

Most dissemination protocols rely on multihop broadcast forwarding. When a node holds information about a hazard, it is responsible for forwarding this information to all vehicles traveling toward the danger. Broadcast is used to cover the entire region in the sender's vicinity, and relaying allows the information to reach all the nodes outside of the vicinity within a geographical region known as the "zone of relevance." The point is to find the most suitable relay node to reliably forward the message. To this end, there are several strategies proposed in the literature that can be classified into five classes, as shown in Fig. 1. Table 3 provides qualitative analysis of these protocols based on different parameters.

2.3.1 Topology-Based Protocols

These protocols rely on neighborhood knowledge. The main idea is that a sender selects the next relay in advance because it knows its neighbors' positions. Generally, it is the farthest one. When receiving the message, the node that finds its identity enclosed in the message recognizes itself as a relay node and repeats the process. The other nodes simply retain the message to stay informed. To the best of our knowledge, the first safety dissemination protocol [17] belongs to this class. Topology-based protocols do not guarantee that the farthest selected node can receive the message correctly and can rebroadcast it successfully because the medium is not reliable. One solution to this problem is proposed in [18]. In this protocol, the portion of road in the senders' vicinity is divided into segments; vehicles located in the furthest nonempty segment contend for the duration of time depending on their contention window and check if the selected relay rebroadcasted the message. If not, they forward the message after executing the backoff algorithm to avoid congestion. In another attempt to implement a reliable data dissemination protocol, the authors of [19] proposed a hierarchical-assisted node-based data dissemination scheme (HADD). In this scheme, the forwarder makes use of dynamic prediction to select the next relay within its neighbor table. The next relay is selected as the farthest node that is more likely to stay in vicinity after Δt, which is the communication delay. The selection takes into account the relative speed of the forwarder and the next relay. Following the same approach, the solution proposed in [20] relies on nodes, future velocities prediction based on their past and current velocities, and then determines the best next relay.

2.3.2 Time-Based Protocols

In this class, neighborhood knowledge is not required; the relay node is self-elected after receiving the safety message. All vehicles that have received the message start a waiting time phase before deciding whether or not to rebroadcast it; the vehicle that waits the shortest duration considers itself to be a relay and decides to rebroadcast the message. The other nodes can hear the sent message while in their waiting time phase and then conclude that some nodes are relaying the message. In [17] which is proposed in the same paper as TRADE, the waiting time is inversely proportional to the distance between the sender and the receiver, so that border nodes retransmit earlier. The same idea, with the main goal of making one relay node at each hop, which is considered sufficient, is discussed in [21, 22]. While these

TABLE 3 Qualitative Analysis of Multihop Dissemination Protocols

Protocol	Simulator	Environment	Propagation Model	Ack	Link Loss	Intersection	Metric
Topology-based protocols							
TRADE [17]	Own	Urban, rural	Not provided	No	No	Yes	Bandwidth utilization, reachability
HADD [19]	Matlab	Urban, bidirectional	Not provided	No	Opposite dir	Yes	Data rate, delay
SFBB [20]	GloMoSim	Highway, bidirectional	Not provided	No	No	No	Delivery ratio, delay
Time-based protocols							
DDT [17]	Own	Urban, rural	Not provided	No	No	Yes	Bandwidth utilization
ODAM [21]	NS2	Highway, unidirectional	Not provided	Yes	Rebroadcast	No	Informed vehicles
SEAD [22]	NS3	Highway, unidirectional	Nakagami	Implicit	No	No	Packet delivery ratio, forwarding ratio, end-to-end delay, link load, packet drop ratio
VSPP [23]	NS2	Highway unidirectional	TwoRayGround	No	No	No	Delay, collision ratio, overhead
Cluster-based protocols							
CBNCR [24]	R console	Not provided	Not provided	No	No	No	Throughput, delivery ratio, reliability, and delay
VMaSC [25]	NS3	Highway, bidirectional	Path loss + Friis models	No	Use of infrastructure	No	CH duration, CM duration, CH change rate, clustering overhead, and number of vehicles in the SE state (selection of next state)
Contention-based protocols							
AMB [27]	CSIM	Urban	Not provided	Yes	No	Yes	Packet delivery, channel load, and dissemination speed
UMBP [28]	Analysis + NS2	Urban	Not provided	Yes	No	Yes	One-hop delay, message propagation speed, and reception rate
BMMB [29]	Analysis + Veins	Urban	Not provided	Yes	No	Yes	One-hop delay, message propagation speed, and time cost
Adaptive protocols							
[30]	OMNET	Manhattan	TwoRayGround	Implicit	No	No	Delivery ratio and total messages transmitted
ZBRP [31]	NS2	Highway, bidirectional	TwoRayGround	No	Rebroadcast	No	Hop count, coverage time, overhead, and delivery ratio

protocols can be efficient in low-density scenarios, they are at a disadvantage in terms of scalability because nodes' waiting time values are highly correlated. To deal with this problem, a virtual slotted p-persistence (VSPP) scheme is proposed in [23]. In VSPP, the authors propose a technique of virtual slots formation based on density around the sender. This assumes that beacons are periodically exchanged between vehicles. When a message is received, each vehicle in the vicinity calculates its slot number and the number of vehicles in its slot N_S. It waits a duration of time T that is attributed to each slot so that the farthest slot has the lowest value of T and forwards the packet with a probability of $\frac{1}{N_S}$ to avoid rebroadcasting from all nodes within the same slot. Unfortunately, it is possible that no node will relay the transmission in this strategy. Furthermore, if the density surrounding the sender is low, the relay, which is likely to be in the region, will need to wait for a given time for no reason because waiting time depends on the relay's distance to the sender. Generally, time-based protocols are not scalable because of the spatial storm problem.

TABLE 4 Secure Data Dissemination Techniques

Protocol	Type of Attack	Security Propriety	Architecture	Strategy	Strength	Weakness
Centralized approach						
[38]	Security and privacy attacks	Authentication, confidentiality, nonrepudiation, message integrity, privacy	Infrastructure-based	Each vehicle is provided with its unique identifier, its public key certificate including a public and private key pair. Vehicles are identified by short-lived authenticated pseudonyms	Anonymous communication (use of pseudonym)	Not suitable for broadcast communications. Total dependency on infrastructure
VBII [36]	Fabrication, falsification	Integrity, authentication	Infrastructure-based and V2V	The central authority computes vehicles' trust score based on previous reported incidents that are validated by the real facts. The trust score is distributed to passing vehicles via RSU	A global view of individual vehicles trustworthiness is constructed by taking advantage of the connectivity with the infrastructure which completes the limited local view obtained in ad hoc fashion	The accuracy of the vehicles's trust score totally depends on infrastructure connection which is not permanent
EBRS [33]	Sybil attack	Authentication, privacy, integrity, nonrepudiation	Infrastructure-based and V2V	Establishing certificate, certificate validation, reputation, and trust values based on neighbors' confirmation on sensed events to avoid message fabrication	Identity validation and setting thresholds for reputation and trust values for each event message make message fabrication difficult	Certificate establishment and validation at each sensed event may not be suitable for real time applications
Location-based trust estimation						
CNPV [40]	False position advertisement, traffic dropping (black-hole attack)	Availability	V2V	Control of the distance through two rounds transmission between nodes	Adaptable to topology-based protocols	Requires two rounds of communication to validate position leading to delayed decision making
[39]	Fabrication, falsification	Integrity	V2V	Probabilistic and deterministic approaches based on past collected observations	No required infrastructure	Collected information is ephemeral and in deterministic approach, considering just distance verification and transmission noise to calculate a node trust level cannot be sufficient to determine its misbehaving
Reputation-based trust estimation						
RITA [41]	Fabrication, falsification	Integrity	V2V	The forwarding strategy takes into account vehicles' trust level based on their locations and their previous communications, and risk estimation	Permanent monitoring of the nodes' behavior to estimate the attack risk. RSU is preferred forwarder if connectivity is established	The ephemeral nature of the network does not allow pertinent information collection about neighbors
Social [42]	Fabrication	Integrity	V2V	A voting scheme where voting vehicles are given weights according to their distance to the reported event	The strategy avoids oversampling caused by an opinion based on neighbors' reports	Multiple incident reports are required to make a decision

2.3.3 Cluster-Based Protocols

In cluster-based dissemination protocols, the network is represented as successive clusters formed by vehicle nodes that are reachable at one or more hops in diameter. This strategy is suitable when the topology of the network does not change quickly. The authors of [24] proposed a one-hop clustering technique where members can have one of three roles, namely cluster head (CH), gateway (GW), and ordinary member. Gateways are common nodes to successive clusters and serve as relays between CHs. In a cluster, the CH is responsible for forwarding messages to its cluster members and to its successive CH. In [24] the cluster formation is initiated by a vehicle that holds information to disseminate on the network. So, there is no need for cluster maintenance. In [25], the authors investigate the usage of the LTE in addition to the IEEE 802.11p technology aiming at achieving a high data packet delivery ratio and low delay. A multihop clustering is proposed where the CH is dynamically elected based on mobility metric considered as the average relative speed among neighboring vehicles. Multihop clustering allows the usage of the cellular communication at a minimum level. Even clustering simplifies some essential processes, such as routing and bandwidth allocation, cluster formation, and its maintenance in a distributed manner, especially in rapidly changing topologies may result in high delay and overhead.

2.3.4 Contention-Based Protocols

These protocols adjust the MAC layer parameters. Some proposed protocols are entirely implemented at the MAC layer and define access methods to make dissemination strategies more reliable because broadcast unreliability affects dissemination performance. One of the most important papers in this scheme is [26], which has been improved in [27]. The aim of this protocol is to maximize message forwarding, alleviate the broadcast storm, and prevent the hidden terminal problem in order to increase reliability. This protocol proposes a handshake sequence, known as request-to-broadcast (RTB)/clear-to-broadcast (CTB). The RTB packet contains the position of the source node and the dissemination direction. When receiving the RTB packet, all nodes in the direction of dissemination transmit a jamming signal known as a black burst with a length proportional to their distance from the source. Therefore, the furthest node sends the longest black burst. After sending the black burst, each node listens to the channel. The farthest node from the source will find the channel idle and conclude that it is responsible for replying by sending a CTB packet to the source, defining itself as a relay. Then the source sends the message to the relay, which acknowledges it afterward. This process is repeated all along the road. The proposed protocol in [28] aims at minimizing the redundancy and the time needed to perform one hop either in a directional broadcast, bidirectional broadcast, or multidirectional broadcast depending on the positions of the senders: a one-way, two-way, or intersection. Considering distance as the lone parameter is not enough; it may lead to the spatial storm problem in case of high density, thereby limiting the scalability of the network. In another attempt to improve this strategy, the authors in [29] propose the use of multichannel system to enable vehicles to transmit and sense black-burst signals at different channels, thus reducing contention. Solutions that rely on the handshake sequence may suffer from high delays in message delivery. Furthermore, the authors of both solutions do not discuss how the proposed mechanisms can be integrated with the existing MAC protocols.

2.3.5 Adaptive Protocols

In this class, the selection of the next relay depends on traffic and communication state. Mostly, mathematic models are used to elect the next relay. The authors of [30] proposed an approach based on social metrics, namely the clustering coefficient and the node degree. The clustering coefficient for a vehicle is given by the number of connections between neighbors over total number of possible connections, while the node degree is based on density. When a vehicle receives a message, it calculates a waiting time base on these two metrics. In [31] the authors propose the use of neighborhood knowledge especially the speed and direction of nodes to calculate the best candidate having the longest one-hop connectivity. The election of relays is a continuous process based on Hello messages. So, a vehicle knows its role at the time of rebroadcasting an emergency message which does not cost additional time delay.

3 SECURE DATA DISSEMINATION

The inherent characteristics of VANETs, such as the use of wireless medium and the vehicles' high speed, in addition to the constraints of safety applications which are mostly time critical and act on wide range areas, make it vulnerable to different security threats. Especially, the multihop broadcast nature of data dissemination process favors different types of attacks. For instance, message falsification or dropping and false message sending resulting in compromising traffic quality and people's lives. Therefore, securing data dissemination is challenging at two essential levels. The first is to provide message authentication and integrity. The second is to ensure the network availability, which can be threatened by attacks such as jamming, sybil, and black holes [32–34]. To guarantee message confidentiality and integrity, the WAVE security services provided by the Standard IEEE1609.2 specify the format of secure messages and their processing [35]. However, the use of symmetric message encryption requires session key establishment between two communicating nodes. Nevertheless, in the context of dissemination, a message is sent equally to several nodes, which make traditional encryption schemes fail meeting low delay requirement. Several works proposed in the literature aim at detecting and excluding misbehaving nodes from the communication system based on infrastructure as a centralized authority [36–38]. This approach seems to be costly and requires total coverage of infrastructure, which is unrealistic in large scale. Fully distributed approaches deal with trust management issue. Solutions proposed [39, 40] attribute a trust level based on information received by neighbors to reveal malicious information. In fact, the challenge with those solutions is to find fair criteria that provide trustworthiness of received information especially in ephemeral networks, such as VANET. Despite the effort made to secure VANET, more work is needed to deal specifically with securing dissemination. In Table 4, we review the most relevant techniques used in the literature to secure data dissemination.

4 CONCLUSION AND FUTURE CHALLENGES

Safety applications are a core component of ITS and dissemination is a key technique to spread critical information to make our roads safer. In this context, the international community has put forth great efforts to lead innovative projects to reduce or eliminate crashes and to provide the best tools for road management. Due to unreliable links, it is difficult to design a highly reliable, scalable, and rapid dissemination protocol without high cost in term of network load. Actually, before real deployment, these applications need more investigation to meet new challenges.

- Create efficient MAC protocols to provide reliable broadcasting techniques with adaptive contention mechanisms.
- Develop efficient and accurate neighborhood service, which does not affect safety applications because sharing the same control channel increases the contention.
- Explore heterogeneous VANET schemes to make use of applications with multiple resources, especially with the emergence of new cellular technologies such as LTE Advanced and the upcoming 5G.
- Adaptive protocols need to be more investigated in the next years. To this end, many solutions can be inspired from existing models in artificial intelligence.
- Develop more realistic mobility generators that take into account different environments related to real road infrastructure and vehicles' behavior by modeling the influence of the communication on the traffic scenarios so that vehicles, according to specific models, react in response to particular events on road. For example, vehicle may slow or change itinerary in reaction of accident announcement.
- Security is still in its early stages with regard to vehicular networks. Yet, there could be no real deployment of VANETs if there are security flaws, especially relating to privacy and trust. With the opening of VANETs toward other technologies such as cellular technologies and clouds the problem of security becomes more complex.

References

[1] S. Bitam, A. Mellouk, Cloud computing-based message dissemination protocol for vehicular ad hoc networks, in: International Conference on Wired/Wireless Internet Communication (WWIC), Springer, 2015, pp. 32–45.

[2] P. Li, T. Zhang, C. Huang, X. Chen, B. Fu, A V2I-based real-time traffic density estimation system, Wirel. Pers. Commun. 83 (1) (2015) 259–280.

[3] G.G.M. Ali, E. Chan, W. Li, On scheduling data access with cooperative load balancing in vehicular ad hoc networks (VANETs), J. Supercomput. 67 (2) (2014) 438–468.

[4] G.N. Ali, P. Chong, S. Samantha, E. Chanc, Efficient data dissemination in cooperative multi-RSU vehicular ad hoc networks (VANETs), J. Syst. Softw. 117 (2016) 508–527.

[5] P. Li, T. Zhang, C. Huang, X. Chen, B. Fu, RSU-assisted geocast in vehicular ad hoc networks, IEEE Wirel. Commun. 24 (1) (2017) 53–59.

[6] J. Barrachina, P. Garrido, M. Fogue, F. Martínez, J. Cano, D. Tavares, C. Calafate, P. Manzoni, On efficient data dissemination using network coding in multi-RSU vehicular ad hoc networks, in: Proc. of the 83rd IEEE Conference on Vehicular Technology (VTC Spring), IEEE, China, 2016, pp. 1–5.

[7] B. Liu, D. Jia, J. Wang, K. Lu, L. Wu, Cloud-assisted safety message dissemination in VANET-cellular heterogeneous wireless network, J. IEEE Syst. 11 (1) (2015) 128–139.

[8] P. Li, T. Zhang, C. Huang, X. Chen, B. Fu, Node density estimation in VANETs using received signal power, RadioEngineering 24 (2) (2015) 489–498.

[9] R. Bauza, J. Gozalvez, Traffic congestion detection in large-scale scenarios using vehicle-to-vehicle communications, J. Netw. Comput. Appl. 36 (5) (2013) 1295–1307.

[10] W.K. Wolterink, G. Heijenk, G. Karagiannis, Information dissemination in VANETS by piggybacking on beacons—an analysis of the impact of network parameters, in: Proc. of IEEE Vehicular Networking Conference (VNC), 2011, pp. 94–101. The Netherlands.

[11] K.Z. Ghafoor, J. Lloret, K.A. Bakar, A.S. Sadiq, S.A.B. Mussa, Beaconing approaches in vehicular ad hoc networks: a survey, Wirel. Pers. Commun. 73 (3) (2014) 885–912.

[12] H. Piao, Y. Park, B. Kim, H. Kim, Safety beaconing rate control based on vehicle counting in WAVE, in: Proc. of IEEE Intelligent Vehicles Symposium (IV), 2015, pp. 1361–1366.

[13] K.Z. Ghafoor, K.A. Bakar, M.V. Eenennaam, R.H. Khokhar, A.J. Gonzalez, A fuzzy logic approach to beaconing for vehicular ad hoc networks, Telecommun. Syst. 52 (1) (2013) 139–149.

[14] B. Ayguna, M. Bobanb, A. Wyglinskia, ECPR: environment-and context-aware combined power and rate distributed congestion control for vehicular communications, Comput. Commun. 93 (2016) 3–16.

[15] G. Weidl, V. Singhal, D. Petrich, G. Breuel, Collision risk prediction and warning at road intersections using an object oriented Bayesian network, in: Proc. of the 5th International Conference Automotive User Interfaces and Interactive Vehicular Applications (Automotive UIa, 13), 2013, pp. 270–277. Eindhoven.

[16] Z. Doukha, S. Moussaoui, An SDMA-based mechanism for accurate and efficient neighborhood-discovery link-layer service, IEEE Trans. Veh. Technol. 65 (2) (2016) 603–613.

[17] M.T. Sun, W.C. Feng, T.H. Lai, K. Yamada, H. Okada, GPS-based message broadcast for adaptive inter-vehicle communications, in: Proc. of the 52nd IEEE Vehicular Technology Conference (VTC), 2000, pp. 2685–2692. 6, Boston, MA, USA.

[18] G. Samara, W.A.H.A. Alsalihy, S. Ramadass, Increase emergency message reception in VANET, J. Appl. Sci. 11 (14) (2011) 2606–2612.

[19] X. Bai, Y. Hong, Y. Du, Z. Gao, Efficient data dissemination scheme for the Urbain vehicular networks: a survey of broadcast protocols for vehicular ad-hoc networks, Inf. Technol. J. 12 (9) (2013) 1696–1706.

[20] J. Yang, Z. Fei, Broadcasting with prediction and selective forwarding in vehicular networks, Int. J. Distrib. Sensor Netw. 2013 (9) (2013) 1–9.

[21] A. Benslimane, Optimized dissemination of alarm messages in vehicular ad hoc networks, in: Proc. of the 7th IEEE International Conference, High Speed Networks and Multimedia Communications (HSNMC), vol. 3079, 2004, pp. 655–666. France.

[22] I. Achour, T. Bejaoui, A. Busson, S. Tabbane, SEAD: a simple and efficient adaptive data dissemination protocol in vehicular ad-hoc networks, Int. J. Wirel. Netw. 22 (5) (2016) 1673–1683.

[23] J. Choi, J. Nam, Y. Cho, Robust broadcast scheme regardless of vehicle distribution in vehicular ad hoc networks, EURASIP J. Wirel. Commun. Netw. 2014 (133) (2014) 1–8.

[24] D. Haritha, R.V.S. Lalitha, Cluster based neighbor coverage relaying (CBNCR): a novel broadcasting mechanism for dissemination of data in VANETs, J. Comput. Eng. Intell. Syst. 5 (9) (2014) 36–43.

[25] S. Ucar, S. Ergen, O. Ozkasap, Multihop-cluster-based IEEE 802.11p and LTE hybrid architecture for VANET safety message dissemination, IEEE Trans. Veh. Technol. 65 (4) (2016) 2621–2636.

[26] G. Korkmaz, E. Ekici, F.O. Zgüner, Urban multi-hop broadcast protocols for inter-vehicle communication systems, in: Proc. of the 1st ACM Workshop on Vehicular Ad-Hoc Networks (VANET), ACM, 2004, pp. 76–85.

[27] G. Korkmaz, E. Ekici, F. Ozguner, An efficient fully ad-hoc multihop broadcast protocol for inter-vehicular communication systems, in: Proc. of IEEE Int. Conf. Commun. (ICC'06), vol. 1, 2006, pp. 423–428. Istanbul.

[28] Y. Bi, X. Shen, A multi-hop broadcast protocol for emergency message dissemination in urban vehicular ad hoc networks, IEEE Trans. Intell. Transp. Syst. 17 (3) (2016) 2606–2612.

[29] W. Libing, N. Lei, F. Jing, H. Yanxiang, L. Qin, W. Dan, An efficient multi-hop broadcast protocol for emergency messages dissemination in VANET, Chin. J. Electron. 26 (3) (2017) 614–623.

[30] F. da Cunha, G. Maia, A. Viana, R.F. Mini, L. Villas, A.F. Loureiro, Socially inspired data dissemination for vehicular ad hoc networks, in: Proceedings of the 17th ACM International Conference on Modeling, Analysis and Simulation of Wireless and Mobile Systems, 2014. Montreal.

[31] G. Aldabbagh, M. Rehan, H. Hasbullah, W. Rehan, O. Chughtai, A driver safety information broadcast protocol for VANET, Int. J. Appl. Math. Inf. Sci. 10 (2) (2016) 451–468.

[32] L. Nikita, V. Alexey, J. Magnus, L. Jonathan, Real-time detection of denial-of-service attacks in IEEE 802.11p vehicular networks, IEEE Commun. Lett. 18 (2014) 110–113.

[33] X. Feng, C. Li, D. Chen, J. Tang, A method for defending against multi-source Sybil attacks in VANET, Peer-to-Peer Netw. Appl. 10 (2) (2017) 305–314.

[34] B. Vimal, K. Roshan, K. Singh, S. Kumar, Performance analysis of black hole attack in VANET, Int. J. Comput. Netw. Inf. Secur. 4 (11) (2012) 47–54.

[35] Intelligent Transportation Systems Committee, IEEE Standard for Wireless Access in Vehicular Environments – Security Services for Applications and Management Messages, IEEE Std 1609.2-2016 (Revision of IEEE Std 1609.2-2013), pp. 1–240, March 2016.

[36] C. Liao, J. Chang, I. Lee, K.K. Venkatasubramanian, A trust model for vehicular network-based incident reports, in: Fifth International Symposium on Wireless Vehicular Communications (WiVeC), IEEE, 2013, pp. 1–5.

[37] T. Khan, N. Ahmad, Y. Cao, J. Asim, A. Muhammad, H. Sana, H. Cruickshank, Certificate revocation in vehicular ad hoc networks techniques and protocols: a survey, Sci. China Inf. Sci. 60 (2017) 1–17.

[38] P. Kamat, A. Baliga, W. Trappe, An identity-based security framework for VANETs, in: Proceedings of the Third International Workshop on Vehicular Ad Hoc Networks, ACM, 2006, pp. 94–95.

[39] D. Rawat, G. Yan, B. Bista, M. Weighle, Trust on the security of wireless vehicular ad-hoc networking, Ad Hoc Sensor Wirel. Netw. 24 (3–4) (2015) 283–305.

[40] M. Fogue, F.J. Martinez, P. Garrido, M. Fiore, Securing warning message dissemination in VANETs using cooperative neighbor position verification, IEEE Trans. Veh. Technol. 64 (6) (2015) 2538–2550.

[41] C. Kerrache, C. Calafate, N. Lagraa, J.C. Cano, P. Manzoni, RITA: RIsk-aware Trust-based Architecture for collaborative multi-hop vehicular communications, Secur. Commun. Netw. 9 (17) (2016) 4428–4442.

[42] Z. Huang, S. Ruj, M.A. Cavenaghi, M. Stojmenovic, A. Nayak, A social network approach to trust management in VANETs, Peer-to-Peer Netw. Appl. 7 (3) (2014) 229–242.

CHAPTER

16

Connected Cars: Automotive Cybersecurity and Privacy for Smart Cities

Habeeb Olufowobi and Gedare Bloom
Howard University, Washington, DC, United States

1 INTRODUCTION

This section introduces the role of automobiles in the Smart City ecosystem. The terminology and the layout of the chapter is described to orient the reader with a roadmap for the sections of this chapter. Here we also explain how the chapter is organized in two parts: smart transportation and intelligent transportation systems (ITS).

Notable attention has been focused on the Internet of Things (IoT) by the academic and industrial communities in the past several years. Increasingly, applications based on the IoT have been deployed in use cases that are significant in the Smart City ecosystem. A fundamental application of the IoT is in smart transportation. Smart transportation describes an application of modern technologies and strategic management to transportation systems. These technologies include low-level sensors and actuators, data gathering and analysis, and wireless network communication. Taken together, these technologies can dynamically adjust traffic behavior through signal manipulation, better inform users on the status of transportation networks, increase efficiency of transportation services, and improve traffic management operations.

The benefits and effectiveness of smart transportation in a Smart City ecosystem cannot be overemphasized. Also, in-vehicle systems and global positioning system (GPS)-based services have inspired innovations. Intelligent transportation has become an essential part of the general IoT landscape when it comes to developing an empowered society. Integrating technology into transportation infrastructure can decrease the associated cost of traffic congestion, increase the safety of users, and also facilitate the development of smarter infrastructure to meet future demands. Furthermore, connecting the car to other smart cars and the transportation infrastructure of the Smart City ecosystem will enable new possibilities for our societies, such as self-monitoring roads that can predict traffic and send information to on-the-road users. ITS have made all these transportation technologies possible. However, these possibilities come with anticipated security and privacy risks.

The modern automobile is a cyber-physical system (CPS) comprising tens to hundreds of computers that control the vehicle's electrical-mechanical components operated by hundreds of millions of software lines of code. Vehicle components are controlled by various electrical control units (ECUs) that are connected together through an internal network, also called an in-vehicle network, which may even be connected to the Internet. Each in-vehicle network typically connects multiple communication networks and protocols, including the industry standard Controller Area Network (CAN), Local Interconnect Network, FlexRay, Media Oriented Systems Transport, and Radio Frequency communication. An in-vehicle network consists of nodes, gateways, and buses. Data is transferred from one network to another through a gateway, and all messages are broadcast on the bus. The vehicle network is a medium that facilitates data exchange in the automobile. These networks can be accessed through the standard on-board diagnostics (OBD)—a vehicle self-diagnostics and reporting port—or via wireless communication interfaces such as Bluetooth, WiFi, and cellular telephone networks.

From the communication bus perspective, modern vehicles contain multiple interfaces that expose the vehicular systems to cyberattacks through physical and wireless access. These interfaces require varying levels of security in order to effectively thwart cybercriminals from gaining access to them. Physical access means that the attacker has

Smart Cities Cybersecurity and Privacy
https://doi.org/10.1016/B978-0-12-815032-0.00016-0

a direct connection to the OBD port of the vehicle that is connected to the CAN bus and all ECUs. This port can be accessed easily by an adversary with the right equipment and a window of opportunity. The attacker can plug a small dongle into the OBD port to gather information or inject messages directly into the vehicle. Also, an attacker can plug a device into the port and access it remotely [1]. Alternatively, an attacker may gain access to the network through the use of the USB port. Using these methods, multiple teams have demonstrated overriding security controls to reflash ECUs [2, 3], providing the opportunity to inject or monitor CAN traffic without leaving any physical traces.

Remote and wireless attack surfaces are more worrying because the attacker does not need to physically connect any dongle to the vehicle. These attack surfaces include in-vehicle Bluetooth and the telematics unit that are common in vehicles for wireless and cellular connectivity. Bluetooth attacks have been demonstrated by Checkoway et al. [1] using various methods of connecting to the communication bus through Bluetooth with malware installed on an already-paired Android phone, and with a method they developed for unauthorized pairing. Miller and Valasek [4] demonstrated unauthorized CAN bus access to a 2015 Jeep Cherokee through its WiFi network that exploits the weakness in its password generation protocol.

The apparent motivations for adversaries to launch cyberattacks against vehicles are shared across the autonomous vehicle (AV), vehicular ad-hoc networks (VANETs), vehicle-to-vehicle (V2V), vehicle-to-infrastructure (V2I), connected car, ITS, and even traditional (nonconnected) automobiles. These motivations, or goals, include:

- *desire* for infamy, vengeance, or twisted pleasure [5];
- *profit* [6];
- *control traffic* [7], so as to create open or congested routes;
- *disrupt traffic* [8] to create congestion or even panic;
- *conduct intelligence, surveillance, and reconnaissance (ISR)* [9], whether targeted or en masse;
- *vehicle theft* [10], usually targeted;
- *remote hijack* [11, 12], to take control of an operating vehicle;
- infecting with *vehicle malware* [13]; and
- creating a *vehicular botnet* [14].

The kinds of attacks that an adversary may launch to achieve their goals are summarized in Table 1. These attacks are many and varied, but they are basically based on compromising the traditional information security objectives of confidentiality, integrity, availability (CIA), and disrupting the security system's implementation of one of Lampson's "gold standards" of authentication, authorization, and audit. Confidentiality may be lost when an adversary can eavesdrop on the information sent through networks, or unauthorized users have access to the information shared within the network, while the integrity of transmitted messages can be compromised by message tampering, injection, replay, masquerading, and deletion. Service availability may be compromised by denying access to use the service, which is typically accomplished by a denial-of-service (DOS) attack or the related distributed DOS (DDOS) attack. In the following list, we briefly describe each kind of attack:

- *Denial of service.* DOS attacks occur when an adversary takes overall control of the network resources or floods the communication channels to deny inflow and outflow of information, making the whole network unusable for all connected nodes. The overall goal is to prevent the legitimate nodes from using the network resources [15]. This attack compromises the availability of the network, which is an essential requirement of normal vehicle operations in the Smart City. This action places the driver and passengers in danger if they solely depend on the information provided by the network.

TABLE 1 Threats and Attacks Against Vehicles Grouped by Targeted Security Objective

Availability	Confidentiality	Integrity	Authentication
Denial of service (DOS)	Traffic analysis	GPS signal spoofing	Sybil
Distributed DOS (DDOS)	Eavesdropping	Replay	Impersonation
Jamming	Tunneling	Wormhole	Masquerade
Black hole	Cryptanalysis	False data injection	Tampering
Spamming		Man-in-the-middle (MitM)	
		Malware	

- *Node impersonation.* An adversarial node broadcasts a message and claims the message is from another node by changing his or her identity to prevent being detected. The node may assume the identity of an authorized node to utilize network resources or to disrupt the normal operations of the network.
- *Sybil attack.* An adversary creates multiple identities of itself to transmit messages to different nodes on the network. Thus, other nodes believe that there are many nodes on the network at the same time, and are forced to use alternate routes. Also, the adversarial node has the potential to inject false information into the networks through the fictional nodes contrived on the network. Sybil attacks have been considered a severe security threat to sensor networks and VANETs, and they can compromise the data integrity, security, and resource utilization of the vehicular networks [16].
- *GPS spoofing.* The adversarial node overrides the signal from a GPS satellite to provide false location and time information to targeted nodes. An adversary makes use of a GPS satellite simulator to generate signals more effectively than the original GPS satellite [17] to deceive vehicles to think they are in different locations.
- *Masquerade.* A malicious node simulates an identity to pretend to be another node. This simulation can be accomplished by message fabrication, replay, and alterations.
- *Black hole.* The adversarial node will not participate in the operation of the routing information when the information is received. This disrupts the routing table and causes packet loss because the network traffic will be redirected.
- *Traffic analysis.* An adversary intercepts and analyzes communication patterns of nodes in order to extract useful information. This attack can be performed even when the messages are encrypted and cannot be decrypted.
- *Malware.* Malicious software is designed to run on a system without the user's consent with the intent of harming the system. Malware is injected into a network to cause disruptions in normal operations, which can lead to serious consequences.
- *Man-in-the-middle (MitM).* An adversary eavesdrops and possibly modifies the communication between two nodes who think they have a direct communication with one another. MitM violates trust between nodes in the network.
- *Timing attacks.* The adversary intentionally creates a delay to prevent messages from reaching the destination node in time.
- *Eavesdropping.* As a passive attacker, an adversary intercepts (listens) to messages sent on the network. Detecting this kind of attack can be difficult, while launching the attack can be easy, both depending on the communication media.

Some of these attacks rely on physical access, for example, GPS spoofing can only be done in (relatively) close proximity to the target, while other attacks can be conducted remotely using only a network connection. In general, any goal that can be achieved through remote attacks is achievable through physical attacks, because with physical access the adversary can control and observe the same data used to launch an attack with remote access. Although physical access may be harder to achieve for an adversary, attacks that rely on physical access tend to be less complex to conduct than those with remote access. Often, physical access may be used to facilitate remote access, for example, by using physical access to install a wireless or radio device that enables future remote access.

1.1 Chapter Layout

This chapter is organized in two parts. Part I consists of Sections 2–6, and addresses the security and privacy of AVs and V2V communication as the underlying technologies for smart transportation. Sections 7–11 compose Part II, which explores the impact on security and privacy caused by the integration of vehicles with the transportation infrastructure via the V2I and infrastructure-to-vehicle (I2V) communications. We conclude in Section 12.

1.1.1 Part I: Smart Transportation

Section 2 describes the current state-of-the-art capabilities in AVs and V2V communication, and discusses some of the expected developments in these capabilities. Primarily, the goal of this section is to give the reader sufficient background and terminology for the remainder of Part I.

Section 3 identifies the range of realistic threat models that should be considered against AVs. Motivations for attacks will be described, along with the attack capabilities of adversaries in the Smart City ecosystem. The impacts of attacks will also be discussed. We will address threats against both the automotive systems, for example, the CAN bus, and the autonomous software, that is, the machine learning and computer vision algorithms. Section 4 surveys the solutions for assuring security and protecting privacy against the threats and attacks on AVs. Gaps in the literature, that is, threats that are inadequately defended against by known approaches, will also be identified here.

Section 5 describes how the introduction of communication between vehicles causes new threat models to be relevant; new motivation and attack capabilities will be identified. We will briefly discuss vehicular ad hoc networks here together with direct communications between cars. Section 6 discusses solutions for security and privacy despite the threats and attacks against V2V communications.

1.1.2 Part II: Vehicle-Infrastructure Integration

Section 7 describes the current state-of-the-art capabilities in communications between vehicles and the transportation infrastructure, and discusses expected evolution in these capabilities. This section provides background and terminology to understand the remainder of Part II.

Section 8 identifies the threats and attacks against connected cars that arise due to the introduction of vehicle-infrastructure communications. Section 9 surveys approaches for providing security and protecting privacy against the threats and attacks targeting vehicles that are introduced by communications between vehicles and transportation infrastructure. We will not discuss in any detail solutions pertaining to known problems with vehicular or infrastructure security that existed prior to such communication capabilities.

Section 10 surveys attacks against transportation infrastructure that are enabled by communication between the infrastructure and vehicles. Section 11 identifies solutions for assuring security and privacy against the threats and attacks targeting civil infrastructure that are introduced by such vehicle-infrastructure communication.

2 AVs AND V2V COMMUNICATION

With the growing numbers of vehicles on the road, driver error often results in car crashes, which sometimes include loss of human lives or bodily injury. AVs and V2V communication aim to reduce driver error while simultaneously bringing the potential to reduce congestion on our roadways by using sensors and in-vehicle technologies to shape how people move around, work, and live in a Smart City ecosystem. Highly automated vehicles are able to navigate using artificial intelligence, sensors, and interconnected computer systems working together to control the vehicle to reach its destination without human operation. In-vehicle sensors generate data that are analyzed by computer software for the vehicle decision-making algorithms that control vehicle operations such as acceleration, braking, and steering in real-time. The sensors are connected to other devices or services within and outside the vehicle using internal and external networks for data communication. Internal connections rely on the existing in-vehicle network structures of modern vehicles. External communications may include V2V or even communicate with the transportation infrastructure (V2I) and the Internet. Together, the communication capabilities provide traffic information and alerts to help ensure the safety of the vehicle, its passengers, and its surrounding environment.

2.1 Overview of AVs

Increasingly, AVs are expected to form a significant part of the automotive industry. The industry and other stakeholders continue to harness advances in technology to develop capabilities that will ease congestion on our roads and provide social welfare benefits to users. Some of the benefits include increased mobility for the disabled, elderly, and the young; improved fuel or energy consumption, and reduced fuel emissions. Traffic flow could be more efficient, because the AVs will obey traffic laws and travel times more diligently than human operators, and vehicles can be used to engage in activities even without a human driver, thereby reducing travel costs. However, important challenges in achieving these benefits include the cybersecurity and privacy protection of this vehicle and its passengers. As the vehicles become more network-connected, they also become more attractive targets for cyberattack. The risk associated with an attacked AV may greatly outweigh its benefit, as the impacts can affect human safety.

2.2 Overview of V2V

V2V facilitates wireless information exchange between vehicles about potential collisions on the road. V2V aims to provide drivers with significant information and warn them about any imminent hazard in real-time. Using dedicated short-range radio communication (DSRC) technology [18], cars will communicate with each other, automatically broadcast data such as current GPS location, the speed of the vehicle, direction, path history, and vehicle control information—brake status, transmission state, and steering wheel angle. By integrating V2V communication services into the vehicle, the technology is expected to enhance the safety and efficiency of the drivers and our roads. The idea is to prevent vehicle collisions.

DSRC protocols [19] are based on the IEEE 802.11 WiFi standard and can accommodate device communication of up to 300 m in range. With this protocol, vehicles will have a 360-degree view of the road, and will be able to share safety messages in their close proximity that can help drivers responds quickly to prevent crashes and save lives. DSRC works in the 5.9 GHz band with a bandwidth of 75 MHz that is assigned separately only for vehicular communication. With a broadcast update of up to 10 times per second, connected vehicles can share basic safety messages that can better pinpoint dangers and warn the drivers about a potential collision. The DSRC protocol has a low communication latency (less than 100 ms) and high data transfer rates (up to 27 Mbps for services and 6 Mbps for safety) [20]. It can also support a multihop network for extended range communications. Devices using this protocol can communicate not only with themselves, but also the road infrastructure.

According to the US Department of Transportation and the National Highway Traffic Safety Administration (NHTSA), V2V addresses the following three different safety applications scenarios for which current vehicle sensors, such as cameras or LIDAR, cannot be utilized [21]:

1. *Intersection movement assist*: This technology alerts the driver when it is unsafe to enter an intersection due to a possible collision with other vehicles at the intersection. Such alerts could help at signalized intersections, and those with stop and yield signs, to avoid potentially dangerous accidents.
2. *Emergency electric brake light*: This technology alerts the driver to apply the brake when a similar V2V-equipped vehicle decelerates quickly. The decelerating vehicle may not be directly in front of the warning vehicle. The warning will be quite helpful in circumstances where the driver's line of sight is obstructed by other vehicles or extreme weather conditions.
3. *Left turn assist*: This technology alerts the driver not to turn left in front of another vehicle traveling in the opposing direction when entering an intersection. When turning across opposite lanes, this warning can help prevent accidents with an approaching vehicle.

Other technologies enabled by V2V include:

1. *Forward collision warning*: This technology is designed to limit and decrease rear-end crashes and to also assist in keeping a reasonably safe distance between vehicles. The warning alerts drivers when an impending frontal collision is about to occur.
2. *Blind spot*: This technology alerts the drivers of the presence of other vehicles in the areas they are unable to see. The system identifies the nearness of another vehicle traveling diagonally behind the driver's vehicle and signals its presence with an indicator.
3. *Lane departure or keep warning*: This technology alerts the drivers whenever the vehicle is veering from the lane by monitoring the lane markings on the roadway. The lane keep warning is able to take corrective actions by keeping the vehicle from drifting, unlike the lane departure warning that just alerts the driver about lane changes.
4. *Do not pass warning*: This technology alerts the driver that it is unsafe to overtake a slower moving vehicle when using a passing zone that is occupied by another vehicle traveling in the opposite direction. This warning alerts the driver to avoid a head-on collision with the oncoming vehicle.

The future of our roads and cars depends on V2V communication technology. Connectivity presents incredible possibilities for growth by decreasing congestion and increasing the efficiency of traffic flow. These technologies can be harnessed to enhance the safety and usage of our roadway infrastructure. However, V2V can also create potential security threats. Adversarial vehicles can use this technology for sending fraudulent messages for their own gain or use it to disrupt the flow of the traffic system. The severity of a potential tampering could have disastrous consequences, and even result in loss of human life. Hence, it is essential to design the V2V system with robust security to ensure seamless communication and trusted data sharing.

3 THREATS AGAINST AVs

Vehicle connectivity is a new sensation among several auto industries and the government, and the use of these technologies continues to develop rapidly. However, any new technology comes with new risks and challenges along with the benefits. Modern vehicles contain multiple interfaces that expose the vehicular systems to cyberattacks. We will consider these cyberattacks in two different perspectives.

From the AV perspective, an adversary may breach the network that facilitates the communications between the control systems of the vehicle, such as the sensors, cameras, GPS, radar, and odometry to have full control, which can threaten human lives. The key control systems could be deactivated remotely to direct or drive the vehicle to an undisclosed destination. Also, the connected technologies, including the laser range finders, LIDAR, cameras, and sensors acting as the vehicle's eyes and ears are attractive targets for cyberattackers, because they contain complex software that may have some bugs that are sometimes vulnerable to a security breach.

Another key area of software attack is on the machine learning and the computer vision algorithms used for the AVs. The machine learning models are vulnerable to adversarial example attacks, which are inputs designed to intentionally confuse the model into producing an incorrect output, such as miscategorizing an object for another [22–25]. This type of attack causes an inherent security threat for practical machine learning applications, and an adversary can perform misclassification attacks on a machine learning system—such as an AV—without access to the underlying machine learning model [22, 26]. In this kind of attack, an adversary may alter the images (traffic signs) used internally by the vehicle by transforming the physical sign to something else, and then use the modified image to mislead the navigation system of the AV or cause the vehicle to behave dangerously. Furthermore, AV-connected technologies generate and collect a vast amount of data through sensing and learning about the vehicle's surrounding environment during operation. Misuse of such data is a threat to the privacy of the drivers, passengers, other vehicles, and other users of the roadways, including pedestrians and cyclists.

Worthy of note are the privacy-related issues of the AVs. Presently, AVs are still in testing phases, and while there are no definite answers to the type of data the vehicles will be collecting and sharing with other AVs and the infrastructure, AVs currently are logging and sharing location-related information about the vehicle itself. This type of information has the potential to be used in tracking and determining the places visited by the vehicle owner, which is privacy invasive. Other privacy-related issues that can be considered in using AVs include owners and passengers information, location tracking, sensor data collection by auto companies, and travel data stored for route planning, point of interest, and location features. Travel and location data leveraged with supplementary information of the owner and passenger of the vehicle could produce such benefits like traffic planning, increased safety, and reducing traffic. But, this kind of combined dataset can be privacy invasive, as it exposes sensitive information about the users of the service, especially if the data is persistently maintained. If an adversary has access to such information, individuals, and society at large may be at risk of information misuse.

The advancement in technology for AVs is generating waves across the automotive and information technology industries, and also excitement among technology enthusiasts, hobbyists, and consumers. However, the risks associated with the use of AVs, as well as cybersecurity threats directed toward them, need to be fully examined and understood before AVs start operating on our roadways.

4 SECURITY AND PRIVACY FOR AVs

Auto manufacturers have been struggling to address security and privacy issues in AVs because the attack surface continues to grow as new functionality for safety and comfort are added to the vehicle. Software-related security solutions are deemed sufficient in some cases, while in other cases, tamper-proof security solutions are required. Security solutions such as message encryption and authentication [27–30], digital signatures [31], intrusion detection systems (IDS) [32–36], and over-the-air (OTA) firmware security updates can provide comprehensive system protection [37]. In the case of privacy, it remains to be seen what kind of personal information the AVs can collect at the moment because they are still in the testing phase. At a minimum, the vehicles will be using the GPS location data—route information, destination information, speed, total trip time—to track their own locations, retaining this data in memory for navigation purposes. This type of data needs to be kept secure to protect the privacy and safety of drivers and passengers.

At the component or device level, the amount of power consumed when in operation, the timing information, electromagnetic radiation, and the sound produced by these components can be another source of information that can be exploited to perform an advanced side-channel attack and physical reverse engineering. Physical security may be employed to protect the components against such threats. For devices that can be accessed remotely, adapting software agents used in distributed real-time can facilitate secure and robust status updates for identifying cyberattacks [38].

Addressing privacy concerns in AVs has been a major topic of discussion for both the government and the automotive industry. Several measures may be taken to ensure the safety and privacy of personal information collected and stored for vehicle operations. This includes legislation guiding the collection and use of data, data anonymization, notice and consent, differential privacy, and so on.

5 THREATS AGAINST V2V

Raya and Hubaux [39] present four different classifications of attackers in VANETs. These are insider versus outsider, malicious versus rationale, active versus passive, and local versus extended attackers. Insiders are the authenticated users of the network, while outsiders are not. With malicious attackers, the intention is to disrupt the functionality of the network with no personal benefits, while a rational attacker seeks to gain some profits from such an attack. A passive attacker monitors and eavesdrops on the network activities, whereas an active attacker is able to generate and send malicious packets on the network. For local attackers, they have a limited reach, and can only perform their attacks within this reach, while extended attackers have a wider reach scattered across the network.

V2V uses the VANET mesh structure to communicate so each node in the network can broadcast and receive signals. VANET aims to enable safe and efficient driving while providing support for infotainment features. Nodes in the network include the vehicles and the roadside infrastructure units. These nodes may physically move freely within the connected network coverage and communicate in single or multihop routing patterns. VANET is designed to ensure continuous and secure communication between all the nodes on the network. Security goals of VANET include ensuring that the source of any message is as claimed, thereby enforcing message integrity, and all the nodes should be obscured from one another and cannot be tracked to enforce privacy. Also, the network should ensure that each node is providing accurate information. However, security concerns and challenges with VANETs can directly affect the vehicle and the infrastructure, while some attacks could also be directed at the applications using the network. These concerns present different levels of threats to the security goals of the network.

Sumra et al. [40] group the threat levels into three categories based on the CIA triad, and the authors consider availability of the network resources to be at the apex and the most significant of the three levels. Attacks against availability include DOS and DDOS attacks. The next level is the integrity of the information. The attacker's goal here is to modify the messages in the network. This compromises the integrity of the network activities, but the network services are still accessible. At the lower level are passive attacks, where the adversary does not interrupt the network services, but analyzes the network activities to gain information, that is, circumvent any confidentiality of message information. The information analyzed can be used in identifying the communicating nodes, their locations, or other key data about them.

6 SECURITY AND PRIVACY FOR V2V

A key area to focus on regarding the security and privacy of V2I is the need for a secure public key infrastructure (PKI) [41] and the proposed security credential management scheme (SCMS) for V2V communication [42, 43]. A vehicular PKI allows each vehicle on the network to have a public-private key pair that allows it to sign messages and verify received messages by relying on a trusted certificate authority [31]. Most important, the deployment of SCMS will have profound and widespread influence, not only on the security of V2V, its intended purpose, but also on the privacy of connected vehicles, with respect to the SCMS infrastructure, and also the security of connected cars in terms of their reliance on the correctness and inviolability of the SCMS and its constituents. An analogy may be seen in the reliance of the Internet on a secure and trustworthy PKI as the first step for establishing secure connections between two parties without using other prior information. If the PKI does not work or is compromised, for example when certificates or signing keys are stolen, then the root of trust is broken, and there can be no security. Similarly, a vehicular PKI as envisioned by the SCMS, or any similar scheme used to establish authority and authenticity, is a lynchpin for secure communications in the V2I and V2V realm, including as a method to provide for secure OTA software updates.

Pseudonym-based authentication has been proposed to avoid unauthorized vehicle traceability and location privacy during communications and preserve both confidential information and privacy of the driver. A key challenge with pseudonyms is the need to refresh them to avoid overuse that can lead to linking long-term pseudonyms to true identities. A common approach to solve this challenge is to change pseudonyms frequently using an algorithm that attempts to ensure privacy while balancing the cost of replacing pseudonyms [44–47]. These algorithms aim to provide location privacy for the vehicles and the users on the network. With pseudonyms, the real identity of the user is obscured, which prevents identity linking.

Another security and location privacy-concealing approach makes use of group signatures. A group signature is a cryptographic primitive that allows the constituent users of a group to share the ability to sign a message on behalf of the entire group. Grouping of vehicles traveling at the same speed toward the same direction was proposed by Sampigethaya et al. [48]. The authors identified that combining neighboring vehicles into groups can reduce the number of

V2I transmissions. With this approach, the vehicle will be provided with an extended silent period that enhances their anonymity in the network. Furthermore, temporary anonymous certified keys based on group signatures was presented by Studer et al. [49] to fulfill the security and privacy management of VANETs. Here, the on-board units provide short-lived keys that are certified by the regional authority for communications. During key updates, a regional authority verifies the requesting on-board unit's validity, but does not determine its identity, thus preserving its privacy and allowing it to acquire a certificate for a temporary key. Guo et al. [50] present a group signature-based scheme that relies on tamper-resistant devices for preventing adversarial attacks. This scheme allows a group member to sign messages on behalf of the group while the single public key can be used to verify the signature without revealing the identity of the signer. An important feature of group signatures is that they make it impossible to determine if two signatures have been issued by the same group member, which efficiently prevents tracking of users subject to a large enough group (i.e., the anonymity set).

K-anonymity, a scheme proposed by Sweeney [51], is another approach to deal with security and privacy risks in VANETs using the DSRC/WAVE standards. K-anonymity requires that an entity must be distinguishable from $k-1$ other entities, in the results of database queries [52], that is, a node cannot be individually identified from a group of k nodes on the network. Feng et al. [53] proposed a privacy-preserving model called (k, R, r)-anonymity that can be implemented on a mobile terminal. The main idea is to replace the physical location of users and the query target by a specific area and a set of location types, respectively. Caballero-Gil et al. [54] also proposed a revocation scheme that detects and eliminates malicious users after a number of complaints have been received while guaranteeing k-anonymity.

While works using differential privacy for privacy preservation in VANETs promise privacy of information [55–58], additional privacy risk needs to be considered at the communication level, as well as the computation that manipulates the data [59].

7 V2I AND I2V COMMUNICATION

Conventional ITSs treat vehicles—and their drivers—as external agents that are monitored and measured through sensors embedded in the infrastructure. The ITS influences vehicles through physical actuation of mutable infrastructure components such as traffic lights and gates that especially are prevalent in ramp metering and traffic flow control applications. Indirect moderation of vehicle behavior is achieved by ITS through visual communication with drivers by way of programmable road signs, such as variable speed zones and congestion alerts. These visual cues require drivers to both observe and honor the warning message for effect. The arrival of V2I/I2V brings active, wireless communication links between vehicles and infrastructure that enable direct messages and the ability of an ITS to treat a vehicle as part of the system by eliciting information from it and by sending targeted warnings and messages—possibly even commands—to it. The inclusion of vehicles within the ITS represents a paradigm shift that will radically change the nature of transportation infrastructure because of the addition of V2I/I2V communication [60].

V2I/I2V is an enabler for VANET and ushers in the next generation of ITS: the era of connected vehicles [61]. Advanced applications in connected vehicles integrate live sensing data embedded in transportation infrastructure with V2I communications and Internet data sources to provide novel safety features, more efficient traffic, and delivery of digital services (i.e., infotainment) [62]. Already deployed capabilities in smart infrastructures include red light violation warning, curve speed warning, weather advisories, traffic signal change warning, congestion and detour warning for navigation planning, and more [63]. New capabilities continue to emerge on a regular basis, and adoption by public communities is encouraged by the possible benefits of ITS [64], which include improved public safety, traffic safety, fuel and travel time efficiency, and job growth due to market expansion.

The role of V2I/I2V in emerging Smart Cities is to increase the data sources available for ITS by collecting from vehicles directly, provide support for VANET security and Internet-connectivity, and to close the loop by communicating feedback to vehicles and drivers [65]. Prior to the widespread adoption of wireless technology, ITS relied upon indirect collection of vehicle data using sensor measurements embedded in the infrastructure, and generated physical signals to mediate vehicle behavior, for example, metering lights and smart road signs. ITS therefore relied on widespread data collection and analysis, but without direct communication over a computer network with external agents.

Problematic to the expansion of V2I/I2V are the joint concerns of security and privacy. The security concerns of ITS in the past were readily solved by traditional network security solutions using standard cryptographic techniques. Connected car security is necessary to prevent remote exploits of moving vehicles, and infrastructure security requires rethinking in order to ensure resilient operations at all times because of new, ubiquitous communication pathways between external agents and infrastructure components. Privacy has also been a well-known concern of ITS [66], and has been recognized as a key challenge since the advent of V2I [67], yet remains a significant issue in practice. Privacy is primarily of concern for vehicle drivers and passengers, but the challenges that impede privacy, and their respective solutions, exist at both ends of the vehicle-infrastructure communication channel.

8 THREATS AGAINST CONNECTED CARS DUE TO V2I/I2V

Existing work in the area of transportation infrastructure cybersecurity focuses primarily on attacks against the infrastructure with the goal of manipulating traffic signals to indirectly influence vehicle behavior [7, 8]. The rise of V2I/I2V introduces new possibilities for attackers to target cyberattacks directly at vehicles using the infrastructure as an attack vector. This section identifies such new threats that arise due to the introduction of communication pathways between vehicles and ITS. Motivations for attacks and attack capabilities are described, along with the potential impacts of attacks. The focus of this section is how communicating with infrastructure opens new attack surfaces against vehicles, after which we will discuss approaches to provide security and privacy before exploring how V2I enables attacks against the infrastructure coming from the connected vehicles. We do not address here the existing attack surfaces, threats, and security solutions for automobiles that predate V2I/I2V, which, while relevant, are not facilitated by the rise of this new communication paradigm.

By itself, V2I/I2V does not introduce any new motivation for attacks, but it does expose three attack vectors relevant to compromise of the connected car:

- components of the physical *transportation infrastructure*;
- media channels and protocols of the V2I/I2V *network infrastructure*; and
- *on-board computers* of the connected car that support V2I/I2V.

Adversaries capable of exploiting vulnerabilities in these attack vectors are varied, but may be broadly categorized according to their level of access, physical or remote, to the respective infrastructure. That is, the ability to access the physical or network infrastructure, or the on-board computers of individual vehicles, may be physically under adversarial control, or the adversary may be limited to making remote accesses through, for example, manipulation of ingested data, as in false data injection attacks, or through passive monitoring or eavesdropping.

Attacks coming through the physical transportation infrastructure leverage the adversaries, ability to control that infrastructure. The sophistication of such an attack is therefore quite high, because the adversary must be able to first subvert components of the infrastructure. Once inside the infrastructure, however, the adversary has the advantage that V2I protocols rely on the infrastructure to be correct. Thus, some motivations for attack, namely those that aim to control, disrupt, or monitor traffic, are met without needing to compromise the connected car, and may even be feasible with remote access to the physical infrastructure. For example, ramp metering attacks that target ITS through remote or physical access [7] could accomplish similar outcomes by influencing the physical infrastructure to not just change traffic signals, but to even send messages to the connected car that alter its behavior. Another example is the "Zombies ahead!" message that was presented by hacked changeable message signs [8], which may cause confusion or even panic for human drivers, while the impact of customized messages broadcast by the infrastructure to automated or semi-AVs could be much worse.

From the adversary's perspective, the network infrastructure is perhaps the most interesting of the three new attack vectors that V2I creates, because the networks are wireless, thus easier to access both physically and remotely in comparison with the other two vectors, and the networks are ubiquitous, with connections not only to connected cars and transportation infrastructure, but also to Internet-connected computer systems, such as the servers used for PKI, databases to store the vast data collected from the transportation infrastructure, and third-party service providers envisioned to support future driver and passenger demands in both the infotainment market segment and the evolution of the Smart City [68].

The third attack vector of on-board computer systems is, perhaps, less enticing to attackers than the other two vectors, but must not be ignored. Of special concern for this vector is that, while traditional vehicular control systems can be isolated from remote network connections that provide infotainment and telematics, the expected development of V2I messages includes the transmission of command-and-control messages that influence the vehicle's driving behavior. In the especially concerning case of AVs, V2I messages may even translate directly into vehicular control. Thus, the interface between the vehicle and the V2I network is an important element of the cybersecurity of connected cars to defend against external attacks. As such, the ability to provide OTA updates in a secure yet prompt fashion for cybersecurity purposes will be important in the connected car.

9 SECURITY AND PRIVACY FOR CONNECTED CARS

Security and privacy solutions proposed for connected cars generally follow traditional information security system architecture design and implementation [69, 70]. The following security mechanisms are particularly being explored in the V2I domain:

- cryptography [71];
- IDS;
- formal methods, modeling, and verification [72, 73];
- antivirus software [13]; and
- hardware-based trusted computing [74, 75].

Novel security solutions also appear in the V2I/I2V space to counter the issues faced by the automotive domain that are not relevant in the information security space. In particular, countermeasures for vehicular theft exist for which no obvious complements are found in the traditional cybersecurity realm [76]. Similarly, the need to balance safety constraints, economic pressures, and privacy concerns with security needs sufficiently restrict the solution space such that, despite the similarity in problems and solution methods, significant work remains in addressing the challenges of automotive security.

10 THREATS AGAINST INTELLIGENT TRANSPORTATION INFRASTRUCTURE DUE TO V2I/I2V

The inclusion of communication channels between connected vehicles and ITS opens new attack surfaces against the transportation infrastructure and its supporting CPS components. In this section, we identify the new threat vectors that V2I/I2V create within civil infrastructure. The motivation for attacks against ITS is essentially a subset of those for attacks against connected cars and vehicles in general:

- *infamy*;
- *control traffic* [7];
- *disrupt traffic* [8]; and
- *collect ISR* [9].

Note that cybersecurity for ITS has long been a concern, especially for public sector agencies and the transportation profession. A lengthy yet accessible introduction to the view of cybersecurity through the lens of transportation operations management can be found in a document prepared by the Transportation Research Board [77]. Vulnerabilities in ITS existed before the introduction of V2I/I2V, but the new communication channels introduce attack vectors through which adversaries may attempt to exploit the ITS and achieve their goals. In particular, the new attack vectors that threaten the transportation infrastructure are

- *vehicles* participating in the V2I/I2V communications;
- *networking* media and protocols of V2I/I2V; and
- *added computing* (hardware and software) that supports V2I/I2V.

Perhaps the most obvious attack vector that V2I introduces is the vehicles themselves. As active participants in the ITS, malicious vehicles now can influence and attack the infrastructure itself through directed cyberattacks within the network that connects vehicles and infrastructure. Attacks against the networking layers also have precedent in the ITS prior to including vehicles in the network. For example, loop detectors embedded in the roadway to detect vehicles communicate wirelessly with a roadside unit that controls traffic signals for stoplights at intersections and in ramp metering applications. A demonstrated attack spoofs a sensor (loop detector) signal, which allows the adversary to trick the roadside unit into altering its behavior with respect to traffic flow control [78, 79]. The inclusion of additional communication—mostly wireless—to roadside units increases their exposure to similar attacks. Even simpler attacks such as jamming are feasible and effective in achieving the disruption of traffic [80]. The inclusion of even more hardware and software within both vehicles and infrastructure to support V2I increases the attack surface of ITS, thus providing more opportunities for adversaries to launch successful cyberattacks against the computer systems themselves. Existing threat characterization for ITS considers these new threat vectors as extensions to those stemming from VANET and V2V, which are usually cast in terms of cryptographic communication security [81, 82]. A comprehensive technical report produced by ETSI identifies a broad set of threats, attacks, and countermeasures in an ITS [83].

11 SECURITY AND PRIVACY FOR INTELLIGENT TRANSPORTATION INFRASTRUCTURE

Generically, the (draft) NIST Cybersecurity Framework for Critical Infrastructure [84] provides a framework to guide organizations in securing their critical infrastructure. The NIST framework adopts a risk management approach consisting of five core functions: identify, protect, detect, respond, and recover. Identify encompasses threat characterization, while protect, detect, and respond address the usual cybersecurity defensive mechanisms and incidence response deployed in (IT) security. Recover is of particular importance in critical infrastructure, because appropriate recovery ensures the resilience of the infrastructure. The NIST framework has been adopted and specialized by multiple ITS domain-specific cybersecurity policies [85].

Much of the prior work in ITS security focuses on V2V and VANET [86], or on threats to the infrastructure that come from other sources besides V2I [87–90]. Much more work needs to be done in examining the threat landscape that V2I introduces against the transportation infrastructure, and then ensuring that cybersecurity approaches for ITS are resilient to attacks coming from any new attack vectors.

The impact on privacy caused by integration of V2I and ITS also has received quite a bit of attention. Cottrill [91] examines the problem and solution space for privacy concerns with respect to the emerging V2I-ITS integration. Glancy [60] discusses, among other topics, the legal and policy issues caused by V2I/I2V, including privacy concerns and security challenges. Privacy is also a repeated theme of concern in the proposed rules for V2V communications, especially as they rely on PKI and network infrastructure [43]. Lederman et al. [92] survey privacy protections in ITS and propose solutions for privacy protection in ITS data collection and storage.

12 CONCLUSIONS AND FUTURE WORK

As the boundary line blurs between vehicle, network, and transportation infrastructure, the security and privacy concerns of all the entities involved in modern transportation will continue to grow in importance. In this chapter, we have dissected how advancements made in autonomy, intervehicle connectivity, and vehicle-infrastructure integration are impacting the security and privacy of vehicle and transportation infrastructure computing systems. None of the concerns in any of these areas are solved, and much work remains to be done, especially in the emerging domains of V2I and AVs. Privacy also is underinvestigated in the research community, despite being valued by the consumer, and solutions to protect privacy could have a high impact on the adoption rate and long-term viability of automotive and transportation technology that enables Smart Cities. As the standards and regulations for vehicular technology change in response to autonomy and ubiquitous connectivity, so too must the security and privacy research community continue to identify problems and propose preventive, reactive, and responsive solutions that are amenable to public use and policy making. Security and privacy of vehicles and transportation critical infrastructure are not just technical problems, but they are also social and international, multicultural problems for which the solutions must meet the security and privacy requirements while also being responsive to human socioeconomic and cross-cultural needs while satisfying the CPS safety constraints. The complexity of this problem ensures that it will remain an active and viable research area for years to come, and that the fundamental problems will persist. Therefore, an important future research direction is on how to evaluate proposed solutions for security and privacy to meet the preceding constraints and also address the fundamental problems. Another area that merits further investigation is building security into the entire components of the automobile used for communication, and determining how to maintain that level of security through the entire lifecycle of the components by remote updates and other security measures.

ACKNOWLEDGMENTS

This material is based upon work supported by the National Science Foundation under Grant No. CNS-1646317 and the US Department of Homeland Security under Grant Award Number 2017-ST-062-000003. Any opinions, findings, and conclusions or recommendations expressed in this material are those of the authors and do not necessarily reflect the views of the National Science Foundation and should not be interpreted as necessarily representing the official policies, either expressed or implied, of the US Department of Homeland Security.

References

[1] S. Checkoway, D. McCoy, B. Kantor, D. Anderson, H. Shacham, S. Savage, K. Koscher, A. Czeskis, F. Roesner, T. Kohno, et al., Comprehensive experimental analyses of automotive attack surfaces, in: USENIX Security Symposium, San Francisco, CA, 2011.

[2] K. Koscher, A. Czeskis, F. Roesner, S. Patel, T. Kohno, S. Checkoway, D. McCoy, B. Kantor, D. Anderson, H. Shacham, et al., Experimental security analysis of a modern automobile, in: 2010 IEEE Symposium on Security and Privacy (SP), IEEE, 2010, pp. 447–462.

[3] C. Miller, C. Valasek, Adventures in automotive networks and control units, DEF CON 21 (2013) 260–264.

[4] C. Miller, C. Valasek, Remote Exploitation of an Unaltered Passenger Vehicle, in: BlackHat USA, 2015.

[5] M. Hamad, M. Nolte, V. Prevelakis, Towards comprehensive threat modeling for vehicles, in: the 1st Workshop on Security and Dependability of Critical Embedded Real-Time Systems, 2016, p. 31.

[6] C. Ventures, Cybercrime Report 2017. Available from: https://cybersecurityventures.com/hackerpocalypse-cybercrime-report-2016/ (Accessed 31 January 2018).

[7] J. Reilly, S. Martin, M. Payer, A.M. Bayen, Creating complex congestion patterns via multi-objective optimal freeway traffic control with application to cyber-security, Transp. Res. B Methodol. 91 (2016) 366–382.

[8] J. Olofsson, "Zombies ahead!" A study of how hacked digital road signs destabilize the physical space of roadways, Vis. Commun. 13 (1) (2014) 75–93.

[9] K. Hill, "God View": uber allegedly stalked users for party-goers' viewing pleasure (Updated). Available from: https://www.forbes.com/sites/kashmirhill/2014/10/03/god-view-uber-allegedly-stalked-users-for-party-goers-viewing-pleasure/ (Accessed 31 January 2018).

[10] N.T. Courtois, G.V. Bard, D. Wagner, Algebraic and slide attacks on KeeLoq, in: Fast Software Encryption, Springer, Berlin, Heidelberg, 2008, pp. 97–115.

[11] S. Checkoway, D. McCoy, B. Kantor, D. Anderson, H. Shacham, S. Savage, K. Koscher, A. Czeskis, F. Roesner, T. Kohno, Comprehensive experimental analyses of automotive attack surfaces, in: Proceedings of the 20th USENIX Conference on Security, USENIX Association, Berkeley, CA, USA, 2011, p. 6.

[12] S. Woo, H.J. Jo, D.H. Lee, A practical wireless attack on the connected car and security protocol for in-vehicle CAN, IEEE Trans. Intell. Transp. Syst. 16 (2) (2015) 993–1006.

[13] T. Zhang, H. Antunes, S. Aggarwal, Defending connected vehicles against malware: challenges and a solution framework, IEEE Internet Things J. 1 (1) (2014) 10–21.

[14] M.T. Garip, M.E. Gursoy, P. Reiher, M. Gerla, Congestion attacks to autonomous cars using vehicular botnets, in: NDSS Workshop on Security of Emerging Networking Technologies (SENT), 2015.

[15] H. Hasbullah, I.A. Soomro, et al., Denial of service (DOS) attack and its possible solutions in VANET, World Acad. Sci. Eng. Technol. 4 (5) (2010) 813–817.

[16] U.S.R.K. Dhamodharan, R. Vayanaperumal, Detecting and preventing sybil attacks in wireless sensor networks using message authentication and passing method, Sci. World J. 2015 (2015) 1–7.

[17] A. Rawat, S. Sharma, R. Sushil, VANET: security attacks and its possible solutions, J. Inf. Oper. Manag. 3 (1) (2012) 301.

[18] J.B. Kenney, Dedicated short-range communications (DSRC) standards in the United States, Proc. IEEE 99 (7) (2011) 1162–1182.

[19] C.V. Consortium, Vehicle safety communications project-final report, NHTSA Publication DOT HS vol. 810 (2006) 591.

[20] R. Roebuck, DSRC Technology and the DSRC Industry Consortium (DIC) Prototype Team, 28 (2005). Prepared by SIRIT Technologies for ARINDC/US DOT.

[21] J. Harding, G. Powell, R. Yoon, J. Fikentscher, C. Doyle, D. Sade, M. Lukuc, J. Simons, J. Wang, Vehicle-to-vehicle communications: readiness of V2V technology for application, 2014. Tech. Rep.

[22] N. Papernot, P. McDaniel, X. Wu, S. Jha, A. Swami, Distillation as a defense to adversarial perturbations against deep neural networks, in: 2016 IEEE Symposium on Security and Privacy (SP), IEEE, 2016, pp. 582–597.

[23] A. Kurakin, I. Goodfellow, S. Bengio, Adversarial machine learning at scale, 2016. ArXiv preprint arXiv:1611.01236.

[24] L. Huang, A.D. Joseph, B. Nelson, B.I. Rubinstein, J. Tygar, Adversarial machine learning, in: Proceedings of the 4th ACM Workshop on Security and Artificial Intelligence, ACM, 2011, pp. 43–58.

[25] A. Madry, A. Makelov, L. Schmidt, D. Tsipras, A. Vladu, Towards deep learning models resistant to adversarial attacks, 2017. ArXiv Preprint arXiv:1706.06083.

[26] N. Papernot, P. McDaniel, I. Goodfellow, S. Jha, Z.B. Celik, A. Swami, Practical black-box attacks against deep learning systems using adversarial examples, 2016. ArXiv preprint.

[27] M. Wolf, A. Weimerskirch, C. Paar, Security in automotive bus systems, in: Workshop on Embedded Security in Cars, 2004.

[28] H. Ueda, R. Kurachi, H. Takada, T. Mizutani, M. Inoue, S. Horihata, Security authentication system for in-vehicle network, SEI Tech. Rev. (81) (2015) 5–9.

[29] J.A. Bruton, Securing CAN Bus Communication: An Analysis of Cryptographic Approaches, National University of Ireland, Galway, 2014.

[30] W.A. Farag, CANTrack: enhancing automotive CAN bus security using intuitive encryption algorithms, in: 2017 7th International Conference on Modeling, Simulation, and Applied Optimization (ICMSAO), IEEE, 2017, pp. 1–5.

[31] M. Raya, P. Papadimitratos, J.-P. Hubaux, Securing vehicular communications, IEEE Wirel. Commun. 13 (5) (2006) 8–15.

[32] M. Müter, N. Asaj, Entropy-based anomaly detection for in-vehicle networks, in: 2011 IEEE Intelligent Vehicles Symposium (IV), IEEE, 2011, pp. 1110–1115.

[33] T. Hoppe, S. Kiltz, J. Dittmann, Security threats to automotive CAN networks—practical examples and selected short-term countermeasures, Reliab. Eng. Syst. Saf. 96 (1) (2011) 11–25.

[34] U.E. Larson, D.K. Nilsson, E. Jonsson, An approach to specification-based attack detection for in-vehicle networks, in: 2008 IEEE Intelligent Vehicles Symposium, 2008, pp. 220–225.

[35] H.M. Song, H.R. Kim, H.K. Kim, Intrusion detection system based on the analysis of time intervals of CAN messages for in-vehicle network, in: 2016 International Conference on Information Networking (ICOIN), 2016, pp. 63–68.

[36] C. Young, J. Zambreno, G. Bloom, Towards a fail-operational intrusion detection system for in-vehicle networks, in: Proceedings of the Workshop on Security and Dependability of Critical Embedded Real-Time Systems (CERTS), 2016. http://par.nsf.gov/biblio/10040592.

[37] P. Pype, G. Daalderop, E. Schulz-Kamm, E. Walters, M. von Grafenstein, Privacy and security in autonomous vehicles, in: Automated Driving, Springer, 2017, pp. 17–27.

[38] E. Yaßdereli, C. Gemci, A.Z. Aktaş, A study on cyber-security of autonomous and unmanned vehicles, J. Def. Model. Simul. 12 (4) (2015) 369–381.

[39] M. Raya, J.-P. Hubaux, Securing vehicular ad hoc networks, J. Comput. Secur. 15 (1) (2007) 39–68.

[40] I.A. Sumra, H.B. Hasbullah, J.-L.B. AbManan, Attacks on security goals (confidentiality, integrity, availability) in VANET: a survey, in: Vehicular Ad-Hoc Networks for Smart Cities, Springer, 2015, pp. 51–61.

[41] N. Alexiou, M. Laganà, S. Gisdakis, M. Khodaei, P. Papadimitratos, Vespa: vehicular security and privacy-preserving architecture, in: Proceedings of the 2nd ACM Workshop on Hot Topics on Wireless Network Security and PrivacyACM, 2013, pp. 19–24.

[42] W. Whyte, A. Weimerskirch, V. Kumar, T. Hehn, A security credential management system for V2V communications, in: 2013 IEEE Vehicular Networking Conference, 2013, pp. 1–8.

[43] 82 FR 3854—Federal Motor Vehicle Safety Standards; V2V Communications, Fed. Regist. 82 (8) (2017) 3854–4019.

[44] A. Adigun, B.A. Bensaber, I. Biskri, Protocol of change pseudonyms for VANETs, in: 2013 IEEE 38th Conference on Local Computer Networks Workshops (LCN Workshops), IEEE, 2013, pp. 162–167.

[45] M. Gerlach, F. Guttler, Privacy in VANETs using changing pseudonyms-ideal and real, in: IEEE 65th Vehicular Technology Conference, 2007, VTC2007-Spring, IEEE, 2007, pp. 2521–2525.

[46] L. Buttyán, T. Holczer, I. Vajda, On the effectiveness of changing pseudonyms to provide location privacy in VANETs, in: European Workshop on Security in Ad-Hoc and Sensor Networks, Springer, 2007, pp. 129–141.

[47] R. Lu, X. Lin, T.H. Luan, X. Liang, X. Shen, Pseudonym changing at social spots: an effective strategy for location privacy in VANETs, IEEE Trans. Veh. Technol. 61 (1) (2012) 86–96.

[48] K. Sampigethaya, L. Huang, M. Li, R. Poovendran, K. Matsuura, K. Sezaki, CARAVAN: providing location privacy for VANET, Department of Electrical Engineering, Washington University, Seattle, 2005. Tech. Rep.

[49] A. Studer, E. Shi, F. Bai, A. Perrig, TACKing together efficient authentication, revocation, and privacy in VANETs, in: 6th Annual IEEE Communications Society Conference on Sensor, Mesh and Ad Hoc Communications and Networks, 2009, SECON'09, IEEE, 2009, pp. 1–9.

[50] J. Guo, J.P. Baugh, S. Wang, A group signature based secure and privacy-preserving vehicular communication framework, in: 2007 Mobile Networking for Vehicular Environments, IEEE, 2007, pp. 103–108.

[51] L. Sweeney, k-Anonymity: a model for protecting privacy, Int. J. Uncertainty Fuzziness Knowledge Based Syst. 10 (05) (2002) 557–570.

[52] G.P. Corser, H. Fu, A. Banihani, Evaluating location privacy in vehicular communications and applications, IEEE Trans. Intell. Transp. Syst. 17 (9) (2016) 2658–2667.

[53] Y. Feng, X. Li, B. Song, (k, R, r)-anonymity: a light-weight and personalized location protection model for LBS query, in: Proceedings of the ACM Turing 50th Celebration Conference, China, ACM, 2017, p. 29.

[54] C. Caballero-Gil, J. Molina-Gil, J. Hernández-Serrano, O. León, M. Soriano-Ibanez, Providing k-anonymity and revocation in ubiquitous VANETs, Ad Hoc Netw. 36 (2016) 482–494.

[55] W.-D. Yang, Z.-M. Gao, K. Wang, H.-Y. Liu, A privacy-preserving data aggregation mechanism for VANETs, J. High Speed Netw. 22 (3) (2016) 223–230.

[56] C.-W. Chen, S.-Y. Chang, Y.-C. Hu, Y.-W. Chen, Protecting vehicular networks privacy in the presence of a single adversarial authority, in: 2017 IEEE Conference on Communications and Network Security (CNS), IEEE, 2017, pp. 1–9.

[57] T. Zhang, Q. Zhu, Distributed privacy-preserving collaborative intrusion detection systems for VANETs, IEEE Trans. Signal Inf. Process. Netw. 4 (1) (2018) 148–161.

[58] M. Han, Z. Duan, Y. Li, Privacy issues for transportation cyber physical systems, in: Secure and Trustworthy Transportation Cyber-Physical Systems, Springer, 2017, pp. 67–86.

[59] C. Dwork, G.J. Pappas, Privacy in information-rich intelligent infrastructure, 2017. ArXiv preprint arXiv:1706.01985.

[60] D.J. Glancy, Sharing the road: smart transportation infrastructure, Fordham Urb. LJ 41 (2013) 1617.

[61] K.C. Dey, A. Rayamajhi, M. Chowdhury, P. Bhavsar, J. Martin, Vehicle-to-vehicle (V2V) and vehicle-to-infrastructure (V2I) communication in a heterogeneous wireless network-performance evaluation, Transp. Res. C Emerg. Technol. 68 (2016) 168–184.

[62] P. Papadimitratos, A. De La Fortelle, K. Evenssen, R. Brignolo, S. Cosenza, Vehicular communication systems: enabling technologies, applications, and future outlook on intelligent transportation, IEEE Commun. Mag. 47 (11) (2009) 84–95.

[63] US Department of Transportation, Intelligent transportation systems—CV pilot deployment program. Available from: https://www.its.dot.gov/pilots/cv_pilot_apps.htm (Accessed 31 January 2018).

[64] K. Dar, M. Bakhouya, J. Gaber, M. Wack, P. Lorenz, Wireless communication technologies for ITS applications [topics in automotive networking], IEEE Commun. Mag. 48 (5) (2010) 156–162.

[65] M. Faezipour, M. Nourani, A. Saeed, S. Addepalli, Progress and challenges in intelligent vehicle area networks, Commun. ACM 55 (2) (2012) 90–100.

[66] S.L. Garfinkel, Why driver privacy must be a part of ITS, in: L.M. Branscomb, J. Keller (Eds.), Converging Infrastructures: Intelligent Transportation and the National Information Infrastructure, MIT Press, Cambridge, MA, 1996, pp. 324–340.

[67] L. Jacobson, VII Privacy Policies Framework, Version 1.0.2, The Institutional Issues Subcommittee of the National VII Coalition, 2007. Tech. Rep.

[68] M. Gerla, E.-K. Lee, G. Pau, U. Lee, Internet of vehicles: from intelligent grid to autonomous cars and vehicular clouds, in: 2014 IEEE World Forum on Internet of Things (WF-IoT), IEEE, 2014, pp. 241–246.

[69] R. Moalla, B. Lonc, H. Labiod, N. Simoni, Towards a cooperative ITS vehicle application oriented security framework, in: 2014 IEEE Intelligent Vehicles Symposium Proceedings, 2014, pp. 1043–1048.

[70] E.G. AbdAllah, M. Zulkernine, Y.X. Gu, C. Liem, Towards defending connected vehicles against attacks, in: Proceedings of the Fifth European Conference on the Engineering of Computer-Based Systems, ACM, New York, NY, 2017, pp. 9:1–9:9.

[71] M. Gerlach, A. Festag, T. Leinmüller, G. Goldacker, C. Harsch, Security architecture for vehicular communication, in: Workshop on Intelligent Transportation, 2007.

[72] F. Sagstetter, M. Lukasiewycz, S. Steinhorst, M. Wolf, A. Bouard, W.R. Harris, S. Jha, T. Peyrin, A. Poschmann, S. Chakraborty, Security challenges in automotive hardware/software architecture design, in: 2013 Design, Automation Test in Europe Conference Exhibition (DATE), 2013, pp. 458–463.

[73] B. Zheng, W. Li, P. Deng, L. Gérard, Q. Zhu, N. Shankar, Design and verification for transportation system security, in: Proceedings of the 52nd Annual Design Automation Conference, ACM, New York, NY, 2015, pp. 96:1–96:6.

[74] S. Duri, M. Gruteser, X. Liu, P. Moskowitz, R. Perez, M. Singh, J.-M. Tang, Framework for security and privacy in automotive telematics, in: Proceedings of the 2nd International Workshop on Mobile Commerce, ACM, New York, NY, 2002, pp. 25–32.

[75] F. Kargl, P. Papadimitratos, L. Buttyan, M. Müter, E. Schoch, B. Wiedersheim, T.V. Thong, G. Calandriello, A. Held, A. Kung, J.P. Hubaux, Secure vehicular communication systems: implementation, performance, and research challenges, IEEE Commun. Mag. 46 (11) (2008) 110–118.

[76] P. Knapik, E. Schoch, F. Kargl, Electronic decal: a security function based on V2X communication, in: 2013 IEEE 77th Vehicular Technology Conference (VTC Spring), 2013, pp. 1–5.

[77] Transportation Research Board and National Academies of Sciences, Engineering, and Medicine, Protection of Transportation Infrastructure from Cyber Attacks: A Primer, The National Academies Press, Washington, DC, 2016.

[78] K. Zetter, Hackers Can Mess With Traffic Lights to Jam Roads and Reroute Cars, 2014. https://www.wired.com/2014/04/traffic-lights-hacking/.

[79] A. Ghafouri, W. Abbas, Y. Vorobeychik, X. Koutsoukos, Vulnerability of fixed-time control of signalized intersections to cyber-tampering, in: 2016 Resilience Week (RWS), 2016, pp. 130–135.

[80] N. Ekedebe, W. Yu, H. Song, C. Lu, On a Simulation Study of Cyber Attacks on Vehicle-to-Infrastructure Communication (V2I) in Intelligent Transportation System (ITS), in: vol. 9497, International Society for Optics and Photonics, 2015, p. 94970B.

[81] M. Zhao, J. Walker, C.-C. Wang, Security challenges for the intelligent transportation system, in: Proceedings of the First International Conference on Security of Internet of Things, ACM, New York, NY, 2012, pp. 107–115.

[82] E.B. Hamida, H. Noura, W. Znaidi, Security of cooperative intelligent transport systems: standards, threats analysis and cryptographic countermeasures, Electronics 4 (3) (2015) 380–423.

[83] ETSI, Intelligent Transport Systems (ITS); Security; Threat, Vulnerability and Risk Analysis (TVRA), (2010). France, http://www.etsi.org/deliver/etsi_tr/102800_102899/102893/01.01.01_60/tr_102893v010101p.pdf Tech. Rep. ETSI TR 102 893.

[84] NIST, Cybersecurity Framework. Available from: https://www.nist.gov/cyberframework (Accessed 31 January 2018).

[85] M.C. Ramon, D.A. Zajac, Cybersecurity Literature Review and Efforts Report, 2018. http://onlinepubs.trb.org/onlinepubs/nchrp/docs/NCHRP03-127_Cybersecurity_Literature_Review.pdf.

[86] M.N. Mejri, J. Ben-Othman, M. Hamdi, Survey on VANET security challenges and possible cryptographic solutions, Veh. Commun. 1 (2) (2014) 53–66.

[87] E.S. Canepa, C.G. Claudel, Spoofing cyber attack detection in probe-based traffic monitoring systems using mixed integer linear programming, in: 2013 International Conference on Computing, Networking and Communications (ICNC), 2013, pp. 327–333.

[88] B. Ghena, W. Beyer, A. Hillaker, J. Pevarnek, J.A. Halderman, Green lights forever: analyzing the security of traffic infrastructure, in: 8th USENIX Workshop on Offensive Technologies (WOOT 14), USENIX Association, San Diego, CA, 2014. https://www.usenix.org/conference/woot14/workshop-program/presentation/ghena.

[89] A. Laszka, B. Potteiger, Y. Vorobeychik, S. Amin, X. Koutsoukos, Vulnerability of transportation networks to traffic-signal tampering, in: 2016 ACM/IEEE 7th International Conference on Cyber-Physical Systems (ICCPS), 2016, pp. 1–10.

[90] Z. Li, D. Jin, C. Hannon, M. Shahidehpour, J. Wang, Assessing and mitigating cybersecurity risks of traffic light systems in smart cities, IET Cyber-Phys. Syst. Theory Appl. 1 (1) (2016) 60–69.

[91] C. Cottrill, Approaches to privacy preservation in intelligent transportation systems and vehicle-infrastructure integration initiative, Transp. Res. Rec. (2129) (2009) 9–15.

[92] J. Lederman, B.D. Taylor, M. Garrett, A private matter: the implications of privacy regulations for intelligent transportation systems, Transp. Plan. Technol. 39 (2) (2016) 115–135.

Fraud Detection Model Based on Multi-Verse Features Extraction Approach for Smart City Applications

Ali Safa Sadiq*, Hossam Faris[†], Ala' M. Al-Zoubi[†], Seyedali Mirjalili[‡], and Kayhan Zrar Ghafoor[§,¶]

*School of Information Technology, Monash University, Bandar Sunway, Malaysia
[†]Business Information Technology Department, King Abdulla II School for Information Technology, The University of Jordan, Amman, Jordan
[‡]Institute for Integrated and Intelligent Systems, Griffith University, Brisbane, Australia
[§]School of Electronic, Information and Electrical Engineering, Shanghai Jiao Tong University, Shanghai, China
[¶]Department of Computer Science, Faculty of Science, Cihan University-Erbil, Kurdistan, Iraq

1 INTRODUCTION

Credit cards are widely used across the world for purchasing online goods. Nowadays, with the expanded concept of the smart city, online purchasing has become very common due to the large number of benefits. In addition, people also use credit cards for various other online transactions. With all these online transactions happening simultaneously, it is no surprise that fraud can take place during these transactions. Because online transactions involve the Internet, a lot of theft of confidential data can take place. Credit card information is prone to being hacked by fraudsters. Once this information is obtained, misuse can take place, and many unauthorized transactions can happen as a result. These unauthorized transactions are known as fraudulent transactions. Sometimes fraudsters do not have to hack to obtain credit card information. If they manage to obtain the physical card of the user, they can pretend to be the real card holder and start making online transactions. No one will be aware of the fraud taking place unless the real card holder complains about this. However, by the time the user realizes this, it might be too late to take any preventive actions. Therefore, it is important to ensure that credit card fraud is minimized.

The main objective of the credit card fraud detection system (CCFDS) is to classify data according to genuine or fraud transactions. Credit card companies or online merchants should aim to have a system that can detect a fraudulent transaction and prevent that transaction from taking place. Some companies have existing systems equipped with algorithms that rely on deep learning or pattern recognition based on the history of given transactions in order to discover relationships leading to the detection of fraud. However, these systems tend to have false positive alarms, whereby the wrong classification could be made [1,2]. For example, a genuine transaction could be mistakenly classified as fraudulent, and vice versa. Hence, to detect fraudulent transactions correctly, the false positive alarms need to be reduced by coming up with a more effective detection model. Therefore, classification of the supplied data samples is important to determine which transactions are genuine and which should be categorized as fraud.

There are several requirements and constraints that CCFDS needs to meet [3]. In terms of requirements, any detection system needs to be able to correctly classify the transactions as genuine or fraudulent. This is the main requirement of the CCFDS, because without fulfilling this requirement, the potential of such a system will fail to meet the objective. In addition, to ensure the efficiency of the detection system, dataset samples should be carefully analyzed to figure out the different set of features that the fraudsters attempt in each attack to ensure that CCFDS can perform its intended function. Finally, the system needs to be able to complete the desired tasks in a timely manner.

A recent e-Commerce merchants' survey that was conducted by [4] highlighted the percentage of rejected orders that respondents believed to actually be valid—which had been determined to be false positives—was found to be 8.6%. This rate is the foundation for fear for two reasons. First, one in every 10 orders was mistakenly turned down, leading to lost revenue, which is mostly noticeable if the transaction amount was significant. Second, a genuine customer in e-Commerce had the bad experience of getting his or her order terminated, which is considered a kind of "customer insult" that can cause a drop in return visits or satisfaction ratings. The main reason behind this substantial problem is the lack of accuracy in identifying fraud in e-Commerce transactions [4,5].

The process of identifying and locating the sources of fraud in e-Commerce is still time consuming; sources are identified long after the fraud is completed. Hence, these strategies are unable to stop cybercrimes, and also unable to prevent further occurrences of such crimes in the future. In order to identify fraudulent cases, an efficient and effective model should be established to figure out the possible detection patterns, which can help in forming an accurate classifier to be used in detecting fraud for e-Commerce security. The open challenge that could be highlighted here is that the detection rate decreases significantly when the number of features and training samples increase [2]. Because features extraction is a process of selecting a set of F features from a data set of N features, $F < N$, the cost of some evaluation function or measure will be optimized over the space of all possible feature subsets of fraudulent cases. There are still many obstacles that the feature extraction procedure must overcome to improve its accuracy in removing the nondominated features, and accordingly, its ability to reduce the training time and mitigate the complexity of the developed classification models.

It is worth mentioning that numerous studies have highlighted that attempting the feature extraction technique usually contributes to enhancements in predictive accuracy, and improvements in the clarity and generality of the developed model, which is still an open research problem [1]. On the other hand, extracting the best subset of features that helps in accurately identifying fraud from all possible 2N subsets is not an easy task, and tends to be a nonpolynomial complex problem during the rise of searching space [1]. By shedding light on SVM, its performance could be significantly enhanced by obtaining a systematic features extraction model. The same is true for data mining and machine learning techniques.

The rest of this chapter is organized as follows: Section 2 delivers related works and the literature review of recent trends in this area, including feature extraction as the main area of this work. The proposed credit card fraud detection system is discussed in Section 3. The results are presented and analyzed in Section 4. Section 5 concludes the chapter and suggests future studies.

2 RELATED WORK

The CCFDS mainly monitors the users' behavior as a way to guess, identify, or prevent undesirable behavior. As a way to come up with an effective CCFDS, it is very important to comprehend the existing techniques used in detecting frauds cases. Thus, there are many techniques that have been looked at in this chapter that have been used to detect credit card fraud. Many researchers have studied the different techniques to determine their effectiveness in detecting fraud. Each technique has its own unique way of determining whether a transaction is genuine or fraudulent. The methods used to detect credit card fraud include decision trees, genetic algorithms, neural networks, and many more. For example, there are artificial neural-network models that fall under the category of artificial intelligence, machine learning, and sequence alignment algorithms, which rely on the expenditure figure of the cardholder [6]. On the other hand, as a way to improve the fraud detection competence and decrease economic loss, some other technologies incorporate a web services-based two-way scheme for CCFD in which involved banks can share the knowledge about fraud patterns in a heterogeneous and disseminated environment. We will now take a closer look at these techniques via the following sub-sections. Before we go in details of related works, we would like to provide the readers with a quick overview on some statistical analysis on the role of e-Commerce cyber security and its implication on the roadmap plan of potential smart city application. Malaysian e-Commerce will be discussed in the following paragraphs to brief this role as a use case.

Customers are increasingly buying more goods and services online with their mobile devices. At the same time, e-Commerce retailers must defend themselves and their customers from the threat of online fraud. Yet most e-Commerce systems are enforced to fight those challenges while drawing on constricted, static fraud management budgets and limited resources. Fraud management is a critical factor of operating an e-Commerce website, because it is essentially tied directly to a merchant's bottom line. To comprehend what merchants in Asia, and Malaysia in

eCommerce contribution to GDP
(RM billion)

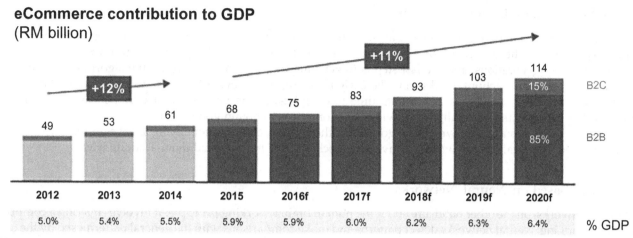

FIG. 1   Malaysia e-Commerce growth.

particular, are concerned with in fraud management, Cyber Source commissioned an inaugural online payment fraud survey for this region. A total of 152 merchants took part, representing an even spread across the top Southeast Asia e-Commerce markets in size and growth rate—Indonesia, Malaysia, the Philippines, Singapore, and Thailand. In terms of e-Commerce revenue, 51.3% have an annual turnover of less than US$5M, while 48.7% have an annual turnover of US$5M or more [4,5].

In Malaysia, there has been tremendous growth in online sales, with the e-Commerce contribution to the Gross Domestic Product GDP estimated to be RM 68 billion in 2015 (see Fig. 1). B2C and B2B are two forms of commercial transactions. B2C, which stands for business-to-consumer, is a process for selling products directly to consumers. B2B, which stands for business-to-business, is a process for selling products or services to other businesses. From this observation of high growth of using e-Commerce, there is an essential desire to provide effective fraud detection for e-commerce security. The following sub-sections discuss different state-of-the-art approaches that are proposed to address the issues of detection accuracy of CCFD models.

2.1 CCFD Based on Decision Trees and SVM

According to P.R. Shimpi in the article titled "Survey on Credit Card Fraud Detection Techniques," the authors have described several techniques that can be used to detect credit card fraud. This includes genetic algorithms. The decision tree is a technique that uses a depth-first, greedy approach to partitioning data until all the data belongs to a special class. The decision tree is one of the techniques that has been applied for fraud detection [7]. It produces a classifier utilizing a tree architecture; the leaf in this technique designates attributes of a given transaction, decision nodes that identify a check on the value of a feature, and a branch for each possible solution, which could produce a sub-tree or a new leaf [8]. Decision trees also have their limitations; for example, they are prone to sampling.

The authors in [9], have proposed a CCFDS based on a number of decision tree and SVM methods. Using their system, each account has been individually monitored via appropriate descriptors, and the transactions were recognized and labelled as fraudulent or normal. They have developed their detection algorithm based on the score gain that indicates the suspicion rate of each given transection that was obtained by the developed classifier models. Thus, whenever a new transection takes place, the classifier predicts whether its fraud or normal. The given scores assist the staff in making further decisions on the transaction to be blocked or not, rather than organizations involving more man-power to filter and make decisions. The authors in [9] reported that the preciseness of obtaining a score in this regard still represents a challenge. Moreover, the use of SVM in training, and in validating huge amounts of transection data to build the classifier model is still challenging due to the fact that tuning SVM parameters is an open issue, including Cost (C), gamma (γ), and Radial Basis Function (RBF) [10].

Although in most cases, obtained scores from these classification algorisms are not directly adopted, they are mostly used to assist the inspection staff within the area of expertise to inspect and attempt to recognize the fraud. Because the organizations have limited staff for this process, the ability of the detection systems to produce accurate suspicion scores helps these staffs in many ways. Nevertheless, the success of the detection systems lies in distinguishing the fraudulent transactions from legitimate ones through producing suspicion scores with high precision.

2.2 CCFD Based on Genetic Algorithms

Genetic algorithms, on the other hand, use an algorithm to detect frauds. There are four main steps, which are: first, to input a group of credit card transaction data, then compute the critical values, generate critical values found after a limited number of generations, and the last step is to generate fraud transactions using the algorithm. By knowing which are the fraud transactions, banks can take early measures and prevent these transactions from taking place. Generic algorithms can sometimes take a long time to complete, as the population size influences the results [7]. If the size of the population is small, then it will take a long time to obtain good results.

To sum up, GA is a successful wrapper algorithm, although it is computationally expensive and likely to impulsively converge into local optima when the diversity mechanism is not adjusted in an accurate way.

2.3 CCFD Based on Neural Networks

Neural networks, on the other hand, are about the human brain's working principle. It involves making a computer capable of thinking. Neural networks detect patterns and make comparisons with the general pattern used by the card holder. If an unusual pattern is detected, then that transaction has a high chance of being fraudulent. An article by R. Patidar and L. Sharma focuses on neural networks in credit card fraud detection. They have done extensive research on neural networks, and have found several problems. One is that before beginning training, several parameters of neural networks need to be set up, such as connection weights, number of neurons in the hidden layer, number of input features, learning rate, momentum, and other factors. The selection of these parameters will determine the success rate at which fraudulent transactions are detected. However, there are no optimal rules on how to set up these parameters [11]. Hence, researchers much continue to work on optimizing the accuracy rate of CCFD. This must be done in addition to combining genetic algorithms with neural networks to determine the types of credit card fraud (Fig. 2).

2.4 CCFD Based on Bayesian Networks

The article titled "Analysis on Credit Card Fraud Detection Methods," discusses Bayesian networks. In the technique described, two Bayesian networks are constructed. One is to model the behavior of the fraud, and the other is to model the behavior of a legitimate user. The fraud network is set up using expert knowledge, and the legitimate user network is set up using data from the nonfraudulent user [12]. The idea is to determine the conditional probability via a directed acyclic graph. However, Bayesian networks have several limitations, as it can be difficult to convert expert knowledge into probability distributions [13].

2.5 CCFD Based on the Hidden Markov Model

The authors of the aforementioned article "Analysis on Credit Card Fraud Detection Methods" have also discussed the Hidden Markov model. This model uses an algorithm to determine fraudulent transactions. The model is trained and tested to determine whether a transaction is fraudulent or not [12]. Hence, when a transaction tends to not be accepted by the Hidden Markov model, by being given a high probability indexed value, the transaction is determined to be fraudulent. The limitation with the Hidden Markov model is that there are often large numbers of unstructured parameters [12]. Fig. 3 presents the state diagram of the proposed Hidden Markov model for CCFD.

2.6 CCFD Based on Parenclitic Networks Reconstruction

Although data mining algorithms are widely used for determining hidden patterns in data, they typically facing a shortcoming in terms of the capability of synthesizing metrics that could provide a clear image of the comprehensive structure

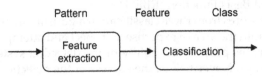

FIG. 2   Pattern recognition in neural network [11].

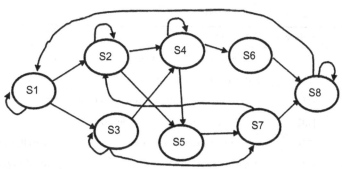

FIG. 3 State diagrams of hidden markov model.

obtained by the relations among the diverse features in data. In the past few years, there was a diverse usage of the complex networks theory as one of the approaches to overcoming this constraint. Therefore, as an attempt to address this challenge, researchers have proposed parenclitic network reconstruction, which is a technique in which the difference between one data instance and another set of standards are highlighted [14]. This means that the real data set is used for verification purposes. Thus, each transaction is compared with the standards of the real data set, which acts as a threshold. This is a type of data mining process. There are several limitations to this method. Mainly, false positive alarms can occur frequently, and it can be difficult to detect them when they occur. False positive alarms can occur when the transaction has related results with the real data set, because they will be deemed valid transactions, although they could be fraudulent. Accordingly, there will be no additional verifications triggered. Hence, false positives alarms can happen. Therefore, it can be said that there are many techniques to detect sources of credit card fraud. Each of these techniques has its own strengths and weaknesses. However, if implemented while taking in consideration of optimizing the features extraction model, they can serve their purpose and more accurately detect fraud transactions while using credit cards in e-Commerce.

2.7 CCFD Based on Meta-Learning

Meta learning is a technique whereby legitimate transactions are filtered out from a dataset containing both legitimate and fraudulent transaction data. There process includes the arbiter and combiner strategies. However, it was discovered that the combining strategy was more efficient in performance compared with the arbiter strategy [15]. Hence, the combining strategy is used in detecting credit card fraud in e-Commerce. Attributes and correct classification of credit card transaction instances are used to train multiple base classifiers. The original attributes and the base classifiers are normally combined, and a new set of features is created for each instance of correct classification. This new set is used as training data to generate meta-level classifiers. The prediction made from the meta-level classifiers is then used as the final detection. The main limitation in this method is the complexity and the difficulty of adapting to new forms of fraud. In another words, the created classifier will be running based on the extracted set of features using an arbitrary strategy, which may lead to fraud detection accuracy issues.

2.8 Summary of CCFD Based on Classification Algorithms

Feature extraction is the procedure of selecting a set of F features from a data set of N features, $F < N$, thus the cost of some evaluation functions or measures will be optimized over the space of all possible feature subsets. The aim of the feature extraction procedure is to remove the nondominant features and accordingly reduce the training time and mitigate the complexity of the developed classification models. Numerous studies have highlighted that attempting the feature extraction technique usually contributes to enhancements in predictive accuracy, and improvements in the clarity and generality of the developed model [1]. On the other hand, extracting the best subset of features that helps in accurately identifying fraud from all possible $2N$ subsets is not an easy task, and tends to be a nonpolynomial complex problem during the increase of searching space [1]. By shedding the light on SVM, its performance could be significantly enhanced by obtaining a systematic feature election model, as the same applies to data mining and machine learning techniques. Each of the preceding methods has its benefits and disadvantages. Table 1 summarizes the methods used in identifying fraud.

TABLE 1   Summary of Credit Card Fraud Detection Models

Technique	Reference	Advantage	Disadvantage
Decision tree	[7]	Powerful detection technique	Tree structure prone to sampling
Genetic algorithm	[7]	Supports multi-objective	May require a lot of time
Neural networks	[11]	Can handle substantial amounts of data	No clear rules to set up parameters
Bayesian networks	[13]	Suitable for small and incomplete data sets	Collecting and structuring expert knowledge
Hidden Markov model	[12]	Strong statistical foundation	Have large numbers of unstructured parameters
Parenclitic networks reconstruction	[14]	Time efficient	False positive alarms can occur
Meta-learning	[16]	High accuracy	Low speed of detection

3 PROPOSED CREDIT CARD FRAUD DETECTION MODEL BASED ON MULTI-VERSE FEATURES EXTRACTION (CCFD-MVFEX)

In this section, our proposed credit card detection model, CCFD-MVFEX, is discussed. The proposed model relies on two main components, which are SVM and Multi-Verse Features Extraction (MVFEX). The model was constructed based on the hybridization of SVM and MVFEX in order to overcome the limitations of SVM in classification and detection. Thus, the following subsections discuss the main concepts of SVM, as well as the technical concept of MVFEX and the use of the hybrid optimizer in building the CCFD model.

3.1 Support Vector Machine

As we have discussed, SVM is considered one of the highly used models to approximate and classify data for a given problem, such as the issue of identifying credit card fraud. SVM was first proposed and developed by Vapnik in [17]. SVM has applications for classification, as well as regression related problems. The authors in [18] have conducted extensive comparative research, and they have highlighted that SVM performs among the best classifiers developed so far. In comparison with the other classifiers, SVM relies mainly on the training process as a way to construct its model. SVM moves across the training data using a nonlinear mapping function, which is a concept known as the kernel trick. Thus, the training data transforms to the higher dimensional space, whereby the data of online transactions can be alienated linearly. Or, to identify the best hyper-planes (support vectors) with the greatest normalized margin, considering the data points that assist in building a general fraud detection model. Hence, the main objective of the learning course of SVM is to find out the optimal linear hype-planes in a given dimension [19]. Fig. 4 illustrates the binary classification of our proposed model in classifying the dataset of online transactions by SVM's optimal hyperplanes.

By assuming that having a dataset $\{Ai, Bi\}i = 1, \dots n$ where the Ai is the inserted dataset with f number of features used in the training set, Bi is the targeted class, (fraud/nonfraud (genuine transaction)). The ultimate goal of the SVM algorithm is to draw the linear decision function specified in Eq. (1):

$$f(x) = (w, \mu_i(x)) + b \tag{1}$$

where w is the weight value and b is the constant value of SVM, which will be projected from the dataset. The μ is a nonlinear function that plots the input features to a higher feature space.

The main challenge when constructing a CCFD model based on SVM is in selection of kernel functions and the values of their parameters, which have a serious influence on the accuracy of the SVM model. The values of SVM parameters have significant influence of its performance. As per argued in Section 2, there are various methods used for optimizing these parameters. Meanwhile, the metaheuristic algorithms have recently proved to be effective in finding the optimal values for optimization problems; hence, we have applied MVFEX optimization to improve the accuracy of identifying the source of credit card fraud, which is considered as the main contribution to CCFD.

3.2 Multi-Verse Feature EXtraction Model (MVFEX)

In this section we present the optimization algorithm called the multi-verse optimizer [20], which is used in developing our MVFEX. The multi-verse optimizer is an evolutionary metaheuristic algorithm that mimics the rules of the common theory known as multi-verse. The robustness of this algorithm comes from the ability of interactions among searching

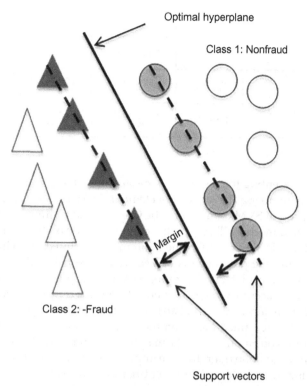

FIG. 4 Optimal hyperplane in support vector machine for classifying credit card fraud.

agents in finding the optimum solution, (in our case it is represented with the best set of features that identify the sources of CCF and the parameter values of the SVM model used in classification). The interaction was simulated using black, white, and worm holes, which has mainly been inspired from the theory of the existence of multiple universes. The main feature of this algorithm is an effective population-based stochastic behavior that helps approximate the global optimum for our optimization for the fraud detection model, and gathering multiple fraudulent detection patterns.

To simulate this algorithm, two factors need be calculated initially as a way to update the obtained set of fraudulent features and SVM parameters: Wormhole Existence Probability (WEP) and Traveling Distance Rate (TDR). These factors assist in indicating how frequently and how much the value of the detection accuracy varies throughout the optimization course. These factors are defined as follows:

$$WEP = \beta + i \times \left(\frac{\partial - \beta}{I}\right)$$

where β is the minimum value, ∂ is the maximum value, i is the current iteration, and I symbolizes the maximum number of iterations allowed.

$$TDR = 1 - \frac{i^{1/\gamma}}{I^{1/\gamma}}$$

To present the research methodology used for identifying the sources of fraud in e-Commerce, Fig. 4 depicts the following phases: fraudulent features extraction, constructing detection patterns, multi-verse model development, model design and implementation, testing and evaluation.

At first, e-Commerce data are captured and analyzed for online merchants (we have initially collected data samples of online merchants from Germany, Taiwan, Australia, and Japan) to trigger anomaly behaviors based on an extracted set of features and their correlation with each class (Fraudulent or Genuine). Then, the extracted subset of features is investigated further upon verifying the confusion matrix (see Fig. 5), which subsequently extracts the possible detection pattern of the recognized fraud. The feature wrapper method is exploited by the proposed model to evaluate subsets of variables, which allows detection of the possible interactions between variables. Features of transactions are, therefore, investigated to extract and collect all possible patterns of fraud in e-Commerce.

The model is constructed in three phases. First, the proposed multi-verse optimization (MVO) algorithm is used for features extraction and SVM parameters optimization for fraud detection in e-Commerce. The second phase is to define the fitness function, and the third is the model architecture. We have applied an encoding scheme for

		Actual class	
		Positive	Negative
Predicted class	Positive	True positive (TP)	False positive (FP)
	Negative	False negative (FN)	True negative (TN)

FIG. 5 Confusion matrix.

representing MVO universes, representing the algorithm's parameters of e-Commerce data samples. The individuals will be encoded as a vector of real numbers. The number of elements in each vector equals the number of features in the dataset, plus two elements to represent SVM parameters: the Cost (C) and Gamma (γ). In order to assess the generated universes (solutions), the developed model will rely on the confusion matrix shown in Fig. 5, which is considered the primary source for evaluating classification models. The main model architecture will be applied to perform fraudulent features extraction and optimize the parameters of SVM simultaneously using the MVO algorithm.

Afterward, the sources of fraudulent detection components are designed based on extracted features and constructed patterns with respect to the accuracy measurement of optimized SVM classifiers. Every generated solution by MVO, which represents the parameters of SVM and an extracted set of selected features, is assessed using the fitness function, which is the accuracy as determined based on the confusion matrix evaluation. The evolutionary cycle of MVO as static until a termination condition is met (a maximum number of iterations as a termination condition was set). Also, in this phase the reproduction operators are implemented, which are applied by MVO in order to evolve the generated universes searching for a better quality identifier of fraudulent sources. The general flowchart of the architecture of the proposed model is shown in Fig. 6.

In the final phase, the proposed model is tested through mathematical model and simulation experiments using the Matlab tool. A separate experiment is conducted to test the capability of the model in extracting fraudulent features to be used in constructing detection patterns, and the accuracy of identified sources of fraud in e-Commerce. Statistical measurements and quantitative evaluation are performed for each experiment to prove the accomplishment of the proposed model. The results will be evaluated using different datasets. The following section demonstrates the results and evaluation of our proposed model.

4 RESULTS AND DISCUSSION

In order to benchmark the performance of the proposed CCFD-MVFEX model, four standard datasets are employed: German, Australian, Taiwanese, and Japanese; which are achieved from the UCI Repository of Machine Learning Databases [21]. For verification, the results of MVO+SVM are compared with those obtained by NB, Multi-Layer Perceptron (MLP), Neural Networks (k-NN), Radial basis function Neural Networks, and a Support Vector Machine equipped with a grid search (SVM+Grid Search). The metric to quantify the performance of these algorithms is the accuracy of the solution obtained at the end of the classification process.

Inspecting the results in Table 2, it is evident that the accuracy of the results obtained by the proposed CCFD-MVFEX is better than other methods in three datasets: German, Australian, and Japanese. In the Taiwan dataset, this algorithm is the third best algorithm. The reason for the better results obtained by the proposed model is due to the use of MVO. The MVO algorithm is one of the recent evolutionary algorithms that has been proven to benefit from high exploration and local optima avoidance. This algorithm has been equipped with adaptive randomized operators that assist it in providing time-varying stochastic behaviors when solving optimization problems. The CFFD classifier is trained using the MVO algorithm to better handle such challenging problems, and with highly multi-modal search landscapes. The stochastic operators of MVO assist SVM to better classify fraud transactions.

The second best algorithm s is the SVM+grid search. However, CCFD using an SVM classifier optimized visa grid search method still suffers from computational time complexity. The reason behind that is the necessity for an enormous amount of potential evaluations [22,23]. Hence, we could observe that our proposed model maintains efficient solutions for improving the performance of SVM, and the factors of its kernel, by extracting the best set of features that help in identifying fraud.

One of the worst training algorithms is MLP as per the results in Table 2. This is due to the Back Propagation (BP), which is the default training algorithm for MLP. The BP algorithm is a conventional optimization technique to find the

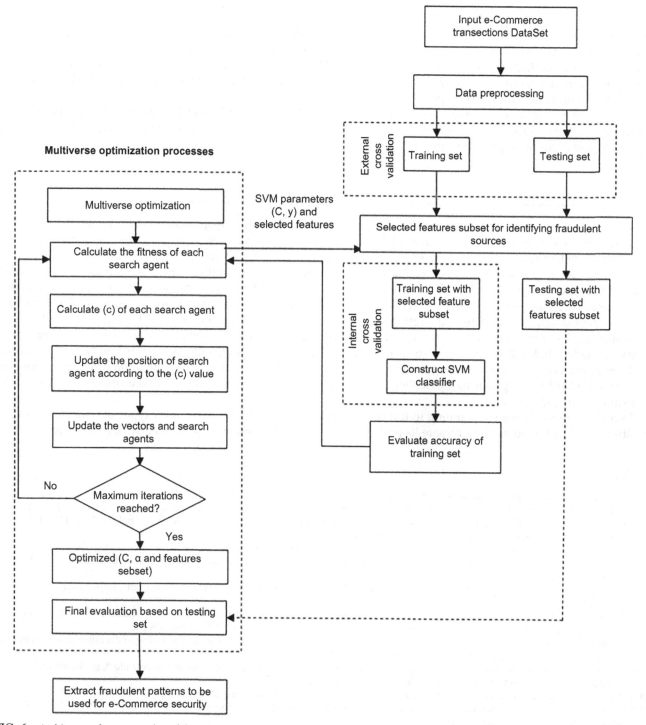

FIG. 6 Architecture for proposed model.

TABLE 2 Benchmark Accuracy Measure of Proposed CCFD-MVFEX

Dataset	CCFD-NB Accuracy	CCFD-MLP Accuracy	CCFD-K-NN Accuracy	CCFD-RbfNetwork Accuracy	CCFD-SVM + Grid search Accuracy	CCFD-MVFEX Accuracy
Germany	72.70	66.00	69.50	73.20	71.47	**74.00**
Australia	77.54	83.77	82.03	80.29	83.33	**85.65**
Taiwan	67.43	80.91	76.92	79.10	**81.80**	79.11
Japan	77.68	83.04	81.01	80.00	85	**86.09**

The highlighted bold accuracy values are the best achieved average accuracy per dataset, which obviously show that our proposed model could obtain with Germany, Australia as well as Japan data sets the best average value in comparison with other benchmarked methods.

optimal values for the connection weights and biases. This algorithm is beneficial when classifying nonlinear and small datasets. However, its performance degrades substantially proportional to the number of features and training samples of e-Commerce data. The search landscapes of the CCFD of training MLP when classifying challenging datasets is highly multi-modal, so most of the conventional techniques get trapped in local solutions of classified transactions. This is the main reason for the poor performance of MLP.

Taken together, these results show that the idea of using the CCFD-MVFEX model is beneficial to designing a more accurate credit card fraud detection system. Classification is one of the main steps in fraud detection systems, so using a reliable and accurate algorithm is essential.

5 CONCLUSION

This chapter has presented a new model called the multi-verse feature extraction model. This model is used to improve the detection accuracy of sources of fraud for e-Commerce security. After an intensive survey, we have observed that identifying fraudulent patterns can be efficiently accomplished via identifying salient features that could assist in constructing a sensitive detection model. Utilizing the best representative subset of features for online transactions, the classification could take place in identifying the attempt to determine whether the transaction is fraudulent or genuine. Therefore, in this chapter we have developed our classifier using the SVM model with an MVO optimizer and features extractor, which achieved an effective detection model that can be applied in detecting credit card fraud in e-Commerce. The proposed model was implemented and evaluated using the Matlab tool, with the following benchmark methods: NB, Multi-Layer Perceptron (MLP), Neural Networks (k-NN), Radial basis function Neural Networks, and a Support Vector Machine equipped with a grid search (SVM+Grid Search). The evaluation proved that our proposed CCFD-MVFEX outperforms the existing methods in an average of tested online datasets of German, Australian, Taiwanese, and Japanese.

In our future work, we are planning to test our proposed model with more complex types of data samples with multi-dimensional features and evaluate its performance with more comparisons of recently developed approaches.

References

[1] G. Chandrashekar, F. Sahin, A survey on feature selection methods, Comput. Electr. Eng. 40 (1) (2014) 16–28.
[2] C.-F. Chao, M.-H. Horng, The construction of support vector machine classifier using the firefly algorithm, Comput. Intell. Neurosci. (2015) 1–8.
[3] D.A. Alejandro Correa Bahnsen, Feature engineering strategies for credit card fraud detection, Expert Syst. Appl. 51 (2016) 134–142.
[4] CyberSource Corporation, North America Online Fraud Benchmark Report, 2017.
[5] CyberSource Corporation, Online Fraud Benchmark Report, Southeast Asia Edition (2016).
[6] A. Kundu, S. Panigrahi, S. Sural, A.K. Majumdar, BLAST-SSAHA hybridization for credit card fraud detection, IEEE Trans. Depend. Secure Comput. 6 (4) (2009) 309–315.
[7] P.R. Shimpi, Survey on credit card fraud detection techniques, Int. J. Eng. Comput. Sci. 4 (11) (2016) 15010–15015, https://doi.org/10.18535/ijecs/v4i11.25.
[8] R.F. Lima, A.C.M. Pereira, Feature selection approaches to fraud detection in e-payment systems, in: International Conference on Electronic Commerce and Web Technologies, Springer, 2017, pp. 111–126, https://doi.org/10.1007/978-3-319-53676-7 9.
[9] Y. Sahin, E. Duman, Detecting credit card fraud by decision trees and support vector machines, in: Proceeding of the International Multi Conference of Engineering's and Computer Scientists, 16–18 March, 2011, pp. 1–6.
[10] A. Rodan, H. Faris, Credit risk evaluation using cycle reservoir neural networks with support vector machines readout, in: Asian Conference on Intelligent Information and Database Systems, Springer, 2016, pp. 595–604.
[11] R. Patidar, L. Sharma, Credit card fraud detection using neural network, Int. J. Soft Comput. Eng. 1 (NCAI2011) (2011) 32–38.
[12] Renu, Suman, Analysis on credit card fraud detection methods, Int. J. Comput. Trends Technol. 8 (1) (2014) 45–51. ISSN: 2231-2803. Seventh Sense Research Group. www.ijcttjournal.org.
[13] L. Uusitalo, Advantages and challenges of Bayesian networks in environmental modelling, Sci. Dir. 203 (2007) 312–318.
[14] M. Zanin, M. Romance, S. Moral, R. Criado, Credit card fraud detection through parenclitic network analysis, Soc. Inf. Netw. 2017 arXiv preprint arXiv:1706.01953.
[15] D.L. Talekar, K. Adhiya, Credit card fraud detection system: a survey, Int. Open Access J. Mod. Eng. Res. 4 (9) (2014) 24–31.
[16] A.G. Neha Sethi, A revived survey of various credit card fraud detection techniques, Int. J. Comput. Sci. Mob. Comput. 3 (2014) 780–791.
[17] V. Vapnik, An overview of statistical learning theory, IEEE Trans. Neural Netw. (5) (1999) 988–999.
[18] M. Fernandez-Delgado, E. Cernadas, S. Barro, D. Amorim, Do we need hundreds of classifiers to solve real world classification problems? J. Mach. Learn. Res. 15 (1) (2014) 3133–3181.
[19] S. Eswaramoorthy, S. Eswaramoorthy, N. Sivakumaran, N. Sivakumaran, S. Sekaran, S. Sekaran, Grey wolf optimization based parameter selection for support vector machines, Int. J. Comput. Math. Electr. Electron. Eng. 35 (5) (2016) 1513–1523.
[20] S. Mirjalili, S.M. Mirjalili, A. Hatamlou, Multi-verse optimizer: a nature-inspired algorithm for global optimization, Neural Comput. & Applic. 27 (2) (2016) 495–513.
[21] M. Lichman, UCI Machine Learning Repository, 2013.

[22] C. Staelin, Parameter selection for support vector machines, Hewlett-Packard Company, 2003. Tech. Rep. HPL-2002-354R1.

[23] X.L. Zhang, X.F. Chen, Z.J. He, An ACO-based algorithm for parameter optimization of support vector machines, Expert Syst. Appl. 37 (9) (2010) 6618–6628.

Further Reading

[24] L. Delamaire, H.A.H. Abdou, J. Pointon, Credit card fraud and detection techniques: a review, Banks Bank Syst. 4 (2) (2009) 57–68.

[25] P. Dostal, P. Pokorny, Cluster Analysis and Neural Network, Department of Informatics, Faculty of Business and Management, Brno University of Technology, 2017.

[26] M.A.T. Mohammed, A.S. Sadiq, R.A. Arshah, F. Ernawan, S. Mirjalili, Soft set decision/forecasting system based on hybrid parameter reduction algorithm, J. Telecommun. Electron. Comput. Eng. 9 (2–7) (2017) 143–148.

[27] D. Das, A.S. Sadiq, N.B. Ahmad, J. Lloret, Stock market prediction with big data through hybridization of data mining and optimized neural network techniques, J. Mult. Valued Log. Soft Comput. 29 (1/2) (2017) 157–181.

18

Privacy Preserving Data Utility Mining Architecture

Yousra Abdul Alsahib S. Aldeen*,† and Mazleena Salleh†

*Department of Computer Science, College of Science for Women, University of Baghdad, Baghdad, Iraq
†Faculty of Computing, University Technology Malaysia, Skudai, Malaysia

1 INTRODUCTION

Creation and innovation in smart cities do not originally lie in the applications, but also in the utilization of implicit technologies that enable them. Numerous technologies usually associated with the smart city are smart cards, ubiquitous connectivity, (participatory) sensor networks, the Internet of Things (IoT), wearable devices, autonomous systems, intelligent vehicles, open data, and cloud computing (CC). CC has emerged as an outstanding service, and has radically transformed the information technology industry [1]. Certainly, it is not only an innovative blending of new Internet services and notions, but also future economic solutions [2, 3]. Stakeholders engaged in computing business chains can reduce their financial investments in hardware, data storage utilization, and computational power by availing themselves of the benefits of this novel electronic-trade model [4]. Literally, customers from every field (academics, science, technology, engineering, and medicine) are taking advantage of the notable benefits of CC [5]. It enables a multitenant environment, where users collaboratively share data. The widespread popularity of CC has prompted the majority of well-known organizations to develop their IT systems on it. Despite several attractive features, CC faces various challenges, such as quality improvement of services, security enhancement, scalability requirements, and so forth.

One of the most significant issues in privacy is to protect sensitive financial and health records from falling into the hands of those committing fraud and phishing incursions [6]. Medical data, which contains sensitive information, is highly useful to the research community for disease analyses, drug development, and subsequent cures. Thus, anonymization mediated privacy preserving data mining appears to be an urgent necessity because it is difficult to extract important and useful information from anonymized data. Anonymization not only assures privacy requirements, but also protects the data utility. Furthermore, it is mandatory to remove the link between sensitive data and individuals prior to publishing. Elimination of the classified information from released data is not enough to impart SSN privacy. Research has revealed that using partial identification and available information (quasiidentifiers) such as individual age, gender, ZIP code, and data records that direct re-identification of dataset information is possible [7]. Various privacy metrics, including adversary models, are accessible to prevent such identification [8–10]. For example, in K-anonymity, each tuple t is required to be anonymitized with at least $(K-1)$ additional tuples. Indistinguishability occurs when two individual records agree with a set of quasiidentifier attributes.

Over the years, many algorithms have been proposed to achieve the fundamental privacy standards by generalized manipulation, where the data values are replaced through general values. These general values characterize the original ones by suggesting other atomic values, such as "rose" being changed to "flower," which is common in numerous proposed algorithms. Unlike the perturbation technique, this generalization applies the noise data cells individually before publishing, and consequently preserves the data truthfulness. Moreover, the occurrence of information loss and overgeneralization limits the privacy requirements. To overcome such shortcomings, various heuristics approaches have been designed. Again, the relatively small output space of these techniques leads to huge data loss in the presence of strict privacy requirements. Thus, utility preservation in generalization-based approaches remains a challenging task. Issues such as overgeneralization of outliers in private datasets and increasing the number of groups are the other concerns [11].

To overcome such limitations, a hybrid K-anonymity data relocation technique is proposed. By combining the generalization technique with a data relocation approach, more utilized anonymizations are achieved. The overall utility is enhanced at the cost of truthfulness. Through data relocation, the number of groups is reduced, and their tuples are populated, and belong to small, equal groups. The overrelocation that leads to localized utility and harmful truthfulness is not considered. This target archives by bounding the number of relocations, and controls the tradeoff between utility and truthfulness. However, small numbers of relocations can stop overgeneralization.

2 PRIVACY CHALLENGES IN CC

While the storage of data on remote servers is not a new development, the present expansion of CC justifies a more careful look at its actual results, including privacy issues. Addressing privacy issues is difficult when there is extensive use of CC [12, 13]. The major reasons and the main issues leading to violations of privacy in CC are described as follows:

(i) Publishing or distributing clients' data in CC has many limitations. One of the key concerns is privacy exposure of the client data and the resulting patterns.
(ii) Privacy preservation for the growing data is still a challenging task, and it needs a thorough investigation. Existing traditional approaches suffer from performance overhead.
(iii) Lately, varieties of data mining techniques on CC have been implemented to aid the decision-making process. These techniques are used to extract the hidden information from huge datasets in the form of new models, trends, and diverse patterns.
(iv) Protection of utility is still considered a primary issue, particularly for generalization-based methods. One of the prime reasons of overgeneralization is the presence of outliers in private datasets.

2.1 Privacy and Security Challenges in CC

Considering the privacy within the cloud, there are numerous threats to the user's sensitive data in cloud storage. Xiao et al. [13] addressed a correlation among five prominent privacy and security attributes, including confidentiality, availability, integrity, accountability, and privacy preservation. The weaknesses, the risk models, and current defense schemes in the cloud computing environment are presented. It confirms the significance of separating privacy from security, where privacy is considered closely linked to security.

Moreover, additional security elements may have negative or positive effects on privacy. Fig. 1 shows the diagram of cloud security and privacy in view of five security/privacy attributes (i.e., confidentiality, integrity, availability, accountability, and privacy-preservation).

Issues related to the privacy, security, and trust in cloud environments are extensively surveyed [14–16] assist users in identifying the threats. Various methods to restrict these potential threats are discussed. Tchifilionova [17] acknowledged that the fact that security and privacy will remain a major concern in the cloud. He identified the biggest threats in current cloud computing. Four active methods are proposed to handle security and privacy issues [18], which dealt with security in the cloud for role-based access control (RBAC). The unauthorized secondary usage of the data is avoided by proposing user control methods and an identification management method. These methods are found to be practical for the generalized CC.

The necessity of CC related data preservation, and privacy laws in the EU, can be of practical importance to the model [19, 20]. The high-level control of security, data protection, transfer, confidentiality, intellectual property, law enforcement access, and risk allocation are recommended. Pauley [21] successfully evaluated privacy menaces in the cloud, where the shortcomings of existing methodologies are addressed.

Svantesson and Clarke [22] confirmed the link of CC with serious risks to privacy, where the existing privacy law might struggle to determine some of those threats. A policy-based authorization infrastructure that a cloud provider could execute as a service to the users is described by [23]. These infrastructure policies ensure that reaching data would always be restricted, despite data movement between services or cloud providers.

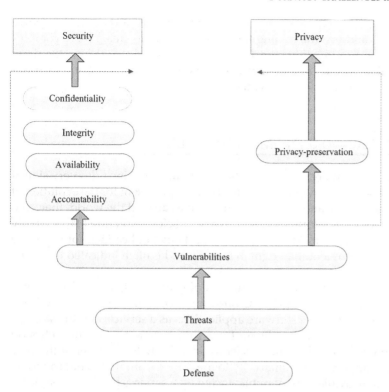

FIG. 1 Cloud security and privacy.

Adrian [24] aimed to control the CC infrastructure for determining the practicality of the privacy rule. A relationship between privacy and personal information is established to determine the effect of the Internet on privacy, and the influence of cloud computing on privacy. Hou et al. [25] addressed the problem of forensic investigation using homomorphic and commutative encryption, where the problem is solved by offering two forensically sound schemes. Concurrently, the service provider could not distinguish the interested information from investigators.

Data privacy issues in CC have been studied by [26, 27]. This concise study on privacy and the security of data perseveration issues is performed through all phases of the data lifecycle. Some solutions are discussed, such as a fully homomorphic encryption scheme, decentralized information flow control (DIFC), a precise method to confirm the integrity of the data, differential privacy protection technology, client-based privacy management, and data integrity (PDI) solution. Patel [28] explored the latest developed intrusion detection and prevention systems (IDPSs) and alarm management techniques. A complete classification is performed to determine the possible solutions against intrusions in CC.

2.2 Privacy Violation and Data Mining

Data mining is the method of digging out hidden information from a database. In fact, there is a trend among businesses to collaborate and share data and mining results to gain mutual benefits due to the development of new technology such as CC. These techniques are used to extract the hidden information from huge datasets in the form of new models, trends, and diverse patterns [29]. However, privacy requires the personal data protection of any individual during data mining. Privacy in CC implies the individual's personal information (called sensitive data) is shielded while publishing [10, 30]. Research has revealed that attackers often observe and target the information efficiently from third-party clouds [30].

Indeed, individuals' sensitive data information requires supreme privacy protection before being outsourced to the cloud [31]. Due to CC's many benefits, the issue of privacy-preserving data mining has become more significant. This relates the cumulative capability to store an individual user's data, and the rising complexity of data mining algorithms to influence this information. An integrative method depends on the characteristic elements of web mining to limit the risk [32].

Two simple classes of web mining projects are refined based on the mining of web logs. The purpose is to improve the navigation experience within a certain web site, and use the mining tools on web data to create more complex implications about an individual's attributes. Dev et al. [33] identified the data mining-based privacy risks in the cloud and designed a distributed architecture to restrict the risks. It combined categorization, fragmentation, and distribution. Data are split into chunks and then sent to appropriate cloud providers.

3 PRIVACY CHALLENGES IN SMART CITIES

Smart cities are complex. Different technologies, applications, and concepts are interacting to include every side of the digital citizen's life. The concept of a privacy-challenging environment is the basic requirement for the evolution of efficient protection techniques. Based on the present studies, and analysis of smart cities around the world, they conclude that, with few exceptions, privacy protection, or even information on privacy policies is still rare [34]. Roughly every aspect of a citizen's privacy is potentially at stake in a smart city because smart city applications spread in the very space in which citizens live. Privacy has been settled as a human right in Europe, and is often indicated to as "the right to be let alone" [35].

However, it is difficult to adapt to a cloud environment where large amounts of private data are collected, processed, and stored. This makes defining privacy a complex issue [34]. CC outsources computational tasks to third parties, which supply the hardware infrastructure, and the entire software applications as a service; and the storage, the operating system, or platform [36]. The one-time cost for IT hardware turns into a running cost that relies on service consumption by CC. Services of CC can progress quickly and efficiently identically to the level of the user request that a cloud client experiences. This matter is important in a smart city to measure the amount of data analysis done on data collected throughout the city, or to ensure availability of public-facing web services [34]. This chapter is aimed at focusing on smart city solutions that are circulated over different types of the cloud environment. Furthermore, it discusses privacy challenges related to the use of cloud computing and preserving the utility of data while achieving the privacy requirement [35].

4 APPLICATIONS OF A SMART CITY

The major goals of smart cities are to improve their citizens' quality of life and to improve their economic growth. To achieve these two goals, efficiency and sustainability should be increased by improving decision making through the increased availability of information, and by permitting citizens to participate. Numerous smart city applications have been proposed to achieve this goal. These applications have already been deployed in nine areas: utilities, environment, mobility, public services, buildings, economy, citizens, health care, and governance. None of the nine areas can be isolated from each other. Rather, services in various areas can be deployed in conjunction [34].

4.1 Data Utility Preserving

Privacy-preserving data mining has arisen as a new research avenue in which several techniques have been developed to anonymize the data for publishing. Still, the protection and truthfulness potency of this generalized technique is limited to a small output space, often leading to unacceptable utility loss in the case of significant privacy requirements. A hybrid generalization data relocation technique is introduced in this chapter to overcome this limitation. The technique is based on the hybridization of the generalization method and the data relocation method to combine the advantages of both. Anonymization is achieved by using the generalization method. Truthfulness is preserved, but information is lost in generalization. Data relocation preserves the utility of the data, but damages the truthfulness of data. For this reason, the hybrid of these two methods results in the trade-off between privacy and the utility of data. Furthermore, the trade-off between truthfulness and utility acts as a control input parameter in data relocation. The feasibility of data relocation is decided by measuring the performance of each K-anonymity's iteration, where data rows are changed into small groups of tuples. Being indistinguishable to each other, these tuples create anonymizations of finer granularity with assured privacy standards. Furthermore, this technique is designed for L-diversity, and (a, K) anonymity. Experimental results demonstrate considerable utility enhancement as a function of a relatively small number of group relocations. Fig. 2 illustrates the main concept related to the privacy preserving data utility mining technique.

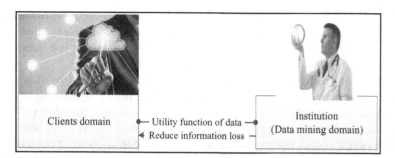

FIG. 2 Main concept of the technique.

The most common feature in all anonymization techniques is the data handling procedure, which applies the generalizations. This requires changing the data values to more general ones. The resultant dataset is comprised of the original and the other atomic values; for example, "Italy" is replaced by "Europe." In addition, more tuples can present analogous meanings. Unlike perturbation techniques (using the noise by collecting the data cells autonomously before publishing), generalizations can protect the data truthfulness. However, generalizations lead to information loss unless they are inhibited. Thus, overgeneralization must be avoided upon fulfilling privacy requirements. Several heuristics techniques have been developed to tackle this problem. Generalization-based techniques suffer from information loss, and the presence of outliers in private datasets originates from overgeneralization. For example, if the neighborhood of the outliers is not deeply occupied in the high dimensional domain, it is difficult for an anonymization to create an equal group of adequate size by increasing the number of groups lower than K. Therefore, efficient and accurate techniques are needed to prevent the destruction of overall datasets. To resolve the negative impacts of outliers and overgeneralization, the hybrid generalization data relocation technique is introduced. It combines the generalization method with data relocation methods to attain more utilized anonymizations. For further population of small equality groups of tuples, changing certain data cells that act as outliers is involved in data relocation. Overrelocation should be avoided, as it harms truthfulness and localized utility. This can be accomplished by limiting the number of relocations that algorithm can apply, thus controlling the trade-off between utility and truthfulness. Even a small number of relocations can prevent overgeneralization. The hybrid generalization can easily overcome the limitations of generalization and the data relocation methods. Furthermore, it can improve the generalization method without being stuck in local optimal solutions. Hybrid generalization permits relocation of groups and enhances the overall utility at the cost of truthfulness. The main idea behind data relocation is to merge the complementary groups with lower K. This reduces the size of groups to further populate small equality groups of tuples. It is customary to provide the following definitions to clarify the hybrid generalization principle.

Definition 1. Generalization: A generalization, written $\{c\} \rightarrow p$, replaces all child values $\{c\}$ with the parent value $\{p\}$. This is valid if all values lower than c are generalized to c. A vid is generalized by $\{c\} \rightarrow p$ if it contains some value in $\{c\}$ [37].

Definition 2. Equality group: The equality group of tuple t in dataset T^* is the set of all its tuples with identical quasiidentifiers to t [37]. The data relocation being a trade-off between trustworthiness and utility acts as a control input parameter. The performance of each K-anonymity's iteration is measured to decide the feasibility of data relocation, where data rows are changed into small groups of tuples. These tuples being indistinguishable to each other creates anonymizations of finer granularity with an assured privacy standard. Furthermore, this technique is designed for L-diversity, and (α, K)-anonymity. The idea of this research is close to Nergiz and Gök, but with an improvement whereby the number of groups is reduced, as well as improved to overcome the limitations of this article by applying other privacy models in this technique, such as L-diversity, and (α, K) anonymity, and it is not limited to only K-anonymity. While Nergiz and Gök's work based on K-anonymity limits identification of tuples, it also fails to enforce constraints on the sensitive attributes in a given equality group. Thus, there is still a risk of sensitive information disclosure.

5 HYBRID GENERALIZATION DATA RELOCATION TECHNIQUE

The proposed hybrid generalization data relocation technique aims at measuring the performance of each K-anonymity's iteration and deciding whether data relocation will be conducted or not. This technique is accomplished in three stages, including initialization, generalization, and data relocation; it also preserves sensitive attributes, which are discussed as follows.

Initialization: Given a dataset (row table), which refers to the anonymized dataset. Assuming the execution of the first operation of K-anonymity, the groups of quasiidentifiers are selected to get the list lower than K, which is called BelowKList as shown in Table 2. Then, the percentage reduction of BelowKList is logged. This percentage is a good indicator of how much one step of generalization or suppression was capable of performing K-anonymity.

Generalization and data relocation: In case this percentage has produced less than 80% of reduction in BelowKList, then data relocation is necessary; this is because any other step of K-anonymity will impact the utility of data significantly. This percentage is chosen based on natural data as a tunable parameter. When data relocation is called, it will be performed according to the flowchart shown in Fig. 3. Initially, a list of groups that complement each other with respect to the value of K will be generated. In order to perform data relocation for uniting, each pair of those groups is under one K group as shown in Table 2. Then, the remaining groups are united by data relocation according to their RowCount as shown in Tables 3–9.

FIG. 3   Flowchart of hybrid generalization data relocation.

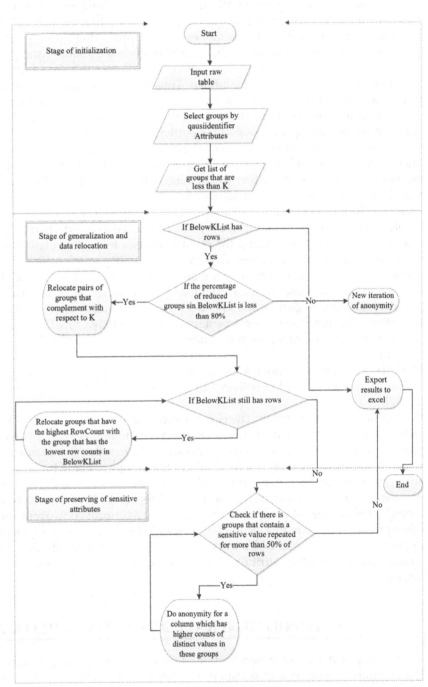

The groups with the lowest row count are united with the groups with the highest counts. This operation is executed iteratively until the BelowKList is empty. It is important to note that this flowchart does not show that the data relocation will be checked after it is performed according to the percentage of data modification in the tables. In case it is more than 10%, then a rollback is called, and new K-anonymity iteration is performed. It is important to avoid losing the truthfulness in the table, and to maintain the utility of the tables. Thus, overrelocation needs to be avoided by limiting the number of relocations that the algorithm can apply.

Preservation of sensitive attributes: This step checks the BelowKList, where the groups with the lowest row count are united with the highest if BelowKList is filled. Otherwise, a data processing step is performed to maintain L-diversity, where the sensitive attribute is checked with respect to their frequency values in one group. If this frequency is more than 50%, then a new K-anonymity iteration is conducted with $(K+1)$ values until there is no sensitive value above this frequency. Fig. 4 illustrates the steps of pseudo-code of hybrid generalization data relocation.

6 RESULTS AND EVALUATION

The present work is based on a bank's direct marketing data set, which is collected from different web sources of the University of California at Irvine (UCI) machine learning repository. This data set is used to implement and estimate the performance of the proposed anonymization technique in terms of preserving the data privacy for publication in the cloud. Earlier, this data set was collected and arranged by Moro and Laureano [38] and also utilized by Elsalamony [39]. The dataset (52,944 records) is associated to different marketing campaigns of a Portuguese banking institution based on phone calls. The data was collected during the period of 2008–13 [40]. Regularly, more than one contact was required with a single client in order to analyze if the product (bank term deposit) has been (or not) subscribed. Bank.csv is shown in 10% of the examples (4521), randomly selected from bank-full.csv.

The bank's direct marketing data set includes 300 data samples with 17 attributes, without any missing values [41]. The data set is comprised of two different attributes; nominal and numeral, as listed in Table 1. Three types of attributes are depicted in Table 1, including numerical (age, balance, day, duration, campaign, pdays, and previous), categorical (job, marital, education, contact, month, and poutcome), and binary, that include yes or no in their classes such as default, housing, loan, and output [39]. Fig. 5 illustrates the data before anonymizing.

This technique is performed on an anonymized dataset after anonymizing them in Phase 1, based on the heuristic anonymization technique. This technique is achieved by selecting groups from these anonymized datasets, which are lower than K values, as shown in Table 2. After testing the groups of quasi-identifiers that are lower than K, the complement groups, with respect to the K value, are united by data relocation, as mentioned in Section 4.

As mentioned before, the main aim of the hybrid generalization technique is to minimize information loss by reducing the size of groups to further populate small, equal groups of tuples. The results of the hybrid generalization technique are displayed in Tables 2–9.

Table 2 shows the creation of BelowKList. After inputting the anonymized dataset, the groups of quasi-identifiers are selected. These groups are checked to get the list lower than the K value, which is called BelowKList. Then, it should

```
1. Input:        Raw Table
2. Output:       Hybrid K_Anonymized Table
3. Main:
4.   Reduced_Percentage=100;
5.   Select Groups by Quasi_Indentifier attributes
6.   BlowKList=Get_LessThatK()
7.     While (Not (Empty(BlowKList)))
8.        If (Reduced_Percentage<%80)
9.          Roll_Back();
10.     Valid=Relocation (BlowKList);
11.   Else
12.      Anonymity_step();
13.      Update (Reduced_Percentage);
14.   End
15.   End
16.  If (Not(Valid))
17.    Roll_Back();
18.  End;
19.   Diversity ();
20.   Export_Results();
21.  End
22.   Relocation(A)
23. Relocate_Complementary(); % relocate groups that K-complement each other
24.     While (Empty(A))
25.        Relocate_Min_Max (A);   % relocate highest and lowest number counts % groups
26.   End
27.  End
```

FIG. 4 Pseudo-code for hybrid generalization data relocation.

TABLE 1 Description of Datasets

No.	Attributes	Kind of attributes	Attributes design	Classification of attributes
1	Age	Numerical	Numerical	QI(secret)
2	Job	Categorical	Admin, unknown, unemployed, management, house main, entrepreneur, student, blue-collar, self-employed, retired, technician services	QI(secret)
3	Marital	Categorical	Married, divorced (widowed), single	QI(secret)
4	Education	Categorical	Unknown, secondary, primary	QI(secret)
5	Default	Binary	Yes, No	None
6	Balance	Numeric	Numeric	Sensitive (top secret)
7	Housing	Binary	Yes, No	None
8	Loan	Binary	Yes, No	None
9	Contact	Categorical	Unknown, telephone, cellular	None
10	Day	Numeric	Numeric	None
11	Month	Categorical	0–12	None
12	Duration	Numeric	Numeric	None
13	Campaign	Numeric	Numeric	None
14	Pdays	Numeric	Contacted, numeric	None
15	Pervious	Numeric	Numeric	None
16	P out come	Categorical	Unknown, failure, success, other	None
17	Output	Binary	Yes, No	None

FIG. 5 Bank data before anonymized.

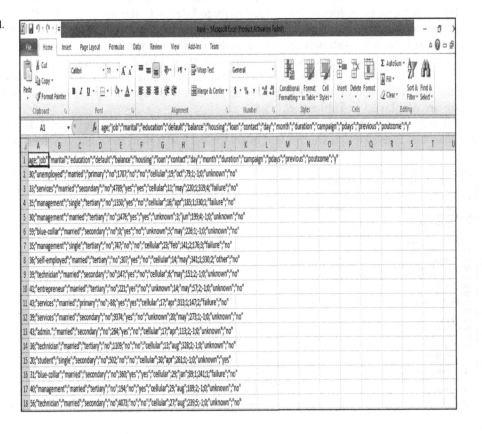

TABLE 2 Creation of BelowKList

Job	Marital	Education	Group count
Unemployed	Divorced	Unknown	1
Student	Divorced	Primary	1
Student	Divorced	Secondary	1
Self-employed	Divorced	Unknown	1
Student	Divorced	Unknown	1
Student	Married	Primary	2
Student	Divorced	Tertiary	3
Unknown	Divorced	Tertiary	3
Unknown	Divorced	Secondary	3
Unknown	Divorced	Primary	4
Blue-collar	Divorced	Tertiary	4
Retired	Single	Unknown	5

TABLE 3 Labeling the BelowKList and the Complementary Groups by A, B, and C

Job	Marital	Education	Group count
Unemployed	Divorced	Unknown	1A
Student	Divorced	Primary	1
Student	Divorced	Secondary	1
Self-employed	Divorced	Unknown	1
Student	Divorced	Unknown	1
Student	Married	Primary	2B
Student	Divorced	Tertiary	3C
Unknown	Divorced	Tertiary	3C
Unknown	Divorced	Secondary	3
Unknown	Divorced	Primary	4B
Blue-collar	Divorced	Tertiary	4
Retired	Single	Unknown	5A

TABLE 4 BelowKList After First Step of Data Relocation

Job	Marital	Education	Group count
Retired	Single	Unknown	1A
Student	Divorced	Primary	1
Student	Divorced	Secondary	1
Self-employed	Divorced	Unknown	1
Student	Divorced	Unknown	1
Unknown	Divorced	Primary	2B
Unknown	Divorced	Tertiary	3C
Unknown	Divorced	Tertiary	3C
Unknown	Divorced	Secondary	3
Unknown	Divorced	Primary	4B
Blue-collar	Divorced	Tertiary	4
Retired	Single	Unknown	5A

TABLE 5   BelowKList New Groups After First Step of Data Relocation

Job	Marital	Education	Group count
Student	Divorced	Primary	1A
Student	Divorced	Secondary	1A
Self-employed	Divorced	Unknown	1B
Student	Divorced	Unknown	1B
Unknown	Divorced	Secondary	3B
Blue-collar	Divorced	Tertiary	4A
Unknown	Divorced	Primary	6
Retired	Single	Unknown	6

TABLE 6   BelowKList After Second Step of Data Relocation

Job	Marital	Education	Group count
Blue-collar	Divorced	Tertiary	1A
Blue-collar	Divorced	Tertiary	1A
Self-unknown	Divorced	Secondary	1B
Unknown	Divorced	Secondary	1B
Unknown	Divorced	Secondary	3B
Blue-collar	Divorced	Tertiary	4A
Unknown	Divorced	Primary	6
Retired	Single	Unknown	6

TABLE 7   BelowKList New Groups' First and Second Step of Data Relocation

Job	Marital	Education	Group count
Unknown	Divorced	Secondary	5A
Blue-collar	Divorced	Tertiary	6A
Unknown	Divorced	Primary	6
Retired	Single	Unknown	6

TABLE 8   BelowKList After the Third Step of Data Relocation

Job	Marital	Education	Group count
Blue-collar	Divorced	Tertiary	5A
Blue-collar	Divorced	Tertiary	6A
Unknown	Divorced	Primary	6
Retired	Single	Unknown	6

TABLE 9   BelowKList New Groups After the Third First Step of Data Relocation

Job	Marital	Education	Group count
Unknown	Divorced	Primary	6
Retired	Single	Unknown	6
Blue-collar	Divorced	Tertiary	11

check the percentage of reduction of BelowKList to achieve the data relocation method. If the percentage is less than 80%, the data relocation is required, as shown in Fig. 3. Otherwise, it should be achieved by anonymization.

Before achieving the data relocation n, a list of groups that complement each other with respect to the value of K will be created. So, the complementing groups are labelled with A, B, and C as listed in Table 3.

After the first step of data relocation, the complementing groups are integrated under one K value, as shown in Table 4. For example, the first row (1A) is integrated with last row (5A) under one K value, so, the first row becomes (Retired, Single, Unknown). Same is for all the remaining complementing groups, for example, the sixth row (2B) is integrated with the tenth one (4B), and the seventh and eighth (3C) are also integrated.

To create the equality groups that contain similar tuples with respect to the K value, the complementing groups are united by achieving the data relocation method under one K value, as shown in Table 5. For that, the first row (1A) is united with the last row (A5). The sixth row (2B) is united with tenth row (4B), and seventh and eighth rows (3C) are also united. Table 5 has outperformed in the preserving utility of data compared with Tables 1–3. It reduces the size of groups compared with other tables. With transformation, the number of groups becomes eight, while the number of groups for other tables is twelve.

To create more equality, groups should be achieved by another step of data relocation. So BelowKList is checked to identify if it still has rows whereby the process will proceed for the relocation method until BelowKList becomes empty. But before achieving the data relocation, it should be checked that the percentage of data relocation is not more than 10% according to the percentage of data modification in the table. If it is more than 10%, then a rollback is called, and a new K-anonymity iteration is performed. Otherwise, the second step of data relocation is shown in Table 6.

Data after application of the second step of data relocation is shown in Table 6. The remaining groups are integrated by applying data relocation according to their RowCount. More specifically, the groups with the lowest row counts are integrated with the groups with highest row counts. The first two groups (1A) that have the lowest rows are integrated with the sixth group (4A), which has the highest rows, by applying the data relocation method to create one group (second group in Table 7). Furthermore, other groups with the lowest row counts are integrated with the ones having the highest row counts. So, the third and fourth groups (1B) are integrated with the fifth group (3B) under one group (first group in Table 7). This operation is executed iteratively until the BelowKList is empty.

After achieving the second step of data relocation, the number of groups has become four, as shown in Table 7. Comparing with Table 6 and other tables, Table 7 is superior in minimizing information loss by reducing the size of the groups to half. The percentage of data relocation will be checked again before performing the third step.

If the percentage is not more than 10%, the third step of data relocation is achieved as shown in Table 8. Also, the remaining groups are integrated by applying data relocation according to their RowCount. So, the first group with the lowest row count is integrated with the second group with highest row count under one K value of the highest row (blue-collar, divorced, and tertiary). To achieve the data relocation method, the first two groups are integrated under one K value, as shown in Table 9 (the last group).

In comparing Table 9 to the other tables, we see that it has outperformed the other tables in preserving the utility of data by reducing the size of groups to be only three. This signifies that Table 9 is superior compared with the other tables, especially Table 2.

The experimental evaluation of hybrid generalization data relocation has been presented. The truthfulness and utility of the hybrid generalization data relocation technique has been evaluated using UTD Anonymization Tool Box software.

Truthfulness evaluation: Fig. 6 shows the percentage of relocation, which is calculated to measure the data truthfulness of the proposed hybrid generalization data relocation technique. The data relocation is found to affect the truthfulness. The percentage of data relocation attained a maximum of 6%, regardless of the value of K, as illustrated in the

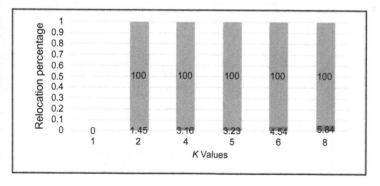

FIG. 6 K-dependent relocation percentage as a measure of truthfulness.

FIG. 7   Relocation percentage as a measure of truthfulness.

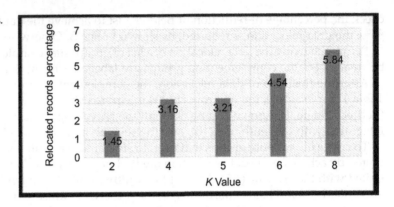

shaded blue band in Fig. 6. This signifies that the truthfulness of the data is more than 94% (dark grey). The measure of truthfulness is observed to depend on the percentage of data relocation. In other words, it is the complementary percentage of data relocation, as depicted in Fig. 7, which is considered a good indicator of the capacity of the hybrid generalization data relocation technique to maintain the data truthfulness relocation percentage.

Utility evaluation: The expression for utility has been described by Eqs. (1)–(4). The metric of utility information gained per privacy loss (IGPL) is written as [42],

$$IGPL = IG(spec)/(PL(spec) + 1) \tag{1}$$

$$IG = R_c - \sum_{c \in child(p)} (R_c/R_p)I(R_c) \tag{2}$$

R_x represents the set of original records having attribute values that can be generalized to x. IR is the entropy of R_x given by,

$$IR = - \sum_{s \in sensitive} (|(R_x, sv)/|R_x|| \cdot \log_2(|R_x, sv|/|R_x|)) \tag{3}$$

Let Ap (spec) mean the anonymity before performing spec. Ap represent the anonymity after performing spec. Privacy loss caused by spec is calculated using the expression,

$$PL = Ap - Ac \tag{4}$$

It is found that to preserve the data utility, the relocation technique is used, but with a limited percentage. However, it is essential to tradeoff between data utility and truthfulness. The utility is measured in terms of two metrics based on the average group size. Fig. 8 displays the K-value dependent average group size as an indicator to data utility. The average group size is observed to reduce significantly using the hybrid generalization data relocation technique. Thus, the application of the hybrid generalization data relocation technique minimized the information loss. Conversely, too big of an average group size in K-anonymity enhanced the information loss. This is equivalent to an increase of the utility of the resulted anonymized data in the hybrid generalization data relocation technique, and acts as a good performance indicator.

FIG. 8   K-value dependent average group size as an indicator to utility.

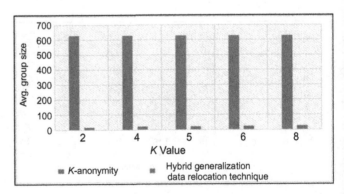

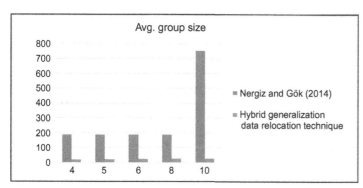

7 DISCUSSION OF VALIDATION

This chapter has focused on preserving the utility of a dataset. It aims to reduce the size of groups to further populate small, equal groups of tuples based on a hybrid generalization data relocation technique. The hybrid generalization data relocation technique is validated and compared with [37] by using UTD Anonymization Tool Box software. The comprehensive open source software for anonymizing the sensitive personal data, including UTD Anonymization ToolBox, is employed to evaluate the merits of the improvement gained from the proposed technique. It is designed to promote research in the area of privacy-preserving data analysis at the UT Dallas Data Security and Privacy Lab. Furthermore, it is prepared based on several anonymization methods into a toolbox to be used by researchers. These algorithms can be applied directly to a dataset that is used as library tasks inside other applications. The toolbox actually contains six various anonymization methods over three various privacy definitions. It can release the source code of a recent study on classifying anonymized data together with the anonymization toolbox [43, 44]. These are used to benchmark the proposed privacy-persevering techniques. The effectiveness of the proposed method to preserve privacy of data to be published in CC is validated using the corrected dataset as used by other researchers [37, 40, 42, 45, 46].

Nergiz and Gök [37] have limited their study to only one privacy model, which is K-anonymity. Meanwhile, the hybrid generalization data relocation is achieved by combining other privacy metrics such as L-diversity and (α, K)-anonymity. Another significant improvement of hybrid generalization data relocation techniques is from the perspective of utility measured by average group size. The main goal of the hybrid generalization data relocation technique is to reduce the size of average groups to preserve the utility of datasets. Fig. 9 displays that the hybrid generalization data relocation technique has successfully preserved low values of group sizes as compared with the work of Nergiz and Gök [37] when K has increased. This means that more utility is sustained regardless of the values of K.

8 SUMMARY

The main goals of this chapter are to highlight how CC is associated with the smart city, how to develop smart city services with CC while achieving privacy requirements, and to reduce the occurrence of information loss and over-generalization that limit privacy in CC data mining. The presence of a relatively small output space and strict privacy requirements of conventional techniques are responsible for huge data losses. The limitations associated with existing generalization-based approaches, such as improper utility loss for stringent privacy requirements for relatively small output spaces is overcome. Thus, achieving utility preservation based on a generalization technique remains a challenging task. Issues such as overgeneralization of outliers in private datasets and increasing the number of groups are the other concerns.

In this view, an enhancement of the privacy preserving data utility mining technique based on hybrid generalization data relocation is introduced to resolve the negative effects of outliers and overgeneralization in data mining. The complete architecture of the technique is discussed, and the experimental results are evaluated to determine its validity. The performance evaluation of the hybrid generalization data relocation technique is performed in terms of data truthfulness and utility. It is asserted that, unlike the perturbation technique, the present generalization preserves truthfulness. Thus, it preserved data truthfulness.

FIG. 10 Hybrid generalization data relocation technique for preserving utility of data [37].

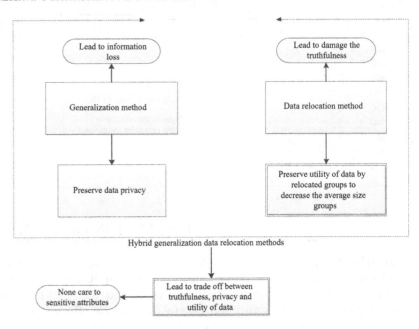

More utilized anonymizations are achieved by combining the technique of generalization with data relocation. The overall utility is enhanced at the cost of truthfulness. Through data relocation, the number of groups is reduced, and their tuples populate small, equal groups. The overrelocation that localizes the utility and damages the truthfulness is excluded. This is attained by bounding the number of relocations and controlling the trade-off between utility and truthfulness, where small numbers of relocations stopped the overgeneralization. Experimental results demonstrated significant utility enhancement as a function of a relatively small number of group relocations [37].

Practical data anonymization should strive to attain two conflicting goals, which are achieving a given privacy requirement, and to preserve the utility of the data. For generalization-based methods, protection of the utility of data is still considered a main issue. The presence of outliers in private datasets is one of the key reasons for overgeneralization. It becomes challenging for an anonymization algorithm to create an equality group of sufficient size due to fewer neighborhood outliers in the high-dimensional domain.

Most of the existing techniques [11, 47–52] are based on generalizations to achieve an anonymity model. Many of them implement generalization as their anonymization solutions. Generalization is applied on the QI, and replaces the QI attribute with the less-specific, but semantically consistent values. Consequently, more tuples will have the same set of QI attributes, thus become indistinguishable from each other. Enough generalization will hide a record in a crowd, with at least K records having the same QI attributes, thus K-anonymity is satisfied. However, generalization preserves the truthfulness of data, but leads to information loss. While Nergiz and Gök [37] proposed the hybrid method of trading-off between privacy and utility of data, they failed to take care of sensitive attributes. Consequently, a good technique preserves the utility of data, and the performance of privacy is measured with minimal information loss. Fig. 10 shows the diagram of preserving the utility of data. With the contributions of this chapter, we plan to achieve privacy in CC by combining privacy preservation as a metric with other integrity and availability metrics among the smart cities.

References

[1] E. Michael Armbrust, I. Stoica, M. Zaharia, A. Fox, A view of cloud computing, Commun. ACM 53 (4) (2009) 50.

[2] I.B. Rajkumar Buyya, C.S. Yeo, S. Venugopal, J. Broberg, Cloud computing and emerging IT platforms: vision, hype, and reality for delivering computing as the 5th utility, Futur. Gener. Comput. Syst. 25 (6) (2009) 17.

[3] W. Cohen, D. Levinthal, Absorptive capacity: a new perspective on learning and innovation, Adm. Sci. Q. 35 (1) (1990) 128–152.

[4] L. Wang, J. Zhan, W. Shi, Y. Liang, In cloud, can scientific communities benefit from the economies of scale? IEEE Trans. Parallel Distrib. Syst. 23 (2) (2012) 296–303.

[5] X. Yang, L. Wang, G. Laszewski, Recent research advances in e-Science, Clust. Comput. 12 (4) (2009) 353–356.

[6] D. Zissis, D. Lekkas, Addressing cloud computing security issues, Futur. Gener. Comput. Syst. 28 (3) (2012) 583–592.

[7] P. Samarati, Protecting respondents' identities in microdata release, IEEE Trans. Knowl. Data Eng. 13 (6) (2001) 1010–1027.

[8] R.C. Wong, J. Li, A.W. Fu, K. Wang, (α, k)-anonymity: an enhanced k-anonymity model for privacy-preserving data publishing, in: International Conference on Knowledge Discovery and Data Mining SIGKDD, 2006, pp. 754–759.

[9] S. Kumara, S. Singhb, A. Singhc, J. Alid, Virtualization, the great thing and issues in cloud computing, Int. J. Curr. Eng. Technol. 2013 (2013) 338–341.

[10] M.E. Nergiz, C. Clifton, Presence without complete world knowledge, IEEE Trans. Knowl. Data Eng. 22 (6) (2010) 868–883.

[11] M.E. Nergiz, M.Z. Gök, U. Özkanli, Preservation of utility through hybrid k-anonymization, in: Trust, Privacy, and Security in Digital Business, 8058, Springer, Berlin, Heidelberg, 2013, pp. 97–111.

[12] Y. Xiao, C. Lin, Y. Jiang, X. Chu, F. Liu, An efficient privacy-preserving publish-subscribe service scheme for cloud computing, in: 2010 IEEE Glob. Telecommun. Conference (GLOBECOM), vol. 1, 2010, pp. 1–5.

[13] Z. Xiao, Y. Xiao, S. Member, Security and privacy in cloud computing, IEEE Commun. Surv. Tutor. 12 (2012) 1–17.

[14] S. Subashini, V. Kavitha, A survey on security issues in service delivery models of cloud computing, J. Netw. Comput. Appl. 34 (1) (2011) 1–11.

[15] R. Gellman, Privacy in the clouds: risks to privacy and confidentiality from cloud computing, in: Proceedings of World Priv. Forum, 2009.

[16] R. Chow, P. Golle, M. Jakobsson, E. Shi, J. Staddon, R. Masuoka, J. Molina, Controlling data in the cloud: outsourcing computation without outsourcing control, in: Proceedings of the 2009 ACM Workshop on Cloud Computing Security (CCSW'09), 2009, pp. 85–90.

[17] V. Tchifilionova, Security and privacy implications of cloud computing–lost in the cloud, Open Res. Probl. Netw. Secur. (2011) 149–158.

[18] Z. Wang, Security and privacy issues within the cloud computing, in: 2011 International Conference Comput. Inf. Science, 2011, pp. 175–178.

[19] S. Porwal, S.K. Nair, T. Dimitrakos, Regulatory impact of data protection and privacy in the cloud, Perspective (2011) 290–299.

[20] N.J. King, V.T. Raja, Protecting the privacy and security of sensitive customer data in the cloud, Comput. Law Secur. Rev. 28 (3) (2012) 308–319.

[21] W.A. Pauley Jr., An Empirical Study of Privacy Risk Assessment Methodologies in Cloud Computing Environments, ProQuest dissertations theses, vol. Ph.D 2012.

[22] D. Svantesson, R. Clarke, Privacy and consumer risks in cloud computing, Comput. Law Secur. Rev. 26 (4) (2010) 391–397.

[23] D.W. Chadwick, K. Fatema, A privacy preserving authorisation system for the cloud, J. Comput. Syst. Sci. 78 (5) (2012) 1359–1373.

[24] A. Adrian, How much privacy do clouds provide? An Australian perspective, Comput. Law Secur. Rev. 29 (1) (2013) 48–57.

[25] S. Hou, T. Uehara, S.M. Yiu, L.C.K. Hui, K.P. Chow, Privacy preserving confidential forensic investigation for shared or remote servers, in: 2011 Seventh International Conference on Intelligent Information Hiding Multimedia Signal Processesing, 2011, pp. 378–383.

[26] A.W. Khan, S.U. Khan, M. Ilyas, M.I. Azeem, A literature survey on data privacy/protection issues and challenges in cloud computing, IOSR J. Comput. Eng. 1 (3) (2012) 28–36.

[27] D. Chen, H. Zhao, Data security and privacy protection issues in cloud computing, in: 2012 International Conference on Computer Science and Electronics Engineering, vol. 973, 2012, pp. 647–651.

[28] A. Patel, et al., An intrusion detection and prevention system in cloud computing: a systematic review, J. Netw. Comput. Appl. 36 (1) (2013) 25–41.

[29] C. Wolf, Privacy and data security in the cloud: what are the issues? IP Litig.: Devoted Intellect. Prop. Litig. Enforc. 18 (6) (2012) 19–29.

[30] M. Prakash, G. Singaravel, An approach for prevention of privacy breach and information leakage in sensitive data mining, Comput. Electr. Eng. (2015) 1–7.

[31] S. Kamara, C. Papamanthou, T. Roeder, Dynamic searchable symmetric encryption, in: 2012 ACM Conference, 2012, pp. 965–976.

[32] J.D. Velásquez, Web mining and privacy concerns: some important legal issues to be consider before applying any data and information extraction technique in web-based environments, Expert Syst. Appl. 40 (13) (2013) 5228–5239.

[33] H. Dev, T. Sen, M. Basak, M.E. Ali, An approach to protect the privacy of cloud data from data mining based attacks, in: 2012 SC Companion High Performance Computing, Networking Storage Analysis, 2012, pp. 1106–1115.

[34] D. Eckhoff, I. Wagner, Privacy in the smart city-application, technologies, challenges and solutions, in: IEEE Commun. Surv. Tutorials, 2017, pp. 1–28.

[35] S. Warren, L. Brandeis, The right to privacy, Harv. Law Rev. 4 (5) (1890) 193–220.

[36] D. Catteddu, G. Hogben, Cloud computing: Benefits, risks and recommendations for information security, in: Web Application Security, vol. 72, Springer, Berlin, Heidelberg, 2009, p. 17. no. 1.

[37] M.E. Nergiz, M.Z. Gök, Hybrid k-anonymity, Comput. Secur. 44 (2014) 51–63.

[38] S. Moro, R.M.S. Laureano, Using data mining for bank direct marketing: an application of the CRISP-DM methodology, in: The European Simulation and Modelling Conference, Figure 1, 2011, pp. 117–121.

[39] H.A. Elsalamony, Bank direct marketing analysis of data mining techniques, Int. J. Comput. Appl. 85 (7) (2014) 12–22.

[40] S. Moro, P. Cortez, P. Rita, A data-driven approach to predict the success of bank telemarketing, Decis. Support. Syst. 62 (2014) 22–31.

[41] K. Bache, M. Lichman, UCI Machine Learning Repository, School of Information and Computer Sciences, University of California, Irvine, CA, 2013.

[42] X. Zhang, C. Liu, S. Nepal, C. Yang, W. Dou, J. Chen, A hybrid approach for scalable sub-tree anonymization over big data using MapReduce on cloud, J. Comput. Syst. Sci. 80 (5) (2014) 1008–1020.

[43] V. Ayala-Rivera, P. McDonagh, T. Cerqueus, L. Murphy, A systematic comparison and evaluation of k-Anonymization algorithms for practitioners, Trans. Data Priv. 7 (3) (2014) 337–370.

[44] O. Sané, F. Camara, S. Ndiaye, Y. Slimani, An approach to overcome inference channels on k-anonymous data, Int. J. Adv. Sci. Technol. 42 (2012) 83–90.

[45] X. Zhang, C. Liu, S. Nepal, J. Chen, An efficient quasi-identifier index based approach for privacy preservation over incremental data sets on cloud, J. Comput. Syst. Sci. 79 (5) (2013) 542–555.

[46] J.J. Yang, J.Q. Li, Y. Niu, A hybrid solution for privacy preserving medical data sharing in the cloud environment, Futur. Gener. Comput. Syst. 43–44 (2014) 74–86.

[47] G. Aggarwal, R. Panigrahy, T. Feder, D. Thomas, K. Kenthapadi, S. Khuller, A. Zhu, Achieving anonymity via clustering, ACM Trans. Algorithms 6 (3) (2005) 1–19.

[48] J.J. Panackal, A.S. Pillai, Adaptive utility-based anonymization model: performance evaluation on big data sets, Procedia Comput. Sci. 50 (2015) 347–352.

[49] V. Rajalakshmi, G.S.A. Mala, Anonymization by data relocation using sub-clustering for privacy preserving data mining, Indian J. Sci. Technol. 7 (July) (2014) 975–980.

[50] G. Loukides, A. Gkoulalas-Divanis, J. Shao, Efficient and flexible anonymization of transaction data, Knowl. Inf. Syst. 36 (1) (2012) 153–210.

[51] X. He, D. Li, Y. Hao, H. Chen, Utility-friendly heterogenous generalization in privacy preserving data publishing, in: Conceptual Modeling. ER 2014, Lecture Notes in Computer Science, vol. 8824, Springer, Cham, 2014, pp. 186–194.

[52] Y. He, S. Barman, J.F. Naughton, Preventing equivalence attacks in updated, anonymized data, in: Proceedings of International Conference on Data Engineering, 2011, pp. 529–540.

19

Smart Megaprojects in Smart Cities, Dimensions, and Challenges

Azadeh Sarkheyli* and Elnaz Sarkheyli†
*Department of Informatics, Dalarna University, Falun, Sweden
†Faculty of Art and Architecture, Kharazmi University, Tehran, Iran

1 INTRODUCTION

One of the main concerns of urban planners in decision-making and policy-making is the lack of access to the necessary information about urban issues. Among the issues is decision-making about the construction of megaprojects, which mostly have extensive consequences on their impact zones. Many urban projects, including highways, intersections, shopping malls, renewal of urban centers, and airports, which are called megaprojects, are built while the estimation of their effects on their surrounding areas is defective, incomplete, or even sometimes plagued with major errors that cause the projects to fail. The failure is usually related to the lack of information and the weak process of the megaproject's management. In fact, because megaprojects are long-term, large-scale, and costly projects engaging a range of various stakeholders with conflicting demands, an appropriate megaproject's management is critical to its success.

In the age of technology and information, there are several digital devices and sensors detecting human behaviors, and controlling buildings, spaces, and transportation vehicles, as well as tracking organizations and people's interactions and functions. In fact, a large amount of data and information exists in digital contexts, and its integration and management are crucial to enhancing achievements and understandings. Smart and digital cities refer to the initiatives in using data, information, digital devices, and related technologies to provide sustainable cities (better environmental conservation leads to a better quality of life and economic growth). So, smart cities can provide the necessary context for better performance of megaprojects. In other words, smart cities can lead to the sort of megaprojects that effectively use data and technologies to provide a sustainable urban environment.

In fact, the concept of a "smart city," which originated from similar concepts such as the "information city" and "intelligent city," focuses on the various methods of data collection and data analysis to develop and distribute services, facilities, and infrastructure in an optimized manner, and still meet urban demands (for example, transportation and energy demands), and control and manage the city's growth, emissions, crises, and changes. Therefore, urban projects are supposed to be more controllable and detectable in smart cities. In fact, information systems have created opportunities to capture information that was never previously accessible [1]. Thus, it is possible to track citizens' behaviors, including transit usage, social interactions, the buildings and urban functions' footprint in energy consumptions and emissions, as well as the amount and quality of urban service delivery, land use and physical changes, and the environmental changes, by using current information technologies and digital devices (such as GIS, RFID tags, satellite images, mobile applications, social web networks).

This chapter intends to contribute to the smart city discourse by identification of the available and required information for a megaproject's management, and providing a framework to increase the efficiency of the megaprojects in economic prosperity, social improvement, and environmental resiliency. Moreover, it seeks to understand the related dimensions and the probable challenges of data management in smart cities. Therefore, the focal point of this research is to find a compatible relationship between the dimensions of smart cities and the dimensions of megaprojects' management.

The next three sections introduce the main concepts of smart cities, including various definitions, dimensions, and components, data and information management, and the megaproject's management. This is followed by a presentation of our conceptual framework regarding the potential role of megaprojects in a smart city. Next, the final section presents future research and conclusions.

2 SMART CITIES SMARTLY USE INFORMATION

Although the smart city is a recent conception, there are many literature studies about the concept and its application in different areas. The first study concerning this topic was carried out in 1994, and the interest in the topic had been quite stable from 1993 to 2010. It has had an exponential increase that could be referred to as: the Kyoto Protocol [2], the rise of widespread use of the Internet all over the world in 2000, the IBM Smart Planer concept, and the Covenant of Mayors of European Cities to reduce CO2 emissions by more than 20% by 2020 in 2008, the Europe 2020 Strategy for smart growth investing in education, research and innovation areas, in technologies and resources low-carbon economy, and job creation and poverty reduction [3].

"Smart cities are nowadays widespread all over the world; in all the continents, cities are moving toward smarter urban spaces, using high technologies to face the crucial problems linked with the urban life like traffic, pollution, city crowding, and poverty." [4]. The current wave of smart and sustainable cities projects proposed numerous proposals related to economic growth through smart and sustainable computational urbanisms [5]. "Smart-city projects are often set up as public–private partnerships between multinational technology companies including Cisco, IBM, and Hewlett Packard, along with city governments, universities, and design and engineering firms" [5].

Dameri [4] writes a comprehensive definition of the smart city: "a smart city is a well-defined geographical area, in which high technologies such as ICT, logistic, energy production, and so on, cooperate to create benefits for citizens in terms of well-being, inclusion and participation, environmental quality, intelligent development; it is governed by a well-defined pool of subjects, able to state the rules and policy for the city government and development."

Currently, several cities use the label "smart city" to describe a strategic direction toward environmentally sustainable development, sound economic growth, and better quality of life. Nam and Pardo [6] state that a smarter city infuses information into its physical infrastructure to improve conveniences, facilitate mobility, add efficiencies, conserve energy, improve the quality of air and water, identify problems and fix them quickly, recover rapidly from disasters, collect data to make better decisions, deploy resources effectively, and share data to enable collaboration across entities and domains. In other words, in the age of information, the smarter cities are the cities that use data sources and their resulting information in a smarter manner.

In a smart city, the efficient information gathering system and data analysis should enable developers, urban planners, urban managers, and policymakers to assess the consumption behavior, demand changes, and the impacts of the new developments to designate the optimal solutions, alleviate the negative consequences, and control the overall urban development. Basically, we need to know how the existing information technologies, social networks, and the related applications can improve the detection of the physical, economic, and social changes caused by urban interventions such as megaprojects. For example, it is important to know how physical developments influence the energy consumption and emissions, the land and building values, the increase in construction and investment, the economic prosperity or the functional decline, the changes in travel behavior and social interactions, and so forth.

In a smart city context, where the access to different information about economic, physical, and social changes is possible, in order to evaluate the results and effectiveness of physical interventions, the main challenge would be adequate data management. This includes the integration of the information, and better monitoring of the information. In other words, many digital devices and the organizations providing the information are dispersed and unrelated, and gather data in different units that are inapplicable for other reasons. The deficiency exists in targeting and coordination for more efficient use of available data and information in the context of smart cities.

As Derrible [7] states: "To become sustainable and resilient, future cities will likely leverage the current proliferation of data and increase computing power to become smart" [7].

3 SMART CITY: DIMENSIONS AND COMPONENTS

"More recent and commercially led proposals for 'smart cities' have focused on how networked urbanisms and participatory media might achieve 'greener' or more efficient cities that are simultaneously engines for economic growth." [5]. While the concept of smart cities is spreading around the world, and many cities, as well as nations, carry out research, infrastructure improvement, and carry out initiatives to become smart, the smart cities produce a new atmosphere, including the changes in urban functions, the relations between cities and urban regions, the location of urban services and land uses, the amount and quality of citizens' relationships, and so forth. Deloitte [8] clustered the major shift associated with the digital economy into five domains: I. Value propositions, II. Customers, Channels and Relationships, III. Activities and Resources, IV. Partners, V. Costs, and Revenues.

However, smart cities face challenges and threats. The challenges in a smart city are:

- the controlled transition of the labor market due to automation,
- winning the war on talent between metropolitan areas,
- social cohesion, inclusiveness, solidarity,
- security and privacy,
- and resilience [8].

On the other hand, the smart city influences the physical and natural environment and social status because it aims to provide an urban context that is more sustainable. Caldwell et al. [9] state that the digital matrix alters human perceptions of the city, informs our behavior, and increasingly influences the urban designs we ultimately inhabit.

The smart city goal would be reliable through an adequate and integrated information infrastructure, and the optimal usage of the information for crisis management, urban growth control, environmental protection, competitiveness promotion, economic growth, and so forth.

Nam and Pardo [6] describe three dimensions for smart cities: technology, people, and community. However, according to Lee and Phaal [10], the concept of the smart city has six main dimensions: a smart economy, smart mobility, a smart environment, smart people, smart living, and smart governance.

On the other hand, Roche [11] states that "A smart city is a city that is able, in a multifaceted territory, to efficiently mobilize technological innovations so as to anticipate, understand, openly discuss, act and serve many actors with a wide range of profits. To do so, a smart city operates in four main dimensions: the intelligent city (its social infrastructure), the digital city (information infrastructure), the open city (open governance), and the live city (a continuously adaptive urban living fabric)" [11].

Some components are mentioned in the empirical implementation of smart initiatives, even if they are not ever really involved in the smart city implementation: the land, the technologies, the citizens, and the government [4].

Harrison and Donelly [1] introduce the Urban Information Model (in order to theorize smart cities) as a very large number of layers representing a common two-dimensional space, the territory of the urban environment, whether that is a single city or a metropolis. The groups of layers (see Fig. 1) are detailed below:

1. The natural environment group, including topography, flora and fauna, natural resources, geology, and so forth.
2. The infrastructure group, including the built environment (roads, bridges, tunnels, buildings, pipelines, electrical and communication lines, and so forth), as well as things that move (trains, boats, buses, and so forth), which is constructed in the natural environment.

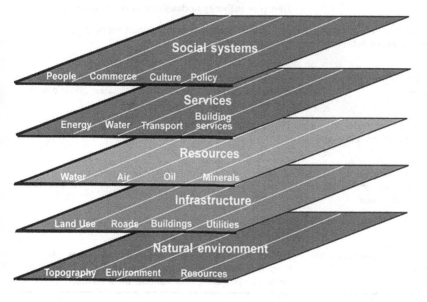

FIG. 1   A simplified view of the Urban Information Model [1].

3. The resources group, representing materials that originate in and eventually return to the natural environment after passing through various processes of refining and consumption in the services group, as well as capacities that are temporarily consumed, for example by the passage of a vehicle over a bridge, and are then re-generated.
4. The services group, representing many kinds of services, including transportation, energy, commerce, healthcare, and so forth. Many of these services consume or transform resources from the resource group.
5. The social systems group, including the locations and actions of people, such as commerce and culture, laws, regulations, governance, and so forth, that exploit the services and resources from these respective groups. This group contains the topmost and most interesting layer, in which we find the people systems.

Zygiaris [12] explains six layers in the definition and application of smart cities and their principal components: the city; the green city layer; the interconnection layer; the instrumentation layer; the open integration layer; the application layer; the innovation layer. However, Anthopoulos and Vakali [13] explain that the smart city's generic architecture contains the user layer, service layer, infrastructure layer and data layer.

Eight critical factors of smart city initiatives include management and organization, technology, governance, policy context, people, and communities, economy, built infrastructure, and the natural environment. These factors form the basis of an integrative framework that can be used to examine how local governments are envisioning smart city initiatives [14].

4 DATA AND INFORMATION MANAGEMENT IN SMART CITIES

Table 1 shows an example of the various categories, domains, and types of data that can be collected from smart cities [15–17]. Moreover, big data, the Internet of Things (IoT), and cloud computing are useful to drive smart city implementation, and they can work with other software and hardware to lead the vision of smart city to achievement.

TABLE 1   A Sample of Data Categories, Domains, and Types in Smart Cities

Data category	Data domain	Data type	Example of application
Infrastructure	Traffic, transport and asset management, built environment	Monitoring data, registration data, geodata	Traffic and congestion patterns, real-time dashboards. Number of vehicles passing between two points, speed Maps of cities (roads, street names, POIs, subway and bus stations, etc.) Public transport schedules Transport authority updates (roadwork, traffic status, etc.)
Sustainability	Energy usage, water, environment, weather, air quality	Sensor and monitoring data, civic measurement data	Air quality monitoring and pollution warnings, particle concentration
Health	Health, quality of life, well-being, life expectancy health	Health data, survey data, lifelogging	Location specific noise levels and social or health problems in specific neighborhoods, relevant information about potential or confirmed sources of health threats
Cohesion	Education, social capital, migration, neighborhoods, housing, crime	Survey data, civic and community web presence data	School quality in specific neighborhoods
Commerce	Business opportunities, marketing, location-based services, municipal services	Social media data, open government data, library data, waste collection data	Investment maps for attracting new business
Experience	City events, leisure, nightlife, tourism, heritage	Social media data, archive data, sensor data	Real-time social media analytics for crowd control, entertainment (movie/theater plays)
Citizen	Individual data	Social media data, survey data, registration data	Tweets, status updates and blog posts, popular places, household energy consumption, parking meters, personal data for service purposes, personal data for surveillance purposes

TABLE 2   A Sample of Data and Their Usage in Smart Cities

Data domain	Smart cities
Traffic	- Singapore: With cameras and sensors embedded throughout the city. Singapore is gathering data on an incomparable scale. This data allows officials to determine traffic density, send out wide-scale emergency signals and prevent crime [18]. - Songdo: The traffic is measured and regulated with the help of RFID tags on the cars. The RFID tags will send the geolocation data to a central monitoring unit that will identify the congested areas. Also, the citizens will always know via their smartphones and mobile devices the exact status of public transportation and its availability [19]. - Melbourne: Intelligent transport systems in the smart city analyze the gathered data and deliver insights into traffic planning, pedestrian flows, public transport efficiency, and freight movements [20].
Transport	- Singapore: In order to mitigate the effects of a heavy population, Singapore has created some amazingly innovative solutions, particularly related to transport via smart mobility policies. The policy concentrates on reducing traffic and ensuring that their public transportation system is an attractive alternative. Owning a car in Singapore is an expensive and complicated process. There are auctions just to get rights to purchase a car. Singapore introduced the world's first Electronic Road Pricing systems (ERPs), which charge drivers more in peak hours. As Chin Kian Keong with Singapore's Land Transport authority asserts, they want to penalize the act of driving: "we want to move people from cars, because cars are not such an efficient use of the limited road space that we have" [18]. - Melbourne: Integrated transport in this smart city aims to combine various modes of travel. Reduced delays, increased safety, and better health can all be achieved by sharing information between users, operators, and network managers. This will optimize mobility and minimize costs for travelers [20].
Health data	- Singapore: Applied big data to address the issue of health quality of their aging population. As part of the Smart Nation initiative, the Singapore government will spend an estimated $250 million SG by 2020 on this initiative. It will include tracking devices such as fitness trackers and sensors that will allow remote access to relatives and medical practitioners, emergency alerts that monitor things such as blood pressure and heart rate, technology that allows the elderly greater independence in their homes, and connected public transportation systems that promote mobility. These technologies will not just help to alleviate the economic strain that an aging population puts on society as a whole, but they also ensure that their elderly citizens are maintaining a good quality of life to the very end [18].
Garbage	- Songdo: Even garbage collection will generate data. Residents who dispose of garbage will need to use a chip card in the containers. The city planners and architects, along with Cisco, are working on the concept of totally eliminating garbage trucks. Garbage trucks will not collect and dispose of garbage anymore. Each house will have garbage disposal units and garbage will be sucked from them to the garbage treatment centers, which will dispose of it in an environmentally-friendly way. The garbage will be used to generate power for the city [19].
Safety	- Songdo: Data will make life more secure for the citizens. For example, children playing in the parks will wear bracelets with sensors that will allow the children to be tracked for safety [19].
Energy, electricity	- Songdo: The smart energy grid can measure the presence of people in a particular area, in a particular moment, and can accordingly adjust the streetlights. It will ensure that areas that are scantly populated will automatically have some of the street lights turned off. This will result in significant energy savings [19].

According to the different data and activities within the concept of smart cities, they can essentially change our lives at many levels, such as improved transportation, less pollution, better waste management, fewer parking problems, and more energy savings. Therefore, several examples of big data and IoT helping to build smart cities are listed in Table 2. Singapore, Songdo, and Melbourne are selected as examples to describe the various data and their usage in smart cities.

5 DIMENSIONS AND CRITERIA FOR THE MEGAPROJECTS' MANAGEMENT

According to the sustainable development approach, the results of megaprojects as urban catalysts should be responsive to three main goals: the economic prosperity, livable and equable cities, and environmental resiliency. In other words, to evaluate the impacts of a megaproject, it is necessary to know how the project is capable of ensuring economic prosperity, the livability and equity, and environmental resiliency. As the information technologies, social networks, and the related applications are initiated and executed, the required infrastructure and services for smart cities are being provided with fairly high speed. Therefore, the distinction of a smart city with other cities will be the smarter use of the extensive available data and information. In fact, the art of smarter cities would be the optimal data and information management, and the effort to maximize the integration and analysis of the data provided by the available data sources (DSs in Fig. 2).

FIG. 2 The relationship between the dimensions of smart cities and megaprojects

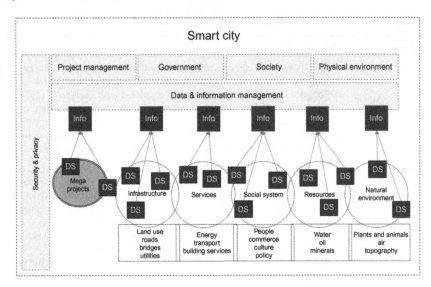

In smart cities, the information is provided by the available data from the existing data sources (such as sensors, RFID tags, cameras, etc.) from various subsystems and information layers. The information layers could be categorized in the infrastructure layer, services layer, social system layer, resource layer, and natural environment layer. In addition, megaprojects provide information as a subsystem in the whole system of the smart city.

As megaprojects usually contain a series of buildings, activities, infrastructures, spaces, transportation systems, and various actors; different kinds of data can be collected from megaprojects, some of which are presented in this section. In order to gather data/information, Internet access is very significant, and plays a key role in communication technologies and IoT. The IoT is applied for data collection through wireless technologies (e.g., mobile devices and sensors), micro-electromechanical systems, and micro-services, for example, in order to manage and control anything that an IT division in a megaproject is responsible for. On the other hand, the Web of Things (WoT) relies on the connectivity service of the IoT to create services and applications exploiting the IoT data. Meanwhile, smart cities present an opportunity for rendering WoT-enabled services.

Megaprojects' management, meaning the stakeholder management, the financial management, the construction and operation management, and the alleviation of the negative impacts on their surroundings, is a critical requisite for the projects' success and the realization of sustainable development. In other words, the long-term construction period, the high costs of construction and operation, the large number of stakeholders, and the extensive consequences of megaprojects make their management necessary. Considering the context of a smart city, a megaproject as an urban catalyst accelerating the sustainable development is a driving force to the realization of the smart city's visions. However, the unforeseen and negative footprint of the megaproject may make major changes to the urban data and the whole urban environment. Thus, megaprojects as urban catalysts can be the approaching and the distracting forces for sustainable development at the same time. A better understanding of the available data sources and better information management of the impacts of megaprojects on the city can lead us to the provision of smarter cities. Fig. 3 shows a conceptual framework of the relationship between megaprojects and a smart city. According to the figure, the connections between the constructs could be clearer. The role of megaprojects in the framework is identified as a moderator construct that will strengthen the relationship between a smart city and the results of it based on the sustainable development approach. In other words, megaprojects as a moderator construct will have a positive effect on their connection.

Using the data and information, as well as technologies, in a smart way, smart megaprojects can be proposed as the mediators in smart cities to reach their goals. Smart megaprojects are able to provide unified and integrable data and information through new and innovative technologies. Smart megaprojects include the effective projects' management in order to adhere to the time and financial plan. In addition, smart megaprojects are able to react in a smart way to unforeseen risks and challenges. Moreover, smart megaprojects can control their effects on the environment in a smart way by accelerating their positive impacts, and alleviation of their negative consequences, which will be done through smarter usage of energies, the infrastructure, and services, as well as the built spaces.

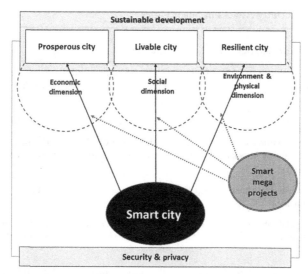

FIG. 3 The conceptual framework of the potential role of megaprojects in a smart city.

However, as more data usage for various reasons raises the risk of loss of security and privacy, the smart megaprojects might succumb to the same risk if the issues are ignored. Therefore, security and privacy should be a major part of the conceptual framework of the smart megaprojects. Hence, in the next section, we discuss security and privacy in smart cities. Consequently, various risks and attacks that are relevant to the megaprojects' management are described as well.

6 SECURITY AND PRIVACY IN A SMART CITY

Security and privacy have to be seen as a critical part of the architecture of a smart city to implement it within all of the layers, including the business layer, the application layer, the cloud layer, the integration layer, and the perception layer [15]. Consequently, it also should be considered for all of the dimensions of a smart city (smart transport, smart energy, smart technology, smart living, smart environment, smart citizens and education, smart economy, and smart government), and also to improve the quality of life [21, 22]. Hence, every smart city should be a secure city, too. In the following, several challenges of security and privacy in smart cities have been discussed within the proposed framework for smart management.

There are many resources in smart cities that are producing various types of data. These urban data are used within different dimensions of the smart cities, such as smart technologies (e.g., IoT, cloud computing, databases, and artificial intelligence), smart governance (e.g., transport, health, education, infrastructure, energy, and environment), and smart economy (e.g., finance, business, and communication) [15, 17, 22, 23]. Hence, data and information security are essential for a smart city in order to achieve the best results of the smart management.

According to the different types of data, there are unlocked data or open data that are available for the public. However, there are locked data that require security and privacy, such as individual data, communication data, and transaction data, and they should be secured in order to decrease the risk of data and information management.

Generally, there are different kinds of risks for data and information management, such as data loss, data disclosure, low quality of data, and low quantity of data that can happen based on various security attacks such as availability attacks, integrity attacks, confidentiality attacks, and accountability attacks [24]. In addition, privacy is implemented in a smart city through protecting several issues that could be related to identities (individual data), transactions (queries and responses), communications (communication channels), mobility (tracking location coordinates), and territories (personal property and space) [15, 17]. Table 3 shows a sample of the privacy in a smart city based on different categories of data and security attacks with an example for each one.

TABLE 3 Privacy-Related Issues and Security Attacks in Smart Cities

Data category	Privacy-related issues	Security attacks	Examples
Infrastructure	Communications	Availability attacks, integrity attacks	Risk of data loss and disclosure via illicit activities that disrupt the normal functioning of devices/networks
Sustainability	Communications	Availability attacks, integrity attacks	Risk of low quality and quantity of data and information via physical damages or changing the smart things' settings or properties
Health	Identities	Confidentiality attacks, availability attacks, integrity attacks	Risk of data disclosure and data loss through software attacks on an operating system, other applications in IoT nodes
Cohesion	Communications, mobility	Availability attacks, integrity attacks	Risk of data loss via accessibility of unauthorized users
Commerce	Identities, transactions, communications	Availability attacks, integrity attacks	Disclosure of different kinds of conversations and recordings and access to communication channels by unauthorized users
Experience	Communications	Availability attacks, integrity attacks	Risk of low quantity and quality data via lack of the accurate information
Citizen	Identities, communications, territories	Confidentiality attacks, accountability attacks	Risk of data disclosure and data loss by stealing the passwords or access keys

7 CONCLUSION

This research investigates how megaprojects can positively influence smart cities. Consistent with the previous finding on the effect of a smart city in sustainable development, a relationship between them has been reported based on the literature. From the perspectives of economies, social issues, and the environment, megaprojects have been found to positively moderate the relationship between a smart city and prosperous, livable, and resilient city. Consequently, it is expected that urban development would be fairly sustained.

According to the framework that is proposed in this research, different types of the provided data based on a smart city and megaprojects should be integrated into each other in order to achieve the best results of a smart city using a sustainable development approach. Therefore, the data will be integrated with metadata and various types of data from various sources, such as static databases and also data that will be aggregated, filtered, and combined via querying, which usually needs to be interpreted, combined with other data sources, and analyzed.

Moreover, data sources of smart cities propose a variety of data that should be aggregated and filtered after collection. Consequently, the data transferred to data representation for interoperable publication and the published data sources are then made discoverable and become available.

Thus, various levels of processing the provided data give rise to challenges in different dimensions. In other words, different domains of data such as health, safety, traffic, and transportation that are provided based on the different sensors and devices have different qualities. Hence, data quality, data validity, and device availability can be different, and their processing results can be changed, also. Furthermore, there are the issues of privacy and security for the sensitive and private data that should be considered in the whole process of data from collection to utilization.

Consequently, the research concludes that to have a successful strategy of urban planning and development, this framework may be considered by managers and researchers. It is helpful to consider the issues and challenges of different types of data that are mentioned herein that can be provided in various smart cities. This could be a useful starting point toward the improvement of urban development using a sustainable development approach.

References

[1] C. Harrison, I.A. Donnelly, A theory of smart cities, in: Proceedings of the 55th Annual Meeting of the ISSS-2011, Hull, UK, Vol. 55, 2011. No. 1.
[2] M. Grubb, C. Vrolijk, D. Brack, The kyoto protocol: A guide and assessment, in: Royal Institute of International Affairs Energy and Environmental Programme, 1997.
[3] A. Cocchia, Smart and digital city: A systematic literature review, in: Smart City, Springer International Publishing, Switzerland, 2014, pp. 13–43.
[4] R.P. Dameri, Searching for smart city definition: a comprehensive proposal, Int. J. Comput. Technol. 11 (5) 2013 2544–2551.

[5] J. Gabrys, Programming environments: environmentality and citizen sensing in the smart city, Environ. Plann. D: Soc. Space 32 (1) 2014 30–48.

[6] T. Nam, T.A. Pardo, Conceptualizing smart city with dimensions of technology, people, and institutions, in: Proceedings of the 12th Annual International Digital Government Research Conference: Digital Government Innovation in Challenging Times, ACM, 2011, pp. 282–291.

[7] S. Derrible, Complexity in future cities: the rise of networked infrastructure, Int. J. Urban Sci. 21 (sup1) 2017 68–86.

[8] M. Deloitte, Smart cities: How rapid advances in technology are reshaping our economy and society?, 2015. Version 1.0, URL: http://www.deloitte.nl/govlab.

[9] G.A. Caldwell, C.H. Smith, E.M. Clift, Digital Futures and the City of Today: New Technologies and Physical Spaces, Mediated Cities Series, Intellect Ltd., Bristol, England, 2016.

[10] J.H. Lee, R. Phaal, S.H. Lee, An integrated service-device-technology roadmap for smart city development, Technol. Forecast. Soc. Chang. 80 (2) 2013 286–306.

[11] S. Roche, Geographic information science I: why does a smart city need to be spatially enabled? Prog. Hum. Geogr. 38 (5) 2014 703–711.

[12] S. Zygiaris, Smart city reference model: assisting planners to conceptualize the building of smart city innovation ecosystems, J. Knowl. Econ. 4 (2) 2013 217–231.

[13] L.G. Anthopoulos, A. Vakali, Urban planning and smart cities: Interrelations and reciprocities, in: The Future Internet Assembly, Springer, Berlin, Heidelberg, 2012, pp. 178–189.

[14] H. Chourabi, T. Nam, S. Walker, J.R. Gil-Garcia, S. Mellouli, K. Nahon, H.J. Scholl, Understanding smart cities: An integrative framework, in: System Science (HICSS), 2012 45th Hawaii International Conference, IEEE, 2012, pp. 2289–2297.

[15] A. AlDairi, Cyber security attacks on smart cities and associated mobile technologies, Procedia Comput. Sci. 109 2017 1086–1091.

[16] S. Bischof, A. Karapantelakis, C.S. Nechifor, A.P. Sheth, A. Mileo, P. Barnaghi, Semantic Modelling of Smart City Data, 2014, http://corescholar.libraries.wright.edu/knoesis/572 (accessed 12 December 2017).

[17] L. Van Zoonen, Privacy concerns in smart cities, Gov. Inf. Q. 33 (3) 2016 472–480.

[18] K.E. Calder, Singapore: Smart City, Smart State, Brookings Institution Press, Washington, DC, 2016.

[19] K. Pal, How big data helps build smart cities, 2015. http://www.kdnuggets.com/2015/10/big-data-smart-cities.html (accessed 15 April 2017).

[20] S. Mattern, Interfacing urban intelligence, in: Code & the City, 2016, pp. 49–60.

[21] E. Bertino, E. Ferrari, Big data security and privacy, in: A Comprehensive Guide Through the Italian Database Research Over the Last 25 Years, Springer, Cham, 2018, pp. 425–439.

[22] M. Lacinák, J. Ristvej, Smart city, safety and security, Procedia Eng. 192 2017 522–527.

[23] A. Cook, M. Robinson, M.A. Ferrag, L.A. Maglaras, Y. He, K. Jones, H. Janicke, Internet of cloud: Security and privacy issues, in: Cloud Computing for Optimization: Foundations, Applications, and Challenges, Springer, Cham, 2018, pp. 271–301.

[24] A. Bartoli, J. Hernández-Serrano, M. Soriano, M. Dohler, A. Kountouris, D. Barthel, Security and privacy in your smart city, in: Proceedings of the Barcelona Smart Cities Congress, vol. 292, 2011.

Index

Note: Page numbers followed by *f* indicate figures, *t* indicate tables, and *b* indicate boxes.

Printed in the United States
By Bookmasters